ISBN: 9781415877210
Item Number: 005557458

The Bible is not like any other book.

The Bible is special because it is God's Word. Many years ago, God told Bible writers what He wanted us to know, and they wrote down God's words for us to read, learn from, and obey. The words you read in the Bible today are the same ones that God told people to write thousands of years ago. Every word in the Bible is absolutely true because it comes from God.

The Bible can help you...

- know God better
- know Jesus as your Savior and Lord
- learn how God wants you to live
- find answers to your questions
- find encouragement
- and much, much more!

Reading the Bible can be an exciting adventure!

Turn to page vi and find the "Day 1" devotion. This is a great place to start reading and learning from the Bible!

Division	Book	Page Number
Gospels	Matthew	1
	Mark	31
	Luke	50
	John	82
History	Acts	106
Paul's Letters	Romans	137
	1 Corinthians	151
	2 Corinthians	164
	Galatians	172
	Ephesians	176
	Philippians	181
	Colossians	184
	1 Thessalonians	187
	2 Thessalonians	189
	1 Timothy	191
	2 Timothy	194
	Titus	197
	Philemon	198
General Letters	Hebrews	199
	James	209
	1 Peter	212
	2 Peter	216
	1 John	219
	2 John	222
	3 John	223
	Jude	223
Prophecy	Revelation	224
Poetry and Wisdom	Psalms	245
	Proverbs	323

"Devotions" is a word that many people use when they talk about reading and studying the Bible. Devotions make it easier to read the Bible and pray every day. They can help you understand and learn from what you read in the Bible. The devotions in this Bible can help you **discover** truth about Jesus, **decide** what to do with the evidence you uncover, and **defend** your faith to anyone who asks why you believe what the Bible says about Jesus. They can help you discover proof that Jesus is who He says He is (God's Son and the only way to heaven) and that He really did die and come back to life. They can also give you the tools you need to be able to tell others about Jesus and answer their questions.

Here's how it works.

Start with Day 1. Even though there are two devotions on each page, read only one per day. Read the verse first. Think about what the verse means. Then read the rest of the devotion. Did it help you better understand what God wants you to learn from that verse? Is there anything you need to change about yourself after reading God's words in the Bible? There are journal pages at the end of each week of devotions. Write down your thoughts or even a prayer as you work through the devotion each day.

Take a few moments to pray.

Prayer is both talking to and listening to God. You won't be able to hear God's voice with your ears, but the Holy Spirit will help you know what God wants to tell you. Each day, tell God what you learned from the Bible. Ask God to forgive you for the ways you sinned today. Ask for His help to do things differently tomorrow. Be still and quiet for a moment. God may help you to think of some other things to talk to Him about.

Once you make it a habit, reading your Bible and praying every day will be easy.

DAY 1

○○○○○○○○○○○○○○○○○○○○○○○○○○○○○

In the
beginning
was the Word.
John 1:1a

"I heard the sun is going to explode tomorrow," said Julian at recess. "That's not true!" Ryan responded. "Sure it is," said Julian. "I saw it on the news."

Would you believe the sun was going to explode just because your friend told you? Or because you heard it on the news or read it on the Internet? Probably not. The same should be true for your faith. Don't just repeat something you've heard or believe something you've read. Think about it for yourself! Do some detective work to discover what facts are true and which ones are false. Learn the difference between someone's opinion and the facts about God, Jesus, and the Bible. The Bible is the most complete source of information about Jesus. Everything you read in the Bible is true. But there are also hundreds of other ancient writings about Jesus, too. These writings help prove the Bible is true.

Think About It: What people and sources do you trust? Make a list of ones you trust and a list of ones that may not always be accurate.

DAY 2

○○○○○○○○○○○○○○○○○○○○○○○○○○

Your word
is truth.
John 17:17b

Historians are people who study events that have taken place in the past. Some historians may be Christians, but some are not. Historians can be sure what things were like in the past by studying the people, events, writings, and culture from long ago. In other words, they use facts about the past to determine what is true.

When you read the Bible you learn about the people, events, writings, and culture from thousands of years ago. Just like a historian! God says everything in the Bible is true. Even today's verse, John 17:17, says that God's Word (the Bible) is true. Did you know that historians have found other writings from the same time as the Bible that prove the things in the Bible are true? By looking at the facts, historians can determine that what the Bible says is true. What the Bible says about God and Jesus is true, too!

Think About It: Do you believe the Bible is true? If you do, write in this Bible: "I know the Bible is true." If you're not sure, write down your questions. Ask an adult to help you investigate the facts and find out the answers.

DAY 3

○○○○○○○○○○○○○○○○○○○○○○○○○○○○

"But you," He asked them, "who do you say that I am?"

Matthew 16:15

When someone gives you a compliment, do you get a little embarrassed? If someone said, "You are the best reader in the entire world!" would you put your head down and say, "Oh, wow, thanks"? Or would you say, "No I'm not"?

When Jesus asked His disciples this question (Matthew 16:15), Simon Peter answered, "You are the Messiah, the Son of the living God!" Peter was saying Jesus is a big deal—a really, really big deal! But Jesus never said, "No, I'm not." He didn't act embarrassed as if Peter was giving Him a compliment that wasn't true. In fact, Jesus was pleased with Peter, because what Peter said was the truth. Jesus knew that God had helped Peter understand who Jesus really was. That knowledge wasn't something that Peter came up with on his own. He knew it because God had told him. Jesus said, "Flesh and blood did not reveal this to you, but My Father in heaven" (Matthew 16:17).

Think About It: Look through your Bible. Make a list of the things Jesus said He was. Here are two to get you started: *Son of the living God, Messiah* ...

DAY 4

○○○○○○○○○○○○○○○○○○○○○○○○○○○○

Those who believe without seeing are blessed.

John 20:29b

Are you a skeptic? A *skeptic* is a person who doesn't believe that something is true. A *skeptic* never believes what anybody else says ... he has to check out the facts for himself.

It is good to check out the facts on your own. Sometimes it's hard to believe what other people say. One of Jesus' disciples was like that. His name was Thomas. Thomas didn't believe Jesus had risen from the dead, even when his friends told him that Jesus was alive again. Thomas said that he would only believe if he got to see and touch the scars on Jesus' hands and feet.

Well, he did! Thomas saw Jesus after He rose from the dead. Thomas got to see the scars on Jesus' hands and feet with his own eyes. Jesus even let Thomas touch them. Then, Thomas definitely believed! Thomas proclaimed that Jesus was "My Lord and my God!"

Think About It: After discovering the evidence for yourself in VBS, will you believe that Jesus is who He says He is? Pray this prayer: *Jesus, help me to discover for myself that You are my Lord and God.*

DAY 5

〇〇〇〇〇〇〇〇〇〇〇〇〇〇〇〇〇〇〇〇〇〇〇〇

Again the high priest questioned Him, "Are You the Messiah, the Son of the Blessed One?" "I am," said Jesus.

Mark 14:61b-62a

Have you ever heard someone brag that he's the best video gamer in the entire world or that he's best friends with the principal? Most of the time, people brag about themselves when they want to feel better about themselves. They stretch the truth so others will give them special attention.

Did Jesus brag about Himself? Did He stretch the truth about being the Son of God? Did He need to feel better about Himself? Did He want others to give Him special attention? When Jesus did acknowledge who He was, He was spit on and beaten. The truth is, Jesus wasn't bragging or stretching the truth. He said those things because they were actually true!

Think About It: Do you know a bragger? Give him a compliment that is true. For example: "It's impossible to be the best gamer in the world, but I really liked how you passed level nine. Can you help me do that?"

DAY 6

〇〇〇〇〇〇〇〇〇〇〇〇〇〇〇〇〇〇〇〇〇〇〇〇

And they all condemned Him to be deserving of death.

Mark 14:64b

What are the consequences when you get in trouble? Consequences are the result of your actions; they can be positive or negative. If you disobey your parents, the negative consequence may be that you cannot watch TV for a week or you have to go to bed early.

Jesus was on trial for His life, even though He had never done anything wrong. He knew that if He claimed to be the Son of God people would try to stone Him, beat Him, and even kill Him. That was the consequence. And that is just what happened! Jesus was put to death because He said that He was God's Son. Would you be willing to die for something you knew was not true? Of course not! Because Jesus was willing to die for what He said, we can believe that it was absolutely true!

Think About It: Words are very powerful. Once spoken, you can't take back words. What did you say today that was good? What words would you take back if you could?

DAY 7 🞊🞊🞊🞊🞊🞊🞊🞊🞊🞊🞊🞊🞊🞊🞊🞊🞊🞊🞊🞊🞊🞊🞊

For I passed on to you as most important what I received: that Christ died for our sins according to the Scriptures, that He was buried, that He was raised on the third day according to the Scriptures.

1 Corinthians 15:3-4

This is the most important truth ever—Jesus died to pay the penalty for your sins, was buried, and rose again. Many people do not believe Jesus really died, so they don't believe He rose from the dead. Some believe He faked His death either with good acting or by taking a drug to make him seem dead.

The truth is, Jesus couldn't have survived the crucifixion. It was a cruel way to die. The Bible says Jesus was brutally beaten before He ever made it to the cross. Jesus' death was not a hoax. He didn't fake it. He wasn't rescued at the last minute. He really died. If He hadn't, His sacrifice would have been meaningless and there would have been nothing miraculous about His resurrection. He went through all the pain and torture because He loves you more than anything!

Think About It: Every day this week, thank Jesus for paying the penalty for your sins. It will start to make a difference in your choices and actions!

DAY 8 🞊🞊🞊🞊🞊🞊🞊🞊🞊🞊🞊🞊🞊🞊🞊🞊🞊🞊🞊🞊🞊🞊🞊

Jesus went up into the temple complex and began to teach.

John 7:14b

Some people claim that Jesus acted like a crazy person so they have an excuse to not believe in Him. But was it true?

Insanity is a mental disorder with specific symptoms (or signs) including unpredictable emotions, difficulty having long conversations, and speaking in a way that makes no sense to others. Did Jesus show these signs of insanity? Was Jesus emotional at strange times? He cried when His friend Lazarus died (John 11:35)… that's perfectly normal. Did Jesus have trouble with long conversations or speaking to others? No, He taught at the temple many times and people came from all over to hear Him teach. In fact, people were amazed at His teaching and wondered how He knew the Scriptures so well (John 7:15). If Jesus was really insane, would He have been able to teach others so well? No way! See how easy it is to debunk that claim when you examine the evidence?

Think About It: Some people make outrageous claims… so be careful. But you can trust the Bible is true and can always believe what it says.

NOTES

DAY 9

Look, I am sending you what My Father promised.

Luke 24:49a

When your grandma is coming to your house, you can hardly wait for her to get there! The Jewish people felt the same way about waiting for the Messiah. They knew He was coming and waited anxiously. The Old Testament even gave them clues to help them know who to look for. For example, they knew the Messiah would be born in Bethlehem, would be descended from David, would not be accepted by people, would suffer and die, and would take the sins of people on Himself. Does Jesus fit that description? Absolutely! Those things were written hundreds of years before Jesus was born and yet every single clue fits Him!

When Grandma finally gets to your house, do you say, "You're not my grandma"? Of course not! But that's what happened with Jesus. The people were waiting for the Messiah, but they didn't know it was Jesus. Look at the clues. Only Jesus could be the Messiah!

Think About It: Which prediction about the Messiah do you think best fits Jesus? If you had lived during Bible times, would you have believed Jesus was the Messiah?

DAY 10

Everything written about Me in the Law of Moses, the Prophets, and the Psalms must be fulfilled.

Luke 24:44b

You can't choose where you are born, who your parents are, or who your ancestors are. Old Testament verses foretold (told ahead of time) that the Messiah would be born in Bethlehem and would come from King David's family. There's no way an ordinary person could have picked his birthplace or family history and pretended he was the Messiah.

But what about the other prophecies about the Messiah? Could it just be coincidence that Jesus fulfilled the hundreds of prophesies from the Old Testament? (A coincidence is like when you and your best friend wear the same shirt, and you didn't even plan it.) Dr. Peter Stoner and 600 students used math equations to find out that the chance of one person (Jesus) fulfilling just eight of the prophesies is one in a hundred million billion![1]

Think About It: Math, science, history, and archaeology prove that Jesus is who He said He is. What evidence helps you believe? Why?

[1] Lee Strobel and Rob Suggs, *The Case for Christ for Kids* (Grand Rapids: Zonderkidz, 2010).

DAY 11

〇〇〇〇〇〇〇〇〇〇〇〇〇〇〇〇〇〇〇〇〇〇〇〇〇〇

We were eyewitnesses of His majesty.

2 Peter 1:16b

Have you ever noticed the crazy headlines in the tabloid magazines at the checkout line at the grocery store? *Wolf Man Attacks Village! President Abducted by Aliens! Three-headed Monster Learns to Read!* These stories may be written down—and even published—but are they true? Of course not! So what makes the Bible true?

One of the major reasons the Bible is considered to be true is that it was written by eyewitnesses. *Eyewitnesses* are people who saw something happen with their own eyes. If there's a car accident, the police want to talk to the people who saw it happen, not the people who heard it from a friend who heard it from a friend. The stories of Jesus in the Bible were written by four eyewitnesses: Matthew, Mark, Luke, and John. Each of these men tells his eyewitness account about Jesus' life in the Bible.

Think About It: Imagine you were an eyewitness to Jesus' life. What parts of His story would you want to tell others about?

DAY 12

〇〇〇〇〇〇〇〇〇〇〇〇〇〇〇〇〇〇〇〇〇〇〇〇

What was from the beginning, what we have heard, what we have seen with our eyes, what we have observed, and have touched with our hands...

1 John 1:1

"I saw the world's biggest candy cane on our trip!" exclaimed Madison. "How big was it? What did it look like?" asked Tyler. "Did it smell good?" Olivia wanted to know. "Did you touch it? What did it feel like?" inquired Sammy.

When we hear a story, we want to know all about it: what, where, when, why, how. We want the person to describe it so that we can imagine being there. We want to know everything our five senses can tell us: how it looked, smelled, tasted, sounded, and felt. That's how it was with Jesus' friends who wrote down what it was like to be with Jesus. Every friend was different—they all had unique personalities and special experiences with Jesus. That's why the Gospels, the first four books of the New Testament (Matthew, Mark, Luke, John), tell the story of Jesus' life just a little bit differently.

Think About It: Close your eyes and imagine being Jesus' friend and walking next to Him. What do you see, smell, taste, hear, and touch?

DAY 13 〔○○○○○○○○○○○○○○○○○○○○○○○○○〕

And there came a voice from heaven: This is My beloved Son.
Matthew 3:17

Jamal told a story about how a shark swam past him while snorkeling on vacation. "We don't believe you! That didn't really happen!" his friends exclaimed. Jamal yelled for his mom: "Hey, Mom! Tell them it's true! That really happened, didn't it?" "Yep, it's true!" Jamal's mom confirmed to his friends.

Sometimes a mother or a father can confirm whether your story is true or false. In Jesus' case, His Father confirmed that Jesus was indeed who He said He was—God's Son. Jesus was getting baptized by John the Baptist. When Jesus came up from the water, the heavens opened up and God's voice was heard by everyone who was there. God said that Jesus was His Son. God also said He takes delight in His Son, Jesus. Jesus pleased His Father.

Think About It: What things do you do that please your mom and dad? Think of something special for your parents to show your love for them. You could clean your room, make a card, or make their favorite dessert.

DAY 14 〔○○○○○○○○○○○○○○○○○○○○○○○○〕

This man really was God's Son!
Matthew 27:54b

Have you ever done a puppet show? You can make a puppet do and say anything you want it to. Without you, the puppet doesn't have any life.

Everything in nature is created by God. The entire earth is under His control. First Corinthians 10:26 says, "The earth is the Lord's, and all that is in it." That's the reason why things in nature happened when Jesus died on the cross. Nature literally mourned. For example, there was an earthquake when Jesus died. No one could have made an earthquake happen. Only God is in control of nature and His creation.

The centurion, after seeing, hearing, and feeling the earthquake, was convinced that Jesus really was God's Son. It took an act of nature for this man to believe Jesus was the Son of God.

Think About It: What made you believe Jesus is God's Son? Was it because of something in nature, reading the Bible, or something else? Write it down so you will always remember when and how you believed in Jesus.

DAY 15 ⎯◯◯◯◯◯◯◯◯◯◯◯◯◯◯◯◯◯◯◯◯◯◯◯◯◯◯⎯

You are the Son of God! You are the King of Israel!
John 1:49b

Jesus knows everything about you. He knows all the good stuff and all the bad—and He loves you anyway! No matter what you do, think, or say, God will always love you. He knows what is in your heart. When Jesus saw Nathanael, He instantly knew he was a good man. Nathanael was amazed! He knew only God could know Him like that! Nathanael called Jesus *Rabbi*, which means "Teacher." By calling Him Rabbi, Nathanael was acknowledging Jesus as his authority. Nathanael was the student, and Jesus was the teacher.

Nathanael also proclaimed that Jesus was the Son of God and the King of Israel. He immediately knew who Jesus was and believed in Him. He was never skeptical about Jesus. How wonderful to have instant faith like Nathanael! How amazing for Jesus to invite Nathanael to walk and talk with Him as a friend!

Think About It: Jesus has called you by name. He wants to be your friend. Will you let Jesus be your teacher? If so, pray a short prayer to Him now.

DAY 16 ⎯◯◯◯◯◯◯◯◯◯◯◯◯◯◯◯◯◯◯◯◯◯◯◯◯◯⎯

Then He got up and rebuked the wind and the raging waves. So they ceased, and there was a calm.
Luke 8:24b

Jesus performed many miracles during His three years of ministry. Some of the miracles were over nature; some of them were over demon powers; some of them were about meeting people's needs; and some of them were about healing people. Some people who don't believe in Jesus say His miracles were just illusions or tricks.

Let's look at the evidence about Jesus calming the wind and waves. Can someone trick nature into doing what he wants? Could someone trick you into believing a violent storm suddenly stopped? Definitely not. The disciples and Jesus were on a boat in the middle of a lake. A violent storm came, and the boat almost sank! Imagine the rough waters and the strong wind. The disciples were afraid they would drown! Jesus told the wind and the waves to stop—and they did. No tricks. No illusions. They stopped because Jesus is the Son of God.

Think About It: Miracles still happen today! People are healed, and God works in situations that seem impossible. What miracles have you seen?

NOTES

DAY 17 [○○○○○○○○○○○○○○○○○○○○○○○○○○○○○]

Jesus took the loaves, and after giving thanks He distributed them.

John 6:11a

What is the difference between needs and wants? *Needs* are the things you must have to live. *Wants* are the things you would like to have. Many times Jesus helped provide people with the things they needed to live, like food.

One day a large crowd followed Jesus. There were over 5,000 people. Jesus was concerned about them having enough food. His disciples said they didn't have enough money to feed all the people. A little boy had five loaves of bread and two fish… not enough to feed thousands of people! But Jesus took the boy's gift, prayed, and began to give the food to the hungry people. The food kept coming and coming—it was a miracle! The people got as much food as they wanted, and there were 12 baskets of leftovers. When the people saw this miracle, they knew Jesus was more than just a good man.

Think About It: You may feel like a kid who has nothing to give Jesus. But He can take anything you have and turn it into much. What talents, skills, or possessions do you have for Jesus to use?

DAY 18 [○○○○○○○○○○○○○○○○○○○○○○○○○○○]

My teaching isn't Mine but is from the One who sent me.

John 7:16

How smart are your teachers? Smarter than you? We learn from people who know more than we do so we can gain from their knowledge. We respect teachers and look up to them.

Jesus was an excellent teacher. He taught in the temple many times. He explained what the Scriptures meant. In Jesus' day, the Bible wasn't yet in a book. The Old Testament Scriptures were written on lots of scrolls, and there weren't many copies for people to read. People went to the temple to hear the priest read from the scrolls because they didn't have their own copies. Many people appreciated how Jesus explained Scriptures. He taught exactly what God wanted Him to teach. Today, we can read the Bible for ourselves. You even have your own copy. Become a student of Jesus by reading it!

Think About It: Reading your Bible every day is important to learn and grow as a Christian. When is the best time for you to read your Bible? Commit to reading it at that time every day.

DAY 19

He must go on to Jerusalem and suffer many things.
Matthew 16:21b

Do you have chores that you must do daily or weekly? Do you look forward to doing those chores? Some kids enjoy the jobs they have to do; others do not. Jesus had a job to do on earth. He knew His mission was to die for everyone's sins. He was given this job by His Father, God. Do you think Jesus looked forward to doing His job on earth? The Bible says that Jesus asked God to take away this mission. But Jesus knew He must do it to complete God's plan. He willingly obeyed.

Jesus told His disciples many times that He would suffer, be killed, and be raised on the third day. The disciples didn't always understand what Jesus meant. Only Jesus could predict the future. He knew God's plan was to save people and give them eternal life.

Think About It: Next time your parents give you a job, complete it willingly, like Jesus did when He accomplished God's plan for Him.

DAY 20

He began to tell them the things that would happen to Him.
Mark 10:32b

This Scripture is the third time Jesus predicted His death to the disciples. He was trying to prepare the disciples for what would happen in the future. When Jesus was crucified on the cross and raised on the third day, the disciples were able to tell others that Jesus had said this would happen. This is more evidence that Jesus was God's Son. Only God knows the future. No man or woman could have predicted this would happen to Jesus. Only Jesus knew because He truly is the Son of God.

Many people predict certain things will happen, like the end of the world. But they are wrong. Although they claim to be like God, they are not. There is only one God, and only He knows the future. You can believe this truth and trust the one and only God for your future.

Think About It: Are you anxious, worried, or uncertain about the future? God is in control and knows the future! Trust Him! Pray and ask God to help you through anything that comes your way today.

DAY 21 ○○○○○○○○○○○○○○○○○○○○○○○○○

She has done a noble thing for Me.
Mark 14:6b

Have you ever saved up your allowance to buy something really special? Was it worth saving your money to buy the thing you wanted? What if you gave that special item to a friend? Somebody might say, "Why did you do that? You saved your money for a long time to buy that!"

A woman in the Bible saved her money to buy an alabaster jar of perfume. She had to save her money for almost a year just to buy that one jar! The woman came to a house where Jesus was visiting. She broke the jar and poured the perfume on Jesus' head. She did this to show respect, love, and humility toward Jesus. Some of the other people got upset with her and wondered why in the world she would waste such expensive perfume. But Jesus knew what this woman did for Him was very special.

Think About It: When you give to others out of love and humility, God sees that as special. Time, money, and gifts are all things you can give away. What can you give to others who are in need?

DAY 22 ○○○○○○○○○○○○○○○○○○○○○○○○

They saw that He was already dead.
John 19:33b

Roman soldiers were at Jesus' crucifixion. Their job was to carry out the crucifixion of Jesus and the other two criminals. They had probably done this many times with many other men who were criminals. The soldiers were not compassionate about people dying. They didn't care what happened to the criminals. They just did their jobs. It didn't matter to them who Jesus was. In fact, they even took Jesus' clothes and split them up among themselves. They saw it as a "bonus" of the job—free clothes!

This is why the soldiers' testimonies about Jesus' death are important. The Roman soldiers would have told just the facts. They didn't care about Jesus or His death. They confirmed that Jesus was dead. Some people think Jesus just fainted on the cross, but the soldiers' eyewitness accounts prove that Jesus actually died on the cross.

Think About It: Many people are like the Roman soldiers who know about Jesus but may never believe in Him. Pray for a friend or family member to believe in Jesus as Savior.

DAY 23 〔○○○○○○○○○○○○○○○○○○○○○○○〕

An angel of the Lord descended from heaven and approached the tomb.
Matthew 28:2b

Have you ever gotten a message from someone? Maybe it was a voicemail, text, letter, or card. It makes you feel special when you get a message!

God sent a special messenger to proclaim that Jesus had risen from the dead—an angel! An angel came from heaven, rolled back the stone to the tomb, and sat on the stone. When Mary Magdalene and the other Mary got to the tomb, they saw the angel. The angel had a special message for them. He said Jesus wasn't there, because He had been resurrected! The angel even let them see the empty tomb. Then the angel told them to tell the disciples that Jesus had risen from the dead. What wonderful news! God didn't just let the women discover the empty tomb and wonder where Jesus was. God sent an angel to tell them the message!

Think About It: Like the angel, you can be a special messenger for God! Make a list of people with whom you can share the news about Jesus' resurrection. Then go proclaim (tell) the message!

DAY 24 〔○○○○○○○○○○○○○○○○○○○○○○○〕

They gave the soldiers a large sum of money and told them, "Say this…"
Matthew 28:12b–13a

The chief priests and elders wanted to make sure nothing happened to Jesus' body. So soldiers were ordered to stand guard outside the tomb. But when the soldiers saw the angel, they fainted from fear! When the chief priests and elders heard that the tomb was found empty, they came up with a plan. They bribed the soldiers to lie! They gave the soldiers a lot of money to say that Jesus' disciples stole His body during the night while the soldiers were sleeping. The soldiers took the money and lied about Jesus.

Some people today believe this lie. But it's not a very good lie. If the soldiers had really fallen asleep, it would have cost them their jobs and possibly even their lives! No soldier would dare to fall asleep on the job! Plus, the stone in front of the tomb was so heavy that it took many men to roll it. If the soldiers had really been asleep, all that noise would certainly have awakened them!

Think About It: Some people lie to make you believe something that isn't true. Don't believe lies. And don't tell them either!

NOTES

DAY 25 〔○○○○○○○○○○○○○○○○○○○○○○○○○〕

So He went
in to stay
with them.
Luke 24:29b

Do you ever hear the phrase, "Okay, but … "? Perhaps you are explaining something to a friend, and your friend says, "Okay, I believe that part, but what about this part of the story?" That is what some people say about Jesus' death and resurrection. Some believe Jesus really died, because there is enough evidence to know that is true. But they don't believe He came back to life. How can you know Jesus' resurrection was real?

The best evidence that proves Jesus is alive is that many people saw Him! Mary Magdalene and the other Mary saw Jesus after they saw the empty tomb. Two men saw Jesus as they walked along the road. They urged Jesus to stay with them, so He did. Then Jesus' eleven disciples saw Him. Later, many more saw Jesus. In fact, over 500 people saw Jesus with their own eyes after He had been resurrected (1 Corinthians 15:6).

Think About It: Over 500 people saw Jesus alive after His resurrection. How do you think their lives were changed after they saw Jesus?

DAY 26 〔○○○○○○○○○○○○○○○○○○○○○○○○○〕

He also
appeared
to me.
1 Corinthians 15:8b

Do you believe that nothing is impossible with God? God was able to raise Jesus from the dead. He also changed Paul's life very dramatically. Paul did not believe Jesus was the Messiah and persecuted people who were Christians. *Persecuted* means he mistreated them—and even had some of them imprisoned or killed! Then one day Jesus actually appeared to Paul. From then on, Paul was a changed man! You would never believe that someone who persecuted Christians would eventually be a Christian. But nothing is impossible with God!

After meeting Jesus, Paul's life radically changed. He was completely different! Paul's testimony about how Jesus changed his life is important evidence. His testimony of seeing Jesus alive helps prove that Jesus really did rise from the dead.

Think About It: Is there something in your life right now that seems impossible? Pray about it and ask God to work it out. Nothing is impossible with God!

DAY 27 ⟦◦◦◦◦◦◦◦◦◦◦◦◦◦◦◦◦◦◦◦◦◦◦⟧

This is the disciple who testifies to these things.
John 21:24a

Whenever you write your name, it is called your signature. Important documents require signatures as a way of saying "I guarantee that everything written in this document is true."

The last two verses in the Gospel of John are like a signature. John, who wrote the book, included his name at the end so that everyone would know that he witnessed everything that he wrote about and that his testimony is true. John and Jesus knew each other well. They were very good friends. John spent a lot of time with Jesus and saw what Jesus did. That's why John could write about it in his book. John said that so much more happened than could fit in his book. In fact, he said that if he tried to write down everything Jesus did and said, the world couldn't hold all of the books it would take!

Think About It: John was a personal friend of Jesus. You can be, too! Consider Jesus a friend and talk to Him like you do your best friend.

DAY 28 ⟦◦◦◦◦◦◦◦◦◦◦◦◦◦◦◦◦◦◦◦◦◦◦◦◦⟧

Honor the Messiah as Lord in your hearts.
1 Peter 3:15a

Do you know you are very special? You are! Being a Christian is special. Once you make Jesus your Savior and Lord, you will never be the same! You are guaranteed to be God's child and live eternally with Him in heaven. Because you will never be the same, you should act, think, and talk differently once you are a Christian.

Nobody is perfect, and nobody can be "good" by themselves. You need God's help every day! *Honor* (some translations say *set apart*) means "to put in a particular position." This verse says you should put God above all other things. He should be more important to you than anything or anybody. When Jesus is Lord of your heart and life, He will help you obey the things God says in the Bible to do. The Holy Spirit will also help guide you every day.

Think About It: A great way to honor God as Lord of your life is to spend time reading the Bible and praying to Him every day. Start a "quiet time" or "devotional time" today!

DAY 29]○○○○○○○○○○○○○○○○○○○○○○○○○[

Jesus told him, "I am the way, the truth, and the life. No ones comes to the Father except through Me."

John 14:6

In a car, there are usually lots of different ways to get to the same place. If you don't know how to get somewhere new, it can be easy to get lost or confused by the many roads, even with a GPS! But Jesus was clear when He gave directions on how to live forever with God in heaven. There's only one way. Read John 14:6 again. What does this verse say?

That's pretty clear, isn't it? There are no alternate routes, no shortcuts, and no other things you can do to get there on your own. You have to believe that Jesus paid for your sin through His death and that He rose again. Then you have to choose to follow and obey Him every day.

Think About It: If you have not asked Jesus to direct your life, ask a parent or teacher to talk with you about becoming a Christian. If you are already a Christian, use this Bible to share the ABCs with someone else. Help him know about the only way to heaven.

DAY 30]○○○○○○○○○○○○○○○○○○○○○○○○[

Always be ready to give a defense to anyone who asks you for a reason for the hope that is within you.

1 Peter 3:15b

You've now spent 30 days digging into God's Word and investigating the facts, evidence, and truth about who Jesus is. What is your verdict? Do you think He was more than just a good man? Do you think He performed miracles? Do you think He died on a cross? Do you think He was raised from the dead?

Although you are young now, the answers to these questions will be the foundation of your faith for the rest of your life. It is wonderful for you to discover these truths on your own so that your faith in Jesus is solid and secure. You know the truth! Nothing is greater than knowing Jesus. You know the Bible is true and in it you can read about the hope Jesus brings. You can share the hope of Jesus with others. When people ask you why you believe in Jesus, you can tell them!

Think About It: Always be ready to explain why you believe in Jesus and why the Bible is true. When you tell others, you are being a missionary for God!

THE
NEW TESTAMENT

MATTHEW

1 The historical record[A] of Jesus Christ, the Son of David, the Son of Abraham:

2 Abraham fathered[B] Isaac,
Isaac fathered Jacob,
Jacob fathered Judah and his brothers,
3 Judah fathered Perez and Zerah by Tamar,
Perez fathered Hezron,
Hezron fathered Aram,
4 Aram fathered Amminadab,
Amminadab fathered Nahshon,
Nahshon fathered Salmon,
5 Salmon fathered Boaz by Rahab,
Boaz fathered Obed by Ruth,
Obed fathered Jesse,
6 and Jesse fathered King David.

Then[C] David fathered Solomon by Uriah's wife,
7 Solomon fathered Rehoboam,
Rehoboam fathered Abijah,
Abijah fathered Asa,[D]
8 Asa[D] fathered Jehoshaphat,
Jehoshaphat fathered Joram,[E]
Joram fathered Uzziah,
9 Uzziah fathered Jotham,
Jotham fathered Ahaz,
Ahaz fathered Hezekiah,
10 Hezekiah fathered Manasseh,
Manasseh fathered Amon,[F]
Amon fathered Josiah,
11 and Josiah fathered Jechoniah and his brothers
at the time of the exile to Babylon.

12 Then after the exile to Babylon Jechoniah fathered Shealtiel,
Shealtiel fathered Zerubbabel,
13 Zerubbabel fathered Abiud,
Abiud fathered Eliakim,
Eliakim fathered Azor,
14 Azor fathered Zadok,
Zadok fathered Achim,
Achim fathered Eliud,
15 Eliud fathered Eleazar,
Eleazar fathered Matthan,
Matthan fathered Jacob,
16 and Jacob fathered Joseph the husband of Mary,
who gave birth to[G] Jesus who is called the Messiah.

17 So all the generations from Abraham to David were 14 generations; and from David until the exile to Babylon, 14 generations; and from the exile to Babylon until the Messiah, 14 generations.

18 The birth of Jesus Christ came about this way: After His mother Mary had been engaged to Joseph, it was discovered before they came together that she was pregnant by the Holy Spirit. 19 So her husband Joseph, being a righteous man, and not wanting to disgrace her publicly, decided to divorce her secretly. 20 But after he had considered these things, an angel of the Lord suddenly appeared to him in a dream, saying, "Joseph, son of David, don't be afraid to take Mary as your wife, because what has been conceived in her is by the Holy Spirit. 21 She will give birth to a son, and you are to name Him Jesus,[H] because He will save His people from their sins."

22 Now all this took place to fulfill what was spoken by the Lord through the prophet:

23 **See, the virgin will become pregnant**
and give birth to a son,
and they will name Him Immanuel,[I]

which is translated "God is with us." 24 When Joseph got up from sleeping, he did as the Lord's angel had commanded him. He married her 25 but did not know her intimately until she gave birth to a son.[J] And he named Him Jesus.

2 After Jesus was born in Bethlehem of Judea in the days of King Herod, wise men from the east arrived unexpectedly in Jerusalem, 2 saying, "Where is He who has been born King of the Jews? For we saw His star in the east[K] and have come to worship Him."[L] 3 When King Herod heard this, he was deeply disturbed, and all Jerusalem with him. 4 So he assembled all the chief priests and scribes of the people and asked them where the Messiah would be born.

A1:1 Or *The book of the genealogy* B1:2 In vv. 2-16 either a son, as here, or a later descendant, as in v. 8 C1:6 Other mss add *King*
D1:7,8 Other mss read *Asaph* E1:8 = Jehoram F1:10 Other mss read *Amos* G1:16 Lit *Mary, from whom was born* H1:21 *Jesus* is the Gk form of the Hb name "Joshua," which = "The LORD saves" or "Yahweh saves." I1:23 Is 7:14 J1:25 Other mss read *to her firstborn son*
K2:2 Or *star at its rising* L2:2 Or *to pay Him homage*

⁵"In Bethlehem of Judea," they told him, "because this is what was written by the prophet:

⁶ **And you, Bethlehem,** in the land of Judah,
are by no means **least**
among the leaders of Judah:
because out of you will come a leader
who will shepherd My people Israel."[A]

⁷Then Herod secretly summoned the wise men and asked them the exact time the star appeared. ⁸He sent them to Bethlehem and said, "Go and search carefully for the child. When you find Him, report back to me so that I too can go and worship Him."[B]

⁹After hearing the king, they went on their way. And there it was—the star they had seen in the east![C] It led them until it came and stopped above the place where the child was. ¹⁰When they saw the star, they were overjoyed beyond measure. ¹¹Entering the house, they saw the child with Mary His mother, and falling to their knees, they worshiped Him.[D] Then they opened their treasures and presented Him with gifts: gold, frankincense, and myrrh. ¹²And being warned in a dream not to go back to Herod, they returned to their own country by another route.

¹³After they were gone, an angel of the Lord suddenly appeared to Joseph in a dream, saying, "Get up! Take the child and His mother, flee to Egypt, and stay there until I tell you. For Herod is about to search for the child to destroy Him." ¹⁴So he got up, took the child and His mother during the night, and escaped to Egypt. ¹⁵He stayed there until Herod's death, so that what was spoken by the Lord through the prophet might be fulfilled: **Out of Egypt I called My Son.**[E]

¹⁶Then Herod, when he saw that he had been outwitted by the wise men, flew into a rage. He gave orders to massacre all the male children in and around Bethlehem who were two years[F] old and under, in keeping with the time he had learned from the wise men. ¹⁷Then what was spoken through Jeremiah the prophet was fulfilled:

¹⁸ **A voice was heard in Ramah,**

weeping,[G] and great mourning,
Rachel weeping for her children;
and she refused to be consoled,
because they were no more.[H]

¹⁹After Herod died, an angel of the Lord suddenly appeared in a dream to Joseph in Egypt, ²⁰saying, "Get up! Take the child and His mother and go to the land of Israel, because those who sought the child's life are dead." ²¹So he got up, took the child and His mother, and entered the land of Israel. ²²But when he heard that Archelaus[I] was ruling over Judea in place of his father Herod, he was afraid to go there. And being warned in a dream, he withdrew to the region of Galilee. ²³Then he went and settled in a town called Nazareth to fulfill what was spoken through the prophets, that He will be called a Nazarene.

3 In those days John the Baptist came, preaching in the Wilderness of Judea ²and saying, "Repent, because the kingdom of heaven has come near!" ³For he is the one spoken of through the prophet Isaiah, who said:

A voice of one crying out
in the wilderness:
Prepare the way for the Lord;
make His paths straight![J]

⁴John himself had a camel-hair garment with a leather belt around his waist, and his food was locusts and wild honey. ⁵Then people from Jerusalem, all Judea, and all the vicinity of the Jordan were flocking to him, ⁶and they were baptized by him in the Jordan River as they confessed their sins.

⁷When he saw many of the Pharisees and Sadducees coming to the place of his baptism,[K] he said to them, "Brood of vipers! Who warned you to flee from the coming wrath? ⁸Therefore produce fruit consistent with[L] repentance. ⁹And don't presume to say to yourselves, 'We have Abraham as our father.' For I tell you that God is able to raise up children for Abraham from these stones! ¹⁰Even now the ax is ready to strike the root of the trees! Therefore, every tree that doesn't produce good fruit will be cut down and thrown into the fire.

¹¹"I baptize you with[M] water for repentance,[N] but the One who is coming after me is more

A2:6 Mc 5:2 B2:8 Or and pay Him homage C2:9 Or star . . . at its rising D2:11 Or they paid Him homage E2:15 Hs 11:1 F2:16 Lit were from two years G2:18 Other mss read Ramah, lamentation, and weeping, H2:18 Jr 31:15 I2:22 A son of Herod the Great who ruled a portion of his father's kingdom 4 B.C.–A.D. 6 J3:3 Is 40:3 K3:7 Lit to his baptism L3:8 Lit fruit worthy of M3:11 Or in N3:11 Baptism was the means by which repentance was expressed publicly.

powerful than I. I am not worthy to remove[A] His sandals. He Himself will baptize you with[B] the Holy Spirit and fire. [12]His winnowing shovel[C] is in His hand, and He will clear His threshing floor and gather His wheat into the barn. But the chaff He will burn up with fire that never goes out."

[13]Then Jesus came from Galilee to John at the Jordan, to be baptized by him. [14]But John tried to stop Him, saying, "I need to be baptized by You, and yet You come to me?" [15]Jesus answered him, "Allow it for now, because this is the way for us to fulfill all righteousness." Then he allowed Him to be baptized.

[16]After Jesus was baptized, He went up immediately from the water. The heavens suddenly opened for Him,[D] and He saw the Spirit of God descending like a dove and coming down on Him. [17]And there came a voice from heaven:

This is My beloved Son.
I take delight in Him!

4 Then Jesus was led up by the Spirit into the wilderness to be tempted by the Devil. [2]After He had fasted 40 days and 40 nights, He was hungry. [3]Then the tempter approached Him and said, "If You are the Son of God, tell these stones to become bread."

[4]But He answered, "It is written:

Man must not live on bread alone
but on every word that comes
from the mouth of God."[E]

[5]Then the Devil took Him to the holy city,[F] had Him stand on the pinnacle of the temple, [6]and said to Him, "If You are the Son of God, throw Yourself down. For it is written:

He will give His angels orders
concerning you,
and they will support you
with their hands
so that you will not strike
your foot against a stone."[G]

[7]Jesus told him, "It is also written: Do not test the Lord your God."[H]

[8]Again, the Devil took Him to a very high mountain and showed Him all the kingdoms of the world and their splendor. [9]And he said to Him, "I will give You all these things if You will fall down and worship me."[I]

[10]Then Jesus told him, "Go away,[J] Satan! For it is written:

Worship the Lord your God,
and serve only Him."[K]

[11]Then the Devil left Him, and immediately angels came and began to serve Him.

[12]When He heard that John had been arrested, He withdrew into Galilee. [13]He left Nazareth behind and went to live in Capernaum by the sea, in the region of Zebulun and Naphtali. [14]This was to fulfill what was spoken through the prophet Isaiah:

[15]   Land of Zebulun and land of Naphtali,
       along the sea road, beyond the Jordan,
       Galilee of the Gentiles!
[16]   The people who live in darkness
       have seen a great light,
       and for those living in the shadowland
           of death,
       light has dawned.[L,M]

[17]From then on Jesus began to preach, "Repent, because the kingdom of heaven has come near!"

[18]As He was walking along the Sea of Galilee, He saw two brothers, Simon, who was called Peter, and his brother Andrew. They were casting a net into the sea, since they were fishermen. [19]"Follow Me," He told them, "and I will make you fish for[N] people!" [20]Immediately they left their nets and followed Him.

[21]Going on from there, He saw two other brothers, James the son of Zebedee, and his brother John. They were in a boat with Zebedee their father, mending their nets, and He called them. [22]Immediately they left the boat and their father and followed Him.

[23]Jesus was going all over Galilee, teaching in their synagogues, preaching the good news of the kingdom, and healing every[O] disease and sickness among the people. [24]Then the news about Him spread throughout Syria. So they brought to Him all those who were afflicted, those suffering from various diseases and intense pains, the demon-possessed, the epileptics, and the paralytics. And He healed them.

[A]3:11 Or to carry   [B]3:11 Or in   [C]3:12 A wooden farm implement used to toss threshed grain into the wind so the lighter chaff would blow away and separate from the heavier grain   [D]3:16 Other mss omit for Him   [E]4:4 Dt 8:3   [F]4:5 = Jerusalem   [G]4:6 Ps 91:11-12   [H]4:7 Dt 6:16   [I]4:9 Or and pay me homage   [J]4:10 Other mss read Get behind Me   [K]4:10 Dt 6:13   [L]4:16 Lit dawned on them   [M]4:15-16 Is 9:1-2   [N]4:19 Lit you fishers of   [O]4:23 Or every kind of

²⁵Large crowds followed Him from Galilee, Decapolis, Jerusalem, Judea, and beyond the Jordan.

5 When He saw the crowds, He went up on the mountain, and after He sat down, His disciples came to Him. ²Then[A] He began to teach them, saying:

³ "The poor in spirit are blessed,
for the kingdom of heaven is theirs.
⁴ Those who mourn are blessed,
for they will be comforted.
⁵ The gentle are blessed,
for they will inherit the earth.
⁶ Those who hunger and thirst
for righteousness are blessed,
for they will be filled.
⁷ The merciful are blessed,
for they will be shown mercy.
⁸ The pure in heart are blessed,
for they will see God.
⁹ The peacemakers are blessed,
for they will be called sons of God.
¹⁰ Those who are persecuted
for righteousness are blessed,
for the kingdom of heaven is theirs.

¹¹"You are blessed when they insult and persecute you and falsely say every kind of evil against you because of Me. ¹²Be glad and rejoice, because your reward is great in heaven. For that is how they persecuted the prophets who were before you.

¹³"You are the salt of the earth. But if the salt should lose its taste, how can it be made salty? It's no longer good for anything but to be thrown out and trampled on by men.

¹⁴"You are the light of the world. A city situated on a hill cannot be hidden. ¹⁵No one lights a lamp and puts it under a basket,[B] but rather on a lampstand, and it gives light for all who are in the house. ¹⁶In the same way, let your light shine[C] before men, so that they may see your good works and give glory to your Father in heaven.

¹⁷"Don't assume that I came to destroy the Law or the Prophets. I did not come to destroy but to fulfill. ¹⁸For I assure you: Until heaven and earth pass away, not the smallest letter[D] or one stroke of a letter will pass from the law

until all things are accomplished. ¹⁹Therefore, whoever breaks one of the least of these commands and teaches people to do so will be called least in the kingdom of heaven. But whoever practices and teaches these commands will be called great in the kingdom of heaven. ²⁰For I tell you, unless your righteousness surpasses that of the scribes and Pharisees, you will never enter the kingdom of heaven.

²¹"You have heard that it was said to our ancestors,[E] Do not murder,[F] and whoever murders will be subject to judgment. ²²But I tell you, everyone who is angry with his brother[G] will be subject to judgment. And whoever says to his brother, 'Fool!'[H] will be subject to the Sanhedrin. But whoever says, 'You moron!' will be subject to hellfire.[I] ²³So if you are offering your gift on the altar, and there you remember that your brother has something against you, ²⁴leave your gift there in front of the altar. First go and be reconciled with your brother, and then come and offer your gift. ²⁵Reach a settlement quickly with your adversary while you're on the way with him, or your adversary will hand you over to the judge, the judge to[J] the officer, and you will be thrown into prison. ²⁶I assure you: You will never get out of there until you have paid the last penny![K]

²⁷"You have heard that it was said, Do not commit adultery.[L] ²⁸But I tell you, everyone who looks at a woman to lust for her has already committed adultery with her in his heart. ²⁹If your right eye causes you to sin, gouge it out and throw it away. For it is better that you lose one of the parts of your body than for your whole body to be thrown into hell. ³⁰And if your right hand causes you to sin, cut it off and throw it away. For it is better that you lose one of the parts of your body than for your whole body to go into hell!

³¹"It was also said, Whoever divorces his wife must give her a written notice of divorce.[M] ³²But I tell you, everyone who divorces his wife, except in a case of sexual immorality,[N] causes her to commit adultery. And whoever marries a divorced woman commits adultery.

³³"Again, you have heard that it was said to our ancestors,[O] You must not break your oath, but you must keep your oaths to the Lord.[P] ³⁴But I tell you, don't take an oath at all: ei-

A5:2 Lit Then opening His mouth   B5:15 A large basket used to measure grain   C5:16 Or way, your light must shine   D5:18 Or not one iota; iota is the smallest letter of the Gk alphabet.   E5:21 Lit to the ancients   F5:21 Ex 20:13; Dt 5:17   G5:22 Other mss add without a cause   H5:22 Lit Raca, an Aram term of abuse similar to "airhead"   I5:22 Lit the gehenna of fire   J5:25 Other mss read judge will hand you over to   K5:26 Lit quadrans, the smallest and least valuable Roman coin, worth ¹/₆₄ of a daily wage   L5:27 Ex 20:14; Dt 5:18   M5:31 Dt 24:1   N5:32 Gk porneia = fornication, or possibly a violation of Jewish marriage laws   O5:33 Lit to the ancients   P5:33 Lv 19:12; Nm 30:2; Dt 23:21

ther by heaven, because it is God's throne; ³⁵or by the earth, because it is His footstool; or by Jerusalem, because it is the city of the great King. ³⁶Neither should you swear by your head, because you cannot make a single hair white or black. ³⁷But let your word 'yes' be 'yes,' and your 'no' be 'no.'ᴬ Anything more than this is from the evil one.

³⁸"You have heard that it was said, **An eye for an eye and a tooth for a tooth.**ᴮ ³⁹But I tell you, don't resistᶜ an evildoer. On the contrary, if anyone slaps you on your right cheek, turn the other to him also. ⁴⁰As for the one who wants to sue you and take away your shirt,ᴰ let him have your coatᴱ as well. ⁴¹And if anyone forcesᶠ you to go one mile, go with him two. ⁴²Give to the one who asks you, and don't turn away from the one who wants to borrow from you.

⁴³"You have heard that it was said, **Love your neighbor**ᴳ and hate your enemy. ⁴⁴But I tell you, love your enemiesᴴ and pray for those whoᴵ persecute you, ⁴⁵so that you may beᴶ sons of your Father in heaven. For He causes His sun to rise on the evil and the good, and sends rain on the righteous and the unrighteous. ⁴⁶For if you love those who love you, what reward will you have? Don't even the tax collectors do the same? ⁴⁷And if you greet only your brothers, what are you doing out of the ordinary?ᴷ Don't even the Gentilesᴸ do the same? ⁴⁸Be perfect, therefore, as your heavenly Father is perfect.

6 "Be careful not to practice your righteousnessᴹ in front of people, to be seen by them. Otherwise, you will have no reward from your Father in heaven. ²So whenever you give to the poor, don't sound a trumpet before you, as the hypocrites do in the synagogues and on the streets, to be applauded by people. I assure you: They've got their reward! ³But when you give to the poor, don't let your left hand know what your right hand is doing, ⁴so that your giving may be in secret. And your Father who sees in secret will reward you.ᴺ

⁵"Whenever you pray, you must not be like the hypocrites, because they love to pray standing in the synagogues and on the street corners to be seen by people. I assure you: They've got their reward! ⁶But when you pray, go into your private room, shut your door, and pray to your Father who is in secret. And your Father who sees in secret will reward you.ᴼ ⁷When you pray, don't babble like the idolaters,ᴾ since they imagine they'll be heard for their many words. ⁸Don't be like them, because your Father knows the things you need before you ask Him.

⁹"Therefore, you should pray like this:

> Our Father in heaven,
> Your name be honored as holy.
> ¹⁰ Your kingdom come.
> Your will be done
> on earth as it is in heaven.
> ¹¹ Give us today our daily bread.ᵠ
> ¹² And forgive us our debts,
> as we also have forgiven
> our debtors.
> ¹³ And do not bring us
> intoᴿ temptation,
> but deliver us from the evil one.ˢ
> [For Yours is the kingdom
> and the power
> and the glory forever. Amen.]ᵀ

¹⁴"For if you forgive people their wrongdoing,ᵁ your heavenly Father will forgive you as well. ¹⁵But if you don't forgive people,ⱽ your Father will not forgive your wrongdoing.ᵁ

¹⁶"Whenever you fast, don't be sad-faced like the hypocrites. For they make their faces unattractiveᵂ so their fasting is obvious to people. I assure you: They've got their reward! ¹⁷But when you fast, put oil on your head, and wash your face, ¹⁸so that you don't show your fasting to people but to your Father who is in secret. And your Father who sees in secret will reward you.ᴼ

¹⁹"Don't collect for yourselves treasuresˣ on earth, where moth and rust destroy and where thieves break in and steal. ²⁰But collect for yourselves treasures in heaven, where neither moth nor rust destroys, and where thieves don't break in and steal. ²¹For where your treasure is, there your heart will be also.

ᴬ**5:37** Say what you mean and mean what you say   ᴮ**5:38** Ex 21:24; Lv 24:20; Dt 19:21   ᶜ**5:39** Or *don't set yourself against,* or *don't retaliate against*   ᴰ**5:40** Lit *tunic;* = inner garment   ᴱ**5:40** Or *garment;* lit *robe;* = outer garment   ᶠ**5:41** Roman soldiers could require people to carry loads for them.   ᴳ**5:43** Lv 19:18   ᴴ**5:44** Other mss add *bless those who curse you, do good to those who hate you,*   ᴵ**5:44** Other mss add *mistreat you and*   ᴶ**5:45** Or *may become,* or *may show yourselves to be*   ᴷ**5:47** Or *doing that is superior;* lit *doing more*   ᴸ**5:47** Other mss read *tax collectors*   ᴹ**6:1** Other mss read *charitable giving*   ᴺ**6:4** Other mss read *will Himself reward you openly*   ᴼ**6:6,18** Other mss add *openly*   ᴾ**6:7** Or *Gentiles, or nations, or heathen, or pagans*   ᵠ**6:11** Or *our necessary bread, our bread for tomorrow*   ᴿ**6:13** Or *do not cause us to come into*   ˢ**6:13** Or *from evil*   ᵀ**6:13** Other mss omit bracketed text   ᵁ**6:14,15** Or *trespasses*   ⱽ**6:15** Other mss add *their wrongdoing*   ᵂ**6:16** Or *unrecognizable,* or *disfigured*   ˣ**6:19** Or *valuables*

²²"The eye is the lamp of the body. If your eye is good, your whole body will be full of light. ²³But if your eye is bad, your whole body will be full of darkness. So if the light within you is darkness—how deep is that darkness!

²⁴"No one can be a slave of two masters, since either he will hate one and love the other, or be devoted to one and despise the other. You cannot be slaves of God and of money.

²⁵"This is why I tell you: Don't worry about your life, what you will eat or what you will drink; or about your body, what you will wear. Isn't life more than food and the body more than clothing? ²⁶Look at the birds of the sky: They don't sow or reap or gather into barns, yet your heavenly Father feeds them. Aren't you worth more than they? ²⁷Can any of you add a single cubit to his height^A by worrying? ²⁸And why do you worry about clothes? Learn how the wildflowers of the field grow: they don't labor or spin thread. ²⁹Yet I tell you that not even Solomon in all his splendor was adorned like one of these! ³⁰If that's how God clothes the grass of the field, which is here today and thrown into the furnace tomorrow, won't He do much more for you—you of little faith? ³¹So don't worry, saying, 'What will we eat?' or 'What will we drink?' or 'What will we wear?' ³²For the idolaters^B eagerly seek all these things, and your heavenly Father knows that you need them. ³³But seek first the kingdom of God^C and His righteousness, and all these things will be provided for you. ³⁴Therefore don't worry about tomorrow, because tomorrow will worry about itself. Each day has enough trouble of its own.

7 "Do not judge, so that you won't be judged. ²For with the judgment you use,^D you will be judged, and with the measure you use,^E it will be measured to you. ³Why do you look at the speck in your brother's eye but don't notice the log in your own eye? ⁴Or how can you say to your brother, 'Let me take the speck out of your eye,' and look, there's a log in your eye? ⁵Hypocrite! First take the log out of your eye, and then you will see clearly to take the speck out of your brother's eye. ⁶Don't give what is holy to dogs or toss your pearls before pigs, or they will trample them with their feet, turn, and tear you to pieces.

⁷"Keep asking,^F and it will be given to you. Keep searching,^G and you will find. Keep knocking,^H and the door^I will be opened to you. ⁸For everyone who asks receives, and the one who searches finds, and to the one who knocks, the door^J will be opened. ⁹What man among you, if his son asks him for bread, will give him a stone? ¹⁰Or if he asks for a fish, will give him a snake? ¹¹If you then, who are evil, know how to give good gifts to your children, how much more will your Father in heaven give good things to those who ask Him! ¹²Therefore, whatever you want others to do for you, do also the same for them—this is the Law and the Prophets.^K

¹³"Enter through the narrow gate. For the gate is wide and the road is broad that leads to destruction, and there are many who go through it. ¹⁴How narrow is the gate and difficult the road that leads to life, and few find it.

¹⁵"Beware of false prophets who come to you in sheep's clothing but inwardly are ravaging wolves. ¹⁶You'll recognize them by their fruit. Are grapes gathered from thornbushes or figs from thistles? ¹⁷In the same way, every good tree produces good fruit, but a bad tree produces bad fruit. ¹⁸A good tree can't produce bad fruit; neither can a bad tree produce good fruit. ¹⁹Every tree that doesn't produce good fruit is cut down and thrown into the fire. ²⁰So you'll recognize them by their fruit.

²¹"Not everyone who says to Me, 'Lord, Lord!' will enter the kingdom of heaven, but only the one who does the will of My Father in heaven. ²²On that day many will say to Me, 'Lord, Lord, didn't we prophesy in Your name, drive out demons in Your name, and do many miracles in Your name?' ²³Then I will announce to them, 'I never knew you! Depart from Me, you lawbreakers!'^LM

²⁴"Therefore, everyone who hears these words of Mine and acts on them will be like a sensible man who built his house on the rock. ²⁵The rain fell, the rivers rose, and the winds blew and pounded that house. Yet it didn't collapse, because its foundation was on the rock. ²⁶But everyone who hears these words of Mine and doesn't act on them will be like a foolish man who built his house on the sand. ²⁷The rain fell, the rivers rose, the winds blew and

^A6:27 Or add one moment to his life-span   ^B6:32 Or Gentiles, or nations, or heathen, or pagans   ^C6:33 Other mss omit of God   ^D7:2 Lit you judge   ^E7:2 Lit you measure   ^F7:7 Or Ask   ^G7:7 Or Search   ^H7:7 Or Knock   ^I7:7 Lit and it   ^J7:8 Lit knocks, it   ^K7:12 When capitalized, the Law and the Prophets = the OT   ^L7:23 Lit you who work lawlessness   ^M7:23 Ps 6:8

pounded that house, and it collapsed. And its collapse was great!"

²⁸When Jesus had finished this sermon,ᴬ the crowds were astonished at His teaching, ²⁹because He was teaching them like one who had authority, and not like their scribes.

8 When He came down from the mountain, large crowds followed Him. ²Right away a man with a serious skin disease came up and knelt before Him, saying, "Lord, if You are willing, You can make me clean."

³Reaching out His hand He touched him, saying, "I am willing; be made clean." Immediately his disease was healed.ᴮ ⁴Then Jesus told him, "See that you don't tell anyone; but go, show yourself to the priest, and offer the gift that Moses prescribed, as a testimony to them."

⁵When He entered Capernaum, a centurion came to Him, pleading with Him, ⁶"Lord, my servant is lying at home paralyzed, in terrible agony!"

⁷"I will come and heal him," He told him.

⁸"Lord," the centurion replied, "I am not worthy to have You come under my roof. But only say the word, and my servant will be cured. ⁹For I too am a man under authority, having soldiers under my command.ᶜ I say to this one, 'Go!' and he goes; and to another, 'Come!' and he comes; and to my slave, 'Do this!' and he does it."

¹⁰Hearing this, Jesus was amazed and said to those following Him, "I assure you: I have not found anyone in Israel with so great a faith! ¹¹I tell you that many will come from east and west, and recline at the table with Abraham, Isaac, and Jacob in the kingdom of heaven. ¹²But the sons of the kingdom will be thrown into the outer darkness. In that place there will be weeping and gnashing of teeth." ¹³Then Jesus told the centurion, "Go. As you have believed, let it be done for you." And his servant was cured that very moment.ᴰ

¹⁴When Jesus went into Peter's house, He saw his mother-in-law lying in bed with a fever. ¹⁵So He touched her hand, and the fever left her. Then she got up and began to serve Him. ¹⁶When evening came, they brought to Him many who were demon-possessed. He drove out the spirits with a word and healed all who

were sick, ¹⁷so that what was spoken through the prophet Isaiah might be fulfilled:

He Himself took our weaknesses and carried our diseases.ᴱ

¹⁸When Jesus saw large crowdsᶠ around Him, He gave the order to go to the other side of the sea.ᴳ ¹⁹A scribe approached Him and said, "Teacher, I will follow You wherever You go!"

²⁰Jesus told him, "Foxes have dens and birds of the sky have nests, but the Son of Man has no place to lay His head."

²¹"Lord," another of His disciples said, "first let me go bury my father."ᴴ

²²But Jesus told him, "Follow Me, and let the dead bury their own dead."

²³As He got into theᴵ boat, His disciples followed Him. ²⁴Suddenly, a violent storm arose on the sea, so that the boat was being swamped by the waves. But He was sleeping. ²⁵So the disciples came and woke Him up, saying, "Lord, save us! We're going to die!"

²⁶But He said to them, "Why are you fearful, you of little faith?" Then He got up and rebuked the winds and the sea. And there was a great calm.

²⁷The men were amazed and asked, "What kind of man is this?—even the winds and the sea obey Him!"

²⁸When He had come to the other side, to the region of the Gadarenes,ᴶ two demon-possessed men met Him as they came out of the tombs. They were so violent that no one could pass that way. ²⁹Suddenly they shouted, "What do You have to do with us,ᴷ,ᴸ Son of God? Have You come here to torment us before the time?"

³⁰Now a long way off from them, a large herd of pigs was feeding. ³¹"If You drive us out," the demons begged Him, "send us into the herd of pigs."

³²"Go!" He told them. So when they had come out, they entered the pigs. And suddenly the whole herd rushed down the steep bank into the sea and perished in the water. ³³Then the men who tended them fled. They went into the city and reported everything—especially what had happened to those who were demon-possessed. ³⁴At that, the whole town went

ᴬ7:28 Lit had ended these words   ᴮ8:3 Lit cleansed   ᶜ8:9 Lit under me   ᴰ8:13 Or that hour; lit very hour   ᴱ8:17 Is 53:4   ᶠ8:18 Other mss read saw a crowd   ᴳ8:18 = Sea of Galilee   ᴴ8:21 Not necessarily meaning his father was already dead   ᴵ8:23 Other mss read to a   ᴶ8:28 Other mss read Gergesenes   ᴷ8:29 Other mss add Jesus   ᴸ8:29 Lit What to us and to You out to meet Jesus. When they saw Him, they begged Him to leave their region.

9 So He got into a boat, crossed over, and came to His own town. [2]Just then some men[A] brought to Him a paralytic lying on a mat. Seeing their faith, Jesus told the paralytic, "Have courage, son, your sins are forgiven."

[3]At this, some of the scribes said among themselves, "He's blaspheming!"

[4]But perceiving their thoughts, Jesus said, "Why are you thinking evil things in your hearts?[B] [5]For which is easier: to say, 'Your sins are forgiven,' or to say, 'Get up and walk'? [6]But so you may know that the Son of Man has authority on earth to forgive sins"—then He told the paralytic, "Get up, pick up your mat, and go home." [7]And he got up and went home. [8]When the crowds saw this, they were awestruck[C,D] and gave glory to God who had given such authority to men.

[9]As Jesus went on from there, He saw a man named Matthew sitting at the tax office, and He said to him, "Follow Me!" So he got up and followed Him.

[10]While He was reclining at the table in the house, many tax collectors and sinners came as guests to eat[E] with Jesus and His disciples. [11]When the Pharisees saw this, they asked His disciples, "Why does your Teacher eat with tax collectors and sinners?"

[12]But when He heard this, He said, "Those who are well don't need a doctor, but the sick do. [13]Go and learn what this means: I desire mercy and not sacrifice.[F] For I didn't come to call the righteous, but sinners."[G]

[14]Then John's disciples came to Him, saying, "Why do we and the Pharisees fast often, but Your disciples do not fast?"

[15]Jesus said to them, "Can the wedding guests[H] be sad while the groom is with them? The time[I] will come when the groom will be taken away from them, and then they will fast. [16]No one patches an old garment with unshrunk cloth, because the patch pulls away from the garment and makes the tear worse. [17]And no one puts[J] new wine into old wineskins. Otherwise, the skins burst, the wine spills out, and the skins are ruined. But they put new wine into fresh wineskins, and both are preserved."

[18]As He was telling them these things, suddenly one of the leaders[K] came and knelt down before Him, saying, "My daughter is near death,[L] but come and lay Your hand on her, and she will live." [19]So Jesus and His disciples got up and followed him.

[20]Just then, a woman who had suffered from bleeding for 12 years approached from behind and touched the tassel on His robe, [21]for she said to herself, "If I can just touch His robe, I'll be made well!"[M]

[22]But Jesus turned and saw her. "Have courage, daughter," He said. "Your faith has made you well."[N] And the woman was made well from that moment.[O]

[23]When Jesus came to the leader's house, He saw the flute players and a crowd lamenting loudly. [24]"Leave," He said, "because the girl isn't dead, but sleeping." And they started laughing at Him. [25]But when the crowd had been put outside, He went in and took her by the hand, and the girl got up. [26]And this news spread throughout that whole area.

[27]As Jesus went on from there, two blind men followed Him, shouting, "Have mercy on us, Son of David!"

[28]When He entered the house, the blind men approached Him, and Jesus said to them, "Do you believe that I can do this?"

"Yes, Lord," they answered Him.

[29]Then He touched their eyes, saying, "Let it be done for you according to your faith!" [30]And their eyes were opened. Then Jesus warned them sternly, "Be sure that no one finds out!"[P] [31]But they went out and spread the news about Him throughout that whole area.

[32]Just as they were going out, a demon-possessed man who was unable to speak was brought to Him. [33]When the demon had been driven out, the man[Q] spoke. And the crowds were amazed, saying, "Nothing like this has ever been seen in Israel!"

[34]But the Pharisees said, "He drives out demons by the ruler of the demons!"

[35]Then Jesus went to all the towns and villages, teaching in their synagogues, preaching the good news of the kingdom, and healing every[R] disease and every sickness.[S] [36]When He saw the crowds, He felt compassion for them, because they were weary and worn out, like

A9:2 Lit then they B9:4 Or minds C9:8 Other mss read amazed D9:8 Lit afraid E9:10 Lit came, they were reclining (at the table); at important meals the custom was to recline on a mat at a low table and lean on the left elbow. F9:13 Hs 6:6 G9:13 Other mss add to repentance H9:15 Lit the sons of the bridal chamber I9:15 Lit days J9:17 Lit And they do not put K9:18 A leader of a synagogue; Mk 5:22 L9:18 Lit daughter has now come to the end M9:21 Or be delivered N9:22 Or has saved you O9:22 Lit hour P9:30 Lit no one knows Q9:33 Lit the man who was unable to speak R9:35 Or every kind of S9:35 Other mss add among the people sheep without a shepherd. [37] Then He said to His disciples, "The harvest is abundant, but the workers are few. [38] Therefore, pray to the Lord of the harvest to send out workers into His harvest."

10 Summoning His 12 disciples, He gave them authority over unclean spirits, to drive them out and to heal every[A] disease and sickness. [2] These are the names of the 12 apostles:

First, Simon, who is called Peter,
and Andrew his brother;
James the son of Zebedee,
and John his brother;
[3] Philip and Bartholomew;[B]
Thomas and Matthew
the tax collector;
James the son of Alphaeus,
and Thaddaeus;[C]
[4] Simon the Zealot,[D] and Judas Iscariot,[E]
who also betrayed Him.

[5] Jesus sent out these 12 after giving them instructions: "Don't take the road leading to other nations, and don't enter any Samaritan town. [6] Instead, go to the lost sheep of the house of Israel. [7] As you go, announce this: 'The kingdom of heaven has come near.' [8] Heal the sick, raise the dead, cleanse those with skin diseases, drive out demons. You have received free of charge; give free of charge. [9] Don't take along gold, silver, or copper for your moneybelts. [10] Don't take a traveling bag for the road, or an extra shirt, sandals, or a walking stick, for the worker is worthy of his food.

[11] "When you enter any town or village, find out who is worthy, and stay there until you leave. [12] Greet a household when you enter it, [13] and if the household is worthy, let your peace be on it. But if it is unworthy, let your peace return to you. [14] If anyone will not welcome you or listen to your words, shake the dust off your feet when you leave that house or town. [15] I assure you: It will be more tolerable on the day of judgment for the land of Sodom and Gomorrah than for that town.

[16] "Look, I'm sending you out like sheep among wolves. Therefore be as shrewd as serpents and as harmless as doves. [17] Because people will hand you over to sanhedrins[F] and flog you in their synagogues, beware of them. [18] You will even be brought before governors and kings because of Me, to bear witness to them and to the nations. [19] But when they hand you over, don't worry about how or what you should speak. For you will be given what to say at that hour, [20] because you are not speaking, but the Spirit of your Father is speaking through you.

[21] "Brother will betray brother to death, and a father his child. Children will even rise up against their parents and have them put to death. [22] You will be hated by everyone because of My name. But the one who endures to the end will be delivered.[G] [23] When they persecute you in one town, escape to another. For I assure you: You will not have covered the towns of Israel before the Son of Man comes. [24] A disciple[H] is not above his teacher, or a slave above his master. [25] It is enough for a disciple to become like his teacher and a slave like his master. If they called the head of the house 'Beelzebul,' how much more the members of his household!

[26] "Therefore, don't be afraid of them, since there is nothing covered that won't be uncovered and nothing hidden that won't be made known. [27] What I tell you in the dark, speak in the light. What you hear in a whisper,[I] proclaim on the housetops. [28] Don't fear those who kill the body but are not able to kill the soul; rather, fear Him who is able to destroy both soul and body in hell. [29] Aren't two sparrows sold for a penny?[J] Yet not one of them falls to the ground without your Father's consent.[K] [30] But even the hairs of your head have all been counted. [31] So don't be afraid therefore; you are worth more than many sparrows.

[32] "Therefore, everyone who will acknowledge Me before men, I will also acknowledge him before My Father in heaven. [33] But whoever denies Me before men, I will also deny him before My Father in heaven. [34] Don't assume that I came to bring peace on the earth. I did not come to bring peace, but a sword. [35] For I came to turn

a man against his father,
a daughter against her mother,

A[10:1] Or every kind of   B[10:3] Probably the Nathanael of Jn 1:45-51   C[10:3] Other mss read and Lebbaeus, whose surname was Thaddaeus   D[10:4] Lit the Cananaean   E[10:4] Iscariot is probably "a man of Kerioth," a town in Judea.   F[10:17] Local Jewish courts or local councils   G[10:22] Or saved   H[10:24] Or student   I[10:27] Lit in the ear   J[10:29] Gk assarion, a small copper coin   K[10:29] Lit ground apart from your Father

a daughter-in-law against
her mother-in-law;
³⁶ and a man's enemies will be
the members of his household.^A

³⁷ The person who loves father or mother more than Me is not worthy of Me; the person who loves son or daughter more than Me is not worthy of Me. ³⁸ And whoever doesn't take up his cross and follow^B Me is not worthy of Me. ³⁹ Anyone finding^C his life will lose it, and anyone losing^D his life because of Me will find it.

⁴⁰ "The one who welcomes you welcomes Me, and the one who welcomes Me welcomes Him who sent Me. ⁴¹ Anyone who^E welcomes a prophet because he is a prophet^F will receive a prophet's reward. And anyone who^G welcomes a righteous person because he's righteous^H will receive a righteous person's reward. ⁴² And whoever gives just a cup of cold water to one of these little ones because he is a disciple^I—I assure you: He will never lose his reward!"

11 When Jesus had finished giving orders to His 12 disciples, He moved on from there to teach and preach in their towns. ² When John heard in prison what the Messiah was doing, he sent a message by his disciples ³ and asked Him, "Are You the One who is to come, or should we expect someone else?"

⁴ Jesus replied to them, "Go and report to John what you hear and see: ⁵ the blind see, the lame walk, those with skin diseases are healed,^J the deaf hear, the dead are raised, and the poor are told the good news. ⁶ And if anyone is not offended because of Me, he is blessed."

⁷ As these men went away, Jesus began to speak to the crowds about John: "What did you go out into the wilderness to see? A reed swaying in the wind? ⁸ What then did you go out to see? A man dressed in soft clothes? Look, those who wear soft clothes are in kings' palaces. ⁹ But what did you go out to see? A prophet? Yes, I tell you, and far more than a prophet. ¹⁰ This is the one it is written about:

Look, I am sending My messenger
ahead of You;^K
he will prepare Your way before You.^L

¹¹ "I assure you: Among those born of women no one greater than John the Baptist has appeared,^M but the least in the kingdom of heaven is greater than he. ¹² From the days of John the Baptist until now, the kingdom of heaven has been suffering violence,^N and the violent have been seizing it by force. ¹³ For all the prophets and the Law prophesied until John; ¹⁴ if you're willing to accept it, he is the Elijah who is to come. ¹⁵ Anyone who has ears^O should listen!

¹⁶ "To what should I compare this generation? It's like children sitting in the marketplaces who call out to each other:

¹⁷ We played the flute for you,
but you didn't dance;
we sang a lament,
but you didn't mourn!^P

¹⁸ For John did not come eating or drinking, and they say, 'He has a demon!' ¹⁹ The Son of Man came eating and drinking, and they say, 'Look, a glutton and a drunkard, a friend of tax collectors and sinners!' Yet wisdom is vindicated^Q by her deeds."^R

²⁰ Then He proceeded to denounce the towns where most of His miracles were done, because they did not repent: ²¹ "Woe to you, Chorazin! Woe to you, Bethsaida! For if the miracles that were done in you had been done in Tyre and Sidon, they would have repented in sackcloth and ashes long ago! ²² But I tell you, it will be more tolerable for Tyre and Sidon on the day of judgment than for you. ²³ And you, Capernaum, will you be exalted to heaven? You will go down to Hades. For if the miracles that were done in you had been done in Sodom, it would have remained until today. ²⁴ But I tell you, it will be more tolerable for the land of Sodom on the day of judgment than for you."

²⁵ At that time Jesus said, "I praise^S You, Father, Lord of heaven and earth, because You have hidden these things from the wise and learned and revealed them to infants. ²⁶ Yes, Father, because this was Your good pleasure.^T ²⁷ All things have been entrusted to Me by My Father. No one knows^U the Son except the Father, and no one knows the Father except the

Son and anyone to whom the Son desires[A] to reveal Him.

[28]"Come to Me, all of you who are weary and burdened, and I will give you rest. [29]All of you, take up My yoke and learn from Me, because I am gentle and humble in heart, and you will find rest for yourselves. [30]For My yoke is easy and My burden is light."

12 At that time Jesus passed through the grainfields on the Sabbath. His disciples were hungry and began to pick and eat some heads of grain. [2]But when the Pharisees saw it, they said to Him, "Look, Your disciples are doing what is not lawful to do on the Sabbath!"

[3]He said to them, "Haven't you read what David did when he and those who were with him were hungry— [4]how he entered the house of God, and they ate[B] the sacred bread, which is not lawful for him or for those with him to eat, but only for the priests? [5]Or haven't you read in the Law[C] that on Sabbath days the priests in the temple violate the Sabbath and are innocent? [6]But I tell you that something greater than the temple is here! [7]If you had known what this means: I desire mercy and not sacrifice,[D] you would not have condemned the innocent. [8]For the Son of Man is Lord of the Sabbath."

[9]Moving on from there, He entered their synagogue. [10]There He saw a man who had a paralyzed hand. And in order to accuse Him they asked Him, "Is it lawful to heal on the Sabbath?"

[11]But He said to them, "What man among you, if he had a sheep[E] that fell into a pit on the Sabbath, wouldn't take hold of it and lift it out? [12]A man is worth far more than a sheep, so it is lawful to do what is good on the Sabbath."

[13]Then He told the man, "Stretch out your hand." So he stretched it out, and it was restored, as good as the other. [14]But the Pharisees went out and plotted against Him, how they might destroy Him.

[15]When Jesus became aware of this, He withdrew from there. Huge crowds[F] followed Him, and He healed them all. [16]He warned them not to make Him known, [17]so that what was spoken through the prophet Isaiah might be fulfilled:

[18]   **Here is My Servant**
        whom I have chosen,

My beloved in whom My soul delights;
I will put My Spirit on Him,
and He will proclaim justice
**   to the nations.**
[19] **He will not argue or shout,**
      and no one will hear His voice
      in the streets.
[20] **He will not break a bruised reed,**
      and He will not put out
      a smoldering wick,
      until He has led justice to victory.[G]
[21] **The nations will put their hope**
      in His name.[H]

[22]Then a demon-possessed man who was blind and unable to speak was brought to Him. He healed him, so that the man[I] could both speak and see. [23]And all the crowds were astounded and said, "Perhaps this is the Son of David!"

[24]When the Pharisees heard this, they said, "The man drives out demons only by Beelzebul, the ruler of the demons."

[25]Knowing their thoughts, He told them: "Every kingdom divided against itself is headed for destruction, and no city or house divided against itself will stand. [26]If Satan drives out Satan, he is divided against himself. How then will his kingdom stand? [27]And if I drive out demons by Beelzebul, who is it your sons drive them out by? For this reason they will be your judges. [28]If I drive out demons by the Spirit of God, then the kingdom of God has come to you. [29]How can someone enter a strong man's house and steal his possessions unless he first ties up the strong man? Then he can rob his house. [30]Anyone who is not with Me is against Me, and anyone who does not gather with Me scatters. [31]Because of this, I tell you, people will be forgiven every sin and blasphemy, but the blasphemy against[J] the Spirit will not be forgiven.[K] [32]Whoever speaks a word against the Son of Man, it will be forgiven him. But whoever speaks against the Holy Spirit, it will not be forgiven him, either in this age or in the one to come.

[33]"Either make the tree good and its fruit good, or make the tree bad[L] and its fruit bad; for a tree is known by its fruit. [34]Brood of vipers! How can you speak good things when you are evil? For the mouth speaks from the overflow of the heart. [35]A good man produces

good things from his storeroom of good,[A] and an evil man produces evil things from his storeroom of evil. [36]I tell you that on the day of judgment people will have to account for every careless word they speak.[B] [37]For by your words you will be acquitted, and by your words you will be condemned."

[38]Then some of the scribes and Pharisees said to Him, "Teacher, we want to see a sign from You."

[39]But He answered them, "An evil and adulterous generation demands a sign, but no sign will be given to it except the sign of the prophet Jonah. [40]For as Jonah was in the belly of the huge fish three days and three nights, so the Son of Man will be in the heart of the earth three days and three nights. [41]The men of Nineveh will stand up at the judgment with this generation and condemn it, because they repented at Jonah's proclamation; and look—something greater than Jonah is here! [42]The queen of the south will rise up at the judgment with this generation and condemn it, because she came from the ends of the earth to hear the wisdom of Solomon; and look—something greater than Solomon is here!

[43]"When an unclean spirit comes out of a man, it roams through waterless places looking for rest but doesn't find any. [44]Then it says, 'I'll go back to my house that I came from.' And returning, it finds the house vacant, swept, and put in order. [45]Then off it goes and brings with it seven other spirits more evil than itself, and they enter and settle down there. As a result, that man's last condition is worse than the first. That's how it will also be with this evil generation."

[46]He was still speaking to the crowds when suddenly His mother and brothers were standing outside wanting to speak to Him. [47]Someone told Him, "Look, Your mother and Your brothers are standing outside, wanting to speak to You."[C]

[48]But He replied to the one who told Him, "Who is My mother and who are My brothers?" [49]And stretching out His hand toward His disciples, He said, "Here are My mother and My brothers! [50]For whoever does the will of My Father in heaven, that person is My brother and sister and mother."

13 On that day Jesus went out of the house and was sitting by the sea. [2]Such large crowds gathered around Him that He got into a boat and sat down, while the whole crowd stood on the shore.

[3]Then He told them many things in parables, saying: "Consider the sower who went out to sow. [4]As he was sowing, some seed fell along the path, and the birds came and ate them up. [5]Others fell on rocky ground, where there wasn't much soil, and they sprang up quickly since the soil wasn't deep. [6]But when the sun came up they were scorched, and since they had no root, they withered. [7]Others fell among thorns, and the thorns came up and choked them. [8]Still others fell on good ground and produced a crop: some 100, some 60, and some 30 times what was sown. [9]Anyone who has ears[D] should listen!"

[10]Then the disciples came up and asked Him, "Why do You speak to them in parables?"

[11]He answered them, "Because the secrets of the kingdom of heaven have been given for you to know, but it has not been given to them. [12]For whoever has, more will be given to him, and he will have more than enough. But whoever does not have, even what he has will be taken away from him. [13]For this reason I speak to them in parables, because looking they do not see, and hearing they do not listen or understand. [14]Isaiah's prophecy is fulfilled in them, which says:

> You will listen and listen,
> yet never understand;
> and you will look and look,
> yet never perceive.
> [15] For this people's heart
> has grown callous;
> their ears are hard of hearing,
> and they have shut their eyes;
> otherwise they might see
> with their eyes
> and hear with their ears,
> understand with their hearts
> and turn back—
> and I would cure them.[E]

[16]"But your eyes are blessed because they do see, and your ears because they do hear! [17]For I assure you: Many prophets and righteous people longed to see the things you see yet

A12:35 Other mss read *from the storehouse of his heart* B12:36 Lit *will speak* C12:47 Other mss omit this v. D13:9 Other mss add *to hear* E13:14-15 Is 6:9-10 didn't see them; to hear the things you hear yet didn't hear them.

¹⁸"You, then, listen to the parable of the sower: ¹⁹When anyone hears the word^A about the kingdom and doesn't understand it, the evil one comes and snatches away what was sown in his heart. This is the one sown along the path. ²⁰And the one sown on rocky ground—this is one who hears the word and immediately receives it with joy. ²¹Yet he has no root in himself, but is short-lived. When pressure or persecution comes because of the word, immediately he stumbles. ²²Now the one sown among the thorns—this is one who hears the word, but the worries of this age and the seduction^B of wealth choke the word, and it becomes unfruitful. ²³But the one sown on the good ground—this is one who hears and understands the word, who does bear fruit and yields: some 100, some 60, some 30 times what was sown."

²⁴He presented another parable to them: "The kingdom of heaven may be compared to a man who sowed good seed in his field. ²⁵But while people were sleeping, his enemy came, sowed weeds^C among the wheat, and left. ²⁶When the plants sprouted and produced grain, then the weeds also appeared. ²⁷The landowner's slaves came to him and said, 'Master, didn't you sow good seed in your field? Then where did the weeds come from?'

²⁸"'An enemy did this!' he told them.

"'So, do you want us to go and gather them up?' the slaves asked him.

²⁹"'No,' he said. 'When you gather up the weeds, you might also uproot the wheat with them. ³⁰Let both grow together until the harvest. At harvest time I'll tell the reapers: Gather the weeds first and tie them in bundles to burn them, but store the wheat in my barn.'"

³¹He presented another parable to them: "The kingdom of heaven is like a mustard seed that a man took and sowed in his field. ³²It's the smallest of all the seeds, but when grown, it's taller than the vegetables and becomes a tree, so that the birds of the sky come and nest in its branches."

³³He told them another parable: "The kingdom of heaven is like yeast that a woman took and mixed into 50 pounds^D of flour until it spread through all of it."^E

³⁴Jesus told the crowds all these things in parables, and He would not speak anything to them without a parable, ³⁵so that what was spoken through the prophet might be fulfilled:

> I will open My mouth in parables;
> I will declare things kept secret
> from the foundation of the world.^F

³⁶Then He dismissed the crowds and went into the house. His disciples approached Him and said, "Explain the parable of the weeds in the field to us."

³⁷He replied: "The One who sows the good seed is the Son of Man; ³⁸the field is the world; and the good seed—these are the sons of the kingdom. The weeds are the sons of the evil one, ³⁹and the enemy who sowed them is the Devil. The harvest is the end of the age, and the harvesters are angels. ⁴⁰Therefore, just as the weeds are gathered and burned in the fire, so it will be at the end of the age. ⁴¹The Son of Man will send out His angels, and they will gather from His kingdom everything that causes sin^G and those guilty of lawlessness.^H ⁴²They will throw them into the blazing furnace where there will be weeping and gnashing of teeth. ⁴³Then the righteous will shine like the sun in their Father's kingdom. Anyone who has ears^I should listen!

⁴⁴"The kingdom of heaven is like treasure, buried in a field, that a man found and reburied. Then in his joy he goes and sells everything he has and buys that field.

⁴⁵"Again, the kingdom of heaven is like a merchant in search of fine pearls. ⁴⁶When he found one priceless^J pearl, he went and sold everything he had, and bought it.

⁴⁷"Again, the kingdom of heaven is like a large net thrown into the sea. It collected every kind of fish, ⁴⁸and when it was full, they dragged it ashore, sat down, and gathered the good fish into containers, but threw out the worthless ones. ⁴⁹So it will be at the end of the age. The angels will go out, separate the evil people from the righteous, ⁵⁰and throw them into the blazing furnace. In that place there will be weeping and gnashing of teeth.

⁵¹"Have you understood all these things?"^K "Yes," they told Him.

---

^A13:19 Gk *logos* = *word*, or *message*, or *saying*, or *thing*   ^B13:22 Or *pleasure*, or *deceitfulness*   ^C13:25 Or *darnel*, a weed similar in appearance to wheat in the early stages   ^D13:33 Lit *3 sata*; about 40 quarts   ^E13:33 Or *until all of it was leavened*   ^F13:35 Ps 78:2   ^G13:41 Or *stumbling*   ^H13:41 Or *those who do lawlessness*   ^I13:43 Other mss add *to hear*   ^J13:46 Or *very precious*   ^K13:51 Other mss add *Jesus asked them*

⁵²"Therefore," He said to them, "every student of Scripture^A instructed in the kingdom of heaven is like a landowner who brings out of his storeroom what is new and what is old." ⁵³When Jesus had finished these parables, He left there.

⁵⁴He went to His hometown and began to teach them in their synagogue, so that they were astonished and said, "How did this wisdom and these miracles come to Him? ⁵⁵Isn't this the carpenter's son? Isn't His mother called Mary, and His brothers James, Joseph,^B Simon, and Judas? ⁵⁶And His sisters, aren't they all with us? So where does He get all these things?" ⁵⁷And they were offended by Him.

But Jesus said to them, "A prophet is not without honor except in his hometown and in his household." ⁵⁸And He did not do many miracles there because of their unbelief.

14 At that time Herod the tetrarch heard the report about Jesus. ²"This is John the Baptist!" he told his servants. "He has been raised from the dead, and that's why supernatural powers are at work in him."

³For Herod had arrested John, chained^C him, and put him in prison on account of Herodias, his brother Philip's wife, ⁴since John had been telling him, "It's not lawful for you to have her!" ⁵Though he wanted to kill him, he feared the crowd, since they regarded him as a prophet.

⁶But when Herod's birthday celebration came, Herodias's daughter danced before them^D and pleased Herod. ⁷So he promised with an oath to give her whatever she might ask. ⁸And prompted by her mother, she answered, "Give me John the Baptist's head here on a platter!" ⁹Although the king regretted it, he commanded that it be granted because of his oaths and his guests. ¹⁰So he sent orders and had John beheaded in the prison. ¹¹His head was brought on a platter and given to the girl, who carried it to her mother. ¹²Then his disciples came, removed the corpse,^E buried it, and went and reported to Jesus.

¹³When Jesus heard about it, He withdrew from there by boat to a remote place to be alone. When the crowds heard this, they followed Him on foot from the towns. ¹⁴As He stepped ashore,^F He saw a huge crowd, felt compassion for them, and healed their sick.

¹⁵When evening came, the disciples approached Him and said, "This place is a wilderness, and it is already late.^G Send the crowds away so they can go into the villages and buy food for themselves."

¹⁶"They don't need to go away," Jesus told them. "You give them something to eat."

¹⁷"But we only have five loaves and two fish here," they said to Him.

¹⁸"Bring them here to Me," He said. ¹⁹Then He commanded the crowds to sit down^H on the grass. He took the five loaves and the two fish, and looking up to heaven, He blessed them. He broke the loaves and gave them to the disciples, and the disciples gave them to the crowds. ²⁰Everyone ate and was filled. Then they picked up 12 baskets full of leftover pieces! ²¹Now those who ate were about 5,000 men, besides women and children.

²²Immediately He^I made the disciples get into the boat and go ahead of Him to the other side, while He dismissed the crowds. ²³After dismissing the crowds, He went up on the mountain by Himself to pray. When evening came, He was there alone. ²⁴But the boat was already over a mile^J from land,^K battered by the waves, because the wind was against them. ²⁵Around three in the morning,^L He came toward them walking on the sea. ²⁶When the disciples saw Him walking on the sea, they were terrified. "It's a ghost!" they said, and cried out in fear.

²⁷Immediately Jesus spoke to them. "Have courage! It is I. Don't be afraid."

²⁸"Lord, if it's You," Peter answered Him, "command me to come to You on the water."

²⁹"Come!" He said.

And climbing out of the boat, Peter started walking on the water and came toward Jesus. ³⁰But when he saw the strength of the wind,^M he was afraid. And beginning to sink he cried out, "Lord, save me!"

³¹Immediately Jesus reached out His hand, caught hold of him, and said to him, "You of little faith, why did you doubt?" ³²When they got into the boat, the wind ceased. ³³Then those in the boat worshiped Him and said, "Truly You are the Son of God!"

A13:52 Or every scribe   **B13:55** Other mss read Joses; Mk 6:3   **C14:3** Or bound   **D14:6** Lit danced in the middle   **E14:12** Other mss read body   **F14:14** Lit Coming out (of the boat)   **G14:15** Lit and the time (for the evening meal) has already passed   **H14:19** Lit to recline   **I14:22** Other mss read Jesus   **J14:24** Lit already many stadia; 1 stadion = 600 feet   **K14:24** Other mss read already in the middle of the sea   **L14:25** Lit fourth watch of the night = 3 to 6 a.m.   **M14:30** Other mss read saw the wind

³⁴Once they crossed over, they came to land at Gennesaret. ³⁵When the men of that place recognized Him, they alerted[A] the whole vicinity and brought to Him all who were sick. ³⁶They were begging Him that they might only touch the tassel on His robe. And as many as touched it were made perfectly well.

15 Then Pharisees and scribes came from Jerusalem to Jesus and asked, ²"Why do Your disciples break the tradition of the elders? For they don't wash their hands when they eat!"[B]

³He answered them, "And why do you break God's commandment because of your tradition? ⁴For God said:[C]

Honor your father
　and your mother;[D] and,
The one who speaks evil of father
　or mother
　must be put to death.[E]

⁵But you say, 'Whoever tells his father or mother, "Whatever benefit you might have received from me is a gift committed to the temple"— ⁶he does not have to honor his father.'[F] In this way, you have revoked God's word[G] because of your tradition. ⁷Hypocrites! Isaiah prophesied correctly about you when he said:

8　These people[H] honor Me with their lips,
　　but their heart is far from Me.
9　They worship Me in vain,
　　teaching as doctrines the commands
　　of men."[I]

¹⁰Summoning the crowd, He told them, "Listen and understand: ¹¹It's not what goes into the mouth that defiles a man, but what comes out of the mouth, this defiles a man."

¹²Then the disciples came up and told Him, "Do You know that the Pharisees took offense when they heard this statement?"

¹³He replied, "Every plant that My heavenly Father didn't plant will be uprooted. ¹⁴Leave them alone! They are blind guides.[J] And if the blind guide the blind, both will fall into a pit."

¹⁵Then Peter replied to Him, "Explain this parable to us."

¹⁶"Are even you still lacking in understanding?" He[K] asked. ¹⁷"Don't you realize[L] that

whatever goes into the mouth passes into the stomach and is eliminated?[M] ¹⁸But what comes out of the mouth comes from the heart, and this defiles a man. ¹⁹For from the heart come evil thoughts, murders, adulteries, sexual immoralities, thefts, false testimonies, blasphemies. ²⁰These are the things that defile a man, but eating with unwashed hands does not defile a man."

²¹When Jesus left there, He withdrew to the area of Tyre and Sidon. ²²Just then a Canaanite woman from that region came and kept crying out,[N] "Have mercy on me, Lord, Son of David! My daughter is cruelly tormented by a demon."

²³Yet He did not say a word to her. So His disciples approached Him and urged Him, "Send her away because she cries out after us."[O]

²⁴He replied, "I was sent only to the lost sheep of the house of Israel."

²⁵But she came, knelt before Him, and said, "Lord, help me!"

²⁶He answered, "It isn't right to take the children's bread and throw it to their dogs."

²⁷"Yes, Lord," she said, "yet even the dogs eat the crumbs that fall from their masters' table!"

²⁸Then Jesus replied to her, "Woman, your faith is great. Let it be done for you as you want." And from that moment[P] her daughter was cured.

²⁹Moving on from there, Jesus passed along the Sea of Galilee. He went up on a mountain and sat there, ³⁰and large crowds came to Him, having with them the lame, the blind, the deformed, those unable to speak, and many others. They put them at His feet, and He healed them. ³¹So the crowd was amazed when they saw those unable to speak talking, the deformed restored, the lame walking, and the blind seeing. And they gave glory to the God of Israel.

³²Now Jesus summoned His disciples and said, "I have compassion on the crowd, because they've already stayed with Me three days and have nothing to eat. I don't want to send them away hungry; otherwise they might collapse on the way."

³³The disciples said to Him, "Where could we get enough bread in this desolate place to fill such a crowd?"

A14:35 Lit sent into   B15:2 Lit eat bread = eat a meal   C15:4 Other mss read commanded, saying   D15:4 Ex 20:12; Dt 5:16   E15:4 Ex 21:17; Lv 20:9   F15:6 Other mss read then he does not have to honor his father or mother   G15:6 Other mss read commandment   H15:8 Other mss add draw near to Me with their mouths, and   I15:8-9 Is 29:13 LXX   J15:14 Other mss add for the blind   K15:16 Other mss read Jesus   L15:17 Other mss add yet   M15:17 Lit and goes out into the toilet   N15:22 Other mss read and cried out to Him   O15:23 Lit she is yelling behind us or after us   P15:28 Lit hour

³⁴"How many loaves do you have?" Jesus asked them.

"Seven," they said, "and a few small fish."

³⁵After commanding the crowd to sit down on the ground, ³⁶He took the seven loaves and the fish, and He gave thanks, broke them, and kept on giving them to the disciples, and the disciples gave them to the crowds. ³⁷They all ate and were filled. Then they collected the leftover pieces—seven large baskets full. ³⁸Now those who ate were 4,000 men, besides women and children. ³⁹After dismissing the crowds, He got into the boat and went to the region of Magadan.ᴬ

16 The Pharisees and Sadducees approached, and as a test, asked Him to show them a sign from heaven.

²He answered them: "When evening comes you say, 'It will be good weather because the sky is red.' ³And in the morning, 'Today will be stormy because the sky is red and threatening.' Youᴮ know how to read the appearance of the sky, but you can't read the signs of the times.ᶜ ⁴An evil and adulterous generation demands a sign, but no sign will be given to it except the sign ofᴰ Jonah." Then He left them and went away.

⁵The disciples reached the other shore,ᴱ and they had forgotten to take bread.

⁶Then Jesus told them, "Watch out and beware of the yeastᶠ of the Pharisees and Sadducees."

⁷And they discussed among themselves, "We didn't bring any bread."

⁸Aware of this, Jesus said, "You of little faith! Why are you discussing among yourselves that you do not have bread? ⁹Don't you understand yet? Don't you remember the five loaves for the 5,000 and how many baskets you collected? ¹⁰Or the seven loaves for the 4,000 and how many large baskets you collected? ¹¹Why is it you don't understand that when I told you, 'Beware of the yeast of the Pharisees and Sadducees,' it wasn't about bread?" ¹²Then they understood that He did not tell them to beware of the yeast in bread, but of the teaching of the Pharisees and Sadducees.

¹³When Jesus came to the region of Caesarea Philippi,ᴳ He asked His disciples, "Who do people say that the Son of Man is?"ᴴ

¹⁴And they said, "Some say John the Baptist; others, Elijah; still others, Jeremiah or one of the prophets."

¹⁵"But you," He asked them, "who do you say that I am?"

¹⁶Simon Peter answered, "You are the Messiah, the Son of the living God!"

¹⁷And Jesus responded, "Simon son of Jonah,ᴵ you are blessed because flesh and blood did not reveal this to you, but My Father in heaven. ¹⁸And I also say to you that you are Peter,ᴶ and on this rockᴷ I will build My church, and the forcesᴸ of Hades will not overpower it. ¹⁹I will give you the keys of the kingdom of heaven, and whatever you bind on earth is already boundᴹ in heaven, and whatever you loose on earth is already loosedᴺ in heaven."

²⁰And He gave the disciples orders to tell no one that He wasᴼ the Messiah.

²¹From then on Jesus began to point out to His disciples that He must go to Jerusalem and suffer many things from the elders, chief priests, and scribes, be killed, and be raised the third day. ²²Then Peter took Him aside and began to rebuke Him, "Oh no,ᴾ Lord! This will never happen to You!"

²³But He turned and told Peter, "Get behind Me, Satan! You are an offense to Me because you're not thinking about God's concerns,� but man's."

²⁴Then Jesus said to His disciples, "If anyone wants to come with Me, he must deny himself, take up his cross, and follow Me. ²⁵For whoever wants to save his life will lose it, but whoever loses his life because of Me will find it. ²⁶What will it benefit a man if he gains the whole world yet loses his life? Or what will a man give in exchange for his life? ²⁷For the Son of Man is going to come with His angels in the glory of His Father, and then He will reward each according to what he has done. ²⁸I assure you: There are some standing here who will not taste death until they see the Son of Man coming in His kingdom."

17 After six days Jesus took Peter, James, and his brother John and led them up on a high mountain by themselves. ²He was

ᴬ15:39 Other mss read *Magdala*   ᴮ16:3 Other mss read *Hypocrites! You*   ᶜ16:2-3 Other mss omit *When* (v. 2) through end of v. 3   ᴰ16:4 Other mss add *the prophet*   ᴱ16:5 Lit *disciples went to the other side*   ᶠ16:6 Or *leaven*   ᴳ16:13 A town north of Galilee at the base of Mount Hermon   ᴴ16:13 Other mss read *that I, the Son of Man, am*   ᴵ16:17 Or *son of John*   ᴶ16:18 *Peter* (Gk *Petros*) = a specific stone or rock   ᴷ16:18 *Rock* (Gk *petra*) = a rocky crag or bedrock   ᴸ16:18 Lit *gates*   ᴹ16:19 Or *earth will be bound*   ᴺ16:19 Or *earth will be loosed*   ᴼ16:20 Other mss add *Jesus*   ᴾ16:22 Lit *Mercy to You = May God have mercy on You*   Q16:23 Lit *about the things of God* transformed[A] in front of them, and His face shine like the sun. Even His clothes became as white as the light. [3]Suddenly, Moses and Elijah appeared to them, talking with Him.

[4]Then Peter said to Jesus, "Lord, it's good for us to be here! If You want, I will make[B] three tabernacles here: one for You, one for Moses, and one for Elijah."

[5]While he was still speaking, suddenly a bright cloud covered[C] them, and a voice from the cloud said:

This is My beloved Son.
I take delight in Him.
Listen to Him!

[6]When the disciples heard it, they fell face-down and were terrified. [7]Then Jesus came up, touched them, and said, "Get up; don't be afraid." [8]When they looked up they saw no one except Him[D]—Jesus alone. [9]As they were coming down from the mountain, Jesus commanded them, "Don't tell anyone about the vision until the Son of Man is raised[E] from the dead."

[10]So the disciples questioned Him, "Why then do the scribes say that Elijah must come first?"

[11]"Elijah is coming[F] and will restore everything," He replied.[G] [12]"But I tell you: Elijah has already come, and they didn't recognize him. On the contrary, they did whatever they pleased to him. In the same way the Son of Man is going to suffer at their hands."[H] [13]Then the disciples understood that He spoke to them about John the Baptist.

[14]When they reached the crowd, a man approached and knelt down before Him. [15]"Lord," he said, "have mercy on my son, because he has seizures[I] and suffers severely. He often falls into the fire and often into the water. [16]I brought him to Your disciples, but they couldn't heal him."

[17]Jesus replied, "You unbelieving and re-bellious[J] generation! How long will I be with you? How long must I put up with you? Bring him here to Me." [18]Then Jesus rebuked the de-mon,[K] and it[L] came out of him, and from that moment[M] the boy was healed.

[19]Then the disciples approached Jesus pri-vately and said, "Why couldn't we drive it out?"

[20]"Because of your little faith," He[N] told them. "For I assure you: If you have faith the size of[O] a mustard seed, you will tell this mountain, 'Move from here to there,' and it will move. Nothing will be impossible for you. [[21]However, this kind does not come out ex-cept by prayer and fasting.]"[P]

[22]As they were meeting[Q] in Galilee, Jesus told them, "The Son of Man is about to be be-trayed into the hands of men. [23]They will kill Him, and on the third day He will be raised up." And they were deeply distressed.

[24]When they came to Capernaum, those who collected the double-drachma tax[R] approached Peter and said, "Doesn't your Teacher pay the double-drachma tax?"

[25]"Yes," he said.

When he went into the house, Jesus spoke to him first,[S] "What do you think, Simon? Who do earthly kings collect tariffs or taxes from? From their sons or from strangers?"[T]

[26]"From strangers," he said.[U]

"Then the sons are free," Jesus told him. [27]"But, so we won't offend them, go to the sea, cast in a fishhook, and take the first fish that you catch. When you open its mouth you'll find a coin.[V] Take it and give it to them for Me and you."

18 At that time[M] the disciples came to Jesus and said, "Who is greatest in the king-dom of heaven?"

[2]Then He called a child to Him and had him stand among them. [3]"I assure you," He said, "unless you are converted[W] and become like children, you will never enter the kingdom of heaven. [4]Therefore, whoever humbles himself like this child—this one is the greatest in the kingdom of heaven. [5]And whoever welcomes[X] one child like this in My name welcomes Me.

[6]"But whoever causes the downfall of one of these little ones who believe in Me—it would be better for him if a heavy millstone[Y] were hung around his neck and he were drowned in the depths of the sea! [7]Woe to the world because of offenses. For offenses must come, but woe to that man by whom the offense

A17:2 Or transfigured   B17:4 Other mss read wish, let's make   C17:5 Or enveloped; Ex 40:34-35   D17:8 Other mss omit Him   E17:9 Other mss read Man has risen   F17:11 Other mss add first   G17:11 Other mss read Jesus said to them   H17:12 Lit suffer by them   I17:15 Lit he is moonstruck; thought to be a form of epilepsy   J17:17 Or corrupt, or perverted, or twisted; Dt 32:5   K17:18 Lit rebuked him or it   L17:18 Lit the demon   M17:18; 18:1 Lit hour   N17:20 Other mss read your unbelief," Jesus   O17:20 Lit faith like   P17:21 Other mss omit bracketed text; Mk 9:29   Q17:22 Other mss read were staying   R17:24 Jewish men paid this tax to support the temple; Ex 30:11-16. A double-drachma could purchase 2 sheep.   S17:25 Lit Jesus anticipated him by saying   T17:25 Or foreigners   U17:26 Other mss read Peter said to Him   V17:27 Gk stater, worth 2 double-drachmas   W18:3 Or are turned around   X18:5 Or receives   Y18:6 A millstone turned by a donkey comes. ⁸If your hand or your foot causes your downfall, cut it off and throw it away. It is better for you to enter life maimed or lame, than to have two hands or two feet and be thrown into the eternal fire. ⁹And if your eye causes your downfall, gouge it out and throw it away. It is better for you to enter life with one eye, rather than to have two eyes and be thrown into hellfire!ᴬ

¹⁰"See that you don't look down on one of these little ones, because I tell you that in heaven their angels continually view the face of My Father in heaven. [¹¹For the Son of Man has come to save the lost.]ᴮ ¹²What do you think? If a man has 100 sheep, and one of them goes astray, won't he leave the 99 on the hillside and go and search for the stray? ¹³And if he finds it, I assure you: He rejoices over that sheepᶜ more than over the 99 that did not go astray. ¹⁴In the same way, it is not the will of your Father in heaven that one of these little ones perish.

¹⁵"If your brother sins against you,ᴰ go and rebuke him in private.ᴱ If he listens to you, you have won your brother. ¹⁶But if he won't listen, take one or two more with you, so that by the testimonyᶠ of two or three witnesses every fact may be established.ᴳ ¹⁷If he pays no attention to them, tell the church.ᴴ But if he doesn't pay attention even to the church, let him be like an unbelieverᴵ and a tax collector to you. ¹⁸I assure you: Whateverᶠ you bind on earth is already boundᴶ in heaven, and whatever you loose on earth is already loosedᴷ in heaven. ¹⁹Again, I assure you: If two of you on earth agree about any matter that youᴸ pray for, it will be done for youᴹ by My Father in heaven. ²⁰For where two or three are gathered together in My name, I am there among them."

²¹Then Peter came to Him and said, "Lord, how many times could my brother sin against me and I forgive him? As many as seven times?"

²²"I tell you, not as many as seven," Jesus said to him, "but 70 times seven.ᴺ ²³For this reason, the kingdom of heaven can be compared to a king who wanted to settle accounts with his slaves. ²⁴When he began to settle accounts, one who owed 10,000 talentsᴼ was brought before him. ²⁵Since he had no way to pay it back, his master commanded that he, his wife, his children, and everything he had be sold to pay the debt.

²⁶"At this, the slave fell facedown before him and said, 'Be patient with me, and I will pay you everything!' ²⁷Then the master of that slave had compassion, released him, and forgave him the loan.

²⁸"But that slave went out and found one of his fellow slaves who owed him 100 denarii.ᴾ He grabbed him, started choking him, and said, 'Pay what you owe!'

²⁹"At this, his fellow slave fell downᵠ and began begging him, 'Be patient with me, and I will pay you back.' ³⁰But he wasn't willing. On the contrary, he went and threw him into prison until he could pay what was owed. ³¹When the other slaves saw what had taken place, they were deeply distressed and went and reported to their master everything that had happened.

³²"Then, after he had summoned him, his master said to him, 'You wicked slave! I forgave you all that debt because you begged me. ³³Shouldn't you also have had mercy on your fellow slave, as I had mercy on you?' ³⁴And his master got angry and handed him over to the jailers to be tortured until he could pay everything that was owed. ³⁵So My heavenly Father will also do to you if each of you does not forgive his brotherᴿ from hisˢ heart."

19 When Jesus had finished this instruction, He departed from Galilee and went to the region of Judea across the Jordan. ²Large crowds followed Him, and He healed them there. ³Some Pharisees approached Him to test Him. They asked, "Is it lawful for a man to divorce his wife on any grounds?"

⁴"Haven't you read," He replied, "that He who createdᵀ them in the beginning made them male and female,"ᵁ ⁵and He also said:

> "For this reason a man will leave
> his father and mother
> and be joined to his wife,
> and the two will become one flesh?ⱽ

⁶So they are no longer two, but one flesh. Therefore, what God has joined together, man must not separate."

ᴬ18:9 Lit gehenna of fire ᴮ18:11 Other mss omit bracketed text ᶜ18:13 Lit over it ᴰ18:15 Other mss omit against you ᴱ18:15 Lit him between you and him alone ᶠ18:16 Lit mouth ᴳ18:16 Dt 19:15 ᴴ18:17 Or congregation ᴵ18:17 Or like a Gentile ᴶ18:18 Or earth will be bound ᴷ18:18 Or earth will be loosed ᴸ18:19 Lit they ᴹ18:19 Lit for them ᴺ18:22 Or but 77 times ᴼ18:24 A huge sum of money that could never be repaid by a slave; a talent = 6,000 denarii ᴾ18:28 A small sum compared to 10,000 talents ᵠ18:29 Other mss add at his feet ᴿ18:35 Other mss add his trespasses ˢ18:35 Lit your ᵀ19:4 Other mss read made ᵁ19:4 Gn 1:27; 5:2 ⱽ19:5 Gn 2:24

⁷"Why then," they asked Him, "did Moses command us to give divorce papers and to send her away?"

⁸He told them, "Moses permitted you to divorce your wives because of the hardness of your hearts. But it was not like that from the beginning. ⁹And I tell you, whoever divorces his wife, except for sexual immorality, and marries another, commits adultery."ᴬ

¹⁰His disciples said to Him, "If the relationship of a man with his wife is like this, it's better not to marry!"

¹¹But He told them, "Not everyone can accept this saying, but only those it has been given to. ¹²For there are eunuchs who were born that way from their mother's womb, there are eunuchs who were made by men, and there are eunuchs who have made themselves that way because of the kingdom of heaven. Let anyone accept this who can."

¹³Then children were brought to Him so He might put His hands on them and pray. But the disciples rebuked them. ¹⁴Then Jesus said, "Leave the children alone, and don't try to keep them from coming to Me, because the kingdom of heaven is made up of people like this."ᴮ ¹⁵After putting His hands on them, He went on from there.

¹⁶Just then someone came up and asked Him, "Teacher, what good must I do to have eternal life?"

¹⁷"Why do you ask Me about what is good?"ᶜ He said to him. "There is only One who is good.ᴰ If you want to enter into life, keep the commandments."

¹⁸"Which ones?" he asked Him. Jesus answered:

Do not murder;
do not commit adultery;
do not steal;
do not bear false witness;
¹⁹ honor your father and your mother;
and love your neighbor as yourself.ᴱ

²⁰"I have kept all these,"ᶠ the young man told Him. "What do I still lack?"

²¹"If you want to be perfect,"ᴳ Jesus said to him, "go, sell your belongings and give to the poor, and you will have treasure in heaven. Then come, follow Me."

²²When the young man heard that command, he went away grieving, because he had many possessions.

²³Then Jesus said to His disciples, "I assure you: It will be hard for a rich person to enter the kingdom of heaven! ²⁴Again I tell you, it is easier for a camel to go through the eye of a needle than for a rich person to enter the kingdom of God."

²⁵When the disciples heard this, they were utterly astonished and asked, "Then who can be saved?"

²⁶But Jesus looked at them and said, "With men this is impossible, but with God all things are possible."

²⁷Then Peter responded to Him, "Look, we have left everything and followed You. So what will there be for us?"

²⁸Jesus said to them, "I assure you: In the Messianic Age,ᴴ when the Son of Man sits on His glorious throne, you who have followed Me will also sit on 12 thrones, judging the 12 tribes of Israel. ²⁹And everyone who has left houses, brothers or sisters, father or mother,ᴵ children, or fields because of My name will receive 100 times more and will inherit eternal life. ³⁰But many who are first will be last, and the last first.

20 "For the kingdom of heaven is like a landowner who went out early in the morning to hire workers for his vineyard. ²After agreeing with the workers on one denarius for the day, he sent them into his vineyard. ³When he went out about nine in the morning,ᴶ he saw others standing in the marketplace doing nothing. ⁴To those men he said, 'You also go to my vineyard, and I'll give you whatever is right.' So off they went. ⁵About noon and at three,ᴷ he went out again and did the same thing. ⁶Then about fiveᴸ he went and found others standing around,ᴹ and said to them, 'Why have you been standing here all day doing nothing?'

⁷"'Because no one hired us,' they said to him.

"'You also go to my vineyard,' he told them.ᴺ ⁸When evening came, the owner of the vineyard told his foreman, 'Call the workers and

ᴬ19:9 Other mss add Also whoever marries a divorced woman commits adultery; Mt 5:32   ᴮ19:14 Lit heaven is of such ones   ᶜ19:17 Other mss read Why do you call Me good?   ᴰ19:17 Other mss read No one is good but One—God   ᴱ19:18-19 Ex 20:12-16; Lv 19:18; Dt 5:16-20   ᶠ19:20 Other mss add from my youth   ᴳ19:21 Or complete   ᴴ19:28 Lit the regeneration   ᴵ19:29 Other mss add or wife   ᴶ20:3 Lit about the third hour   ᴷ20:5 Lit about the sixth hour and the ninth hour   ᴸ20:6 Lit about the eleventh hour   ᴹ20:6 Other mss add doing nothing   ᴺ20:7 Other mss add 'and you'll get whatever is right.'

give them their pay, starting with the last and ending with the first.'[A]

[9] "When those who were hired about five[B] came, they each received one denarius. [10] So when the first ones came, they assumed they would get more, but they also received a denarius each. [11] When they received it, they began to complain to the landowner: [12] 'These last men put in one hour, and you made them equal to us who bore the burden of the day and the burning heat!'

[13] "He replied to one of them, 'Friend, I'm doing you no wrong. Didn't you agree with me on a denarius? [14] Take what's yours and go. I want to give this last man the same as I gave you. [15] Don't I have the right to do what I want with my business?[C] Are you jealous[D] because I'm generous?'[E]

[16] "So the last will be first, and the first last."[F]

[17] While going up to Jerusalem, Jesus took the 12 disciples aside privately and said to them on the way: [18] "Listen! We are going up to Jerusalem. The Son of Man will be handed over to the chief priests and scribes, and they will condemn Him to death. [19] Then they will hand Him over to the Gentiles to be mocked, flogged,[G] and crucified, and He will be resurrected[H] on the third day."

[20] Then the mother of Zebedee's sons approached Him with her sons. She knelt down to ask Him for something. [21] "What do you want?" He asked her.

"Promise,"[I] she said to Him, "that these two sons of mine may sit, one on Your right and the other on Your left, in Your kingdom."

[22] But Jesus answered, "You don't know what you're asking. Are you able to drink the cup[J] that I am about to drink?"[K]

"We are able," they said to Him.

[23] He told them, "You will indeed drink My cup.[L] But to sit at My right and left is not Mine to give; instead, it belongs to those for whom it has been prepared by My Father." [24] When the 10 disciples heard this, they became indignant with the two brothers. [25] But Jesus called them over and said, "You know that the rulers of the Gentiles dominate them, and the men of high position exercise power over them. [26] It must not be like that among you. On the contrary, whoever wants to become great among you

must be your servant, [27] and whoever wants to be first among you must be your slave; [28] just as the Son of Man did not come to be served, but to serve, and to give His life—a ransom for many."

[29] As they were leaving Jericho, a large crowd followed Him. [30] There were two blind men sitting by the road. When they heard that Jesus was passing by, they cried out, "Lord, have mercy on us, Son of David!" [31] The crowd told them to keep quiet, but they cried out all the more, "Lord, have mercy on us, Son of David!"

[32] Jesus stopped, called them, and said, "What do you want Me to do for you?"

[33] "Lord," they said to Him, "open our eyes!" [34] Moved with compassion, Jesus touched their eyes. Immediately they could see, and they followed Him.

21 When they approached Jerusalem and came to Bethphage at the Mount of Olives, Jesus then sent two disciples, [2] telling them, "Go into the village ahead of you. At once you will find a donkey tied there, and a colt with her. Untie them and bring them to Me. [3] If anyone says anything to you, you should say that the Lord needs them, and immediately he will send them."

[4] This took place so that what was spoken through the prophet might be fulfilled:

[5]   **Tell Daughter Zion,**
       "Look, your King is coming to you,
       gentle, and mounted on a donkey,
       even on a colt,
       the foal of a beast of burden."[M]

[6] The disciples went and did just as Jesus directed them. [7] They brought the donkey and the colt; then they laid their robes on them, and He sat on them. [8] A very large crowd spread their robes on the road; others were cutting branches from the trees and spreading them on the road. [9] Then the crowds who went ahead of Him and those who followed kept shouting:

       Hosanna **to the Son of David!**
       He who comes in the name
       of the Lord is the blessed One![N]
       Hosanna **in the highest heaven!**

A20:8 Lit *starting from the last until the first*   B20:9 Lit *about the eleventh hour*   C20:15 Lit *with what is mine*   D20:15 Lit *Is your eye evil; an idiom for jealousy or stinginess*   E20:15 Lit *good*   F20:16 Other mss add *For many are called, but few are chosen.*   G20:19 Or *scourged*   H20:19 Other mss read *will rise again*   I20:21 Lit *Say*   J20:22 Figurative language referring to His coming suffering; Mt 26:39; Jn 18:11   K20:22 Other mss add *and (or) to be baptized with the baptism that I am baptized with?"*   L20:23 Other mss add *and be baptized with the baptism that I am baptized with.*   M21:5 Is 62:11; Zch 9:9   N21:9 Ps 118:25-26

[10] When He entered Jerusalem, the whole city was shaken, saying, "Who is this?" [11] And the crowds kept saying, "This is the prophet Jesus from Nazareth in Galilee!"

[12] Jesus went into the temple complex[A] and drove out all those buying and selling in the temple. He overturned the money changers' tables and the chairs of those selling doves. [13] And He said to them, "It is written, My house will be called a house of prayer.[B] But you are making it a den of thieves!"[C]

[14] The blind and the lame came to Him in the temple complex, and He healed them. [15] When the chief priests and the scribes saw the wonders that He did and the children shouting in the temple complex, "*Hosanna* to the Son of David!" they were indignant [16] and said to Him, "Do You hear what these children are saying?"

"Yes," Jesus told them. "Have you never read:

> You have prepared[D] praise
> from the mouths of children
> and nursing infants?"[E]

[17] Then He left them, went out of the city to Bethany, and spent the night there.

[18] Early in the morning, as He was returning to the city, He was hungry. [19] Seeing a lone fig tree by the road, He went up to it and found nothing on it except leaves. And He said to it, "May no fruit ever come from you again!" At once the fig tree withered.

[20] When the disciples saw it, they were amazed and said, "How did the fig tree wither so quickly?"

[21] Jesus answered them, "I assure you: If you have faith and do not doubt, you will not only do what was done to the fig tree, but even if you tell this mountain, 'Be lifted up and thrown into the sea,' it will be done. [22] And if you believe, you will receive whatever you ask for in prayer."

[23] When He entered the temple complex, the chief priests and the elders of the people came up to Him as He was teaching and said, "By what authority are You doing these things? Who gave You this authority?"

[24] Jesus answered them, "I will also ask you one question, and if you answer it for Me, then I will tell you by what authority I do these things. [25] Where did John's baptism come from? From heaven or from men?"

They began to argue among themselves, "If we say, 'From heaven,' He will say to us, 'Then why didn't you believe him?' [26] But if we say, 'From men,' we're afraid of the crowd, because everyone thought John was a prophet." [27] So they answered Jesus, "We don't know."

And He said to them, "Neither will I tell you by what authority I do these things.

[28] "But what do you think? A man had two sons. He went to the first and said, 'My son, go, work in the vineyard today.'

[29] "He answered, 'I don't want to!' Yet later he changed his mind and went. [30] Then the man went to the other and said the same thing.

"'I will, sir,' he answered. But he didn't go.

[31] "Which of the two did his father's will?"

"The first," they said.

Jesus said to them, "I assure you: Tax collectors and prostitutes are entering the kingdom of God before you! [32] For John came to you in the way of righteousness, and you didn't believe him. Tax collectors and prostitutes did believe him, but you, when you saw it, didn't even change your minds then and believe him.

[33] "Listen to another parable: There was a man, a landowner, who planted a vineyard, put a fence around it, dug a winepress in it, and built a watchtower. He leased it to tenant farmers and went away. [34] When the grape harvest[F] drew near, he sent his slaves to the farmers to collect his fruit. [35] But the farmers took his slaves, beat one, killed another, and stoned a third. [36] Again, he sent other slaves, more than the first group, and they did the same to them. [37] Finally, he sent his son to them. 'They will respect my son,' he said.

[38] "But when the tenant farmers saw the son, they said among themselves, 'This is the heir. Come, let's kill him and take his inheritance!' [39] So they seized him, threw him out of the vineyard, and killed him. [40] Therefore, when the owner of the vineyard comes, what will he do to those farmers?"

[41] "He will completely destroy those terrible men," they told Him, "and lease his vineyard to other farmers who will give him his produce at the harvest."[G]

[42] Jesus said to them, "Have you never read in the Scriptures:

> The stone that the builders rejected
> has become the cornerstone.[H]

A21:12 Other mss add *of God*   B21:13 Is 56:7   C21:13 Jr 7:11   D21:16 Or *restored*   E21:16 Ps 8:2   F21:34 Lit *the season of fruits*
G21:41 Lit *him the fruits in their seasons*   H21:42 Lit *the head of the corner*

This came from the Lord
and is wonderful in our eyes?[A]

[43] Therefore I tell you, the kingdom of God will be taken away from you and given to a nation producing its[B] fruit. [[44] Whoever falls on this stone will be broken to pieces; but on whoever it falls, it will grind him to powder!]"[C]

[45] When the chief priests and the Pharisees heard His parables, they knew He was speaking about them. [46] Although they were looking for a way to arrest Him, they feared the crowds, because they[D] regarded Him as a prophet.

22 Once more Jesus spoke to them in parables: [2] "The kingdom of heaven may be compared to a king who gave a wedding banquet for his son. [3] He sent out his slaves to summon those invited to the banquet, but they didn't want to come. [4] Again, he sent out other slaves, and said, 'Tell those who are invited: Look, I've prepared my dinner; my oxen and fattened cattle have been slaughtered, and everything is ready. Come to the wedding banquet.'

[5] "But they paid no attention and went away, one to his own farm, another to his business. [6] And the others seized his slaves, treated them outrageously and killed them. [7] The king[E] was enraged, so he sent out his troops, destroyed those murderers, and burned down their city.

[8] "Then he told his slaves, 'The banquet is ready, but those who were invited were not worthy. [9] Therefore go to where the roads exit the city and invite everyone you find to the banquet.' [10] So those slaves went out on the roads and gathered everyone they found, both evil and good. The wedding banquet was filled with guests.[F] [11] But when the king came in to view the guests, he saw a man there who was not dressed for a wedding. [12] So he said to him, 'Friend, how did you get in here without wedding clothes?' The man was speechless. [13] "Then the king told the attendants, 'Tie him up hand and foot,[G] and throw him into the outer darkness, where there will be weeping and gnashing of teeth.'

[14] "For many are invited, but few are chosen."

[15] Then the Pharisees went and plotted how to trap Him by what He said.[H] [16] They sent their disciples to Him, with the Herodians. "Teacher," they said, "we know that You are truthful and teach truthfully the way of God. You defer to no one, for You don't show partiality.[I] [17] Tell us, therefore, what You think. Is it lawful to pay taxes to Caesar or not?"

[18] But perceiving their malice, Jesus said, "Why are you testing Me, hypocrites? [19] Show Me the coin used for the tax." So they brought Him a denarius. [20] "Whose image and inscription is this?" He asked them.

[21] "Caesar's," they said to Him.

Then He said to them, "Therefore give back to Caesar the things that are Caesar's, and to God the things that are God's." [22] When they heard this, they were amazed. So they left Him and went away.

[23] The same day some Sadducees, who say there is no resurrection, came up to Him and questioned Him: [24] "Teacher, Moses said, **if a man dies, having no children, his brother is to marry his wife and raise up offspring for his brother.**[J] [25] Now there were seven brothers among us. The first got married and died. Having no offspring, he left his wife to his brother. [26] The same happened to the second also, and the third, and so to all seven.[K] [27] Then last of all the woman died. [28] In the resurrection, therefore, whose wife will she be of the seven? For they all had married her."[L]

[29] Jesus answered them, "You are deceived, because you don't know the Scriptures or the power of God. [30] For in the resurrection they neither marry nor are given in marriage but are like[M] angels in heaven. [31] Now concerning the resurrection of the dead, haven't you read what was spoken to you by God: [32] I am the God of Abraham and the God of Isaac and the God of Jacob?[N] He[O] is not the God of the dead, but of the living."

[33] And when the crowds heard this, they were astonished at His teaching.

[34] When the Pharisees heard that He had silenced the Sadducees, they came together. [35] And one of them, an expert in the law, asked a question to test Him: [36] "Teacher, which command in the law is the greatest?"[P]

[37] He said to him, "Love the Lord your God with all your heart, with all your soul, and with all your mind.[Q] [38] This is the greatest and most

A21:42 Ps 118:22-23   B21:43 = the kingdom's   C21:44 Other mss omit bracketed text   D21:46 = the crowds   E22:7 Other mss read But when the (that) king heard about it he   F22:10 Lit those reclining (to eat)   G22:13 Other mss add take him away   H22:15 Lit trap Him in a word   I22:16 Lit don't look on the face of men; that is, on the outward appearance   J22:24 Dt 25:5   K22:26 Lit so until the seven   L22:28 Lit all had her   M22:30 Other mss add God's   N22:32 Ex 3:6,15-16   O22:32 Other mss read God   P22:36 Lit is great   Q22:37 Dt 6:5

important[A] command. [39] The second is like it: Love your neighbor as yourself.[B] [40] All the Law and the Prophets depend[C] on these two commands."

[41] While the Pharisees were together, Jesus questioned them, [42] "What do you think about the Messiah? Whose Son is He?"

"David's," they told Him.

[43] He asked them, "How is it then that David, inspired by the Spirit,[D] calls Him 'Lord':

[44]   The Lord declared to my Lord,
        'Sit at My right hand
        until I put Your enemies
        under Your feet'?[E,F]

[45] "If David calls Him 'Lord,' how then can the Messiah be his Son?" [46] No one was able to answer Him at all,[G] and from that day no one dared to question Him anymore.

23 Then Jesus spoke to the crowds and to His disciples: [2] "The scribes and the Pharisees are seated in the chair of Moses.[H] [3] Therefore do whatever they tell you, and observe it. But don't do what they do,[I] because they don't practice what they teach. [4] They tie up heavy loads that are hard to carry[J] and put them on people's shoulders, but they themselves aren't willing to lift a finger[K] to move them. [5] They do everything[L] to be observed by others: They enlarge their phylacteries[M] and lengthen their tassels.[N] [6] They love the place of honor at banquets, the front seats in the synagogues, [7] greetings in the marketplaces, and to be called 'Rabbi' by people.

[8] "But as for you, do not be called 'Rabbi,' because you have one Teacher,[O] and you are all brothers. [9] Do not call anyone on earth your father, because you have one Father, who is in heaven. [10] And do not be called masters either, because you have one Master,[P] the Messiah. [11] The greatest among you will be your servant. [12] Whoever exalts himself will be humbled, and whoever humbles himself will be exalted.

[13] "But woe to you, scribes and Pharisees, hypocrites! You lock up the kingdom of heaven from people. For you don't go in, and you don't allow those entering to go in.

[[14] "Woe to you, scribes and Pharisees, hypocrites! You devour widows' houses and make long prayers just for show.[Q] This is why you will receive a harsher punishment.][R]

[15] "Woe to you, scribes and Pharisees, hypocrites! You travel over land and sea to make one proselyte, and when he becomes one, you make him twice as fit for hell[S] as you are!

[16] "Woe to you, blind guides, who say, 'Whoever takes an oath by the sanctuary, it means nothing. But whoever takes an oath by the gold of the sanctuary is bound by his oath.'[T] [17] Blind fools![U] For which is greater, the gold or the sanctuary that sanctified the gold? [18] Also, 'Whoever takes an oath by the altar, it means nothing. But whoever takes an oath by the gift that is on it is bound by his oath.'[T] [19] Blind people![V] For which is greater, the gift or the altar that sanctifies the gift? [20] Therefore, the one who takes an oath by the altar takes an oath by it and by everything on it. [21] The one who takes an oath by the sanctuary takes an oath by it and by Him who dwells in it. [22] And the one who takes an oath by heaven takes an oath by God's throne and by Him who sits on it.

[23] "Woe to you, scribes and Pharisees, hypocrites! You pay a tenth of[W] mint, dill, and cumin,[X] yet you have neglected the more important matters of the law—justice, mercy, and faith. These things should have been done without neglecting the others. [24] Blind guides! You strain out a gnat, yet gulp down a camel!

[25] "Woe to you, scribes and Pharisees, hypocrites! You clean the outside of the cup and dish, but inside they are full of greed[Y] and self-indulgence! [26] Blind Pharisee! First clean the inside of the cup,[Z] so the outside of it[AA] may also become clean.

[27] "Woe to you, scribes and Pharisees, hypocrites! You are like whitewashed tombs, which appear beautiful on the outside, but inside are full of dead men's bones and every impurity. [28] In the same way, on the outside you seem righteous to people, but inside you are full of hypocrisy and lawlessness.

[29] "Woe to you, scribes and Pharisees, hypocrites! You build the tombs of the prophets

[A]22:38 Lit and first   [B]22:39 Lv 19:18   [C]22:40 Or hang   [D]22:43 Lit David in Spirit   [E]22:44 Other mss read until I make Your enemies Your footstool   [F]22:44 Ps 110:1   [G]22:46 Lit answer Him a word   [H]23:2 Perhaps a special chair for teaching in synagogues, or a metaphorical phrase for teaching with Moses' authority   [I]23:3 Lit do according to their works   [J]23:4 Other mss omit that are hard to carry   [K]23:4 Lit lift with their finger   [L]23:5 Lit do all their works   [M]23:5 Small leather boxes containing OT texts, worn by Jews on their arms and foreheads   [N]23:5 Other mss add on their robes   [O]23:8 Other mss add the Messiah   [P]23:10 Or Teacher   [Q]23:14 Or prayers with false motivation   [R]23:14 Other mss omit bracketed text   [S]23:15 Lit twice the son of gehenna   [T]23:16,18 Lit is obligated   [U]23:17 Lit Fools and blind   [V]23:19 Other mss read Fools and blind   [W]23:23 Or You tithe   [X]23:23 A plant whose seeds are used as a seasoning   [Y]23:25 Or full of violence   [Z]23:26 Other mss add and dish   [AA]23:26 Other mss read of them and decorate the monuments of the righteous, [30] and you say, 'If we had lived in the days of our fathers, we wouldn't have taken part with them in shedding the prophets' blood.'[A] [31] You, therefore, testify against yourselves that you are sons of those who murdered the prophets. [32] Fill up, then, the measure of your fathers' sins![B]

[33] "Snakes! Brood of vipers! How can you escape being condemned to hell?[C] [34] This is why I am sending you prophets, sages, and scribes. Some of them you will kill and crucify, and some of them you will flog in your synagogues and hound from town to town. [35] So all the righteous blood shed on the earth will be charged to you,[D] from the blood of righteous Abel to the blood of Zechariah, son of Berechiah, whom you murdered between the sanctuary and the altar. [36] I assure you: All these things will come on this generation!

[37] "Jerusalem, Jerusalem! She who kills the prophets and stones those who are sent to her. How often I wanted to gather your children together, as a hen gathers her chicks[E] under her wings, yet you were not willing! [38] See, your house is left to you desolate. [39] For I tell you, you will never see Me again until you say, 'He who comes in the name of the Lord is the blessed One'!"[F]

24 As Jesus left and was going out of the temple complex, His disciples came up and called His attention to the temple buildings. [2] Then He replied to them, "Don't you see all these things? I assure you: Not one stone will be left here on another that will not be thrown down!"

[3] While He was sitting on the Mount of Olives, the disciples approached Him privately and said, "Tell us, when will these things happen? And what is the sign of Your coming and of the end of the age?"

[4] Then Jesus replied to them: "Watch out that no one deceives you. [5] For many will come in My name, saying, 'I am the Messiah,' and they will deceive many. [6] You are going to hear of wars and rumors of wars. See that you are not alarmed, because these things must take place, but the end is not yet. [7] For nation will rise up against nation, and kingdom against kingdom. There will be famines[G] and earth-

quakes in various places. [8] All these events are the beginning of birth pains.

[9] "Then they will hand you over for persecution,[H] and they will kill you. You will be hated by all nations because of My name. [10] Then many will take offense, betray one another and hate one another. [11] Many false prophets will rise up and deceive many. [12] Because lawlessness will multiply, the love of many will grow cold. [13] But the one who endures to the end will be delivered.[I] [14] This good news of the kingdom will be proclaimed in all the world[J] as a testimony to all nations. And then the end will come.

[15] "So when you see the abomination that causes desolation,[K,L] spoken of by the prophet Daniel, standing in the holy place" (let the reader understand[M]), [16] "then those in Judea must flee to the mountains! [17] A man on the housetop[N] must not come down to get things out of his house. [18] And a man in the field must not go back to get his clothes. [19] Woe to pregnant women and nursing mothers in those days! [20] Pray that your escape may not be in winter or on a Sabbath. [21] For at that time there will be great tribulation, the kind that hasn't taken place from the beginning of the world until now and never will again! [22] Unless those days were limited, no one would[O] survive.[P] But those days will be limited because of the elect.

[23] "If anyone tells you then, 'Look, here is the Messiah!' or, 'Over here!' do not believe it! [24] False messiahs[Q] and false prophets will arise and perform great signs and wonders to lead astray, if possible, even the elect. [25] Take note: I have told you in advance. [26] So if they tell you, 'Look, He's in the wilderness!' don't go out; 'Look, He's in the inner rooms!' do not believe it. [27] For as the lightning comes from the east and flashes as far as the west, so will be the coming of the Son of Man. [28] Wherever the carcass is, there the vultures[R] will gather.

[29] "Immediately after the tribulation of those days:

> The sun will be darkened,
> and the moon will not shed its light;
> the stars will fall from the sky,
> and the celestial powers will be shaken.

[A] 23:30 Lit have been partakers with them in the blood of the prophets [B] 23:32 Lit the measure of your fathers [C] 23:33 Lit escape from the judgment of gehenna [D] 23:35 Lit will come on you [E] 23:37 Or as a mother bird gathers her young [F] 23:39 Ps 118:26 [G] 24:7 Other mss add epidemics [H] 24:9 Or tribulation, or distress [I] 24:13 Or be saved [J] 24:14 Or in all the inhabited earth [K] 24:15 Or abomination of desolation, or desolating sacrilege [L] 24:15 Dn 9:27 [M] 24:15 These are, most likely, Matthew's words to his readers. [N] 24:17 Or roof [O] 24:22 Lit short, all flesh would not [P] 24:22 Or be saved or delivered [Q] 24:24 Or False christs [R] 24:28 Or eagles

³⁰"Then the sign of the Son of Man will appear in the sky, and then all the peoples of the earthᴬ will mourn;ᴮ and they will see the Son of Man coming on the clouds of heaven with power and great glory. ³¹He will send out His angels with a loud trumpet, and they will gather His elect from the four winds, from one end of the sky to the other.

³²"Now learn this parable from the fig tree: As soon as its branch becomes tender and sprouts leaves, you know that summer is near. ³³In the same way, when you see all these things, recognizeᶜ that Heᴰ is near—at the door! ³⁴I assure you: This generation will certainly not pass away until all these things take place. ³⁵Heaven and earth will pass away, but My words will never pass away.

³⁶"Now concerning that day and hour no one knows—neither the angels in heaven, nor the Sonᴱ—except the Father only. ³⁷As the days of Noah were, so the coming of the Son of Man will be. ³⁸For in those days before the flood they were eating and drinking, marrying and giving in marriage, until the day Noah boarded the ark. ³⁹They didn't knowᶠ until the flood came and swept them all away. So this is the way the coming of the Son of Man will be: ⁴⁰Then two men will be in the field: one will be taken and one left. ⁴¹Two women will be grinding at the mill: one will be taken and one left. ⁴²Therefore be alert, since you don't know what dayᴳ your Lord is coming. ⁴³But know this: If the homeowner had known what timeᴴ the thief was coming, he would have stayed alert and not let his house be broken into. ⁴⁴This is why you also must be ready, because the Son of Man is coming at an hour you do not expect.

⁴⁵"Who then is a faithful and sensible slave, whom his master has put in charge of his household, to give them food at the proper time? ⁴⁶That slave whose master finds him working when he comes will be rewarded. ⁴⁷I assure you: He will put him in charge of all his possessions. ⁴⁸But if that wicked slave says in his heart, 'My master is delayed,' ⁴⁹and starts to beat his fellow slaves, and eats and drinks with drunkards, ⁵⁰that slave's master will come on a day he does not expect and at an hour he does not know. ⁵¹He will cut him to piecesᴵ and

assign him a place with the hypocrites. In that place there will be weeping and gnashing of teeth.

25 "Then the kingdom of heaven will be like 10 virginsᴶ who took their lamps and went out to meet the groom. ²Five of them were foolish and five were sensible. ³When the foolish took their lamps, they didn't take olive oil with them. ⁴But the sensible ones took oil in their flasks with their lamps. ⁵Since the groom was delayed, they all became drowsy and fell asleep.

⁶"In the middle of the night there was a shout: 'Here's the groom! Come out to meet him.'

⁷"Then all those virgins got up and trimmed their lamps. ⁸But the foolish ones said to the sensible ones, 'Give us some of your oil, because our lamps are going out.'

⁹"The sensible ones answered, 'No, there won't be enough for us and for you. Go instead to those who sell, and buy oil for yourselves.'

¹⁰"When they had gone to buy some, the groom arrived. Then those who were ready went in with him to the wedding banquet, and the door was shut.

¹¹"Later the rest of the virgins also came and said, 'Master, master, open up for us!'

¹²"But he replied, 'I assure you: I do not know you!'

¹³"Therefore be alert, because you don't know either the day or the hour.ᴷ

¹⁴"For it is just like a man going on a journey. He called his own slaves and turned over his possessions to them. ¹⁵To one he gave five talents;ᴸ to another, two; and to another, one—to each according to his own ability. Then he went on a journey. Immediately ¹⁶the man who had received five talents went, put them to work, and earned five more. ¹⁷In the same way the man with two earned two more. ¹⁸But the man who had received one talent went off, dug a hole in the ground, and hid his master's money.

¹⁹"After a long time the master of those slaves came and settled accounts with them. ²⁰The man who had received five talents approached, presented five more talents, and said, 'Master, you gave me five talents. Look, I've earned five more talents.'

ᴬ24:30 Or all the tribes of the land   ᴮ24:30 Lit will beat; that is, beat their breasts   ᶜ24:33 Or things, you know   ᴰ24:33 Or it; that is, summer   ᴱ24:36 Other mss omit nor the Son   ᶠ24:39 They didn't know the day and hour of the coming judgment.   ᴳ24:42 Other mss read hour; = time   ᴴ24:43 Lit watch; a division of the night in ancient times   ᴵ24:51 Lit him in two   ᴶ25:1 Or bridesmaids   ᴷ25:13 Other mss add in which the Son of Man is coming.   ᴸ25:15 Worth a very large sum of money; a talent = 6,000 denarii

²¹"His master said to him, 'Well done, good and faithful slave! You were faithful over a few things; I will put you in charge of many things. Share your master's joy!'

²²"Then the man with two talents also approached. He said, 'Master, you gave me two talents. Look, I've earned two more talents.'

²³"His master said to him, 'Well done, good and faithful slave! You were faithful over a few things; I will put you in charge of many things. Share your master's joy!'

²⁴"Then the man who had received one talent also approached and said, 'Master, I know you. You're a difficult man, reaping where you haven't sown and gathering where you haven't scattered seed. ²⁵So I was afraid and went off and hid your talent in the ground. Look, you have what is yours.'

²⁶"But his master replied to him, 'You evil, lazy slave! If you knew that I reap where I haven't sown and gather where I haven't scattered, ²⁷then^A you should have deposited my money with the bankers. And when I returned I would have received my money^B back with interest.

²⁸"'So take the talent from him and give it to the one who has 10 talents. ²⁹For to everyone who has, more will be given, and he will have more than enough. But from the one who does not have, even what he has will be taken away from him. ³⁰And throw this good-for-nothing slave into the outer darkness. In that place there will be weeping and gnashing of teeth.'

³¹"When the Son of Man comes in His glory, and all the angels^C with Him, then He will sit on the throne of His glory. ³²All the nations^D will be gathered before Him, and He will separate them one from another, just as a shepherd separates the sheep from the goats. ³³He will put the sheep on His right and the goats on the left. ³⁴Then the King will say to those on His right, 'Come, you who are blessed by My Father, inherit the kingdom prepared for you from the foundation of the world.

³⁵   For I was hungry
     and you gave Me something to eat;
     I was thirsty
     and you gave Me something to drink;
     I was a stranger and you took Me in;
³⁶   I was naked and you clothed Me;

     I was sick and you took care of Me;
     I was in prison and you visited Me.'

³⁷"Then the righteous will answer Him, 'Lord, when did we see You hungry and feed You, or thirsty and give You something to drink? ³⁸When did we see You a stranger and take You in, or without clothes and clothe You? ³⁹When did we see You sick, or in prison, and visit You?'

⁴⁰"And the King will answer them, 'I assure you: Whatever you did for one of the least of these brothers of Mine, you did for Me.' ⁴¹Then He will also say to those on the left, 'Depart from Me, you who are cursed, into the eternal fire prepared for the Devil and his angels!

⁴²   For I was hungry
     and you gave Me nothing to eat;
     I was thirsty
     and you gave Me nothing to drink;
⁴³   I was a stranger
     and you didn't take Me in;
     I was naked
     and you didn't clothe Me,
     sick and in prison
     and you didn't take care of Me.'

⁴⁴"Then they too will answer, 'Lord, when did we see You hungry, or thirsty, or a stranger, or without clothes, or sick, or in prison, and not help You?'

⁴⁵"Then He will answer them, 'I assure you: Whatever you did not do for one of the least of these, you did not do for Me either.'

⁴⁶"And they will go away into eternal punishment, but the righteous into eternal life."

26 When Jesus had finished saying all this, He told His disciples, ²"You know^E that the Passover takes place after two days, and the Son of Man will be handed over to be crucified."

³Then the chief priests^F and the elders of the people assembled in the palace of the high priest, who was called Caiaphas, ⁴and they conspired to arrest Jesus in a treacherous way and kill Him. ⁵"Not during the festival," they said, "so there won't be rioting among the people."

⁶While Jesus was in Bethany at the house of Simon, a man who had a serious skin disease, ⁷a woman approached Him with an alabaster jar of very expensive fragrant oil. She poured it on His head as He was reclining at the table. ⁸When the disciples saw it, they were indig-

nant. "Why this waste?" they asked. [9]"This might have been sold for a great deal and given to the poor."

[10]But Jesus, aware of this, said to them, "Why are you bothering this woman? She has done a noble thing for Me. [11]You always have the poor with you, but you do not always have Me. [12]By pouring this fragrant oil on My body, she has prepared Me for burial. [13]I assure you: Wherever this gospel is proclaimed in the whole world, what this woman has done will also be told in memory of her."

[14]Then one of the Twelve—the man called Judas Iscariot—went to the chief priests [15]and said, "What are you willing to give me if I hand Him over to you?" So they weighed out 30 pieces of silver for him. [16]And from that time he started looking for a good opportunity to betray Him.

[17]On the first day of Unleavened Bread the disciples came to Jesus and asked, "Where do You want us to prepare the Passover so You may eat it?"

[18]"Go into the city to a certain man," He said, "and tell him, 'The Teacher says: My time is near; I am celebrating the Passover at your place[A] with My disciples.'" [19]So the disciples did as Jesus had directed them and prepared the Passover. [20]When evening came, He was reclining at the table with the Twelve. [21]While they were eating, He said, "I assure you: One of you will betray Me."

[22]Deeply distressed, each one began to say to Him, "Surely not I, Lord?"

[23]He replied, "The one who dipped his hand with Me in the bowl—he will betray Me. [24]The Son of Man will go just as it is written about Him, but woe to that man by whom the Son of Man is betrayed! It would have been better for that man if he had not been born."

[25]Then Judas, His betrayer, replied, "Surely not I, Rabbi?"

"You have said it," He told him.

[26]As they were eating, Jesus took bread, blessed and broke it, gave it to the disciples, and said, "Take and eat it; this is My body." [27]Then He took a cup, and after giving thanks, He gave it to them and said, "Drink from it, all of you. [28]For this is My blood that establishes the covenant;[B] it is shed for many for the

forgiveness of sins. [29]But I tell you, from this moment I will not drink of this fruit of the vine until that day when I drink it in a new way[C] in My Father's kingdom with you." [30]After singing psalms,[D] they went out to the Mount of Olives.

[31]Then Jesus said to them, "Tonight all of you will run away[E] because of Me, for it is written:

> I will strike the shepherd,
> and the sheep of the flock
> will be scattered.[F]

[32]But after I have been resurrected, I will go ahead of you to Galilee."

[33]Peter told Him, "Even if everyone runs away because of You, I will never run away!"

[34]"I assure you," Jesus said to him, "tonight, before the rooster crows, you will deny Me three times!"

[35]"Even if I have to die with You," Peter told Him, "I will never deny You!" And all the disciples said the same thing.

[36]Then Jesus came with them to a place called Gethsemane,[G] and He told the disciples, "Sit here while I go over there and pray." [37]Taking along Peter and the two sons of Zebedee, He began to be sorrowful and deeply distressed. [38]Then He said to them, "My soul is swallowed up in sorrow[H]—to the point of death.[I] Remain here and stay awake with Me." [39]Going a little farther,[J] He fell facedown and prayed, "My Father! If it is possible, let this cup pass from Me. Yet not as I will, but as You will."

[40]Then He came to the disciples and found them sleeping. He asked Peter, "So, couldn't you[K] stay awake with Me one hour? [41]Stay awake and pray, so that you won't enter into temptation. The spirit is willing, but the flesh is weak."

[42]Again, a second time, He went away and prayed, "My Father, if this[L] cannot pass[M] unless I drink it, Your will be done." [43]And He came again and found them sleeping, because they could not keep their eyes open.[N]

[44]After leaving them, He went away again and prayed a third time, saying the same thing once more. [45]Then He came to the disciples and said to them, "Are you still sleeping and

---

[A]26:18 Lit *Passover with you*   [B]26:28 Other mss read *new covenant*   [C]26:29 Or *drink new wine*; lit *drink it new*   [D]26:30 Pss 113–118 were sung during and after the Passover meal.   [E]26:31 Or *stumble*   [F]26:31 Zch 13:7   [G]26:36 A garden east of Jerusalem at the base of the Mount of Olives; Gethsemane = olive oil press   [H]26:38 Or *I am deeply grieved*, or *I am overwhelmed by sorrow*; Ps 42:6,11; 43:5   [I]26:38 Lit *unto death*   [J]26:39 Other mss read *Drawing nearer*   [K]26:40 = all 3 disciples because the verb in Gk is pl   [L]26:42 Other mss add *cup*   [M]26:42 Other mss add *from Me*   [N]26:43 Lit *because their eyes were weighed down* resting?[A] Look, the time is near. The Son of Man is being betrayed into the hands of sinners. [46]Get up; let's go! See, My betrayer is near."

[47]While He was still speaking, Judas, one of the Twelve, suddenly arrived. A large mob, with swords and clubs, was with him from the chief priests and elders of the people. [48]His betrayer had given them a sign: "The One I kiss, He's the One; arrest Him!" [49]So he went right up to Jesus and said, "Greetings, Rabbi!" and kissed Him.

[50]"Friend," Jesus asked him, "why have you come?"[B]

Then they came up, took hold of Jesus, and arrested Him. [51]At that moment one of those with Jesus reached out his hand and drew his sword. He struck the high priest's slave and cut off his ear.

[52]Then Jesus told him, "Put your sword back in its place because all who take up a sword will perish by a sword. [53]Or do you think that I cannot call on My Father, and He will provide Me at once with more than 12 legions[C] of angels? [54]How, then, would the Scriptures be fulfilled that say it must happen this way?"

[55]At that time Jesus said to the crowds, "Have you come out with swords and clubs, as if I were a criminal,[D] to capture Me? Every day I used to sit, teaching in the temple complex, and you didn't arrest Me. [56]But all this has happened so that the prophetic Scriptures[E] would be fulfilled." Then all the disciples deserted Him and ran away.

[57]Those who had arrested Jesus led Him away to Caiaphas the high priest, where the scribes and the elders had convened. [58]Meanwhile, Peter was following Him at a distance right to the high priest's courtyard.[F] He went in and was sitting with the temple police[G] to see the outcome.[H]

[59]The chief priests and the whole Sanhedrin were looking for false testimony against Jesus so they could put Him to death. [60]But they could not find any, even though many false witnesses came forward.[I] Finally, two[J] who came forward [61]stated, "This man said, 'I can demolish God's sanctuary and rebuild it in three days.'"

[62]The high priest then stood up and said to Him, "Don't You have an answer to what these men are testifying against You?" [63]But Jesus kept silent. Then the high priest said to Him, "By the living God I place You under oath: tell us if You are the Messiah, the Son of God!"

[64]"You have said it,"[K] Jesus told him. "But I tell you, in the future[L] you will see the Son of Man seated at the right hand of the Power and coming on the clouds of heaven."[M]

[65]Then the high priest tore his robes and said, "He has blasphemed! Why do we still need witnesses? Look, now you've heard the blasphemy! [66]What is your decision?"[N]

They answered, "He deserves death!" [67]Then they spit in His face and beat Him; others slapped Him [68]and said, "Prophesy to us, Messiah! Who hit You?"

[69]Now Peter was sitting outside in the courtyard. A servant approached him and she said, "You were with Jesus the Galilean too."

[70]But he denied it in front of everyone: "I don't know what you're talking about!"

[71]When he had gone out to the gateway, another woman saw him and told those who were there, "This man was with Jesus the Nazarene!"

[72]And again he denied it with an oath, "I don't know the man!"

[73]After a little while those standing there approached and said to Peter, "You certainly are one of them, since even your accent[O] gives you away."

[74]Then he started to curse[P] and to swear with an oath, "I do not know the man!" Immediately a rooster crowed, [75]and Peter remembered the words Jesus had spoken, "Before the rooster crows, you will deny Me three times." And he went outside and wept bitterly.

27 When daybreak came, all the chief priests and the elders of the people plotted against Jesus to put Him to death. [2]After tying Him up, they led Him away and handed Him over to Pilate,[Q] the governor.

[3]Then Judas, His betrayer, seeing that He had been condemned, was full of remorse and returned the 30 pieces of silver to the chief priests and elders. [4]"I have sinned by betraying innocent blood," he said.

A26:45 Or Sleep on now and take your rest.　B26:50 Or Jesus told him, "do what you have come for." (as a statement)　C26:53 A Roman legion contained up to 6,000 soldiers.　D26:55 Lit as against a criminal　E26:56 Or the Scriptures of the prophets　F26:58 Or high priest's palace　G26:58 Or the officers, or the servants　H26:58 Lit end　I26:60 Other mss add they found none　J26:60 Other mss add false witnesses　K26:64 Or That is true, an affirmative oath; Mt 27:11; Mk 15:2　L26:64 Lit you, from now　M26:64 Ps 110:1; Dn 7:13　N26:66 Lit What does it seem to you?　O26:73 Or speech　P26:74 To call down curses on himself if what he said weren't true　Q27:2 Other mss read Pontius Pilate

"What's that to us?" they said. "See to it yourself!"

[5] So he threw the silver into the sanctuary and departed. Then he went and hanged himself.

[6] The chief priests took the silver and said, "It's not lawful to put it into the temple treasury,[A] since it is blood money."[B] [7] So they conferred together and bought the potter's field with it as a burial place for foreigners. [8] Therefore that field has been called "Blood Field" to this day. [9] Then what was spoken through the prophet Jeremiah was fulfilled:

They took the 30 pieces of silver, the price of Him whose price was set by the Israelites, [10] and they gave them for the potter's field, as the Lord directed me.[C]

[11] Now Jesus stood before the governor. "Are You the King of the Jews?" the governor asked Him.

Jesus answered, "You have said it."[D] [12] And while He was being accused by the chief priests and elders, He didn't answer.

[13] Then Pilate said to Him, "Don't You hear how much they are testifying against You?" [14] But He didn't answer him on even one charge, so that the governor was greatly amazed.

[15] At the festival the governor's custom was to release to the crowd a prisoner they wanted. [16] At that time they had a notorious prisoner called Barabbas.[E] [17] So when they had gathered together, Pilate said to them, "Who is it you want me to release for you—Barabbas,[E] or Jesus who is called Messiah?" [18] For he knew they had handed Him over because of envy.

[19] While he was sitting on the judge's bench, his wife sent word to him, "Have nothing to do with that righteous man, for today I've suffered terribly in a dream because of Him!"

[20] The chief priests and the elders, however, persuaded the crowds to ask for Barabbas and to execute Jesus. [21] The governor asked them, "Which of the two do you want me to release for you?"

"Barabbas!" they answered.

[22] Pilate asked them, "What should I do then with Jesus, who is called Messiah?"

They all answered, "Crucify Him!"[F] [23] Then he said, "Why? What has He done wrong?"

But they kept shouting, "Crucify Him!" all the more.

[24] When Pilate saw that he was getting nowhere,[G] but that a riot was starting instead, he took some water, washed his hands in front of the crowd, and said, "I am innocent of this man's blood.[H] See to it yourselves!"

[25] All the people answered, "His blood be on us and on our children!" [26] Then he released Barabbas to them. But after having Jesus flogged,[I] he handed Him over to be crucified.

[27] Then the governor's soldiers took Jesus into headquarters and gathered the whole company around Him. [28] They stripped Him and dressed Him in a scarlet military robe. [29] They twisted together a crown of thorns, put it on His head, and placed a reed in His right hand. And they knelt down before Him and mocked Him: "Hail, King of the Jews!" [30] Then they spit on Him, took the reed, and kept hitting Him on the head. [31] When they had mocked Him, they stripped Him of the robe, put His clothes on Him, and led Him away to crucify Him.

[32] As they were going out, they found a Cyrenian man named Simon. They forced this man to carry His cross. [33] When they came to a place called *Golgotha* (which means Skull Place), [34] they gave Him wine[J] mixed with gall to drink. But when He tasted it, He would not drink it. [35] After crucifying Him they divided His clothes by casting lots.[K] [36] Then they sat down and were guarding Him there. [37] Above His head they put up the charge against Him in writing:

THIS IS JESUS THE KING OF THE JEWS.

[38] Then two criminals[L] were crucified with Him, one on the right and one on the left. [39] Those who passed by were yelling insults at[M] Him, shaking their heads [40] and saying, "The One who would demolish the sanctuary and rebuild it in three days, save Yourself! If You are the Son of God, come down from the cross!" [41] In the same way the chief priests,

A27:6 See Mk 7:11 where the same Gk word (Corban) means a gift pledged to the temple.   B27:6 Lit the price of blood   C27:9-10 Jr 32:6-9; Zch 11:12-13   D27:11 Or That is true, an affirmative oath; Mt 26:64; Mk 15:2   E27:16,17 Other mss read Jesus Barabbas   F27:22 Lit "Him—be crucified!"   G27:24 Lit that it availed nothing   H27:24 Other mss read this righteous man's blood   I27:26 Roman flogging was done with a whip made of leather strips embedded with pieces of bone or metal that brutally tore the flesh.   J27:34 Other mss read sour wine   K27:35 Other mss add that what was spoken by the prophet might be fulfilled: "They divided My clothes among them, and for My clothing they cast lots."   L27:38 Or revolutionaries   M27:39 Lit passed by blasphemed or were blaspheming with the scribes and elders,[A] mocked Him and said, [42] "He saved others, but He cannot save Himself! He is the King of Israel! Let Him[B] come down now from the cross, and we will believe in Him. [43] He has put His trust in God; let God rescue Him now—if He wants Him!"[C] For He said, 'I am God's Son.'" [44] In the same way even the criminals who were crucified with Him kept taunting Him.

[45] From noon until three in the afternoon[D] darkness came over the whole land.[E] [46] About three in the afternoon Jesus cried out with a loud voice, *"Elí, Elí, lemá[F] sabachtháni?"* that is, "My God, My God, why have You forsaken[G] Me?"[H]

[47] When some of those standing there heard this, they said, "He's calling for Elijah!"

[48] Immediately one of them ran and got a sponge, filled it with sour wine, fixed it on a reed, and offered Him a drink. [49] But the rest said, "Let's see if Elijah comes to save Him!"

[50] Jesus shouted again with a loud voice and gave up His spirit. [51] Suddenly, the curtain of the sanctuary[I] was split in two from top to bottom; the earth quaked and the rocks were split. [52] The tombs were also opened and many bodies of the saints who had fallen asleep were raised. [53] And they came out of the tombs after His resurrection, entered the holy city, and appeared to many.

[54] When the centurion and those with him, who were guarding Jesus, saw the earthquake and the things that had happened, they were terrified and said, "This man really was God's Son!"[J]

[55] Many women who had followed Jesus from Galilee and ministered to Him were there, looking on from a distance. [56] Among them were Mary Magdalene, Mary the mother of James and Joseph, and the mother of Zebedee's sons.

[57] When it was evening, a rich man from Arimathea named Joseph came, who himself had also become a disciple of Jesus. [58] He approached Pilate and asked for Jesus' body. Then Pilate ordered that it[K] be released. [59] So Joseph took the body, wrapped it in clean, fine linen, [60] and placed it in his new tomb, which he had cut into the rock. He left after rolling a great stone against the entrance of the tomb. [61] Mary Magdalene and the other Mary were seated there, facing the tomb.

[62] The next day, which followed the preparation day, the chief priests and the Pharisees gathered before Pilate [63] and said, "Sir, we remember that while this deceiver was still alive He said, 'After three days I will rise again.' [64] Therefore give orders that the tomb be made secure until the third day. Otherwise, His disciples may come, steal Him, and tell the people, 'He has been raised from the dead.' Then the last deception will be worse than the first."

[65] "You have[L] a guard of soldiers,"[M] Pilate told them. "Go and make it as secure as you know how." [66] Then they went and made the tomb secure by sealing the stone and setting the guard.[N]

28 After the Sabbath, as the first day of the week was dawning, Mary Magdalene and the other Mary went to view the tomb. [2] Suddenly there was a violent earthquake, because an angel of the Lord descended from heaven and approached the tomb. He rolled back the stone and was sitting on it. [3] His appearance was like lightning, and his robe was as white as snow. [4] The guards were so shaken from fear of him that they became like dead men.

[5] But the angel told the women, "Don't be afraid, because I know you are looking for Jesus who was crucified. [6] He is not here! For He has been resurrected, just as He said. Come and see the place where He lay. [7] Then go quickly and tell His disciples, 'He has been raised from the dead. In fact, He is going ahead of you to Galilee; you will see Him there.' Listen, I have told you."

[8] So, departing quickly from the tomb with fear and great joy, they ran to tell His disciples the news. [9] Just then[O] Jesus met them and said, "Good morning!" They came up, took hold of His feet, and worshiped Him. [10] Then Jesus told them, "Do not be afraid. Go and tell My brothers to leave for Galilee, and they will see Me there."

[11] As they were on their way, some of the guards came into the city and reported to the chief priests everything that had happened. [12] After the priests[P] had assembled with the

A27:41 Other mss add *and Pharisees*   B27:42 Other mss read *If He . . . Israel, let Him*   C27:43 Or *if He takes pleasure in Him*   D27:45 Lit *From the sixth hour to the ninth hour*   E27:45 Or *whole earth*   F27:46 Some mss read *lama*; other mss read *lima*   G27:46 Or *abandoned*   H27:46 Ps 22:1   I27:51 A heavy curtain separated the inner room of the temple from the outer.   J27:54 Or *the Son of God*   K27:58 Other mss read *that the body*   L27:65 Or *"Take*   M27:65 It is uncertain whether this guard consisted of temple police or Roman soldiers.   N27:66 Lit *stone with the guard*   O28:9 Other mss add *as they were on their way to tell the news to His disciples*   P28:12 Lit *After they* elders and agreed on a plan, they gave the soldiers a large sum of money [13]and told them, "Say this, 'His disciples came during the night and stole Him while we were sleeping.' [14]If this reaches the governor's ears,[A] we will deal with[B] him and keep you out of trouble." [15]So they took the money and did as they were instructed. And this story has been spread among Jewish people to this day.

[16] The 11 disciples traveled to Galilee, to the mountain where Jesus had directed them.

[17]When they saw Him, they worshiped,[C] but some doubted. [18]Then Jesus came near and said to them, "All authority has been given to Me in heaven and on earth. [19]Go, therefore, and make disciples of [D] all nations, baptizing them in the name of the Father and of the Son and of the Holy Spirit, [20]teaching them to observe everything I have commanded you. And remember,[E] I am with you always,[F] to the end of the age."

MARK

1 The beginning of the gospel of Jesus Christ, the Son of God. [2]As it is written in Isaiah the prophet:[G]

**Look, I am sending My messenger ahead of You,
who will prepare Your way.**[H]
[3] **A voice of one crying out
in the wilderness:
Prepare the way for the Lord;
make His paths straight!**[I]

[4]John came baptizing[J] in the wilderness and preaching a baptism of repentance[K] for the forgiveness of sins. [5]The whole Judean countryside and all the people of Jerusalem were flocking to him, and they were baptized by him in the Jordan River as they confessed their sins. [6]John wore a camel-hair garment with a leather belt around his waist and ate locusts and wild honey. [7]He was preaching: "Someone more powerful than I will come after me. I am not worthy to stoop down and untie the strap of His sandals. [8]I have baptized you with[L] water, but He will baptize you with the Holy Spirit."

[9]In those days Jesus came from Nazareth in Galilee and was baptized in the Jordan by John. [10]As soon as He came up out of the water, He saw the heavens being torn open and the Spirit descending to Him like a dove. [11]And a voice came from heaven:

You are My beloved Son;
I take delight in You![M]

[12]Immediately the Spirit drove Him into the wilderness. [13]He was in the wilderness 40 days, being tempted by Satan. He was with the wild animals, and the angels began to serve Him.

[14]After John was arrested, Jesus went to Galilee, preaching the good news[N,O] of God:[P] [15]"The time is fulfilled, and the kingdom of God has come near. Repent and believe in the good news!"

[16]As He was passing along by the Sea of Galilee, He saw Simon and Andrew, Simon's brother. They were casting a net into the sea, since they were fishermen. [17]"Follow Me," Jesus told them, "and I will make you fish for[Q] people!" [18]Immediately they left their nets and followed Him. [19]Going on a little farther, He saw James the son of Zebedee and his brother John. They were in their boat mending their nets. [20]Immediately He called them, and they left their father Zebedee in the boat with the hired men and followed Him.

[21]Then they went into Capernaum, and right away He entered the synagogue on the Sabbath and began to teach. [22]They were astonished at His teaching because, unlike the scribes, He was teaching them as one having authority.

[23]Just then a man with an unclean spirit was in their synagogue. He cried out,[R] [24]"What do You have to do with us,[S] Jesus—Nazarene? Have You come to destroy us? I know who You are—the Holy One of God!"

[25]But Jesus rebuked him and said, "Be quiet,[T] and come out of him!" [26]And the unclean spirit

[A]**28:14** Lit *this is heard by the governor*   [B]**28:14** Lit *will persuade*   [C]**28:17** Other mss add *Him*   [D]**28:19** Or *disciple; lit and instruct*   [E]**28:20** Lit *look*   [F]**28:20** Lit *all the days*   [G]**1:2** Other mss read *in the prophets*   [H]**1:2** Other mss add *before You*   [I]**1:2-3** Is 40:3; Mal 3:1   [J]**1:4** Or *John the Baptist came,* or *John the Baptizer came*   [K]**1:4** Or *a baptism based on repentance*   [L]**1:8** Or *in*   [M]**1:11** Or *In You I am well pleased*   [N]**1:14** Other mss add *of the kingdom*   [O]**1:14** Or *gospel*   [P]**1:14** Either *from God* or *about God*   [Q]**1:17** Lit *you to become fishers of*   [R]**1:23** Other mss add to the beginning of v. 24: *"Leave us alone.*   [S]**1:24** Lit *What to us and to You*   [T]**1:25** Or *Be muzzled* convulsed him, shouted with a loud voice, and came out of him.

²⁷Then they were all amazed, so they began to argue with one another, saying, "What is this? A new teaching with authority!ᴬ He commands even the unclean spirits, and they obey Him." ²⁸News about Him then spread throughout the entire vicinity of Galilee.

²⁹As soon as they left the synagogue, they went into Simon and Andrew's house with James and John. ³⁰Simon's mother-in-law was lying in bed with a fever, and they told Him about her at once. ³¹So He went to her, took her by the hand, and raised her up. The fever left her,ᴮ and she began to serve them.

³²When evening came, after the sun had set, they began bringing to Him all those who were sick and those who were demon-possessed. ³³The whole town was assembled at the door, ³⁴and He healed many who were sick with various diseases and drove out many demons. But He would not permit the demons to speak, because they knew Him.

³⁵Very early in the morning, while it was still dark, He got up, went out, and made His way to a deserted place. And He was praying there. ³⁶Simon and his companions went searching for Him. ³⁷They found Him and said, "Everyone's looking for You!"

³⁸And He said to them, "Let's go on to the neighboring villages so that I may preach there too. This is why I have come." ³⁹So He went into all of Galilee, preaching in their synagogues and driving out demons.

⁴⁰Then a man with a serious skin disease came to Him and, on his knees,ᶜ begged Him: "If You are willing, You can make me clean."

⁴¹Moved with compassion, Jesus reached out His hand and touched him. "I am willing," He told him. "Be made clean." ⁴²Immediately the disease left him, and he was healed.ᴰ ⁴³Then He sternly warned him and sent him away at once, ⁴⁴telling him, "See that you say nothing to anyone; but go and show yourself to the priest, and offer what Moses prescribed for your cleansing, as a testimony to them." ⁴⁵Yet he went out and began to proclaim it widely and to spread the news, with the result that Jesus could no longer enter a town openly. But

He was out in deserted places, and they would come to Him from everywhere.

2 When He entered Capernaum again after some days, it was reported that He was at home. ²So many people gathered together that there was no more room, not even in the doorway, and He was speaking the message to them. ³Then they came to Him bringing a paralytic, carried by four men. ⁴Since they were not able to bring him toᴱ Jesus because of the crowd, they removed the roof above where He was. And when they had broken through, they lowered the mat on which the paralytic was lying.

⁵Seeing their faith, Jesus told the paralytic, "Son, your sins are forgiven."

⁶But some of the scribes were sitting there, thinking to themselves:ᶠ ⁷"Why does He speak like this? He's blaspheming! Who can forgive sins but God alone?"

⁸Right away Jesus understood in His spirit that they were thinking like this within themselves and said to them, "Why are you thinking these things in your hearts?ᴳ ⁹Which is easier: to say to the paralytic, 'Your sins are forgiven,' or to say, 'Get up, pick up your mat, and walk'? ¹⁰But so you may know that the Son of Man has authority on earth to forgive sins," He told the paralytic, ¹¹"I tell you: get up, pick up your mat, and go home."

¹²Immediately he got up, picked up the mat, and went out in front of everyone. As a result, they were all astounded and gave glory to God, saying, "We have never seen anything like this!"

¹³Then Jesus went out again beside the sea. The whole crowd was coming to Him, and He taught them. ¹⁴Then, moving on, He saw Levi the son of Alphaeus sitting at the tax office, and He said to him, "Follow Me!" So he got up and followed Him.

¹⁵While He was reclining at the table in Levi's house, many tax collectors and sinners were also guestsᴴ with Jesus and His disciples, because there were many who were following Him. ¹⁶When the scribes of the Phariseesᴵ saw that He was eating with sinners and tax collectors, they asked His disciples, "Why does He eatᴶ with tax collectors and sinners?"

[17] When Jesus heard this, He told them, "Those who are well don't need a doctor, but the sick do need one. I didn't come to call the righteous, but sinners."

[18] Now John's disciples and the Pharisees[A] were fasting. People came and asked Him, "Why do John's disciples and the Pharisees' disciples fast, but Your disciples do not fast?"

[19] Jesus said to them, "The wedding guests[B] cannot fast while the groom is with them, can they? As long as they have the groom with them, they cannot fast. [20] But the time[C] will come when the groom is taken away from them, and then they will fast in that day. [21] No one sews a patch of unshrunk cloth on an old garment. Otherwise, the new patch pulls away from the old cloth, and a worse tear is made. [22] And no one puts new wine into old wineskins. Otherwise, the wine will burst the skins, and the wine is lost as well as the skins.[D] But new wine is for fresh wineskins."

[23] On the Sabbath He was going through the grainfields, and His disciples began to make their way picking some heads of grain. [24] The Pharisees said to Him, "Look, why are they doing what is not lawful on the Sabbath?"

[25] He said to them, "Have you never read what David and those who were with him did when he was in need and hungry— [26] how he entered the house of God in the time of Abiathar the high priest and ate the sacred bread—which is not lawful for anyone to eat except the priests—and also gave some to his companions?" [27] Then He told them, "The Sabbath was made for[E] man and not man for[E] the Sabbath. [28] Therefore, the Son of Man is Lord even of the Sabbath."

3 Now He entered the synagogue again, and a man was there who had a paralyzed hand. [2] In order to accuse Him, they were watching Him closely to see whether He would heal him on the Sabbath. [3] He told the man with the paralyzed hand, "Stand before us."[F] [4] Then He said to them, "Is it lawful on the Sabbath to do what is good or to do what is evil, to save life or to kill?" But they were silent. [5] After looking around at them with anger and sorrow at the hardness of their hearts, He told the man, "Stretch out your hand." So he stretched it out, and his hand was restored. [6] Immediately the Pharisees went out and started plotting with the Herodians against Him, how they might destroy Him.

[7] Jesus departed with His disciples to the sea, and a large crowd followed from Galilee, Judea, [8] Jerusalem, Idumea, beyond the Jordan, and around Tyre and Sidon. The large crowd came to Him because they heard about everything He was doing. [9] Then He told His disciples to have a small boat ready for Him, so the crowd would not crush Him. [10] Since He had healed many, all who had diseases were pressing toward Him to touch Him. [11] Whenever the unclean spirits saw Him, those possessed fell down before Him and cried out, "You are the Son of God!" [12] And He would strongly warn them not to make Him known.

[13] Then He went up the mountain and summoned those He wanted, and they came to Him. [14] He also appointed 12—He also named them apostles[G]—to be with Him, to send them out to preach, [15] and to have authority to[H] drive out demons.

[16] He appointed the Twelve:[I]

To Simon, He gave the name Peter;
[17] and to James the son of Zebedee,
and to his brother John,
He gave the name "Boanerges"
(that is, "Sons of Thunder");
[18] Andrew;
Philip and Bartholomew;
Matthew and Thomas;
James the son of Alphaeus,
and Thaddaeus;
Simon the Zealot,[J]
[19] and Judas Iscariot,[K]
who also betrayed Him.

[20] Then He went home, and the crowd gathered again so that they were not even able to eat.[L] [21] When His family heard this, they set out to restrain Him, because they said, "He's out of His mind."

[22] The scribes who had come down from Jerusalem said, "He has Beelzebul in Him!" and, "He drives out demons by the ruler of the demons!"

[23] So He summoned them and spoke to them in parables: "How can Satan drive out Satan? [24] If a kingdom is divided against itself, that kingdom cannot stand. [25] If a house is divided

against itself, that house cannot stand. [26] And if Satan rebels against himself and is divided, he cannot stand but is finished![A]

[27] "On the other hand, no one can enter a strong man's house and rob his possessions unless he first ties up the strong man. Then he will rob his house. [28] I assure you: People will be forgiven for all sins[B] and whatever blasphemies they may blaspheme. [29] But whoever blasphemes against the Holy Spirit never has forgiveness, but is guilty of an eternal sin"[C]— [30] because they were saying, "He has an unclean spirit."

[31] Then His mother and His brothers came, and standing outside, they sent word to Him and called Him. [32] A crowd was sitting around Him and told Him, "Look, Your mother, Your brothers, and Your sisters[D] are outside asking for You."

[33] He replied to them, "Who are My mother and My brothers?" [34] And looking about at those who were sitting in a circle around Him, He said, "Here are My mother and My brothers! [35] Whoever does the will of God is My brother and sister and mother."

4 Again He began to teach by the sea, and a very large crowd gathered around Him. So He got into a boat on the sea and sat down, while the whole crowd was on the shore facing the sea. [2] He taught them many things in parables, and in His teaching He said to them: [3] "Listen! Consider the sower who went out to sow. [4] As he sowed, this occurred: Some seed fell along the path, and the birds came and ate it up. [5] Other seed fell on rocky ground where it didn't have much soil, and it sprang up right away, since it didn't have deep soil. [6] When the sun came up, it was scorched, and since it didn't have a root, it withered. [7] Other seed fell among thorns, and the thorns came up and choked it, and it didn't produce a crop. [8] Still others fell on good ground and produced a crop that increased 30, 60, and 100 times what was sown." [9] Then He said, "Anyone who has ears to hear should listen!"

[10] When He was alone with the Twelve, those who were around Him asked Him about the parables. [11] He answered them, "The secret of the kingdom of God has been given to you, but to those outside, everything comes in parables [12] so that

> they may look and look,
> yet not perceive;
> they may listen and listen,
> yet not understand;
> otherwise, they might turn back—
> and be forgiven."[E,F]

[13] Then He said to them: "Don't you understand this parable? How then will you understand any of the parables? [14] The sower sows the word. [15] These[G] are the ones along the path where the word is sown: when they hear, immediately Satan comes and takes away the word sown in them.[H] [16] And these are[I] the ones sown on rocky ground: when they hear the word, immediately they receive it with joy. [17] But they have no root in themselves; they are short-lived. When pressure or persecution comes because of the word, they immediately stumble. [18] Others are sown among thorns; these are the ones who hear the word, [19] but the worries of this age, the seduction[J] of wealth, and the desires for other things enter in and choke the word, and it becomes unfruitful. [20] But the ones sown on good ground are those who hear the word, welcome it, and produce a crop: 30, 60, and 100 times what was sown."

[21] He also said to them, "Is a lamp brought in to be put under a basket or under a bed? Isn't it to be put on a lampstand? [22] For nothing is concealed except to be revealed, and nothing hidden except to come to light. [23] If anyone has ears to hear, he should listen!" [24] Then He said to them, "Pay attention to what you hear. By the measure you use,[K] it will be measured and added to you. [25] For to the one who has, it will be given, and from the one who does not have, even what he has will be taken away."

[26] "The kingdom of God is like this," He said. "A man scatters seed on the ground; [27] he sleeps and rises—night and day, and the seed sprouts and grows—he doesn't know how. [28] The soil produces a crop by itself—first the blade, then the head, and then the ripe grain on the head. [29] But as soon as the crop is ready, he sends for the sickle, because the harvest has come."

A3:26 Lit but he has an end   B3:28 Lit All things will be forgiven the sons of men   C3:29 Other mss read is subject to eternal judgment
D3:32 Other mss omit and Your sisters   E4:12 Other mss read and their sins be forgiven them   F4:12 Is 6:9-10   G4:15 Some people
H4:15 Other mss read in their hearts   I4:16 Other mss read are like   J4:19 Or pleasure, or deceitfulness   K4:24 Lit you measure

³⁰And He said: "How can we illustrate the kingdom of God, or what parable can we use to describe it? ³¹It's like a mustard seed that, when sown in the soil, is smaller than all the seeds on the ground. ³²And when sown, it comes up and grows taller than all the vegetables, and produces large branches, so that the birds of the sky can nest in its shade."

³³He would speak the word to them with many parables like these, as they were able to understand. ³⁴And He did not speak to them without a parable. Privately, however, He would explain everything to His own disciples.

³⁵On that day, when evening had come, He told them, "Let's cross over to the other side of the sea." ³⁶So they left the crowd and took Him along since He was already in the boat. And other boats were with Him. ³⁷A fierce windstorm arose, and the waves were breaking over the boat, so that the boat was already being swamped. ³⁸But He was in the stern, sleeping on the cushion. So they woke Him up and said to Him, "Teacher! Don't You care that we're going to die?"

³⁹He got up, rebuked the wind, and said to the sea, "Silence! Be still!" The wind ceased, and there was a great calm. ⁴⁰Then He said to them, "Why are you fearful? Do you still have no faith?"

⁴¹And they were terrified and asked one another, "Who then is this? Even the wind and the sea obey Him!"

5 Then they came to the other side of the sea, to the region of the Gerasenes.ᴬ ²As soon as He got out of the boat, a man with an unclean spirit came out of the tombs and met Him. ³He lived in the tombs. No one was able to restrain him anymore—even with chains— ⁴because he often had been bound with shackles and chains, but had snapped off the chains and smashed the shackles. No one was strong enough to subdue him. ⁵And always, night and day, he was crying out among the tombs and in the mountains and cutting himself with stones.

⁶When he saw Jesus from a distance, he ran and knelt down before Him. ⁷And he cried out with a loud voice, "What do You have to do with me,ᴮ Jesus, Son of the Most High God? I begᶜ You before God, don't torment me!" ⁸For

He had told him, "Come out of the man, you unclean spirit!"

⁹"What is your name?" He asked him.

"My name is Legion,"ᴰ he answered Him, "because we are many." ¹⁰And he kept begging Him not to send them out of the region.

¹¹Now a large herd of pigs was there, feeding on the hillside. ¹²The demonsᴱ begged Him, "Send us to the pigs, so we may enter them." ¹³And He gave them permission. Then the unclean spirits came out and entered the pigs, and the herd of about 2,000 rushed down the steep bank into the sea and drowned there. ¹⁴The men who tended themᶠ ran off and reported it in the town and the countryside, and people went to see what had happened. ¹⁵They came to Jesus and saw the man who had been demon-possessed by the legion, sitting there, dressed and in his right mind; and they were afraid. ¹⁶The eyewitnesses described to them what had happened to the demon-possessed man and told about the pigs. ¹⁷Then they began to beg Him to leave their region.

¹⁸As He was getting into the boat, the man who had been demon-possessed kept begging Him to be with Him. ¹⁹But He would not let him; instead, He told him, "Go back home to your own people, and report to them how much the Lord has done for you and how He has had mercy on you." ²⁰So he went out and began to proclaim in the Decapolis how much Jesus had done for him, and they were all amazed.

²¹When Jesus had crossed over again by boat to the other side, a large crowd gathered around Him while He was by the sea. ²²One of the synagogue leaders, named Jairus, came, and when he saw Jesus, he fell at His feet ²³and kept begging Him, "My little daughter is at death's door.ᴳ Come and lay Your hands on her so she can get well and live."

²⁴So Jesus went with him, and a large crowd was following and pressing against Him. ²⁵A woman suffering from bleeding for 12 years ²⁶had endured much under many doctors. She had spent everything she had and was not helped at all. On the contrary, she became worse. ²⁷Having heard about Jesus, she came behind Him in the crowd and touched His robe. ²⁸For she said, "If I can just touch His robes, I'll be made well!" ²⁹Instantly her flow

ᴬ5:1 Some mss read *Gadarenes*; other mss read *Gergesenes* ᴮ5:7 Lit *What to me and to You* ᶜ5:7 Or *adjure* ᴰ5:9 A Roman legion contained up to 6,000 soldiers; here legion indicates a large number. ᴱ5:12 Other mss read *All the demons* ᶠ5:14 Other mss read *tended the pigs* ᴳ5:23 Lit *My little daughter has it finally*; = to be at the end of life of blood ceased, and she sensed in her body that she was cured of her affliction.

³⁰ At once Jesus realized in Himself that power had gone out from Him. He turned around in the crowd and said, "Who touched My robes?"

³¹ His disciples said to Him, "You see the crowd pressing against You, and You say, 'Who touched Me?'"

³² So He was looking around to see who had done this. ³³ Then the woman, knowing what had happened to her, came with fear and trembling, fell down before Him, and told Him the whole truth. ³⁴ "Daughter," He said to her, "your faith has made you well.ᴬ Go in peace and be freeᴮ from your affliction."

³⁵ While He was still speaking, people came from the synagogue leader's house and said, "Your daughter is dead. Why bother the Teacher anymore?"

³⁶ But when Jesus overheard what was said, He told the synagogue leader, "Don't be afraid. Only believe." ³⁷ He did not let anyone accompany Him except Peter, James, and John, James's brother. ³⁸ They came to the leader's house, and He saw a commotion—people weeping and wailing loudly. ³⁹ He went in and said to them, "Why are you making a commotion and weeping? The child is not dead but asleep."

⁴⁰ They started laughing at Him, but He put them all outside. He took the child's father, mother, and those who were with Him, and entered the place where the child was. ⁴¹ Then He took the child by the hand and said to her, *"Talitha koum!"*ᶜ (which is translated, "Little girl, I say to you, get up!"). ⁴² Immediately the girl got up and began to walk. (She was 12 years old.) At this they were utterly astounded. ⁴³ Then He gave them strict orders that no one should know about this and said that she should be given something to eat.

6 He went away from there and came to His hometown, and His disciples followed Him. ² When the Sabbath came, He began to teach in the synagogue, and many who heard Him were astonished. "Where did this man get these things?" they said. "What is this wisdom given to Him, and how are these miracles performed by His hands? ³ Isn't this the carpenter, the son of Mary, and the brother of James, Jo-

ses, Judas, and Simon? And aren't His sisters here with us?" So they were offended by Him.

⁴ Then Jesus said to them, "A prophet is not without honor except in his hometown, among his relatives, and in his household." ⁵ So He was not able to do any miraclesᴰ there, except that He laid His hands on a few sick people and healed them. ⁶ And He was amazed at their unbelief.

Now He was going around the villages in a circuit, teaching. ⁷ He summoned the Twelve and began to send them out in pairs and gave them authority over unclean spirits. ⁸ He instructed them to take nothing for the road except a walking stick: no bread, no traveling bag, no money in their belts. ⁹ They were to wear sandals, but not put on an extra shirt. ¹⁰ Then He said to them, "Whenever you enter a house, stay there until you leave that place. ¹¹ If any place does not welcome you and people refuse to listen to you, when you leave there, shake the dust off your feet as a testimony against them."ᴱ

¹² So they went out and preached that people should repent. ¹³ And they were driving out many demons, anointing many sick people with olive oil, and healing them.

¹⁴ King Herod heard of this, because Jesus' name had become well known. Someᶠ said, "John the Baptist has been raised from the dead, and that's why supernatural powers are at work in him." ¹⁵ But others said, "He's Elijah." Still others said, "He's a prophetᴳ—like one of the prophets."

¹⁶ When Herod heard of it, he said, "John, the one I beheaded, has been raised!" ¹⁷ For Herod himself had given orders to arrest John and to chain him in prison on account of Herodias, his brother Philip's wife, whom he had married. ¹⁸ John had been telling Herod, "It is not lawful for you to have your brother's wife!" ¹⁹ So Herodias held a grudge against him and wanted to kill him. But she could not, ²⁰ because Herod was in awe ofᴴ John and was protecting him, knowing he was a righteous and holy man. When Herod heard him he would be very disturbed,ⁱ yet would hear him gladly.

²¹ Now an opportune time came on his birthday, when Herod gave a banquet for his nobles, military commanders, and the leading men of Galilee. ²² When Herodias's own daughterᴶ

ᴬ5:34 Or *has saved you*   ᴮ5:34 Lit *healthy*   ᶜ5:41 An Aram expression   ᴰ6:5 Lit *miracle*   ᴱ6:11 Other mss add *I assure you, it will be more tolerable for Sodom or Gomorrah on judgment day than for that town.*   ᶠ6:14 Other mss read *He*   ᴳ6:15 Lit *Others said, "A prophet*   ᴴ6:20 Or *Herod feared*   ⁱ6:20 Other mss read *When he heard him, he did many things*   ᴶ6:22 Other mss read *When his daughter Herodias* came in and danced, she pleased Herod and his guests. The king said to the girl, "Ask me whatever you want, and I'll give it to you." [23] So he swore oaths to her: "Whatever you ask me I will give you, up to half my kingdom."

[24] Then she went out and said to her mother, "What should I ask for?"

"John the Baptist's head!" she said.

[25] Immediately she hurried to the king and said, "I want you to give me John the Baptist's head on a platter—right now!"

[26] Though the king was deeply distressed, because of his oaths and the guests[A] he did not want to refuse her. [27] The king immediately sent for an executioner and commanded him to bring John's head. So he went and beheaded him in prison, [28] brought his head on a platter, and gave it to the girl. Then the girl gave it to her mother. [29] When his disciples[B] heard about it, they came and removed his corpse and placed it in a tomb.

[30] The apostles gathered around Jesus and reported to Him all that they had done and taught. [31] He said to them, "Come away by yourselves to a remote place and rest for a while." For many people were coming and going, and they did not even have time to eat. [32] So they went away in the boat by themselves to a remote place, [33] but many saw them leaving and recognized them. People ran there by land from all the towns and arrived ahead of them.[C] [34] So as He stepped ashore, He saw a huge crowd and had compassion on them, because they were like sheep without a shepherd. Then He began to teach them many things.

[35] When it was already late, His disciples approached Him and said, "This place is a wilderness, and it is already late! [36] Send them away, so they can go into the surrounding countryside and villages to buy themselves something to eat."

[37] "You give them something to eat," He responded.

They said to Him, "Should we go and buy 200 denarii worth of bread and give them something to eat?"

[38] And He asked them, "How many loaves do you have? Go look."

When they found out they said, "Five, and two fish."

[39] Then He instructed them to have all the people sit down[D] in groups on the green grass. [40] So they sat down in ranks of hundreds and fifties. [41] Then He took the five loaves and the two fish, and looking up to heaven, He blessed and broke the loaves. He kept giving them to His disciples to set before the people. He also divided the two fish among them all. [42] Everyone ate and was filled. [43] Then they picked up 12 baskets full of pieces of bread and fish. [44] Now those who ate the loaves were 5,000 men.

[45] Immediately He made His disciples get into the boat and go ahead of Him to the other side, to Bethsaida, while He dismissed the crowd. [46] After He said good-bye to them, He went away to the mountain to pray. [47] When evening came, the boat was in the middle of the sea, and He was alone on the land. [48] He saw them being battered as they rowed,[E] because the wind was against them. Around three in the morning[F] He came toward them walking on the sea and wanted to pass by them. [49] When they saw Him walking on the sea, they thought it was a ghost and cried out; [50] for they all saw Him and were terrified. Immediately He spoke with them and said, "Have courage! It is I. Don't be afraid." [51] Then He got into the boat with them, and the wind ceased. They were completely astounded,[G] [52] because they had not understood about the loaves. Instead, their hearts were hardened.

[53] When they had crossed over, they came to land at Gennesaret and beached the boat. [54] As they got out of the boat, people immediately recognized Him. [55] They hurried throughout that vicinity and began to carry the sick on mats to wherever they heard He was. [56] Wherever He would go, into villages, towns, or the country, they laid the sick in the marketplaces and begged Him that they might touch just the tassel of His robe. And everyone who touched it was made well.

7 The Pharisees and some of the scribes who had come from Jerusalem gathered around Him. [2] They observed that some of His disciples were eating their bread with unclean—that is, unwashed—hands. [3] (For the Pharisees, in fact all the Jews, will not eat unless they wash their hands ritually, keeping the tradition of the elders. [4] When they come from the marketplace,

---

[A]6:26 Lit and those reclining at the table [B]6:29 = John's disciples [C]6:33 Other mss add and gathered around Him [D]6:39 Lit people recline [E]6:48 Or them struggling as they rowed [F]6:48 Lit Around the fourth watch of the night = 3 to 6 a.m. [G]6:51 Lit were astounded in themselves they do not eat unless they have washed. And there are many other customs they have received and keep, like the washing of cups, jugs, copper utensils, and dining couches.^A) ⁵Then the Pharisees and the scribes asked Him, "Why don't Your disciples live according to the tradition of the elders, instead of eating bread with ritually unclean^B hands?"

⁶He answered them, "Isaiah prophesied correctly about you hypocrites, as it is written:

These people honor Me with their lips,
but their heart is far from Me.
⁷ They worship Me in vain,
teaching as doctrines the commands
of men.^C

⁸Disregarding the command of God, you keep the tradition of men."^D ⁹He also said to them, "You completely invalidate God's command in order to maintain^E your tradition! ¹⁰For Moses said:

Honor your father
and your mother;^F and
Whoever speaks evil of father
or mother
must be put to death.^G

¹¹But you say, 'If a man tells his father or mother: Whatever benefit you might have received from me is Corban'" (that is, a gift committed to the temple), ¹²"you no longer let him do anything for his father or mother. ¹³You revoke God's word by your tradition that you have handed down. And you do many other similar things." ¹⁴Summoning the crowd again, He told them, "Listen to Me, all of you, and understand: ¹⁵Nothing that goes into a person from outside can defile him, but the things that come out of a person are what defile him. [¹⁶If anyone has ears to hear, he should listen!]"^H

¹⁷When He went into the house away from the crowd, the disciples asked Him about the parable. ¹⁸And He said to them, "Are you also as lacking in understanding? Don't you realize that nothing going into a man from the outside can defile him? ¹⁹For it doesn't go into his heart but into the stomach and is eliminated."^I (As a result, He made all foods clean.^J) ²⁰Then He said, "What comes out of a person—that defiles him. ²¹For from within, out of people's

hearts, come evil thoughts, sexual immoralities, thefts, murders, ²²adulteries, greed, evil actions, deceit, promiscuity, stinginess,^K blasphemy, pride, and foolishness. ²³All these evil things come from within and defile a person."

²⁴He got up and departed from there to the region of Tyre and Sidon.^L He entered a house and did not want anyone to know it, but He could not escape notice. ²⁵Instead, immediately after hearing about Him, a woman whose little daughter had an unclean spirit came and fell at His feet. ²⁶Now the woman was Greek, a Syrophoenician by birth, and she kept asking Him to drive the demon out of her daughter. ²⁷He said to her, "Allow the children to be satisfied first, because it isn't right to take the children's bread and throw it to the dogs."

²⁸But she replied to Him, "Lord, even the dogs under the table eat the children's crumbs."

²⁹Then He told her, "Because of this reply, you may go. The demon has gone out of your daughter." ³⁰When she went back to her home, she found her child lying on the bed, and the demon was gone.

³¹Again, leaving the region of Tyre, He went by way of Sidon to the Sea of Galilee, through^M the region of the Decapolis. ³²They brought to Him a deaf man who also had a speech difficulty, and begged Jesus to lay His hand on him. ³³So He took him away from the crowd privately. After putting His fingers in the man's ears and spitting, He touched his tongue. ³⁴Then, looking up to heaven, He sighed deeply and said to him, "Ephphatha!"^N (that is, "Be opened!"). ³⁵Immediately his ears were opened, his speech difficulty was removed,^O and he began to speak clearly. ³⁶Then He ordered them to tell no one, but the more He would order them, the more they would proclaim it.

³⁷They were extremely astonished and said, "He has done everything well! He even makes deaf people hear, and people unable to speak, talk!"

8 In those days there was again a large crowd, and they had nothing to eat. He summoned the disciples and said to them, ²"I have compassion on the crowd, because they've already stayed with Me three days and have nothing to eat. ³If I send them home

^A7:4 Other mss omit and dining couches   ^B7:5 Other mss read with unwashed   ^C7:6-7 Is 29:13   ^D7:8 Other mss add The washing of jugs, and cups, and many other similar things you practice.   ^E7:9 Other mss read to establish   ^F7:10 Ex 20:12; Dt 5:16   ^G7:10 Ex 21:17; Lv 20:9   ^H7:16 Other mss omit bracketed text   ^I7:19 Lit goes out into the toilet   ^J7:19 Other mss read is eliminated, making all foods clean."   ^K7:22 Lit evil eye   ^L7:24 Other mss omit and Sidon   ^M7:31 Or into   ^N7:34 An Aram expression   ^O7:35 Lit opened, the bond of his tongue was untied hungry,[A] they will collapse on the way, and some of them have come a long distance."

⁴His disciples answered Him, "Where can anyone get enough bread here in this desolate place to fill these people?"

⁵"How many loaves do you have?" He asked them.

"Seven," they said. ⁶Then He commanded the crowd to sit down on the ground. Taking the seven loaves, He gave thanks, broke the loaves, and kept on giving them to His disciples to set before the people. So they served the loaves to the crowd. ⁷They also had a few small fish, and when He had blessed them, He said these were to be served as well. ⁸They ate and were filled. Then they collected seven large baskets of leftover pieces. ⁹About 4,000 men were there. He dismissed them ¹⁰and immediately got into the boat with His disciples and went to the district of Dalmanutha.[B]

¹¹The Pharisees came out and began to argue with Him, demanding of Him a sign from heaven to test Him. ¹²But sighing deeply in His spirit, He said, "Why does this generation demand a sign? I assure you: No sign will be given to this generation!" ¹³Then He left them, got on board the boat again, and went to the other side.

¹⁴They had forgotten to take bread and had only one loaf with them in the boat. ¹⁵Then He commanded them: "Watch out! Beware of the yeast of the Pharisees and the yeast of Herod."

¹⁶They were discussing among themselves that they did not have any bread. ¹⁷Aware of this, He said to them, "Why are you discussing that you do not have any bread? Don't you understand or comprehend? Is your heart hardened? ¹⁸Do you have eyes, and not see, and do you have ears, and not hear?[C] And do you not remember? ¹⁹When I broke the five loaves for the 5,000, how many baskets full of pieces of bread did you collect?"

"Twelve," they told Him.

²⁰"When I broke the seven loaves for the 4,000, how many large baskets full of pieces of bread did you collect?"

"Seven," they said.

²¹And He said to them, "Don't you understand yet?"

²²Then they came to Bethsaida. They brought a blind man to Him and begged Him to touch him. ²³He took the blind man by the hand and brought him out of the village. Spitting on his eyes and laying His hands on him, He asked him, "Do you see anything?"

²⁴He looked up and said, "I see people—they look to me like trees walking."

²⁵Again Jesus placed His hands on the man's eyes, and he saw distinctly. He was cured and could see everything clearly. ²⁶Then He sent him home, saying, "Don't even go into the village."[D]

²⁷Jesus went out with His disciples to the villages of Caesarea Philippi. And on the road He asked His disciples, "Who do people say that I am?"

²⁸They answered Him, "John the Baptist; others, Elijah; still others, one of the prophets."

²⁹"But you," He asked them again, "who do you say that I am?"

Peter answered Him, "You are the Messiah!"

³⁰And He strictly warned them to tell no one about Him.

³¹Then He began to teach them that the Son of Man must suffer many things and be rejected by the elders, the chief priests, and the scribes, be killed, and rise after three days. ³²He was openly talking about this. So Peter took Him aside and began to rebuke Him.

³³But turning around and looking at His disciples, He rebuked Peter and said, "Get behind Me, Satan, because you're not thinking about God's concerns,[E] but man's!"

³⁴Summoning the crowd along with His disciples, He said to them, "If anyone wants to be My follower, he must deny himself, take up his cross, and follow Me. ³⁵For whoever wants to save his life will lose it, but whoever loses his life because of Me and the gospel will save it. ³⁶For what does it benefit a man to gain the whole world yet lose his life? ³⁷What can a man give in exchange for his life? ³⁸For whoever is ashamed of Me and of My words in this adulterous and sinful generation, the Son of Man will also be ashamed of him when He comes in the glory of His Father with the holy angels."

9 Then He said to them, "I assure you: There are some standing here who will not taste death until they see the kingdom of God come in power."

²After six days Jesus took Peter, James, and John and led them up on a high mountain by themselves to be alone. He was transformed[F]

ᴬ8:3 Or fasting   ᴮ8:10 Probably on the western shore of the Sea of Galilee   ᶜ8:18 Jr 5:21; Ezk 12:2   ᴰ8:26 Other mss add or tell anyone in the village   ᴱ8:33 Lit about the things of God   ᶠ9:2 Or transfigured in front of them, ³and His clothes became dazzling—extremely white as no launderer on earth could whiten them. ⁴Elijah appeared to them with Moses, and they were talking with Jesus.

⁵Then Peter said to Jesus, "Rabbi, it's good for us to be here! Let us make three tabernacles: one for You, one for Moses, and one for Elijah"— ⁶because he did not know what he should say, since they were terrified.

⁷A cloud appeared, overshadowing them, and a voice came from the cloud:

This is My beloved Son;
listen to Him!

⁸Then suddenly, looking around, they no longer saw anyone with them except Jesus alone.

⁹As they were coming down from the mountain, He ordered them to tell no one what they had seen until the Son of Man had risen from the dead. ¹⁰They kept this word to themselves, discussing what "rising from the dead" meant. ¹¹Then they began to question Him, "Why do the scribes say that Elijah must come first?"

¹²"Elijah does come first and restores everything," He replied. "How then is it written about the Son of Man that He must suffer many things and be treated with contempt? ¹³But I tell you that Elijah really has come, and they did whatever they pleased to him, just as it is written about him."

¹⁴When they came to the disciples, they saw a large crowd around them and scribes disputing with them. ¹⁵All of a sudden, when the whole crowd saw Him, they were amazed^A and ran to greet Him. ¹⁶Then He asked them, "What are you arguing with them about?"

¹⁷Out of the crowd, one man answered Him, "Teacher, I brought my son to You. He has a spirit that makes him unable to speak. ¹⁸Wherever it seizes him, it throws him down, and he foams at the mouth, grinds his teeth, and becomes rigid. So I asked Your disciples to drive it out, but they couldn't."

¹⁹He replied to them, "You unbelieving generation! How long will I be with you? How long must I put up with you? Bring him to Me." ²⁰So they brought him to Him. When the spirit saw Him, it immediately convulsed the boy. He fell to the ground and rolled around, foaming

at the mouth. ²¹"How long has this been happening to him?" Jesus asked his father.

"From childhood," he said. ²²"And many times it has thrown him into fire or water to destroy him. But if You can do anything, have compassion on us and help us."

²³Then Jesus said to him, "'If You can'?^B,^C Everything is possible to the one who believes."

²⁴Immediately the father of the boy cried out, "I do believe! Help my unbelief."

²⁵When Jesus saw that a crowd was rapidly coming together, He rebuked the unclean spirit, saying to it, "You mute and deaf spirit,^D I command you: come out of him and never enter him again!"

²⁶Then it came out, shrieking and convulsing him^E violently. The boy became like a corpse, so that many said, "He's dead." ²⁷But Jesus, taking him by the hand, raised him, and he stood up.

²⁸After He went into a house, His disciples asked Him privately, "Why couldn't we drive it out?"

²⁹And He told them, "This kind can come out by nothing but prayer [and fasting]."^F

³⁰Then they left that place and made their way through Galilee, but He did not want anyone to know it. ³¹For He was teaching His disciples and telling them, "The Son of Man is being betrayed^G into the hands of men. They will kill Him, and after He is killed, He will rise three days later." ³²But they did not understand this statement, and they were afraid to ask Him.

³³Then they came to Capernaum. When He was in the house, He asked them, "What were you arguing about on the way?" ³⁴But they were silent, because on the way they had been arguing with one another about who was the greatest. ³⁵Sitting down, He called the Twelve and said to them, "If anyone wants to be first, he must be last of all and servant of all." ³⁶Then He took a child, had him stand among them, and taking him in His arms, He said to them, ³⁷"Whoever welcomes^H one little child such as this in My name welcomes Me. And whoever welcomes Me does not welcome Me, but Him who sent Me."

³⁸John said to Him, "Teacher, we saw someone^I driving out demons in Your name, and we

tried to stop him because he wasn't following us."

³⁹"Don't stop him," said Jesus, "because there is no one who will perform a miracle in My name who can soon afterward speak evil of Me. ⁴⁰For whoever is not against us is for us. ⁴¹And whoever gives you a cup of water to drink because of My name,ᴬ since you belong to the Messiah—I assure you: He will never lose his reward.

⁴²"But whoever causes the downfall of one of these little ones who believe in Me—it would be better for him if a heavy millstoneᴮ were hung around his neck and he were thrown into the sea. ⁴³And if your hand causes your downfall, cut it off. It is better for you to enter life maimed than to have two hands and go to hell—the unquenchable fire, [⁴⁴where

> Their worm does not die,
> and the fire is not quenched.]ᶜ·ᴰ

⁴⁵And if your foot causes your downfall, cut it off. It is better for you to enter life lame than to have two feet and be thrown into hell— [the unquenchable fire, ⁴⁶where

> Their worm does not die,
> and the fire is not quenched.]ᶜ·ᴰ

⁴⁷And if your eye causes your downfall, gouge it out. It is better for you to enter the kingdom of God with one eye than to have two eyes and be thrown into hell, ⁴⁸where

> Their worm does not die,
> and the fire is not quenched.ᴰ

⁴⁹For everyone will be salted with fire.ᴱ·ᶠ ⁵⁰Salt is good, but if the salt should lose its flavor, how can you make it salty? Have salt among yourselves and be at peace with one another."

10 He set out from there and went to the region of Judea and across the Jordan. Then crowds converged on Him again and, as He usually did, He began teaching them once more. ²Some Pharisees approached Him to test Him. They asked, "Is it lawful for a man to divorce his wife?"

³He replied to them, "What did Moses command you?"

⁴They said, "Moses permitted us to write divorce papers and send her away."

⁵But Jesus told them, "He wrote this command for you because of the hardness of your hearts. ⁶But from the beginning of creation Godᴳ made them male and female.ᴴ

⁷   For this reason a man will leave
    his father and mother
    [and be joined to his wife],ᶜ
⁸   and the two will become one flesh.ᴵ

So they are no longer two, but one flesh. ⁹Therefore what God has joined together, man must not separate."

¹⁰Now in the house the disciples questioned Him again about this matter. ¹¹And He said to them, "Whoever divorces his wife and marries another commits adultery against her. ¹²Also, if she divorces her husband and marries another, she commits adultery."

¹³Some people were bringing little children to Him so He might touch them, but His disciples rebuked them. ¹⁴When Jesus saw it, He was indignant and said to them, "Let the little children come to Me. Don't stop them, for the kingdom of God belongs to such as these. ¹⁵I assure you: Whoever does not welcomeᴶ the kingdom of God like a little child will never enter it." ¹⁶After taking them in His arms, He laid His hands on them and blessed them.

¹⁷As He was setting out on a journey, a man ran up, knelt down before Him, and asked Him, "Good Teacher, what must I do to inherit eternal life?"

¹⁸"Why do you call Me good?" Jesus asked him. "No one is good but One—God. ¹⁹You know the commandments:

> Do not murder;
> do not commit adultery;
> do not steal;
> do not bear false witness;
> do not defraud;
> honor your father and mother."ᴷ

²⁰He said to Him, "Teacher, I have kept all these from my youth."

²¹Then, looking at him, Jesus loved him and said to him, "You lack one thing: Go, sell all you have and give to the poor, and you will have treasure in heaven. Then come,ᴸ follow Me." ²²But he was stunnedᴹ at this demand,

ᴬ9:41 Lit drink in the name   ᴮ9:42 A millstone turned by a donkey   ᶜ9:44,46; 10:7 Other mss omit bracketed text   ᴰ9:44,46,48 Is 66:24   ᴱ9:49 Other mss add and every sacrifice will be salted with salt   ᶠ9:49 Lv 2:13; Ezk 43:24   ᴳ10:6 Other mss omit God   ᴴ10:6 Gn 1:27; 5:2   ᴵ10:7-8 Gn 2:24   ᴶ10:15 Or not receive   ᴷ10:19 Ex 20:12-16; Dt 5:16-20   ᴸ10:21 Other mss add taking up the cross, and   ᴹ10:22 Or he became gloomy and he went away grieving, because he had many possessions.

²³ Jesus looked around and said to His disciples, "How hard it is for those who have wealth to enter the kingdom of God!" ²⁴ But the disciples were astonished at His words. Again Jesus said to them, "Children, how hard it is^A to enter the kingdom of God! ²⁵ It is easier for a camel to go through the eye of a needle than for a rich person to enter the kingdom of God."

²⁶ So they were even more astonished, saying to one another, "Then who can be saved?"

²⁷ Looking at them, Jesus said, "With men it is impossible, but not with God, because all things are possible with God."

²⁸ Peter began to tell Him, "Look, we have left everything and followed You."

²⁹ "I assure you," Jesus said, "there is no one who has left house, brothers or sisters, mother or father,^B children, or fields because of Me and the gospel, ³⁰ who will not receive 100 times more, now at this time—houses, brothers and sisters, mothers and children, and fields, with persecutions—and eternal life in the age to come. ³¹ But many who are first will be last, and the last first."

³² They were on the road, going up to Jerusalem, and Jesus was walking ahead of them. They were astonished, but those who followed Him were afraid. Taking the Twelve aside again, He began to tell them the things that would happen to Him.

³³ "Listen! We are going up to Jerusalem. The Son of Man will be handed over to the chief priests and the scribes, and they will condemn Him to death. Then they will hand Him over to the Gentiles, ³⁴ and they will mock Him, spit on Him, flog^C Him, and kill Him, and He will rise after three days."

³⁵ Then James and John, the sons of Zebedee, approached Him and said, "Teacher, we want You to do something for us if we ask You."

³⁶ "What do you want Me to do for you?" He asked them.

³⁷ They answered Him, "Allow us to sit at Your right and at Your left in Your glory."

³⁸ But Jesus said to them, "You don't know what you're asking. Are you able to drink the cup I drink or to be baptized with the baptism I am baptized with?"

³⁹ "We are able," they told Him.

Jesus said to them, "You will drink the cup I drink, and you will be baptized with the baptism I am baptized with. ⁴⁰ But to sit at My right or left is not Mine to give; instead, it is for those it has been prepared for." ⁴¹ When the other 10 disciples heard this, they began to be indignant with James and John.

⁴² Jesus called them over and said to them, "You know that those who are regarded as rulers of the Gentiles dominate them, and their men of high positions exercise power over them. ⁴³ But it must not be like that among you. On the contrary, whoever wants to become great among you must be your servant, ⁴⁴ and whoever wants to be first among you must be a slave to all. ⁴⁵ For even the Son of Man did not come to be served, but to serve, and to give His life—a ransom for many."^D

⁴⁶ They came to Jericho. And as He was leaving Jericho with His disciples and a large crowd, Bartimaeus (the son of Timaeus), a blind beggar, was sitting by the road. ⁴⁷ When he heard that it was Jesus the Nazarene, he began to cry out, "Son of David, Jesus, have mercy on me!" ⁴⁸ Many people told him to keep quiet, but he was crying out all the more, "Have mercy on me, Son of David!"

⁴⁹ Jesus stopped and said, "Call him."

So they called the blind man and said to him, "Have courage! Get up; He's calling for you." ⁵⁰ He threw off his coat, jumped up, and came to Jesus.

⁵¹ Then Jesus answered him, "What do you want Me to do for you?"

"*Rabbouni,*"^E the blind man told Him, "I want to see!"

⁵² "Go your way," Jesus told him. "Your faith has healed you." Immediately he could see and began to follow Him on the road.

11 When they approached Jerusalem, at Bethphage and Bethany near the Mount of Olives, He sent two of His disciples ² and told them, "Go into the village ahead of you. As soon as you enter it, you will find a young donkey tied there, on which no one has ever sat. Untie it and bring it here. ³ If anyone says to you, 'Why are you doing this?' say, 'The Lord needs it and will send it back here right away.'"

⁴ So they went and found a young donkey outside in the street, tied by a door. They untied it, ⁵ and some of those standing there said to them, "What are you doing, untying the

---

^A10:24 Other mss add *for those trusting in wealth*   ^B10:29 Other mss add *or wife*   ^C10:34 Or *scourge*   ^D10:45 Or *in the place of many*; Is 53:10-12   ^E10:51 Hb word for *my teacher* donkey?" ⁶They answered them just as Jesus had said, so they let them go. ⁷Then they brought the donkey to Jesus and threw their robes on it, and He sat on it.

⁸Many people spread their robes on the road, and others spread leafy branches cut from the fields.ᴬ ⁹Then those who went ahead and those who followed kept shouting:

> **Hosanna!**
> **He who comes in the name**
> **of the Lord is the blessed One!**ᴮ
> 10   The coming kingdom
>   of our father David is blessed!
>   **Hosanna** in the highest heaven!

¹¹And He went into Jerusalem and into the temple complex. After looking around at everything, since it was already late, He went out to Bethany with the Twelve.

¹²The next day when they came out from Bethany, He was hungry. ¹³After seeing in the distance a fig tree with leaves, He went to find out if there was anything on it. When He came to it, He found nothing but leaves, because it was not the season for figs. ¹⁴He said to it, "May no one ever eat fruit from you again!" And His disciples heard it.

¹⁵They came to Jerusalem, and He went into the temple complex and began to throw out those buying and selling in the temple. He overturned the money changers' tables and the chairs of those selling doves, ¹⁶and would not permit anyone to carry goods through the temple complex.

¹⁷Then He began to teach them: "Is it not written, **My house will be called a house of prayer for all nations?**ᶜ But you have made it **a den of thieves!**"ᴰ ¹⁸Then the chief priests and the scribes heard it and started looking for a way to destroy Him. For they were afraid of Him, because the whole crowd was astonished by His teaching.

¹⁹And whenever evening came, they would go out of the city.

²⁰Early in the morning, as they were passing by, they saw the fig tree withered from the roots up. ²¹Then Peter remembered and said to Him, "Rabbi, look! The fig tree that You cursed is withered."

²²Jesus replied to them, "Have faith in God. ²³I assure you: If anyone says to this mountain, 'Be lifted up and thrown into the sea,' and does not doubt in his heart, but believes that what he says will happen, it will be done for him. ²⁴Therefore I tell you, all the things you pray and ask for—believe that you have receivedᴱ them, and you will have them. ²⁵And whenever you stand praying, if you have anything against anyone, forgive him, so that your Father in heaven will also forgive you your wrongdoing. [²⁶But if you don't forgive, neither will your Father in heaven forgive your wrongdoing.]ᶠ˒ᴳ

²⁷They came again to Jerusalem. As He was walking in the temple complex, the chief priests, the scribes, and the elders came ²⁸and asked Him, "By what authority are You doing these things? Who gave You this authority to do these things?"

²⁹Jesus said to them, "I will ask you one question; then answer Me, and I will tell you by what authority I am doing these things. ³⁰Was John's baptism from heaven or from men? Answer Me."

³¹They began to argue among themselves: "If we say, 'From heaven,' He will say, 'Then why didn't you believe him?' ³²But if we say, 'From men'"—they were afraid of the crowd, because everyone thought that John was a genuine prophet. ³³So they answered Jesus, "We don't know."

And Jesus said to them, "Neither will I tell you by what authority I do these things."

12 Then He began to speak to them in parables: "A man planted a vineyard, put a fence around it, dug out a pit for a winepress, and built a watchtower. Then he leased it to tenant farmers and went away. ²At harvest time he sent a slave to the farmers to collect some of the fruit of the vineyard from the farmers. ³But they took him, beat him, and sent him away empty-handed. ⁴Again he sent another slave to them, and theyᴴ hit him on the head and treated him shamefully.ᴵ ⁵Then he sent another, and they killed that one. He also sent many others; they beat some and they killed some.

⁶"He still had one to send, a beloved son. Finally he sent him to them, saying, 'They will respect my son.'

ᴬ11:8 Other mss read *others were cutting leafy branches from the trees and spreading them on the road*   ᴮ11:9 Ps 118:26   ᶜ11:17 Is 56:7
ᴰ11:17 Jr 7:11   ᴱ11:24 Some mss read *you receive*; other mss read *you will receive*   ᶠ11:26 Other mss omit bracketed text   ᴳ11:25-26 These are the only uses of this word in Mk. It means "the violation of the Law" or "stepping over a boundary" or "departing from the path" or "trespass."   ᴴ12:4 Other mss add *threw stones and*   ᴵ12:4 Other mss add *and sent him off*

[7] "But those tenant farmers said among themselves, 'This is the heir. Come, let's kill him, and the inheritance will be ours!' [8] So they seized him, killed him, and threw him out of the vineyard.

[9] "Therefore, what will the owner[A] of the vineyard do? He will come and destroy the farmers and give the vineyard to others. [10] Haven't you read this Scripture:

> The stone that the builders rejected
> has become the cornerstone.[B]
> [11]   This came from the Lord
> and is wonderful in our eyes?"[C]

[12] Because they knew He had said this parable against them, they were looking for a way to arrest Him, but they were afraid of the crowd. So they left Him and went away.

[13] Then they sent some of the Pharisees and the Herodians to Him to trap Him by what He said.[D] [14] When they came, they said to Him, "Teacher, we know You are truthful and defer to no one, for You don't show partiality[E] but teach truthfully the way of God. Is it lawful to pay taxes to Caesar or not? [15] Should we pay, or should we not pay?"

But knowing their hypocrisy, He said to them, "Why are you testing Me? Bring Me a denarius to look at." [16] So they brought one. "Whose image and inscription is this?" He asked them.

"Caesar's," they said.

[17] Then Jesus told them, "Give back to Caesar the things that are Caesar's, and to God the things that are God's." And they were amazed at Him.

[18] Some Sadducees, who say there is no resurrection, came to Him and questioned Him: [19] "Teacher, Moses wrote for us that **if a man's brother dies**, leaves his wife behind, and **leaves no child, his brother should take the wife and produce offspring for his brother.**[F] [20] There were seven brothers. The first took a wife, and dying, left no offspring. [21] The second also took her, and he died, leaving no offspring. And the third likewise. [22] So the seven[G] left no offspring. Last of all, the woman died too. [23] In the resurrection, when they rise,[H] whose wife will she be, since the seven had married her?"[I]

[24] Jesus told them, "Are you not deceived because you don't know the Scriptures or the power of God? [25] For when they rise from the dead, they neither marry nor are given in marriage but are like angels in heaven. [26] Now concerning the dead being raised—haven't you read in the book of Moses, in the passage about the burning bush, how God spoke to him: I am the God of Abraham and the God of Isaac and the God of Jacob?[J] [27] He is not God of the dead but of the living. You are badly deceived."

[28] One of the scribes approached. When he heard them debating and saw that Jesus answered them well, he asked Him, "Which command is the most important of all?"[K]

[29] "This is the most important,"[L] Jesus answered:

> Listen, Israel! The Lord our God, the Lord is One.[M] [30] Love the Lord your God with all your heart, with all your soul, with all your mind, and with all your strength.[N,O]

[31] "The second is: Love your neighbor as yourself.[P] There is no other command greater than these."

[32] Then the scribe said to Him, "You are right, Teacher! You have correctly said that He is One, and there is no one else except Him. [33] And to love Him with all your heart, with all your understanding,[Q] and with all your strength, and to love your neighbor as yourself, is far more important than all the burnt offerings and sacrifices."

[34] When Jesus saw that he answered intelligently, He said to him, "You are not far from the kingdom of God." And no one dared to question Him any longer.

[35] So Jesus asked this question as He taught in the temple complex, "How can the scribes say that the Messiah is the Son of David? [36] David himself says by the Holy Spirit:

> The Lord declared to my Lord,
> 'Sit at My right hand
> until I put Your enemies
> under Your feet.'[R]

A12:9 Or lord B12:10 Lit the head of the corner C12:10-11 Ps 118:22-23 D12:13 Lit trap Him in (a) word E12:14 Lit don't look on the face of men; that is, on the outward appearance F12:19 Gn 38:8; Dt 25:5 G12:22 Other mss add had taken her and H12:23 Other mss omit when they rise I12:23 Lit the seven had her as a wife J12:26 Ex 3:6,15-16 K12:28 Lit Which command is first of all? L12:29 Other mss add of all the commands M12:29 Or The Lord our God is one Lord. N12:30 Other mss add This is the first commandment. O12:30 Dt 6:4-5; Jos 22:5 P12:31 Lv 19:18 Q12:33 Other mss add with all your soul R12:36 Ps 110:1

[37] David himself calls Him 'Lord'; how then can the Messiah be his Son?" And the large crowd was listening to Him with delight.

[38] He also said in His teaching, "Beware of the scribes, who want to go around in long robes, and who want greetings in the marketplaces, [39] the front seats in the synagogues, and the places of honor at banquets. [40] They devour widows' houses and say long prayers just for show. These will receive harsher punishment."

[41] Sitting across from the temple treasury, He watched how the crowd dropped money into the treasury. Many rich people were putting in large sums. [42] And a poor widow came and dropped in two tiny coins worth very little.[A] [43] Summoning His disciples, He said to them, "I assure you: This poor widow has put in more than all those giving to the temple treasury. [44] For they all gave out of their surplus, but she out of her poverty has put in everything she possessed—all she had to live on."

13 As He was going out of the temple complex, one of His disciples said to Him, "Teacher, look! What massive stones! What impressive buildings!"

[2] Jesus said to him, "Do you see these great buildings? Not one stone will be left here on another that will not be thrown down!"

[3] While He was sitting on the Mount of Olives across from the temple complex, Peter, James, John, and Andrew asked Him privately, [4] "Tell us, when will these things happen? And what will be the sign when all these things are about to take place?"

[5] Then Jesus began by telling them: "Watch out that no one deceives you. [6] Many will come in My name, saying, 'I am He,' and they will deceive many. [7] When you hear of wars and rumors of wars, don't be alarmed; these things must take place, but the end is not yet. [8] For nation will rise up against nation, and kingdom against kingdom. There will be earthquakes in various places, and famines.[B] These are the beginning of birth pains.

[9] "But you, be on your guard! They will hand you over to sanhedrins,[C] and you will be flogged in the synagogues. You will stand before governors and kings because of Me, as a witness to them. [10] And the good news[D] must first be proclaimed to all nations. [11] So when

they arrest you and hand you over, don't worry beforehand what you will say. On the contrary, whatever is given to you in that hour—say it. For it isn't you speaking, but the Holy Spirit. [12] Then brother will betray brother to death, and a father his child. Children will rise up against parents and put them to death. [13] And you will be hated by everyone because of My name. But the one who endures to the end will be delivered.[E]

[14] "When you see the **abomination that causes desolation**[F] standing where it should not" (let the reader understand[G]), "then those in Judea must flee to the mountains! [15] A man on the housetop must not come down or go in to get anything out of his house. [16] And a man in the field must not go back to get his clothes. [17] Woe to pregnant women and nursing mothers in those days! [18] Pray it[H] won't happen in winter. [19] For those will be days of tribulation, the kind that hasn't been from the beginning of the world,[I] which God created, until now and never will be again! [20] Unless the Lord limited those days, no one would survive.[J] But He limited those days because of the elect, whom He chose.

[21] "Then if anyone tells you, 'Look, here is the Messiah! Look—there!' do not believe it! [22] For false messiahs[K] and false prophets will rise up and will perform signs and wonders to lead astray, if possible, the elect. [23] And you must watch! I have told you everything in advance.

[24] "But in those days, after that tribulation:

The sun will be darkened,
and the moon will not shed its light;
[25]   the stars will be falling from the sky,
and the celestial powers will be shaken.

[26] Then they will see the Son of Man coming in clouds with great power and glory. [27] He will send out the angels and gather His elect from the four winds, from the end of the earth to the end of the sky.

[28] "Learn this parable from the fig tree: As soon as its branch becomes tender and sprouts leaves, you know that summer is near. [29] In the same way, when you see these things happening, know[L] that He[M] is near—at the door! [30] I assure you: This generation will certainly

---

A **12:42** Lit *dropped in two lepta, which is a quadrans;* the *lepton* was the smallest and least valuable Gk coin in use. The *quadrans,* 1/64 of a daily wage, was the smallest Roman coin.   B **13:8** Other mss add *and disturbances*   C **13:9** Local Jewish courts or local councils   D **13:10** Or *the gospel*   E **13:13** Or *saved*   F **13:14** Dn 9:27   G **13:14** These are, most likely, Mark's words to his readers.   H **13:18** Other mss read *pray that your escape*   I **13:19** Lit *creation*   J **13:20** Lit *days, all flesh would not survive*   K **13:22** Or *false christs*   L **13:29** Or *you know*   M **13:29** Or *it;* = *summer* not pass away until all these things take place. ³¹Heaven and earth will pass away, but My words will never pass away.

³²"Now concerning that day or hour no one knows—neither the angels in heaven nor the Son—except the Father. ³³Watch! Be alert!ᴬ For you don't know when the time is coming. ³⁴It is like a man on a journey, who left his house, gave authority to his slaves, gave each one his work, and commanded the doorkeeper to be alert. ³⁵Therefore be alert, since you don't know when the master of the house is coming—whether in the evening or at midnight or at the crowing of the rooster or early in the morning. ³⁶Otherwise, he might come suddenly and find you sleeping. ³⁷And what I say to you, I say to everyone: Be alert!"

14 After two days it was the Passover and the Festival of Unleavened Bread. The chief priests and the scribes were looking for a treacherous way to arrest and kill Him. ²"Not during the festival," they said, "or there may be rioting among the people."

³While He was in Bethany at the house of Simon who had a serious skin disease, as He was reclining at the table, a woman came with an alabaster jar of pure and expensive fragrant oil of nard. She broke the jar and poured it on His head. ⁴But some were expressing indignation to one another: "Why has this fragrant oil been wasted? ⁵For this oil might have been sold for more than 300 denarii and given to the poor." And they began to scold her.

⁶Then Jesus said, "Leave her alone. Why are you bothering her? She has done a noble thing for Me. ⁷You always have the poor with you, and you can do what is good for them whenever you want, but you do not always have Me. ⁸She has done what she could; she has anointed My body in advance for burial. ⁹I assure you: Wherever the gospel is proclaimed in the whole world, what this woman has done will also be told in memory of her."

¹⁰Then Judas Iscariot, one of the Twelve, went to the chief priests to hand Him over to them. ¹¹And when they heard this, they were glad and promised to give him silver.ᴮ So he started looking for a good opportunity to betray Him.

¹²On the first day of Unleavened Bread, when they sacrifice the Passover lamb, His disciples asked Him, "Where do You want us to go and prepare the Passover so You may eat it?"

¹³So He sent two of His disciples and told them, "Go into the city, and a man carrying a water jug will meet you. Follow him. ¹⁴Wherever he enters, tell the owner of the house, 'The Teacher says, "Where is the guest room for Me to eat the Passover with My disciples?"' ¹⁵He will show you a large room upstairs, furnished and ready. Make the preparations for us there." ¹⁶So the disciples went out, entered the city, and found it just as He had told them, and they prepared the Passover.

¹⁷When evening came, He arrived with the Twelve. ¹⁸While they were reclining and eating, Jesus said, "I assure you: One of you will betray Me—one who is eating with Me!"

¹⁹They began to be distressed and to say to Him one by one, "Surely not I?"

²⁰He said to them, "It is one of the Twelve—the one who is dipping bread with Me in the bowl. ²¹For the Son of Man will go just as it is written about Him, but woe to that man by whom the Son of Man is betrayed! It would have been better for that man if he had not been born."

²²As they were eating, He took bread, blessed and broke it, gave it to them, and said, "Take it;ᶜ this is My body."

²³Then He took a cup, and after giving thanks, He gave it to them, and so they all drank from it. ²⁴He said to them, "This is My blood that establishes the covenant;ᴰ it is shed for many. ²⁵I assure you: I will no longer drink of the fruit of the vine until that day when I drink it in a new wayᴱ in the kingdom of God." ²⁶After singing psalms,ᶠ they went out to the Mount of Olives.

²⁷Then Jesus said to them, "All of you will run away,ᴳ,ᴴ because it is written:

I will strike the shepherd,
and the sheep will be scattered.ᴵ

²⁸But after I have been resurrected, I will go ahead of you to Galilee."

²⁹Peter told Him, "Even if everyone runs away, I will certainly not!"

³⁰"I assure you," Jesus said to him, "today, this very night, before the rooster crows twice, you will deny Me three times!"

ᴬ13:33 Other mss add and pray   ᴮ14:11 Or money; in Mt 26:15 it is specified as 30 pieces of silver; see Zch 11:12-13   ᶜ14:22 Other mss add eat;   ᴰ14:24 Other mss read the new covenant   ᴱ14:25 Or drink new wine; lit drink it new   ᶠ14:26 Pss 113–118 were sung during and after the Passover meal.   ᴳ14:27 Other mss add because of Me this night   ᴴ14:27 Or stumble   ᴵ14:27 Zch 13:7

[31] But he kept insisting, "If I have to die with You, I will never deny You!" And they all said the same thing.

[32] Then they came to a place named Gethsemane, and He told His disciples, "Sit here while I pray." [33] He took Peter, James, and John with Him, and He began to be deeply distressed and horrified. [34] Then He said to them, "My soul is swallowed up in sorrow[A]—to the point of death. Remain here and stay awake." [35] Then He went a little farther, fell to the ground, and began to pray that if it were possible, the hour might pass from Him. [36] And He said, *"Abba,* Father! All things are possible for You. Take this cup away from Me. Nevertheless, not what I will, but what You will."

[37] Then He came and found them sleeping. "Simon, are you sleeping?" He asked Peter. "Couldn't you stay awake one hour? [38] Stay awake and pray so that you won't enter into temptation. The spirit is willing, but the flesh is weak."

[39] Once again He went away and prayed, saying the same thing. [40] And He came again and found them sleeping, because they could not keep their eyes open.[B] They did not know what to say to Him. [41] Then He came a third time and said to them, "Are you still sleeping and resting? Enough! The time has come. Look, the Son of Man is being betrayed into the hands of sinners. [42] Get up; let's go! See—My betrayer is near."

[43] While He was still speaking, Judas, one of the Twelve, suddenly arrived. With him was a mob, with swords and clubs, from the chief priests, the scribes, and the elders. [44] His betrayer had given them a signal. "The One I kiss," he said, "He's the One; arrest Him and take Him away under guard." [45] So when he came, he went right up to Him and said, "Rabbi!"—and kissed Him. [46] Then they took hold of Him and arrested Him. [47] And one of those who stood by drew his sword, struck the high priest's slave, and cut off his ear.

[48] But Jesus said to them, "Have you come out with swords and clubs, as though I were a criminal,[C] to capture Me? [49] Every day I was among you, teaching in the temple complex, and you didn't arrest Me. But the Scriptures must be fulfilled." [50] Then they all deserted Him and ran away.

[51] Now a certain young man,[D] having a linen cloth wrapped around his naked body, was following Him. They caught hold of him, [52] but he left the linen cloth behind and ran away naked.

[53] They led Jesus away to the high priest, and all the chief priests, the elders, and the scribes convened. [54] Peter followed Him at a distance, right into the high priest's courtyard. He was sitting with the temple police,[E] warming himself by the fire.[F]

[55] The chief priests and the whole Sanhedrin were looking for testimony against Jesus to put Him to death, but they could find none. [56] For many were giving false testimony against Him, but the testimonies did not agree. [57] Some stood up and were giving false testimony against Him, stating, [58] "We heard Him say, 'I will demolish this sanctuary made by human hands, and in three days I will build another not made by hands.'" [59] Yet their testimony did not agree even on this.

[60] Then the high priest stood up before them all and questioned Jesus, "Don't You have an answer to what these men are testifying against You?" [61] But He kept silent and did not answer anything. Again the high priest questioned Him, "Are You the Messiah, the Son of the Blessed One?"

[62] "I am," said Jesus, "and all of you[G] will see the Son of Man seated at the right hand of the Power and coming with the clouds of heaven."[H]

[63] Then the high priest tore his robes and said, "Why do we still need witnesses? [64] You have heard the blasphemy! What is your decision?"[I]

And they all condemned Him to be deserving of death. [65] Then some began to spit on Him, to blindfold Him, and to beat Him, saying, "Prophesy!" The temple police also took Him and slapped Him.

[66] While Peter was in the courtyard below, one of the high priest's servants came. [67] When she saw Peter warming himself, she looked at him and said, "You also were with that Nazarene, Jesus."

[68] But he denied it: "I don't know or understand what you're talking about!" Then he went out to the entryway, and a rooster crowed.[J]

A14:34 Or *I am deeply grieved*   B14:40 Lit *because their eyes were weighed down*   C14:48 Lit *as against a criminal*   D14:51 Perhaps John Mark who later wrote this Gospel   E14:54 Or *the officers;* lit *the servants*   F14:54 Lit *light*   G14:62 Lit *and you*   H14:62 Ps 110:1; Dn 7:13   I14:64 Lit *How does it appear to you?*   J14:68 Other mss omit *and a rooster crowed*

⁶⁹When the servant saw him again she began to tell those standing nearby, "This man is one of them!"

⁷⁰But again he denied it. After a little while those standing there said to Peter again, "You certainly are one of them, since you're also a Galilean!"ᴬ

⁷¹Then he started to curseᴮ and to swear with an oath, "I don't know this man you're talking about!"

⁷²Immediately a rooster crowed a second time, and Peter remembered when Jesus had spoken the word to him, "Before the rooster crows twice, you will deny Me three times." When he thought about it, he began to weep.ᶜ

15 As soon as it was morning, the chief priests had a meeting with the elders, scribes, and the whole Sanhedrin. After tying Jesus up, they led Him away and handed Him over to Pilate.

²So Pilate asked Him, "Are You the King of the Jews?"

He answered him, "You have said it."ᴰ

³And the chief priests began to accuse Him of many things. ⁴Then Pilate questioned Him again, "Are You not answering anything? Look how many things they are accusing You of!" ⁵But Jesus still did not answer anything, so Pilate was amazed.

⁶At the festival it was Pilate's custom to release for the people a prisoner they requested. ⁷There was one named Barabbas, who was in prison with rebels who had committed murder during the rebellion. ⁸The crowd came up and began to ask Pilate to do for them as was his custom. ⁹So Pilate answered them, "Do you want me to release the King of the Jews for you?" ¹⁰For he knew it was because of envy that the chief priests had handed Him over. ¹¹But the chief priests stirred up the crowd so that he would release Barabbas to them instead.

¹²Pilate asked them again, "Then what do you want me to do with the One you call the King of the Jews?"

¹³Again they shouted, "Crucify Him!"

¹⁴Then Pilate said to them, "Why? What has He done wrong?"

But they shouted, "Crucify Him!" all the more.

¹⁵Then, willing to gratify the crowd, Pilate released Barabbas to them. And after having Jesus flogged,ᴱ he handed Him over to be crucified.

¹⁶Then the soldiers led Him away into the courtyard (that is, headquarters) and called the whole company together. ¹⁷They dressed Him in a purple robe, twisted together a crown of thorns, and put it on Him. ¹⁸And they began to salute Him, "Hail, King of the Jews!" ¹⁹They kept hitting Him on the head with a reed and spitting on Him. Getting down on their knees, they were paying Him homage. ²⁰When they had mocked Him, they stripped Him of the purple robe, put His clothes on Him, and led Him out to crucify Him.

²¹They forced a man coming in from the country, who was passing by, to carry Jesus' cross. He was Simon, a Cyrenian, the father of Alexander and Rufus. ²²And they brought Jesus to the place called *Golgotha* (which means Skull Place). ²³They tried to give Him wine mixed with myrrh, but He did not take it. ²⁴Then they crucified Him and divided His clothes, casting lots for them to decide what each would get. ²⁵Now it was nine in the morningᶠ when they crucified Him. ²⁶The inscription of the charge written against Him was:

THE KING OF THE JEWS.

²⁷They crucified two criminalsᴳ with Him, one on His right and one on His left. [²⁸So the Scripture was fulfilled that says: **And He was counted among outlaws.**]ᴴ,ᴵ ²⁹Those who passed by were yelling insults atᴶ Him, shaking their heads, and saying, "Ha! The One who would demolish the sanctuary and build it in three days, ³⁰save Yourself by coming down from the cross!" ³¹In the same way, the chief priests with the scribes were mocking Him to one another and saying, "He saved others; He cannot save Himself! ³²Let the Messiah, the King of Israel, come down now from the cross, so that we may see and believe." Even those who were crucified with Him were taunting Him.

³³When it was noon,ᴷ darkness came over the whole landᴸ until three in the afternoon.ᴹ ³⁴And at threeᴹ Jesus cried out with a loud

voice, *"Eloi, Eloi, lemá*^A *sabachtháni?"* which is translated, "My God, My God, why have You forsaken Me?"^B

³⁵ When some of those standing there heard this, they said, "Look, He's calling for Elijah!" ³⁶ Someone ran and filled a sponge with sour wine, fixed it on a reed, offered Him a drink, and said, "Let's see if Elijah comes to take Him down!"

³⁷ But Jesus let out a loud cry and breathed His last. ³⁸ Then the curtain of the sanctuary^C was split in two from top to bottom. ³⁹ When the centurion, who was standing opposite Him, saw the way He^D breathed His last, he said, "This man really was God's Son!"^E

⁴⁰ There were also women looking on from a distance. Among them were Mary Magdalene, Mary the mother of James the younger and of Joses, and Salome. ⁴¹ When He was in Galilee, they would follow Him and help Him. Many other women had come up with Him to Jerusalem.

⁴² When it was already evening, because it was preparation day (that is, the day before the Sabbath), ⁴³ Joseph of Arimathea, a prominent member of the Sanhedrin who was himself looking forward to the kingdom of God, came and boldly went in to Pilate and asked for Jesus' body. ⁴⁴ Pilate was surprised that He was already dead. Summoning the centurion, he asked him whether He had already died. ⁴⁵ When he found out from the centurion, he gave the corpse to Joseph. ⁴⁶ After he bought some fine linen, he took Him down and wrapped Him in the linen. Then he placed Him in a tomb cut out of the rock, and rolled a stone against the entrance to the tomb. ⁴⁷ Now Mary Magdalene and Mary the mother of Joses were watching where He was placed.

16 When the Sabbath was over, Mary Magdalene, Mary the mother of James, and Salome bought spices, so they could go and anoint Him. ² Very early in the morning, on the first day of the week, they went to the tomb at sunrise. ³ They were saying to one another, "Who will roll away the stone from the entrance to the tomb for us?" ⁴ Looking up, they observed that the stone—which was very large—had been rolled away. ⁵ When they entered the tomb, they saw a young man^F dressed in a long white robe sitting on the right side; they were amazed and alarmed.

⁶ "Don't be alarmed," he told them. "You are looking for Jesus the Nazarene, who was crucified. He has been resurrected! He is not here! See the place where they put Him. ⁷ But go, tell His disciples and Peter, 'He is going ahead of you to Galilee; you will see Him there just as He told you.'"

⁸ So they went out and started running from the tomb, because trembling and astonishment overwhelmed them. And they said nothing to anyone, since they were afraid.

[⁹ Early on the first day of the week, after He had risen, He appeared first to Mary Magdalene, out of whom He had driven seven demons. ¹⁰ She went and reported to those who had been with Him, as they were mourning and weeping. ¹¹ Yet, when they heard that He was alive and had been seen by her, they did not believe it. ¹² Then after this, He appeared in a different form to two of them walking on their way into the country. ¹³ And they went and reported it to the rest, who did not believe them either.

¹⁴ Later, He appeared to the Eleven themselves as they were reclining at the table. He rebuked their unbelief and hardness of heart, because they did not believe those who saw Him after He had been resurrected. ¹⁵ Then He said to them, "Go into all the world and preach the gospel to the whole creation. ¹⁶ Whoever believes and is baptized will be saved, but whoever does not believe will be condemned. ¹⁷ And these signs will accompany those who believe: In My name they will drive out demons; they will speak in new languages; ¹⁸ they will pick up snakes;^G if they should drink anything deadly, it will never harm them; they will lay hands on the sick, and they will get well."

¹⁹ Then after speaking to them, the Lord Jesus was taken up into heaven and sat down at the right hand of God. ²⁰ And they went out and preached everywhere, the Lord working with them and confirming the word by the accompanying signs.]^H

---

^A15:34 Some mss read *lama;* other mss read *lima*   ^B15:34 Ps 22:1   ^C15:38 A heavy curtain separated the inner room of the temple from the outer.   ^D15:39 Other mss read *saw that He cried out like this and*   ^E15:39 Or *the Son of God;* Mk 1:1   ^F16:5 In Mt 28:2, the young man = an angel   ^G16:18 Other mss add *with their hands*   ^H16:9-20 Other mss omit bracketed text

LUKE

1 Many have undertaken to compile a narrative about the events that have been fulfilled^A among us, ²just as the original eyewitnesses and servants of the word handed them down to us. ³It also seemed good to me, since I have carefully investigated everything from the very first, to write to you in an orderly sequence, most honorable Theophilus, ⁴so that you may know the certainty of the things about which you have been instructed.^B

⁵In the days of King Herod of Judea, there was a priest of Abijah's division^C named Zechariah. His wife was from the daughters of Aaron, and her name was Elizabeth. ⁶Both were righteous in God's sight, living without blame according to all the commands and requirements of the Lord. ⁷But they had no children^D because Elizabeth could not conceive,^E and both of them were well along in years.^F

⁸When his division was on duty and he was serving as priest before God, ⁹it happened that he was chosen by lot, according to the custom of the priesthood, to enter the sanctuary of the Lord and burn incense. ¹⁰At the hour of incense the whole assembly of the people was praying outside. ¹¹An angel of the Lord appeared to him, standing to the right of the altar of incense. ¹²When Zechariah saw him, he was startled and overcome with fear.^G ¹³But the angel said to him:

Do not be afraid, Zechariah,
because your prayer has been heard.
Your wife Elizabeth will bear you a son,
and you will name him John.
¹⁴ There will be joy and delight for you,
and many will rejoice at his birth.
¹⁵ For he will be great in the sight
of the Lord
and will never drink wine or beer.
He will be filled with the Holy Spirit
while still in his mother's womb.
¹⁶ He will turn many of the sons of Israel
to the Lord their God.
¹⁷ And he will go before Him
in the spirit and power of Elijah,
to turn the hearts of fathers
to their children,

and the disobedient
to the understanding of the righteous,
to make ready for the Lord
a prepared people.

¹⁸"How can I know this?" Zechariah asked the angel. "For I am an old man, and my wife is well along in years."^H

¹⁹The angel answered him, "I am Gabriel, who stands in the presence of God, and I was sent to speak to you and tell you this good news. ²⁰Now listen! You will become silent and unable to speak until the day these things take place, because you did not believe my words, which will be fulfilled in their proper time."

²¹Meanwhile, the people were waiting for Zechariah, amazed that he stayed so long in the sanctuary. ²²When he did come out, he could not speak to them. Then they realized that he had seen a vision in the sanctuary. He kept making signs to them and remained speechless. ²³When the days of his ministry were completed, he went back home.

²⁴After these days his wife Elizabeth conceived and kept herself in seclusion for five months. She said, ²⁵"The Lord has done this for me. He has looked with favor in these days to take away my disgrace among the people."

²⁶In the sixth month, the angel Gabriel was sent by God to a town in Galilee called Nazareth, ²⁷to a virgin engaged to a man named Joseph, of the house of David. The virgin's name was Mary. ²⁸And the angel came to her and said, "Rejoice, favored woman! The Lord is with you."^I ²⁹But she was deeply troubled by this statement, wondering what kind of greeting this could be. ³⁰Then the angel told her:

Do not be afraid, Mary,
for you have found favor with God.
³¹ Now listen:
You will conceive and give birth to
a son,
and you will call His name Jesus.
³² He will be great
and will be called the Son of
the Most High,
and the Lord God will give Him
the throne of His father David.

³³ He will reign over the house of Jacob
forever,
and His kingdom will have no end.

³⁴ Mary asked the angel, "How can this be,
since I have not been intimate with a man?"^A
³⁵ The angel replied to her:

"The Holy Spirit will come upon you,
and the power of the Most High
will overshadow you.
Therefore, the holy One to be born
will be called the Son of God.

³⁶ And consider your relative Elizabeth—even
she has conceived a son in her old age, and
this is the sixth month for her who was called
childless. ³⁷ For nothing will be impossible
with God."
³⁸ "I am the Lord's slave,"^B said Mary. "May it
be done to me according to your word." Then
the angel left her.
³⁹ In those days Mary set out and hurried to a
town in the hill country of Judah ⁴⁰ where she
entered Zechariah's house and greeted Elizabeth. ⁴¹ When Elizabeth heard Mary's greeting,
the baby leaped inside her,^C and Elizabeth was
filled with the Holy Spirit. ⁴² Then she exclaimed with a loud cry:

"You are the most blessed of women,
and your child will be blessed!^D

⁴³ How could this happen to me, that the moth-
er of my Lord should come to me? ⁴⁴ For you
see, when the sound of your greeting reached
my ears, the baby leaped for joy inside me!^E
⁴⁵ She who has believed is blessed because what
was spoken to her by the Lord will be fulfilled!"
⁴⁶ And Mary said:

My soul proclaims the greatness
of^F the Lord,
⁴⁷   and my spirit has rejoiced in God
my Savior,
⁴⁸   because He has looked with favor
on the humble condition of His slave.
Surely, from now on all generations
will call me blessed,
⁴⁹   because the Mighty One
has done great things for me,
and His name is holy.

⁵⁰   His mercy is from generation
to generation
on those who fear Him.
⁵¹   He has done a mighty deed
with His arm;
He has scattered the proud
because of the thoughts of their hearts;
⁵²   He has toppled the mighty
from their thrones
and exalted the lowly.
⁵³   He has satisfied the hungry
with good things
and sent the rich away empty.
⁵⁴   He has helped His servant Israel,
mindful of His mercy,^G
⁵⁵   just as He spoke to our ancestors,
to Abraham and his
descendants^H forever.

⁵⁶ And Mary stayed with her about three
months; then she returned to her home.
⁵⁷ Now the time had come for Elizabeth
to give birth, and she had a son. ⁵⁸ Then her
neighbors and relatives heard that the Lord
had shown her His great mercy,^I and they rejoiced with her.
⁵⁹ When they came to circumcise the child on
the eighth day, they were going to name him
Zechariah, after his father. ⁶⁰ But his mother
responded, "No! He will be called John."
⁶¹ Then they said to her, "None of your rela-
tives has that name." ⁶² So they motioned to
his father to find out what he wanted him to
be called. ⁶³ He asked for a writing tablet and
wrote:

HIS NAME IS JOHN.

And they were all amazed. ⁶⁴ Immediately his
mouth was opened and his tongue set free, and
he began to speak, praising God. ⁶⁵ Fear came
on all those who lived around them, and all
these things were being talked about throughout the hill country of Judea. ⁶⁶ All who heard
about him took it to heart, saying, "What then
will this child become?" For, indeed, the Lord's
hand was with him.
⁶⁷ Then his father Zechariah was filled with
the Holy Spirit and prophesied:

⁶⁸   Praise the Lord, the God of Israel,
because He has visited

---

^A**1:34** Lit *since I do not know a man*   ^B**1:38** Lit *Look, the Lord's slave*   ^C**1:41** Lit *leaped in her abdomen or womb*   ^D**1:42** Lit *and the fruit of your
abdomen* (or *womb*) *is blessed*   ^E**1:44** Lit *in my abdomen or womb*   ^F**1:46** Or *soul magnifies*   ^G**1:54** Because He remembered His mercy;
Ps 98:3   ^H**1:55** Or *offspring*; lit *seed*   ^I**1:58** Lit *the Lord magnified His mercy with her*

and provided redemption
for His people.

⁶⁹ He has raised up a horn of salvation^A
for us
in the house of His servant David,

⁷⁰ just as He spoke by the mouth
of His holy prophets in ancient times;

⁷¹ salvation from our enemies
and from the clutches^B of those
who hate us.

⁷² He has dealt mercifully
with our fathers
and remembered His holy covenant—

⁷³ the oath that He swore to our father
Abraham.
He has given us the privilege,

⁷⁴ since we have been rescued
from our enemies' clutches,^C
to serve Him without fear

⁷⁵ in holiness and righteousness
in His presence all our days.

⁷⁶ And child, you will be called
a prophet of the Most High,
for you will go before the Lord
to prepare His ways,

⁷⁷ to give His people knowledge
of salvation
through the forgiveness of their sins.

⁷⁸ Because of our God's merciful
compassion,
the Dawn from on high will visit us

⁷⁹ to shine on those who live in darkness
and the shadow of death,
to guide our feet into the way of peace.

⁸⁰ The child grew up and became spiritually strong, and he was in the wilderness until the day of his public appearance to Israel.

2 In those days a decree went out from Caesar Augustus^D that the whole empire^E should be registered. ²This first registration took place while^F Quirinius was governing Syria. ³So everyone went to be registered, each to his own town.

⁴And Joseph also went up from the town of Nazareth in Galilee, to Judea, to the city of David, which is called Bethlehem, because he was of the house and family line of David, ⁵to be registered along with Mary, who was engaged

to him^G and was pregnant. ⁶While they were there, the time came for her to give birth. ⁷Then she gave birth to her firstborn Son, and she wrapped Him snugly in cloth and laid Him in a feeding trough—because there was no room for them at the lodging place.

⁸In the same region, shepherds were staying out in the fields and keeping watch at night over their flock. ⁹Then an angel of the Lord stood before^H them, and the glory of the Lord shone around them, and they were terrified.^I ¹⁰But the angel said to them, "Don't be afraid, for look, I proclaim to you good news of great joy that will be for all the people:^J ¹¹Today a Savior, who is Messiah the Lord, was born for you in the city of David. ¹²This will be the sign for you: You will find a baby wrapped snugly in cloth and lying in a feeding trough."

¹³Suddenly there was a multitude of the heavenly host with the angel, praising God and saying:

¹⁴ Glory to God in the highest heaven,
and peace on earth to people
He favors!^{K L}

¹⁵When the angels had left them and returned to heaven, the shepherds said to one another, "Let's go straight to Bethlehem and see what has happened, which the Lord has made known to us."

¹⁶They hurried off and found both Mary and Joseph, and the baby who was lying in the feeding trough. ¹⁷After seeing them, they reported the message they were told about this child, ¹⁸and all who heard it were amazed at what the shepherds said to them. ¹⁹But Mary was treasuring up all these things^M in her heart and meditating on them. ²⁰The shepherds returned, glorifying and praising God for all they had seen and heard, just as they had been told.

²¹When the eight days were completed for His circumcision, He was named Jesus—the name given by the angel before He was conceived.^N ²²And when the days of their purification according to the law of Moses were finished, they brought Him up to Jerusalem to present Him to the Lord ²³(just as it is written in the law of the Lord: **Every firstborn male**^O **will be dedicated**^P **to the Lord**^Q) ²⁴and to offer

A1:69 = a strong Savior   B1:71 Lit the hand   C1:74 Lit from the hand of enemies   D2:1 Emperor who ruled the Roman Empire 27 B.C.–A.D. 14; also known as Octavian, he established the peaceful era known as the Pax Romana; Caesar was a title of Roman emperors.   E2:1 Or the whole inhabited world   F2:2 Or This registration was the first while, or This registration was before   G2:5 Other mss read was his engaged wife   H2:9 Or Lord appeared to   I2:9 Lit they feared a great fear   J2:10 Or the whole nation   K2:14 Other mss read earth good will to people   L2:14 Or earth to men of good will   M2:19 Lit these words   N2:21 Or conceived in the womb   O2:23 Lit "Every male that opens a womb   P2:23 Lit be called holy   Q2:23 Ex 13:2,12 a sacrifice (according to what is stated in the law of the Lord: **a pair of turtledoves or two young pigeons**[A]).

[25] There was a man in Jerusalem whose name was Simeon. This man was righteous and devout, looking forward to Israel's consolation,[B] and the Holy Spirit was on him. [26] It had been revealed to him by the Holy Spirit that he would not see death before he saw the Lord's Messiah. [27] Guided by the Spirit, he entered[C] the temple complex. When the parents brought in the child Jesus to perform for Him what was customary under the law, [28] Simeon took Him up in his arms, praised God, and said:

[29] Now, Master,
   You can dismiss Your slave in peace,
   as You promised.
[30] For my eyes have seen Your salvation.
[31] You have prepared it
   in the presence of all peoples—
[32] a light for revelation to the Gentiles[D]
   and glory to Your people Israel.

[33] His father and mother[E] were amazed at what was being said about Him. [34] Then Simeon blessed them and told His mother Mary: "Indeed, this child is destined to cause the fall and rise of many in Israel and to be a sign that will be opposed[F]— [35] and a sword will pierce your own soul—that the thoughts[G] of many hearts may be revealed."

[36] There was also a prophetess, Anna, a daughter of Phanuel, of the tribe of Asher. She was well along in years,[H] having lived with her husband seven years after her marriage,[I] [37] and was a widow for 84 years.[J] She did not leave the temple complex, serving God night and day with fasting and prayers. [38] At that very moment,[K] she came up and began to thank God and to speak about Him to all who were looking forward to the redemption of Jerusalem.[L]

[39] When they had completed everything according to the law of the Lord, they returned to Galilee, to their own town of Nazareth. [40] The boy grew up and became strong, filled with wisdom, and God's grace was on Him.

[41] Every year His parents traveled to Jerusalem for the Passover Festival. [42] When He was 12 years old, they went up according to the custom of the festival. [43] After those days were over, as they were returning, the boy Jesus stayed behind in Jerusalem, but His parents[M] did not know it. [44] Assuming He was in the traveling party, they went a day's journey. Then they began looking for Him among their relatives and friends. [45] When they did not find Him, they returned to Jerusalem to search for Him. [46] After three days, they found Him in the temple complex sitting among the teachers, listening to them and asking them questions. [47] And all those who heard Him were astounded at His understanding and His answers. [48] When His parents saw Him, they were astonished, and His mother said to Him, "Son, why have You treated us like this? Your father and I have been anxiously searching for You."

[49] "Why were you searching for Me?" He asked them. "Didn't you know that I had to be in My Father's house?"[N] [50] But they did not understand what He said to them.

[51] Then He went down with them and came to Nazareth and was obedient to them. His mother kept all these things in her heart. [52] And Jesus increased in wisdom and stature, and in favor with God and with people.

3 In the fifteenth year of the reign of Tiberius Caesar,[O] while Pontius Pilate was governor of Judea, Herod was tetrarch[P] of Galilee, his brother Philip tetrarch of the region of Iturea[Q] and Trachonitis,[Q] and Lysanias tetrarch of Abilene,[R] [2] during the high priesthood of Annas and Caiaphas, God's word came to John the son of Zechariah in the wilderness. [3] He went into all the vicinity of the Jordan, preaching a baptism of repentance[S] for the forgiveness of sins, [4] as it is written in the book of the words of the prophet Isaiah:

   **A voice of one crying out
      in the wilderness:
   Prepare the way for the Lord;
      make His paths straight!**
[5]   **Every valley will be filled,
      and every mountain and hill will be
         made low;**[T]
   **the crooked will become straight,
   the rough ways smooth,**

A2:24 Lv 5:11; 12:8   **B2:25** The coming of the Messiah with His salvation for the nation; Is 40:1; 61:2; Lk 2:26,30   **C2:27** Lit *And in the Spirit, he came into*   **D2:32** Or *the nations*   **E2:33** Other mss read *But Joseph and His mother*   **F2:34** Or *spoken against*   **G2:35** Or *schemes*   **H2:36** Lit *in many days*   **I2:36** Lit *years from her virginity*   **J2:37** Or *she was a widow until the age of 84*   **K2:38** Lit *very hour*   **L2:38** Other mss read *in Jerusalem*   **M2:43** Other mss read *Joseph and His mother*   **N2:49** Or *be involved in My Father's interests (or things), or be among My Father's people*   **O3:1** Emperor who ruled the Roman Empire A.D. 14–37   **P3:1** Or *ruler*   **Q3:1** A small province northeast of Galilee   **R3:1** A small Syrian province   **S3:3** Or *baptism based on repentance*   **T3:5** Lit *be humbled*

⁶ **and everyone**^A **will see the salvation of God.**^B

⁷ He then said to the crowds who came out to be baptized by him, "Brood of vipers! Who warned you to flee from the coming wrath? ⁸ Therefore produce fruit consistent with repentance. And don't start saying to yourselves, 'We have Abraham as our father,' for I tell you that God is able to raise up children for Abraham from these stones! ⁹ Even now the ax is ready to strike^C the root of the trees! Therefore, every tree that doesn't produce good fruit will be cut down and thrown into the fire."

¹⁰ "What then should we do?" the crowds were asking him.

¹¹ He replied to them, "The one who has two shirts^D must share with someone who has none, and the one who has food must do the same."

¹² Tax collectors also came to be baptized, and they asked him, "Teacher, what should we do?"

¹³ He told them, "Don't collect any more than what you have been authorized."

¹⁴ Some soldiers also questioned him: "What should we do?"

He said to them, "Don't take money from anyone by force or false accusation; be satisfied with your wages."

¹⁵ Now the people were waiting expectantly, and all of them were debating in their minds^E whether John might be the Messiah. ¹⁶ John answered them all, "I baptize you with^F water, but One is coming who is more powerful than I. I am not worthy to untie the strap of His sandals. He will baptize you with^F the Holy Spirit and fire. ¹⁷ His winnowing shovel^G is in His hand to clear His threshing floor and gather the wheat into His barn, but the chaff He will burn up with a fire that never goes out." ¹⁸ Then, along with many other exhortations, he proclaimed good news to the people. ¹⁹ But Herod the tetrarch, being rebuked by him about Herodias, his brother's wife, and about all the evil things Herod had done, ²⁰ added this to everything else—he locked John up in prison.

²¹ When all the people were baptized, Jesus also was baptized. As He was praying, heaven opened, ²² and the Holy Spirit descended on Him in a physical appearance like a dove. And a voice came from heaven:

> You are My beloved Son.
> I take delight in You!

²³ As He began His ministry, Jesus was about 30 years old and was thought to be^H the

    son of Joseph, son^I of Heli,
²⁴ son of Matthat, son of Levi,
    son of Melchi, son of Jannai,
    son of Joseph, ²⁵ son of Mattathias,
    son of Amos, son of Nahum,
    son of Esli, son of Naggai,
²⁶ son of Maath, son of Mattathias,
    son of Semein, son of Josech,
    son of Joda, ²⁷ son of Joanan,
    son of Rhesa, son of Zerubbabel,
    son of Shealtiel, son of Neri,
²⁸ son of Melchi, son of Addi,
    son of Cosam, son of Elmadam,
    son of Er, ²⁹ son of Joshua,
    son of Eliezer, son of Jorim,
    son of Matthat, son of Levi,
³⁰ son of Simeon, son of Judah,
    son of Joseph, son of Jonam,
    son of Eliakim, ³¹ son of Melea,
    son of Menna, son of Mattatha,
    son of Nathan, son of David,
³² son of Jesse, son of Obed,
    son of Boaz, son of Salmon,^J
    son of Nahshon, ³³ son of Amminadab,
    son of Ram,^K son of Hezron,
    son of Perez, son of Judah,
³⁴ son of Jacob, son of Isaac,
    son of Abraham, son of Terah,
    son of Nahor, ³⁵ son of Serug,
    son of Reu, son of Peleg,
    son of Eber, son of Shelah,
³⁶ son of Cainan, son of Arphaxad,
    son of Shem, son of Noah,
    son of Lamech, ³⁷ son of Methuselah,
    son of Enoch, son of Jared,
    son of Mahalaleel, son of Cainan,
³⁸ son of Enos, son of Seth,
    son of Adam, son of God.

4 Then Jesus returned from the Jordan, full of the Holy Spirit, and was led by the Spirit in the wilderness ² for 40 days to be tempted by the Devil. He ate nothing during those days,

---

^A **3:6** Lit *all flesh*   ^B **3:4-6** Is 40:3-5   ^C **3:9** Lit *the ax lies at*   ^D **3:11** Lit *tunics*   ^E **3:15** Or *hearts*   ^F **3:16** Or *in*   ^G **3:17** A wooden farm implement used to toss threshed grain into the wind so the lighter chaff would blow away and separate from the heavier grain   ^H **3:23** People did not know about His virgin birth; Mt 1:18-25; Lk 1:26-38   ^I **3:23** The relationship in some cases may be more distant than a son.   ^J **3:32** Other mss read *Sala*   ^K **3:33** Other mss read *Amminadab, son of Aram, son of Joram*; other mss read *Amminadab, son of Admin, son of Arni* and when they were over,^A He was hungry. ³The Devil said to Him, "If You are the Son of God, tell this stone to become bread."

⁴But Jesus answered him, "It is written: Man must not live on bread alone."^B,C

⁵So he took Him up^D and showed Him all the kingdoms of the world in a moment of time. ⁶The Devil said to Him, "I will give You their splendor and all this authority, because it has been given over to me, and I can give it to anyone I want. ⁷If You, then, will worship me,^E all will be Yours."

⁸And Jesus answered him,^F "It is written:

Worship the Lord your God,
and serve Him only."^G

⁹So he took Him to Jerusalem, had Him stand on the pinnacle of the temple, and said to Him, "If You are the Son of God, throw Yourself down from here. ¹⁰For it is written:

He will give His angels orders
    concerning you,
to protect you,^H ¹¹and
they will support you with their hands,
so that you will not strike
    your foot against a stone."^I

¹²And Jesus answered him, "It is said: Do not test the Lord your God."^J

¹³After the Devil had finished every temptation, he departed from Him for a time.

¹⁴Then Jesus returned to Galilee in the power of the Spirit, and news about Him spread throughout the entire vicinity. ¹⁵He was teaching in their synagogues, being acclaimed^K by everyone.

¹⁶He came to Nazareth, where He had been brought up. As usual, He entered the synagogue on the Sabbath day and stood up to read. ¹⁷The scroll of the prophet Isaiah was given to Him, and unrolling the scroll, He found the place where it was written:

¹⁸ The Spirit of the Lord is on Me,
    because He has anointed Me
    to preach good news to the poor.
    He has sent Me^L
    to proclaim freedom^M to the captives
    and recovery of sight to the blind,
    to set free the oppressed,

¹⁹ to proclaim the year
    of the Lord's favor.^N,O

²⁰He then rolled up the scroll, gave it back to the attendant, and sat down. And the eyes of everyone in the synagogue were fixed on Him. ²¹He began by saying to them, "Today as you listen, this Scripture has been fulfilled."

²²They were all speaking well of Him^P and were amazed by the gracious words that came from His mouth, yet they said, "Isn't this Joseph's son?"

²³Then He said to them, "No doubt you will quote this proverb^Q to Me: 'Doctor, heal yourself. So all we've heard that took place in Capernaum, do here in Your hometown also.'"

²⁴He also said, "I assure you: No prophet is accepted in his hometown. ²⁵But I say to you, there were certainly many widows in Israel in Elijah's days, when the sky was shut up for three years and six months while a great famine came over all the land. ²⁶Yet Elijah was not sent to any of them—but to a widow at Zarephath in Sidon. ²⁷And in the prophet Elisha's time, there were many in Israel who had serious skin diseases, yet not one of them was healed^R—only Naaman the Syrian."

²⁸When they heard this, everyone in the synagogue was enraged. ²⁹They got up, drove Him out of town, and brought Him to the edge^S of the hill that their town was built on, intending to hurl Him over the cliff. ³⁰But He passed right through the crowd and went on His way.

³¹Then He went down to Capernaum, a town in Galilee, and was teaching them on the Sabbath. ³²They were astonished at His teaching because His message had authority. ³³In the synagogue there was a man with an unclean demonic spirit who cried out with a loud voice, ³⁴"Leave us alone!^T What do You have to do with us,^U Jesus—Nazarene? Have You come to destroy us? I know who You are—the Holy One of God!"

³⁵But Jesus rebuked him and said, "Be quiet and come out of him!"

And throwing him down before them, the demon came out of him without hurting him at all. ³⁶Amazement came over them all, and they kept saying to one another, "What is this message? For He commands the unclean

A4:2 Lit were completed   B4:4 Other mss add but on every word of God   C4:4 Dt 8:3   D4:5 Other mss read So the Devil took Him up on a high mountain   E4:7 Lit will fall down before me   F4:8 Other mss add "Get behind Me, Satan!   G4:8 Dt 6:13   H4:10 Ps 91:11   I4:11 Ps 91:12   J4:12 Dt 6:16   K4:15 Or glorified   L4:18 Other mss add to heal the brokenhearted,   M4:18 Or release, or forgiveness   N4:19 The time of messianic grace   O4:18-19 Is 61:1-2   P4:22 Or They were testifying against Him   Q4:23 Or parable   R4:27 Lit cleansed   S4:29 Lit brow   T4:34 Or Ha!, or Ah!   U4:34 Lit What to us and to You spirits with authority and power, and they come out!" [37] And news about Him began to go out to every place in the vicinity.

[38] After He left the synagogue, He entered Simon's house. Simon's mother-in-law was suffering from a high fever, and they asked Him about her. [39] So He stood over her and rebuked the fever, and it left her. She got up immediately and began to serve them.

[40] When the sun was setting, all those who had anyone sick with various diseases brought them to Him. As He laid His hands on each one of them, He would heal them. [41] Also, demons were coming out of many, shouting and saying, "You are the Son of God!" But He rebuked them and would not allow them to speak, because they knew He was the Messiah.

[42] When it was day, He went out and made His way to a deserted place. But the crowds were searching for Him. They came to Him and tried to keep Him from leaving them. [43] But He said to them, "I must proclaim the good news about the kingdom of God to the other towns also, because I was sent for this purpose." [44] And He was preaching in the synagogues of Galilee.[A]

[5] As the crowd was pressing in on Jesus to hear God's word, He was standing by Lake Gennesaret.[B] [2] He saw two boats at the edge of the lake;[C] the fishermen had left them and were washing their nets. [3] He got into one of the boats, which belonged to Simon, and asked him to put out a little from the land. Then He sat down and was teaching the crowds from the boat.

[4] When He had finished speaking, He said to Simon, "Put out into deep water and let down[D] your nets for a catch."

[5] "Master," Simon replied, "we've worked hard all night long and caught nothing! But at Your word, I'll let down the nets."[E]

[6] When they did this, they caught a great number of fish, and their nets[E] began to tear. [7] So they signaled to their partners in the other boat to come and help them; they came and filled both boats so full that they began to sink.

[8] When Simon Peter saw this, he fell at Jesus' knees and said, "Go away from me, because I'm a sinful man, Lord!" [9] For he and all those with him were amazed[F] at the catch of fish they took, [10] and so were James and John, Zebedee's sons, who were Simon's partners.

"Don't be afraid," Jesus told Simon. "From now on you will be catching people!" [11] Then they brought the boats to land, left everything, and followed Him.

[12] While He was in one of the towns, a man was there who had a serious skin disease all over him. He saw Jesus, fell facedown, and begged Him: "Lord, if You are willing, You can make me clean."

[13] Reaching out His hand, He touched him, saying, "I am willing; be made clean," and immediately the disease left him. [14] Then He ordered him to tell no one: "But go and show yourself to the priest, and offer what Moses prescribed for your cleansing as a testimony to them."

[15] But the news[G] about Him spread even more, and large crowds would come together to hear Him and to be healed of their sicknesses. [16] Yet He often withdrew to deserted places and prayed.

[17] On one of those days while He was teaching, Pharisees and teachers of the law were sitting there who had come from every village of Galilee and Judea, and also from Jerusalem. And the Lord's power to heal was in Him. [18] Just then some men came, carrying on a mat a man who was paralyzed. They tried to bring him in and set him down before Him. [19] Since they could not find a way to bring him in because of the crowd, they went up on the roof and lowered him on the mat through the roof tiles into the middle of the crowd before Jesus. [20] Seeing their faith He said, "Friend,[H] your sins are forgiven you."

[21] Then the scribes and the Pharisees began to think: "Who is this man who speaks blasphemies? Who can forgive sins but God alone?"

[22] But perceiving their thoughts, Jesus replied to them, "Why are you thinking this in your hearts?[I] [23] Which is easier: to say, 'Your sins are forgiven you,' or to say, 'Get up and walk'? [24] But so you may know that the Son of Man has authority on earth to forgive sins"—He told the paralyzed man, "I tell you: Get up, pick up your mat, and go home."

[25] Immediately he got up before them, picked up what he had been lying on, and went home glorifying God. [26] Then everyone was astounded, and they were giving glory to God.

And they were filled with awe and said, "We have seen incredible things today!"

²⁷ After this, Jesus went out and saw a tax collector named Levi sitting at the tax office, and He said to him, "Follow Me!" ²⁸ So, leaving everything behind, he got up and began to follow Him.

²⁹ Then Levi hosted a grand banquet for Him at his house. Now there was a large crowd of tax collectors and others who were guests^A with them. ³⁰ But the Pharisees and their scribes were complaining to His disciples, "Why do you eat and drink with tax collectors and sinners?"

³¹ Jesus replied to them, "The healthy don't need a doctor, but the sick do. ³² I have not come to call the righteous, but sinners to repentance."

³³ Then they said to Him, "John's disciples fast often and say prayers, and those of the Pharisees do the same, but Yours eat and drink."^B

³⁴ Jesus said to them, "You can't make the wedding guests^C fast while the groom is with them, can you? ³⁵ But the time^D will come when the groom will be taken away from them—then they will fast in those days."

³⁶ He also told them a parable: "No one tears a patch from a new garment and puts it on an old garment. Otherwise, not only will he tear the new, but also the piece from the new garment will not match the old. ³⁷ And no one puts new wine into old wineskins. Otherwise, the new wine will burst the skins, it will spill, and the skins will be ruined. ³⁸ But new wine should be put into fresh wineskins.^E ³⁹ And no one, after drinking old wine, wants new, because he says, 'The old is better.'"^F

6 On a Sabbath,^G He passed through the grainfields. His disciples were picking heads of grain, rubbing them in their hands, and eating them. ² But some of the Pharisees said, "Why are you doing what is not lawful on the Sabbath?"

³ Jesus answered them, "Haven't you read what David and those who were with him did when he was hungry— ⁴ how he entered the house of God, and took and ate the sacred bread, which is not lawful for any but the priests to eat? He even gave some to those who

were with him." ⁵ Then He told them, "The Son of Man is Lord of the Sabbath."

⁶ On another Sabbath He entered the synagogue and was teaching. A man was there whose right hand was paralyzed. ⁷ The scribes and Pharisees were watching Him closely, to see if He would heal on the Sabbath, so that they could find a charge against Him. ⁸ But He knew their thoughts and told the man with the paralyzed hand, "Get up and stand here."^H So he got up and stood there. ⁹ Then Jesus said to them, "I ask you: Is it lawful on the Sabbath to do what is good or to do what is evil, to save life or to destroy it?" ¹⁰ After looking around at them all, He told him, "Stretch out your hand." He did so, and his hand was restored.^I ¹¹ They, however, were filled with rage and started discussing with one another what they might do to Jesus.

¹² During those days He went out to the mountain to pray and spent all night in prayer to God. ¹³ When daylight came, He summoned His disciples, and He chose 12 of them—He also named them apostles:

¹⁴ Simon, whom He also named Peter,
    and Andrew his brother;
    James and John;
    Philip and Bartholomew;
¹⁵ Matthew and Thomas;
    James the son of Alphaeus,
    and Simon called the Zealot;
¹⁶ Judas the son of James,
    and Judas Iscariot, who became
    a traitor.

¹⁷ After coming down with them, He stood on a level place with a large crowd of His disciples and a great number of people from all Judea and Jerusalem and from the seacoast of Tyre and Sidon. ¹⁸ They came to hear Him and to be healed of their diseases; and those tormented by unclean spirits were made well. ¹⁹ The whole crowd was trying to touch Him, because power was coming out from Him and healing them all.

²⁰ Then looking up at^J His disciples, He said:

    You who are poor are blessed,
      because the kingdom of God is yours.
²¹ You who are now hungry are blessed,

---

^A5:29 Lit were reclining (at the table); at important meals the custom was to recline on a mat at a low table and lean on the left elbow. ^B5:33 Other mss read "Why do John's . . . drink?" (as a question) ^C5:34 Or the friends of the groom; lit sons of the bridal chamber ^D5:35 Lit days ^E5:38 Other mss add And so both are preserved. ^F5:39 Other mss read is good ^G6:1 Other mss read a second-first Sabbath; perhaps a special Sabbath ^H6:8 Lit stand in the middle ^I6:10 Other mss add as sound as the other ^J6:20 Lit Then lifting up His eyes to

because you will be filled.
You who now weep are blessed,
    because you will laugh.
²² You are blessed when people hate you,
    when they exclude you, insult you,
    and slander your name as evil
    because of the Son of Man.

²³ "Rejoice in that day and leap for joy! Take note—your reward is great in heaven, for this is the way their ancestors used to treat the prophets.

²⁴   But woe to you who are rich,
        for you have received your comfort.
²⁵   Woe to you who are now full,
        for you will be hungry.
    Woe to youᴬ who are now laughing,
        for you will mourn and weep.
²⁶   Woe to youᴬ
        when all people speak well of you,
        for this is the way their ancestors
        used to treat the false prophets.

²⁷ "But I say to you who listen: Love your enemies, do what is good to those who hate you, ²⁸ bless those who curse you, pray for those who mistreat you. ²⁹ If anyone hits you on the cheek, offer the other also. And if anyone takes away your coat, don't hold back your shirt either. ³⁰ Give to everyone who asks you, and from one who takes your things, don't ask for them back. ³¹ Just as you want others to do for you, do the same for them. ³² If you love those who love you, what credit is that to you? Even sinners love those who love them. ³³ If you do what is good to those who are good to you, what credit is that to you? Even sinners do that. ³⁴ And if you lend to those from whom you expect to receive, what credit is that to you? Even sinners lend to sinners to be repaid in full. ³⁵ But love your enemies, do what is good, and lend, expecting nothing in return. Then your reward will be great, and you will be sons of the Most High. For He is gracious to the ungrateful and evil. ³⁶ Be merciful, just as your Father also is merciful.

³⁷ "Do not judge, and you will not be judged. Do not condemn, and you will not be condemned. Forgive, and you will be forgiven. ³⁸ Give, and it will be given to you; a good measure—pressed down, shaken together, and running over—will be poured into your lap.

For with the measure you use,ᴮ it will be measured back to you."

³⁹ He also told them a parable: "Can the blind guide the blind? Won't they both fall into a pit? ⁴⁰ A disciple is not above his teacher, but everyone who is fully trained will be like his teacher.

⁴¹ "Why do you look at the speck in your brother's eye, but don't notice the log in your own eye? ⁴² Or how can you say to your brother, 'Brother, let me take out the speck that is in your eye,' when you yourself don't see the log in your eye? Hypocrite! First take the log out of your eye, and then you will see clearly to take out the speck in your brother's eye.

⁴³ "A good tree doesn't produce bad fruit; on the other hand, a bad tree doesn't produce good fruit. ⁴⁴ For each tree is known by its own fruit. Figs aren't gathered from thornbushes, or grapes picked from a bramble bush. ⁴⁵ A good man produces good out of the good storeroom of his heart. An evil man produces evil out of the evil storeroom, for his mouth speaks from the overflow of the heart.

⁴⁶ "Why do you call Me 'Lord, Lord,' and don't do the things I say? ⁴⁷ I will show you what someone is like who comes to Me, hears My words, and acts on them: ⁴⁸ He is like a man building a house, who dug deepᶜ and laid the foundation on the rock. When the flood came, the river crashed against that house and couldn't shake it, because it was well built. ⁴⁹ But the one who hears and does not act is like a man who built a house on the ground without a foundation. The river crashed against it, and immediately it collapsed. And the destruction of that house was great!"

7 When He had concluded all His sayings in the hearing of the people, He entered Capernaum. ² A centurion's slave, who was highly valued by him, was sick and about to die. ³ When the centurion heard about Jesus, he sent some Jewish elders to Him, requesting Him to come and save the life of his slave. ⁴ When they reached Jesus, they pleaded with Him earnestly, saying, "He is worthy for You to grant this, ⁵ because he loves our nation and has built us a synagogue." ⁶ Jesus went with them, and when He was not far fromᴰ the house, the centurion sent friends to tell Him, "Lord, don't trouble Yourself, since I am not worthy to have You come under my roof. ⁷ That is why I didn't even consider myself worthy to

ᴬ6:25,26 Other mss omit *to you*   ᴮ6:38 Lit *you measure*   ᶜ6:48 Lit *dug and went deep*   ᴰ7:6 Lit *and He already was not far from* come to You. But say the word, and my servant will be cured.[A] [8] For I too am a man placed under authority, having soldiers under my command.[B] I say to this one, 'Go!' and he goes; and to another, 'Come!' and he comes; and to my slave, 'Do this!' and he does it."

[9] Jesus heard this and was amazed at him, and turning to the crowd following Him, He said, "I tell you, I have not found so great a faith even in Israel!" [10] When those who had been sent returned to the house, they found the slave in good health.

[11] Soon afterward He was on His way to a town called Nain. His disciples and a large crowd were traveling with Him. [12] Just as He neared the gate of the town, a dead man was being carried out. He was his mother's only son, and she was a widow. A large crowd from the city was also with her. [13] When the Lord saw her, He had compassion on her and said, "Don't cry." [14] Then He came up and touched the open coffin,[C] and the pallbearers stopped. And He said, "Young man, I tell you, get up!"

[15] The dead man sat up and began to speak, and Jesus gave him to his mother. [16] Then fear[D] came over everyone, and they glorified God, saying, "A great prophet has risen among us," and "God has visited[E] His people." [17] This report about Him went throughout Judea and all the vicinity.

[18] Then John's disciples told him about all these things. So John summoned two of his disciples [19] and sent them to the Lord, asking, "Are You the One who is to come, or should we look for someone else?"

[20] When the men reached Him, they said, "John the Baptist sent us to ask You, 'Are You the One who is to come, or should we look for someone else?'"

[21] At that time Jesus healed many people of diseases, plagues, and evil spirits, and He granted sight to many blind people. [22] He replied to them, "Go and report to John the things you have seen and heard: The blind receive their sight, the lame walk, those with skin diseases are healed,[F] the deaf hear, the dead are raised, and the poor are told the good news. [23] And anyone who is not offended because of Me is blessed." [24] After John's messengers left, He began to speak to the crowds about John: "What did you go out into the wilderness to

see? A reed swaying in the wind? [25] What then did you go out to see? A man dressed in soft robes? Look, those who are splendidly dressed[G] and live in luxury are in royal palaces. [26] What then did you go out to see? A prophet? Yes, I tell you, and far more than a prophet. [27] This is the one it is written about:

> Look, I am sending My messenger
> ahead of You;[H]
> he will prepare Your way before You.[I]

[28] I tell you, among those born of women no one is greater than John,[J] but the least in the kingdom of God is greater than he."

[29] (And when all the people, including the tax collectors, heard this, they acknowledged God's way of righteousness,[K] because they had been baptized with John's baptism. [30] But since the Pharisees and experts in the law had not been baptized by him, they rejected the plan of God for themselves.)

[31] "To what then should I compare the people of this generation, and what are they like? [32] They are like children sitting in the marketplace and calling to each other:

> We played the flute for you,
> but you didn't dance;
> we sang a lament,
> but you didn't weep!

[33] For John the Baptist did not come eating bread or drinking wine, and you say, 'He has a demon!' [34] The Son of Man has come eating and drinking, and you say, 'Look, a glutton and a drunkard, a friend of tax collectors and sinners!' [35] Yet wisdom is vindicated[L] by all her children."

[36] Then one of the Pharisees invited Him to eat with him. He entered the Pharisee's house and reclined at the table. [37] And a woman in the town who was a sinner found out that Jesus was reclining at the table in the Pharisee's house. She brought an alabaster jar of fragrant oil [38] and stood behind Him at His feet, weeping, and began to wash His feet with her tears. She wiped His feet with the hair of her head, kissing them and anointing them with the fragrant oil.

[39] When the Pharisee who had invited Him saw this, he said to himself, "This man, if He were a prophet, would know who and what kind

---

[A]**7:7** Other mss read *and let my servant be cured* [B]**7:8** Lit *under me* [C]**7:14** Or *the bier* [D]**7:16** Or *awe* [E]**7:16** Or *come to help* [F]**7:22** Lit *cleansed* [G]**7:25** Or *who have glorious robes* [H]**7:27** Lit *messenger before Your face* [I]**7:27** Mal 3:1 [J]**7:28** Other mss read *women is not a greater prophet than John the Baptist* [K]**7:29** Lit *they justified God* [L]**7:35** Or *wisdom is declared right* of woman this is who is touching Him—she's a sinner!"

⁴⁰Jesus replied to him, "Simon, I have something to say to you."

"Teacher," he said, "say it."

⁴¹"A creditor had two debtors. One owed 500 denarii, and the other 50. ⁴²Since they could not pay it back, he graciously forgave them both. So, which of them will love him more?"

⁴³Simon answered, "I suppose the one he forgave more."

"You have judged correctly," He told him. ⁴⁴Turning to the woman, He said to Simon, "Do you see this woman? I entered your house; you gave Me no water for My feet, but she, with her tears, has washed My feet and wiped them with her hair. ⁴⁵You gave Me no kiss, but she hasn't stopped kissing My feet since I came in. ⁴⁶You didn't anoint My head with olive oil, but she has anointed My feet with fragrant oil. ⁴⁷Therefore I tell you, her many sins have been forgiven; that's whyᴬ she loved much. But the one who is forgiven little, loves little." ⁴⁸Then He said to her, "Your sins are forgiven."

⁴⁹Those who were at the table with Him began to say among themselves, "Who is this man who even forgives sins?"

⁵⁰And He said to the woman, "Your faith has saved you. Go in peace."

8 Soon afterward He was traveling from one town and village to another, preaching and telling the good news of the kingdom of God. The Twelve were with Him, ²and also some women who had been healed of evil spirits and sicknesses: Mary, called Magdalene (seven demons had come out of her); ³Joanna the wife of Chuza, Herod's steward; Susanna; and many others who were supporting them from their possessions.

⁴As a large crowd was gathering, and people were flocking to Him from every town, He said in a parable: ⁵"A sower went out to sow his seed. As he was sowing, some fell along the path; it was trampled on, and the birds of the sky ate it up. ⁶Other seed fell on the rock; when it sprang up, it withered, since it lacked moisture. ⁷Other seed fell among thorns; the thorns sprang up with it and choked it. ⁸Still other seed fell on good ground; when it sprang up, it produced a crop: 100 times what was sown." As He said this, He called out, "Anyone who has ears to hear should listen!"

⁹Then His disciples asked Him, "What does this parable mean?" ¹⁰So He said, "The secrets of the kingdom of God have been given for you to know, but to the rest it is in parables, so that

Looking they may not see,
and hearing they may not understand.ᴮ

¹¹"This is the meaning of the parable:ᶜ The seed is the word of God. ¹²The seed along the path are those who have heard and then the Devil comes and takes away the word from their hearts, so that they may not believe and be saved. ¹³And the seed on the rock are those who, when they hear, welcome the word with joy. Having no root, these believe for a while and depart in a time of testing. ¹⁴As for the seed that fell among thorns, these are the ones who, when they have heard, go on their way and are choked with worries, riches, and pleasures of life, and produce no mature fruit. ¹⁵But the seed in the good ground—these are the ones who,ᴰ having heard the word with an honest and good heart, hold on to it and by enduring, bear fruit.

¹⁶"No one, after lighting a lamp, covers it with a basket or puts it under a bed, but puts it on a lampstand so that those who come in may see its light. ¹⁷For nothing is concealed that won't be revealed, and nothing hidden that won't be made known and come to light. ¹⁸Therefore take care how you listen. For whoever has, more will be given to him; and whoever does not have, even what he thinks he has will be taken away from him."

¹⁹Then His mother and brothers came to Him, but they could not meet with Him because of the crowd. ²⁰He was told, "Your mother and Your brothers are standing outside, wanting to see You."

²¹But He replied to them, "My mother and My brothers are those who hear and do the word of God."

²²One day He and His disciples got into a boat, and He told them, "Let's cross over to the other side of the lake." So they set out, ²³and as they were sailing He fell asleep. Then a fierce windstorm came down on the lake; they were being swamped and were in danger. ²⁴They came and woke Him up, saying, "Master, Master, we're going to die!" Then He got up and rebuked the wind and the raging waves. So

---

ᴬ7:47 Her love shows that she has been forgiven   ᴮ8:10 Is 6:9   ᶜ8:11 Lit But this is the parable: ᴰ8:15 Or these are the kind who they ceased, and there was a calm. ²⁵He said to them, "Where is your faith?"

They were fearful and amazed, asking one another, "Who can this be?ᴬ He commands even the winds and the waves, and they obey Him!"

²⁶Then they sailed to the region of the Gerasenes,ᴮ which is opposite Galilee. ²⁷When He got out on land, a demon-possessed man from the town met Him. For a long time he had worn no clothes and did not stay in a house but in the tombs. ²⁸When he saw Jesus, he cried out, fell down before Him, and said in a loud voice, "What do You have to do with me,ᶜ Jesus, You Son of the Most High God? I beg You, don't torment me!" ²⁹For He had commanded the unclean spirit to come out of the man. Many times it had seized him, and though he was guarded, bound by chains and shackles, he would snap the restraints and be driven by the demon into deserted places.

³⁰"What is your name?" Jesus asked him.

"Legion," he said—because many demons had entered him. ³¹And they begged Him not to banish them to the abyss.

³²A large herd of pigs was there, feeding on the hillside. The demons begged Him to permit them to enter the pigs, and He gave them permission. ³³The demons came out of the man and entered the pigs, and the herd rushed down the steep bank into the lake and drowned. ³⁴When the men who tended them saw what had happened, they ran off and reported it in the town and in the countryside. ³⁵Then people went out to see what had happened. They came to Jesus and found the man the demons had departed from, sitting at Jesus' feet, dressed and in his right mind. And they were afraid. ³⁶Meanwhile, the eyewitnesses reported to them how the demon-possessed man was delivered. ³⁷Then all the people of the Gerasene regionᴮ asked Him to leave them, because they were gripped by great fear. So getting into the boat, He returned.

³⁸The man from whom the demons had departed kept begging Him to be with Him. But He sent him away and said, ³⁹"Go back to your home, and tell all that God has done for you." And off he went, proclaiming throughout the town all that Jesus had done for him.

⁴⁰When Jesus returned, the crowd welcomed Him, for they were all expecting Him. ⁴¹Just then, a man named Jairus came. He was a leader of the synagogue. He fell down at Jesus' feet and pleaded with Him to come to his house, ⁴²because he had an only daughter about 12 years old, and she was at death's door.ᴰ

While He was going, the crowds were nearly crushing Him. ⁴³A woman suffering from bleeding for 12 years, who had spent all she had on doctorsᴱ yet could not be healed by any, ⁴⁴approached from behind and touched the tassel of His robe. Instantly her bleeding stopped.

⁴⁵"Who touched Me?" Jesus asked.

When they all denied it, Peterᶠ said, "Master, the crowds are hemming You in and pressing against You."ᴳ

⁴⁶"Someone did touch Me," said Jesus. "I know that power has gone out from Me." ⁴⁷When the woman saw that she was discovered,ᴴ she came trembling and fell down before Him. In the presence of all the people, she declared the reason she had touched Him and how she was instantly cured. ⁴⁸"Daughter," He said to her, "your faith has made you well.ᴵ Go in peace."

⁴⁹While He was still speaking, someone came from the synagogue leader's house, saying, "Your daughter is dead. Don't bother the Teacher anymore."

⁵⁰When Jesus heard it, He answered him, "Don't be afraid. Only believe, and she will be made well." ⁵¹After He came to the house, He let no one enter with Him except Peter, John, James, and the child's father and mother. ⁵²Everyone was crying and mourning for her. But He said, "Stop crying, for she is not dead but asleep."

⁵³They started laughing at Him, because they knew she was dead. ⁵⁴So Heᴶ took her by the hand and called out, "Child, get up!" ⁵⁵Her spirit returned, and she got up at once. Then He gave orders that she be given something to eat. ⁵⁶Her parents were astounded, but He instructed them to tell no one what had happened.

9 Summoning the Twelve, He gave them power and authority over all the demons, and power to healᴷ diseases. ²Then He sent

---

ᴬ8:25 Lit Who then is this?   ᴮ8:26,37 Other mss read the Gadarenes   ᶜ8:28 Lit What to me and to You   ᴰ8:42 Lit she was dying   ᴱ8:43 Other mss omit who had spent all she had on doctors   ᶠ8:45 Other mss add and those with him   ᴳ8:45 Other mss add And You say, 'Who touched Me?'   ᴴ8:47 Lit she had not escaped notice   ᴵ8:48 Or has saved you   ᴶ8:54 Other mss add having put them all outside   ᴷ9:1 In this passage, different Gk words are translated as heal. In Eng, "to heal" or "to cure" are synonyms with little distinction in meaning. Technically, we do not heal or cure diseases. People are healed or cured from diseases.

them to proclaim the kingdom of God and to heal the sick.

³"Take nothing for the road," He told them, "no walking stick, no traveling bag, no bread, no money; and don't take an extra shirt. ⁴Whatever house you enter, stay there and leave from there. ⁵If they do not welcome you, when you leave that town, shake off the dust from your feet as a testimony against them." ⁶So they went out and traveled from village to village, proclaiming the good news and healing everywhere.

⁷Herod the tetrarch heard about everything that was going on. He was perplexed, because some said that John had been raised from the dead, ⁸some that Elijah had appeared, and others that one of the ancient prophets had risen. ⁹"I beheaded John," Herod said, "but who is this I hear such things about?" And he wanted to see Him.

¹⁰When the apostles returned, they reported to Jesus all that they had done. He took them along and withdrew privately to a^A town called Bethsaida. ¹¹When the crowds found out, they followed Him. He welcomed them, spoke to them about the kingdom of God, and cured^B those who needed healing.

¹²Late in the day,^C the Twelve approached and said to Him, "Send the crowd away, so they can go into the surrounding villages and countryside to find food and lodging, because we are in a deserted place here."

¹³"You give them something to eat," He told them.

"We have no more than five loaves and two fish," they said, "unless we go and buy food for all these people." ¹⁴(For about 5,000 men were there.)

Then He told His disciples, "Have them sit down^D in groups of about 50 each." ¹⁵They did so, and had them all sit down. ¹⁶Then He took the five loaves and the two fish, and looking up to heaven, He blessed and broke them. He kept giving them to the disciples to set before the crowd. ¹⁷Everyone ate and was filled. Then they picked up^E 12 baskets of leftover pieces.

¹⁸While He was praying in private and His disciples were with Him, He asked them, "Who do the crowds say that I am?"

¹⁹They answered, "John the Baptist; others, Elijah; still others, that one of the ancient prophets has come back."^F

²⁰"But you," He asked them, "who do you say that I am?"

Peter answered, "God's Messiah!"

²¹But He strictly warned and instructed them to tell this to no one, ²²saying, "The Son of Man must suffer many things and be rejected by the elders, chief priests, and scribes, be killed, and be raised the third day."

²³Then He said to them all, "If anyone wants to come with^G Me, he must deny himself, take up his cross daily,^H and follow Me. ²⁴For whoever wants to save his life will lose it, but whoever loses his life because of Me will save it. ²⁵What is a man benefited if he gains the whole world, yet loses or forfeits himself? ²⁶For whoever is ashamed of Me and My words, the Son of Man will be ashamed of him when He comes in His glory and that of the Father and the holy angels. ²⁷I tell you the truth: There are some standing here who will not taste death until they see the kingdom of God."

²⁸About eight days after these words, He took along Peter, John, and James and went up on the mountain to pray. ²⁹As He was praying, the appearance of His face changed, and His clothes became dazzling white. ³⁰Suddenly, two men were talking with Him—Moses and Elijah. ³¹They appeared in glory and were speaking of His death,^I which He was about to accomplish in Jerusalem.

³²Peter and those with him were in a deep sleep,^J and when they became fully awake, they saw His glory and the two men who were standing with Him. ³³As the two men were departing from Him, Peter said to Jesus, "Master, it's good for us to be here! Let us make three tabernacles: one for You, one for Moses, and one for Elijah"—not knowing what he said.

³⁴While he was saying this, a cloud appeared and overshadowed them. They became afraid as they entered the cloud. ³⁵Then a voice came from the cloud, saying:

This is My Son, the Chosen One;^K
listen to Him!

A9:10 Other mss add *deserted place near a*   B9:11 Or *healed*; in this passage, different Gk words are translated as heal. In Eng, "to heal" or "to cure" are synonyms with little distinction in meaning. Technically, we do not heal or cure diseases. People are healed or cured from diseases. C9:12 Lit *When the day began to decline*   D9:14 Lit them recline   E9:17 Lit *Then were picked up by them*   F9:19 Lit *has risen*   G9:23 Lit *come after*   H9:23 Other mss omit *daily*   I9:31 Or *departure*; Gk *exodus*   J9:32 Lit *were weighed down with sleep*   K9:35 Other mss read *the Beloved*

³⁶After the voice had spoken, only Jesus was found. They kept silent, and in those days told no one what they had seen.

³⁷The next day, when they came down from the mountain, a large crowd met Him. ³⁸Just then a man from the crowd cried out, "Teacher, I beg You to look at my son, because he's my only child. ³⁹Often a spirit seizes him; suddenly he shrieks, and it throws him into convulsions until he foams at the mouth;ᴬ woundingᴮ him, it hardly ever leaves him. ⁴⁰I begged Your disciples to drive it out, but they couldn't."

⁴¹Jesus replied, "You unbelieving and rebelliousᶜ generation! How long will I be with you and put up with you? Bring your son here."

⁴²As the boy was still approaching, the demon knocked him down and threw him into severe convulsions. But Jesus rebuked the unclean spirit, cured the boy, and gave him back to his father. ⁴³And they were all astonished at the greatness of God.

While everyone was amazed at all the things He was doing, He told His disciples, ⁴⁴"Let these words sink in:ᴰ The Son of Man is about to be betrayed into the hands of men."

⁴⁵But they did not understand this statement; it was concealed from them so that they could not grasp it, and they were afraid to ask Him about it.ᴱ

⁴⁶Then an argument started among them about who would be the greatest of them. ⁴⁷But Jesus, knowing the thoughts of their hearts, took a little child and had him stand next to Him. ⁴⁸He told them, "Whoever welcomesᶠ this little child in My name welcomes Me. And whoever welcomes Me welcomes Him who sent Me. For whoever is least among you—this one is great."

⁴⁹John responded, "Master, we saw someone driving out demons in Your name, and we tried to stop him because he does not follow us."

⁵⁰"Don't stop him," Jesus told him, "because whoever is not against you is for you."ᴳ

⁵¹When the days were coming to a close for Him to be taken up,ᴴ He determinedᴵ to journey to Jerusalem. ⁵²He sent messengers ahead of Him, and on the way they entered a village of the Samaritans to make preparations for

Him. ⁵³But they did not welcome Him, because He determined to journey to Jerusalem. ⁵⁴When the disciples James and John saw this, they said, "Lord, do You want us to call down fire from heaven to consume them?"ᴶ

⁵⁵But He turned and rebuked them,ᴷ ⁵⁶and they went to another village.

⁵⁷As they were traveling on the road someone said to Him, "I will follow You wherever You go!"

⁵⁸Jesus told him, "Foxes have dens, and birds of the skyᴸ have nests, but the Son of Man has no place to lay His head." ⁵⁹Then He said to another, "Follow Me."

"Lord," he said, "first let me go bury my father."ᴹ

⁶⁰But He told him, "Let the dead bury their own dead, but you go and spread the news of the kingdom of God."

⁶¹Another also said, "I will follow You, Lord, but first let me go and say good-bye to those at my house."

⁶²But Jesus said to him, "No one who puts his hand to the plow and looks back is fit for the kingdom of God."

10 After this, the Lord appointed 70ᴺ others, and He sent them ahead of Him in pairs to every town and place where He Himself was about to go. ²He told them: "The harvest is abundant, but the workers are few. Therefore, pray to the Lord of the harvest to send out workers into His harvest. ³Now go; I'm sending you out like lambs among wolves. ⁴Don't carry a money-bag, traveling bag, or sandals; don't greet anyone along the road. ⁵Whatever house you enter, first say, 'Peace to this household.' ⁶If a son of peaceᴼ is there, your peace will rest on him; but if not, it will return to you. ⁷Remain in the same house, eating and drinking what they offer, for the worker is worthy of his wages. Don't be moving from house to house. ⁸When you enter any town, and they welcome you, eat the things set before you. ⁹Heal the sick who are there, and tell them, 'The kingdom of God has come near you.' ¹⁰When you enter any town, and they don't welcome you, go out into its streets and say, ¹¹'We are wiping off as a witness against you even the dust of your

ᴬ9:39 Lit convulsions with foam   ᴮ9:39 Or bruising, or mauling   ᶜ9:41 Or corrupt, or perverted, or twisted; Dt 32:5   ᴰ9:44 Lit Put these words in your ears   ᴱ9:45 Lit about this statement   ᶠ9:48 Or receives, throughout the verse   ᴳ9:50 Other mss read against us is for us   ᴴ9:51 His ascension   ᴵ9:51 Lit He stiffened His face to go; Is 50:7   ᴶ9:54 Other mss add as Elijah also did   ᴷ9:55-56 Other mss add and said, "You don't know what kind of spirit you belong to. ⁵⁶For the Son of Man did not come to destroy people's lives but to save them,"   ᴸ9:58 Wild birds, as opposed to domestic birds   ᴹ9:59 Not necessarily meaning his father was already dead   ᴺ10:1 Other mss read 72   ᴼ10:6 A peaceful person; one open to the message of the kingdom town that clings to our feet. Know this for certain: The kingdom of God has come near.' [12]I tell you, on that day it will be more tolerable for Sodom than for that town.

[13]"Woe to you, Chorazin! Woe to you, Bethsaida! For if the miracles that were done in you had been done in Tyre and Sidon, they would have repented long ago, sitting in sackcloth and ashes! [14]But it will be more tolerable for Tyre and Sidon at the judgment than for you. [15]And you, Capernaum, will you be exalted to heaven? No, you will go down to Hades! [16]Whoever listens to you listens to Me. Whoever rejects you rejects Me. And whoever rejects Me rejects the One who sent Me."

[17]The Seventy[A] returned with joy, saying, "Lord, even the demons submit to us in Your name."

[18]He said to them, "I watched Satan fall from heaven like a lightning flash. [19]Look, I have given you the authority to trample on snakes and scorpions and over all the power of the enemy; nothing will ever harm you. [20]However, don't rejoice that[B] the spirits submit to you, but rejoice that your names are written in heaven."

[21]In that same hour He[C] rejoiced in the Holy[D] Spirit and said, "I praise[E] You, Father, Lord of heaven and earth, because You have hidden these things from the wise and the learned and have revealed them to infants. Yes, Father, because this was Your good pleasure.[F] [22]All things have[G] been entrusted to Me by My Father. No one knows who the Son is except the Father, and who the Father is except the Son, and anyone to whom the Son desires[H] to reveal Him."

[23]Then turning to His disciples He said privately, "The eyes that see the things you see are blessed! [24]For I tell you that many prophets and kings wanted to see the things you see yet didn't see them; to hear the things you hear yet didn't hear them."

[25]Just then an expert in the law stood up to test Him, saying, "Teacher, what must I do to inherit eternal life?"

[26]"What is written in the law?" He asked him. "How do you read it?"

[27]He answered:

Love the Lord your God with all your heart, with all your soul, with all your strength, and with all your mind; and **your neighbor as yourself.**[I]

[28]"You've answered correctly," He told him. "Do this and you will live."

[29]But wanting to justify himself, he asked Jesus, "And who is my neighbor?"

[30]Jesus took up the question and said: "A man was going down from Jerusalem to Jericho and fell into the hands of robbers. They stripped him, beat him up, and fled, leaving him half dead. [31]A priest happened to be going down that road. When he saw him, he passed by on the other side. [32]In the same way, a Levite, when he arrived at the place and saw him, passed by on the other side. [33]But a Samaritan on his journey came up to him, and when he saw the man, he had compassion. [34]He went over to him and bandaged his wounds, pouring on olive oil and wine. Then he put him on his own animal, brought him to an inn, and took care of him. [35]The next day[J] he took out two denarii, gave them to the innkeeper, and said, 'Take care of him. When I come back I'll reimburse you for whatever extra you spend.'

[36]"Which of these three do you think proved to be a neighbor to the man who fell into the hands of the robbers?"

[37]"The one who showed mercy to him," he said.

Then Jesus told him, "Go and do the same."

[38]While they were traveling, He entered a village, and a woman named Martha welcomed Him into her home.[K] [39]She had a sister named Mary, who also sat at the Lord's[L] feet and was listening to what He said.[M] [40]But Martha was distracted by her many tasks, and she came up and asked, "Lord, don't You care that my sister has left me to serve alone? So tell her to give me a hand."[N]

[41]The Lord[C] answered her, "Martha, Martha, you are worried and upset about many things, [42]but one thing is necessary. Mary has made the right choice,[O] and it will not be taken away from her."

A10:17 Other mss read The Seventy-two   B10:20 Lit don't rejoice in this, that   C10:21,41 Other mss read Jesus   D10:21 Other mss omit Holy   E10:21 Or thank, or confess   F10:21 Lit was well-pleasing in Your sight   G10:22 Other mss read And turning to the disciples, He said, "Everything has   H10:22 Or wills, or chooses   I10:27 Lv 19:18; Dt 6:5   J10:35 Other mss add as he was leaving   K10:38 Other mss omit into her home   L10:39 Other mss read at Jesus'   M10:39 Lit to His word or message   N10:40 Or tell her to help me   O10:42 Lit has chosen the good part

11 He was praying in a certain place, and when He finished, one of His disciples said to Him, "Lord, teach us to pray, just as John also taught his disciples."

² He said to them, "Whenever you pray, say:

Father,^A
Your name be honored as holy.
Your kingdom come.^B
³ Give us each day our daily bread.^C
⁴ And forgive us our sins,
for we ourselves also forgive everyone
in debt to us.^D
And do not bring us into temptation."^E

⁵ He also said to them: "Suppose one of you^F has a friend and goes to him at midnight and says to him, 'Friend, lend me three loaves of bread, ⁶ because a friend of mine on a journey has come to me, and I don't have anything to offer him.'^G ⁷ Then he will answer from inside and say, 'Don't bother me! The door is already locked, and my children and I have gone to bed. I can't get up to give you anything.' ⁸ I tell you, even though he won't get up and give him anything because he is his friend, yet because of his friend's persistence,^H he will get up and give him as much as he needs.

⁹ "So I say to you, keep asking,^I and it will be given to you. Keep searching,^J and you will find. Keep knocking,^K and the door will be opened to you. ¹⁰ For everyone who asks receives, and the one who searches finds, and to the one who knocks, the door will be opened. ¹¹ What father among you, if his son^L asks for a fish, will give him a snake instead of a fish? ¹² Or if he asks for an egg, will give him a scorpion? ¹³ If you then, who are evil, know how to give good gifts to your children, how much more will the heavenly Father give^M the Holy Spirit to those who ask Him?"

¹⁴ Now He was driving out a demon that was mute.^N When the demon came out, the man who had been mute, spoke, and the crowds were amazed. ¹⁵ But some of them said, "He drives out demons by Beelzebul, the ruler of the demons!" ¹⁶ And others, as a test, were demanding of Him a sign from heaven.

¹⁷ Knowing their thoughts, He told them: "Every kingdom divided against itself is head-ed for destruction, and a house divided against itself falls. ¹⁸ If Satan also is divided against himself, how will his kingdom stand? For you say I drive out demons by Beelzebul. ¹⁹ And if I drive out demons by Beelzebul, who is it your sons^O drive them out by? For this reason they will be your judges. ²⁰ If I drive out demons by the finger of God, then the kingdom of God has come to you. ²¹ When a strong man, fully armed, guards his estate, his possessions are secure.^P ²² But when one stronger than he attacks and overpowers him, he takes from him all his weapons^Q he trusted in, and divides up his plunder. ²³ Anyone who is not with Me is against Me, and anyone who does not gather with Me scatters.

²⁴ "When an unclean spirit comes out of a man, it roams through waterless places looking for rest, and not finding rest, it then^R says, 'I'll go back to my house where I came from.' ²⁵ And returning, it finds the house swept and put in order. ²⁶ Then it goes and brings seven other spirits more evil than itself, and they enter and settle down there. As a result, that man's last condition is worse than the first."

²⁷ As He was saying these things, a woman from the crowd raised her voice and said to Him, "The womb that bore You and the one who nursed You are blessed!"

²⁸ He said, "Even more, those who hear the word of God and keep it are blessed!"

²⁹ As the crowds were increasing, He began saying: "This generation is an evil generation. It demands a sign, but no sign will be given to it except the sign of Jonah.^S ³⁰ For just as Jonah became a sign to the people of Nineveh, so also the Son of Man will be to this generation. ³¹ The queen of the south will rise up at the judgment with the men of this generation and condemn them, because she came from the ends of the earth to hear the wisdom of Solomon, and look—something greater than Solomon is here! ³² The men of Nineveh will rise up at the judgment with this generation and condemn it, because they repented at Jonah's proclamation, and look—something greater than Jonah is here!

³³ "No one lights a lamp and puts it in the cellar or under a basket,^T but on a lampstand,

---

A 11:2 Other mss read *Our Father in heaven*   B 11:2 Other mss add *Your will be done on earth as it is in heaven*   C 11:3 *Or our bread for tomorrow*   D 11:4 Or *everyone who wrongs us*   E 11:4 Other mss add *But deliver us from the evil one*   F 11:5 Lit *Who of you*   G 11:6 Lit *I have nothing to set before him*   H 11:8 Or *annoying persistence, or shamelessness*   I 11:9 Or *you, ask*   J 11:9 Or *Search*   K 11:9 Or *Knock*   L 11:11 Other mss read *son asks for bread, would give him a stone? Or if he*   M 11:13 Lit *the Father from heaven will give*   N 11:14 A demon that caused the man to be mute   O 11:19 *Your exorcists*   P 11:21 Lit *his possessions are in peace*   Q 11:22 Gk *panoplia*, the armor and weapons of a foot soldier; Eph 6:11,13   R 11:24 Other mss omit *then*   S 11:29 Other mss add *the prophet*   T 11:33 Other mss omit *or under a basket* so that those who come in may see its light. ³⁴Your eye is the lamp of the body. When your eye is good, your whole body is also full of light. But when it is bad, your body is also full of darkness. ³⁵Take care then, that the light in you is not darkness. ³⁶If, therefore, your whole body is full of light, with no part of it in darkness, it will be entirely illuminated, as when a lamp shines its light on you."ᴬ

³⁷As He was speaking, a Pharisee asked Him to dine with him. So He went in and reclined at the table. ³⁸When the Pharisee saw this, he was amazed that He did not first perform the ritual washingᴮ before dinner. ³⁹But the Lord said to him: "Now you Pharisees clean the outside of the cup and dish, but inside you are full of greed and evil. ⁴⁰Fools! Didn't He who made the outside make the inside too? ⁴¹But give from what is within to the poor,ᶜ and then everything is clean for you.

⁴²"But woe to you Pharisees! You give a tenthᴰ of mint, rue, and every kind of herb, and you bypassᴱ justice and love for God.ᶠ These things you should have done without neglecting the others.

⁴³"Woe to you Pharisees! You love the front seat in the synagogues and greetings in the marketplaces.

⁴⁴"Woe to you!ᴳ You are like unmarked graves; the people who walk over them don't know it."

⁴⁵One of the experts in the law answered Him, "Teacher, when You say these things You insult us too."

⁴⁶Then He said: "Woe also to you experts in the law! You load people with burdens that are hard to carry, yet you yourselves don't touch these burdens with one of your fingers.

⁴⁷"Woe to you! You build monumentsᴴ to the prophets, and your fathers killed them. ⁴⁸Therefore, you are witnesses that you approveᴵ the deeds of your fathers, for they killed them, and you build their monuments.ᴶ ⁴⁹Because of this, the wisdom of God said, 'I will send them prophets and apostles, and some of them they will kill and persecute,' ⁵⁰so that this generation may be held responsible for the blood of all the prophets shed since the foundation of the worldᴷ— ⁵¹from the blood of

Abel to the blood of Zechariah, who perished between the altar and the sanctuary.

"Yes, I tell you, this generation will be held responsible.ᴸ

⁵²"Woe to you experts in the law! You have taken away the key of knowledge! You didn't go in yourselves, and you hindered those who were going in."

⁵³When He left there,ᴹ the scribes and the Pharisees began to oppose Him fiercely and to cross-examine Him about many things; ⁵⁴they were lying in wait for Him to trap Him in something He said.ᴺ

12 In these circumstances,ᴼ a crowd of many thousands came together, so that they were trampling on one another. He began to say to His disciples first: "Be on your guard against the yeastᴾ of the Pharisees, which is hypocrisy. ²There is nothing covered that won't be uncovered, nothing hidden that won't be made known. ³Therefore, whatever you have said in the dark will be heard in the light, and what you have whispered in an ear in private rooms will be proclaimed on the housetops.

⁴"And I say to you, My friends, don't fear those who kill the body, and after that can do nothing more. ⁵But I will show you the One to fear: Fear Him who has authority to throw people into hell after death. Yes, I say to you, this is the One to fear! ⁶Aren't five sparrows sold for two pennies?ᵠ Yet not one of them is forgotten in God's sight. ⁷Indeed, the hairs of your head are all counted. Don't be afraid; you are worth more than many sparrows!

⁸"And I say to you, anyone who acknowledges Me before men, the Son of Man will also acknowledge him before the angels of God, ⁹but whoever denies Me before men will be denied before the angels of God. ¹⁰Anyone who speaks a word against the Son of Man will be forgiven, but the one who blasphemes against the Holy Spirit will not be forgiven. ¹¹Whenever they bring you before synagogues and rulers and authorities, don't worry about how you should defend yourselves or what you should say. ¹²For the Holy Spirit will teach you at that very hour what must be said."

ᴬ11:36 Or shines on you with its rays   ᴮ11:38 Lit He did not first wash   ᶜ11:41 Or But donate from the heart as charity   ᴰ11:42 Or a tithe   ᴱ11:42 Or neglect   ᶠ11:42 Lit the justice and the love of God   ᴳ11:44 Other mss read you scribes and Pharisees, hypocrites!   ᴴ11:47 Or graves   ᴵ11:48 Lit witnesses and approve   ᴶ11:48 Other mss omit their monuments   ᴷ11:50 Lit so that the blood of all . . . world may be required of this generation,   ᴸ11:51 Lit you, it will be required of this generation   ᴹ11:53 Other mss read And as He was saying these things to them   ᴺ11:54 Other mss add so that they might bring charges against Him   ᴼ12:1 Or Meanwhile, or At this time, or During this period   ᴾ12:1 Or leaven   ᵠ12:6 Lit two assaria; the assarion (sg) was a small copper coin

¹³Someone from the crowd said to Him, "Teacher, tell my brother to divide the inheritance with me."

¹⁴"Friend,"ᴬ He said to him, "who appointed Me a judge or arbitrator over you?" ¹⁵He then told them, "Watch out and be on guard against all greed because one's life is not in the abundance of his possessions."

¹⁶Then He told them a parable: "A rich man's land was very productive. ¹⁷He thought to himself, 'What should I do, since I don't have anywhere to store my crops? ¹⁸I will do this,' he said. 'I'll tear down my barns and build bigger ones and store all my grain and my goods there. ¹⁹Then I'll say to myself, "Youᴮ have many goods stored up for many years. Take it easy; eat, drink, and enjoy yourself."'

²⁰"But God said to him, 'You fool! This very night your life is demanded of you. And the things you have prepared—whose will they be?'

²¹"That's how it is with the one who stores up treasure for himself and is not rich toward God."

²²Then He said to His disciples: "Therefore I tell you, don't worry about your life, what you will eat; or about the body, what you will wear. ²³For life is more than food and the body more than clothing. ²⁴Consider the ravens: They don't sow or reap; they don't have a storeroom or a barn; yet God feeds them. Aren't you worth much more than the birds? ²⁵Can any of you add a cubit to his heightᶜ by worrying? ²⁶If then you're not able to do even a little thing, why worry about the rest?

²⁷"Consider how the wildflowers grow: They don't labor or spin thread. Yet I tell you, not even Solomon in all his splendor was adorned like one of these! ²⁸If that's how God clothes the grass, which is in the field today and is thrown into the furnace tomorrow, how much more will He do for you—you of little faith? ²⁹Don't keep striving for what you should eat and what you should drink, and don't be anxious. ³⁰For the Gentile world eagerly seeks all these things, and your Father knows that you need them.

³¹"But seek His kingdom, and these things will be provided for you. ³²Don't be afraid, little flock, because your Father delights to give you the kingdom. ³³Sell your possessions and give to the poor. Make money-bags for yourselves that won't grow old, an inexhaustible treasure in heaven, where no thief comes near and no moth destroys. ³⁴For where your treasure is, there your heart will be also.

³⁵"Be ready for serviceᴰ and have your lamps lit. ³⁶You must be like people waiting for their master to returnᴱ from the wedding banquet so that when he comes and knocks, they can open the door for him at once. ³⁷Those slaves the master will find alert when he comes will be blessed. I assure you: He will get ready,ᶠ have them recline at the table, then come and serve them. ³⁸If he comes in the middle of the night, or even near dawn,ᴳ and finds them alert, those slaves are blessed. ³⁹But know this: If the homeowner had known at what hour the thief was coming, he would not have let his house be broken into. ⁴⁰You also be ready, because the Son of Man is coming at an hour that you do not expect."

⁴¹"Lord," Peter asked, "are You telling this parable to us or to everyone?"

⁴²The Lord said: "Who then is the faithful and sensible manager his master will put in charge of his household servants to give them their allotted food at the proper time? ⁴³That slave whose master finds him working when he comes will be rewarded. ⁴⁴I tell you the truth: He will put him in charge of all his possessions. ⁴⁵But if that slave says in his heart, 'My master is delaying his coming,' and starts to beat the male and female slaves, and to eat and drink and get drunk, ⁴⁶that slave's master will come on a day he does not expect him and at an hour he does not know. He will cut him to piecesᴴ and assign him a place with the unbelievers.ᴵ ⁴⁷And that slave who knew his master's will and didn't prepare himself or do itᴶ will be severely beaten. ⁴⁸But the one who did not know and did things deserving of blows will be beaten lightly. Much will be required of everyone who has been given much. And even more will be expected of the one who has been entrusted with more.ᴷ

⁴⁹"I came to bring fire on the earth, and how I wish it were already set ablaze! ⁵⁰But I have a baptism to be baptized with, and how it consumes Me until it is finished! ⁵¹Do you think

ᴬ12:14 Lit Man   ᴮ12:19 Lit say to my soul, "Soul, you   ᶜ12:25 Or add one moment to his life-span   ᴰ12:35 Lit Let your loins be girded; an idiom for tying up loose outer clothing in preparation for action; Ex 12:11   ᴱ12:36 Lit master, when he should return   ᶠ12:37 Lit will gird himself   ᴳ12:38 Lit even in the second or third watch   ᴴ12:46 Lit him in two   ᴵ12:46 Or unfaithful, or untrustworthy   ᴶ12:47 Lit or do toward his will   ᴷ12:48 Or much that I came here to give peace to the earth? No, I tell you, but rather division! [52]From now on, five in one household will be divided: three against two, and two against three.

[53] They will be divided, father against son,
son against father,
mother against daughter,
daughter against mother,
mother-in-law against
her daughter-in-law,
and daughter-in-law
against mother-in-law."[A]

[54]He also said to the crowds: "When you see a cloud rising in the west, right away you say, 'A storm is coming,' and so it does. [55]And when the south wind is blowing, you say, 'It's going to be a scorcher!' and it is. [56]Hypocrites! You know how to interpret the appearance of the earth and the sky, but why don't you know how to interpret this time?

[57]"Why don't you judge for yourselves what is right? [58]As you are going with your adversary to the ruler, make an effort to settle with him on the way. Then he won't drag you before the judge, the judge hand you over to the bailiff, and the bailiff throw you into prison. [59]I tell you, you will never get out of there until you have paid the last cent."[B]

13 At that time, some people came and reported to Him about the Galileans whose blood Pilate had mixed with their sacrifices. [2]And He[C] responded to them, "Do you think that these Galileans were more sinful than all Galileans because they suffered these things? [3]No, I tell you; but unless you repent, you will all perish as well! [4]Or those 18 that the tower in Siloam fell on and killed—do you think they were more sinful than all the people who live in Jerusalem? [5]No, I tell you; but unless you repent, you will all perish as well!"

[6]And He told this parable: "A man had a fig tree that was planted in his vineyard. He came looking for fruit on it and found none. [7]He told the vineyard worker, 'Listen, for three years I have come looking for fruit on this fig tree and haven't found any. Cut it down! Why should it even waste the soil?'

[8]"But he replied to him, 'Sir,[D] leave it this year also, until I dig around it and fertilize it.

[9]Perhaps it will bear fruit next year, but if not, you can cut it down.'"

[10]As He was teaching in one of the synagogues on the Sabbath, [11]a woman was there who had been disabled by a spirit[E] for over 18 years. She was bent over and could not straighten up at all.[F] [12]When Jesus saw her, He called out to her,[G] "Woman, you are free of your disability." [13]Then He laid His hands on her, and instantly she was restored and began to glorify God.

[14]But the leader of the synagogue, indignant because Jesus had healed on the Sabbath, responded by telling the crowd, "There are six days when work should be done; therefore come on those days and be healed and not on the Sabbath day."

[15]But the Lord answered him and said, "Hypocrites! Doesn't each one of you untie his ox or donkey from the feeding trough on the Sabbath and lead it to water? [16]Satan has bound this woman, a daughter of Abraham, for 18 years—shouldn't she be untied from this bondage on the Sabbath day?"

[17]When He had said these things, all His adversaries were humiliated, but the whole crowd was rejoicing over all the glorious things He was doing.

[18]He said, therefore, "What is the kingdom of God like, and what can I compare it to? [19]It's like a mustard seed that a man took and sowed in his garden. It grew and became a tree, and the birds of the sky nested in its branches."

[20]Again He said, "What can I compare the kingdom of God to? [21]It's like yeast that a woman took and mixed into 50 pounds[H] of flour until it spread through the entire mixture."[I]

[22]He went through one town and village after another, teaching and making His way to Jerusalem. [23]"Lord," someone asked Him, "are there few being saved?"[J]

He said to them, [24]"Make every effort to enter through the narrow door, because I tell you, many will try to enter and won't be able [25]once the homeowner gets up and shuts the door. Then you will stand[K] outside and knock on the door, saying, 'Lord, open up for us!' He will answer you, 'I don't know you or where you're from.' [26]Then you will say,[L] 'We ate and drank in Your presence, and You taught

A12:53 Mc 7:6   B12:59 Gk lepton, the smallest and least valuable copper coin in use   C13:2 Other mss read Jesus   D13:8 Or Lord   E13:11 Lit had a spirit of disability   F13:11 Or straighten up completely   G13:12 Or He summoned her   H13:21 Lit 3 sata; about 40 quarts   I13:21 Or until all of it was leavened   J13:23 Or are the saved few? (in number); lit are those being saved few?   K13:25 Lit you will begin to stand   L13:26 Lit you will begin to say in our streets!' ²⁷But He will say, 'I tell you, I don't know you or where you're from. Get away from Me, all you workers of unrighteousness!' ²⁸There will be weeping and gnashing of teeth in that place, when you see Abraham, Isaac, Jacob, and all the prophets in the kingdom of God, but yourselves thrown out. ²⁹They will come from east and west, from north and south, and recline at the table in the kingdom of God. ³⁰Note this: Some are last who will be first, and some are first who will be last."

³¹At that time some Pharisees came and told Him, "Go, get out of here! Herod wants to kill You!"

³²He said to them, "Go tell that fox, 'Look! I'm driving out demons and performing healings today and tomorrow, and on the third day[A] I will complete My work.'[B] ³³Yet I must travel today, tomorrow, and the next day, because it is not possible for a prophet to perish outside of Jerusalem!

³⁴"Jerusalem, Jerusalem! She who kills the prophets and stones those who are sent to her. How often I wanted to gather your children together, as a hen gathers her chicks under her wings, but you were not willing! ³⁵See, your house[C] is abandoned to you. And I tell you, you will not see Me until the time comes when you say, 'He who comes in the name of the Lord is the blessed One'!"[D]

14 One Sabbath, when He went to eat[E] at the house of one of the leading Pharisees, they were watching Him closely. ²There in front of Him was a man whose body was swollen with fluid.[F] ³In response, Jesus asked the law experts and the Pharisees, "Is it lawful to heal on the Sabbath or not?" ⁴But they kept silent. He took the man, healed him, and sent him away. ⁵And to them, He said, "Which of you whose son or ox falls into a well, will not immediately pull him out on the Sabbath day?" ⁶To this they could find no answer.

⁷He told a parable to those who were invited, when He noticed how they would choose the best places for themselves: ⁸"When you are invited by someone to a wedding banquet, don't recline at the best place, because a more distinguished person than you may have been invited by your host.[G] ⁹The one who invited both of you may come and say to you, 'Give

your place to this man,' and then in humiliation, you will proceed to take the lowest place.

¹⁰"But when you are invited, go and recline in the lowest place, so that when the one who invited you comes, he will say to you, 'Friend, move up higher.' You will then be honored in the presence of all the other guests. ¹¹For everyone who exalts himself will be humbled, and the one who humbles himself will be exalted."

¹²He also said to the one who had invited Him, "When you give a lunch or a dinner, don't invite your friends, your brothers, your relatives, or your rich neighbors, because they might invite you back, and you would be repaid. ¹³On the contrary, when you host a banquet, invite those who are poor, maimed, lame, or blind. ¹⁴And you will be blessed, because they cannot repay you; for you will be repaid at the resurrection of the righteous."

¹⁵When one of those who reclined at the table with Him heard these things, he said to Him, "The one who will eat bread in the kingdom of God is blessed!"

¹⁶Then He told him: "A man was giving a large banquet and invited many. ¹⁷At the time of the banquet, he sent his slave to tell those who were invited, 'Come, because everything is now ready.'

¹⁸"But without exception[H] they all began to make excuses. The first one said to him, 'I have bought a field, and I must go out and see it. I ask you to excuse me.'

¹⁹"Another said, 'I have bought five yoke of oxen, and I'm going to try them out. I ask you to excuse me.'

²⁰"And another said, 'I just got married,[I] and therefore I'm unable to come.'

²¹"So the slave came back and reported these things to his master. Then in anger, the master of the house told his slave, 'Go out quickly into the streets and alleys of the city, and bring in here the poor, maimed, blind, and lame!'

²²"'Master,' the slave said, 'what you ordered has been done, and there's still room.'

²³"Then the master told the slave, 'Go out into the highways and lanes and make them come in, so that my house may be filled. ²⁴For I tell you, not one of those men who were invited will enjoy my banquet!'"

A13:32 Very shortly B13:32 Lit *I will be finished* C13:35 Probably the temple; Jr 12:7; 22:5 D13:35 Ps 118:26 E14:1 Lit *eat bread*; = eat a meal F14:2 Afflicted with dropsy or edema G14:8 Lit *by him* H14:18 Lit *And from one* (voice) I14:20 Lit *I have married a woman*

²⁵Now great crowds were traveling with Him. So He turned and said to them: ²⁶"If anyone comes to Me and does not hate his own father and mother, wife and children, brothers and sisters—yes, and even his own life—he cannot be My disciple. ²⁷Whoever does not bear his own cross and come after Me cannot be My disciple.

²⁸"For which of you, wanting to build a tower, doesn't first sit down and calculate the cost to see if he has enough to complete it? ²⁹Otherwise, after he has laid the foundation and cannot finish it, all the onlookers will begin to make fun of him, ³⁰saying, 'This man started to build and wasn't able to finish.'

³¹"Or what king, going to war against another king, will not first sit down and decide if he is able with 10,000 to oppose the one who comes against him with 20,000? ³²If not, while the other is still far off, he sends a delegation and asks for terms of peace. ³³In the same way, therefore, every one of you who does not say good-bye to^A all his possessions cannot be My disciple.

³⁴"Now, salt is good, but if salt should lose its taste, how will it be made salty? ³⁵It isn't fit for the soil or for the manure pile; they throw it out. Anyone who has ears to hear should listen!"

15 All the tax collectors and sinners were approaching to listen to Him. ²And the Pharisees and scribes were complaining, "This man welcomes sinners and eats with them!"

³So He told them this parable: ⁴"What man among you, who has 100 sheep and loses one of them, does not leave the 99 in the open field^B and go after the lost one until he finds it? ⁵When he has found it, he joyfully puts it on his shoulders, ⁶and coming home, he calls his friends and neighbors together, saying to them, 'Rejoice with me, because I have found my lost sheep!' ⁷I tell you, in the same way, there will be more joy in heaven over one sinner who repents than over 99 righteous people who don't need repentance.

⁸"Or what woman who has 10 silver coins,^C if she loses one coin, does not light a lamp, sweep the house, and search carefully until she finds it? ⁹When she finds it, she calls her women friends and neighbors together, saying, 'Rejoice with me, because I have found

the silver coin I lost!' ¹⁰I tell you, in the same way, there is joy in the presence of God's angels over one sinner who repents."

¹¹He also said: "A man had two sons. ¹²The younger of them said to his father, 'Father, give me the share of the estate I have coming to me.' So he distributed the assets^D to them. ¹³Not many days later, the younger son gathered together all he had and traveled to a distant country, where he squandered his estate in foolish living. ¹⁴After he had spent everything, a severe famine struck that country, and he had nothing.^E ¹⁵Then he went to work for^F one of the citizens of that country, who sent him into his fields to feed pigs. ¹⁶He longed to eat his fill from^G the carob pods^H the pigs were eating, but no one would give him any. ¹⁷When he came to his senses,^I he said, 'How many of my father's hired hands have more than enough food, and here I am dying of hunger!^J ¹⁸I'll get up, go to my father, and say to him, Father, I have sinned against heaven and in your sight. ¹⁹I'm no longer worthy to be called your son. Make me like one of your hired hands.' ²⁰So he got up and went to his father. But while the son was still a long way off, his father saw him and was filled with compassion. He ran, threw his arms around his neck,^K and kissed him. ²¹The son said to him, 'Father, I have sinned against heaven and in your sight. I'm no longer worthy to be called your son.'

²²"But the father told his slaves, 'Quick! Bring out the best robe and put it on him; put a ring on his finger^L and sandals on his feet. ²³Then bring the fattened calf and slaughter it, and let's celebrate with a feast, ²⁴because this son of mine was dead and is alive again; he was lost and is found!' So they began to celebrate.

²⁵"Now his older son was in the field; as he came near the house, he heard music and dancing. ²⁶So he summoned one of the servants and asked what these things meant. ²⁷'Your brother is here,' he told him, 'and your father has slaughtered the fattened calf because he has him back safe and sound.'^M

²⁸"Then he became angry and didn't want to go in. So his father came out and pleaded with him. ²⁹But he replied to his father, 'Look, I have been slaving many years for you, and

^A14:33 Or does not renounce or leave   ^B15:4 Or the wilderness   ^C15:8 Gk 10 drachmas; a drachma was a silver coin = a denarius   ^D15:12 Or living; lit livelihood   ^E15:14 Lit and he began to be in need   ^F15:15 Lit went and joined with   ^G15:16 Other mss read to fill his stomach with ^H15:16 Seed casings of a tree used as food for cattle, pigs, and sometimes the poor   ^I15:17 Lit to himself   ^J15:17 Or dying in the famine; v. 14 ^K15:20 Lit He ran, fell on his neck   ^L15:22 Lit hand   ^M15:27 Lit him back healthy

I have never disobeyed your orders, yet you never gave me a young goat so I could celebrate with my friends. ³⁰But when this son of yours came, who has devoured your assets^A with prostitutes, you slaughtered the fattened calf for him.'

³¹"'Son,'^B he said to him, 'you are always with me, and everything I have is yours. ³²But we had to celebrate and rejoice, because this brother of yours was dead and is alive again; he was lost and is found.'"

16 He also said to the disciples: "There was a rich man who received an accusation that his manager was squandering his possessions. ²So he called the manager in and asked, 'What is this I hear about you? Give an account of your management, because you can no longer be my manager.'

³"Then the manager said to himself, 'What should I do, since my master is taking the management away from me? I'm not strong enough to dig; I'm ashamed to beg. ⁴I know what I'll do so that when I'm removed from management, people will welcome me into their homes.'

⁵"So he summoned each one of his master's debtors. 'How much do you owe my master?' he asked the first one.

⁶"'A hundred measures of olive oil,' he said.

"'Take your invoice,' he told him, 'sit down quickly, and write 50.'

⁷"Next he asked another, 'How much do you owe?'

"'A hundred measures of wheat,' he said.

"'Take your invoice,' he told him, 'and write 80.'

⁸"The master praised the unrighteous manager because he had acted astutely. For the sons of this age are more astute than the sons of light in dealing with their own people.^C ⁹And I tell you, make friends for yourselves by means of the unrighteous money so that when it fails,^D they may welcome you into eternal dwellings. ¹⁰Whoever is faithful in very little is also faithful in much, and whoever is unrighteous in very little is also unrighteous in much. ¹¹So if you have not been faithful with the unrighteous money, who will trust you with what is genuine? ¹²And if you have not been faithful with what belongs to someone else, who will give you what is your own? ¹³No household

slave can be the slave of two masters, since either he will hate one and love the other, or he will be devoted to one and despise the other. You can't be slaves to both God and money."

¹⁴The Pharisees, who were lovers of money, were listening to all these things and scoffing at Him. ¹⁵And He told them: "You are the ones who justify yourselves in the sight of others, but God knows your hearts. For what is highly admired by people is revolting in God's sight.

¹⁶"The Law and the Prophets were^E until John; since then, the good news of the kingdom of God has been proclaimed, and everyone is strongly urged to enter it.^F ¹⁷But it is easier for heaven and earth to pass away than for one stroke of a letter in the law to drop out.

¹⁸"Everyone who divorces his wife and marries another woman commits adultery, and everyone who marries a woman divorced from her husband commits adultery.

¹⁹"There was a rich man who would dress in purple and fine linen, feasting lavishly every day. ²⁰But a poor man named Lazarus, covered with sores, was left at his gate. ²¹He longed to be filled with what fell from the rich man's table, but instead the dogs would come and lick his sores. ²²One day the poor man died and was carried away by the angels to Abraham's side.^G The rich man also died and was buried. ²³And being in torment in Hades, he looked up and saw Abraham a long way off, with Lazarus at his side. ²⁴'Father Abraham!' he called out, 'Have mercy on me and send Lazarus to dip the tip of his finger in water and cool my tongue, because I am in agony in this flame!'

²⁵"'Son,'^H Abraham said, 'remember that during your life you received your good things, just as Lazarus received bad things, but now he is comforted here, while you are in agony. ²⁶Besides all this, a great chasm has been fixed between us and you, so that those who want to pass over from here to you cannot; neither can those from there cross over to us.'

²⁷"'Father,' he said, 'then I beg you to send him to my father's house— ²⁸because I have five brothers—to warn them, so they won't also come to this place of torment.'

²⁹"But Abraham said, 'They have Moses and the prophets; they should listen to them.'

---

^A15:30 Lit *livelihood*, or *living*   ^B15:31 Or *Child*   ^C16:8 Lit *own generation*   ^D16:9 Other mss read *when you fail* or *pass away*   ^E16:16 Perhaps *were proclaimed*, or *were in effect*   ^F16:16 Or *everyone is forcing his way into it*   ^G16:22 Or *to Abraham's bosom*; lit *to the fold of Abraham's robe*; Jn 13:23   ^H16:25 Lit *Child*

³⁰"'No, father Abraham,' he said. 'But if someone from the dead goes to them, they will repent.'

³¹"But he told him, 'If they don't listen to Moses and the prophets, they will not be persuaded if someone rises from the dead.'"

17 He said to His disciples, "Offenses^A will certainly come,^B but woe to the one they come through! ²It would be better for him if a millstone^C were hung around his neck and he were thrown into the sea than for him to cause one of these little ones to stumble. ³Be on your guard. If your brother sins,^D rebuke him, and if he repents, forgive him. ⁴And if he sins against you seven times in a day, and comes back to you seven times, saying, 'I repent,' you must forgive him."

⁵The apostles said to the Lord, "Increase our faith."

⁶"If you have faith the size of^E a mustard seed," the Lord said, "you can say to this mulberry tree, 'Be uprooted and planted in the sea,' and it will obey you.

⁷"Which one of you having a slave tending sheep or plowing will say to him when he comes in from the field, 'Come at once and sit down to eat'? ⁸Instead, will he not tell him, 'Prepare something for me to eat, get ready,^F and serve me while I eat and drink; later you can eat and drink'? ⁹Does he thank that slave because he did what was commanded?^G ¹⁰In the same way, when you have done all that you were commanded, you should say, 'We are good-for-nothing slaves; we've only done our duty.'"

¹¹While traveling to Jerusalem, He passed between^H Samaria and Galilee. ¹²As He entered a village, 10 men with serious skin diseases met Him. They stood at a distance ¹³and raised their voices, saying, "Jesus, Master, have mercy on us!"

¹⁴When He saw them, He told them, "Go and show yourselves to the priests." And while they were going, they were healed.^I

¹⁵But one of them, seeing that he was healed, returned and, with a loud voice, gave glory to God. ¹⁶He fell facedown at His feet, thanking Him. And he was a Samaritan.

¹⁷Then Jesus said, "Were not 10 cleansed? Where are the nine? ¹⁸Didn't any return^J to give glory to God except this foreigner?" ¹⁹And He told him, "Get up and go on your way. Your faith has made you well."^K

²⁰Being asked by the Pharisees when the kingdom of God will come, He answered them, "The kingdom of God is not coming with something observable; ²¹no one will say,^L 'Look here!' or 'There!' For you see, the kingdom of God is among you."

²²Then He told the disciples: "The days are coming when you will long to see one of the days of the Son of Man, but you won't see it. ²³They will say to you, 'Look there!' or 'Look here!' Don't follow or run after them. ²⁴For as the lightning flashes from horizon to horizon and lights up the sky, so the Son of Man will be in His day. ²⁵But first He must suffer many things and be rejected by this generation.

²⁶"Just as it was in the days of Noah, so it will be in the days of the Son of Man: ²⁷People went on eating, drinking, marrying and giving in marriage until the day Noah boarded the ark, and the flood came and destroyed them all. ²⁸It will be the same as it was in the days of Lot: People went on eating, drinking, buying, selling, planting, building. ²⁹But on the day Lot left Sodom, fire and sulfur rained from heaven and destroyed them all. ³⁰It will be like that on the day the Son of Man is revealed. ³¹On that day, a man on the housetop, whose belongings are in the house, must not come down to get them. Likewise the man who is in the field must not turn back. ³²Remember Lot's wife! ³³Whoever tries to make his life secure^M,N will lose it, and whoever loses his life will preserve it. ³⁴I tell you, on that night two will be in one bed: One will be taken and the other will be left. ³⁵Two women will be grinding grain together: One will be taken and the other left. [³⁶Two will be in a field: One will be taken, and the other will be left.]^O

³⁷"Where, Lord?" they asked Him.

He said to them, "Where the corpse is, there also the vultures will be gathered."

18 He then told them a parable on the need for them to pray always and not become discouraged: ²"There was a judge in a certain town who didn't fear God or respect man. ³And a widow in that town kept coming to him, saying, 'Give me justice against my adversary.'

^A17:1 Or Traps, or Bait-sticks, or Causes of stumbling, or Causes of sin   ^B17:1 Lit It is impossible for offenses not to come   ^C17:2 Large stone used for grinding grains into flour   ^D17:3 Other mss add against you   ^E17:6 Lit faith like   ^F17:8 Or eat, gird yourself; lit eat, tuck in your robe   ^G17:9 Other mss add I don't think so   ^H17:11 Or through the middle of   ^I17:14 Lit cleansed   ^J17:18 Lit Were they not found returning   ^K17:19 Or faith has saved you   ^L17:21 Lit they will not say   ^M17:33 Other mss read to save his life   ^N17:33 Or tries to retain his life   ^O17:36 Other mss omit bracketed text

⁴"For a while he was unwilling, but later he said to himself, 'Even though I don't fear God or respect man, ⁵yet because this widow keeps pestering me,^A I will give her justice, so she doesn't wear me out^B by her persistent coming.'"

⁶Then the Lord said, "Listen to what the unjust judge says. ⁷Will not God grant justice to His elect who cry out to Him day and night? Will He delay to help them?^C ⁸I tell you that He will swiftly grant them justice. Nevertheless, when the Son of Man comes, will He find that faith^D on earth?"

⁹He also told this parable to some who trusted in themselves that they were righteous and looked down on everyone else: ¹⁰"Two men went up to the temple complex to pray, one a Pharisee and the other a tax collector. ¹¹The Pharisee took his stand^E and was praying like this: 'God, I thank You that I'm not like other people^F—greedy, unrighteous, adulterers, or even like this tax collector. ¹²I fast twice a week; I give a tenth^G of everything I get.'

¹³"But the tax collector, standing far off, would not even raise his eyes to heaven but kept striking his chest^H and saying, 'God, turn Your wrath from me^I—a sinner!' ¹⁴I tell you, this one went down to his house justified rather than the other; because everyone who exalts himself will be humbled, but the one who humbles himself will be exalted."

¹⁵Some people were even bringing infants to Him so He might touch them, but when the disciples saw it, they rebuked them. ¹⁶Jesus, however, invited them: "Let the little children come to Me, and don't stop them, because the kingdom of God belongs to such as these. ¹⁷I assure you: Whoever does not welcome the kingdom of God like a little child will never enter it."

¹⁸A ruler asked Him, "Good Teacher, what must I do to inherit eternal life?"

¹⁹"Why do you call Me good?" Jesus asked him. "No one is good but One—God. ²⁰You know the commandments:

> Do not commit adultery;
> do not murder;
> do not steal;
> do not bear false witness;
> honor your father and mother."^J

²¹"I have kept all these from my youth," he said.

²²When Jesus heard this, He told him, "You still lack one thing: Sell all that you have and distribute it to the poor, and you will have treasure in heaven. Then come, follow Me."

²³After he heard this, he became extremely sad, because he was very rich.

²⁴Seeing that he became sad,^K Jesus said, "How hard it is for those who have wealth to enter the kingdom of God! ²⁵For it is easier for a camel to go through the eye of a needle than for a rich person to enter the kingdom of God."

²⁶Those who heard this asked, "Then who can be saved?"

²⁷He replied, "What is impossible with men is possible with God."

²⁸Then Peter said, "Look, we have left what we had and followed You."

²⁹So He said to them, "I assure you: There is no one who has left a house, wife or brothers, parents or children because of the kingdom of God, ³⁰who will not receive many times more at this time, and eternal life in the age to come."

³¹Then He took the Twelve aside and told them, "Listen! We are going up to Jerusalem. Everything that is written through the prophets about the Son of Man will be accomplished. ³²For He will be handed over to the Gentiles, and He will be mocked, insulted, spit on; ³³and after they flog Him, they will kill Him, and He will rise on the third day."

³⁴They understood none of these things. This saying^L was hidden from them, and they did not grasp what was said.

³⁵As He drew near Jericho, a blind man was sitting by the road begging. ³⁶Hearing a crowd passing by, he inquired what this meant. ³⁷"Jesus the Nazarene is passing by," they told him.

³⁸So he called out, "Jesus, Son of David, have mercy on me!" ³⁹Then those in front told him to keep quiet,^M but he kept crying out all the more, "Son of David, have mercy on me!"

⁴⁰Jesus stopped and commanded that he be brought to Him. When he drew near, He asked him, ⁴¹"What do you want Me to do for you?"

"Lord," he said, "I want to see!"

⁴²"Receive your sight!" Jesus told him. "Your faith has healed you."^N ⁴³Instantly he could

---

^A**18:5** Lit *widow causes me trouble*   ^B**18:5** Or *doesn't give me a black eye,* or *doesn't ruin my reputation*   ^C**18:7** Or *Will He put up with them?*   ^D**18:8** Or *faith,* or *that kind of faith,* or *any faith,* or *the faith,* or *faithfulness;* the faith that persists in prayer for God's vindication   ^E**18:11** Or *Pharisee stood by himself*   ^F**18:11** Or *like the rest of men*   ^G**18:12** Or *give tithes*   ^H**18:13** = *mourning*   ^I**18:13** Lit *God, be propitious to me;* = *May Your wrath be turned aside by the sacrifice*   ^J**18:20** Ex 20:12-16; Dt 5:16-20   ^K**18:24** Other mss omit *he became sad*   ^L**18:34** The meaning of the saying   ^M**18:39** Or *those in front rebuked him*   ^N**18:42** Or *has saved you* see, and he began to follow Him, glorifying God. All the people, when they saw it, gave praise to God.

19 He entered Jericho and was passing through. ²There was a man named Zacchaeus who was a chief tax collector, and he was rich. ³He was trying to see who Jesus was, but he was not able because of the crowd, since he was a short man. ⁴So running ahead, he climbed up a sycamore tree to see Jesus, since He was about to pass that way. ⁵When Jesus came to the place, He looked up and said to him, "Zacchaeus, hurry and come down because today I must stay at your house."

⁶So he quickly came down and welcomed Him joyfully. ⁷All who saw it began to complain, "He's gone to lodge with a sinful man!"

⁸But Zacchaeus stood there and said to the Lord, "Look, I'll give^A half of my possessions to the poor, Lord! And if I have extorted anything from anyone, I'll pay^B back four times as much!"

⁹"Today salvation has come to this house," Jesus told him, "because he too is a son of Abraham. ¹⁰For the Son of Man has come to seek and to save the lost."^C

¹¹As they were listening to this, He went on to tell a parable because He was near Jerusalem, and they thought the kingdom of God was going to appear right away. ¹²Therefore He said: "A nobleman traveled to a far country to receive for himself authority to be king^D and then return. ¹³He called 10 of his slaves, gave them 10 minas,^E and told them, 'Engage in business until I come back.'

¹⁴"But his subjects hated him and sent a delegation after him, saying, 'We don't want this man to rule over us!'

¹⁵"At his return, having received the authority to be king,^F he summoned those slaves he had given the money to, so he could find out how much they had made in business. ¹⁶The first came forward and said, 'Master, your mina has earned 10 more minas.'

¹⁷"'Well done, good^G slave!' he told him. 'Because you have been faithful in a very small matter, have authority over 10 towns.'

¹⁸"The second came and said, 'Master, your mina has made five minas.'

¹⁹"So he said to him, 'You will be over five towns.'

²⁰"And another came and said, 'Master, here is your mina. I have kept it hidden away in a cloth ²¹because I was afraid of you, for you're a tough man: you collect what you didn't deposit and reap what you didn't sow.'

²²"He told him, 'I will judge you by what you have said,^H you evil slave! If you knew I was a tough man, collecting what I didn't deposit and reaping what I didn't sow, ²³why didn't you put my money in the bank? And when I returned, I would have collected it with interest!' ²⁴So he said to those standing there, 'Take the mina away from him and give it to the one who has 10 minas.'

²⁵"But they said to him, 'Master, he has 10 minas.'

²⁶"'I tell you, that to everyone who has, more will be given; and from the one who does not have, even what he does have will be taken away. ²⁷But bring here these enemies of mine, who did not want me to rule over them, and slaughter^I them in my presence.'"

²⁸When He had said these things, He went on ahead, going up to Jerusalem. ²⁹As He approached Bethphage and Bethany, at the place called the Mount of Olives, He sent two of the disciples ³⁰and said, "Go into the village ahead of you. As you enter it, you will find a young donkey tied there, on which no one has ever sat. Untie it and bring it here. ³¹If anyone asks you, 'Why are you untying it?' say this: 'The Lord needs it.'"

³²So those who were sent left and found it just as He had told them. ³³As they were untying the young donkey, its owners said to them, "Why are you untying the donkey?"

³⁴"The Lord needs it," they said. ³⁵Then they brought it to Jesus, and after throwing their robes on the donkey, they helped Jesus get on it. ³⁶As He was going along, they were spreading their robes on the road. ³⁷Now He came near the path down the Mount of Olives, and the whole crowd of the disciples began to praise God joyfully with a loud voice for all the miracles they had seen:

³⁸   **The King who comes
    in the name of the Lord**^J,K
    is the blessed One.
    Peace in heaven
    and glory in the highest heaven!

^A19:8 Or I give   ^B19:8 Or I pay   ^C19:10 Or save what was lost   ^D19:12 Lit to receive for himself a kingdom or sovereignty   ^E19:13 = Gk coin worth 100 drachmas or about 100 days' wages   ^F19:15 Lit to receive for himself a kingdom or sovereignty   ^G19:17 Or capable   ^H19:22 Lit you out of your mouth   ^I19:27 Or execute   ^J19:38 Luke substitutes "the King" for "He" in Ps 118:26.   ^K19:38 Ps 118:26

[39] Some of the Pharisees from the crowd told Him, "Teacher, rebuke Your disciples."

[40] He answered, "I tell you, if they were to keep silent, the stones would cry out!"

[41] As He approached and saw the city, He wept over it, [42] saying, "If you knew this day what would bring peace—but now it is hidden from your eyes. [43] For the days will come on you when your enemies will build an embankment against you, surround you, and hem you in on every side. [44] They will crush you and your children within you to the ground, and they will not leave one stone on another in you, because you did not recognize the time of your visitation."

[45] He went into the temple complex and began to throw out those who were selling,[A] [46] and He said, "It is written, My house will be a house of prayer, but you have made it a den of thieves!"[B]

[47] Every day He was teaching in the temple complex. The chief priests, the scribes, and the leaders of the people were looking for a way to destroy Him, [48] but they could not find a way to do it, because all the people were captivated by what they heard.[C]

20 One day[D] as He was teaching the people in the temple complex and proclaiming the good news, the chief priests and the scribes, with the elders, came up [2] and said to Him: "Tell us, by what authority are You doing these things? Who is it who gave You this authority?"

[3] He answered them, "I will also ask you a question. Tell Me, [4] was the baptism of John from heaven or from men?"

[5] They discussed it among themselves: "If we say, 'From heaven,' He will say, 'Why didn't you believe him?' [6] But if we say, 'From men,' all the people will stone us, because they are convinced that John was a prophet."

[7] So they answered that they did not know its origin.[E]

[8] And Jesus said to them, "Neither will I tell you by what authority I do these things."

[9] Then He began to tell the people this parable: "A man planted a vineyard, leased it to tenant farmers, and went away for a long time. [10] At harvest time he sent a slave to the farmers so that they might give him some fruit from the vineyard. But the farmers beat him and sent him away empty-handed. [11] He sent yet another slave, but they beat that one too, treated him shamefully, and sent him away empty-handed. [12] And he sent yet a third, but they wounded this one too and threw him out.

[13] "Then the owner of the vineyard said, 'What should I do? I will send my beloved son. Perhaps[F] they will respect him.'

[14] "But when the tenant farmers saw him, they discussed it among themselves and said, 'This is the heir. Let's kill him, so the inheritance will be ours!' [15] So they threw him out of the vineyard and killed him.

"Therefore, what will the owner of the vineyard do to them? [16] He will come and destroy those farmers and give the vineyard to others."

But when they heard this they said, "No—never!"

[17] But He looked at them and said, "Then what is the meaning of this Scripture:[G]

> The stone that the builders rejected—
> this has become the cornerstone?[H,I]

[18] Everyone who falls on that stone will be broken to pieces, and if it falls on anyone, it will grind him to powder!"

[19] Then the scribes and the chief priests looked for a way to get their hands on Him that very hour, because they knew He had told this parable against them, but they feared the people.

[20] They[J] watched closely and sent spies who pretended to be righteous,[K] so they could catch Him in what He said,[L] to hand Him over to the governor's rule and authority. [21] They questioned Him, "Teacher, we know that You speak and teach correctly, and You don't show partiality,[M] but teach truthfully the way of God. [22] Is it lawful for us to pay taxes to Caesar or not?"

[23] But detecting their craftiness, He said to them,[N] [24] "Show Me a denarius. Whose image and inscription does it have?"

"Caesar's," they said.

[25] "Well then," He told them, "give back to Caesar the things that are Caesar's and to God the things that are God's."

A19:45 Other mss add and buying in it   B19:46 Is 56:7; Jr 7:11   C19:48 Lit people hung on what they heard   D20:1 Lit It happened on one of the days   E20:7 Or know where it was from   F20:13 Other mss add when they see him   G20:17 Lit When then is this that is written   H20:17 Lit the head of the corner   I20:17 Ps 118:22   J20:20 The scribes and chief priests of v. 19   K20:20 Or upright; that is, loyal to God's law   L20:20 Lit catch Him in a word   M20:21 Lit You don't receive a face   N20:23 Other mss add "Why are you testing Me?

²⁶They were not able to catch Him in what He said^A in public,^B and being amazed at His answer, they became silent.

²⁷Some of the Sadducees, who say there is no resurrection, came up and questioned Him: ²⁸"Teacher, Moses wrote for us that **if a man's brother** has a wife, and **dies childless, his brother should take the wife and produce offspring for his brother.**^C ²⁹Now there were seven brothers. The first took a wife and died without children. ³⁰Also the second^D ³¹and the third took her. In the same way, all seven died and left no children. ³²Finally, the woman died too. ³³In the resurrection, therefore, whose wife will the woman be? For all seven had married her."^E

³⁴Jesus told them, "The sons of this age marry and are given in marriage. ³⁵But those who are counted worthy to take part in that age and in the resurrection from the dead neither marry nor are given in marriage. ³⁶For they cannot die anymore, because they are like angels and are sons of God, since they are sons of the resurrection. ³⁷Moses even indicated in the passage about the burning bush that the dead are raised, where he calls the Lord the God of Abraham and the God of Isaac and the God of Jacob.^F ³⁸He is not God of the dead but of the living, because all are living to^G Him."

³⁹Some of the scribes answered, "Teacher, You have spoken well." ⁴⁰And they no longer dared to ask Him anything.

⁴¹Then He said to them, "How can they say that the Messiah is the Son of David? ⁴²For David himself says in the Book of Psalms:

The Lord declared to my Lord,
'Sit at My right hand
⁴³   until I make Your enemies
Your footstool.'^H

⁴⁴David calls Him 'Lord'; how then can the Messiah be his Son?"

⁴⁵While all the people were listening, He said to His disciples, ⁴⁶"Beware of the scribes, who want to go around in long robes and who love greetings in the marketplaces, the front seats in the synagogues, and the places of honor at banquets. ⁴⁷They devour widows'

houses and say long prayers just for show. These will receive greater punishment."^I

21 He looked up and saw the rich dropping their offerings into the temple treasury. ²He also saw a poor widow dropping in two tiny coins.^J ³"I tell you the truth," He said. "This poor widow has put in more than all of them. ⁴For all these people have put in gifts out of their surplus, but she out of her poverty has put in all she had to live on."

⁵As some were talking about the temple complex, how it was adorned with beautiful stones and gifts dedicated to God,^K He said, ⁶"These things that you see—the days will come when not one stone will be left on another that will not be thrown down!"

⁷"Teacher," they asked Him, "so when will these things be? And what will be the sign when these things are about to take place?"

⁸Then He said, "Watch out that you are not deceived. For many will come in My name, saying, 'I am He,' and, 'The time is near.' Don't follow them. ⁹When you hear of wars and rebellions,^L don't be alarmed. Indeed, these things must take place first, but the end won't come right away."

¹⁰Then He told them: "Nation will be raised up against nation, and kingdom against kingdom. ¹¹There will be violent earthquakes, and famines and plagues in various places, and there will be terrifying sights and great signs from heaven. ¹²But before all these things, they will lay their hands on you and persecute you. They will hand you over to the synagogues and prisons, and you will be brought before kings and governors because of My name. ¹³It will lead to an opportunity for you to witness.^M ¹⁴Therefore make up your minds^N not to prepare your defense ahead of time, ¹⁵for I will give you such words^O and a wisdom that none of your adversaries will be able to resist or contradict. ¹⁶You will even be betrayed by parents, brothers, relatives, and friends. They will kill some of you. ¹⁷You will be hated by everyone because of My name, ¹⁸but not a hair of your head will be lost. ¹⁹By your endurance gain^P your lives.

²⁰"When you see Jerusalem surrounded by armies, then recognize that its desolation has come near. ²¹Then those in Judea must flee

^A20:26 Lit catch Him in a word   ^B20:26 Lit in front of the people   ^C20:28 Dt 25:5   ^D20:30 Other mss add took her as wife, and he died without children   ^E20:33 Lit had her as wife   ^F20:37 Ex 3:6,15   ^G20:38 Or with   ^H20:42-43 Ps 110:1   ^I20:47 Or judgment   ^J21:2 Lit two lepta; the lepton was the smallest and least valuable Gk coin in use.   ^K21:5 Gifts given to the temple in fulfillment of vows to God   ^L21:9 Or insurrections, or revolutions   ^M21:13 Lit lead to a testimony for you   ^N21:14 Lit Therefore place (determine) in your hearts   ^O21:15 Lit you a mouth   ^P21:19 Other mss read endurance you will gain to the mountains! Those inside the city[A] must leave it, and those who are in the country must not enter it, [22]because these are days of vengeance to fulfill all the things that are written. [23]Woe to pregnant women and nursing mothers in those days, for there will be great distress in the land[B] and wrath against this people. [24]They will fall by the edge of the sword and be led captive into all the nations, and Jerusalem will be trampled by the Gentiles[C] until the times of the Gentiles are fulfilled.

[25]"Then there will be signs in the sun, moon, and stars; and there will be anguish on the earth among nations bewildered by the roaring sea and waves. [26]People will faint from fear and expectation of the things that are coming on the world, because the celestial powers will be shaken. [27]Then they will see the Son of Man coming in a cloud with power and great glory. [28]But when these things begin to take place, stand up and lift up your heads, because your redemption is near!"

[29]Then He told them a parable: "Look at the fig tree, and all the trees. [30]As soon as they put out leaves you can see for yourselves and recognize that summer is already near. [31]In the same way, when you see these things happening, recognize[D] that the kingdom of God is near. [32]I assure you: This generation will certainly not pass away until all things take place. [33]Heaven and earth will pass away, but My words will never pass away.

[34]"Be on your guard, so that your minds are not dulled[E] from carousing,[F] drunkenness, and worries of life, or that day will come on you unexpectedly [35]like a trap. For it will come on all who live on the face of the whole earth. [36]But be alert at all times, praying that you may have strength[G] to escape all these things that are going to take place and to stand before the Son of Man."

[37]During the day, He was teaching in the temple complex, but in the evening He would go out and spend the night on what is called the Mount of Olives. [38]Then all the people would come early in the morning to hear Him in the temple complex.

22 The Festival of Unleavened Bread, which is called Passover, was drawing near. [2]The chief priests and the scribes were looking for a way to put Him to death, because they were afraid of the people.

[3]Then Satan entered Judas, called Iscariot, who was numbered among the Twelve. [4]He went away and discussed with the chief priests and temple police how he could hand Him over to them. [5]They were glad and agreed to give him silver.[H] [6]So he accepted the offer and started looking for a good opportunity to betray Him to them when the crowd was not present.

[7]Then the Day of Unleavened Bread came when the Passover lamb had to be sacrificed. [8]Jesus sent Peter and John, saying, "Go and prepare the Passover meal for us, so we can eat it."

[9]"Where do You want us to prepare it?" they asked Him.

[10]"Listen," He said to them, "when you've entered the city, a man carrying a water jug will meet you. Follow him into the house he enters. [11]Tell the owner of the house, 'The Teacher asks you, "Where is the guest room where I can eat the Passover with My disciples?"' [12]Then he will show you a large, furnished room upstairs. Make the preparations there."

[13]So they went and found it just as He had told them, and they prepared the Passover.

[14]When the hour came, He reclined at the table, and the apostles with Him. [15]Then He said to them, "I have fervently desired to eat this Passover with you before I suffer. [16]For I tell you, I will not eat it again[I] until it is fulfilled in the kingdom of God." [17]Then He took a cup, and after giving thanks, He said, "Take this and share it among yourselves. [18]For I tell you, from now on I will not drink of the fruit of the vine until the kingdom of God comes."

[19]And He took bread, gave thanks, broke it, gave it to them, and said, "This is My body, which is given for you. Do this in remembrance of Me."

[20]In the same way He also took the cup after supper and said, "This cup is the new covenant established by My blood; it is shed for you.[J] [21]But look, the hand of the one betraying Me is at the table with Me! [22]For the Son of Man will go away as it has been determined, but woe to that man by whom He is betrayed!"

[A]21:21 Lit inside her   [B]21:23 Or the earth   [C]21:24 Or nations   [D]21:31 Or you know   [E]21:34 Lit your hearts are not weighed down   [F]21:34 Or hangovers   [G]21:36 Other mss read you may be counted worthy   [H]22:5 Or money; Mt 26:15 specifies 30 pieces of silver; Zch 11:12-13   [I]22:16 Other mss omit again   [J]22:19-20 Other mss omit which is given for you [v. 19] through the end of v. 20

²³So they began to argue among themselves which of them it could be who was going to do this thing.

²⁴Then a dispute also arose among them about who should be considered the greatest. ²⁵But He said to them, "The kings of the Gentiles dominate them, and those who have authority over them are calledᴬ 'Benefactors.'ᴮ ²⁶But it must not be like that among you. On the contrary, whoever is greatest among you must become like the youngest, and whoever leads, like the one serving. ²⁷For who is greater, the one at the table or the one serving? Isn't it the one at the table? But I am among you as the One who serves. ²⁸You are the ones who stood by Me in My trials. ²⁹I bestow on you a kingdom, just as My Father bestowed one on Me, ³⁰so that you may eat and drink at My table in My kingdom. And you will sit on thrones judging the 12 tribes of Israel.

³¹"Simon, Simon,ᶜ look out! Satan has asked to sift youᴰ like wheat. ³²But I have prayed for youᴱ that your faith may not fail. And you, when you have turned back, strengthen your brothers."

³³"Lord," he told Him, "I'm ready to go with You both to prison and to death!"

³⁴"I tell you, Peter," He said, "the rooster will not crow today untilᶠ you deny three times that you know Me!"

³⁵He also said to them, "When I sent you out without money-bag, traveling bag, or sandals, did you lack anything?"

"Not a thing," they said.

³⁶Then He said to them, "But now, whoever has a money-bag should take it, and also a traveling bag. And whoever doesn't have a sword should sell his robe and buy one. ³⁷For I tell you, what is written must be fulfilled in Me: And He was counted among the outlaws.ᴳ Yes, what is written about Me is coming to its fulfillment."

³⁸"Lord," they said, "look, here are two swords."

"Enough of that!"ᴴ He told them.

³⁹He went out and made His way as usual to the Mount of Olives, and the disciples followed Him. ⁴⁰When He reached the place, He told them, "Pray that you may not enter into temptation." ⁴¹Then He withdrew from them about a stone's throw, knelt down, and began to pray, ⁴²"Father, if You are willing, take this cup away from Me—nevertheless, not My will, but Yours, be done."

[⁴³Then an angel from heaven appeared to Him, strengthening Him. ⁴⁴Being in anguish, He prayed more fervently, and His sweat became like drops of blood falling to the ground.]ᴵ ⁴⁵When He got up from prayer and came to the disciples, He found them sleeping, exhausted from their grief.ᴶ ⁴⁶"Why are you sleeping?" He asked them. "Get up and pray, so that you won't enter into temptation."

⁴⁷While He was still speaking, suddenly a mob was there, and one of the Twelve named Judas was leading them. He came near Jesus to kiss Him, ⁴⁸but Jesus said to him, "Judas, are you betraying the Son of Man with a kiss?"

⁴⁹When those around Him saw what was going to happen, they asked, "Lord, should we strike with the sword?" ⁵⁰Then one of them struck the high priest's slave and cut off his right ear.

⁵¹But Jesus responded, "No more of this!"ᴷ And touching his ear, He healed him. ⁵²Then Jesus said to the chief priests, temple police, and the elders who had come for Him, "Have you come out with swords and clubs as if I were a criminal?ᴸ ⁵³Every day while I was with you in the temple complex, you never laid a hand on Me. But this is your hour—and the dominion of darkness."

⁵⁴They seized Him, led Him away, and brought Him into the high priest's house. Meanwhile Peter was following at a distance. ⁵⁵They lit a fire in the middle of the courtyard and sat down together, and Peter sat among them. ⁵⁶When a servant saw him sitting in the firelight, and looked closely at him, she said, "This man was with Him too."

⁵⁷But he denied it: "Woman, I don't know Him!"

⁵⁸After a little while, someone else saw him and said, "You're one of them too!"

"Man, I am not!" Peter said.

⁵⁹About an hour later, another kept insisting, "This man was certainly with Him, since he's also a Galilean."

⁶⁰But Peter said, "Man, I don't know what you're talking about!" Immediately, while he

---

ᴬ22:25 Or them call themselves   ᴮ22:25 Title of honor given to those who benefited the public good   ᶜ22:31 Other mss read Then the Lord said, "Simon, Simon   ᴰ22:31 In Gk, the word you is pl   ᴱ22:32 In Gk, the word you is sg   ᶠ22:34 Other mss read before   ᴳ22:37 Is 53:12   ᴴ22:38 Or It is enough!   ᴵ22:43-44 Other mss omit bracketed text   ᴶ22:45 Lit sleeping from grief   ᴷ22:51 Lit Permit as far as this   ᴸ22:52 Lit as against a criminal was still speaking, a rooster crowed. ⁶¹Then the Lord turned and looked at Peter. So Peter remembered the word of the Lord, how He had said to him, "Before the rooster crows today, you will deny Me three times." ⁶²And he went outside and wept bitterly.

⁶³The men who were holding Jesus started mocking and beating Him. ⁶⁴After blindfolding Him, they kept^A asking, "Prophesy! Who hit You?" ⁶⁵And they were saying many other blasphemous things against Him.

⁶⁶When daylight came, the elders^B of the people, both the chief priests and the scribes, convened and brought Him before their Sanhedrin. ⁶⁷They said, "If You are the Messiah, tell us."

But He said to them, "If I do tell you, you will not believe. ⁶⁸And if I ask you, you will not answer. ⁶⁹But from now on, the Son of Man will be seated at the right hand of the Power of God."

⁷⁰They all asked, "Are You, then, the Son of God?"

And He said to them, "You say that I am."

⁷¹"Why do we need any more testimony," they said, "since we've heard it ourselves from His mouth?"

23 Then their whole assembly rose up and brought Him before Pilate. ²They began to accuse Him, saying, "We found this man subverting our nation, opposing payment of taxes to Caesar, and saying that He Himself is the Messiah, a King."

³So Pilate asked Him, "Are You the King of the Jews?"

He answered him, "You have said it."^C

⁴Pilate then told the chief priests and the crowds, "I find no grounds for charging this man."

⁵But they kept insisting, "He stirs up the people, teaching throughout all Judea, from Galilee where He started even to here."

⁶When Pilate heard this,^D he asked if the man was a Galilean. ⁷Finding that He was under Herod's jurisdiction, he sent Him to Herod, who was also in Jerusalem during those days. ⁸Herod was very glad to see Jesus; for a long time he had wanted to see Him because he had heard about Him and was hoping to see some miracle^E performed by Him. ⁹So he kept ask-

ing Him questions, but Jesus did not answer him. ¹⁰The chief priests and the scribes stood by, vehemently accusing Him. ¹¹Then Herod, with his soldiers, treated Him with contempt, mocked Him, dressed Him in a brilliant robe, and sent Him back to Pilate. ¹²That very day Herod and Pilate became friends.^F Previously, they had been hostile toward each other.

¹³Pilate called together the chief priests, the leaders, and the people, ¹⁴and said to them, "You have brought me this man as one who subverts the people. But in fact, after examining Him in your presence, I have found no grounds to charge this man with those things you accuse Him of. ¹⁵Neither has Herod, because he sent Him back to us. Clearly, He has done nothing to deserve death. ¹⁶Therefore, I will have Him whipped^G and then release Him." [¹⁷For according to the festival he had to release someone to them.]^H

¹⁸Then they all cried out together, "Take this man away! Release Barabbas to us!" ¹⁹(He had been thrown into prison for a rebellion that had taken place in the city, and for murder.)

²⁰Pilate, wanting to release Jesus, addressed them again, ²¹but they kept shouting, "Crucify! Crucify Him!"

²²A third time he said to them, "Why? What has this man done wrong? I have found in Him no grounds for the death penalty. Therefore, I will have Him whipped and then release Him."

²³But they kept up the pressure, demanding with loud voices that He be crucified. And their voices^I won out. ²⁴So Pilate decided to grant their demand ²⁵and released the one they were asking for, who had been thrown into prison for rebellion and murder. But he handed Jesus over to their will.

²⁶As they led Him away, they seized Simon, a Cyrenian, who was coming in from the country, and laid the cross on him to carry behind Jesus. ²⁷A large crowd of people followed Him, including women who were mourning and lamenting Him. ²⁸But turning to them, Jesus said, "Daughters of Jerusalem, do not weep for Me, but weep for yourselves and your children. ²⁹Look, the days are coming when they will say, 'The women without children, the wombs that never bore and the breasts that never nursed, are fortunate!' ³⁰Then they will

begin to say to the mountains, 'Fall on us!' and to the hills, 'Cover us!'[A] [31] For if they do these things when the wood is green, what will happen when it is dry?"

[32] Two others—criminals—were also led away to be executed with Him. [33] When they arrived at the place called The Skull, they crucified Him there, along with the criminals, one on the right and one on the left. [[34] Then Jesus said, "Father, forgive them, because they do not know what they are doing."][B] And they divided His clothes and cast lots.

[35] The people stood watching, and even the leaders kept scoffing: "He saved others; let Him save Himself if this is God's Messiah, the Chosen One!" [36] The soldiers also mocked Him. They came offering Him sour wine [37] and said, "If You are the King of the Jews, save Yourself!"

[38] An inscription was above Him:[C]

THIS IS
THE KING OF THE JEWS.

[39] Then one of the criminals hanging there began to yell insults at[D] Him: "Aren't You the Messiah? Save Yourself and us!"

[40] But the other answered, rebuking him: "Don't you even fear God, since you are undergoing the same punishment? [41] We are punished justly, because we're getting back what we deserve for the things we did, but this man has done nothing wrong." [42] Then he said, "Jesus, remember me[E] when You come into Your kingdom!"

[43] And He said to him, "I assure you: Today you will be with Me in paradise."

[44] It was now about noon,[F] and darkness came over the whole land[G] until three,[H] [45] because the sun's light failed.[I] The curtain of the sanctuary was split down the middle. [46] And Jesus called out with a loud voice, "Father, into Your hands I entrust My spirit."[J] Saying this, He breathed His last.

[47] When the centurion saw what happened, he began to glorify God, saying, "This man really was righteous!" [48] All the crowds that had gathered for this spectacle, when they saw what had taken place, went home, striking their chests.[K] [49] But all who knew Him, including the women who had followed Him from Galilee, stood at a distance, watching these things.

[50] There was a good and righteous man named Joseph, a member of the Sanhedrin, [51] who had not agreed with their plan and action. He was from Arimathea, a Judean town, and was looking forward to the kingdom of God. [52] He approached Pilate and asked for Jesus' body. [53] Taking it down, he wrapped it in fine linen and placed it in a tomb cut into the rock, where no one had ever been placed.[L] [54] It was preparation day, and the Sabbath was about to begin.[M] [55] The women who had come with Him from Galilee followed along and observed the tomb and how His body was placed. [56] Then they returned and prepared spices and perfumes. And they rested on the Sabbath according to the commandment.

24 On the first day of the week, very early in the morning, they[N] came to the tomb, bringing the spices they had prepared. [2] They found the stone rolled away from the tomb. [3] They went in but did not find the body of the Lord Jesus. [4] While they were perplexed about this, suddenly two men stood by them in dazzling clothes. [5] So the women were terrified and bowed down to the ground.[O]

"Why are you looking for the living among the dead?" asked the men. [6] "He is not here, but He has been resurrected! Remember how He spoke to you when He was still in Galilee, [7] saying, 'The Son of Man must be betrayed into the hands of sinful men, be crucified, and rise on the third day'?" [8] And they remembered His words.

[9] Returning from the tomb, they reported all these things to the Eleven and to all the rest. [10] Mary Magdalene, Joanna, Mary the mother of James, and the other women with them were telling the apostles these things. [11] But these words seemed like nonsense to them, and they did not believe the women. [12] Peter, however, got up and ran to the tomb. When he stooped to look in, he saw only the linen cloths.[P] So he went home, amazed at what had happened.

[13] Now that same day two of them were on their way to a village called[Q] Emmaus, which was about seven miles[R] from Jerusalem. [14] Together they were discussing everything that had taken place. [15] And while they were

A23:30 Hs 10:8   B23:34 Other mss omit bracketed text   C23:38 Other mss add written in Greek, Latin, and Hebrew letters   D23:39 Or began to blaspheme   E23:42 Other mss add Lord   F23:44 Lit about the sixth hour   G23:44 Or whole earth   H23:44 Lit the ninth hour   I23:45 Other mss read three, and the sun was darkened   J23:46 Ps 31:5   K23:48 = mourning   L23:53 Or interred, or laid   M23:54 Lit was dawning; not in the morning but at sundown Friday   N24:1 Other mss add and other women with them   O24:5 Lit and inclined their faces to the ground   P24:12 Other mss add lying there   Q24:13 Lit village, which name is   R24:13 Lit about 60 stadia; 1 stadion = 600 feet discussing and arguing, Jesus Himself came near and began to walk along with them. [16]But they[A] were prevented from recognizing Him. [17]Then He asked them, "What is this dispute that you're having[B] with each other as you are walking?" And they stopped walking and looked discouraged.

[18]The one named Cleopas answered Him, "Are You the only visitor in Jerusalem who doesn't know the things that happened there in these days?"

[19]"What things?" He asked them.

So they said to Him, "The things concerning Jesus the Nazarene, who was a Prophet powerful in action and speech before God and all the people, [20]and how our chief priests and leaders handed Him over to be sentenced to death, and they crucified Him. [21]But we were hoping that He was the One who was about to redeem Israel. Besides all this, it's the third day since these things happened. [22]Moreover, some women from our group astounded us. They arrived early at the tomb, [23]and when they didn't find His body, they came and reported that they had seen a vision of angels who said He was alive. [24]Some of those who were with us went to the tomb and found it just as the women had said, but they didn't see Him."

[25]He said to them, "How unwise and slow you are to believe in your hearts all that the prophets have spoken! [26]Didn't the Messiah have to suffer these things and enter into His glory?" [27]Then beginning with Moses and all the Prophets, He interpreted for them the things concerning Himself in all the Scriptures.

[28]They came near the village where they were going, and He gave the impression that He was going farther. [29]But they urged Him: "Stay with us, because it's almost evening, and now the day is almost over." So He went in to stay with them.

[30]It was as He reclined at the table with them that He took the bread, blessed and broke it, and gave it to them. [31]Then their eyes were opened, and they recognized Him, but He disappeared from their sight. [32]So they said to each other, "Weren't our hearts ablaze within us while He was talking with us on the road and explaining the Scriptures to us?" [33]That very hour they got up and returned to Jerusalem. They found the Eleven and those with them gathered together, [34]who said,[C] "The Lord has certainly been raised, and has appeared to Simon!" [35]Then they began to describe what had happened on the road and how He was made known to them in the breaking of the bread.

[36]And as they were saying these things, He Himself stood among them. He said to them, "Peace to you!" [37]But they were startled and terrified and thought they were seeing a ghost. [38]"Why are you troubled?" He asked them. "And why do doubts arise in your hearts? [39]Look at My hands and My feet, that it is I Myself! Touch Me and see, because a ghost does not have flesh and bones as you can see I have." [40]Having said this, He showed them His hands and feet. [41]But while they still were amazed and unbelieving because of their joy, He asked them, "Do you have anything here to eat?" [42]So they gave Him a piece of a broiled fish,[D] [43]and He took it and ate in their presence.

[44]Then He told them, "These are My words that I spoke to you while I was still with you—that everything written about Me in the Law of Moses, the Prophets, and the Psalms must be fulfilled." [45]Then He opened their minds to understand the Scriptures. [46]He also said to them, "This is what is written:[E] The Messiah would suffer and rise from the dead the third day, [47]and repentance for[F] forgiveness of sins would be proclaimed in His name to all the nations, beginning at Jerusalem. [48]You are witnesses of these things. [49]And look, I am sending you[G] what My Father promised. As for you, stay in the city[H] until you are empowered[I] from on high."

[50]Then He led them out as far as Bethany, and lifting up His hands He blessed them. [51]And while He was blessing them, He left them and was carried up into heaven. [52]After worshiping Him, they returned to Jerusalem with great joy. [53]And they were continually in the temple complex praising God.[J]

[A]24:16 Lit their eyes   [B]24:17 Lit What are these words that you are exchanging   [C]24:34 Gk is specific that this refers to the Eleven and those with them.   [D]24:42 Other mss add and some honeycomb   [E]24:46 Other mss add and thus it was necessary that   [F]24:47 Other mss read repentance and   [G]24:49 Lit upon you   [H]24:49 Other mss add of Jerusalem   [I]24:49 Lit clothed with power   [J]24:53 Other mss read praising and blessing God. Amen.

JOHN

1 In the beginning was the Word,^A
and the Word was with God,
and the Word was God.
² He was with God in the beginning.
³ All things were created
    through Him,
and apart from Him not one thing
    was created
that has been created.
⁴ Life was in Him,^B
and that life was the light of men.
⁵ That light shines in the darkness,
yet the darkness did not overcome^C it.

⁶ There was a man named John
who was sent from God.
⁷ He came as a witness
to testify about the light,
so that all might believe through him.^D
⁸ He was not the light,
but he came to testify about the light.
⁹ The true light, who gives light
    to everyone,
was coming into the world.^E

¹⁰ He was in the world,
and the world was created
    through Him,
yet the world did not
    recognize Him.
¹¹ He came to His own,^F
and His own people^F
    did not receive Him.
¹² But to all who did receive Him,
He gave them the right to be^G
    children of God,
to those who believe in His name,
¹³ who were born,
not of blood,^H
or of the will of the flesh,
or of the will of man,^I
but of God.

¹⁴ The Word became flesh^J
and took up residence^K among us.
We observed His glory,
the glory as the One and Only Son^L
    from the Father,
full of grace and truth.
¹⁵ (John testified concerning Him
    and exclaimed,
"This was the One of whom I said,
'The One coming after me
    has surpassed me,
because He existed before me.'")
¹⁶ Indeed, we have all received grace
    after grace
from His fullness,
¹⁷ for the law was given through Moses,
grace and truth came
    through Jesus Christ.
¹⁸ No one has ever seen God.^M
The One and Only Son^N—
the One who is at the Father's side^O—
He has revealed Him.

¹⁹This is John's testimony when the Jews from Jerusalem sent priests and Levites to ask him, "Who are you?"

²⁰He did not refuse to answer, but he declared: "I am not the Messiah."

²¹"What then?" they asked him. "Are you Elijah?"

"I am not," he said.

"Are you the Prophet?"^P

"No," he answered.

²²"Who are you, then?" they asked. "We need to give an answer to those who sent us. What can you tell us about yourself?"

²³He said, "I am a **voice of one crying out in the wilderness: Make straight the way of the Lord**^Q—just as Isaiah the prophet said."

²⁴Now they had been sent from the Pharisees. ²⁵So they asked him, "Why then do you baptize if you aren't the Messiah, or Elijah, or the Prophet?"

^A1:1 The *Word* (Gk *Logos*) is a title for Jesus as the communication and the revealer of God the Father; Jn 1:14,18; Rv 19:13.   ^B1:3-4 Other punctuation is possible: . . . *not one thing was created. What was created in Him was life*   ^C1:5 Or *grasp*, or *comprehend*, or *overtake*; Jn 12:35   ^D1:7 Or *through it* (the light)   ^E1:9 Or *The true light who comes into the world gives light to everyone*, or *The true light enlightens everyone coming into the world.*   ^F1:11 The same Gk adjective is used twice in this verse: the first refers to all that Jesus owned as Creator (*to His own*); the second refers to the Jews (*His own people*).   ^G1:12 Or *become*   ^H1:13 Lit *bloods*; the pl form of *blood* occurs only here in the NT. It may refer either to lineal descent (that is, blood from one's father and mother) or to the OT sacrificial system (that is, the various blood sacrifices). Neither is the basis for birth into the family of God.   ^I1:13 Or *not of human lineage, or of human capacity, or of human volition*   ^J1:14 The eternally existent Word (vv. 1-2) took on full humanity but without sin; Heb 4:15.   ^K1:14 Or *and dwelt in a tent*; lit *and tabernacled*; this word occurs only here in John. A related word, referring to the Festival of Tabernacles, occurs only in 7:2; Ex 40:34-38.   ^L1:14 *Son* is implied from the reference to the Father and from Gk usage.   ^M1:18 Since God is an infinite being, no one can see Him in His absolute essential nature; Ex 33:18-23.   ^N1:18 Other mss read *God*   ^O1:18 Lit *is in the bosom of the Father*   ^P1:21 Probably the Prophet in Dt 18:15   ^Q1:23 Is 40:3

Turn to page 145 and find Romans 10:9-10,13.

[26] "I baptize with[A] water," John answered them. "Someone stands among you, but you don't know Him. [27] He is the One coming after me,[B] whose sandal strap I'm not worthy to untie."

[28] All this happened in Bethany[C] across the Jordan,[D] where John was baptizing.

[29] The next day John saw Jesus coming toward him and said, "Here is the Lamb of God, who takes away the sin of the world! [30] This is the One I told you about: 'After me comes a man who has surpassed me, because He existed before me.' [31] I didn't know Him, but I came baptizing with[A] water so He might be revealed to Israel."

[32] And John testified, "I watched the Spirit descending from heaven like a dove, and He rested on Him. [33] I didn't know Him, but He[E] who sent me to baptize with[A] water told me, 'The One you see the Spirit descending and resting on—He is the One who baptizes with[A] the Holy Spirit.' [34] I have seen and testified that He is the Son of God!"[F]

[35] Again the next day, John was standing with two of his disciples. [36] When he saw Jesus passing by, he said, "Look! The Lamb of God!"

[37] The two disciples heard him say this and followed Jesus. [38] When Jesus turned and noticed them following Him, He asked them, "What are you looking for?"

They said to Him, "Rabbi" (which means "Teacher"), "where are You staying?"

[39] "Come and you'll see," He replied. So they went and saw where He was staying, and they stayed with Him that day. It was about 10 in the morning.[G]

[40] Andrew, Simon Peter's brother, was one of the two who heard John and followed Him. [41] He first found his own brother Simon and told him, "We have found the Messiah!"[H] (which means "Anointed One"), [42] and he brought Simon to Jesus.

When Jesus saw him, He said, "You are Simon, son of John.[I] You will be called Cephas" (which means "Rock").

[43] The next day He[J] decided to leave for Galilee. Jesus found Philip and told him, "Follow Me!"

[44] Now Philip was from Bethsaida, the hometown of Andrew and Peter. [45] Philip found Nathanael[K] and told him, "We have found the One Moses wrote about in the Law (and so did the prophets): Jesus the son of Joseph, from Nazareth!"

[46] "Can anything good come out of Nazareth?" Nathanael asked him.

"Come and see," Philip answered.

[47] Then Jesus saw Nathanael coming toward Him and said about him, "Here is a true Israelite; no deceit is in him."

[48] "How do you know me?" Nathanael asked.

"Before Philip called you, when you were under the fig tree, I saw you," Jesus answered.

[49] "Rabbi," Nathanael replied, "You are the Son of God! You are the King of Israel!"

[50] Jesus responded to him, "Do you believe only because I told you I saw you under the fig tree? You[L] will see greater things than this." [51] Then He said, "I assure you: You[M] will see heaven opened and the angels of God ascending and descending on the Son of Man."

2 On the third day a wedding took place in Cana of Galilee. Jesus' mother was there, and [2] Jesus and His disciples were invited to the wedding as well. [3] When the wine ran out, Jesus' mother told Him, "They don't have any wine."

[4] "What has this concern of yours to do with Me,[N] woman?" Jesus asked. "My hour[O] has not yet come."

[5] "Do whatever He tells you," His mother told the servants.

[6] Now six stone water jars had been set there for Jewish purification. Each contained 20 or 30 gallons.[P]

[7] "Fill the jars with water," Jesus told them. So they filled them to the brim. [8] Then He said to them, "Now draw some out and take it to the chief servant."[Q] And they did.

A1:26,31,33 Or in B1:27 Other mss add who came before me C1:28 Other mss read in Bethabara D1:28 Another Bethany, near Jerusalem, was the home of Lazarus, Martha, and Mary; Jn 11:1. E1:33 He refers to God the Father, who gave John a sign to help him identify the Messiah. Vv. 32-34 indicate that John did not know that Jesus was the Messiah until the Spirit descended upon Him at His baptism. F1:34 Other mss read is the Chosen One of God G1:39 Lit about the tenth hour. Various methods of reckoning time were used in the ancient world. John probably used a different method from the other 3 Gospels. If John used the same method of time reckoning as the other 3 Gospels, the translation would be: It was about four in the afternoon. H1:41 In the NT, the word Messiah translates the Gk word Christos ("Anointed One"), except here and in Jn 4:25 where it translates Messias. I1:42 Other mss read Simon, son of Jonah J1:43 Or he, referring either to Simon Peter (vv. 41-42) or Andrew (vv. 40-41) K1:45 Probably the Bartholomew of the other Gospels and Acts L1:50 In Gk, the word you is sg and refers to Nathanael. M1:51 In Gk, the word you is pl and refers to Nathanael and the other disciples. N2:4 Or You and I see things differently; lit What to Me and to you; Mt 8:29; Mk 1:24; 5:7; Lk 8:28 O2:4 The time of His sacrificial death and exaltation; Jn 7:30; 8:20; 12:23,27; 13:1; 17:1 P2:6 Lit 2 or 3 measures Q2:8 Lit ruler of the table; perhaps master of the feast, or headwaiter

⁹When the chief servant tasted the water (after it had become wine), he did not know where it came from—though the servants who had drawn the water knew. He called the groom ¹⁰and told him, "Everyone sets out the fine wine first, then, after people have drunk freely, the inferior. But you have kept the fine wine until now."

¹¹Jesus performed this first sign^A in Cana of Galilee. He displayed His glory, and His disciples believed in Him.

¹²After this, He went down to Capernaum, together with His mother, His brothers, and His disciples, and they stayed there only a few days.

¹³The Jewish Passover was near, so Jesus went up to Jerusalem. ¹⁴In the temple complex He found people selling oxen, sheep, and doves, and He also found the money changers sitting there. ¹⁵After making a whip out of cords, He drove everyone out of the temple complex with their sheep and oxen. He also poured out the money changers' coins and overturned the tables. ¹⁶He told those who were selling doves, "Get these things out of here! Stop turning My Father's house into a marketplace!"^B

¹⁷And His disciples remembered that it is written: **Zeal for Your house will consume Me.**^C

¹⁸So the Jews replied to Him, "What sign of authority will You show us for doing these things?"

¹⁹Jesus answered, "Destroy this sanctuary, and I will raise it up in three days."

²⁰Therefore the Jews said, "This sanctuary took 46 years to build, and will You raise it up in three days?"

²¹But He was speaking about the sanctuary of His body. ²²So when He was raised from the dead, His disciples remembered that He had said this. And they believed the Scripture and the statement Jesus had made.

²³While He was in Jerusalem at the Passover Festival, many trusted in His name when they saw the signs He was doing. ²⁴Jesus, however, would not entrust Himself to them, since He knew them all ²⁵and because He did not need

anyone to testify about man; for He Himself knew what was in man.

3 There was a man from the Pharisees named Nicodemus, a ruler of the Jews. ²This man came to Him at night and said, "Rabbi, we know that You have come from God as a teacher, for no one could perform these signs You do unless God were with him."

³Jesus replied, "I assure you: Unless someone is born again,^D he cannot see the kingdom of God."

⁴"But how can anyone be born when he is old?" Nicodemus asked Him. "Can he enter his mother's womb a second time and be born?"

⁵Jesus answered, "I assure you: Unless someone is born of water and the Spirit,^E he cannot enter the kingdom of God. ⁶Whatever is born of the flesh is flesh, and whatever is born of the Spirit is spirit. ⁷Do not be amazed that I told you that you^F must be born again. ⁸The wind^G blows where it pleases, and you hear its sound, but you don't know where it comes from or where it is going. So it is with everyone born of the Spirit."

⁹"How can these things be?" asked Nicodemus.

¹⁰"Are you a teacher^H of Israel and don't know these things?" Jesus replied. ¹¹"I assure you: We speak what We know and We testify to what We have seen, but you^I do not accept Our testimony.^J ¹²If I have told you about things that happen on earth and you don't believe, how will you believe if I tell you about things of heaven? ¹³No one has ascended into heaven except the One who descended from heaven—the Son of Man.^K ¹⁴Just as Moses lifted up the snake in the wilderness, so the Son of Man must be lifted up, ¹⁵so that everyone who believes in Him will^L have eternal life.

¹⁶"For God loved the world in this way:^M He gave His One and Only Son, so that everyone who believes in Him will not perish but have eternal life. ¹⁷For God did not send His Son into the world that He might condemn the world, but that the world might be saved through Him. ¹⁸Anyone who believes in Him is not condemned, but anyone who does not

^A2:11 Lit *this beginning of the signs*; Jn 4:54; 20:30. Seven miraculous signs occur in John's Gospel and are so noted in the headings. ^B2:16 Lit *a house of business*   ^C2:17 Ps 69:9   ^D3:3 The same Gk word can mean *again* or *from above* (also in v. 7).   ^E3:5 Or *spirit*, or *wind*; the Gk word *pneuma* can mean *wind*, *spirit*, or *Spirit*, each of which occurs in this context.   ^F3:7 The pronoun is pl in Gk.   ^G3:8 The Gk word *pneuma* can mean wind, spirit, or Spirit, each of which occurs in this context.   ^H3:10 Or *the teacher*   ^I3:11 In Gk, the word *you* is pl here and throughout v. 12.   ^J3:11 The pronouns *we* and *our* refer to Jesus and His authority to speak for the Father.   ^K3:13 Other mss add *who is in heaven*   ^L3:15 Other mss add *not perish, but*   ^M3:16 The Gk word *houtos*, commonly translated in Jn 3:16 as "so" or "so much," occurs over 200 times in the NT. Almost without exception it is an adverb of manner, not degree (for example, see Mt 1:18). It only means "so much" when modifying an adjective (see Gl 3:3; Rv 16:18). Manner seems primarily in view in Jn 3:16, which explains the HCSB's rendering.

Turn to page 98 and find John 14:6.

believe is already condemned, because he has not believed in the name of the One and Only Son of God.

¹⁹"This, then, is the judgment: The light has come into the world, and people loved darkness rather than the light because their deeds were evil. ²⁰For everyone who practices wicked things hates the light and avoids it,ᴬ so that his deeds may not be exposed. ²¹But anyone who lives byᴮ the truth comes to the light, so that his works may be shown to be accomplished by God."ᶜ

²²After this, Jesus and His disciples went to the Judean countryside, where He spent time with them and baptized. ²³John also was baptizing in Aenon near Salim, because there was plenty of water there. People were coming and being baptized, ²⁴since John had not yet been thrown into prison.

²⁵Then a dispute arose between John's disciples and a Jewᴰ about purification. ²⁶So they came to John and told him, "Rabbi, the One you testified about, and who was with you across the Jordan, is baptizing—and everyone is flocking to Him."

²⁷John responded, "No one can receive a single thing unless it's given to him from heaven. ²⁸You yourselves can testify that I said, 'I am not the Messiah, but I've been sent ahead of Him.' ²⁹He who has the bride is the groom. But the groom's friend, who stands by and listens for him, rejoices greatlyᴱ at the groom's voice. So this joy of mine is complete. ³⁰He must increase, but I must decrease."

³¹The One who comes from above is above all. The one who is from the earth is earthly and speaks in earthly terms.ᶠ The One who comes from heaven is above all. ³²He testifies to what He has seen and heard, yet no one accepts His testimony. ³³The one who has accepted His testimony has affirmed that God is true. ³⁴For God sent Him, and He speaks God's words, since Heᴳ gives the Spirit without measure. ³⁵The Father loves the Son and has given all things into His hands. ³⁶The one who believes in the Son has eternal life, but the one who refuses to believe in the Son will not see life; instead, the wrath of God remains on him.

4 When Jesusᴴ knew that the Pharisees heard He was making and baptizing more disciples than John ²(though Jesus Himself was not baptizing, but His disciples were), ³He left Judea and went again to Galilee. ⁴He had to travel through Samaria, ⁵so He came to a town of Samaria called Sychar near the propertyᴵ that Jacob had given his son Joseph. ⁶Jacob's well was there, and Jesus, worn out from His journey, sat down at the well. It was about six in the evening.ᴶ

⁷A woman of Samaria came to draw water.

"Give Me a drink," Jesus said to her, ⁸for His disciples had gone into town to buy food.

⁹"How is it that You, a Jew, ask for a drink from me, a Samaritan woman?" she asked Him. For Jews do not associate withᴷ Samaritans.ᴸ

¹⁰Jesus answered, "If you knew the gift of God, and who is saying to you, 'Give Me a drink,' you would ask Him, and He would give you living water."

¹¹"Sir," said the woman, "You don't even have a bucket, and the well is deep. So where do You get this 'living water'? ¹²You aren't greater than our father Jacob, are You? He gave us the well and drank from it himself, as did his sons and livestock."

¹³Jesus said, "Everyone who drinks from this water will get thirsty again. ¹⁴But whoever drinks from the water that I will give him will never get thirsty again—ever! In fact, the water I will give him will become a wellᴹ of water springing up within him for eternal life."

¹⁵"Sir," the woman said to Him, "give me this water so I won't get thirsty and come here to draw water."

¹⁶"Go call your husband," He told her, "and come back here."

¹⁷"I don't have a husband," she answered.

"You have correctly said, 'I don't have a husband,'" Jesus said. ¹⁸"For you've had five husbands, and the man you now have is not your husband. What you have said is true."

¹⁹"Sir," the woman replied, "I see that You are a prophet. ²⁰Our fathers worshiped on this mountain,ᴺ yet you Jews say that the place to worship is in Jerusalem."

ᴬ3:20 Lit and does not come to the light   ᴮ3:21 Lit who does   ᶜ3:21 It is possible that Jesus' words end at v. 15. Ancient Gk did not have quotation marks.   ᴰ3:25 Other mss read and the Jews   ᴱ3:29 Lit with joy rejoices   ᶠ3:31 Or of earthly things   ᴳ3:34 Other mss read since God   ᴴ4:1 Other mss read the Lord   ᴵ4:5 Lit piece of land   ᴶ4:6 Lit the sixth hour; see note at Jn 1:39; an alt time reckoning would be noon   ᴷ4:9 Or do not share vessels with   ᴸ4:9 Other mss omit For Jews do not associate with Samaritans.   ᴹ4:14 Or spring   ᴺ4:20 Mount Gerizim, where there had been a Samaritan temple that rivaled Jerusalem's

²¹Jesus told her, "Believe Me, woman, an hour is coming when you will worship the Father neither on this mountain nor in Jerusalem. ²²You Samaritans[A] worship what you do not know. We worship what we do know, because salvation is from the Jews. ²³But an hour is coming, and is now here, when the true worshipers will worship the Father in spirit and truth. Yes, the Father wants such people to worship Him. ²⁴God is spirit, and those who worship Him must worship in spirit and truth."

²⁵The woman said to Him, "I know that Messiah[B] is coming" (who is called Christ). "When He comes, He will explain everything to us."

²⁶"I am He," Jesus told her, "the One speaking to you."

²⁷Just then His disciples arrived, and they were amazed that He was talking with a woman. Yet no one said, "What do You want?" or "Why are You talking with her?"

²⁸Then the woman left her water jar, went into town, and told the men, ²⁹"Come, see a man who told me everything I ever did! Could this be the Messiah?" ³⁰They left the town and made their way to Him.

³¹In the meantime the disciples kept urging Him, "Rabbi, eat something."

³²But He said, "I have food to eat that you don't know about."

³³The disciples said to one another, "Could someone have brought Him something to eat?"

³⁴"My food is to do the will of Him who sent Me and to finish His work," Jesus told them. ³⁵"Don't you say, 'There are still four more months, then comes the harvest'? Listen to what I'm telling you: Open[C] your eyes and look at the fields, for they are ready[D] for harvest. ³⁶The reaper is already receiving pay and gathering fruit for eternal life, so the sower and reaper can rejoice together. ³⁷For in this case the saying is true: 'One sows and another reaps.' ³⁸I sent you to reap what you didn't labor for; others have labored, and you have benefited from[E] their labor."

³⁹Now many Samaritans from that town believed in Him because of what the woman said[F] when she testified, "He told me everything I ever did." ⁴⁰Therefore, when the Samaritans came to Him, they asked Him to stay with them, and He stayed there two days. ⁴¹Many more believed because of what He said.[G] ⁴²And they told the woman, "We no longer believe because of what you said, for we have heard for ourselves and know that this really is the Savior of the world."[H]

⁴³After two days He left there for Galilee. ⁴⁴Jesus Himself testified that a prophet has no honor in his own country. ⁴⁵When they entered Galilee, the Galileans welcomed Him because they had seen everything He did in Jerusalem during the festival. For they also had gone to the festival.

⁴⁶Then He went again to Cana of Galilee, where He had turned the water into wine. There was a certain royal official whose son was ill at Capernaum. ⁴⁷When this man heard that Jesus had come from Judea into Galilee, he went to Him and pleaded with Him to come down and heal his son, for he was about to die.

⁴⁸Jesus told him, "Unless you people see signs and wonders, you will not believe."

⁴⁹"Sir," the official said to Him, "come down before my boy dies!"

⁵⁰"Go," Jesus told him, "your son will live." The man believed what[I] Jesus said to him and departed.

⁵¹While he was still going down, his slaves met him saying that his boy was alive. ⁵²He asked them at what time he got better. "Yesterday at seven in the morning[J] the fever left him," they answered. ⁵³The father realized this was the very hour at which Jesus had told him, "Your son will live." Then he himself believed, along with his whole household.

⁵⁴This, therefore, was the second sign Jesus performed after He came from Judea to Galilee.

5 After this, a Jewish festival took place, and Jesus went up to Jerusalem. ²By the Sheep Gate in Jerusalem there is a pool, called Bethesda[K] in Hebrew, which has five colonnades.[L] ³Within these lay a large number of the sick—blind, lame, and paralyzed [—waiting for the moving of the water, ⁴because an angel would go down into the pool from time to time and stir up the water. Then the first one who got in after the water was stirred up recovered from whatever ailment he had].[M]

⁵One man was there who had been sick for 38 years. ⁶When Jesus saw him lying there and

A4:22 *Samaritans* is implied since the Gk verb and pronoun are pl.   B4:25 In the NT, the word *Messiah* translates the Gk word *Christos* ["Anointed One"], except here and in Jn 1:41 where it translates *Messias*.   C4:35 Lit *Raise*   D4:35 Lit *white*   E4:38 Lit *you have entered into*   F4:39 Lit *because of the woman's word*   G4:41 Lit *because of His word*   H4:42 Other mss add *the Messiah*   I4:50 Lit *the word*   J4:52 Or *seven in the evening; lit at the seventh hour*; see note at Jn 1:39; an alt time reckoning would be *at one in the afternoon*   K5:2 Other mss read *Bethzatha*; other mss read *Bethsaida*   L5:2 Rows of columns supporting a roof   M5:3-4 Other mss omit bracketed text knew he had already been there a long time, He said to him, "Do you want to get well?"

⁷"Sir," the sick man answered, "I don't have a man to put me into the pool when the water is stirred up, but while I'm coming, someone goes down ahead of me."

⁸"Get up," Jesus told him, "pick up your mat and walk!" ⁹Instantly the man got well, picked up his mat, and started to walk.

Now that day was the Sabbath, ¹⁰so the Jews said to the man who had been healed, "This is the Sabbath! It's illegal for you to pick up your mat."

¹¹He replied, "The man who made me well told me, 'Pick up your mat and walk.'"

¹²"Who is this man who told you, 'Pick up your mat and walk'?" they asked. ¹³But the man who was cured did not know who it was, because Jesus had slipped away into the crowd that was there.ᴬ

¹⁴After this, Jesus found him in the temple complex and said to him, "See, you are well. Do not sin anymore, so that something worse doesn't happen to you." ¹⁵The man went and reported to the Jews that it was Jesus who had made him well.

¹⁶Therefore, the Jews began persecuting Jesusᴮ because He was doing these things on the Sabbath. ¹⁷But Jesus responded to them, "My Father is still working, and I am working also." ¹⁸This is why the Jews began trying all the more to kill Him: Not only was He breaking the Sabbath, but He was even calling God His own Father, making Himself equal with God.

¹⁹Then Jesus replied, "I assure you: The Son is not able to do anything on His own, but only what He sees the Father doing. For whatever the Fatherᶜ does, the Son also does these things in the same way. ²⁰For the Father loves the Son and shows Him everything He is doing, and He will show Him greater works than these so that you will be amazed. ²¹And just as the Father raises the dead and gives them life, so the Son also gives life to anyone He wants to. ²²The Father, in fact, judges no one but has given all judgment to the Son, ²³so that all people will honor the Son just as they honor the Father. Anyone who does not honor the Son does not honor the Father who sent Him.

²⁴"I assure you: Anyone who hears My word and believes Him who sent Me has eternal life and will not come under judgment but has passed from death to life.

²⁵"I assure you: An hour is coming, and is now here, when the dead will hear the voice of the Son of God, and those who hear will live. ²⁶For just as the Father has life in Himself, so also He has granted to the Son to have life in Himself. ²⁷And He has granted Him the right to pass judgment, because He is the Son of Man. ²⁸Do not be amazed at this, because a time is coming when all who are in the graves will hear His voice ²⁹and come out—those who have done good things, to the resurrection of life, but those who have done wicked things, to the resurrection of judgment.

³⁰"I can do nothing on My own. I judge only as I hear, and My judgment is righteous, because I do not seek My own will, but the will of Him who sent Me.

³¹"If I testify about Myself, My testimony is not valid.ᴰ ³²There is Another who testifies about Me, and I know that the testimony He gives about Me is valid.ᴱ ³³You have sent messengers to John, and he has testified to the truth. ³⁴I don't receive man's testimony, but I say these things so that you may be saved. ³⁵Johnᶠ was a burning and shining lamp, and for a time you were willing to enjoy his light.

³⁶"But I have a greater testimony than John's because of the works that the Father has given Me to accomplish. These very works I am doing testify about Me that the Father has sent Me. ³⁷The Father who sent Me has Himself testified about Me. You have not heard His voice at any time, and you haven't seen His form. ³⁸You don't have His word living in you, because you don't believe the One He sent. ³⁹You pore overᴳ the Scriptures because you think you have eternal life in them, yet they testify about Me. ⁴⁰And you are not willing to come to Me so that you may have life.

⁴¹"I do not accept glory from men, ⁴²but I know you—that you have no love for God within you. ⁴³I have come in My Father's name, yet you don't accept Me. If someone else comes in his own name, you will accept him. ⁴⁴How can you believe? While accepting glory from one another, you don't seek the glory that comes from the only God. ⁴⁵Do not think that I will accuse you to the Father. Your accuser is Moses, on whom you have set your hope. ⁴⁶For if you believed Moses, you would

---

ᴬ5:13 Lit slipped away, there being a crowd in that place   ᴮ5:16 Other mss add and trying to kill Him   ᶜ5:19 Lit whatever that One   ᴰ5:31 Or not true   ᴱ5:32 Or true   ᶠ5:35 Lit That man   ᴳ5:39 In Gk this could be a command: Pore over . . .

believe Me, because he wrote about Me. ⁴⁷But if you don't believe his writings, how will you believe My words?"

6 After this, Jesus crossed the Sea of Galilee (or Tiberias). ²And a huge crowd was following Him because they saw the signs that He was performing by healing the sick. ³So Jesus went up a mountain and sat down there with His disciples.

⁴Now the Passover, a Jewish festival, was near. ⁵Therefore, when Jesus looked up and noticed a huge crowd coming toward Him, He asked Philip, "Where will we buy bread so these people can eat?" ⁶He asked this to test him, for He Himself knew what He was going to do.

⁷Philip answered, "Two hundred denarii worth of bread wouldn't be enough for each of them to have a little."

⁸One of His disciples, Andrew, Simon Peter's brother, said to Him, ⁹"There's a boy here who has five barley loaves and two fish—but what are they for so many?"

¹⁰Then Jesus said, "Have the people sit down."

There was plenty of grass in that place, so they sat down. The men numbered about 5,000. ¹¹Then Jesus took the loaves, and after giving thanks He distributed them to those who were seated—so also with the fish, as much as they wanted.

¹²When they were full, He told His disciples, "Collect the leftovers so that nothing is wasted." ¹³So they collected them and filled 12 baskets with the pieces from the five barley loaves that were left over by those who had eaten.

¹⁴When the people saw the signᴬ He had done, they said, "This really is the Prophet who was to come into the world!" ¹⁵Therefore, when Jesus knew that they were about to come and take Him by force to make Him king, He withdrew againᴮ to the mountain by Himself.

¹⁶When evening came, His disciples went down to the sea, ¹⁷got into a boat, and started across the sea to Capernaum. Darkness had already set in, but Jesus had not yet come to them. ¹⁸Then a high wind arose, and the sea began to churn. ¹⁹After they had rowed about three or four miles,ᶜ they saw Jesus walking on the sea. He was coming near the boat, and they were afraid.

²⁰But He said to them, "It is I.ᴰ Don't be afraid!" ²¹Then they were willing to take Him on board, and at once the boat was at the shore where they were heading.

²²The next day, the crowd that had stayed on the other side of the sea knew there had been only one boat.ᴱ They also knew that Jesus had not boarded the boat with His disciples, but that His disciples had gone off alone. ²³Some boats from Tiberias came near the place where they ate the bread after the Lord gave thanks. ²⁴When the crowd saw that neither Jesus nor His disciples were there, they got into the boats and went to Capernaum looking for Jesus.

²⁵When they found Him on the other side of the sea, they said to Him, "Rabbi, when did You get here?"

²⁶Jesus answered, "I assure you: You are looking for Me, not because you sawᶠ the signs, but because you ate the loaves and were filled. ²⁷Don't work for the food that perishes but for the food that lasts for eternal life, which the Son of Man will give you, because God the Father has set His seal of approval on Him."

²⁸"What can we do to perform the works of God?" they asked.

²⁹Jesus replied, "This is the work of God—that you believe in the One He has sent."

³⁰"What sign then are You going to do so we may see and believe You?" they asked. "What are You going to perform? ³¹Our fathers ate the manna in the wilderness, just as it is written: **He gave them bread from heaven to eat.**"ᴳ,ᴴ

³²Jesus said to them, "I assure you: Moses didn't give you the bread from heaven, but My Father gives you the real bread from heaven. ³³For the bread of God is the One who comes down from heaven and gives life to the world."

³⁴Then they said, "Sir, give us this bread always!"

³⁵"I am the bread of life," Jesus told them. "No one who comes to Me will ever be hungry, and no one who believes in Me will ever be thirsty again. ³⁶But as I told you, you've seen Me,ᴵ and yet you do not believe. ³⁷Everyone the Father gives Me will come to Me, and the one who comes to Me I will never cast out. ³⁸For I have come down from heaven, not to do My will, but the will of Him who sent Me. ³⁹This is the will of Him who sent Me: that I should lose

none of those He has given Me but should raise them up on the last day. ⁴⁰For this is the will of My Father: that everyone who sees the Son and believes in Him may have eternal life, and I will raise him up on the last day."

⁴¹Therefore the Jews started complaining about Him because He said, "I am the bread that came down from heaven." ⁴²They were saying, "Isn't this Jesus the son of Joseph, whose father and mother we know? How can He now say, 'I have come down from heaven'?"

⁴³Jesus answered them, "Stop complaining among yourselves. ⁴⁴No one can come to Me unless the Father who sent Me draws^A him, and I will raise him up on the last day. ⁴⁵It is written in the Prophets: And they will all be taught by God.^B Everyone who has listened to and learned from the Father comes to Me— ⁴⁶not that anyone has seen the Father except the One who is from God. He has seen the Father.

⁴⁷"I assure you: Anyone who believes^C has eternal life. ⁴⁸I am the bread of life. ⁴⁹Your fathers ate the manna in the wilderness, and they died. ⁵⁰This is the bread that comes down from heaven so that anyone may eat of it and not die. ⁵¹I am the living bread that came down from heaven. If anyone eats of this bread he will live forever. The bread that I will give for the life of the world is My flesh."

⁵²At that, the Jews argued among themselves, "How can this man give us His flesh to eat?"

⁵³So Jesus said to them, "I assure you: Unless you eat the flesh of the Son of Man and drink His blood, you do not have life in yourselves. ⁵⁴Anyone who eats My flesh and drinks My blood has eternal life, and I will raise him up on the last day, ⁵⁵because My flesh is real food and My blood is real drink. ⁵⁶The one who eats My flesh and drinks My blood lives in Me, and I in him. ⁵⁷Just as the living Father sent Me and I live because of the Father, so the one who feeds on Me will live because of Me. ⁵⁸This is the bread that came down from heaven; it is not like the manna^D your fathers ate—and they died. The one who eats this bread will live forever."

⁵⁹He said these things while teaching in the synagogue in Capernaum.

⁶⁰Therefore, when many of His disciples heard this, they said, "This teaching is hard! Who can accept^E it?"

⁶¹Jesus, knowing in Himself that His disciples were complaining about this, asked them, "Does this offend you? ⁶²Then what if you were to observe the Son of Man ascending to where He was before? ⁶³The Spirit is the One who gives life. The flesh doesn't help at all. The words that I have spoken to you are spirit and are life. ⁶⁴But there are some among you who don't believe." (For Jesus knew from the beginning those who would not^F believe and the one who would betray Him.) ⁶⁵He said, "This is why I told you that no one can come to Me unless it is granted to him by the Father."

⁶⁶From that moment many of His disciples turned back and no longer accompanied Him. ⁶⁷Therefore Jesus said to the Twelve, "You don't want to go away too, do you?"

⁶⁸Simon Peter answered, "Lord, who will we go to? You have the words of eternal life. ⁶⁹We have come to believe and know that You are the Holy One of God!"^G

⁷⁰Jesus replied to them, "Didn't I choose you, the Twelve? Yet one of you is the Devil!" ⁷¹He was referring to Judas, Simon Iscariot's son,^H,I one of the Twelve, because he was going to betray Him.

7 After this, Jesus traveled in Galilee, since He did not want to travel in Judea because the Jews were trying to kill Him. ²The Jewish Festival of Tabernacles^J,K was near, ³so His brothers said to Him, "Leave here and go to Judea so Your disciples can see Your works that You are doing. ⁴For no one does anything in secret while he's seeking public recognition. If You do these things, show Yourself to the world." ⁵(For not even His brothers believed in Him.)

⁶Jesus told them, "My time has not yet arrived, but your time is always at hand. ⁷The world cannot hate you, but it does hate Me because I testify about it—that its deeds are evil. ⁸Go up to the festival yourselves. I'm not going up to the festival yet,^L because My time has not yet fully come." ⁹After He had said these things, He stayed in Galilee.

¹⁰After His brothers had gone up to the festival, then He also went up, not openly but

A6:44 Or brings, or leads; see the use of this Gk verb in Jn 12:32; 21:6; Ac 16:19; Jms 2:6.   B6:45 Is 54:13   C6:47 Other mss add in Me   D6:58 Other mss omit the manna   E6:60 Lit hear   F6:64 Other mss omit not   G6:69 Other mss read You are the Messiah, the Son of the Living God   H6:71 Other mss read Judas Iscariot, Simon's son   I6:71 Lit Judas, of Simon Iscariot   J7:2 Or Booths   K7:2 One of 3 great Jewish religious festivals, along with Passover and Pentecost; Ex 23:14; Dt 16:16   L7:8 Other mss omit yet secretly. [11] The Jews were looking for Him at the festival and saying, "Where is He?" [12] And there was a lot of discussion about Him among the crowds. Some were saying, "He's a good man." Others were saying, "No, on the contrary, He's deceiving the people." [13] Still, nobody was talking publicly about Him because they feared the Jews.

[14] When the festival was already half over, Jesus went up into the temple complex and began to teach. [15] Then the Jews were amazed and said, "How does He know the Scriptures, since He hasn't been trained?"

[16] Jesus answered them, "My teaching isn't Mine but is from the One who sent Me. [17] If anyone wants to do His will, he will understand whether the teaching is from God or if I am speaking on My own. [18] The one who speaks for himself seeks his own glory. But He who seeks the glory of the One who sent Him is true, and there is no unrighteousness in Him. [19] Didn't Moses give you the law? Yet none of you keeps the law! Why do you want to kill Me?"

[20] "You have a demon!" the crowd responded. "Who wants to kill You?"

[21] "I did one work, and you are all amazed," Jesus answered. [22] "Consider this: Moses has given you circumcision—not that it comes from Moses but from the fathers—and you circumcise a man on the Sabbath. [23] If a man receives circumcision on the Sabbath so that the law of Moses won't be broken, are you angry at Me because I made a man entirely well on the Sabbath? [24] Stop judging according to outward appearances; rather judge according to righteous judgment."

[25] Some of the people of Jerusalem were saying, "Isn't this the man they want to kill? [26] Yet, look! He's speaking publicly and they're saying nothing to Him. Can it be true that the authorities know He is the Messiah? [27] But we know where this man is from. When the Messiah comes, nobody will know where He is from."

[28] As He was teaching in the temple complex, Jesus cried out, "You know Me and you know where I am from. Yet I have not come on My own, but the One who sent Me is true. You don't know Him; [29] I know Him because I am from Him, and He sent Me."

[30] Then they tried to seize Him. Yet no one laid a hand on Him because His hour[A] had not yet come. [31] However, many from the crowd believed in Him and said, "When the Messiah comes, He won't perform more signs than this man has done, will He?"

[32] The Pharisees heard the crowd muttering these things about Him, so the chief priests and the Pharisees sent temple police to arrest Him.

[33] Then Jesus said, "I am only with you for a short time. Then I'm going to the One who sent Me. [34] You will look for Me, but you will not find Me; and where I am, you cannot come."

[35] Then the Jews said to one another, "Where does He intend to go so we won't find Him? He doesn't intend to go to the Dispersion[B] among the Greeks and teach the Greeks, does He? [36] What is this remark He made: 'You will look for Me, and you will not find Me; and where I am, you cannot come'?"

[37] On the last and most important day of the festival, Jesus stood up and cried out, "If anyone is thirsty, he should come to Me[C] and drink! [38] The one who believes in Me, as the Scripture has said,[D] will have streams of living water flow from deep within him." [39] He said this about the Spirit. Those who believed in Jesus were going to receive the Spirit, for the Spirit[E] had not yet been received[F,G] because Jesus had not yet been glorified.

[40] When some from the crowd heard these words, they said, "This really is the Prophet!"[H] [41] Others said, "This is the Messiah!" But some said, "Surely the Messiah doesn't come from Galilee, does He? [42] Doesn't the Scripture say that the Messiah comes from David's offspring[I] and from the town of Bethlehem, where David once lived?" [43] So a division occurred among the crowd because of Him. [44] Some of them wanted to seize Him, but no one laid hands on Him.

[45] Then the temple police came to the chief priests and Pharisees, who asked them, "Why haven't you brought Him?"

[46] The police answered, "No man ever spoke like this!"[J]

[47] Then the Pharisees responded to them: "Are you fooled too? [48] Have any of the rulers or

---

[A]7:30 The time of His sacrificial death and exaltation; Jn 2:4; 8:20; 12:23,27; 13:1; 17:1   [B]7:35 Jewish people scattered throughout Gentile lands who spoke Gk culture   [C]7:37 Other mss omit *to Me*   [D]7:38 Jesus may have had several OT passages in mind; Is 58:11; Ezk 47:1-12; Zch 14:8   [E]7:39 Other mss read *Holy Spirit*   [F]7:39 Other mss read *had not yet been given*   [G]7:39 Lit *the Spirit was not yet*; the word *received* is implied from the previous clause.   [H]7:40 Probably the Prophet in Dt 18:15   [I]7:42 Lit *seed*   [J]7:46 Other mss read *like this man*

Pharisees believed in Him? ⁴⁹But this crowd, which doesn't know the law, is accursed!"

⁵⁰Nicodemus—the one who came to Him previously, being one of them—said to them, ⁵¹"Our law doesn't judge a man before it hears from him and knows what he's doing, does it?"

⁵²"You aren't from Galilee too, are you?" they replied. "Investigate and you will see that no prophet arises from Galilee."ᴬ

8 [⁵³So each one went to his house. ¹But Jesus went to the Mount of Olives.

²At dawn He went to the temple complex again, and all the people were coming to Him. He sat down and began to teach them.

³Then the scribes and the Pharisees brought a woman caught in adultery, making her stand in the center. ⁴"Teacher," they said to Him, "this woman was caught in the act of committing adultery. ⁵In the law Moses commanded us to stone such women. So what do You say?" ⁶They asked this to trap Him, in order that they might have evidence to accuse Him.

Jesus stooped down and started writing on the ground with His finger. ⁷When they persisted in questioning Him, He stood up and said to them, "The one without sin among you should be the first to throw a stone at her."

⁸Then He stooped down again and continued writing on the ground. ⁹When they heard this, they left one by one, starting with the older men. Only He was left, with the woman in the center. ¹⁰When Jesus stood up, He said to her, "Woman, where are they? Has no one condemned you?"

¹¹"No one, Lord,"ᴮ she answered.

"Neither do I condemn you," said Jesus. "Go, and from now on do not sin anymore."]ᶜ

¹²Then Jesus spoke to them again: "I am the light of the world. Anyone who follows Me will never walk in the darkness but will have the light of life."

¹³So the Pharisees said to Him, "You are testifying about Yourself. Your testimony is not valid."ᴰ

¹⁴"Even if I testify about Myself," Jesus replied, "My testimony is valid,ᴱ because I know where I came from and where I'm going. But you don't know where I come from or where I'm going. ¹⁵You judge by human standards.ᶠ I judge no one. ¹⁶And if I do judge, My judg-

ment is true, because I am not alone, but I and the Father who sent Me judge together. ¹⁷Even in your law it is written that the witness of two men is valid. ¹⁸I am the One who testifies about Myself, and the Father who sent Me testifies about Me."

¹⁹Then they asked Him, "Where is Your Father?"

"You know neither Me nor My Father," Jesus answered. "If you knew Me, you would also know My Father." ²⁰He spoke these words by the treasury,ᴳ while teaching in the temple complex. But no one seized Him, because His hourᴴ had not come.

²¹Then He said to them again, "I'm going away; you will look for Me, and you will die in your sin. Where I'm going, you cannot come."

²²So the Jews said again, "He won't kill Himself, will He, since He says, 'Where I'm going, you cannot come'?"

²³"You are from below," He told them, "I am from above. You are of this world; I am not of this world. ²⁴Therefore I told you that you will die in your sins. For if you do not believe that I am He,ᴵ you will die in your sins."

²⁵"Who are You?" they questioned.

"Precisely what I've been telling you from the very beginning," Jesus told them. ²⁶"I have many things to say and to judge about you, but the One who sent Me is true, and what I have heard from Him—these things I tell the world."

²⁷They did not know He was speaking to them about the Father. ²⁸So Jesus said to them, "When you lift up the Son of Man, then you will know that I am He, and that I do nothing on My own. But just as the Father taught Me, I say these things. ²⁹The One who sent Me is with Me. He has not left Me alone, because I always do what pleases Him."

³⁰As He was saying these things, many believed in Him. ³¹So Jesus said to the Jews who had believed Him, "If you continue in My word,ᴶ you really are My disciples. ³²You will know the truth, and the truth will set you free."

³³"We are descendantsᴷ of Abraham," they answered Him, "and we have never been enslaved to anyone. How can You say, 'You will become free'?"

ᴬ7:52 Jonah and probably other prophets did come from Galilee; 2Kg 14:25   ᴮ8:11 Or *Sir*; Jn 4:15,49; 5:7; 6:34; 9:36   ᶜ8:11 Other mss omit bracketed text   ᴰ8:13 The law of Moses required at least 2 witnesses to make a claim legally valid (v. 17).   ᴱ8:14 Or *true*   ᶠ8:15 Lit *You judge according to the flesh*   ᴳ8:20 A place for offerings to be given, perhaps in the court of women   ᴴ8:20 The time of His sacrificial death and exaltation; Jn 2:4; 7:30; 12:23,27; 13:1; 17:1   ᴵ8:24 Jesus claimed to be deity, but the Pharisees didn't understand His meaning.   ᴶ8:31 Or *My teaching*, or *My message*   ᴷ8:33 Or *offspring*; lit *seed*; Jn 7:42

³⁴Jesus responded, "I assure you: Everyone who commits sin is a slave of sin. ³⁵A slave does not remain in the household forever, but a son does remain forever. ³⁶Therefore, if the Son sets you free, you really will be free. ³⁷I know you are descendants^A of Abraham, but you are trying to kill Me because My word^B is not welcome among you. ³⁸I speak what I have seen in the presence of the Father;^C therefore, you do what you have heard from your father."

³⁹"Our father is Abraham!" they replied.

"If you were Abraham's children," Jesus told them, "you would do what Abraham did. ⁴⁰But now you are trying to kill Me, a man who has told you the truth that I heard from God. Abraham did not do this! ⁴¹You're doing what your father does."

"We weren't born of sexual immorality," they said. "We have one Father—God."

⁴²Jesus said to them, "If God were your Father, you would love Me, because I came from God and I am here. For I didn't come on My own, but He sent Me. ⁴³Why don't you understand what I say? Because you cannot listen to^D My word. ⁴⁴You are of your father the Devil, and you want to carry out your father's desires. He was a murderer from the beginning and has not stood in the truth, because there is no truth in him. When he tells a lie, he speaks from his own nature,^E because he is a liar and the father of liars.^F ⁴⁵Yet because I tell the truth, you do not believe Me. ⁴⁶Who among you can convict Me of sin? If I tell the truth, why don't you believe Me? ⁴⁷The one who is from God listens to God's words. This is why you don't listen, because you are not from God."

⁴⁸The Jews responded to Him, "Aren't we right in saying that You're a Samaritan and have a demon?"

⁴⁹"I do not have a demon," Jesus answered. "On the contrary, I honor My Father and you dishonor Me. ⁵⁰I do not seek My glory; the One who seeks it also judges. ⁵¹I assure you: If anyone keeps My word, he will never see death—ever!"

⁵²Then the Jews said, "Now we know You have a demon. Abraham died and so did the prophets. You say, 'If anyone keeps My word, he will never taste death—ever!' ⁵³Are You

greater than our father Abraham who died? Even the prophets died. Who do You pretend to be?"^G

⁵⁴"If I glorify Myself," Jesus answered, "My glory is nothing. My Father—you say about Him, 'He is our God'—He is the One who glorifies Me. ⁵⁵You've never known Him, but I know Him. If I were to say I don't know Him, I would be a liar like you. But I do know Him, and I keep His word. ⁵⁶Your father Abraham was overjoyed that he would see My day; he saw it and rejoiced."

⁵⁷The Jews replied, "You aren't 50 years old yet, and You've seen Abraham?"^H

⁵⁸Jesus said to them, "I assure you: Before Abraham was, I am."^I

⁵⁹At that, they picked up stones to throw at Him. But Jesus was hidden^J and went out of the temple complex.^K

9 As He was passing by, He saw a man blind from birth. ²His disciples questioned Him: "Rabbi, who sinned, this man or his parents, that he was born blind?"

³"Neither this man nor his parents sinned," Jesus answered. "This came about so that God's works might be displayed in him. ⁴We^L must do the works of Him who sent Me^M while it is day. Night is coming when no one can work. ⁵As long as I am in the world, I am the light of the world."

⁶After He said these things He spit on the ground, made some mud from the saliva, and spread the mud on his eyes. ⁷"Go," He told him, "wash in the pool of Siloam" (which means "Sent"). So he left, washed, and came back seeing.

⁸His neighbors and those who formerly had seen him as a beggar said, "Isn't this the man who sat begging?" ⁹Some said, "He's the one." "No," others were saying, "but he looks like him."

He kept saying, "I'm the one!"

¹⁰Therefore they asked him, "Then how were your eyes opened?"

¹¹He answered, "The man called Jesus made mud, spread it on my eyes, and told me, 'Go to Siloam and wash.' So when I went and washed I received my sight."

¹²"Where is He?" they asked.

"I don't know," he said.

^A8:37 Or offspring; lit seed; Jn 7:42 ^B8:37 Or My teaching, or My message ^C8:38 Other mss read of My Father ^D8:43 Or cannot hear ^E8:44 Lit from his own things ^F8:44 Lit of it ^G8:53 Lit Who do You make Yourself? ^H8:57 Other mss read and Abraham has seen You? ^I8:58 I AM is the name God gave Himself at the burning bush; Ex 3:13-14; see note at Jn 8:24. ^J8:59 Or Jesus hid Himself ^K8:59 Other mss add and having gone through their midst, He passed by ^L9:4 Other mss read I ^M9:4 Other mss read sent us

¹³They brought the man who used to be blind to the Pharisees. ¹⁴The day that Jesus made the mud and opened his eyes was a Sabbath. ¹⁵So again the Pharisees asked him how he received his sight.

"He put mud on my eyes," he told them. "I washed and I can see."

¹⁶Therefore some of the Pharisees said, "This man is not from God, for He doesn't keep the Sabbath!" But others were saying, "How can a sinful man perform such signs?" And there was a division among them.

¹⁷Again they asked the blind man,ᴬ "What do you say about Him, since He opened your eyes?"

"He's a prophet," he said.

¹⁸The Jews did not believe this about him —that he was blind and received sight—until they summoned the parents of the one who had received his sight. ¹⁹They asked them, "Is this your son, the one you say was born blind? How then does he now see?"

²⁰"We know this is our son and that he was born blind," his parents answered. ²¹"But we don't know how he now sees, and we don't know who opened his eyes. Ask him; he's of age. He will speak for himself." ²²His parents said these things because they were afraid of the Jews, since the Jews had already agreed that if anyone confessed Him as Messiah, he would be banned from the synagogue. ²³This is why his parents said, "He's of age; ask him."

²⁴So a second time they summoned the man who had been blind and told him, "Give glory to God.ᴮ We know that this man is a sinner!"

²⁵He answered, "Whether or not He's a sinner, I don't know. One thing I do know: I was blind, and now I can see!"

²⁶Then they asked him, "What did He do to you? How did He open your eyes?"

²⁷"I already told you," he said, "and you didn't listen. Why do you want to hear it again? You don't want to become His disciples too, do you?"

²⁸They ridiculed him: "You're that man's disciple, but we're Moses' disciples. ²⁹We know that God has spoken to Moses. But this man—we don't know where He's from!"

³⁰"This is an amazing thing," the man told them. "You don't know where He is from, yet He opened my eyes! ³¹We know that God doesn't listen to sinners, but if anyone is God-fearing and does His will, He listens to him. ³²Throughout historyᶜ no one has ever heard of someone opening the eyes of a person born blind. ³³If this man were not from God, He wouldn't be able to do anything."

³⁴"You were born entirely in sin," they replied, "and are you trying to teach us?" Then they threw him out.ᴰ

³⁵When Jesus heard that they had thrown the man out, He found him and asked, "Do you believe in the Son of Man?"ᴱ

³⁶"Who is He, Sir, that I may believe in Him?" he asked.

³⁷Jesus answered, "You have seen Him; in fact, He is the One speaking with you."

³⁸"I believe, Lord!" he said, and he worshiped Him.

³⁹Jesus said, "I came into this world for judgment, in order that those who do not see will see and those who do see will become blind."

⁴⁰Some of the Pharisees who were with Him heard these things and asked Him, "We aren't blind too, are we?"

⁴¹"If you were blind," Jesus told them, "you wouldn't have sin.ᶠ But now that you say, 'We see'—your sin remains.

10 "I assure you: Anyone who doesn't enter the sheep pen by the door but climbs in some other way, is a thief and a robber. ²The one who enters by the door is the shepherd of the sheep. ³The doorkeeper opens it for him, and the sheep hear his voice. He calls his own sheep by name and leads them out. ⁴When he has brought all his own outside, he goes ahead of them. The sheep follow him because they recognize his voice. ⁵They will never follow a stranger; instead they will run away from him, because they don't recognize the voice of strangers."

⁶Jesus gave them this illustration, but they did not understand what He was telling them.

⁷So Jesus said again, "I assure you: I am the door of the sheep. ⁸All who came before Meᴳ are thieves and robbers, but the sheep didn't listen to them. ⁹I am the door. If anyone enters by Me, he will be saved and will come in and go out and find pasture. ¹⁰A thief comes only to steal and to kill and to destroy. I have come so that they may have life and have it in abundance.

ᴬ9:17 = the man who had been blind   ᴮ9:24 *Give glory to God* was a solemn charge to tell the truth; Jos 7:19.   ᶜ9:32 Lit *From the age*
ᴰ9:34 = they banned him from the synagogue; v. 22   ᴱ9:35 Other mss read *the Son of God*   ᶠ9:41 To *have sin* is an idiom that refers to guilt caused by sin.   ᴳ10:8 Other mss omit *before Me*

¹¹"I am the good shepherd. The good shepherd lays down his life for the sheep. ¹²The hired man, since he is not the shepherd and doesn't own the sheep, leaves them^A and runs away when he sees a wolf coming. The wolf then snatches and scatters them. ¹³This happens because he is a hired man and doesn't care about the sheep.

¹⁴"I am the good shepherd. I know My own sheep, and they know Me, ¹⁵as the Father knows Me, and I know the Father. I lay down My life for the sheep. ¹⁶But I have other sheep that are not of this fold; I must bring them also, and they will listen to My voice. Then there will be one flock, one shepherd. ¹⁷This is why the Father loves Me, because I am laying down My life so I may take it up again. ¹⁸No one takes it from Me, but I lay it down on My own. I have the right to lay it down, and I have the right to take it up again. I have received this command from My Father."

¹⁹Again a division took place among the Jews because of these words. ²⁰Many of them were saying, "He has a demon and He's crazy! Why do you listen to Him?" ²¹Others were saying, "These aren't the words of someone demon-possessed. Can a demon open the eyes of the blind?"

²²Then the Festival of Dedication^B took place in Jerusalem, and it was winter. ²³Jesus was walking in the temple complex in Solomon's Colonnade.^C ²⁴Then the Jews surrounded Him and asked, "How long are You going to keep us in suspense?^D If You are the Messiah, tell us plainly."^E

²⁵"I did tell you and you don't believe," Jesus answered them. "The works that I do in My Father's name testify about Me. ²⁶But you don't believe because you are not My sheep.^F ²⁷My sheep hear My voice, I know them, and they follow Me. ²⁸I give them eternal life, and they will never perish—ever! No one will snatch them out of My hand. ²⁹My Father, who has given them to Me, is greater than all. No one is able to snatch them out of the Father's hand. ³⁰The Father and I are one."^G

³¹Again the Jews picked up rocks to stone Him.

³²Jesus replied, "I have shown you many good works from the Father. Which of these works are you stoning Me for?"

³³"We aren't stoning You for a good work," the Jews answered, "but for blasphemy, because You—being a man—make Yourself God."

³⁴Jesus answered them, "Isn't it written in your scripture,^H I said, you are gods?¹ ³⁵If He called those whom the word of God came to 'gods'—and the Scripture cannot be broken— ³⁶do you say, 'You are blaspheming' to the One the Father set apart and sent into the world, because I said: I am the Son of God? ³⁷If I am not doing My Father's works, don't believe Me. ³⁸But if I am doing them and you don't believe Me, believe the works. This way you will know and understand^J that the Father is in Me and I in the Father." ³⁹Then they were trying again to seize Him, yet He eluded their grasp.

⁴⁰So He departed again across the Jordan to the place where John had been baptizing earlier, and He remained there. ⁴¹Many came to Him and said, "John never did a sign, but everything John said about this man was true." ⁴²And many believed in Him there.

11 Now a man was sick, Lazarus, from Bethany, the village of Mary and her sister Martha. ²Mary was the one who anointed the Lord with fragrant oil and wiped His feet with her hair, and it was her brother Lazarus who was sick. ³So the sisters sent a message to Him: "Lord, the one You love is sick." ⁴When Jesus heard it, He said, "This sickness will not end in death but is for the glory of God, so that the Son of God may be glorified through it." ⁵Now Jesus loved Martha, her sister, and Lazarus. ⁶So when He heard that he was sick, He stayed two more days in the place where He was. ⁷Then after that, He said to the disciples, "Let's go to Judea again."

⁸"Rabbi," the disciples told Him, "just now the Jews tried to stone You, and You're going there again?"

⁹"Aren't there 12 hours in a day?" Jesus answered. "If anyone walks during the day, he doesn't stumble, because he sees the light of this world. ¹⁰If anyone walks during the night, he does stumble, because the light is not in him." ¹¹He said this, and then He told them, "Our friend Lazarus has fallen asleep, but I'm on My way to wake him up."

^A10:12 Lit leaves the sheep   ^B10:22 Or Hanukkah, also called the Feast of Lights; this festival commemorated the rededication of the temple in 164 B.C.   ^C10:23 Rows of columns supporting a roof   ^D10:24 Lit How long are you taking away our life?   ^E10:24 Or openly, or publicly   ^F10:26 Other mss add just as I told you   ^G10:30 Lit I and the Father—We are one.   ^H10:34 Other mss read in the scripture   ^I10:34 Ps 82:6   ^J10:38 Other mss read know and believe

¹²Then the disciples said to Him, "Lord, if he has fallen asleep, he will get well."

¹³Jesus, however, was speaking about his death, but they thought He was speaking about natural sleep. ¹⁴So Jesus then told them plainly, "Lazarus has died. ¹⁵I'm glad for you that I wasn't there so that you may believe. But let's go to him."

¹⁶Then Thomas (called "Twin") said to his fellow disciples, "Let's go so that we may die with Him."

¹⁷When Jesus arrived, He found that Lazarus had already been in the tomb four days. ¹⁸Bethany was near Jerusalem (about two miles[A] away). ¹⁹Many of the Jews had come to Martha and Mary to comfort them about their brother. ²⁰As soon as Martha heard that Jesus was coming, she went to meet Him. But Mary remained seated in the house.

²¹Then Martha said to Jesus, "Lord, if You had been here, my brother wouldn't have died. ²²Yet even now I know that whatever You ask from God, God will give You."

²³"Your brother will rise again," Jesus told her.

²⁴Martha said, "I know that he will rise again in the resurrection at the last day."

²⁵Jesus said to her, "I am the resurrection and the life. The one who believes in Me, even if he dies, will live. ²⁶Everyone who lives and believes in Me will never die—ever. Do you believe this?"

²⁷"Yes, Lord," she told Him, "I believe You are the Messiah, the Son of God, who comes into the world."

²⁸Having said this, she went back and called her sister Mary, saying in private, "The Teacher is here and is calling for you."

²⁹As soon as she heard this, she got up quickly and went to Him. ³⁰Jesus had not yet come into the village but was still in the place where Martha had met Him. ³¹The Jews who were with her in the house consoling her saw that Mary got up quickly and went out. So they followed her, supposing that she was going to the tomb to cry there.

³²When Mary came to where Jesus was and saw Him, she fell at His feet and told Him, "Lord, if You had been here, my brother would not have died!"

³³When Jesus saw her crying, and the Jews who had come with her crying, He was angry[B] in His spirit and deeply moved. ³⁴"Where have you put him?" He asked.

"Lord," they told Him, "come and see."

³⁵Jesus wept.

³⁶So the Jews said, "See how He loved him!" ³⁷But some of them said, "Couldn't He who opened the blind man's eyes also have kept this man from dying?"

³⁸Then Jesus, angry[C] in Himself again, came to the tomb. It was a cave, and a stone was lying against it. ³⁹"Remove the stone," Jesus said.

Martha, the dead man's sister, told Him, "Lord, he's already decaying.[D] It's been four days."

⁴⁰Jesus said to her, "Didn't I tell you that if you believed you would see the glory of God?"

⁴¹So they removed the stone. Then Jesus raised His eyes and said, "Father, I thank You that You heard Me. ⁴²I know that You always hear Me, but because of the crowd standing here I said this, so they may believe You sent Me." ⁴³After He said this, He shouted with a loud voice, "Lazarus, come out!" ⁴⁴The dead man came out bound hand and foot with linen strips and with his face wrapped in a cloth. Jesus said to them, "Loose him and let him go."

⁴⁵Therefore, many of the Jews who came to Mary and saw what He did believed in Him. ⁴⁶But some of them went to the Pharisees and told them what Jesus had done.

⁴⁷So the chief priests and the Pharisees convened the Sanhedrin and said, "What are we going to do since this man does many signs? ⁴⁸If we let Him continue in this way, everyone will believe in Him! Then the Romans will come and remove both our place[E] and our nation."

⁴⁹One of them, Caiaphas, who was high priest that year, said to them, "You know nothing at all! ⁵⁰You're not considering that it is to your[F] advantage that one man should die for the people rather than the whole nation perish." ⁵¹He did not say this on his own, but being high priest that year he prophesied that Jesus was going to die for the nation, ⁵²and not for the nation only, but also to unite the scattered children of God. ⁵³So from that day on

---

A11:18 Lit *15 stadia*; 1 *stadion* = 600 feet   B11:33 The Gk word is very strong and probably indicates Jesus' anger against sin's tyranny and death.   C11:38 See note at 11:33.   D11:39 Lit *he already stinks*   E11:48 The temple or possibly all of Jerusalem   F11:50 Other mss read *to our* they plotted to kill Him. ⁵⁴ Therefore Jesus no longer walked openly among the Jews but departed from there to the countryside near the wilderness, to a town called Ephraim. And He stayed there with the disciples.

⁵⁵ The Jewish Passover was near, and many went up to Jerusalem from the country to purify^A themselves before the Passover. ⁵⁶ They were looking for Jesus and asking one another as they stood in the temple complex: "What do you think? He won't come to the festival, will He?" ⁵⁷ The chief priests and the Pharisees had given orders that if anyone knew where He was, he should report it so they could arrest Him.

12 Six days before the Passover, Jesus came to Bethany where Lazarus^B was, the one Jesus had raised from the dead. ² So they gave a dinner for Him there; Martha was serving them, and Lazarus was one of those reclining at the table with Him. ³ Then Mary took a pound of fragrant oil—pure and expensive nard—anointed Jesus' feet, and wiped His feet with her hair. So the house was filled with the fragrance of the oil.

⁴ Then one of His disciples, Judas Iscariot (who was about to betray Him), said, ⁵ "Why wasn't this fragrant oil sold for 300 denarii^C and given to the poor?" ⁶ He didn't say this because he cared about the poor but because he was a thief. He was in charge of the money-bag and would steal part of what was put in it.

⁷ Jesus answered, "Leave her alone; she has kept it for the day of My burial. ⁸ For you always have the poor with you, but you do not always have Me."

⁹ Then a large crowd of the Jews learned He was there. They came not only because of Jesus, but also to see Lazarus the one He had raised from the dead. ¹⁰ Therefore the chief priests decided to kill Lazarus also ¹¹ because he was the reason many of the Jews were deserting them^D and believing in Jesus.

¹² The next day, when the large crowd that had come to the festival heard that Jesus was coming to Jerusalem, ¹³ they took palm branches and went out to meet Him. They kept shouting: "*Hosanna!* **He who comes in the name of the Lord is the blessed One**^E—the King of Israel!"

¹⁴ Jesus found a young donkey and sat on it, just as it is written: ¹⁵ **Fear no more, Daughter Zion. Look, your King is coming, sitting on a donkey's colt.**^F

¹⁶ His disciples did not understand these things at first. However, when Jesus was glorified, then they remembered that these things had been written about Him and that they had done these things to Him. ¹⁷ Meanwhile, the crowd, which had been with Him when He called Lazarus out of the tomb and raised him from the dead, continued to testify.^G ¹⁸ This is also why the crowd met Him, because they heard He had done this sign.

¹⁹ Then the Pharisees said to one another, "You see? You've accomplished nothing. Look—the world has gone after Him!"

²⁰ Now some Greeks were among those who went up to worship at the festival. ²¹ So they came to Philip, who was from Bethsaida in Galilee, and requested of him, "Sir, we want to see Jesus."

²² Philip went and told Andrew; then Andrew and Philip went and told Jesus. ²³ Jesus replied to them, "The hour has come for the Son of Man to be glorified.

²⁴ "I assure you: Unless a grain of wheat falls to the ground and dies, it remains by itself. But if it dies, it produces a large crop.^H ²⁵ The one who loves his life will lose it, and the one who hates his life in this world will keep it for eternal life. ²⁶ If anyone serves Me, he must follow Me. Where I am, there My servant also will be. If anyone serves Me, the Father will honor him.

²⁷ "Now My soul is troubled. What should I say—Father, save Me from this hour? But that is why I came to this hour. ²⁸ Father, glorify Your name!"^I

Then a voice came from heaven: "I have glorified it, and I will glorify it again!"

²⁹ The crowd standing there heard it and said it was thunder. Others said that an angel had spoken to Him.

³⁰ Jesus responded, "This voice came, not for Me, but for you. ³¹ Now is the judgment of this world. Now the ruler of this world will be cast out. ³² As for Me, if I am lifted up^J from the earth I will draw all people to Myself." ³³ He

^A11:55 The law of Moses required God's people to purify or cleanse themselves so they could celebrate the Passover. Jews often came to Jerusalem a week early to do this; Nm 9:4-11.   ^B12:1 Other mss read *Lazarus who died*   ^C12:5 This amount was about a year's wages for a common worker.   ^D12:11 Lit *going away*   ^E12:13 Ps 118:25-26   ^F12:15 Zch 9:9   ^G12:17 Other mss read *Meanwhile the crowd, which had been with Him, continued to testify that He had called Lazarus out of the tomb and raised him from the dead.*   ^H12:24 Lit *produces much fruit*   ^I12:28 Other mss read *Your Son*   ^J12:32 Or *exalted* said this to signify what kind of death He was about to die.

³⁴ Then the crowd replied to Him, "We have heard from the scripture that the Messiah will remain forever. So how can You say, 'The Son of Man must be lifted up'?ᴬ Who is this Son of Man?"

³⁵ Jesus answered, "The light will be with you only a little longer. Walk while you have the light so that darkness doesn't overtake you. The one who walks in darkness doesn't know where he's going. ³⁶ While you have the light, believe in the light so that you may become sons of light." Jesus said this, then went away and hid from them.

³⁷ Even though He had performed so many signs in their presence, they did not believe in Him. ³⁸ But this was to fulfill the word of Isaiah the prophet, who said:ᴮ

> **Lord, who has believed
> our message?
> And who has the arm of the Lord
> been revealed to?**ᶜ

³⁹ This is why they were unable to believe, because Isaiah also said:

> ⁴⁰ **He has blinded their eyes
> and hardened their hearts,
> so that they would not see
> with their eyes
> or understand with their hearts,
> and be converted,
> and I would heal them.**ᴰ

⁴¹ Isaiah said these things becauseᴱ he saw His glory and spoke about Him.

⁴² Nevertheless, many did believe in Him even among the rulers, but because of the Pharisees they did not confess Him, so they would not be banned from the synagogue. ⁴³ For they loved praise from men more than praise from God.ᶠ

⁴⁴ Then Jesus cried out, "The one who believes in Me believes not in Me, but in Him who sent Me. ⁴⁵ And the one who sees Me sees Him who sent Me. ⁴⁶ I have come as a light into the world, so that everyone who believes in Me would not remain in darkness. ⁴⁷ If anyone hears My words and doesn't keep them, I do not judge him; for I did not come to judge the world but to save the world. ⁴⁸ The one who

rejects Me and doesn't accept My sayings has this as his judge:ᴳ The word I have spoken will judge him on the last day. ⁴⁹ For I have not spoken on My own, but the Father Himself who sent Me has given Me a command as to what I should say and what I should speak. ⁵⁰ I know that His command is eternal life. So the things that I speak, I speak just as the Father has told Me."

13 Before the Passover Festival, Jesus knew that His hour had come to depart from this world to the Father. Having loved His own who were in the world, He loved them to the end.ᴴ

² Now by the time of supper, the Devil had already put it into the heart of Judas, Simon Iscariot's son, to betray Him. ³ Jesus knew that the Father had given everything into His hands, that He had come from God, and that He was going back to God. ⁴ So He got up from supper, laid aside His robe, took a towel, and tied it around Himself. ⁵ Next, He poured water into a basin and began to wash His disciples' feet and to dry them with the towel tied around Him.

⁶ He came to Simon Peter, who asked Him, "Lord, are You going to wash my feet?"

⁷ Jesus answered him, "What I'm doing you don't understand now, but afterward you will know."

⁸ "You will never wash my feet—ever!" Peter said.

Jesus replied, "If I don't wash you, you have no part with Me."

⁹ Simon Peter said to Him, "Lord, not only my feet, but also my hands and my head."

¹⁰ "One who has bathed," Jesus told him, "doesn't need to wash anything except his feet, but he is completely clean. You are clean, but not all of you." ¹¹ For He knew who would betray Him. This is why He said, "You are not all clean."

¹² When Jesus had washed their feet and put on His robe, He reclinedᴵ again and said to them, "Do you know what I have done for you? ¹³ You call Me Teacher and Lord. This is well said, for I am. ¹⁴ So if I, your Lord and Teacher, have washed your feet, you also ought to wash one another's feet. ¹⁵ For I have given you an example that you also should do just as I have done for you.

¹⁶"I assure you: A slave is not greater than his master,ᴬ and a messenger is not greater than the one who sent him. ¹⁷If you know these things, you are blessed if you do them. ¹⁸I'm not speaking about all of you; I know those I have chosen. But the Scripture must be fulfilled: The one who eats My breadᴮ has raised his heel against Me.ᶜ

¹⁹"I am telling you now before it happens, so that when it does happen you will believe that I am He. ²⁰I assure you: Whoever receives anyone I send receives Me, and the one who receives Me receives Him who sent Me."

²¹When Jesus had said this, He was troubled in His spirit and testified, "I assure you: One of you will betray Me!"

²²The disciples started looking at one another—uncertain which one He was speaking about. ²³One of His disciples, the one Jesus loved, was reclining close beside Jesus.ᴰ ²⁴Simon Peter motioned to him to find out who it was He was talking about. ²⁵So he leaned back against Jesus and asked Him, "Lord, who is it?"

²⁶Jesus replied, "He's the one I give the piece of bread to after I have dipped it." When He had dipped the bread, He gave it to Judas, Simon Iscariot's son.ᴱ ²⁷After Judas ate the piece of bread, Satan entered him. Therefore Jesus told him, "What you're doing, do quickly."

²⁸None of those reclining at the table knew why He told him this. ²⁹Since Judas kept the money-bag, some thought that Jesus was telling him, "Buy what we need for the festival," or that he should give something to the poor. ³⁰After receiving the piece of bread, he went out immediately. And it was night.

³¹When he had gone out, Jesus said, "Now the Son of Man is glorified, and God is glorified in Him. ³²If God is glorified in Him,ᶠ God will also glorify Him in Himself and will glorify Him at once.

³³"Children, I am with you a little while longer. You will look for Me, and just as I told the Jews, 'Where I am going you cannot come,' so now I tell you.

³⁴"I give you a new command: Love one another. Just as I have loved you, you must also love one another. ³⁵By this all people will know

that you are My disciples, if you have love for one another."

³⁶"Lord," Simon Peter said to Him, "where are You going?"

Jesus answered, "Where I am going you cannot follow Me now, but you will follow later."

³⁷"Lord," Peter asked, "why can't I follow You now? I will lay down my life for You!"

³⁸Jesus replied, "Will you lay down your life for Me? I assure you: A rooster will not crow until you have denied Me three times.

14 "Your heart must not be troubled. Believeᴳ in God; believe also in Me. ²In My Father's house are many dwelling places;ᴴ if not, I would have told you. I am going away to prepare a place for you. ³If I go away and prepare a place for you, I will come back and receive you to Myself, so that where I am you may be also. ⁴You know the way to where I am going."ᴵ

⁵"Lord," Thomas said, "we don't know where You're going. How can we know the way?"

⁶Jesus told him, "I am the way, the truth, and the life. No one comes to the Father except through Me.

⁷"If you know Me, you will also knowᴶ My Father. From now on you do know Him and have seen Him."

⁸"Lord," said Philip, "show us the Father, and that's enough for us."

⁹Jesus said to him, "Have I been among you all this time without your knowing Me, Philip? The one who has seen Me has seen the Father. How can you say, 'Show us the Father'? ¹⁰Don't you believe that I am in the Father and the Father is in Me? The words I speak to you I do not speak on My own. The Father who lives in Me does His works. ¹¹Believe Me that I am in the Father and the Father is in Me. Otherwise, believeᴷ because of the works themselves.

¹²"I assure you: The one who believes in Me will also do the works that I do. And he will do even greater works than these, because I am going to the Father. ¹³Whatever you ask in My name, I will do it so that the Father may be glorified in the Son. ¹⁴If you ask Meᴸ anything in My name, I will do it.ᴹ

¹⁵"If you love Me, you will keepᴺ My commands. ¹⁶And I will ask the Father, and He will

---

ᴬ13:16 Or lord   ᴮ13:18 Other mss read eats bread with Me   ᶜ13:18 Ps 41:9   ᴰ13:23 Lit reclining at Jesus' breast; that is, on His right; Jn 1:18   ᴱ13:26 Other mss read Judas Iscariot, Simon's son   ᶠ13:32 Other mss omit If God is glorified in Him   ᴳ14:1 Or You believe   ᴴ14:2 The Vg used the Lat term mansio, a traveler's resting place. The Gk word is related to the verb meno, meaning remain or stay, which occurs 40 times in John.   ᴵ14:4 Other mss read this verse: And you know where I am going, and you know the way   ᴶ14:7 Other mss read If you had known Me, you would have known   ᴷ14:11 Other mss read believe Me   ᴸ14:14 Other mss omit Me   ᴹ14:14 Other mss omit all of v. 14   ᴺ14:15 Other mss read If you love Me, keep (as a command)

Turn to page 110 and find Acts 4:12.

give you another Counselor to be with you forever. [17] He is the Spirit of truth. The world is unable to receive Him because it doesn't see Him or know Him. But you do know Him, because He remains with you and will be[A] in you. [18] I will not leave you as orphans; I am coming to you.

[19] "In a little while the world will see Me no longer, but you will see Me. Because I live, you will live too. [20] In that day you will know that I am in My Father, you are in Me, and I am in you. [21] The one who has My commands and keeps them is the one who loves Me. And the one who loves Me will be loved by My Father. I also will love him and will reveal Myself to him."

[22] Judas (not Iscariot) said to Him, "Lord, how is it You're going to reveal Yourself to us and not to the world?"

[23] Jesus answered, "If anyone loves Me, he will keep My word. My Father will love him, and We will come to him and make Our home with him. [24] The one who doesn't love Me will not keep My words. The word that you hear is not Mine but is from the Father who sent Me.

[25] "I have spoken these things to you while I remain with you. [26] But the Counselor, the Holy Spirit—the Father will send Him in My name—will teach you all things and remind you of everything I have told you.

[27] "Peace I leave with you. My peace I give to you. I do not give to you as the world gives. Your heart must not be troubled or fearful. [28] You have heard Me tell you, 'I am going away and I am coming to you.' If you loved Me, you would have rejoiced that I am going to the Father, because the Father is greater than I. [29] I have told you now before it happens so that when it does happen you may believe. [30] I will not talk with you much longer, because the ruler of the world is coming. He has no power over Me.[B] [31] On the contrary, I am going away[C] so that the world may know that I love the Father. Just as the Father commanded Me, so I do.

"Get up; let's leave this place.

15 "I am the true vine, and My Father is the vineyard keeper. [2] Every branch in Me that does not produce fruit He removes, and He prunes every branch that produces fruit so that it will produce more fruit. [3] You are already clean because of the word I have spoken

to you. [4] Remain in Me, and I in you. Just as a branch is unable to produce fruit by itself unless it remains on the vine, so neither can you unless you remain in Me.

[5] "I am the vine; you are the branches. The one who remains in Me and I in him produces much fruit, because you can do nothing without Me. [6] If anyone does not remain in Me, he is thrown aside like a branch and he withers. They gather them, throw them into the fire, and they are burned. [7] If you remain in Me and My words remain in you, ask whatever you want and it will be done for you. [8] My Father is glorified by this: that you produce much fruit and prove to be[D] My disciples.

[9] "As the Father has loved Me, I have also loved you. Remain in My love. [10] If you keep My commands you will remain in My love, just as I have kept My Father's commands and remain in His love.

[11] "I have spoken these things to you so that My joy may be in you and your joy may be complete. [12] This is My command: Love one another as I have loved you. [13] No one has greater love than this, that someone would lay down his life for his friends. [14] You are My friends if you do what I command you. [15] I do not call you slaves anymore, because a slave doesn't know what his master[E] is doing. I have called you friends, because I have made known to you everything I have heard from My Father. [16] You did not choose Me, but I chose you. I appointed you that you should go out and produce fruit and that your fruit should remain, so that whatever you ask the Father in My name, He will give you. [17] This is what I command you: Love one another.

[18] "If the world hates you, understand that it hated Me before it hated you. [19] If you were of the world, the world would love you as its own. However, because you are not of the world, but I have chosen you out of it, the world hates you. [20] Remember the word I spoke to you: 'A slave is not greater than his master.' If they persecuted Me, they will also persecute you. If they kept My word, they will also keep yours. [21] But they will do all these things to you on account of My name, because they don't know the One who sent Me. [22] If I had not come and spoken to them, they would not have sin.[F] Now they have no excuse for their sin. [23] The one who hates Me also hates My Father. [24] If I had not done the

works among them that no one else has done, they would not have sin. Now they have seen and hated both Me and My Father. ²⁵But this happened so that the statement written in their scripture might be fulfilled: **They hated Me for no reason.**ᴬ

²⁶"When the Counselor comes, the One I will send to you from the Father—the Spirit of truth who proceeds from the Father—He will testify about Me. ²⁷You also will testify, because you have been with Me from the beginning.

16 "I have told you these things to keep you from stumbling. ²They will ban you from the synagogues. In fact, a time is coming when anyone who kills you will think he is offering service to God. ³They will do these things because they haven't known the Father or Me. ⁴But I have told you these things so that when their timeᴮ comes you may remember I told them to you. I didn't tell you these things from the beginning, because I was with you.

⁵"But now I am going away to Him who sent Me, and not one of you asks Me, 'Where are You going?' ⁶Yet, because I have spoken these things to you, sorrow has filled your heart. ⁷Nevertheless, I am telling you the truth. It is for your benefit that I go away, because if I don't go away the Counselor will not come to you. If I go, I will send Him to you. ⁸When He comes, He will convict the world about sin, righteousness, and judgment: ⁹About sin, because they do not believe in Me; ¹⁰about righteousness, because I am going to the Father and you will no longer see Me; ¹¹and about judgment, because the ruler of this world has been judged.

¹²"I still have many things to tell you, but you can't bear them now. ¹³When the Spirit of truth comes, He will guide you into all the truth. For He will not speak on His own, but He will speak whatever He hears. He will also declare to you what is to come. ¹⁴He will glorify Me, because He will take from what is Mine and declare it to you. ¹⁵Everything the Father has is Mine. This is why I told you that He takes from what is Mine and will declare it to you.

¹⁶"A little while and you will no longer see Me; again a little while and you will see Me."ᶜ

¹⁷Therefore some of His disciples said to one another, "What is this He tells us: 'A little while and you will not see Me; again a little while and

you will see Me'; and, 'because I am going to the Father'?" ¹⁸They said, "What is this He is saying,ᴰ 'A little while'? We don't know what He's talking about!"

¹⁹Jesus knew they wanted to question Him, so He said to them, "Are you asking one another about what I said, 'A little while and you will not see Me; again a little while and you will see Me'?

²⁰"I assure you: You will weep and wail, but the world will rejoice. You will become sorrowful, but your sorrow will turn to joy. ²¹When a woman is in labor she has pain because her time has come. But when she has given birth to a child, she no longer remembers the suffering because of the joy that a person has been born into the world. ²²So you also have sorrowᴱ now. But I will see you again. Your hearts will rejoice, and no one will rob you of your joy. ²³In that day you will not ask Me anything.

"I assure you: Anything you ask the Father in My name, He will give you. ²⁴Until now you have asked for nothing in My name. Ask and you will receive, so that your joy may be complete.

²⁵"I have spoken these things to you in figures of speech. A time is coming when I will no longer speak to you in figures, but I will tell you plainly about the Father. ²⁶In that day you will ask in My name. I am not telling you that I will make requests to the Father on your behalf. ²⁷For the Father Himself loves you, because you have loved Me and have believed that I came from God.ᶠ ²⁸I came from the Father and have come into the world. Again, I am leaving the world and going to the Father."

²⁹"Ah!" His disciples said. "Now You're speaking plainly and not using any figurative language. ³⁰Now we know that You know everything and don't need anyone to question You. By this we believe that You came from God."

³¹Jesus responded to them, "Do you now believe? ³²Look: An hour is coming, and has come, when each of you will be scattered to his own home, and you will leave Me alone. Yet I am not alone, because the Father is with Me. ³³I have told you these things so that in Me you may have peace. You will have suffering in this world. Be courageous! I have conquered the world."

17 Jesus spoke these things, looked up to heaven, and said:

Father,
the hour has come.
Glorify Your Son
so that the Son may glorify You,
² for You gave Him authority
over all flesh;^A
so He may give eternal life
to all You have given Him.
³ This is eternal life:
that they may know You,
  the only true God,
and the One You have sent—
  Jesus Christ.
⁴ I have glorified You on the earth
by completing the work You gave Me
  to do.
⁵ Now, Father, glorify Me
  in Your presence
with that glory I had with You
before the world existed.

⁶ I have revealed Your name
to the men You gave Me
  from the world.
They were Yours, You gave them to Me,
and they have kept Your word.
⁷ Now they know that all things
You have given to Me are from You,
⁸ because the words that You gave Me,
I have given them.
They have received them
and have known for certain
that I came from You.
They have believed that You sent Me.
⁹ I pray^B for them.
I am not praying for the world
but for those You have given Me,
because they are Yours.
¹⁰ Everything I have is Yours,
and everything You have is Mine,
and I have been glorified in them.
¹¹ I am no longer in the world,
but they are in the world,
and I am coming to You.
Holy Father,
protect^C them by Your name
that You have given Me,
so that they may be one as We are one.
¹² While I was with them,

I was protecting them by Your name
that You have given Me.
I guarded them and not one of them
  is lost,
except the son of destruction,^D
so that the Scripture may be fulfilled.
¹³ Now I am coming to You,
and I speak these things in the world
so that they may have My joy
  completed in them.
¹⁴ I have given them Your word.
The world hated them
because they are not of the world,
as I am not of the world.
¹⁵ I am not praying
that You take them out of the world
but that You protect them
  from the evil one.
¹⁶ They are not of the world,
as I am not of the world.
¹⁷ Sanctify^E them by the truth;
Your word is truth.
¹⁸ As You sent Me into the world,
I also have sent them into the world.
¹⁹ I sanctify Myself for them,
so they also may be sanctified
  by the truth.

²⁰ I pray not only for these,
but also for those who believe in Me
through their message.
²¹ May they all be one,
as You, Father, are in Me and I am
  in You.
May they also be one^F in Us,
so the world may believe You sent Me.
²² I have given them the glory
  You have given Me.
May they be one as We are one.
²³ I am in them and You are in Me.
May they be made completely one,
so the world may know You have
  sent Me
and have loved them as
  You have loved Me.
²⁴ Father,
I desire those You have given Me
to be with Me where I am.
Then they will see My glory,
which You have given Me
because You loved Me
  before the world's foundation.

A17:2 Or *people*   B17:9 Lit *ask* (throughout this passage)   C17:11 Lit *keep* (throughout this passage)   D17:12 The one destined for destruction, loss, or perdition   E17:17 Set apart for special use   F17:21 Other mss omit *one*

²⁵ Righteous Father!
The world has not known You.
However, I have known You,
and these have known
    that You sent Me.

²⁶ I made Your name known to them
and will make it known,
so the love You have loved Me with
may be in them and I may be in them.

18 After Jesus had said these things, He went out with His disciples across the Kidron Valley, where there was a garden, and He and His disciples went into it. ² Judas, who betrayed Him, also knew the place, because Jesus often met there with His disciples. ³ So Judas took a company of soldiers and some temple police from the chief priests and the Pharisees and came there with lanterns, torches, and weapons.

⁴ Then Jesus, knowing everything that was about to happen to Him, went out and said to them, "Who is it you're looking for?"

⁵ "Jesus the Nazarene," they answered.

"I am He,"ᴬ Jesus told them.

Judas, who betrayed Him, was also standing with them. ⁶ When He told them, "I am He," they stepped back and fell to the ground.

⁷ Then He asked them again, "Who is it you're looking for?"

"Jesus the Nazarene," they said.

⁸ "I told you I am He," Jesus replied. "So if you're looking for Me, let these men go." ⁹ This was to fulfill the words He had said: "I have not lost one of those You have given Me."

¹⁰ Then Simon Peter, who had a sword, drew it, struck the high priest's slave, and cut off his right ear. (The slave's name was Malchus.)

¹¹ At that, Jesus said to Peter, "Sheathe your sword! Am I not to drink the cup the Father has given Me?"

¹² Then the company of soldiers, the commander, and the Jewish temple police arrested Jesus and tied Him up. ¹³ First they led Him to Annas, for he was the father-in-law of Caiaphas, who was high priest that year. ¹⁴ Caiaphas was the one who had advised the Jews that it was advantageous that one man should die for the people.

¹⁵ Meanwhile, Simon Peter was following Jesus, as was another disciple. That disciple was an acquaintance of the high priest; so he went with Jesus into the high priest's courtyard.

¹⁶ But Peter remained standing outside by the door. So the other disciple, the one known to the high priest, went out and spoke to the girl who was the doorkeeper and brought Peter in.

¹⁷ Then the slave girl who was the doorkeeper said to Peter, "You aren't one of this man's disciples too, are you?"

"I am not!" he said. ¹⁸ Now the slaves and the temple police had made a charcoal fire, because it was cold. They were standing there warming themselves, and Peter was standing with them, warming himself.

¹⁹ The high priest questioned Jesus about His disciples and about His teaching.

²⁰ "I have spoken openly to the world," Jesus answered him. "I have always taught in the synagogue and in the temple complex, where all the Jews congregate, and I haven't spoken anything in secret. ²¹ Why do you question Me? Question those who heard what I told them. Look, they know what I said."

²² When He had said these things, one of the temple police standing by slapped Jesus, saying, "Is this the way you answer the high priest?"

²³ "If I have spoken wrongly," Jesus answered him, "give evidenceᴮ about the wrong; but if rightly, why do you hit Me?"

²⁴ Then Annas sent Him bound to Caiaphas the high priest.

²⁵ Now Simon Peter was standing and warming himself. They said to him, "You aren't one of His disciples too, are you?"

He denied it and said, "I am not!"

²⁶ One of the high priest's slaves, a relative of the man whose ear Peter had cut off, said, "Didn't I see you with Him in the garden?"

²⁷ Peter then denied it again. Immediately a rooster crowed.

²⁸ Then they took Jesus from Caiaphas to the governor's headquarters. It was early morning. They did not enter the headquarters themselves; otherwise they would be defiled and unable to eat the Passover.

²⁹ Then Pilate came out to them and said, "What charge do you bring against this man?"

³⁰ They answered him, "If this man weren't a criminal,ᶜ we wouldn't have handed Him over to you."

³¹ So Pilate told them, "Take Him yourselves and judge Him according to your law."

"It's not legalᴰ for us to put anyone to death," the Jews declared. ³² They said this so

---

ᴬ**18:5** Lit *I am*; see note at Jn 8:58.　ᴮ**18:23** Or *him, testify*　ᶜ**18:30** Lit *an evil doer*　ᴰ**18:31** According to Roman law that Jesus' words might be fulfilled signifying what kind of death He was going to die.

³³ Then Pilate went back into the headquarters, summoned Jesus, and said to Him, "Are You the King of the Jews?"

³⁴ Jesus answered, "Are you asking this on your own, or have others told you about Me?"

³⁵ "I'm not a Jew, am I?" Pilate replied. "Your own nation and the chief priests handed You over to me. What have You done?"

³⁶ "My kingdom is not of this world," said Jesus. "If My kingdom were of this world, My servantsᴬ would fight, so that I wouldn't be handed over to the Jews. As it is, My kingdom does not have its origin here."ᴮ

³⁷ "You are a king then?" Pilate asked.

"You say that I'm a king," Jesus replied. "I was born for this, and I have come into the world for this: to testify to the truth. Everyone who is of the truth listens to My voice."

³⁸ "What is truth?" said Pilate.

After he had said this, he went out to the Jews again and told them, "I find no grounds for charging Him. ³⁹ You have a custom that I release one prisoner to you at the Passover. So, do you want me to release to you the King of the Jews?"

⁴⁰ They shouted back, "Not this man, but Barabbas!" Now Barabbas was a revolutionary.ᶜ

19 Then Pilate took Jesus and had Him flogged. ² The soldiers also twisted together a crown of thorns, put it on His head, and threw a purple robe around Him. ³ And they repeatedly came up to Him and said, "Hail, King of the Jews!" and were slapping His face.

⁴ Pilate went outside again and said to them, "Look, I'm bringing Him outside to you to let you know I find no grounds for charging Him."

⁵ Then Jesus came out wearing the crown of thorns and the purple robe. Pilate said to them, "Here is the man!"

⁶ When the chief priests and the temple police saw Him, they shouted, "Crucify! Crucify!"

Pilate responded, "Take Him and crucify Him yourselves, for I find no grounds for charging Him."

⁷ "We have a law," the Jews replied to him, "and according to that law He must die, because He made Himselfᴰ the Son of God."

⁸ When Pilate heard this statement, he was more afraid than ever. ⁹ He went back into the headquarters and asked Jesus, "Where are You from?" But Jesus did not give him an answer. ¹⁰ So Pilate said to Him, "You're not talking to me? Don't You know that I have the authority to release You and the authority to crucify You?"

¹¹ "You would have no authority over Me at all," Jesus answered him, "if it hadn't been given you from above. This is why the one who handed Me over to you has the greater sin."ᴱ

¹² From that moment Pilate made every effortᶠ to release Him. But the Jews shouted, "If you release this man, you are not Caesar's friend. Anyone who makes himself a king opposes Caesar!"

¹³ When Pilate heard these words, he brought Jesus outside. He sat down on the judge's bench in a place called the Stone Pavement (but in Hebrew *Gabbatha*). ¹⁴ It was the preparation day for the Passover, and it was about six in the morning.ᴳ Then he told the Jews, "Here is your king!"

¹⁵ But they shouted, "Take Him away! Take Him away! Crucify Him!"

Pilate said to them, "Should I crucify your king?"

"We have no king but Caesar!" the chief priests answered.

¹⁶ So then, because of them, he handed Him over to be crucified.

Therefore they took Jesus away.ᴴ ¹⁷ Carrying His own cross, He went out to what is called Skull Place, which in Hebrew is called *Golgotha*. ¹⁸ There they crucified Him and two others with Him, one on either side, with Jesus in the middle. ¹⁹ Pilate also had a sign lettered and put on the cross. The inscription was:

JESUS THE NAZARENE
THE KING OF THE JEWS.

²⁰ Many of the Jews read this sign, because the place where Jesus was crucified was near the city, and it was written in Hebrew,ᴵ Latin, and Greek. ²¹ So the chief priests of the Jews said to Pilate, "Don't write, 'The King of the

---

ᴬ**18:36** Or *attendants,* or *helpers*   ᴮ**18:36** Lit *My kingdom is not from here*   ᶜ**18:40** Or *robber;* see Jn 10:1,8 for the same Gk word used here   ᴰ**19:7** He claimed to be   ᴱ**19:11** To *have sin* is an idiom that refers to guilt caused by sin.   ᶠ**19:12** Lit *Pilate was trying*   ᴳ**19:14** Lit *the sixth hour;* see note at Jn 1:39; an alt time reckoning would be *about noon*   ᴴ**19:16** Other mss add *and led Him out*   ᴵ**19:20** Or *Aramaic*

Jews,' but that He said, 'I am the King of the Jews.'"

²²Pilate replied, "What I have written, I have written."

²³When the soldiers crucified Jesus, they took His clothes and divided them into four parts, a part for each soldier. They also took the tunic, which was seamless, woven in one piece from the top. ²⁴So they said to one another, "Let's not tear it, but cast lots for it, to see who gets it." They did this to fulfill the Scripture that says: **They divided My clothes among themselves, and they cast lots for My clothing.**ᴬ And this is what the soldiers did.

²⁵Standing by the cross of Jesus were His mother, His mother's sister, Mary the wife of Clopas, and Mary Magdalene. ²⁶When Jesus saw His mother and the disciple He loved standing there, He said to His mother, "Woman, here is your son." ²⁷Then He said to the disciple, "Here is your mother." And from that hour the disciple took her into his home.

²⁸After this, when Jesus knew that everything was now accomplished that the Scripture might be fulfilled, He said, "I'm thirsty!" ²⁹A jar full of sour wine was sitting there; so they fixed a sponge full of sour wine on hyssopᴮ and held it up to His mouth.

³⁰When Jesus had received the sour wine, He said, "It is finished!" Then bowing His head, He gave up His spirit.

³¹Since it was the preparation day, the Jews did not want the bodies to remain on the cross on the Sabbath (for that Sabbath was a specialᶜ day). They requested that Pilate have the men's legs broken and that their bodies be taken away. ³²So the soldiers came and broke the legs of the first man and of the other one who had been crucified with Him. ³³When they came to Jesus, they did not break His legs since they saw that He was already dead. ³⁴But one of the soldiers pierced His side with a spear, and at once blood and water came out. ³⁵He who saw this has testified so that you also may believe. His testimony is true, and he knows he is telling the truth. ³⁶For these things happened so that the Scripture would be fulfilled: **Not one of His bones will be broken.**ᴰ ³⁷Also, another Scripture says: **They will look at the One they pierced.**ᴱ

³⁸After this, Joseph of Arimathea, who was a disciple of Jesus—but secretly because of his fear of the Jews—asked Pilate that he might remove Jesus' body. Pilate gave him permission, so he came and took His body away. ³⁹Nicodemus (who had previously come to Him at night) also came, bringing a mixture of about 75 poundsᶠ of myrrh and aloes. ⁴⁰Then they took Jesus' body and wrapped it in linen cloths with the aromatic spices, according to the burial custom of the Jews. ⁴¹There was a garden in the place where He was crucified. A new tomb was in the garden; no one had yet been placed in it. ⁴²They placed Jesus there because of the Jewish preparation and since the tomb was nearby.

20 On the first day of the week Mary Magdalene came to the tomb early, while it was still dark. She saw that the stone had been removedᴳ from the tomb. ²So she ran to Simon Peter and to the other disciple, the one Jesus loved, and said to them, "They have taken the Lord out of the tomb, and we don't know where they have put Him!"

³At that, Peter and the other disciple went out, heading for the tomb. ⁴The two were running together, but the other disciple outran Peter and got to the tomb first. ⁵Stooping down, he saw the linen cloths lying there, yet he did not go in. ⁶Then, following him, Simon Peter came also. He entered the tomb and saw the linen cloths lying there. ⁷The wrapping that had been on His head was not lying with the linen cloths but was folded up in a separate place by itself. ⁸The other disciple, who had reached the tomb first, then entered the tomb, saw, and believed. ⁹For they still did not understand the Scripture that He must rise from the dead. ¹⁰Then the disciples went home again.

¹¹But Mary stood outside facing the tomb, crying. As she was crying, she stooped to look into the tomb. ¹²She saw two angels in white sitting there, one at the head and one at the feet, where Jesus' body had been lying. ¹³They said to her, "Woman, why are you crying?"

"Because they've taken away my Lord," she told them, "and I don't know where they've put Him." ¹⁴Having said this, she turned around and saw Jesus standing there, though she did not know it was Jesus.

¹⁵"Woman," Jesus said to her, "why are you crying? Who is it you are looking for?"

ᴬ19:24 Ps 22:18   ᴮ19:29 Or with hyssop   ᶜ19:31 Lit great   ᴰ19:36 Ex 12:46; Nm 9:12; Ps 34:20   ᴱ19:37 Zch 12:10   ᶠ19:39 Lit 100 litrai; a Roman litrai = 12 ounces   ᴳ20:1 Lit She saw the stone removed

Supposing He was the gardener, she replied, "Sir, if you've removed Him, tell me where you've put Him, and I will take Him away."

[16] Jesus said, "Mary."

Turning around, she said to Him in Hebrew, *"Rabbouni!"*[A]—which means "Teacher."

[17] "Don't cling to Me," Jesus told her, "for I have not yet ascended to the Father. But go to My brothers and tell them that I am ascending to My Father and your Father—to My God and your God."

[18] Mary Magdalene went and announced to the disciples, "I have seen the Lord!" And she told them what[B] He had said to her.

[19] In the evening of that first day of the week, the disciples were gathered together with the doors locked because of their fear of the Jews. Then Jesus came, stood among them, and said to them, "Peace to you!"

[20] Having said this, He showed them His hands and His side. So the disciples rejoiced when they saw the Lord.

[21] Jesus said to them again, "Peace to you! As the Father has sent Me, I also send you."
[22] After saying this, He breathed on them and said,[C] "Receive the Holy Spirit. [23] If you forgive the sins of any, they are forgiven them; if you retain the sins of any, they are retained."

[24] But one of the Twelve, Thomas (called "Twin"), was not with them when Jesus came. [25] So the other disciples kept telling him, "We have seen the Lord!"

But he said to them, "If I don't see the mark of the nails in His hands, put my finger into the mark of the nails, and put my hand into His side, I will never believe!"

[26] After eight days His disciples were indoors again, and Thomas was with them. Even though the doors were locked, Jesus came and stood among them. He said, "Peace to you!"

[27] Then He said to Thomas, "Put your finger here and observe My hands. Reach out your hand and put it into My side. Don't be an unbeliever, but a believer."

[28] Thomas responded to Him, "My Lord and my God!"

[29] Jesus said, "Because you have seen Me, you have believed.[D] Those who believe without seeing are blessed."

[30] Jesus performed many other signs in the presence of His disciples that are not written in this book. [31] But these are written so that you may believe Jesus is the Messiah, the Son of God,[E] and by believing you may have life in His name.

21 After this, Jesus revealed Himself again to His disciples by the Sea of Tiberias.[F] He revealed Himself in this way:

[2] Simon Peter, Thomas (called "Twin"), Nathanael from Cana of Galilee, Zebedee's sons, and two others of His disciples were together.

[3] "I'm going fishing," Simon Peter said to them.

"We're coming with you," they told him. They went out and got into the boat, but that night they caught nothing.

[4] When daybreak came, Jesus stood on the shore. However, the disciples did not know it was Jesus.

[5] "Men,"[G] Jesus called to them, "you don't have any fish, do you?"

"No," they answered.

[6] "Cast the net on the right side of the boat," He told them, "and you'll find some." So they did,[H] and they were unable to haul it in because of the large number of fish. [7] Therefore the disciple, the one Jesus loved, said to Peter, "It is the Lord!"

When Simon Peter heard that it was the Lord, he tied his outer garment around him[I] (for he was stripped) and plunged into the sea. [8] But since they were not far from land (about 100 yards[J] away), the other disciples came in the boat, dragging the net full of fish. [9] When they got out on land, they saw a charcoal fire there, with fish lying on it, and bread.

[10] "Bring some of the fish you've just caught," Jesus told them. [11] So Simon Peter got up and hauled the net ashore, full of large fish—153 of them. Even though there were so many, the net was not torn.

[12] "Come and have breakfast," Jesus told them. None of the disciples dared ask Him, "Who are You?" because they knew it was the Lord. [13] Jesus came, took the bread, and gave it to them. He did the same with the fish.

[14] This was now the third time[K] Jesus appeared[L] to the disciples after He was raised from the dead.

A 20:16 *Rabbouni* is also used in Mk 10:51   B 20:18 Lit *these things*   C 20:22 Lit *He breathed and said to them*   D 20:29 Or *have you believed?* (as a question)   E 20:31 Or *that the Messiah, the Son of God, is Jesus*   F 21:1 The Sea of Galilee; *Sea of Tiberias* is used only in John; Jn 6:1,23   G 21:5 Lit *Children*   H 21:6 Lit *they cast*   I 21:7 Lit *he girded his garment*   J 21:8 Lit *about 200 cubits*   K 21:14 The other two are in Jn 20:19-29.   L 21:14 Lit *was revealed* (see v. 1)

¹⁵When they had eaten breakfast, Jesus asked Simon Peter, "Simon, son of John,ᴬ do you loveᴮ Me more than these?"

"Yes, Lord," he said to Him, "You know that I love You."

"Feed My lambs," He told him.

¹⁶A second time He asked him, "Simon, son of John, do you love Me?"

"Yes, Lord," he said to Him, "You know that I love You."

"Shepherd My sheep," He told him.

¹⁷He asked him the third time, "Simon, son of John, do you love Me?"

Peter was grieved that He asked him the third time, "Do you love Me?" He said, "Lord, You know everything! You know that I love You."

"Feed My sheep," Jesus said. ¹⁸"I assure you: When you were young, you would tie your belt and walk wherever you wanted. But when you grow old, you will stretch out your hands and someone else will tie you and carry you where you don't want to go." ¹⁹He said this to signify by what kind of death he would glorify God.ᶜ After saying this, He told him, "Follow Me!"

²⁰So Peter turned around and saw the disciple Jesus loved following them. That disciple was the one who had leaned back against Jesus at the supper and asked, "Lord, who is the one that's going to betray You?" ²¹When Peter saw him, he said to Jesus, "Lord—what about him?"

²²"If I want him to remain until I come," Jesus answered, "what is that to you? As for you, follow Me."

²³So this reportᴰ spread to the brothersᴱ that this disciple would not die. Yet Jesus did not tell him that he would not die, but, "If I want him to remain until I come, what is that to you?"

²⁴This is the disciple who testifies to these things and who wrote them down. We know that his testimony is true.

²⁵And there are also many other things that Jesus did, which, if they were written one by one, I suppose not even the world itself could contain the booksᶠ that would be written.

ACTS

1 I wrote the first narrative, Theophilus, about all that Jesus began to do and teach ²until the day He was taken up, after He had given orders through the Holy Spirit to the apostles He had chosen. ³After He had suffered, He also presented Himself alive to them by many convincing proofs, appearing to them during 40 days and speaking about the kingdom of God.

⁴While He was togetherᴳ with them, He commanded them not to leave Jerusalem, but to wait for the Father's promise. "This," He said, "is what you heard from Me; ⁵for John baptized with water, but you will be baptized with the Holy Spirit not many days from now."

⁶So when they had come together, they asked Him, "Lord, are You restoring the kingdom to Israel at this time?"

⁷He said to them, "It is not for you to know times or periods that the Father has set by His own authority. ⁸But you will receive power when the Holy Spirit has come on you, and you will be My witnesses in Jerusalem, in all Judea and Samaria, and to the endsᴴ of the earth."

⁹After He had said this, He was taken up as they were watching, and a cloud took Him out of their sight. ¹⁰While He was going, they were gazing into heaven, and suddenly two men in white clothes stood by them. ¹¹They said, "Men of Galilee, why do you stand looking up into heaven? This Jesus, who has been taken from you into heaven, will come in the same way that you have seen Him going into heaven."

¹²Then they returned to Jerusalem from the mount called the Mount of Olives, which is near Jerusalem—a Sabbath day's journey

ᴬ21:15-17 Other mss read *Simon, son of Jonah*; Mt 16:17; Jn 1:42   ᴮ21:15-17 Two synonyms are translated *love* in this conversation: *agapao*, the first 2 times by Jesus (vv. 15-16); and *phileo*, the last time by Jesus (v. 17) and all 3 times by Peter (vv. 15-17). Peter's threefold confession of love for Jesus corresponds to his earlier threefold denial of Jesus; Jn 18:15-18,25-27.   ᶜ21:19 Jesus predicts that Peter would be martyred. Church tradition says that Peter was crucified upside down.   ᴰ21:23 Lit *this word*   ᴱ21:23 The word *brothers* refers to the late first century Christian community.   ᶠ21:25 Lit *scroll*   ᴳ1:4 Or *He was eating*, or *He was lodging*   ᴴ1:8 Lit *the end* away. ¹³When they arrived, they went to the room upstairs where they were staying:

> Peter, John,
> James, Andrew,
> Philip, Thomas,
> Bartholomew, Matthew,
> James the son of Alphaeus,
> Simon the Zealot,
> and Judas the son of James.

¹⁴All these were continually united in prayer,ᴬ along with the women, including Maryᴮ the mother of Jesus, and His brothers.

¹⁵During these days Peter stood up among the brothersᶜ—the number of people who were together was about 120—and said: ¹⁶"Brothers, the Scripture had to be fulfilled that the Holy Spirit through the mouth of David spoke in advance about Judas, who became a guide to those who arrested Jesus. ¹⁷For he was one of our number and was allotted a share in this ministry." ¹⁸Now this man acquired a field with his unrighteous wages. He fell headfirst and burst open in the middle, and all his insides spilled out. ¹⁹This became known to all the residents of Jerusalem, so that in their own language that field is called *Hakeldama* (that is, Field of Blood). ²⁰"For it is written in the Book of Psalms:

> **Let his dwelling become desolate;**
> **let no one live in it;**ᴰ and
> **Let someone else take**
> **his position.**ᴱ

²¹"Therefore, from among the men who have accompanied us during the whole time the Lord Jesus went in and out among us— ²²beginning from the baptism of John until the day He was taken up from us—from among these, it is necessary that one become a witness with us of His resurrection."

²³So they proposed two: Joseph, called Barsabbas, who was also known as Justus, and Matthias. ²⁴Then they prayed, "You, Lord, know the hearts of all; show which of these two You have chosen ²⁵to take the placeᶠ in this apostolic service that Judas left to go to his own place." ²⁶Then they cast lots for them, and the lot fell to Matthias. So he was numbered with the 11 apostles.

2 When the day of Pentecost had arrived, they were all together in one place. ²Suddenly a sound like that of a violent rushing wind came from heaven, and it filled the whole house where they were staying. ³And tongues, like flames of fire that were divided, appeared to them and rested on each one of them. ⁴Then they were all filled with the Holy Spirit and began to speak in different languages, as the Spirit gave them ability for speech.

⁵There were Jews living in Jerusalem, devout men from every nation under heaven. ⁶When this sound occurred, a crowd came together and was confused because each one heard them speaking in his own language. ⁷And they were astounded and amazed, saying,ᴳ "Look, aren't all these who are speaking Galileans? ⁸How is it that each of us can hear in our own native language? ⁹Parthians, Medes, Elamites; those who live in Mesopotamia, in Judea and Cappadocia, Pontus and Asia, ¹⁰Phrygia and Pamphylia, Egypt and the parts of Libya near Cyrene; visitors from Rome, both Jews and proselytes, ¹¹Cretans and Arabs—we hear them speaking the magnificent acts of God in our own languages." ¹²They were all astounded and perplexed, saying to one another, "What could this be?" ¹³But some sneered and said, "They're full of new wine!"

¹⁴But Peter stood up with the Eleven, raised his voice, and proclaimed to them: "Men of Judah and all you residents of Jerusalem, let me explain thisᴴ to you and pay attention to my words. ¹⁵For these people are not drunk, as you suppose, since it's only nine in the morning.ᴵ ¹⁶On the contrary, this is what was spoken through the prophet Joel:

> ¹⁷ **And it will be** in the last days, says God,
> that **I will pour out My Spirit**
> **on all humanity;**
> **then your sons and your daughters**
> **will prophesy,**
> **your young men will see visions,**
> **and your old men will dream dreams.**
> ¹⁸ **I will even pour out My Spirit**
> **on My male and female slaves**
> **in those days,**
> and they will prophesy.
> ¹⁹ **I will display wonders**
> **in the heaven** above

ᴬ1:14 Other mss add *and petition*   ᴮ1:14 Or *prayer, with their wives and Mary*   ᶜ1:15 Other mss read *disciples*   ᴰ1:20 Ps 69:25   ᴱ1:20 Ps 109:8   ᶠ1:25 Other mss read *to share*   ᴳ2:7 Other mss add *to one another*   ᴴ2:14 Lit *let this be known*   ᴵ2:15 Lit *it's the third hour of the day*

and signs on the earth below:
blood and fire and a cloud of smoke.
20 The sun will be turned to darkness
and the moon to blood
before the great and remarkable Day
of the Lord comes.
21 Then everyone who calls
on the name of the Lord
will be saved.^A

22 "Men of Israel, listen to these words: This Jesus the Nazarene was a man pointed out to you by God with miracles, wonders, and signs that God did among you through Him, just as you yourselves know. 23 Though He was delivered up according to God's determined plan and foreknowledge, you used^B lawless people^C to nail Him to a cross and kill Him. 24 God raised Him up, ending the pains of death, because it was not possible for Him to be held by it. 25 For David says of Him:

I saw the Lord ever before me;
because He is at my right hand,
I will not be shaken.
26 Therefore my heart was glad,
and my tongue rejoiced.
Moreover, my flesh will rest in hope,
27 because You will not leave me
in Hades
or allow Your Holy One to see decay.
28 You have revealed the paths of life
to me;
You will fill me with gladness
in Your presence.^D

29 "Brothers, I can confidently speak to you about the patriarch David: He is both dead and buried, and his tomb is with us to this day. 30 Since he was a prophet, he knew that God had sworn an oath to him to seat one of his descendants^E,F on his throne. 31 Seeing this in advance, he spoke concerning the resurrection of the Messiah:

He^G was not left in Hades,
and His flesh did not
experience decay.^H

32 "God has resurrected this Jesus. We are all witnesses of this. 33 Therefore, since He has been exalted to the right hand of God and has

received from the Father the promised Holy Spirit, He has poured out what you both see and hear. 34 For it was not David who ascended into the heavens, but he himself says:

The Lord declared to my Lord,
'Sit at My right hand
35 until I make Your enemies
Your footstool.'^I

36 "Therefore let all the house of Israel know with certainty that God has made this Jesus, whom you crucified, both Lord and Messiah!"

37 When they heard this, they came under deep conviction^J and said to Peter and the rest of the apostles: "Brothers, what must we do?"

38 "Repent," Peter said to them, "and be baptized, each of you, in the name of Jesus Christ for the forgiveness of your sins, and you will receive the gift of the Holy Spirit. 39 For the promise is for you and for your children, and for all who are far off,^K as many as the Lord our God will call." 40 And with many other words he testified and strongly urged them, saying, "Be saved from this corrupt^L generation!"

41 So those who accepted his message were baptized, and that day about 3,000 people were added to them. 42 And they devoted themselves to the apostles' teaching, to the fellowship, to the breaking of bread, and to the prayers.

43 Then fear came over everyone, and many wonders and signs were being performed through the apostles. 44 Now all the believers were together and held all things in common. 45 They sold their possessions and property and distributed the proceeds to all, as anyone had a need.^M 46 Every day they devoted themselves to meeting together in the temple complex, and broke bread from house to house. They ate their food with a joyful and humble attitude, 47 praising God and having favor with all the people. And every day the Lord added to them^N those who were being saved.

3 Now Peter and John were going up together to the temple complex at the hour of prayer at three in the afternoon.^O 2 And a man who was lame from birth was carried there and placed every day at the temple gate called Beautiful, so he could beg from those entering the temple complex. 3 When he saw Peter and John about to enter the temple complex, he asked for help.

^A2:17-21 Jl 2:28-32   ^B2:23 Other mss read you have taken   ^C2:23 Or used the hand of lawless ones   ^D2:25-28 Ps 16:8-11   ^E2:30 Other mss add according to the flesh to raise up the Messiah   ^F2:30 Lit one from the fruit of his loin   ^G2:31 Other mss read His soul   ^H2:31 Ps 16:10   ^I2:34-35 Ps 110:1   ^J2:37 Lit they were pierced to the heart   ^K2:39 For distant generations or perhaps Gentiles   ^L2:40 Or crooked, or twisted   ^M2:45 Or to all, according to one's needs   ^N2:47 Other mss read to the church   ^O3:1 Lit at the ninth hour

⁴Peter, along with John, looked at him intently and said, "Look at us." ⁵So he turned to them,ᴬ expecting to get something from them. ⁶But Peter said, "I don't have silver or gold, but what I have, I give you: In the name of Jesus Christ the Nazarene, get up and walk!" ⁷Then, taking him by the right hand he raised him up, and at once his feet and ankles became strong. ⁸So he jumped up, stood, and started to walk, and he entered the temple complex with them—walking, leaping, and praising God. ⁹All the people saw him walking and praising God, ¹⁰and they recognized that he was the one who used to sit and beg at the Beautiful Gate of the temple complex. So they were filled with awe and astonishment at what had happened to him.

¹¹While heᴮ was holding on to Peter and John, all the people, greatly amazed, ran toward them in what is called Solomon's Colonnade. ¹²When Peter saw this, he addressed the people: "Men of Israel, why are you amazed at this? Or why do you stare at us, as though we had made him walk by our own power or godliness? ¹³The God of Abraham, Isaac, and Jacob, the God of our fathers, has glorified His Servant Jesus, whom you handed over and denied in the presence of Pilate, when he had decided to release Him. ¹⁴But you denied the Holy and Righteous One and asked to have a murderer given to you. ¹⁵You killed the sourceᶜ of life, whom God raised from the dead; we are witnesses of this. ¹⁶By faith in His name, His name has made this man strong, whom you see and know. So the faith that comes through Him has given him this perfect health in front of all of you.

¹⁷"And now, brothers, I know that you did it in ignorance, just as your leaders also did. ¹⁸But what God predicted through the mouth of all the prophets—that His Messiah would suffer—He has fulfilled in this way. ¹⁹Therefore repent and turn back, so that your sins may be wiped out, that seasons of refreshing may come from the presence of the Lord,ᴰ ²⁰and that He may send Jesus, who has been appointed for you as the Messiah. ²¹Heaven must welcomeᴱ Him until the times of the restoration of all things, which God spoke about by the mouth of His holy prophets from the beginning. ²²Moses said:ᶠ

The Lord your God will raise up for you a Prophet like me from among your brothers. You must listen to Him in everything He will say to you. ²³**And everyone who will not listen to that Prophet will be completely cut off from the people.**ᴳ

²⁴"In addition, all the prophets who have spoken, from Samuel and those after him, have also announced these days. ²⁵You are the sons of the prophets and of the covenant that God made with your ancestors, saying to Abraham, **And all the families of the earth will be blessed through your offspring.**ᴴ ²⁶God raised up His Servantⁱ and sent Him first to you to bless you by turning each of you from your evil ways."

4 Now as they were speaking to the people, the priests, the commander of the temple police, and the Sadducees confronted them, ²because they were provoked that they were teaching the people and proclaiming the resurrection from the dead, using Jesus as the example.ᴶ ³So they seized them and put them in custody until the next day, since it was already evening. ⁴But many of those who heard the message believed, and the number of the men came to about 5,000.

⁵The next day, their rulers, elders, and scribes assembled in Jerusalem ⁶with Annas the high priest, Caiaphas, John and Alexander, and all the members of the high-priestly family.ᴷ ⁷After they had Peter and John stand before them, they asked the question: "By what power or in what name have you done this?"

⁸Then Peter was filled with the Holy Spirit and said to them, "Rulers of the people and elders:ᴸ ⁹If we are being examined today about a good deed done to a disabled man—by what means he was healed— ¹⁰let it be known to all of you and to all the people of Israel, that by the name of Jesus Christ the Nazarene—whom you crucified and whom God raised from the dead—by Him this man is standing here before you healthy. ¹¹This Jesus is

the stone rejected by you builders, which has become the cornerstone.ᴹ,ᴺ

ᴬ**3:5** Or *he paid attention to them*   ᴮ**3:11** Other mss read *the lame man who was healed*   ᶜ**3:15** Or *the Prince,* or *the Ruler*   ᴰ**3:19** Some editors or translators put *that seasons . . . the Lord* in v. 20   ᴱ**3:21** Or *receive,* or *retain*   ᶠ**3:22** Other mss add *to the fathers*   ᴳ**3:22-23** Dt 18:15-19   ᴴ**3:25** Gn 12:3; 18:18; 22:18; 26:4   ⁱ**3:26** Other mss add *Jesus*   ᴶ**4:2** Lit *proclaiming in Jesus the resurrection from the dead*   ᴷ**4:6** Or *high-priestly class,* or *high-priestly clan*   ᴸ**4:8** Other mss add *of Israel*   ᴹ**4:11** Lit *the head of the corner*   ᴺ**4:11** Ps 118:22

Turn to page 219 and find 1 John 1:9.

¹²There is salvation in no one else, for there is no other name under heaven given to people, and we must be saved by it."

¹³When they observed the boldness of Peter and John and realized that they were uneducated and untrained men, they were amazed and recognized that they had been with Jesus. ¹⁴And since they saw the man who had been healed standing with them, they had nothing to say in response. ¹⁵After they had ordered them to leave the Sanhedrin, they conferred among themselves, ¹⁶saying, "What should we do with these men? For an obvious sign, evident to all who live in Jerusalem, has been done through them, and we cannot deny it! ¹⁷However, so this does not spread any further among the people, let's threaten them against speaking to anyone in this name again." ¹⁸So they called for them and ordered them not to preach or teach at all in the name of Jesus.

¹⁹But Peter and John answered them, "Whether it's right in the sight of God for us to listen to you rather than to God, you decide; ²⁰for we are unable to stop speaking about what we have seen and heard."

²¹After threatening them further, they released them. They found no way to punish them, because the people were all giving glory to God over what had been done; ²²for this sign of healing had been performed on a man over 40 years old.

²³After they were released, they went to their own people and reported everything the chief priests and the elders had said to them. ²⁴When they heard this, they all raised their voices to God and said, "Master, You are the One who made the heaven, the earth, and the sea, and everything in them. ²⁵You said through the Holy Spirit, by the mouth of our father David Your servant:ᴬ

> Why did the Gentiles rage
> and the peoples plot futile things?
> ²⁶ The kings of the earth took their stand
> and the rulers assembled together
> against the Lord and
> against His Messiah.ᴮ

²⁷"For, in fact, in this city both Herod and Pontius Pilate, with the Gentiles and the peopleᶜ of Israel, assembled together against Your holy Servant Jesus, whom You anointed, ²⁸to do whatever Your hand and Your plan had predestined to take place. ²⁹And now, Lord, consider their threats, and grant that Your slaves may speak Your message with complete boldness, ³⁰while You stretch out Your hand for healing, signs, and wonders to be performed through the name of Your holy Servant Jesus." ³¹When they had prayed, the place where they were assembled was shaken, and they were all filled with the Holy Spirit and began to speak God's message with boldness.

³²Now the large group of those who believed were of one heart and mind, and no one said that any of his possessions was his own, but instead they held everything in common. ³³And the apostles were giving testimony with great power to the resurrection of the Lord Jesus, and great grace was on all of them. ³⁴For there was not a needy person among them, because all those who owned lands or houses sold them, brought the proceeds of the things that were sold, ³⁵and laid them at the apostles' feet. This was then distributed for each person's basic needs.ᴰ

³⁶Joseph, a Levite and a Cypriot by birth, the one the apostles called Barnabas, which is translated Son of Encouragement, ³⁷sold a field he owned, brought the money, and laid it at the apostles' feet.

5 But a man named Ananias, with his wife Sapphira, sold a piece of property. ²However, he kept back part of the proceeds with his wife's knowledge, and brought a portion of it and laid it at the apostles' feet.

³Then Peter said, "Ananias, why has Satan filled your heart to lie to the Holy Spirit and keep back part of the proceeds from the field? ⁴Wasn't it yours while you possessed it? And after it was sold, wasn't it at your disposal? Why is it that you planned this thing in your heart? You have not lied to men but to God!" ⁵When he heard these words, Ananias dropped dead, and a great fear came on all who heard. ⁶The young men got up, wrapped his body, carried him out, and buried him.

⁷There was an interval of about three hours; then his wife came in, not knowing what had happened. ⁸"Tell me," Peter asked her, "did you sell the field for this price?"

"Yes," she said, "for that price."

⁹Then Peter said to her, "Why did you agree to test the Spirit of the Lord? Look! The feet of

---

ᴬ4:25 Other mss read *through the mouth of David Your servant*   ᴮ4:25-26 Ps 2:1-2   ᶜ4:27 Lit *peoples*   ᴰ4:35 Lit *person as anyone had need*

Turn to page 140 and find Romans 5:8.

those who have buried your husband are at the door, and they will carry you out!"

[10] Instantly she dropped dead at his feet. When the young men came in, they found her dead, carried her out, and buried her beside her husband. [11] Then great fear came on the whole church and on all who heard these things.

[12] Many signs and wonders were being done among the people through the hands of the apostles. By common consent they would all meet in Solomon's Colonnade. [13] None of the rest dared to join them, but the people praised them highly. [14] Believers were added to the Lord in increasing numbers—crowds of both men and women. [15] As a result, they would carry the sick out into the streets and lay them on cots and mats so that when Peter came by, at least his shadow might fall on some of them. [16] In addition, a large group came together from the towns surrounding Jerusalem, bringing sick people and those who were tormented by unclean spirits, and they were all healed. [17] Then the high priest took action. He and all his colleagues, those who belonged to the party of the Sadducees, were filled with jealousy. [18] So they arrested[A] the apostles and put them in the city jail. [19] But an angel of the Lord opened the doors of the jail during the night, brought them out, and said, [20] "Go and stand in the temple complex, and tell the people all about this life." [21] In obedience to this, they entered the temple complex at daybreak and began to teach.

When the high priest and those who were with him arrived, they convened the Sanhedrin—the full Senate of the sons of Israel—and sent orders to the jail to have them brought. [22] But when the temple police got there, they did not find them in the jail, so they returned and reported, [23] "We found the jail securely locked, with the guards standing in front of the doors, but when we opened them, we found no one inside!" [24] As[B] the commander of the temple police and the chief priests heard these things, they were baffled about them, as to what could come of this.

[25] Someone came and reported to them, "Look! The men you put in jail are standing in the temple complex and teaching the people." [26] Then the commander went with the temple police and brought them in without force, be-

cause they were afraid the people might stone them. [27] After they brought them in, they had them stand before the Sanhedrin, and the high priest asked, [28] "Didn't we strictly order you not to teach in this name? And look, you have filled Jerusalem with your teaching and are determined to bring this man's blood on us!"

[29] But Peter and the apostles replied, "We must obey God rather than men. [30] The God of our fathers raised up Jesus, whom you had murdered by hanging Him on a tree. [31] God exalted this man to His right hand as ruler and Savior, to grant repentance to Israel, and forgiveness of sins. [32] We are witnesses of these things, and so is the Holy Spirit whom God has given to those who obey Him."

[33] When they heard this, they were enraged and wanted to kill them. [34] A Pharisee named Gamaliel, a teacher of the law who was respected by all the people, stood up in the Sanhedrin and ordered the men[C] to be taken outside for a little while. [35] He said to them, "Men of Israel, be careful about what you're going to do to these men. [36] Not long ago Theudas rose up, claiming to be somebody, and a group of about 400 men rallied to him. He was killed, and all his partisans were dispersed and came to nothing. [37] After this man, Judas the Galilean rose up in the days of the census and attracted a following.[D] That man also perished, and all his partisans were scattered. [38] And now, I tell you, stay away from these men and leave them alone. For if this plan or this work is of men, it will be overthrown; [39] but if it is of God, you will not be able to overthrow them. You may even be found fighting against God." So they were persuaded by him. [40] After they called in the apostles and had them flogged, they ordered them not to speak in the name of Jesus and released them. [41] Then they went out from the presence of the Sanhedrin, rejoicing that they were counted worthy to be dishonored on behalf of the Name.[E] [42] Every day in the temple complex, and in various homes, they continued teaching and proclaiming the good news that Jesus is the Messiah.

6 In those days, as the number of the disciples was multiplying, there arose a complaint by the Hellenistic Jews[F] against the Hebraic Jews[G] that their widows were being overlooked in the daily distribution. [2] Then the Twelve summoned the whole company

A5:18 Lit laid hands on   B5:24 Other mss add the high priest and   C5:34 Other mss read apostles   D5:37 Lit and drew people after him
E5:41 Other mss add of Jesus, or of Christ   F6:1 Jews of Gk language and culture   G6:1 Jews of Aram or Hb language and culture

of the disciples and said, "It would not be right for us to give up preaching about God to handle financial matters.[A] ³Therefore, brothers, select from among you seven men of good reputation, full of the Spirit and wisdom, whom we can appoint to this duty. ⁴But we will devote ourselves to prayer and to the preaching ministry." ⁵The proposal pleased the whole company. So they chose Stephen, a man full of faith and the Holy Spirit, and Philip, Prochorus, Nicanor, Timon, Parmenas, and Nicolaus, a proselyte from Antioch. ⁶They had them stand before the apostles, who prayed and laid their hands on them.[B]

⁷So the preaching about God flourished, the number of the disciples in Jerusalem multiplied greatly, and a large group of priests became obedient to the faith.

⁸Stephen, full of grace and power, was performing great wonders and signs among the people. ⁹Then some from what is called the Freedmen's Synagogue, composed of both Cyrenians and Alexandrians, and some from Cilicia and Asia, came forward and disputed with Stephen. ¹⁰But they were unable to stand up against his wisdom and the Spirit by whom he was speaking.

¹¹Then they persuaded some men to say, "We heard him speaking blasphemous words against Moses and God!" ¹²They stirred up the people, the elders, and the scribes; so they came, dragged him off, and took him to the Sanhedrin. ¹³They also presented false witnesses who said, "This man does not stop speaking blasphemous words against this holy place and the law. ¹⁴For we heard him say that Jesus, this Nazarene, will destroy this place and change the customs that Moses handed down to us." ¹⁵And all who were sitting in the Sanhedrin looked intently at him and saw that his face was like the face of an angel.

7 "Is this true?"[C] the high priest asked.
²"Brothers and fathers," he said, "listen: The God of glory appeared to our father Abraham when he was in Mesopotamia, before he settled in Haran, ³and said to him:

Get out of your country
and away from your relatives,
and come to the land
that I will show you.[D]

⁴"Then he came out of the land of the Chaldeans and settled in Haran. From there, after his father died, God had him move to this land you now live in. ⁵He didn't give him an inheritance in it, not even a foot of ground, but He promised to give it to him as a possession, and to his descendants after him, even though he was childless. ⁶God spoke in this way:

His descendants would be strangers
in a foreign country,
and they would enslave
and oppress them 400 years.
⁷ I will judge the nation
that they will serve as slaves, God said.
After this, they will come out
and worship Me in this place.[E]

⁸Then He gave him the covenant of circumcision. After this, he fathered Isaac and circumcised him on the eighth day; Isaac did the same with Jacob, and Jacob with the 12 patriarchs.

⁹"The patriarchs became jealous of Joseph and sold him into Egypt, but God was with him ¹⁰and rescued him out of all his troubles. He gave him favor and wisdom in the sight of Pharaoh, king of Egypt, who appointed him ruler over Egypt and over his whole household. ¹¹Then a famine and great suffering came over all of Egypt and Canaan, and our ancestors could find no food. ¹²When Jacob heard there was grain in Egypt, he sent our ancestors the first time. ¹³The second time, Joseph was revealed to his brothers, and Joseph's family became known to Pharaoh. ¹⁴Joseph then invited his father Jacob and all his relatives, 75 people in all, ¹⁵and Jacob went down to Egypt. He and our ancestors died there, ¹⁶were carried back to Shechem, and were placed in the tomb that Abraham had bought for a sum of silver from the sons of Hamor in Shechem.

¹⁷"As the time was drawing near to fulfill the promise that God had made to Abraham, the people flourished and multiplied in Egypt ¹⁸until a different king who did not know Joseph ruled over Egypt.[F] ¹⁹He dealt deceitfully with our race and oppressed our ancestors by making them leave their infants outside, so they wouldn't survive.[G] ²⁰At this time Moses was born, and he was beautiful in God's sight. He was cared for in his father's home three months, ²¹and when he was left outside, Pha-

raoh's daughter adopted and raised him as her own son. ²²So Moses was educated in all the wisdom of the Egyptians and was powerful in his speech and actions.

²³"As he was approaching the age of 40, he decided^A to visit his brothers, the Israelites. ²⁴When he saw one of them being mistreated, he came to his rescue and avenged the oppressed man by striking down the Egyptian. ²⁵He assumed his brothers would understand that God would give them deliverance through him, but they did not understand. ²⁶The next day he showed up while they were fighting and tried to reconcile them peacefully, saying, 'Men, you are brothers. Why are you mistreating each other?'

²⁷"But the one who was mistreating his neighbor pushed him^B away, saying:

Who appointed you a ruler and a judge over us? ²⁸Do you want to kill me, the same way you killed the Egyptian yesterday?^C

²⁹"At this disclosure, Moses fled and became an exile in the land of Midian, where he fathered two sons. ³⁰After 40 years had passed, an angel^D appeared to him in the wilderness of Mount Sinai, in the flame of a burning bush. ³¹When Moses saw it, he was amazed at the sight. As he was approaching to look at it, the voice of the Lord came: ³²**I am the God of your fathers—the God of Abraham, of Isaac, and of Jacob.^E** So Moses began to tremble and did not dare to look.

³³"Then the Lord said to him:

Remove the sandals from your feet, for the place where you are standing is holy ground. ³⁴I have observed the oppression of My people in Egypt; I have heard their groaning and have come down to rescue them. And now, come, I will send you to Egypt.^F

³⁵"This Moses, whom they rejected when they said, **Who appointed you a ruler and a judge?^C**—this one God sent as a ruler and a redeemer by means of the angel who appeared to him in the bush. ³⁶This man led them out and performed wonders and signs in the land

of Egypt, at the Red Sea, and in the wilderness 40 years.

³⁷"This is the Moses who said to the Israelites, **God^G will raise up for you a Prophet like me from among your brothers.^H ³⁸**He is the one who was in the congregation in the wilderness together with the angel who spoke to him on Mount Sinai, and with our ancestors. He received living oracles to give to us. ³⁹Our ancestors were unwilling to obey him, but pushed him away, and in their hearts turned back to Egypt. ⁴⁰They told Aaron:

Make us gods who will go before us. As for this Moses who brought us out of the land of Egypt, we don't know what's happened to him.^I

⁴¹They even made a calf in those days, offered sacrifice to the idol, and were celebrating what their hands had made. ⁴²Then God turned away and gave them up to worship the host of heaven, as it is written in the book of the prophets:

House of Israel, did you bring Me offerings and sacrifices 40 years in the wilderness?
⁴³ **No, you took up the tent of Moloch^J and the star of your god Rephan,^K the images that you made to worship. So I will deport you beyond Babylon!^L**

⁴⁴"Our ancestors had the tabernacle of the testimony in the wilderness, just as He who spoke to Moses commanded him to make it according to the pattern he had seen. ⁴⁵Our ancestors in turn received it and with Joshua brought it in when they dispossessed the nations that God drove out before our fathers, until the days of David. ⁴⁶He found favor in God's sight and asked that he might provide a dwelling place for the God^M of Jacob. ⁴⁷But it was Solomon who built Him a house. ⁴⁸However, the Most High does not dwell in sanctuaries made with hands, as the prophet says:

⁴⁹ **Heaven is My throne, and earth My footstool. What sort of house will you build for Me? says the Lord, or what is My resting place?**

^A**7:23** Lit 40, it came into his heart   ^B**7:27** Moses   ^C**7:27-28,35** Ex 2:14   ^D**7:30** Other mss add of the Lord   ^E**7:32** Ex 3:6,15   ^F**7:33-34** Ex 3:5,7-8,10   ^G**7:37** Other mss read 'The Lord your God   ^H**7:37** Dt 18:15   ^I**7:40** Ex 32:1,23   ^J**7:43** Canaanite or Phoenician sky or sun god   ^K**7:43** Perhaps an Assyrian star god—the planet Saturn   ^L**7:42-43** Am 5:25-27   ^M**7:46** Other mss read house

⁵⁰ **Did not My hand make all
these things?**ᴬ

⁵¹"You stiff-necked people with uncircumcised hearts and ears! You are always resisting the Holy Spirit; as your ancestors did, so do you. ⁵²Which of the prophets did your fathers not persecute? They even killed those who announced beforehand the coming of the Righteous One, whose betrayers and murderers you have now become. ⁵³You received the law under the direction of angels and yet have not kept it."

⁵⁴When they heard these things, they were enraged in their heartsᴮ and gnashed their teeth at him. ⁵⁵But Stephen, filled by the Holy Spirit, gazed into heaven. He saw God's glory, withᶜ Jesus standing at the right hand of God, and he said, ⁵⁶"Look! I see the heavens opened and the Son of Man standing at the right hand of God!"

⁵⁷Then they screamed at the top of their voices, covered their ears, and together rushed against him. ⁵⁸They threw him out of the city and began to stone him. And the witnesses laid their robes at the feet of a young man named Saul. ⁵⁹They were stoning Stephen as he called out: "Lord Jesus, receive my spirit!" ⁶⁰Then he knelt down and cried out with a loud voice, "Lord, do not charge them with this sin!" And saying this, he fell asleep.

8 Saul agreed with putting him to death. On that day a severe persecution broke out against the church in Jerusalem, and all except the apostles were scattered throughout the land of Judea and Samaria. ²Devout men buried Stephen and mourned deeply over him. ³Saul, however, was ravaging the church. He would enter house after house, drag off men and women, and put them in prison.

⁴So those who were scattered went on their way preaching the message of good news. ⁵Philip went down to aᴰ city in Samaria and proclaimed the Messiah to them. ⁶The crowds paid attention with one mind to what Philip said, as they heard and saw the signs he was performing. ⁷For unclean spirits, crying out with a loud voice, came out of many who were possessed, and many who were paralyzed and lame were healed. ⁸So there was great joy in that city.

⁹A man named Simon had previously practiced sorcery in that city and astounded the Samaritan people, while claiming to be somebody great. ¹⁰They all paid attention to him, from the least of them to the greatest, and they said, "This man is called the Great Power of God!"ᴱ ¹¹They were attentive to him because he had astounded them with his sorceries for a long time. ¹²But when they believed Philip, as he preached the good news about the kingdom of God and the name of Jesus Christ, both men and women were baptized. ¹³Then even Simon himself believed. And after he was baptized, he went around constantly withᶠ Philip and was astounded as he observed the signs and great miracles that were being performed.

¹⁴When the apostles who were at Jerusalem heard that Samaria had welcomed God's message, they sent Peter and John to them. ¹⁵After they went down there, they prayed for them, so the Samaritans might receive the Holy Spirit. ¹⁶For He had not yet come down onᴳ any of them; they had only been baptized in the name of the Lord Jesus. ¹⁷Then Peter and John laid their hands on them, and they received the Holy Spirit.

¹⁸When Simon saw that the Holyᴴ Spirit was given through the laying on of the apostles' hands, he offered them money, ¹⁹saying, "Give me this power too, so that anyone I lay hands on may receive the Holy Spirit."

²⁰But Peter told him, "May your silver be destroyed with you, because you thought the gift of God could be obtained with money! ²¹You have no part or share in this matter, because your heart is not right before God. ²²Therefore repent of this wickedness of yours, and pray to the Lord that the intent of your heart may be forgiven you. ²³For I see you are poisoned by bitterness and bound by iniquity."

²⁴"Please prayᴵ to the Lord for me," Simon replied, "so that nothing you have said may happen to me."

²⁵Then, after they had testified and spoken the message of the Lord, they traveled back to Jerusalem, evangelizing many villages of the Samaritans.

²⁶An angel of the Lord spoke to Philip: "Get up and go south to the road that goes down from Jerusalem to Gaza." (This is the desert road.)ᴶ ²⁷So he got up and went. There was an

Ethiopian man, a eunuch and high official of Candace, queen of the Ethiopians,[A] who was in charge of her entire treasury. He had come to worship in Jerusalem [28] and was sitting in his chariot on his way home, reading the prophet Isaiah aloud. [29] The Spirit told Philip, "Go and join that chariot."

[30] When Philip ran up to it, he heard him reading the prophet Isaiah, and said, "Do you understand what you're reading?"

[31] "How can I," he said, "unless someone guides me?" So he invited Philip to come up and sit with him. [32] Now the Scripture passage he was reading was this:

> He was led like a sheep
>   to the slaughter,
> and as a lamb is silent
>   before its shearer,
> so He does not open His mouth.
> [33]   In His humiliation justice
>   was denied Him.
> Who will describe His generation?
> For His life is taken
>   from the earth.[B]

[34] The eunuch replied to Philip, "I ask you, who is the prophet saying this about—himself or another person?" [35] So Philip proceeded[C] to tell him the good news about Jesus, beginning from that Scripture.

[36] As they were traveling down the road, they came to some water. The eunuch said, "Look, there's water! What would keep me from being baptized?" [[37] And Philip said, "If you believe with all your heart you may." And he replied, "I believe that Jesus Christ is the Son of God."][D] [38] Then he ordered the chariot to stop, and both Philip and the eunuch went down into the water, and he baptized him. [39] When they came up out of the water, the Spirit of the Lord carried Philip away, and the eunuch did not see him any longer. But he went on his way rejoicing. [40] Philip appeared in[E] Azotus,[F] and he was traveling and evangelizing all the towns until he came to Caesarea.

9 Meanwhile, Saul was still breathing threats and murder against the disciples of the Lord. He went to the high priest [2] and requested letters from him to the synagogues in Damascus, so that if he found any men or women who belonged to the Way, he might

bring them as prisoners to Jerusalem. [3] As he traveled and was nearing Damascus, a light from heaven suddenly flashed around him. [4] Falling to the ground, he heard a voice saying to him, "Saul, Saul, why are you persecuting Me?"

[5] "Who are You, Lord?" he said.

"I am Jesus, the One you are persecuting," He replied. [6] "But get up and go into the city, and you will be told what you must do."

[7] The men who were traveling with him stood speechless, hearing the sound but seeing no one. [8] Then Saul got up from the ground, and though his eyes were open, he could see nothing. So they took him by the hand and led him into Damascus. [9] He was unable to see for three days and did not eat or drink.

[10] There was a disciple in Damascus named Ananias. And the Lord said to him in a vision, "Ananias!"

"Here I am, Lord!" he said.

[11] "Get up and go to the street called Straight," the Lord said to him, "to the house of Judas, and ask for a man from Tarsus named Saul, since he is praying there. [12] In a vision[G] he has seen a man named Ananias coming in and placing his hands on him so he can regain his sight."

[13] "Lord," Ananias answered, "I have heard from many people about this man, how much harm he has done to Your saints in Jerusalem. [14] And he has authority here from the chief priests to arrest all who call on Your name."

[15] But the Lord said to him, "Go! For this man is My chosen instrument to take My name to Gentiles, kings, and the Israelites. [16] I will show him how much he must suffer for My name!"

[17] So Ananias left and entered the house. Then he placed his hands on him and said, "Brother Saul, the Lord Jesus, who appeared to you on the road you were traveling, has sent me so that you can regain your sight and be filled with the Holy Spirit."

[18] At once something like scales fell from his eyes, and he regained his sight. Then he got up and was baptized. [19] And after taking some food, he regained his strength.

Saul was with the disciples in Damascus for some days. [20] Immediately he began proclaiming Jesus in the synagogues: "He is the Son of God."

^A 8:27 = Nubia   ^B 8:32-33 Is 53:7-8   ^C 8:35 Lit Philip opened his mouth   ^D 8:37 Other mss omit bracketed text   ^E 8:40 Or Philip was found at, or Philip found himself in   ^F 8:40 Or Ashdod   ^G 9:12 Other mss omit In a vision

²¹But all who heard him were astounded and said, "Isn't this the man who, in Jerusalem, was destroying those who called on this name and then came here for the purpose of taking them as prisoners to the chief priests?"

²²But Saul grew more capable and kept confounding the Jews who lived in Damascus by proving that this One is the Messiah.

²³After many days had passed, the Jews conspired to kill him, ²⁴but their plot became known to Saul. So they were watching the gates day and night intending to kill him, ²⁵but his disciples took him by night and lowered him in a large basket through an opening in the wall.

²⁶When he arrived in Jerusalem, he tried to associate with the disciples, but they were all afraid of him, since they did not believe he was a disciple. ²⁷Barnabas, however, took him and brought him to the apostles and explained to them how Saul had seen the Lord on the road and that He had talked to him, and how in Damascus he had spoken boldly in the name of Jesus. ²⁸Saul was coming and going with them in Jerusalem, speaking boldly in the name of the Lord. ²⁹He conversed and debated with the Hellenistic Jews,ᴬ but they attempted to kill him. ³⁰When the brothers found out, they took him down to Caesarea and sent him off to Tarsus.

³¹So the church throughout all Judea, Galilee, and Samaria had peace, being built up and walking in the fear of the Lord and in the encouragement of the Holy Spirit, and it increased in numbers.

³²As Peter was traveling from place to place,ᴮ he also came down to the saints who lived in Lydda. ³³There he found a man named Aeneas, who was paralyzed and had been bedridden for eight years. ³⁴Peter said to him, "Aeneas, Jesus Christ heals you. Get up and make your bed,"ᶜ and immediately he got up. ³⁵So all who lived in Lydda and Sharon saw him and turned to the Lord.

³⁶In Joppa there was a disciple named Tabitha, which is translated Dorcas.ᴰ She was always doing good works and acts of charity. ³⁷In those days she became sick and died. After washing her, they placed her in a room upstairs. ³⁸Since Lydda was near Joppa, the disciples heard that Peter was there and sent two men to him who begged him, "Don't

delay in coming with us." ³⁹So Peter got up and went with them. When he arrived, they led him to the room upstairs. And all the widows approached him, weeping and showing him the robes and clothes that Dorcas had made while she was with them. ⁴⁰Then Peter sent them all out of the room. He knelt down, prayed, and turning toward the body said, "Tabitha, get up!" She opened her eyes, saw Peter, and sat up. ⁴¹He gave her his hand and helped her stand up. Then he called the saints and widows and presented her alive. ⁴²This became known throughout Joppa, and many believed in the Lord. ⁴³And Peter stayed on many days in Joppa with Simon, a leather tanner.ᴱ

10 There was a man in Caesarea named Cornelius, a centurion of what was called the Italian Regiment. ²He was a devout man and feared God along with his whole household. He did many charitable deeds for the Jewish people and always prayed to God. ³About three in the afternoonᶠ he distinctly saw in a vision an angel of God who came in and said to him, "Cornelius!"

⁴Looking intently at him, he became afraid and said, "What is it, lord?"

The angel told him, "Your prayers and your acts of charity have come up as a memorial offering before God. ⁵Now send men to Joppa and call for Simon, who is also named Peter. ⁶He is lodging with Simon, a tanner, whose house is by the sea."

⁷When the angel who spoke to him had gone, he called two of his household slaves and a devout soldier, who was one of those who attended him. ⁸After explaining everything to them, he sent them to Joppa.

⁹The next day, as they were traveling and nearing the city, Peter went up to pray on the housetop about noon.ᴳ ¹⁰Then he became hungry and wanted to eat, but while they were preparing something, he went into a visionary state. ¹¹He saw heaven opened and an object that resembled a large sheet coming down, being lowered by its four corners to the earth. ¹²In it were all the four-footed animals and reptiles of the earth, and the birds of the sky. ¹³Then a voice said to him, "Get up, Peter; kill and eat!"

ᴬ9:29 Lit Hellenists; that is, Gk-speaking Jews   ᴮ9:32 Lit Peter was passing through all   ᶜ9:34 Or and get ready to eat   ᴰ9:36 = Gazelle
ᴱ9:43 Tanners were considered ritually unclean because of their occupation.   ᶠ10:3 Lit About the ninth hour   ᴳ10:9 Lit about the sixth hour

¹⁴"No, Lord!" Peter said. "For I have never eaten anything common^A and ritually unclean!"

¹⁵Again, a second time, a voice said to him, "What God has made clean, you must not call common." ¹⁶This happened three times, and then the object was taken up into heaven.

¹⁷While Peter was deeply perplexed about what the vision he had seen might mean, the men who had been sent by Cornelius, having asked directions to Simon's house, stood at the gate. ¹⁸They called out, asking if Simon, who was also named Peter, was lodging there.

¹⁹While Peter was thinking about the vision, the Spirit told him, "Three men are here looking for you. ²⁰Get up, go downstairs, and accompany them with no doubts at all, because I have sent them."

²¹Then Peter went down to the men and said, "Here I am, the one you're looking for. What is the reason you're here?"

²²They said, "Cornelius, a centurion, an upright and God-fearing man, who has a good reputation with the whole Jewish nation, was divinely directed by a holy angel to call you to his house and to hear a message from you." ²³Peter then invited them in and gave them lodging.

The next day he got up and set out with them, and some of the brothers from Joppa went with him. ²⁴The following day he entered Caesarea. Now Cornelius was expecting them and had called together his relatives and close friends. ²⁵When Peter entered, Cornelius met him, fell at his feet, and worshiped him.

²⁶But Peter helped him up and said, "Stand up! I myself am also a man." ²⁷While talking with him, he went on in and found that many had come together there. ²⁸Peter said to them, "You know it's forbidden for a Jewish man to associate with or visit a foreigner. But God has shown me that I must not call any person common or unclean. ²⁹That's why I came without any objection when I was sent for. So I ask: Why did you send for me?"

³⁰Cornelius replied, "Four days ago at this hour, at three in the afternoon,^B I was^C praying in my house. Just then a man in a dazzling robe stood before me ³¹and said, 'Cornelius, your prayer has been heard, and your acts of charity have been remembered in God's sight. ³²Therefore send someone to Joppa and invite Simon here, who is also named Peter. He is lodging in Simon the tanner's house by the sea.'^D ³³Therefore I immediately sent for you, and you did the right thing in coming. So we are all present before God, to hear everything you have been commanded by the Lord."

³⁴Then Peter began to speak: "Now I really understand that God doesn't show favoritism, ³⁵but in every nation the person who fears Him and does righteousness is acceptable to Him. ³⁶He sent the message to the Israelites, proclaiming the good news of peace through Jesus Christ—He is Lord of all. ³⁷You know the events^E that took place throughout Judea, beginning from Galilee after the baptism that John preached: ³⁸how God anointed Jesus of Nazareth with the Holy Spirit and with power, and how He went about doing good and healing all who were under the tyranny of the Devil, because God was with Him. ³⁹We ourselves are witnesses of everything He did in both the Judean country and in Jerusalem, yet they killed Him by hanging Him on a tree. ⁴⁰God raised up this man on the third day and permitted Him to be seen, ⁴¹not by all the people, but by us, witnesses appointed beforehand by God, who ate and drank with Him after He rose from the dead. ⁴²He commanded us to preach to the people and to solemnly testify that He is the One appointed by God to be the Judge of the living and the dead. ⁴³All the prophets testify about Him that through His name everyone who believes in Him will receive forgiveness of sins."

⁴⁴While Peter was still speaking these words, the Holy Spirit came down on all those who heard the message. ⁴⁵The circumcised believers^F who had come with Peter were astounded because the gift of the Holy Spirit had been poured out on the Gentiles also. ⁴⁶For they heard them speaking in other languages and declaring the greatness of^G God.

Then Peter responded, ⁴⁷"Can anyone withhold water and prevent these people from being baptized, who have received the Holy Spirit just as we have?" ⁴⁸And he commanded them to be baptized in the name of Jesus Christ. Then they asked him to stay for a few days.

---

^A**10:14** Perhaps *profane*, or *non-sacred*; Jews ate distinctive food according to OT law and their traditions, similar to modern kosher or non-kosher foods.   ^B**10:30** Lit *at the ninth hour*   ^C**10:30** Other mss add *fasting and*   ^D**10:32** Other mss add *When he arrives, he will speak to you.*   ^E**10:37** Or *word*; lit *thing*   ^F**10:45** Jewish Christians who stressed circumcision; Ac 11:2; 15:5; Gl 2:12; Col 4:11; Ti 1:10   ^G**10:46** Or *and magnifying*

11 The apostles and the brothers who were throughout Judea heard that the Gentiles had welcomed God's message also. ²When Peter went up to Jerusalem, those who stressed circumcision[A] argued with him, ³saying, "You visited uncircumcised men and ate with them!"

⁴Peter began to explain to them in an orderly sequence, saying: ⁵"I was in the town of Joppa praying, and I saw, in a visionary state, an object that resembled a large sheet coming down, being lowered by its four corners from heaven, and it came to me. ⁶When I looked closely and considered it, I saw the four-footed animals of the earth, the wild beasts, the reptiles, and the birds of the sky. ⁷Then I also heard a voice telling me, 'Get up, Peter; kill and eat!'

⁸"'No, Lord!' I said. 'For nothing common or ritually unclean has ever entered my mouth!' ⁹But a voice answered from heaven a second time, 'What God has made clean, you must not call common.'

¹⁰"Now this happened three times, and then everything was drawn up again into heaven. ¹¹At that very moment, three men who had been sent to me from Caesarea arrived at the house where we were. ¹²Then the Spirit told me to accompany them with no doubts at all. These six brothers accompanied me, and we went into the man's house. ¹³He reported to us how he had seen the angel standing in his house and saying, 'Send[B] to Joppa, and call for Simon, who is also named Peter. ¹⁴He will speak a message[C] to you that you and all your household will be saved by.'

¹⁵"As I began to speak, the Holy Spirit came down on them, just as on us at the beginning. ¹⁶Then I remembered the word of the Lord, how He said, 'John baptized with water, but you will be baptized with the Holy Spirit.' ¹⁷Therefore, if God gave them the same gift that He also gave to us when we believed on the Lord Jesus Christ, how could I possibly hinder God?"

¹⁸When they heard this they became silent. Then they glorified God, saying, "So God has granted repentance resulting in life[D] even to the Gentiles!"

¹⁹Those who had been scattered as a result of the persecution that started because of Stephen made their way as far as Phoenicia, Cyprus, and Antioch, speaking the message to no one except Jews. ²⁰But there were some of them, Cypriot and Cyrenian men, who came to Antioch and began speaking to the Hellenists,[E,F] proclaiming the good news about the Lord Jesus. ²¹The Lord's hand was with them, and a large number who believed turned to the Lord. ²²Then the report about them was heard by the church that was at Jerusalem, and they sent out Barnabas to travel[G] as far as Antioch. ²³When he arrived and saw the grace of God, he was glad and encouraged all of them to remain true to the Lord with a firm resolve of the heart, ²⁴for he was a good man, full of the Holy Spirit and of faith. And large numbers of people were added to the Lord. ²⁵Then he[H] went to Tarsus to search for Saul, ²⁶and when he found him he brought him to Antioch. For a whole year they met with the church and taught large numbers. The disciples were first called Christians at Antioch.

²⁷In those days some prophets came down from Jerusalem to Antioch. ²⁸Then one of them, named Agabus, stood up and predicted by the Spirit that there would be a severe famine throughout the Roman world.[I] This took place during the time of Claudius.[J] ²⁹So each of the disciples, according to his ability, determined to send relief to the brothers who lived in Judea. ³⁰They did this, sending it to the elders by means of Barnabas and Saul.

12 About that time King Herod cruelly attacked some who belonged to the church, ²and he killed James, John's brother, with the sword. ³When he saw that it pleased the Jews, he proceeded to arrest Peter too, during the days of Unleavened Bread. ⁴After the arrest, he put him in prison and assigned four squads of four soldiers each to guard him, intending to bring him out to the people after the Passover. ⁵So Peter was kept in prison, but prayer was being made earnestly to God for him by the church.

⁶On the night before Herod was to bring him out for execution, Peter, bound with two chains, was sleeping between two soldiers, while the sentries in front of the door guarded the prison. ⁷Suddenly an angel of the Lord appeared, and a light shone in the cell. Striking Peter on the side, he woke him up and said,

"Quick, get up!" Then the chains fell off his wrists. ⁸"Get dressed," the angel told him, "and put on your sandals." And he did so. "Wrap your cloak around you," he told him, "and follow me." ⁹So he went out and followed, and he did not know that what took place through the angel was real, but thought he was seeing a vision. ¹⁰After they passed the first and second guard posts, they came to the iron gate that leads into the city, which opened to them by itself. They went outside and passed one street, and immediately the angel left him.

¹¹Then Peter came to himself and said, "Now I know for certain that the Lord has sent His angel and rescued me from Herod's grasp and from all that the Jewish people expected." ¹²When he realized this, he went to the house of Mary, the mother of John Mark,ᴬ where many had assembled and were praying. ¹³He knocked at the door in the gateway, and a servant named Rhoda came to answer. ¹⁴She recognized Peter's voice, and because of her joy, she did not open the gate but ran in and announced that Peter was standing at the gateway.

¹⁵"You're crazy!" they told her. But she kept insisting that it was true. Then they said, "It's his angel!" ¹⁶Peter, however, kept on knocking, and when they opened the door and saw him, they were astounded.

¹⁷Motioning to them with his hand to be silent, he explained to them how the Lord had brought him out of the prison. "Report these things to Jamesᴮ and the brothers," he said. Then he departed and went to a different place.

¹⁸At daylight, there was a great commotionᶜ among the soldiers as to what could have become of Peter. ¹⁹After Herod had searched and did not find him, he interrogated the guards and ordered their execution. Then Herod went down from Judea to Caesarea and stayed there. ²⁰He had been very angry with the Tyrians and Sidonians.ᴰ Together they presented themselves before him. They won over Blastus, who was in charge of the king's bedroom, and through him they asked for peace, because their country was supplied with food from the king's country. ²¹So on an appointed day, dressed in royal robes and seated on the throne, Herod delivered a public address to them. ²²The assembled people began to shout, "It's the voice of a god and not of a man!" ²³At

once an angel of the Lord struck him because he did not give the glory to God, and he became infected with worms and died. ²⁴Then God's message flourished and multiplied. ²⁵After they had completed their relief mission, Barnabas and Saul returned toᴱ Jerusalem, taking along John who is called Mark.

13 In the church that was at Antioch there were prophets and teachers: Barnabas, Simeon who was called Niger, Lucius the Cyrenian, Manaen, a close friend of Herod the tetrarch, and Saul.

²As they were ministering toᶠ the Lord and fasting, the Holy Spirit said, "Set apart for Me Barnabas and Saul for the work I have called them to." ³Then after they had fasted, prayed, and laid hands on them, they sent them off.

⁴Being sent out by the Holy Spirit, they came down to Seleucia, and from there they sailed to Cyprus. ⁵Arriving in Salamis, they proclaimed God's message in the Jewish synagogues. They also had John as their assistant. ⁶When they had gone through the whole island as far as Paphos, they came across a sorcerer, a Jewish false prophet named Bar-Jesus. ⁷He was with the proconsul, Sergius Paulus, an intelligent man. This man summoned Barnabas and Saul and desired to hear God's message. ⁸But Elymas the sorcerer (this is the meaning of his name) opposed them and tried to turn the proconsul away from the faith.

⁹Then Saul—also called Paul—filled with the Holy Spirit, stared straight at the sorcerer ¹⁰and said, "You son of the Devil, full of all deceit and all fraud, enemy of all righteousness! Won't you ever stop perverting the straight paths of the Lord? ¹¹Now, look! The Lord's hand is against you. You are going to be blind, and will not see the sun for a time." Suddenly a mist and darkness fell on him, and he went around seeking someone to lead him by the hand.

¹²Then the proconsul, seeing what happened, believed and was astonished at the teaching about the Lord.

¹³Paul and his companions set sail from Paphos and came to Perga in Pamphylia. John, however, left them and went back to Jerusalem. ¹⁴They continued their journey from Perga and reached Antioch in Pisidia. On the Sabbath day they went into the synagogue and sat down. ¹⁵After the reading of the Law and

ᴬ12:12 Lit John who was called Mark   ᴮ12:17 This was James, the Lord's brother; Mk 6:3. This was not James the apostle; Ac 12:2.   ᶜ12:18 Or was no small disturbance   ᴰ12:20 The people of the area of modern Lebanon   ᴱ12:25 Other mss read from   ᶠ13:2 Or were worshiping the Prophets, the leaders of the synagogue sent word to them, saying, "Brothers, if you have any message of encouragement for the people, you can speak."

[16] Then Paul stood up and motioned with his hand and said: "Men of Israel, and you who fear God, listen! [17] The God of this people Israel chose our ancestors, exalted the people during their stay in the land of Egypt, and led them out of it with a mighty[A] arm. [18] And for about 40 years He put up with them[B] in the wilderness; [19] then after destroying seven nations in the land of Canaan, He gave their land to them as an inheritance. [20] This all took about 450 years. After this, He gave them judges until Samuel the prophet. [21] Then they asked for a king, so God gave them Saul the son of Kish, a man of the tribe of Benjamin, for 40 years. [22] After removing him, He raised up David as their king and testified about him: '**I have found David** the son of Jesse, **a man loyal to Me**,[C] who will carry out all My will.'

[23] "From this man's descendants, according to the promise, God brought the Savior, Jesus,[D] to Israel. [24] Before He came to public attention,[E] John had previously proclaimed a baptism of repentance to all the people of Israel. [25] Then as John was completing his life's work, he said, 'Who do you think I am? I am not the One. But look! Someone is coming after me, and I am not worthy to untie the sandals on His feet.'

[26] "Brothers, sons of Abraham's race, and those among you who fear God, the message of this salvation has been sent to us. [27] For the residents of Jerusalem and their rulers, since they did not recognize Him or the voices of the prophets that are read every Sabbath, have fulfilled their words[F] by condemning Him. [28] Though they found no grounds for the death penalty, they asked Pilate to have Him killed. [29] When they had fulfilled all that had been written about Him, they took Him down from the tree and put Him in a tomb. [30] But God raised Him from the dead, [31] and He appeared for many days to those who came with Him from Galilee to Jerusalem, who are now His witnesses to the people. [32] And we ourselves proclaim to you the good news of the promise that was made to our ancestors. [33] God has

fulfilled this for us, their children, by raising up Jesus, as it is written in the second Psalm:

> **You are My Son;**
> **today I have become Your Father.**[G,H]

[34] Since He raised Him from the dead, never to return to decay, He has spoken in this way, **I will grant you the faithful covenant blessings**[I] **made to David.**[J] [35] Therefore He also says in another passage, **You will not allow Your Holy One to see decay.**[K] [36] For David, after serving his own generation in God's plan, fell asleep, was buried with his fathers, and decayed. [37] But the One God raised up did not decay. [38] Therefore, let it be known to you, brothers, that through this man forgiveness of sins is being proclaimed to you, [39] and everyone who believes in Him is justified from everything that you could not be justified from through the law of Moses. [40] So beware that what is said in the prophets does not happen to you:

> [41] Look, you scoffers,
>   marvel and vanish away,
>   because I am doing a work
>   in your days,
>   a work that you will never believe,
>   even if someone were to explain it
>   to you."[L]

[42] As they[M] were leaving, the people[N] begged that these matters be presented to them the following Sabbath. [43] After the synagogue had been dismissed, many of the Jews and devout proselytes followed Paul and Barnabas, who were speaking with them and persuading them to continue in the grace of God.

[44] The following Sabbath almost the whole town assembled to hear the message of the Lord.[O] [45] But when the Jews saw the crowds, they were filled with jealousy and began to oppose what Paul was saying by insulting him.

[46] Then Paul and Barnabas boldly said: "It was necessary that God's message be spoken to you first. But since you reject it and consider yourselves unworthy of eternal life, we now turn to the Gentiles! [47] For this is what the Lord has commanded us:

> **I have made you**
> **a light for the Gentiles**

A13:17 Lit with an uplifted   B13:18 Other mss read He cared for them   C13:22 1Sm 13:14; Ps 89:20   D13:23 Other mss read brought salvation   E13:24 Lit Before the face of His entrance   F13:27 Lit fulfilled them   G13:33 Or I have begotten You   H13:33 Ps 2:7   I13:34 Lit faithful holy things   J13:34 Is 55:3   K13:35 Ps 16:10   L13:41 Hab 1:5   M13:42 Paul and Barnabas   N13:42 Other mss read they were leaving the synagogue of the Jews, the Gentiles   O13:44 Other mss read of God

**to bring salvation
to the ends**^{A} **of the earth."**^{B}

^{48}When the Gentiles heard this, they rejoiced and glorified the message of the Lord, and all who had been appointed to eternal life believed. ^{49}So the message of the Lord spread through the whole region. ^{50}But the Jews incited the prominent women, who worshiped God, and the leading men of the city. They stirred up persecution against Paul and Barnabas and expelled them from their district. ^{51}But they shook the dust off their feet against them and went to Iconium. ^{52}And the disciples were filled with joy and the Holy Spirit.

14 The same thing happened in Iconium; they entered the Jewish synagogue and spoke in such a way that a great number of both Jews and Greeks believed. ^{2}But the Jews who refused to believe stirred up and poisoned the minds of the Gentiles against the brothers. ^{3}So they stayed there for some time and spoke boldly in reliance on the Lord, who testified to the message of His grace by granting that signs and wonders be performed through them. ^{4}But the people of the city were divided, some siding with the Jews and some with the apostles. ^{5}When an attempt was made by both the Gentiles and Jews, with their rulers, to assault and stone them, ^{6}they found out about it and fled to the Lycaonian towns called Lystra and Derbe, and to the surrounding countryside. ^{7}And there they kept evangelizing.

^{8}In Lystra a man without strength in his feet, lame from birth,^{C} and who had never walked, sat ^{9}and heard Paul speaking. After observing him closely and seeing that he had faith to be healed, ^{10}Paul said in a loud voice, "Stand upright on your feet!" And he jumped up and started to walk around.

^{11}When the crowds saw what Paul had done, they raised their voices, saying in the Lycaonian language, "The gods have come down to us in the form of men!" ^{12}And they started to call Barnabas, Zeus, and Paul, Hermes, because he was the main speaker. ^{13}Then the priest of Zeus, whose temple was just outside the town, brought oxen and garlands to the gates. He, with the crowds, intended to offer sacrifice.

^{14}The apostles Barnabas and Paul tore their robes when they heard this and rushed into the crowd, shouting: ^{15}"Men! Why are you doing these things? We are men also, with the same nature as you, and we are proclaiming good news to you, that you should turn from these worthless things to the living God, **who made the heaven, the earth, the sea, and everything in them.**^{D} ^{16}In past generations He allowed all the nations to go their own way, ^{17}although He did not leave Himself without a witness, since He did what is good by giving you rain from heaven and fruitful seasons and satisfying your^E hearts with food and happiness." ^{18}Even though they said these things, they barely stopped the crowds from sacrificing to them.

^{19}Then some Jews came from Antioch and Iconium, and when they had won over the crowds and stoned Paul, they dragged him out of the city, thinking he was dead. ^{20}After the disciples surrounded him, he got up and went into the town. The next day he left with Barnabas for Derbe.

^{21}After they had evangelized that town and made many disciples, they returned to Lystra, to Iconium, and to Antioch, ^{22}strengthening the^F disciples by encouraging them to continue in the faith and by telling them, "It is necessary to pass through many troubles on our way into the kingdom of God."

^{23}When they had appointed elders in every church and prayed with fasting, they committed them to the Lord in whom they had believed. ^{24}Then they passed through Pisidia and came to Pamphylia. ^{25}After they spoke the message in Perga, they went down to Attalia. ^{26}From there they sailed back to Antioch where they had been entrusted to the grace of God for the work they had now completed. ^{27}After they arrived and gathered the church together, they reported everything God had done with them and that He had opened the door of faith to the Gentiles. ^{28}And they spent a considerable time^G with the disciples.

15 Some men came down from Judea and began to teach the brothers: "Unless you are circumcised according to the custom prescribed by Moses, you cannot be saved!" ^{2}But after Paul and Barnabas had engaged them in serious argument and debate, the church arranged for Paul and Barnabas and some others of them to go up to the apostles and elders in Jerusalem concerning this controversy.

^{A}**13:47** Lit the end ^{B}**13:47** Is 49:6 ^{C}**14:8** Lit from his mother's womb the souls of the ^{G}**14:28** Or spent no little time ^{D}**14:15** Ex 20:11; Ps 146:6 ^{E}**14:17** Other mss read our ^{F}**14:22** Lit

³When they had been sent on their way by the church, they passed through both Phoenicia and Samaria, explaining in detail the conversion of the Gentiles, and they created great joy among all the brothers.

⁴When they arrived at Jerusalem, they were welcomed by the church, the apostles, and the elders, and they reported all that God had done with them. ⁵But some of the believers from the party of the Pharisees stood up and said, "It is necessary to circumcise them and to command them to keep the law of Moses!"

⁶Then the apostles and the elders assembled to consider this matter. ⁷After there had been much debate, Peter stood up and said to them: "Brothers, you are aware that in the early days God made a choice among you,ᴬ that by my mouth the Gentiles would hear the gospel message and believe. ⁸And God, who knows the heart, testified to them by givingᴮ the Holy Spirit, just as He also did to us. ⁹He made no distinction between us and them, cleansing their hearts by faith. ¹⁰Now then, why are you testing God by putting a yoke on the disciples' necks that neither our ancestors nor we have been able to bear? ¹¹On the contrary, we believe we are saved through the grace of the Lord Jesus in the same way they are."

¹²Then the whole assembly fell silent and listened to Barnabas and Paul describing all the signs and wonders God had done through them among the Gentiles. ¹³After they stopped speaking, James responded: "Brothers, listen to me! ¹⁴Simeonᶜ has reported how God first intervened to take from the Gentiles a people for His name. ¹⁵And the words of the prophets agree with this, as it is written:

¹⁶   **After these things I will return
       and rebuild David's fallen tent.
       I will rebuild its ruins
       and set it up again,**
¹⁷   **so the rest of humanity
       may seek the Lord—
       even all the Gentiles
       who are called by My name,
       declares the Lord who does
          these things,**
¹⁸   **known from long ago.**ᴰ'ᴱ

¹⁹Therefore, in my judgment, we should not cause difficulties for those among the Gentiles who turn to God, ²⁰but instead we should write to them to abstain from things polluted by idols, from sexual immorality, from eating anything that has been strangled, and from blood. ²¹For since ancient times, Moses has had those who proclaim him in every city, and every Sabbath day he is read aloud in the synagogues."

²²Then the apostles and the elders, with the whole church, decided to select men who were among them and to send them to Antioch with Paul and Barnabas: Judas, called Barsabbas, and Silas, both leading men among the brothers. ²³They wrote this letter to be delivered by them:ᶠ

From the apostles and the elders, your brothers,
To the brothers among the Gentiles in Antioch, Syria, and Cilicia:
Greetings.
²⁴Because we have heard that some without our authorization went out from us and troubled you with their words and unsettled your hearts,ᴳ ²⁵we have unanimously decided to select men and send them to you along with our dearly loved Barnabas and Paul, ²⁶who have risked their lives for the name of our Lord Jesus Christ. ²⁷Therefore we have sent Judas and Silas, who will personally report the same things by word of mouth.ᴴ ²⁸For it was the Holy Spirit's decision—and ours—to put no greater burden on you than these necessary things: ²⁹that you abstain from food offered to idols, from blood, from eating anything that has been strangled, and from sexual immorality. You will do well if you keep yourselves from these things.
Farewell.

³⁰Then, being sent off, they went down to Antioch, and after gathering the assembly, they delivered the letter. ³¹When they read it, they rejoiced because of its encouragement. ³²Both Judas and Silas, who were also prophets themselves, encouraged the brothers and strengthened them with a long message. ³³After spending some time there, they were sent

---

ᴬ15:7 Other mss read us   ᴮ15:8 Other mss add them   ᶜ15:14 Simon (Peter)   ᴰ15:17-18 Other mss read says the Lord who does all these things. Known to God from long ago are all His works.   ᴱ15:16-18 Am 9:11-12; Is 45:21   ᶠ15:23 Lit Writing by their hand: ᴳ15:24 Other mss add by saying, "Be circumcised and keep the law,"   ᴴ15:27 Lit things through word back in peace by the brothers to those who had sent them.[A,B] [35]But Paul and Barnabas, along with many others, remained in Antioch teaching and proclaiming the message of the Lord.

[36]After some time had passed, Paul said to Barnabas, "Let's go back and visit the brothers in every town where we have preached the message of the Lord and see how they're doing." [37]Barnabas wanted to take along John Mark.[C] [38]But Paul did not think it appropriate to take along this man who had deserted them in Pamphylia and had not gone on with them to the work. [39]There was such a sharp disagreement that they parted company, and Barnabas took Mark with him and sailed off to Cyprus. [40]Then Paul chose Silas and departed, after being commended to the grace of the Lord by the brothers. [41]He traveled through Syria and Cilicia, strengthening the churches.

16 Then he went on to Derbe and Lystra, where there was a disciple named Timothy, the son of a believing Jewish woman, but his father was a Greek. [2]The brothers at Lystra and Iconium spoke highly of him. [3]Paul wanted Timothy[D] to go with him, so he took him and circumcised him because of the Jews who were in those places, since they all knew that his father was a Greek. [4]As they traveled through the towns, they delivered the decisions reached by the apostles and elders at Jerusalem for them to observe. [5]So the churches were strengthened in the faith and increased in number daily.

[6]They went through the region of Phrygia and Galatia and were prevented by the Holy Spirit from speaking the message in Asia. [7]When they came to Mysia, they tried to go into Bithynia, but the Spirit of Jesus did not allow them. [8]So, bypassing Mysia, they came down to Troas. [9]During the night a vision appeared to Paul: A Macedonian man was standing and pleading with him, "Cross over to Macedonia and help us!" [10]After he had seen the vision, we[E] immediately made efforts to set out for Macedonia, concluding that God had called us to evangelize them.

[11]Then, setting sail from Troas, we ran a straight course to Samothrace, the next day to Neapolis, [12]and from there to Philippi, a Roman colony, which is a leading city of that district of Macedonia. We stayed in that city

for a number of days. [13]On the Sabbath day we went outside the city gate by the river, where we thought there was a place of prayer. We sat down and spoke to the women gathered there. [14]A woman named Lydia, a dealer in purple cloth from the city of Thyatira, who worshiped God, was listening. The Lord opened her heart to pay attention to what was spoken by Paul. [15]After she and her household were baptized, she urged us, "If you consider me a believer in the Lord, come and stay at my house." And she persuaded us.

[16]Once, as we were on our way to prayer, a slave girl met us who had a spirit of prediction.[F] She made a large profit for her owners by fortune-telling. [17]As she followed Paul and us she cried out, "These men, who are proclaiming to you[G] the way of salvation, are the slaves of the Most High God." [18]And she did this for many days.

But Paul was greatly aggravated and turning to the spirit, said, "I command you in the name of Jesus Christ to come out of her!" And it came out right away.[H]

[19]When her owners saw that their hope of profit was gone, they seized Paul and Silas and dragged them into the marketplace to the authorities. [20]Bringing them before the chief magistrates, they said, "These men are seriously disturbing our city. They are Jews [21]and are promoting customs that are not legal for us as Romans to adopt or practice."

[22]Then the mob joined in the attack against them, and the chief magistrates stripped off their clothes and ordered them to be beaten with rods. [23]After they had inflicted many blows on them, they threw them in jail, ordering the jailer to keep them securely guarded. [24]Receiving such an order, he put them into the inner prison and secured their feet in the stocks.

[25]About midnight Paul and Silas were praying and singing hymns to God, and the prisoners were listening to them. [26]Suddenly there was such a violent earthquake that the foundations of the jail were shaken, and immediately all the doors were opened, and everyone's chains came loose. [27]When the jailer woke up and saw the doors of the prison open, he drew his sword and was going to kill himself, since he thought the prisoners had escaped.

A15:33 Other mss read the brothers to the apostles   B15:33 Other mss add v. 34: But Silas decided to stay there.   C15:37 Lit John who was called Mark   D16:3 Lit wanted this one   E16:10 The use of we in this passage probably indicates that the author Luke is joining Paul's missionary team here.   F16:16 Or a spirit by which she predicted the future   G16:17 Other mss read us   H16:18 Lit out this hour

[28] But Paul called out in a loud voice, "Don't harm yourself, because all of us are here!"

[29] Then the jailer called for lights, rushed in, and fell down trembling before Paul and Silas. [30] Then he escorted them out and said, "Sirs, what must I do to be saved?"

[31] So they said, "Believe on the Lord Jesus, and you will be saved—you and your household." [32] Then they spoke the message of the Lord to him along with everyone in his house. [33] He took them the same hour of the night and washed their wounds. Right away he and all his family were baptized. [34] He brought them into his house, set a meal before them, and rejoiced because he had believed God with his entire household.

[35] When daylight came, the chief magistrates sent the police to say, "Release those men!"

[36] The jailer reported these words to Paul: "The magistrates have sent orders for you to be released. So come out now and go in peace."

[37] But Paul said to them, "They beat us in public without a trial, although we are Roman citizens, and threw us in jail. And now are they going to smuggle us out secretly? Certainly not! On the contrary, let them come themselves and escort us out!"

[38] Then the police reported these words to the magistrates. They were afraid when they heard that Paul and Silas were Roman citizens. [39] So they came and apologized to them, and escorting them out, they urged them to leave town. [40] After leaving the jail, they came to Lydia's house where they saw and encouraged the brothers, and departed.

17 Then they traveled through Amphipolis and Apollonia and came to Thessalonica, where there was a Jewish synagogue. [2] As usual, Paul went to the synagogue, and on three Sabbath days reasoned with them from the Scriptures, [3] explaining and showing that the Messiah had to suffer and rise from the dead: "This Jesus I am proclaiming to you is the Messiah." [4] Then some of them were persuaded and joined Paul and Silas, including a great number of God-fearing Greeks, as well as a number[A] of the leading women.

[5] But the Jews became jealous, and they brought together some scoundrels from the marketplace, formed a mob, and started a riot in the city. Attacking Jason's house, they searched for them to bring them out to the public assembly. [6] When they did not find them, they dragged Jason and some of the brothers before the city officials, shouting, "These men who have turned the world upside down have come here too, [7] and Jason has received them as guests! They are all acting contrary to Caesar's decrees, saying that there is another king—Jesus!" [8] The Jews stirred up the crowd and the city officials who heard these things. [9] So taking a security bond from Jason and the others, they released them.

[10] As soon as it was night, the brothers sent Paul and Silas off to Berea. On arrival, they went into the synagogue of the Jews. [11] The people here were more open-minded than those in Thessalonica, since they welcomed the message with eagerness and examined the Scriptures daily to see if these things were so. [12] Consequently, many of them believed, including a number of the prominent Greek women as well as men. [13] But when the Jews from Thessalonica found out that God's message had been proclaimed by Paul at Berea, they came there too, agitating and disturbing[B] the crowds. [14] Then the brothers immediately sent Paul away to go to the sea, but Silas and Timothy stayed on there. [15] Those who escorted Paul brought him as far as Athens, and after receiving instructions for Silas and Timothy to come to him as quickly as possible, they departed.

[16] While Paul was waiting for them in Athens, his spirit was troubled within him when he saw that the city was full of idols. [17] So he reasoned in the synagogue with the Jews and with those who worshiped God and in the marketplace every day with those who happened to be there. [18] Then also, some of the Epicurean and Stoic philosophers argued with him. Some said, "What is this pseudo-intellectual[C] trying to say?"

Others replied, "He seems to be a preacher of foreign deities"—because he was telling the good news about Jesus and the Resurrection.[D]

[19] They took him and brought him to the Areopagus,[E] and said, "May we learn about this new teaching you're speaking of? [20] For what you say sounds strange to us, and we want to know what these ideas mean." [21] Now all the Athenians and the foreigners residing there spent their time on nothing else but telling or hearing something new.

A17:4 Lit *as well as not a few*   B17:13 Other mss omit *and disturbing*   C17:18 Lit *this seed picker; =* one who picks up scraps   D17:18 = Gk *Anastasis*   E17:19 Or *Mars Hill*, the oldest and most famous court in Athens with jurisdiction in moral, religious, and civil matters

²²Then Paul stood in the middle of the Areopagus and said: "Men of Athens! I see that you are extremely religious in every respect. ²³For as I was passing through and observing the objects of your worship, I even found an altar on which was inscribed:

TO AN UNKNOWN GOD.

Therefore, what you worship in ignorance, this I proclaim to you. ²⁴The God who made the world and everything in it—He is Lord of heaven and earth and does not live in shrines made by hands. ²⁵Neither is He served by human hands, as though He needed anything, since He Himself gives everyone life and breath and all things. ²⁶From one man[A] He has made every nationality to live over the whole earth and has determined their appointed times and the boundaries of where they live. ²⁷He did this so they might seek God, and perhaps they might reach out and find Him, though He is not far from each one of us. ²⁸For in Him we live and move and exist, as even some of your own poets have said, 'For we are also His offspring.'[B] ²⁹Being God's offspring then, we shouldn't think that the divine nature is like gold or silver or stone, an image fashioned by human art and imagination.

³⁰"Therefore, having overlooked the times of ignorance, God now commands all people everywhere to repent, ³¹because He has set a day when He is going to judge the world in righteousness by the Man He has appointed. He has provided proof of this to everyone by raising Him from the dead."

³²When they heard about resurrection of the dead, some began to ridicule him. But others said, "We'd like to hear from you again about this." ³³Then Paul left their presence. ³⁴However, some men joined him and believed, including Dionysius the Areopagite, a woman named Damaris, and others with them.

18 After this, he[C] left Athens and went to Corinth, ²where he found a Jewish man named Aquila, a native of Pontus, who had recently come from Italy with his wife Priscilla because Claudius[D] had ordered all the Jews to leave Rome. Paul came to them, ³and being of the same occupation, stayed with them and worked, for they were tentmakers[E] by trade.

⁴He reasoned in the synagogue every Sabbath and tried to persuade both Jews and Greeks.

⁵When Silas and Timothy came down from Macedonia, Paul was occupied with preaching the message[F] and solemnly testified to the Jews that Jesus is the Messiah. ⁶But when they resisted and blasphemed, he shook his robe[G] and told them, "Your blood is on your own heads! I am innocent.[H] From now on I will go to the Gentiles." ⁷So he left there and went to the house of a man named Titius Justus, a worshiper of God, whose house was next door to the synagogue. ⁸Crispus, the leader of the synagogue, believed the Lord, along with his whole household. Many of the Corinthians, when they heard, believed and were baptized.

⁹Then the Lord said to Paul in a night vision, "Don't be afraid, but keep on speaking and don't be silent. ¹⁰For I am with you, and no one will lay a hand on you to hurt you, because I have many people in this city." ¹¹And he stayed there a year and six months, teaching the word of God among them.

¹²While Gallio was proconsul of Achaia, the Jews made a united attack against Paul and brought him to the judge's bench. ¹³"This man," they said, "persuades people to worship God contrary to the law!"

¹⁴As Paul was about to open his mouth, Gallio said to the Jews, "If it were a matter of a crime or of moral evil, it would be reasonable for me to put up with you Jews. ¹⁵But if these are questions about words, names, and your own law, see to it yourselves. I don't want to be a judge of such things." ¹⁶So he drove them from the judge's bench. ¹⁷Then they all[I] seized Sosthenes, the leader of the synagogue, and beat him in front of the judge's bench. But none of these things concerned Gallio.

¹⁸So Paul, having stayed on for many days, said good-bye to the brothers and sailed away to Syria. Priscilla and Aquila were with him. He shaved his head at Cenchreae because he had taken a vow. ¹⁹When they reached Ephesus he left them there, but he himself entered the synagogue and engaged in discussion with[J] the Jews. ²⁰And though they asked him to stay for a longer time, he declined, ²¹but he said good-bye

---

A17:26 Other mss read *one blood*   B17:28 This citation is from Aratus, a third-century B.C. Gk poet.   C18:1 Other mss read *Paul*
D18:2 Roman emperor A.D. 41–54; he expelled all Jews from Rome in A.D. 49.   E18:3 Or *leatherworkers*, or less likely *manufacturers of theatrical properties*   F18:5 Other mss read *was urged by the Spirit*   G18:6 A symbolic display of protest; Mt 10:14; Ac 13:51   H18:6 Lit *clean*
I18:17 Other mss read *Then all the Greeks*   J18:19 Or *and addressed*

and stated,^A "I'll come back to you again, if God wills." Then he set sail from Ephesus.

²² On landing at Caesarea, he went up and greeted the church^B and went down to Antioch. ²³ And after spending some time there, he set out, traveling through one place after another in the Galatian territory and Phrygia, strengthening all the disciples.

²⁴ A Jew named Apollos, a native Alexandrian, an eloquent man who was powerful in the use of the Scriptures, arrived in Ephesus. ²⁵ This man had been instructed in the way of the Lord; and being fervent in spirit,^C he spoke and taught the things about Jesus accurately, although he knew only John's baptism. ²⁶ He began to speak boldly in the synagogue. After Priscilla and Aquila heard him, they took him home^D and explained the way of God to him more accurately. ²⁷ When he wanted to cross over to Achaia, the brothers wrote to the disciples urging them to welcome him. After he arrived, he greatly helped those who had believed through grace. ²⁸ For he vigorously refuted the Jews in public, demonstrating through the Scriptures that Jesus is the Messiah.

19 While Apollos was in Corinth, Paul traveled through the interior regions and came to Ephesus. He found some disciples ² and asked them, "Did you receive the Holy Spirit when you believed?"

"No," they told him, "we haven't even heard that there is a Holy Spirit."

³ "Then what baptism were you baptized with?" he asked them.

"With John's baptism," they replied.

⁴ Paul said, "John baptized with a baptism of repentance, telling the people that they should believe in the One who would come after him, that is, in Jesus."

⁵ When they heard this, they were baptized in the name of the Lord Jesus. ⁶ And when Paul had laid his hands on them, the Holy Spirit came on them, and they began to speak in other languages and to prophesy. ⁷ Now there were about 12 men in all.

⁸ Then he entered the synagogue and spoke boldly over a period of three months, engaging in discussion and trying to persuade them about the things of the kingdom of God. ⁹ But when some became hardened and would not believe, slandering the Way in front of the crowd, he withdrew from them and met separately with the disciples, conducting discussions every day in the lecture hall of Tyrannus. ¹⁰ And this went on for two years, so that all the inhabitants of Asia, both Jews and Greeks, heard the message about the Lord.

¹¹ God was performing extraordinary miracles by Paul's hands, ¹² so that even facecloths or work aprons^E that had touched his skin were brought to the sick, and the diseases left them, and the evil spirits came out of them.

¹³ Then some of the itinerant Jewish exorcists attempted to pronounce the name of the Lord Jesus over those who had evil spirits, saying, "I command you by the Jesus that Paul preaches!" ¹⁴ Seven sons of Sceva, a Jewish chief priest, were doing this. ¹⁵ The evil spirit answered them, "I know Jesus, and I recognize Paul—but who are you?" ¹⁶ Then the man who had the evil spirit leaped on them, overpowered them all, and prevailed against them, so that they ran out of that house naked and wounded. ¹⁷ This became known to everyone who lived in Ephesus, both Jews and Greeks. Then fear fell on all of them, and the name of the Lord Jesus was magnified. ¹⁸ And many who had become believers came confessing and disclosing their practices, ¹⁹ while many of those who had practiced magic collected their books and burned them in front of everyone. So they calculated their value and found it to be 50,000 pieces of silver. ²⁰ In this way the Lord's message flourished and prevailed.

²¹ When these events were over, Paul resolved in the Spirit to pass through Macedonia and Achaia and go to Jerusalem. "After I've been there," he said, "I must see Rome as well!" ²² So after sending two of those who assisted him, Timothy and Erastus, to Macedonia, he himself stayed in Asia for a while.

²³ During that time there was a major^F disturbance about the Way. ²⁴ For a person named Demetrius, a silversmith who made silver shrines of Artemis,^G provided a great deal of^H business for the craftsmen. ²⁵ When he had assembled them, as well as the workers engaged in this type of business, he said: "Men, you know that our prosperity is derived

^A18:21 Other mss add "By all means it is necessary to keep the coming festival in Jerusalem. But   ^B18:22 The church in Jerusalem   ^C18:25 Or in the Spirit   ^D18:26 Lit they received him   ^E19:12 Or that also sweatbands and sweatcloths or handkerchiefs   ^F19:23 Lit was not a little   ^G19:24 Artemis was the ancient Gk mother goddess believed to control all fertility.   ^H19:24 Lit provided not a little from this business. ²⁶ You both see and hear that not only in Ephesus, but in almost all of Asia, this man Paul has persuaded and misled a considerable number of people by saying that gods made by hand are not gods! ²⁷ So not only do we run a risk that our business may be discredited, but also that the temple of the great goddess Artemis may be despised and her magnificence come to the verge of ruin—the very one all of Asia and the world adore."

²⁸ When they had heard this, they were filled with rage and began to cry out, "Great is Artemis of the Ephesians!" ²⁹ So the city was filled with confusion, and they rushed all together into the amphitheater, dragging along Gaius and Aristarchus, Macedonians who were Paul's traveling companions. ³⁰ Though Paul wanted to go in before the people, the disciples did not let him. ³¹ Even some of the provincial officials of Asia, who were his friends, sent word to him, pleading with him not to take a chance by going^A into the amphitheater. ³² Meanwhile, some were shouting one thing and some another, because the assembly was in confusion, and most of them did not know why they had come together. ³³ Then some of the crowd gave Alexander advice when the Jews pushed him to the front. So motioning with his hand, Alexander wanted to make his defense to the people. ³⁴ But when they recognized that he was a Jew, a united cry went up from all of them for about two hours: "Great is Artemis of the Ephesians!"

³⁵ However, when the city clerk had calmed the crowd down, he said, "Men of Ephesus! What man is there who doesn't know that the city of the Ephesians is the temple guardian of the great^B Artemis, and of the image that fell from heaven? ³⁶ Therefore, since these things are undeniable, you must keep calm and not do anything rash. ³⁷ For you have brought these men here who are not temple robbers or blasphemers of our^C goddess. ³⁸ So if Demetrius and the craftsmen who are with him have a case against anyone, the courts are in session, and there are proconsuls. Let them bring charges against one another. ³⁹ But if you want something else, it must be decided in a legal assembly. ⁴⁰ In fact, we run a risk of being charged with rioting for what

happened today, since there is no justification that we can give as a reason for this disorderly gathering." ⁴¹ After saying this, he dismissed the assembly.

20 After the uproar was over, Paul sent for the disciples, encouraged them, and after saying good-bye, departed to go to Macedonia. ² And when he had passed through those areas and exhorted them at length, he came to Greece ³ and stayed three months. When he was about to set sail for Syria, a plot was devised against him by the Jews, so a decision was made to go back through Macedonia. ⁴ He was accompanied^D by Sopater son of Pyrrhus^E from Berea, Aristarchus and Secundus from Thessalonica, Gaius from Derbe, Timothy, and Tychicus and Trophimus from Asia. ⁵ These men went on ahead and waited for us in Troas, ⁶ but we sailed away from Philippi after the days of Unleavened Bread. In five days we reached them at Troas, where we spent seven days.

⁷ On the first day of the week, we^F assembled to break bread. Paul spoke to them, and since he was about to depart the next day, he extended his message until midnight. ⁸ There were many lamps in the room upstairs where we were assembled, ⁹ and a young man named Eutychus was sitting on a window sill and sank into a deep sleep as Paul kept on speaking. When he was overcome by sleep, he fell down from the third story and was picked up dead. ¹⁰ But Paul went down, fell on him, embraced him, and said, "Don't be alarmed, for his life is in him!" ¹¹ After going upstairs, breaking the bread, and eating, Paul conversed a considerable time until dawn. Then he left. ¹² They brought the boy home alive and were greatly comforted.

¹³ Then we went on ahead to the ship and sailed for Assos, intending to take Paul on board there. For these were his instructions, since he himself was going by land. ¹⁴ When he met us at Assos, we took him on board and came to Mitylene. ¹⁵ Sailing from there, the next day we arrived off Chios. The following day we crossed over to Samos, and^G the day after, we came to Miletus. ¹⁶ For Paul had decided to sail past Ephesus so he would not have to spend time in Asia, because he was hurrying to be in Jerusalem, if possible, for the day of Pentecost.

---

^A 19:31 Lit not to give himself   ^B 19:35 Other mss add goddess   ^C 19:37 Other mss read your   ^D 20:4 Other mss add to Asia   ^E 20:4 Other mss omit son of Pyrrhus   ^F 20:7 Other mss read the disciples   ^G 20:15 Other mss add after staying at Trogyllium

¹⁷ Now from Miletus, he sent to Ephesus and called for the elders of the church. ¹⁸ And when they came to him, he said to them: "You know, from the first day I set foot in Asia, how I was with you the whole time— ¹⁹ serving the Lord with all humility, with tears, and with the trials that came to me through the plots of the Jews— ²⁰ and that I did not shrink back from proclaiming to you anything that was profitable or from teaching it to you in public and from house to house. ²¹ I testified to both Jews and Greeks about repentance toward God and faith in our Lord Jesus.

²² "And now I am on my way to Jerusalem, bound in my spirit,ᴬ not knowing what I will encounter there, ²³ except that in town after town the Holy Spirit testifies to me that chains and afflictions are waiting for me. ²⁴ But I count my life of no value to myself, so that I may finish my courseᴮ and the ministry I received from the Lord Jesus, to testify to the gospel of God's grace.

²⁵ "And now I know that none of you will ever see my face again—everyone I went about preaching the kingdom to. ²⁶ Therefore I testify to you this day that I am innocentᶜ of everyone's blood, ²⁷ for I did not shrink back from declaring to you the whole plan of God. ²⁸ Be on guard for yourselves and for all the flock that the Holy Spirit has appointed you to as overseers, to shepherd the church of God,ᴰ which He purchased with His own blood. ²⁹ I know that after my departure savage wolves will come in among you, not sparing the flock. ³⁰ And men will rise up from your own number with deviant doctrines to lure the disciples into following them. ³¹ Therefore be on the alert, remembering that night and day for three years I did not stop warning each one of you with tears.

³² "And nowᴱ I commit you to God and to the message of His grace, which is able to build you up and to give you an inheritance among all who are sanctified. ³³ I have not coveted anyone's silver or gold or clothing. ³⁴ You yourselves know that these hands have provided for my needs and for those who were with me. ³⁵ In every way I've shown you that by laboring like this, it is necessary to help the weak and to keep in mind the words of the Lord Jesus, for He said, 'It is more blessed to give than to receive.'"

³⁶ After he said this, he knelt down and prayed with all of them. ³⁷ There was a great deal of weeping by everyone. They embraced Paul and kissed him, ³⁸ grieving most of all over his statement that they would never see his face again. Then they escorted him to the ship.

21 After we tore ourselves away from them and set sail, we came by a direct route to Cos, the next day to Rhodes, and from there to Patara. ² Finding a ship crossing over to Phoenicia, we boarded and set sail. ³ After we sighted Cyprus, leaving it on the left, we sailed on to Syria and arrived at Tyre, because the ship was to unload its cargo there. ⁴ So we found some disciples and stayed there seven days. Through the Spirit they told Paul not to go to Jerusalem. ⁵ When our days there were over, we left to continue our journey, while all of them, with their wives and children, escorted us out of the city. After kneeling down on the beach to pray, ⁶ we said good-bye to one another. Then we boarded the ship, and they returned home.

⁷ When we completed our voyage from Tyre, we reached Ptolemais, where we greeted the brothers and stayed with them one day. ⁸ The next day we left and came to Caesarea, where we entered the house of Philip the evangelist, who was one of the Seven, and stayed with him. ⁹ This man had four virgin daughters who prophesied.

¹⁰ While we were staying there many days, a prophet named Agabus came down from Judea. ¹¹ He came to us, took Paul's belt, tied his own feet and hands, and said, "This is what the Holy Spirit says: 'In this way the Jews in Jerusalem will bind the man who owns this belt and deliver him into Gentile hands.'" ¹² When we heard this, both we and the local people begged him not to go up to Jerusalem. ¹³ Then Paul replied, "What are you doing, weeping and breaking my heart? For I am ready not only to be bound but also to die in Jerusalem for the name of the Lord Jesus." ¹⁴ Since he would not be persuaded, we stopped talking and simply said, "The Lord's will be done!"

¹⁵ After these days we got ready and went up to Jerusalem. ¹⁶ Some of the disciples from Caesarea also went with us and brought us to

ᴬ20:22 Or in the Spirit ᴮ20:24 Other mss add with joy ᶜ20:26 Lit clean ᴰ20:28 Other mss read church of the Lord; other mss read church of the Lord and God ᴱ20:32 Other mss add brothers,

Mnason, a Cypriot and an early disciple, with whom we were to stay.

¹⁷ When we reached Jerusalem, the brothers welcomed us gladly. ¹⁸ The following day Paul went in with us to James, and all the elders were present. ¹⁹ After greeting them, he related in detail what God did among the Gentiles through his ministry.

²⁰ When they heard it, they glorified God and said, "You see, brother, how many thousands of Jews there are who have believed, and they are all zealous for the law. ²¹ But they have been told about you that you teach all the Jews who are among the Gentiles to abandon Moses, by telling them not to circumcise their children or to walk in our customs. ²² So what is to be done?ᴬ They will certainly hear that you've come. ²³ Therefore do what we tell you: We have four men who have obligated themselves with a vow. ²⁴ Take these men, purify yourself along with them, and pay for them to get their heads shaved. Then everyone will know that what they were told about you amounts to nothing, but that you yourself are also careful about observing the law. ²⁵ With regard to the Gentiles who have believed, we have written a letter containing our decision thatᴮ they should keep themselves from food sacrificed to idols, from blood, from what is strangled, and from sexual immorality."

²⁶ Then the next day, Paul took the men, having purified himself along with them, and entered the temple, announcing the completion of the purification days when the offering for each of them would be made. ²⁷ As the seven days were about to end, the Jews from Asia saw him in the temple complex, stirred up the whole crowd, and seized him, ²⁸ shouting, "Men of Israel, help! This is the man who teaches everyone everywhere against our people, our law, and this place. What's more, he also brought Greeks into the temple and has profaned this holy place." ²⁹ For they had previously seen Trophimus the Ephesian in the city with him, and they supposed that Paul had brought him into the temple complex.ᶜ

³⁰ The whole city was stirred up, and the people rushed together. They seized Paul, dragged him out of the temple complex, and at once the gates were shut. ³¹ As they were

trying to kill him, word went up to the commander of the regiment that all Jerusalem was in chaos. ³² Taking along soldiers and centurions, he immediately ran down to them. Seeing the commander and the soldiers, they stopped beating Paul. ³³ Then the commander came up, took him into custody, and ordered him to be bound with two chains. He asked who he was and what he had done. ³⁴ Some in the mob were shouting one thing and some another. Since he was not able to get reliable information because of the uproar, he ordered him to be taken into the barracks. ³⁵ When Paul got to the steps, he had to be carried by the soldiers because of the mob's violence, ³⁶ for the mass of people followed, yelling, "Take him away!"

³⁷ As he was about to be brought into the barracks, Paul said to the commander, "Am I allowed to say something to you?"

He replied, "Do you know Greek? ³⁸ Aren't you the Egyptian who raised a rebellion some time ago and led 4,000 Assassinsᴰ,ᴱ into the wilderness?"

³⁹ Paul said, "I am a Jewish man from Tarsus of Cilicia, a citizen of an important city.ᶠ Now I ask you, let me speak to the people."

⁴⁰ After he had given permission, Paul stood on the steps and motioned with his hand to the people. When there was a great hush, he addressed them in the Hebrew language:

22 ¹ "Brothers and fathers, listen now to my defense before you." ² When they heard that he was addressing them in the Hebrew language, they became even quieter. ³ He continued, "I am a Jewish man, born in Tarsus of Cilicia but brought up in this cityᴳ at the feet of Gamaliel and educated according to the strict view of our patriarchal law. Being zealous for God, just as all of you are today, ⁴ I persecuted this Way to the death, binding and putting both men and women in jail, ⁵ as both the high priest and the whole council of elders can testify about me. After I received letters from them to the brothers, I traveled to Damascus to bring those who were prisoners there to be punished in Jerusalem.

⁶ "As I was traveling and near Damascus, about noon an intense light from heaven suddenly flashed around me. ⁷ I fell to the ground

---

ᴬ21:22 Other mss add *A multitude has to come together, since*   ᴮ21:25 Other mss add *they should observe no such thing, except that*
ᶜ21:29 The inner temple court for Jewish men   ᴰ21:38 Lit *4,000 men of the Assassins*   ᴱ21:38 In Lat, the word *Sicarii* is similar to the Eng
word "cut-throats."   ᶠ21:39 Lit *of no insignificant city*   ᴳ22:3 Probably Jerusalem, but others think Tarsus

and heard a voice saying to me, 'Saul, Saul, why are you persecuting Me?'

⁸ "I answered, 'Who are You, Lord?'

"He said to me, 'I am Jesus the Nazarene, the One you are persecuting!' ⁹ Now those who were with me saw the light,ᴬ but they did not hear the voice of the One who was speaking to me.

¹⁰ "Then I said, 'What should I do, Lord?'

"And the Lord told me, 'Get up and go into Damascus, and there you will be told about everything that is assigned for you to do.'

¹¹ "Since I couldn't see because of the brightness of that light, I was led by the hand by those who were with me, and came into Damascus. ¹² Someone named Ananias, a devout man according to the law, having a good reputation with all the Jews residing there, ¹³ came and stood by me and said, 'Brother Saul, regain your sight.' And in that very hour I looked up and saw him. ¹⁴ Then he said, 'The God of our fathers has appointed you to know His will, to see the Righteous One, and to hear the sound of His voice.ᴮ ¹⁵ For you will be a witness for Him to all people of what you have seen and heard. ¹⁶ And now, why delay? Get up and be baptized, and wash away your sins by calling on His name.'

¹⁷ "After I came back to Jerusalem and was praying in the temple complex, I went into a visionary state ¹⁸ and saw Him telling me, 'Hurry and get out of Jerusalem quickly, because they will not accept your testimony about Me!'

¹⁹ "But I said, 'Lord, they know that in synagogue after synagogue I had those who believed in You imprisoned and beaten. ²⁰ And when the blood of Your witness Stephen was being shed, I was standing by and approving,ᶜ and I guarded the clothes of those who killed him.'

²¹ "Then He said to me, 'Go, because I will send you far away to the Gentiles.'"

²² They listened to him up to this word. Then they raised their voices, shouting, "Wipe this person off the earth—it's a disgrace for him to live!"

²³ As they were yelling and flinging aside their robes and throwing dust into the air, ²⁴ the commander ordered him to be brought into the barracks, directing that he be examined with the scourge, so he could discover

the reason they were shouting against him like this. ²⁵ As they stretched him out for the lash, Paul said to the centurion standing by, "Is it legal for you to scourge a man who is a Roman citizen and is uncondemned?"

²⁶ When the centurion heard this, he went and reported to the commander, saying, "What are you going to do? For this man is a Roman citizen."

²⁷ The commander came and said to him, "Tell me—are you a Roman citizen?"

"Yes," he said.

²⁸ The commander replied, "I bought this citizenship for a large amount of money."

"But I was born a citizen," Paul said.

²⁹ Therefore, those who were about to examine him withdrew from him at once. The commander too was alarmed when he realized Paul was a Roman citizen and he had bound him.

³⁰ The next day, since he wanted to find out exactly why Paul was being accused by the Jews, he released himᴰ and instructed the chief priests and all the Sanhedrin to convene. Then he brought Paul down and placed him before them. ¹ Paul looked intently at the Sanhedrin and said, "Brothers, I have lived my life before God in all good conscience until this day." ² But the high priest Ananias ordered those who were standing next to him to strike him on the mouth. ³ Then Paul said to him, "God is going to strike you, you whitewashed wall! You are sitting there judging me according to the law, and in violation of the law are you ordering me to be struck?"

⁴ And those standing nearby said, "Do you dare revile God's high priest?"

⁵ "I did not know, brothers, that he was the high priest," replied Paul. "For it is written, **You must not speak evil of a ruler of your people.**ᴱ ⁶ When Paul realized that one part of them were Sadducees and the other part were Pharisees, he cried out in the Sanhedrin, "Brothers, I am a Pharisee, a son of Pharisees! I am being judged because of the hope of the resurrection of the dead!" ⁷ When he said this, a dispute broke out between the Pharisees and the Sadducees, and the assembly was divided. ⁸ For the Sadducees say there is no resurrection, and no angel or spirit, but the Pharisees affirm them all.

ᴬ22:9 Other mss add *and were afraid* ᴮ22:14 Lit *to hear a voice from His mouth* ᶜ22:20 Other mss add *of his murder* ᴰ22:30 Other mss add *from his chains* ᴱ23:5 Ex 22:28

⁹ The shouting grew loud, and some of the scribes of the Pharisees' party got up and argued vehemently: "We find nothing evil in this man. What if a spirit or an angel has spoken to him?"ᴬ ¹⁰ When the dispute became violent, the commander feared that Paul might be torn apart by them and ordered the troops to go down, rescue him from them, and bring him into the barracks.

¹¹ The following night, the Lord stood by him and said, "Have courage! For as you have testified about Me in Jerusalem, so you must also testify in Rome."

¹² When it was day, the Jews formed a conspiracy and bound themselves under a curse: neither to eat nor to drink until they had killed Paul. ¹³ There were more than 40 who had formed this plot. ¹⁴ These men went to the chief priests and elders and said, "We have bound ourselves under a solemn curse that we won't eat anything until we have killed Paul. ¹⁵ So now you, along with the Sanhedrin, make a request to the commander that he bring him down to youᴮ as if you were going to investigate his case more thoroughly. However, before he gets near, we are ready to kill him."

¹⁶ But the son of Paul's sister, hearing about their ambush, came and entered the barracks and reported it to Paul. ¹⁷ Then Paul called one of the centurions and said, "Take this young man to the commander, because he has something to report to him."

¹⁸ So he took him, brought him to the commander, and said, "The prisoner Paul called me and asked me to bring this young man to you, because he has something to tell you."

¹⁹ Then the commander took him by the hand, led him aside, and inquired privately, "What is it you have to report to me?"

²⁰ "The Jews," he said, "have agreed to ask you to bring Paul down to the Sanhedrin tomorrow, as though they are going to hold a somewhat more careful inquiry about him. ²¹ Don't let them persuade you, because there are more than 40 of them arranging to ambush him, men who have bound themselves under a curse not to eat or drink until they kill him. Now they are ready, waiting for a commitment from you."

²² So the commander dismissed the young man and instructed him, "Don't tell anyone that you have informed me about this."

²³ He summoned two of his centurions and said, "Get 200 soldiers ready with 70 cavalry and 200 spearmen to go to Caesarea at nine tonight.ᶜ ²⁴ Also provide mounts so they can put Paul on them and bring him safely to Felix the governor."

²⁵ He wrote a letter of this kind:

²⁶ Claudius Lysias,
To the most excellent governor Felix: Greetings.

²⁷ When this man had been seized by the Jews and was about to be killed by them, I arrived with my troops and rescued him because I learned that he is a Roman citizen. ²⁸ Wanting to know the charge they were accusing him of, I brought him down before their Sanhedrin. ²⁹ I found out that the accusations were about disputed matters in their law, and that there was no charge that merited death or chains. ³⁰ When I was informed that there was a plot against the man,ᴰ I sent him to you right away. I also ordered his accusers to state their case against him in your presence.ᴱ

³¹ Therefore, the soldiers took Paul during the night and brought him to Antipatris as they were ordered. ³² The next day, they returned to the barracks, allowing the cavalry to go on with him. ³³ When these men entered Caesarea and delivered the letter to the governor, they also presented Paul to him. ³⁴ After heᶠ read it, he asked what province he was from. So when he learned he was from Cilicia, ³⁵ he said, "I will give you a hearing whenever your accusers get here too." And he ordered that he be kept under guard in Herod's palace.

24 After five days Ananias the high priest came down with some elders and a lawyerᴳ named Tertullus. These men presented their case against Paul to the governor. ² When he was called in, Tertullus began to accuse him and said: "Since we enjoy great peace because of you, and reforms are taking place for the benefit of this nation by your foresight, ³ we acknowledge this in every way

ᴬ23:9 Other mss add *Let us not fight God.* ᴮ23:15 Other mss add *tomorrow* ᶜ23:23 Lit *at the third hour tonight* ᴰ23:30 Other mss add *by the Jews* ᴱ23:30 Other mss add *Farewell* ᶠ23:34 Other mss read *the governor* ᴳ24:1 In Gk, the word *rhetor* is similar to the Eng "rhetoric." In this situation, a rhetorician who was skilled in public speaking in the Gk language was needed.

and everywhere, most excellent Felix, with utmost gratitude. [4] However, so that I will not burden you any further, I beg you in your graciousness to give us a brief hearing. [5] For we have found this man to be a plague, an agitator among all the Jews throughout the Roman world, and a ringleader of the sect of the Nazarenes! [6] He even tried to desecrate the temple, so we apprehended him [and wanted to judge him according to our law. [7] But Lysias the commander came and took him from our hands with great force, [8] commanding his accusers to come to you.][A] By examining him yourself you will be able to discern all these things we are accusing him of." [9] The Jews also joined in the attack, alleging that these things were so.

[10] When the governor motioned to him to speak, Paul replied: "Because I know you have been a judge of this nation for many years, I am glad to offer my defense in what concerns me. [11] You are able to determine that it is no more than 12 days since I went up to worship in Jerusalem. [12] They didn't find me disputing with anyone or causing a disturbance among the crowd, either in the temple complex or in the synagogues or anywhere in the city. [13] Neither can they provide evidence to you of what they now bring against me. [14] But I confess this to you: I worship my fathers' God according to the Way, which they call a sect, believing all the things that are written in the Law and in the Prophets. [15] And I have a hope in God, which these men themselves also accept, that there is going to be a resurrection,[B] both of the righteous and the unrighteous. [16] I always do my best to have a clear conscience toward God and men. [17] After many years, I came to bring charitable gifts and offerings to my nation, [18] and while I was doing this, some Jews from Asia found me ritually purified in the temple, without a crowd and without any uproar. [19] It is they who ought to be here before you to bring charges, if they have anything against me. [20] Either let these men here state what wrongdoing they found in me when I stood before the Sanhedrin, [21] or about this one statement I cried out while standing among them, 'Today I am being judged before you concerning the resurrection of the dead.'"

[22] Since Felix was accurately informed about the Way, he adjourned the hearing, saying, "When Lysias the commander comes down, I will decide your case." [23] He ordered that the centurion keep Paul[C] under guard, though he could have some freedom, and that he should not prevent any of his friends from serving[D] him.

[24] After some days, when Felix came with his wife Drusilla, who was Jewish, he sent for Paul and listened to him on the subject of faith in Christ Jesus. [25] Now as he spoke about righteousness, self-control, and the judgment to come, Felix became afraid and replied, "Leave for now, but when I find time I'll call for you." [26] At the same time he was also hoping that money would be given to him by Paul.[E] For this reason he sent for him quite often and conversed with him.

[27] After two years had passed, Felix received a successor, Porcius Festus, and because he wished to do a favor for the Jews, Felix left Paul in prison.

25 Three days after Festus arrived in the province, he went up to Jerusalem from Caesarea. [2] Then the chief priests and the leaders of the Jews presented their case against Paul to him; and they appealed, [3] asking him to do them a favor against Paul,[F] that he might summon him to Jerusalem. They were preparing an ambush along the road to kill him. [4] However, Festus answered that Paul should be kept at Caesarea, and that he himself was about to go there shortly. [5] "Therefore," he said, "let the men of authority among you go down with me and accuse him, if there is any wrong in this man."

[6] When he had spent not more than eight or 10 days among them, he went down to Caesarea. The next day, seated at the judge's bench, he commanded Paul to be brought in. [7] When he arrived, the Jews who had come down from Jerusalem stood around him and brought many serious charges that they were not able to prove, [8] while Paul made the defense that, "Neither against the Jewish law, nor against the temple, nor against Caesar have I sinned at all."

[9] Then Festus, wanting to do a favor for the Jews, replied to Paul, "Are you willing to go up to Jerusalem, there to be tried before me on these charges?"

A 24:6-8 Other mss omit bracketed text   B 24:15 Other mss add of the dead   C 24:23 Lit him   D 24:23 Other mss add or visiting   E 24:26 Other mss add so that he might release him   F 25:3 Lit asking a favor against him

[10] But Paul said: "I am standing at Caesar's tribunal, where I ought to be tried. I have done no wrong to the Jews, as even you can see very well. [11] If then I am doing wrong, or have done anything deserving of death, I do not refuse to die, but if there is nothing to what these men accuse me of, no one can give me up to them. I appeal to Caesar!"

[12] After Festus conferred with his council, he replied, "You have appealed to Caesar; to Caesar you will go!"

[13] After some days had passed, King Agrippa[A] and Bernice arrived in Caesarea and paid a courtesy call on Festus. [14] Since they stayed there many days, Festus presented Paul's case to the king, saying, "There's a man who was left as a prisoner by Felix. [15] When I was in Jerusalem, the chief priests and the elders of the Jews presented their case and asked for a judgment against him. [16] I answered them that it's not the Romans' custom to give any man up[B] before the accused confronts the accusers face to face and has an opportunity to give a defense concerning the charges. [17] Therefore, when they had assembled here, I did not delay. The next day I sat at the judge's bench and ordered the man to be brought in. [18] Concerning him, the accusers stood up and brought no charge of the sort I was expecting. [19] Instead they had some disagreements with him about their own religion and about a certain Jesus, a dead man Paul claimed to be alive. [20] Since I was at a loss in a dispute over such things, I asked him if he wished to go to Jerusalem and be tried there concerning these matters. [21] But when Paul appealed to be held for trial by the Emperor, I ordered him to be kept in custody until I could send him to Caesar."

[22] Then Agrippa said to Festus, "I would like to hear the man myself."

"Tomorrow you will hear him," he replied.

[23] So the next day, Agrippa and Bernice came with great pomp and entered the auditorium with the commanders and prominent men of the city. When Festus gave the command, Paul was brought in. [24] Then Festus said: "King Agrippa and all men present with us, you see this man about whom the whole Jewish community has appealed to me, both in Jerusalem and here, shouting that he should not live any longer. [25] Now I realized

that he had not done anything deserving of death, but when he himself appealed to the Emperor, I decided to send him. [26] I have nothing definite to write to my lord about him. Therefore, I have brought him before all of you, and especially before you, King Agrippa, so that after this examination is over, I may have something to write. [27] For it seems unreasonable to me to send a prisoner and not to indicate the charges against him."

26 Agrippa said to Paul, "It is permitted for you to speak for yourself."

Then Paul stretched out his hand and began his defense: [2] "I consider myself fortunate, King Agrippa, that today I am going to make a defense before you about everything I am accused of by the Jews, [3] especially since you are an expert in all the Jewish customs and controversies. Therefore I beg you to listen to me patiently.

[4] "All the Jews know my way of life from my youth, which was spent from the beginning among my own nation and in Jerusalem. [5] They have previously known me for quite some time, if they were willing to testify, that according to the strictest party of our religion I lived as a Pharisee. [6] And now I stand on trial for the hope of the promise made by God to our fathers, [7] the promise our 12 tribes hope to attain as they earnestly serve Him night and day. King Agrippa, I am being accused by the Jews because of this hope. [8] Why is it considered incredible by any of you that God raises the dead? [9] In fact, I myself supposed it was necessary to do many things in opposition to the name of Jesus the Nazarene. [10] I actually did this in Jerusalem, and I locked up many of the saints in prison, since I had received authority for that from the chief priests. When they were put to death, I cast my vote against them. [11] In all the synagogues I often tried to make them blaspheme by punishing them. I even pursued them to foreign cities since I was greatly enraged at them.

[12] "I was traveling to Damascus under these circumstances with authority and a commission from the chief priests. [13] King Agrippa, while on the road at midday, I saw a light from heaven brighter than the sun, shining around me and those traveling with me. [14] We all fell to the ground, and I heard a voice speaking to me in the Hebrew language, 'Saul, Saul, why

A25:13 Herod Agrippa II ruled Palestine A.D. 52–ca 95.   B25:16 Other mss add to destruction are you persecuting Me? It is hard for you to kick against the goads.'[A]

[15] "Then I said, 'Who are You, Lord?'

"And the Lord replied: 'I am Jesus, the One you are persecuting. [16] But get up and stand on your feet. For I have appeared to you for this purpose, to appoint you as a servant and a witness of what you have seen[B] and of what I will reveal to you. [17] I will rescue you from the people and from the Gentiles. I now send you to them [18] to open their eyes so they may turn from darkness to light and from the power of Satan to God, that by faith in Me they may receive forgiveness of sins and a share among those who are sanctified.'

[19] "Therefore, King Agrippa, I was not disobedient to the heavenly vision. [20] Instead, I preached to those in Damascus first, and to those in Jerusalem and in all the region of Judea, and to the Gentiles, that they should repent and turn to God, and do works worthy of repentance. [21] For this reason the Jews seized me in the temple complex and were trying to kill me. [22] To this very day, I have obtained help that comes from God, and I stand and testify to both small and great, saying nothing else than what the prophets and Moses said would take place— [23] that the Messiah must suffer, and that as the first to rise from the dead, He would proclaim light to our people and to the Gentiles."

[24] As he was making his defense this way, Festus exclaimed in a loud voice, "You're out of your mind, Paul! Too much study is driving you mad!"

[25] But Paul replied, "I'm not out of my mind, most excellent Festus. On the contrary, I'm speaking words of truth and good judgment. [26] For the king knows about these matters. It is to him I am actually speaking boldly. For I am convinced that none of these things escapes his notice, since this was not done in a corner. [27] King Agrippa, do you believe the prophets? I know you believe."

[28] Then Agrippa said to Paul, "Are you going to persuade me to become a Christian so easily?"

[29] "I wish before God," replied Paul, "that whether easily or with difficulty, not only you but all who listen to me today might become as I am—except for these chains."

[30] So the king, the governor, Bernice, and those sitting with them got up, [31] and when they had left they talked with each other and said, "This man is doing nothing that deserves death or chains."

[32] Then Agrippa said to Festus, "This man could have been released if he had not appealed to Caesar."

27 When it was decided that we were to sail to Italy, they handed over Paul and some other prisoners to a centurion named Julius, of the Imperial Regiment. [2] So when we had boarded a ship of Adramyttium, we put to sea, intending to sail to ports along the coast of Asia. Aristarchus, a Macedonian of Thessalonica, was with us. [3] The next day we put in at Sidon, and Julius treated Paul kindly and allowed him to go to his friends to receive their care. [4] When we had put out to sea from there, we sailed along the northern coast[C] of Cyprus because the winds were against us. [5] After sailing through the open sea off Cilicia and Pamphylia, we reached Myra in Lycia. [6] There the centurion found an Alexandrian ship sailing for Italy and put us on board. [7] Sailing slowly for many days, we came with difficulty as far as Cnidus. Since the wind did not allow us to approach it, we sailed along the south side[C] of Crete off Salmone. [8] With yet more difficulty we sailed along the coast and came to a place called Fair Havens near the city of Lasea.

[9] By now much time had passed, and the voyage was already dangerous. Since the Fast[D] was already over, Paul gave his advice [10] and told them, "Men, I can see that this voyage is headed toward damage and heavy loss, not only of the cargo and the ship but also of our lives." [11] But the centurion paid attention to the captain and the owner of the ship rather than to what Paul said. [12] Since the harbor was unsuitable to winter in, the majority decided to set sail from there, hoping somehow to reach Phoenix, a harbor on Crete open to the southwest and northwest, and to winter there.

[13] When a gentle south wind sprang up, they thought they had achieved their purpose. They weighed anchor and sailed along the shore of Crete. [14] But not long afterward, a fierce wind called the "northeaster"[E] rushed down from the island. [15] Since the ship was

caught and was unable to head into the wind, we gave way to it and were driven along. ¹⁶ After running under the shelter of a little island called Cauda,ᴬ we were barely able to get control of the skiff. ¹⁷ After hoisting it up, they used ropes and tackle and girded the ship. Then, fearing they would run aground on the Syrtis,ᴮ they lowered the drift-anchor, and in this way they were driven along. ¹⁸ Because we were being severely battered by the storm, they began to jettison the cargo the next day. ¹⁹ On the third day, they threw the ship's gear overboard with their own hands.

²⁰ For many days neither sun nor stars appeared, and the severe storm kept raging. Finally all hope that we would be saved was disappearing. ²¹ Since many were going without food, Paul stood up among them and said, "You men should have followed my advice not to sail from Crete and sustain this damage and loss. ²² Now I urge you to take courage, because there will be no loss of any of your lives, but only of the ship. ²³ For this night an angel of the God I belong to and serve stood by me, ²⁴ and said, 'Don't be afraid, Paul. You must stand before Caesar. And, look! God has graciously given you all those who are sailing with you.' ²⁵ Therefore, take courage, men, because I believe God that it will be just the way it was told to me. ²⁶ However, we must run aground on a certain island."

²⁷ When the fourteenth night came, we were drifting in the Adriatic Sea,ᶜ and in the middle of the night the sailors thought they were approaching land.ᴰ ²⁸ They took a sounding and found it to be 120 feetᴱ deep; when they had sailed a little farther and sounded again, they found it to be 90 feetᶠ deep. ²⁹ Then, fearing we might run aground in some rocky place, they dropped four anchors from the stern and prayed for daylight to come.

³⁰ Some sailors tried to escape from the ship; they had let down the skiff into the sea, pretending that they were going to put out anchors from the bow. ³¹ Paul said to the centurion and the soldiers, "Unless these men stay in the ship, you cannot be saved." ³² Then the soldiers cut the ropes holding the skiff and let it drop away.

³³ When it was about daylight, Paul urged them all to take food, saying, "Today is the fourteenth day that you have been waiting and going without food, having eaten nothing. ³⁴ Therefore I urge you to take some food. For this has to do with your survival, since none of you will lose a hair from your head." ³⁵ After he said these things and had taken some bread, he gave thanks to God in the presence of all of them, and when he broke it, he began to eat. ³⁶ They all became encouraged and took food themselves. ³⁷ In all there were 276 of us on the ship. ³⁸ When they had eaten enough, they began to lighten the ship by throwing the grain overboard into the sea.

³⁹ When daylight came, they did not recognize the land but sighted a bay with a beach. They planned to run the ship ashore if they could. ⁴⁰ After casting off the anchors, they left them in the sea, at the same time loosening the ropes that held the rudders. Then they hoisted the foresail to the wind and headed for the beach. ⁴¹ But they struck a sandbar and ran the ship aground. The bow jammed fast and remained immovable, while the stern began to break up by the pounding of the waves.

⁴² The soldiers' plan was to kill the prisoners so that no one could swim away and escape. ⁴³ But the centurion kept them from carrying out their plan because he wanted to save Paul, so he ordered those who could swim to jump overboard first and get to land. ⁴⁴ The rest were to follow, some on planks and some on debris from the ship. In this way, everyone safely reached the shore.

28 Once ashore, we then learned that the island was called Malta. ² The local people showed us extraordinary kindness, for they lit a fire and took us all in, since it was raining and cold. ³ As Paul gathered a bundle of brushwood and put it on the fire, a viper came out because of the heat and fastened itself to his hand. ⁴ When the local people saw the creature hanging from his hand, they said to one another, "This man is probably a murderer, and though he has escaped the sea, Justiceᴳ does not allow him to live!" ⁵ However, he shook the creature off into the fire and suffered no harm. ⁶ They expected that he would swell up or suddenly drop dead. But after they

---

ᴬ27:16 Or *Clauda*   ᴮ27:17 = sandbanks or sandbars near North Africa   ᶜ27:27 Part of the northern Mediterranean Sea; not the modern Adriatic Sea east of Italy   ᴰ27:27 Lit *thought there was land approaching them*   ᴱ27:28 Lit *20 fathoms*   ᶠ27:28 Lit *15 fathoms*   ᴳ28:4 Gk *Dike*, a goddess of justice waited a long time and saw nothing unusual happen to him, they changed their minds and said he was a god.

⁷ Now in the area around that place was an estate belonging to the leading man of the island, named Publius, who welcomed us and entertained us hospitably for three days. ⁸ Publius's father was in bed suffering from fever and dysentery. Paul went to him, and praying and laying his hands on him, he healed him. ⁹ After this, the rest of those on the island who had diseases also came and were cured. ¹⁰ So they heaped many honors on us, and when we sailed, they gave us what we needed.

¹¹ After three months we set sail in an Alexandrian ship that had wintered at the island, with the Twin Brothers^A as its figurehead. ¹² Putting in at Syracuse, we stayed three days. ¹³ From there, after making a circuit along the coast,^B we reached Rhegium. After one day a south wind sprang up, and the second day we came to Puteoli. ¹⁴ There we found believers^C and were invited to stay with them for seven days.

And so we came to Rome. ¹⁵ Now the believers^C from there had heard the news about us and had come to meet us as far as the Forum of Appius and the Three Taverns. When Paul saw them, he thanked God and took courage. ¹⁶ When we entered Rome,^D Paul was permitted to stay by himself with the soldier who guarded him.

¹⁷ After three days he called together the leaders of the Jews. When they had gathered he said to them: "Brothers, although I have done nothing against our people or the customs of our ancestors, I was delivered as a prisoner from Jerusalem into the hands of the Romans. ¹⁸ After they examined me, they wanted to release me, since I had not committed a capital offense. ¹⁹ Because the Jews objected, I was compelled to appeal to Caesar; it was not as though I had any accusation against my nation. ²⁰ For this reason I've asked to see you and speak to you. In fact, it is for the hope of Israel that I'm wearing this chain."

²¹ Then they said to him, "We haven't received any letters about you from Judea. None of the brothers has come and reported or spoken anything evil about you. ²² But we would like to hear from you what you think. For concerning this sect, we are aware that it is spoken against everywhere."

²³ After arranging a day with him, many came to him at his lodging. From dawn to dusk he expounded and witnessed about the kingdom of God. He tried to persuade them concerning Jesus from both the Law of Moses and the Prophets. ²⁴ Some were persuaded by what he said, but others did not believe.

²⁵ Disagreeing among themselves, they began to leave after Paul made one statement: "The Holy Spirit correctly spoke through the prophet Isaiah to your^E ancestors ²⁶ when He said,

> **Go to these people and say:**
> **You will listen and listen,**
> **yet never understand;**
> **and you will look and look,**
> **yet never perceive.**
> 27 **For the hearts of these people**
> **have grown callous,**
> **their ears are hard of hearing,**
> **and they have shut their eyes;**
> **otherwise they might see**
> **   with their eyes**
> **and hear with their ears,**
> **understand with their heart,**
> **and be converted,**
> **and I would heal them.**^F

²⁸ Therefore, let it be known to you that this saving work of God has been sent to the Gentiles; they will listen!" [²⁹ After he said these things, the Jews departed, while engaging in a prolonged debate among themselves.]^G

³⁰ Then he stayed two whole years in his own rented house. And he welcomed all who visited him, ³¹ proclaiming the kingdom of God and teaching the things concerning the Lord Jesus Christ with full boldness and without hindrance.

---

^A 28:11 Gk Dioscuri, twin sons of Zeus   ^B 28:13 Other mss read From there, casting off,   ^C 28:14,15 Lit brothers   ^D 28:16 Other mss add the centurion turned the prisoners over to the military commander; but   ^E 28:25 Other mss read our   ^F 28:26-27 Is 6:9-10   ^G 28:29 Other mss omit bracketed text

ROMANS

1 Paul, a slave of Christ Jesus, called as an apostle[A] and singled out for God's good news— [2] which He promised long ago through His prophets in the Holy Scriptures— [3] concerning His Son, Jesus Christ our Lord, who was a descendant of David[B] according to the flesh [4] and who has been declared to be the powerful Son of God by the resurrection from the dead according to the Spirit of holiness.[C] [5] We have received grace and apostleship through Him to bring about[D] the obedience of faith[E] among all the nations,[F] on behalf of His name, [6] including yourselves who also belong to Jesus Christ by calling:

[7] To all who are in Rome, loved by God, called as saints.

Grace to you and peace from God our Father and the Lord Jesus Christ.

[8] First, I thank my God through Jesus Christ for all of you because the news of your faith[G] is being reported in all the world. [9] For God, whom I serve with my spirit in telling the good news about His Son, is my witness that I constantly mention you, [10] always asking in my prayers that if it is somehow in God's will, I may now at last succeed in coming to you. [11] For I want very much to see you, so I may impart to you some spiritual gift to strengthen you, [12] that is, to be mutually encouraged by each other's faith, both yours and mine.

[13] Now I want you to know,[H] brothers, that I often planned to come to you (but was prevented until now) in order that I might have a fruitful ministry[I] among you, just as among the rest of the Gentiles. [14] I am obligated both to Greeks and barbarians,[J] both to the wise and the foolish. [15] So I am eager to preach the good news to you also who are in Rome.

[16] For I am not ashamed of the gospel,[K] because it is God's power for salvation to everyone who believes, first to the Jew, and also to the Greek. [17] For in it God's righteousness is revealed from faith to faith,[L] just as it is written: **The righteous will live by faith.**[M,N]

[18] For God's wrath is revealed from heaven against all godlessness and unrighteousness of people who by their unrighteousness suppress the truth, [19] since what can be known[O] about God is evident among them, because God has shown it to them. [20] For His invisible attributes, that is, His eternal power and divine nature, have been clearly seen since the creation of the world, being understood through what He has made. As a result, people are without excuse. [21] For though they knew God, they did not glorify Him as God or show gratitude. Instead, their thinking became nonsense, and their senseless minds were darkened. [22] Claiming to be wise, they became fools [23] and exchanged the glory of the immortal God for images resembling mortal man, birds, four-footed animals, and reptiles.

[24] Therefore God delivered them over in the cravings of their hearts to sexual impurity, so that their bodies were degraded among themselves. [25] They exchanged the truth of God for a lie, and worshiped and served something created instead of the Creator, who is praised forever. Amen.

[26] This is why God delivered them over to degrading passions. For even their females exchanged natural sexual relations[P] for unnatural ones. [27] The males in the same way also left natural relations[P] with females and were inflamed in their lust for one another. Males committed shameless acts with males and received in their own persons[Q] the appropriate penalty of their error.

[28] And because they did not think it worthwhile to acknowledge God, God delivered them over to a worthless mind to do what is morally wrong. [29] They are filled with all unrighteousness,[R] evil, greed, and wickedness. They are full of envy, murder, quarrels, deceit, and malice. They are gossips, [30] slanderers, God-haters, arrogant, proud, boastful, inventors of evil, disobedient to parents, [31] undiscerning, untrustworthy, unloving,[S] and unmerciful. [32] Although they know full well

---

A1:1 Or *Jesus, a called apostle*   **B1:3** Lit *was of the seed of David*   **C1:4** Or *the spirit of holiness,* or *the Holy Spirit*   **D1:5** Or *Him for;* lit *Him into*   **E1:5** Or *the obedience that is faith,* or *the faithful obedience,* or *the obedience that comes from faith;* Rm 16:26   **F1:5** Or *Gentiles*   **G1:8** Or *because your faith*   **H1:13** Lit *I don't want you to be unaware*   **I1:13** Lit *have some fruit*   **J1:14** Or *non-Greeks*   **K1:16** Other mss add *of Christ*   **L1:17** Or *revealed out of faith into faith*   **M1:17** Or *The one who is righteous by faith will live*   **N1:17** Hab 2:4   **O1:19** Or *what is known*   **P1:26,27** Lit *natural use*   **Q1:27** Or *in themselves*   **R1:29** Other mss add *sexual immorality*   **S1:31** Other mss add *unforgiving*

God's just sentence—that those who practice such things deserve to die[A]—they not only do them, but even applaud[B] others who practice them.

2 Therefore, any one of you[C] who judges is without excuse. For when you judge another, you condemn yourself, since you, the judge, do the same things. [2] We know that God's judgment on those who do such things is based on the truth. [3] Do you really think—anyone of you who judges those who do such things yet do the same—that you will escape God's judgment? [4] Or do you despise the riches of His kindness, restraint, and patience, not recognizing[D] that God's kindness is intended to lead you to repentance? [5] But because of your hardness and unrepentant heart you are storing up wrath for yourself in the day of wrath, when God's righteous judgment is revealed. [6] **He will repay each one according to his works:**[E] [7] eternal life to those who by persistence in doing good seek glory, honor, and immortality; [8] but wrath and indignation to those who are self-seeking and disobey the truth but are obeying unrighteousness; [9] affliction and distress for every human being who does evil, first to the Jew, and also to the Greek; [10] but glory, honor, and peace for everyone who does what is good, first to the Jew, and also to the Greek. [11] There is no favoritism with God.

[12] All those who sinned without the law will also perish without the law, and all those who sinned under the law will be judged by the law. [13] For the hearers of the law are not righteous before God, but the doers of the law will be declared righteous.[F] [14] So, when Gentiles, who do not have the law, instinctively do what the law demands, they are a law to themselves even though they do not have the law. [15] They show that the work of the law[G] is written on their hearts. Their consciences confirm this. Their competing thoughts will either accuse or excuse them[H] [16] on the day when God judges what people have kept secret, according to my gospel through Christ Jesus.

[17] Now if[I] you call yourself a Jew, and rest in the law, boast in God, [18] know His will, and approve the things that are superior, being instructed from the law, [19] and if you are convinced that you are a guide for the blind, a light to those in darkness, [20] an instructor of the ignorant, a teacher of the immature, having the full expression[J] of knowledge and truth in the law— [21] you then, who teach another, don't you teach yourself? You who preach, "You must not steal"—do you steal? [22] You who say, "You must not commit adultery"—do you commit adultery? You who detest idols, do you rob their temples? [23] You who boast in the law, do you dishonor God by breaking the law? [24] For, as it is written: **The name of God is blasphemed among the Gentiles because of you.**[K]

[25] For circumcision benefits you if you observe the law, but if you are a lawbreaker, your circumcision has become uncircumcision. [26] Therefore if an uncircumcised man keeps the law's requirements, will his uncircumcision not be counted as circumcision? [27] A man who is physically uncircumcised, but who fulfills the law, will judge you who are a lawbreaker in spite of having the letter of the law and circumcision. [28] For a person is not a Jew who is one outwardly, and true circumcision is not something visible in the flesh. [29] On the contrary, a person is a Jew who is one inwardly, and circumcision is of the heart—by the Spirit, not the letter.[L] That man's praise[M] is not from men but from God.

3 So what advantage does the Jew have? Or what is the benefit of circumcision? [2] Considerable in every way. First, they were entrusted with the spoken words of God. [3] What then? If some did not believe, will their unbelief cancel God's faithfulness? [4] Absolutely not! God must be true, even if everyone is a liar, as it is written:

> That You may be justified
> in Your words
> and triumph when You judge.[N]

⁵But if our unrighteousness highlights[A] God's righteousness, what are we to say? I use a human argument:[B] Is God unrighteous to inflict wrath? ⁶Absolutely not! Otherwise, how will God judge the world? ⁷But if by my lie God's truth is amplified to His glory, why am I also still judged as a sinner? ⁸And why not say, just as some people slanderously claim we say, "Let us do what is evil so that good may come"? Their condemnation is deserved!

⁹What then? Are we any better?[C] Not at all! For we have previously charged that both Jews and Gentiles[D] are all under sin,[E] ¹⁰as it is written:[F]

> There is no one righteous,
>   not even one.
> ¹¹ There is no one who understands;
>   there is no one who seeks God.
> ¹² All have turned away;
>   all alike have become useless.
>   There is no one who does
>   what is good,
>   not even one.[G]
> ¹³ Their throat is an open grave;
>   they deceive with their tongues.[H]
>   Vipers' venom is under their lips.[I]
> ¹⁴ Their mouth is full of cursing
>   and bitterness.[J]
> ¹⁵ Their feet are swift to shed blood;
> ¹⁶ ruin and wretchedness are
>   in their paths,
> ¹⁷ and the path of peace
>   they have not known.[K]
> ¹⁸ There is no fear of God
>   before their eyes.[L]

¹⁹Now we know that whatever the law says speaks to those who are subject to the law,[M] so that every mouth may be shut and the whole world may become subject to God's judgment.[N] ²⁰For no one will be justified[O] in His sight by the works of the law, because the knowledge of sin comes through the law.

²¹But now, apart from the law, God's righteousness has been revealed—attested by the Law and the Prophets[P] ²²—that is, God's righteousness through faith in Jesus Christ,[Q] to all who believe, since there is no distinction. ²³For all have sinned and fall short of the[R] glory of God. ²⁴They are justified freely by His grace through the redemption that is in Christ Jesus. ²⁵God presented Him as a propitiation[S] through faith in His blood, to demonstrate His righteousness, because in His restraint God passed over the sins previously committed. ²⁶God presented Him to demonstrate His righteousness at the present time, so that He would be righteous and declare righteous[T] the one who has faith in Jesus.

²⁷Where then is boasting? It is excluded. By what kind of law?[U] By one of works? No, on the contrary, by a law[V] of faith. ²⁸For we conclude that a man is justified by faith apart from the works of the law. ²⁹Or is God for Jews only? Is He not also for Gentiles? Yes, for Gentiles too, ³⁰since there is one God who will justify the circumcised by faith and the uncircumcised through faith. ³¹Do we then cancel the law through faith? Absolutely not! On the contrary, we uphold the law.

4 What then can we say that Abraham, our physical ancestor,[W] has found? ²If Abraham was justified[X] by works, he has something to brag about—but not before God.[Y] ³For what does the Scripture say?

> Abraham believed God,
>   and it was credited to him
>   for righteousness.[Z]

⁴Now to the one who works, pay is not considered as a gift, but as something owed. ⁵But to the one who does not work, but believes on Him who declares the ungodly to be righteous,[AA] his faith is credited for righteousness.

⁶Likewise, David also speaks of the blessing of the man God credits righteousness to apart from works:

> ⁷ How joyful are those whose lawless acts
>   are forgiven

A3:5 Or shows, or demonstrates   B3:5 Lit I speak as a man   C3:9 Are we Jews any better than the Gentiles?   D3:9 Lit Greeks   E3:9 Under sin's power or dominion   F3:10 Paul constructs this charge from a chain of OT quotations, mainly from the Psalms.   G3:10-12 Ps 14:1-3; 53:1-3; Ec 7:20   H3:13 Ps 5:9   I3:13 Ps 140:3   J3:14 Ps 10:7   K3:15-17 Is 59:7-8   L3:18 Ps 36:1   M3:19 Lit those in the law   N3:19 Or become guilty before God, or may be accountable to God   O3:20 Or will be declared righteous, or will be acquitted   P3:21 When capitalized, the Law and the Prophets = OT   Q3:22 Or through the faithfulness of Jesus Christ   R3:23 Or and lack the   S3:25 Or as a propitiatory sacrifice, or as an offering of atonement, or as a mercy seat; 2Co 5:21; Heb 9:5   T3:26 Or and justify, or and acquit   U3:27 Or what principle?   V3:27 Or a principle   W4:1 Lit our ancestor according to the flesh   X4:2 Or was declared righteous, or was acquitted   Y4:2 He has no reason for boasting in God's presence.   Z4:3 Gn 15:6   AA4:5 Or who acquits, or who justifies

Turn to page 141 and find Romans 6:23.

and whose sins are covered!
8 How joyful is the man
the Lord will never charge with sin!^A

⁹Is this blessing only for the circumcised, then? Or is it also for the uncircumcised? For we say, **Faith was credited to Abraham for righteousness.**^B ¹⁰In what way then was it credited—while he was circumcised, or uncircumcised? Not while he was circumcised, but uncircumcised. ¹¹And he received the sign of circumcision as a seal of the righteousness that he had by faith^C while still uncircumcised. This was to make him the father of all who believe but are not circumcised, so that righteousness may be credited to them also. ¹²And he became the father of the circumcised, who are not only circumcised but who also follow in the footsteps of the faith our father Abraham had while he was still uncircumcised.

¹³For the promise to Abraham or to his descendants that he would inherit the world was not through the law, but through the righteousness that comes by faith.^C ¹⁴If those who are of the law are heirs, faith is made empty and the promise is canceled. ¹⁵For the law produces wrath. And where there is no law, there is no transgression.

¹⁶This is why the promise is by faith, so that it may be according to grace, to guarantee it to all the descendants—not only to those who are of the law^D but also to those who are of Abraham's faith. He is the father of us all ¹⁷in God's sight. As it is written: **I have made you the father of many nations.**^E He believed in God, who gives life to the dead and calls things into existence that do not exist. ¹⁸He believed, hoping against hope, so that he became **the father of many nations**^E according to what had been spoken: **So will your descendants be.**^F ¹⁹He considered^G his own body to be already dead (since he was about 100 years old) and also considered the deadness of Sarah's womb, without weakening in the faith. ²⁰He did not waver in unbelief at God's promise but was strengthened in his faith and gave glory to God, ²¹because he was

fully convinced that what He had promised He was also able to perform. ²²Therefore, **it was credited to him for righteousness.**^B ²³Now **it was credited to him** was not written for Abraham alone, ²⁴but also for us. It will be credited to us who believe in Him who raised Jesus our Lord from the dead. ²⁵He was delivered up for^H our trespasses and raised for^H our justification.^I

5 Therefore, since we have been declared righteous by faith, we have peace^J with God through our Lord Jesus Christ. ²We have also obtained access through Him by faith^K into this grace in which we stand, and we rejoice in the hope of the glory of God. ³And not only that, but we also rejoice in our afflictions, because we know that affliction produces endurance, ⁴endurance produces proven character, and proven character produces hope. ⁵This hope will not disappoint us, because God's love has been poured out in our hearts through the Holy Spirit who was given to us.

⁶For while we were still helpless, at the appointed moment, Christ died for the ungodly. ⁷For rarely will someone die for a just person—though for a good person perhaps someone might even dare to die. ⁸But God proves His own love for us in that while we were still sinners, Christ died for us! ⁹Much more then, since we have now been declared righteous by His blood, we will be saved through Him from wrath. ¹⁰For if, while we were enemies, we were reconciled to God through the death of His Son, then how much more, having been reconciled, will we be saved by His life! ¹¹And not only that, but we also rejoice in God through our Lord Jesus Christ. We have now received this reconciliation through Him.

¹²Therefore, just as sin entered the world through one man, and death through sin, in this way death spread to all men, because all sinned.^L ¹³In fact, sin was in the world before the law, but sin is not charged to a person's account when there is no law. ¹⁴Nevertheless, death reigned from Adam to Moses, even over those who did not sin in the likeness of

A4:7-8 Ps 32:1-2 B4:9,22 Gn 15:6 C4:11,13 Lit righteousness of faith D4:16 Or not to those who are of the law only E4:17,18 Gn 17:5
F4:18 Gn 15:5 G4:19 Other mss read He did not consider H4:25 Or because of I4:25 Or acquittal J5:1 Other mss read faith, let us have
peace, which can also be translated faith, let us grasp the fact that we have peace K5:2 Other mss omit by faith L5:12 Or have sinned

Turn to page 177 and find Ephesians 2:8-9.

Adam's transgression. He is a prototype[A] of the Coming One.

[15] But the gift is not like the trespass. For if by the one man's trespass the many died, how much more have the grace of God and the gift overflowed to the many by the grace of the one man, Jesus Christ. [16] And the gift is not like the one man's sin, because from one sin came the judgment, resulting in condemnation, but from many trespasses came the gift, resulting in justification.[B] [17] Since by the one man's trespass, death reigned through that one man, how much more will those who receive the overflow of grace and the gift of righteousness reign in life through the one man, Jesus Christ.

[18] So then, as through one trespass there is condemnation for everyone, so also through one righteous act there is life-giving justification[C] for everyone. [19] For just as through one man's disobedience the many were made sinners, so also through the one man's obedience the many will be made righteous. [20] The law came along to multiply the trespass. But where sin multiplied, grace multiplied even more [21] so that, just as sin reigned in death, so also grace will reign through righteousness, resulting in eternal life through Jesus Christ our Lord.

6 What should we say then? Should we continue in sin so that grace may multiply? [2] Absolutely not! How can we who died to sin still live in it? [3] Or are you unaware that all of us who were baptized into Christ Jesus were baptized into His death? [4] Therefore we were buried with Him by baptism into death, in order that, just as Christ was raised from the dead by the glory of the Father, so we too may walk in a new way[D] of life. [5] For if we have been joined with Him in the likeness of His death, we will certainly also be[E] in the likeness of His resurrection. [6] For we know that our old self[F] was crucified with Him in order that sin's dominion over the body[G] may be abolished, so that we may no longer be enslaved to sin, [7] since a person who has died is freed[H] from sin's claims.[I] [8] Now if we died

with Christ, we believe that we will also live with Him, [9] because we know that Christ, having been raised from the dead, will not die again. Death no longer rules over Him. [10] For in light of the fact that He died, He died to sin once for all; but in light of the fact that He lives, He lives to God. [11] So, you too consider yourselves dead to sin but alive to God in Christ Jesus.[J]

[12] Therefore do not let sin reign in your mortal body, so that you obey[K] its desires. [13] And do not offer any parts[L] of it to sin as weapons for unrighteousness. But as those who are alive from the dead, offer yourselves to God, and all the parts[L] of yourselves to God as weapons for righteousness. [14] For sin will not rule over you, because you are not under law but under grace.

[15] What then? Should we sin because we are not under law but under grace? Absolutely not! [16] Don't you know that if you offer yourselves to someone[M] as obedient slaves, you are slaves of that one you obey—either of sin leading to death or of obedience leading to righteousness? [17] But thank God that, although you used to be slaves of sin, you obeyed from the heart that pattern of teaching you were transferred[N] to, [18] and having been liberated from sin, you became enslaved to righteousness. [19] I am using a human analogy[O] because of the weakness of your flesh.[P] For just as you offered the parts[L] of yourselves as slaves to moral impurity, and to greater and greater lawlessness, so now offer them as slaves to righteousness, which results in sanctification. [20] For when you were slaves of sin, you were free from allegiance to righteousness.[Q] [21] So what fruit was produced[R] then from the things you are now ashamed of? For the end of those things is death. [22] But now, since you have been liberated from sin and have become enslaved to God, you have your fruit, which results in sanctification[S]—and the end is eternal life! [23] For the wages of sin is death, but the gift of God is eternal life in Christ Jesus our Lord.

A5:14 Or *figure*, or *pattern*; = an OT person or thing that prefigures a NT person or thing   **B5:16** Or *acquittal*   **C5:18** Lit *is justification of life*   **D6:4** Or *in newness*   **E6:5** Be joined with Him   **F6:6** Lit *man*; = the person before conversion   **G6:6** Lit *that the body of sin*   **H6:7** Or *justified*; lit *acquitted*   **I6:7** Lit *from sin*   **J6:11** Other mss add *our Lord*   **K6:12** Other mss add *sin* (lit *it*) in   **L6:13,19** Or *members*   **M6:16** Lit *that to whom you offer yourselves*   **N6:17** Or *entrusted*   **O6:19** Lit *I speak humanly*; Paul is personifying sin and righteousness as slave masters.   **P6:19** Or *your human nature*   **Q6:20** Lit *free to righteousness*   **R6:21** Lit *what fruit do you have*   **S6:22** Or *holiness*

Turn to page 109 and find Acts 3:19.

7 Since I am speaking to those who understand law, brothers, are you unaware that the law has authority over someone as long as he lives? ²For example, a married woman is legally bound to her husband while he lives. But if her husband dies, she is released from the law regarding the husband. ³So then, if she gives herself to another man while her husband is living, she will be called an adulteress. But if her husband dies, she is free from that law. Then, if she gives herself to another man, she is not an adulteress.

⁴Therefore, my brothers, you also were put to death in relation to the law through the crucified body of the Messiah, so that you may belong to another—to Him who was raised from the dead—that we may bear fruit for God. ⁵For when we were in the flesh,ᴬ the sinful passions operated through the law in every part of usᴮ and bore fruit for death. ⁶But now we have been released from the law, since we have died to what held us, so that we may serve in the new wayᶜ of the Spirit and not in the old letter of the law.

⁷What should we say then? Is the law sin? Absolutely not! On the contrary, I would not have known sin if it were not for the law. For example, I would not have known what it is to covet if the law had not said, **Do not covet.**ᴰ ⁸And sin, seizing an opportunity through the commandment, produced in me coveting of every kind. For apart from the law sin is dead. ⁹Once I was alive apart from the law, but when the commandment came, sin sprang to life ¹⁰and I died. The commandment that was meant for life resulted in death for me. ¹¹For sin, seizing an opportunity through the commandment, deceived me, and through it killed me. ¹²So then, the law is holy, and the commandment is holy and just and good.

¹³Therefore, did what is good cause my death?ᴱ Absolutely not! On the contrary, sin, in order to be recognized as sin, was producing death in me through what is good, so that through the commandment, sin might become sinful beyond measure. ¹⁴For we know that the law is spiritual, but I am made out

of flesh,ᶠ sold into sin's power. ¹⁵For I do not understand what I am doing, because I do not practice what I want to do, but I do what I hate. ¹⁶And if I do what I do not want to do, I agree with the law that it is good. ¹⁷So now I am no longer the one doing it, but it is sin living in me. ¹⁸For I know that nothing good lives in me, that is, in my flesh. For the desire to do what is good is with me, but there is no ability to do it. ¹⁹For I do not do the good that I want to do, but I practice the evil that I do not want to do. ²⁰Now if I do what I do not want, I am no longer the one doing it, but it is the sin that lives in me. ²¹So I discover this principle:ᴳ When I want to do what is good, evil is with me. ²²For in my inner selfᴴ I joyfully agree with God's law. ²³But I see a different law in the parts of my body,ᴵ waging war against the law of my mind and taking me prisoner to the law of sin in the parts of my body.ᴵ ²⁴What a wretched man I am! Who will rescue me from this dying body? ²⁵I thank God through Jesus Christ our Lord!ᴶ So then, with my mind I myself am a slave to the law of God, but with my flesh, to the law of sin.

8 Therefore, no condemnation now exists for those in Christ Jesus,ᴷ ²because the Spirit's law of life in Christ Jesus has set youᴸ free from the law of sin and of death. ³What the law could not do since it was limitedᴹ by the flesh, God did. He condemned sin in the flesh by sending His own Son in flesh like ours under sin's domain,ᴺ and as a sin offering, ⁴in order that the law's requirement would be accomplished in us who do not walk according to the flesh but according to the Spirit. ⁵For those who liveᴼ according to the flesh think about the things of the flesh, but those who liveᴼ according to the Spirit, about the things of the Spirit. ⁶For the mindset of the flesh is death, but the mind-set of the Spirit is life and peace. ⁷For the mindset of the flesh is hostile to God because it does not submit itself to God's law, for it is unable to do so. ⁸Those who are in the flesh cannot please God. ⁹You, however, are not in the flesh, but in the Spirit, sinceᴾ the Spirit

ᴬ**7:5** = a person's life before accepting Christ   ᴮ**7:5** Lit *of our members*   ᶜ**7:6** Lit *in newness*   ᴰ**7:7** Ex 20:17   ᴱ**7:13** Lit *good become death to me?*   ᶠ**7:14** Other mss read *I am carnal*   ᴳ**7:21** Or *law*   ᴴ**7:22** Lit *inner man*   ᴵ**7:23** Lit *my members*   ᴶ**7:25** Or *Thanks be to God*—(it is done) *through Jesus Christ our Lord!*   ᴷ**8:1** Other mss add *who do not walk according to the flesh but according to the Spirit*   ᴸ**8:2** Other mss read *me*   ᴹ**8:3** Or *weak*   ᴺ**8:3** Lit *in the likeness of sinful flesh*   ᴼ**8:5** Or *those who are*   ᴾ**8:9** Or *provided that* of God lives in you. But if anyone does not have the Spirit of Christ, he does not belong to Him. [10]Now if Christ is in you, the body is dead[A] because of sin, but the Spirit[B] is life because of righteousness. [11]And if the Spirit of Him who raised Jesus from the dead lives in you, then He who raised Christ from the dead will also bring your mortal bodies to life through[C] His Spirit who lives in you.

[12]So then, brothers, we are not obligated to the flesh to live according to the flesh, [13]for if you live according to the flesh, you are going to die. But if by the Spirit you put to death the deeds of the body, you will live. [14]All those led by God's Spirit are God's sons. [15]For you did not receive a spirit of slavery to fall back into fear, but you received the Spirit of adoption, by whom we cry out, *"Abba*, Father!" [16]The Spirit Himself testifies together with our spirit that we are God's children, [17]and if children, also heirs—heirs of God and coheirs with Christ—seeing that[D] we suffer with Him so that we may also be glorified with Him.

[18]For I consider that the sufferings of this present time are not worth comparing with the glory that is going to be revealed to us. [19]For the creation eagerly waits with anticipation for God's sons to be revealed. [20]For the creation was subjected to futility—not willingly, but because of Him who subjected it—in the hope [21]that the creation itself will also be set free from the bondage of corruption into the glorious freedom of God's children. [22]For we know that the whole creation has been groaning together with labor pains until now. [23]And not only that, but we ourselves who have the Spirit as the firstfruits—we also groan within ourselves, eagerly waiting for adoption, the redemption of our bodies. [24]Now in this hope we were saved, yet hope that is seen is not hope, because who hopes for what he sees? [25]But if we hope for what we do not see, we eagerly wait for it with patience.

[26]In the same way the Spirit also joins to help in our weakness, because we do not know what to pray for as we should, but the Spirit Himself intercedes for us[E] with unspoken groanings. [27]And He who searches the hearts knows the Spirit's mind-set, because He intercedes for the saints according to the will of God.

[28]We know that all things work together[F] for the good[G] of those who love God: those who are called according to His purpose. [29]For those He foreknew He also predestined to be conformed to the image of His Son, so that He would be the firstborn among many brothers. [30]And those He predestined, He also called; and those He called, He also justified; and those He justified, He also glorified.

[31]   What then are we to say
         about these things?
      If God is for us, who is against us?
[32]   He did not even spare His own Son
         but offered Him up for us all;
      how will He not also with Him grant
         us everything?
[33]   Who can bring an accusation
         against God's elect?
      God is the One who justifies.
[34]   Who is the one who condemns?
      Christ Jesus is the One who died,
      but even more, has been raised;
      He also is at the right hand
         of God
      and intercedes for us.
[35]   Who can separate us from the love
         of Christ?
      Can affliction or anguish
         or persecution
      or famine or nakedness or danger
         or sword?
[36]   As it is written:
      Because of You
      we are being put to death all day long;
      we are counted as sheep
         to be slaughtered.[H]
[37]   No, in all these things we are
         more than victorious
      through Him who loved us.
[38]   For I am persuaded that not even death
         or life,
      angels or rulers,
      things present or things to come,
         hostile powers,
[39]   height or depth, or any other
         created thing

[A]8:10 Or *the body will die*   [B]8:10 Or *spirit*   [C]8:11 Other mss read *because of*   [D]8:17 Or *provided that*   [E]8:26 Some mss omit *for us*
[F]8:28 Other mss read *that God works together in all things*   [G]8:28 The ultimate good   [H]8:36 Ps 44:22

will have the power
to separate us
from the love of God that is
in Christ Jesus our Lord!

9 I speak the truth in Christ—I am not lying; my conscience is testifying to me with the Holy Spirit[A]— ²that I have intense sorrow and continual anguish in my heart. ³For I could almost wish to be cursed and cut off[B] from the Messiah for the benefit of my brothers, my own flesh and blood. ⁴They are Israelites, and to them belong the adoption, the glory, the covenants, the giving of the law, the temple service, and the promises. ⁵The ancestors are theirs, and from them, by physical descent,[C] came the Messiah, who is God over all, praised forever.[D] Amen.

⁶But it is not as though the word of God has failed. For not all who are descended from Israel are Israel. ⁷Neither are they all children because they are Abraham's descendants.[E] On the contrary, **your offspring will be traced**[F] **through Isaac.**[G] ⁸That is, it is not the children by physical descent[H] who are God's children, but the children of the promise are considered to be the offspring. ⁹For this is the statement of the promise: **At this time I will come, and Sarah will have a son.**[I] ¹⁰And not only that, but also Rebekah received a promise when she became pregnant[J] by one man, our ancestor Isaac. ¹¹For though her sons had not been born yet or done anything good or bad, so that God's purpose according to election might stand— ¹²not from works but from the One who calls—she was told: **The older will serve the younger.**[K] ¹³As it is written: **I have loved Jacob, but I have hated Esau.**[L]

¹⁴What should we say then? Is there injustice with God? Absolutely not! ¹⁵For He tells Moses:

I will show mercy
to whom I will show mercy,
and I will have compassion
on whom I will have compassion.[M]

¹⁶So then it does not depend on human will or effort[N] but on God who shows mercy. ¹⁷For the Scripture tells Pharaoh:

I raised you up for this reason
so that I may display My power
in you
and that My name may be proclaimed
in all the earth.[O]

¹⁸So then, He shows mercy to those He wants to, and He hardens those He wants to harden.

¹⁹You will say to me, therefore, "Why then does He still find fault? For who can resist His will?" ²⁰But who are you, a mere man, to talk back to God? Will what is formed say to the one who formed it, "Why did you make me like this?" ²¹Or has the potter no right over the clay, to make from the same lump one piece of pottery for honor and another for dishonor? ²²And what if God, desiring to display His wrath and to make His power known, endured with much patience objects of wrath ready for destruction? ²³And what if He did this to make known the riches of His glory on objects of mercy that He prepared beforehand for glory— ²⁴on us, the ones He also called, not only from the Jews but also from the Gentiles? ²⁵As He also says in Hosea:

I will call Not My People, My People,
and who is Unloved, Beloved.[P]
²⁶   And it will be in the place where
they were told,
you are not My people,
there they will be called sons
of the living God.[Q]

²⁷But Isaiah cries out concerning Israel:

Though the number of Israel's sons
is like the sand of the sea,
only the remnant will be saved;
²⁸   for the Lord will execute His sentence
completely and decisively
on the earth.[R,S]

²⁹And just as Isaiah predicted:

A9:1 Or testifying with me by the Holy Spirit   B9:3 Lit were anathema   C9:5 Lit them, according to the flesh   D9:5 Or the Messiah, the One who is over all, the God who is blessed forever, or Messiah. God, who is over all, be blessed forever   E9:7 Lit seed   F9:7 Lit called   G9:7 Gn 21:12   H9:8 Lit children of the flesh   I9:9 Gn 18:10,14   J9:10 Or Rebekah conceived by the one act of sexual intercourse   K9:12 Gn 25:23   L9:13 Mal 1:2-3   M9:15 Ex 33:19   N9:16 Or on the one running; lit on the one willing   O9:17 Ex 9:16   P9:25 Hs 2:23   Q9:26 Hs 1:10   R9:28 Or land   S9:27-28 Is 10:22-23; 28:22; Hs 1:10

If the Lord of Hosts[A] had not left
us offspring,
we would have become like Sodom,
and we would have been made
like Gomorrah.[B]

[30] What should we say then? Gentiles, who did not pursue righteousness, have obtained righteousness—namely the righteousness that comes from faith. [31] But Israel, pursuing the law for righteousness, has not achieved the righteousness of the law.[C] [32] Why is that? Because they did not pursue it by faith, but as if it were by works.[D] They stumbled over the stumbling stone. [33] As it is written:

Look! I am putting a stone in Zion
to stumble over
and a rock to trip over,
yet the one who believes on Him
will not be put to shame.[E]

10 Brothers, my heart's desire and prayer to God concerning them[F] is for their salvation! [2] I can testify about them that they have zeal for God, but not according to knowledge. [3] Because they disregarded the righteousness from God and attempted to establish their own righteousness, they have not submitted themselves to God's righteousness. [4] For Christ is the end[G] of the law for righteousness to everyone who believes. [5] For Moses writes about the righteousness that is from the law: **The one who does these things will live by them.**[H] [6] But the righteousness that comes from faith speaks like this: **Do not say in your heart, "Who will go up to heaven?"**[I] that is, to bring Christ down [7] or, **"Who will go down into the abyss?"**[J] that is, to bring Christ up from the dead. [8] On the contrary, what does it say? **The message is near you, in your mouth and in your heart.**[K] This is the message of faith that we proclaim: [9] If you confess with your mouth, "Jesus is Lord," and believe in your heart that God raised Him from the dead, you will be saved. [10] One believes with the heart, resulting in righteousness, and one confesses with the mouth, resulting in salvation. [11] Now the Scripture says, **Everyone who believes on Him will not be put to shame,**[L] [12] for there is no distinction between Jew and Greek, since the same Lord of all is rich to all who call on Him. [13] For **everyone who calls on the name of the Lord will be saved.**[M]

[14] But how can they call on Him they have not believed in? And how can they believe without hearing about Him? And how can they hear without a preacher? [15] And how can they preach unless they are sent? As it is written: **How beautiful[N] are the feet of those[O] who announce the gospel of good things!**[P] [16] But all did not obey the gospel. For Isaiah says, **Lord, who has believed our message?**[Q] [17] So faith comes from what is heard, and what is heard comes through the message about Christ.[R] [18] But I ask, "Did they not hear?" Yes, they did:

Their voice has gone out to all
the earth,
and their words to the ends
of the inhabited world.[S]

[19] But I ask, "Did Israel not understand?" First, Moses said:

I will make you jealous
of those who are not a nation;
I will make you angry by a nation
that lacks understanding.[T]

[20] And Isaiah says boldly:

I was found
by those who were not looking
for Me;
I revealed Myself
to those who were not asking
for Me.[U]

[21] But to Israel he says: **All day long I have spread out My hands to a disobedient and defiant people.**[V]

11 I ask, then, has God rejected His people? Absolutely not! For I too am an Israelite, a descendant of Abraham, from the tribe of Benjamin. [2] God has not rejected His people

---

[A]9:29 Gk *Sabaoth*; this word is a transliteration of the Hb word for *Hosts*, or *Armies*.   [B]9:29 Is 1:9   [C]9:31 Other mss read *the law for righteousness*   [D]9:32 Other mss add *of the law*   [E]9:33 Is 8:14; 28:16   [F]10:1 Other mss read *God for Israel*   [G]10:4 Or *goal*   [H]10:5 Lv 18:5   [I]10:6 Dt 9:4; 30:12   [J]10:7 Dt 30:13   [K]10:8 Dt 30:14   [L]10:11 Is 28:16   [M]10:13 Jl 2:32   [N]10:15 Or *welcome*, or *timely*   [O]10:15 Other mss read *feet of those who announce the gospel of peace, of those*   [P]10:15 Is 52:7; Nah 1:15   [Q]10:16 Is 53:1   [R]10:17 Other mss read *God*   [S]10:18 Ps 19:4   [T]10:19 Dt 32:21   [U]10:20 Is 65:1   [V]10:21 Is 65:2

Turn to page 352.

whom He foreknew. Or don't you know what the Scripture says in the passage about Elijah—how he pleads with God against Israel?

> ³ **Lord, they have killed**
> **Your prophets**
> **and torn down Your altars.**
> **I am the only one left,**
> **and they are trying to take my life!**ᴬ

⁴But what was God's reply to him? **I have left 7,000 men for Myself who have not bowed down to Baal.**ᴮ ⁵In the same way, then, there is also at the present time a remnant chosen by grace. ⁶Now if by grace, then it is not by works; otherwise grace ceases to be grace.ᶜ

⁷What then? Israel did not find what it was looking for, but the elect did find it. The rest were hardened, ⁸as it is written:

> **God gave them a spirit**
> **of insensitivity,**ᴰ
> **eyes that cannot see**
> **and ears that cannot hear,**
> **to this day.**ᴱ

⁹And David says:

> **Let their feasting**ᶠ **become a snare**
> **and a trap,**
> **a pitfall and a retribution to them.**
> ¹⁰ **Let their eyes be darkened**
> **so they cannot see,**
> **and their backs be bent**
> **continually.**ᴳ

¹¹I ask, then, have they stumbled in order to fall? Absolutely not! On the contrary, by their stumbling,ᴴ salvation has come to the Gentiles to make Israel jealous. ¹²Now if their stumblingᴴ brings riches for the world, and their failure riches for the Gentiles, how much more will their full number bring!

¹³Now I am speaking to you Gentiles. In view of the fact that I am an apostle to the Gentiles, I magnify my ministry, ¹⁴if I can somehow make my own peopleᴵ jealous and save some of them. ¹⁵For if their rejection brings reconciliation to the world, what will their acceptance mean but life from the dead? ¹⁶Now if the firstfruits offered up are holy, so

is the whole batch. And if the root is holy, so are the branches.

¹⁷Now if some of the branches were broken off, and you, though a wild olive branch, were grafted in among them and have come to share in the rich rootᴶ of the cultivated olive tree, ¹⁸do not brag that you are better than those branches. But if you do brag—you do not sustain the root, but the root sustains you. ¹⁹Then you will say, "Branches were broken off so that I might be grafted in." ²⁰True enough; they were broken off by unbelief, but you stand by faith. Do not be arrogant, but be afraid. ²¹For if God did not spare the natural branches, He will not spare you either. ²²Therefore, consider God's kindness and severity: severity toward those who have fallen but God's kindness toward you—if you remain in His kindness. Otherwise you too will be cut off. ²³And even they, if they do not remain in unbelief, will be grafted in, because God has the power to graft them in again. ²⁴For if you were cut off from your native wild olive and against nature were grafted into a cultivated olive tree, how much more will these—the natural branches—be grafted into their own olive tree?

²⁵So that you will not be conceited, brothers, I do not want you to be unaware of this mystery: A partial hardening has come to Israel until the full number of the Gentiles has come in. ²⁶And in this way allᴷ Israel will be saved, as it is written:

> **The Liberator will come**
> **from Zion;**
> **He will turn away godlessness**
> **from Jacob.**
> ²⁷ **And this will be My covenant**
> **with them**ᴸ
> **when I take away their sins.**ᴹ

²⁸Regarding the gospel, they are enemies for your advantage, but regarding election, they are loved because of the patriarchs, ²⁹since God's gracious gifts and calling are irrevocable.ᴺ ³⁰As you once disobeyed God, but now have received mercy through their disobedience, ³¹so they too have now disobeyed,

ᴬ11:3 1Kg 19:10,14   ᴮ11:4 1Kg 19:18   ᶜ11:6 Other mss add *But if of works it is no longer grace; otherwise work is no longer work.*   ᴰ11:8 Lit *stupification*   ᴱ11:8 Dt 29:4; Is 29:10   ᶠ11:9 Lit *table*   ᴳ11:9-10 Ps 69:22-23   ᴴ11:11,12 Or *transgression*   ᴵ11:14 Lit *flesh*   ᴶ11:17 Other mss read *the root and the richness*   ᴷ11:26 Or *And then all*   ᴸ11:26-27 Is 59:20-21   ᴹ11:27 Jr 31:31-34   ᴺ11:29 Or *are not taken back* resulting in mercy to you, so that they also now[A] may receive mercy. [32] For God has imprisoned all in disobedience, so that He may have mercy on all.

[33]   Oh, the depth of the riches
          both of the wisdom and the knowledge
               of God!
          How unsearchable His judgments
          and untraceable His ways!
[34]   **For who has known the mind
               of the Lord?**
          Or who has been His counselor?
[35]   **Or who has ever first given to Him,
               and has to be repaid?**[B]
[36]   For from Him and through Him
          and to Him are all things.
          To Him be the glory forever. Amen.

12 Therefore, brothers, by the mercies of God, I urge you to present your bodies as a living sacrifice, holy and pleasing to God; this is your spiritual worship.[C] [2] Do not be conformed to this age, but be transformed by the renewing of your mind, so that you may discern what is the good, pleasing, and perfect will of God.

[3] For by the grace given to me, I tell everyone among you not to think of himself more highly than he should think. Instead, think sensibly, as God has distributed a measure of faith to each one. [4] Now as we have many parts in one body, and all the parts do not have the same function, [5] in the same way we who are many are one body in Christ and individually members of one another. [6] According to the grace given to us, we have different gifts:

          If prophecy,
          use it according to the standard
               of one's[D] faith;
[7]   if service, in service;
          if teaching, in teaching;
[8]   if exhorting, in exhortation;
          giving, with generosity;
          leading, with diligence;
          showing mercy, with cheerfulness.

[9] Love must be without hypocrisy. Detest evil; cling to what is good. [10] Show family affection to one another with brotherly love. Outdo one another in showing honor. [11] Do not lack diligence; be fervent in spirit; serve the Lord. [12] Rejoice in hope; be patient in affliction; be persistent in prayer. [13] Share with the saints in their needs; pursue hospitality. [14] Bless those who persecute you; bless and do not curse. [15] Rejoice with those who rejoice; weep with those who weep. [16] Be in agreement with one another. Do not be proud; instead, associate with the humble. Do not be wise in your own estimation. [17] Do not repay anyone evil for evil. Try to do what is honorable in everyone's eyes. [18] If possible, on your part, live at peace with everyone. [19] Friends, do not avenge yourselves; instead, leave room for His[E] wrath. For it is written: **Vengeance belongs to Me; I will repay,**[F] says the Lord. [20] But

          If your enemy is hungry, feed him.
          **If he is thirsty, give him something
               to drink.**
          **For in so doing
          you will be heaping fiery coals
               on his head.**[G]

[21] Do not be conquered by evil, but conquer evil with good.

13 Everyone must submit to the governing authorities, for there is no authority except from God, and those that exist are instituted by God. [2] So then, the one who resists the authority is opposing God's command, and those who oppose it will bring judgment on themselves. [3] For rulers are not a terror to good conduct, but to bad. Do you want to be unafraid of the authority? Do what is good, and you will have its approval. [4] For government is God's servant for your good. But if you do wrong, be afraid, because it does not carry the sword for no reason. For government is God's servant, an avenger that brings wrath on the one who does wrong. [5] Therefore, you must submit, not only because of wrath, but also because of your conscience. [6] And for this reason you pay taxes, since the authorities are God's public servants, continually attending to these tasks.[H] [7] Pay your obligations to everyone: taxes to those you owe taxes, tolls to those you owe tolls, respect

A11:31 Other mss omit now   B11:34-35 Jb 41:11; Is 40:13; Jr 23:18   C12:1 Or your reasonable service   D12:6 Or the   E12:19 Lit the
F12:19 Dt 32:35   G12:20 Pr 25:21-22   H13:6 Lit to this very thing

to those you owe respect, and honor to those you owe honor.

⁸Do not owe anyone anything,ᴬ except to love one another, for the one who loves another has fulfilled the law. ⁹The commandments:

> **Do not commit adultery;**
> **do not murder;**
> **do not steal;**ᴮ
> **do not covet;**ᶜ

and whatever other commandment—all are summed up by this: **Love your neighbor as yourself.**ᴰ

¹⁰Love does no wrong to a neighbor. Love, therefore, is the fulfillment of the law.

¹¹Besides this, knowing the time, it is already the hour for youᴱ to wake up from sleep, for now our salvation is nearer than when we first believed. ¹²The night is nearly over, and the daylight is near, so let us discard the deeds of darkness and put on the armor of light. ¹³Let us walk with decency, as in the daylight: not in carousing and drunkenness; not in sexual impurity and promiscuity; not in quarreling and jealousy. ¹⁴But put on the Lord Jesus Christ, and make no plans to satisfy the fleshly desires.

14 Accept anyone who is weak in faith,ᶠ but don't argue about doubtful issues. ²One person believes he may eat anything, but one who is weak eats only vegetables. ³One who eats must not look down on one who does not eat, and one who does not eat must not criticize one who does, because God has accepted him. ⁴Who are you to criticize another's household slave? Before his own Lord he stands or falls. And he will stand. For the Lord is ableᴳ to make him stand.

⁵One person considers one day to be above another day. Someone else considers every day to be the same. Each one must be fully convinced in his own mind. ⁶Whoever observes the day, observes it for the honor of the Lord.ᴴ Whoever eats, eats for the Lord, since he gives thanks to God; and whoever does not eat, it is for the Lord that he does not eat it, yet he thanks God. ⁷For none of us lives to himself, and no one dies to himself. ⁸If we live, we live for the Lord; and if we die, we die for the Lord. Therefore, whether we live or die, we belong to the Lord. ⁹Christ died and came to life for this: that He might rule over both the dead and the living. ¹⁰But you, why do you criticize your brother? Or you, why do you look down on your brother? For we will all stand before the tribunal of God.ᴵ ¹¹For it is written:

> **As I live, says the Lord,**
> **every knee will bow to Me,**
> **and every tongue will give praise**
> **to God.**ᴶ

¹²So then, each of us will give an account of himself to God.

¹³Therefore, let us no longer criticize one another. Instead decide never to put a stumbling block or pitfall in your brother's way. ¹⁴(I know and am persuaded by the Lord Jesus that nothing is unclean in itself. Still, to someone who considers a thing to be unclean, to that one it is unclean.) ¹⁵For if your brother is hurt by what you eat, you are no longer walking according to love. Do not destroy that one Christ died for by what you eat. ¹⁶Therefore, do not let your good be slandered, ¹⁷for the kingdom of God is not eating and drinking, but righteousness, peace, and joy in the Holy Spirit. ¹⁸Whoever serves Christ in this way is acceptable to God and approved by men.

¹⁹So then, we must pursue what promotes peace and what builds up one another. ²⁰Do not tear down God's work because of food. Everything is clean, but it is wrong for a man to cause stumbling by what he eats. ²¹It is a noble thing not to eat meat, or drink wine, or do anything that makes your brother stumble.ᴷ ²²Do you have a conviction?ᴸ Keep it to yourself before God. The man who does not condemn himself by what he approves is blessed. ²³But whoever doubts stands condemned if he eats, because his eating is not from a conviction,ᴹ and everything that is not from a convictionᴹ is sin.

15 Now we who are strong have an obligation to bear the weaknesses of those without strength, and not to please ourselves. [2] Each one of us must please his neighbor for his good, to build him up. [3] For even the Messiah did not please Himself. On the contrary, as it is written, **The insults of those who insult You have fallen on Me.**[A] [4] For whatever was written in the past was written for our instruction, so that we may have hope through endurance and through the encouragement from the Scriptures. [5] Now may the God who gives[B] endurance and encouragement allow you to live in harmony with one another, according to the command of Christ Jesus, [6] so that you may glorify the God and Father of our Lord Jesus Christ with a united mind and voice.

[7] Therefore accept one another, just as the Messiah also accepted you, to the glory of God. [8] For I say that the Messiah became a servant of the circumcised[C] on behalf of God's truth, to confirm the promises to the fathers, [9] and so that Gentiles may glorify God for His mercy. As it is written:

> **Therefore I will praise You**
>   **among the Gentiles,**
> **and I will sing psalms**
>   **to Your name.**[D]

[10] Again it says: **Rejoice, you Gentiles, with His people!**[E] [11] And again:

> **Praise the Lord, all you Gentiles;**
> **all the peoples should praise Him!**[F]

[12] And again, Isaiah says:

> **The root of Jesse will appear,**
> **the One who rises to rule**
>   **the Gentiles;**
> **the Gentiles will hope in Him.**[G]

[13] Now may the God of hope fill you with all joy and peace as you believe in Him so that you may overflow with hope by the power of the Holy Spirit.

[14] My brothers, I myself am convinced about you that you also are full of goodness, filled with all knowledge, and able to instruct one another. [15] Nevertheless, I have written to remind you more boldly on some points[H] because of the grace given me by God [16] to be a minister of Christ Jesus to the Gentiles, serving as a priest of God's good news. My purpose is that the offering of the Gentiles may be acceptable, sanctified by the Holy Spirit. [17] Therefore I have reason to boast in Christ Jesus regarding what pertains to God. [18] For I would not dare say anything except what Christ has accomplished through me to make the Gentiles obedient by word and deed, [19] by the power of miraculous signs and wonders, and by the power of God's Spirit. As a result, I have fully proclaimed the good news about the Messiah from Jerusalem all the way around to Illyricum.[I] [20] My aim is to evangelize where Christ has not been named, so that I will not build on someone else's foundation, [21] but, as it is written:

> **Those who were not told about Him**
>   **will see,**
> **and those who have not heard**
>   **will understand.**[J]

[22] That is why I have been prevented many times from coming to you. [23] But now I no longer have any work to do in these provinces,[K] and I have strongly desired for many years to come to you [24] whenever I travel to Spain.[L] For I hope to see you when I pass through, and to be assisted by you for my journey there, once I have first enjoyed your company for a while. [25] Right now I am traveling to Jerusalem to serve the saints, [26] for Macedonia and Achaia[M] were pleased to make a contribution for the poor among the saints in Jerusalem. [27] Yes, they were pleased, and indeed are indebted to them. For if the Gentiles have shared in their spiritual benefits, then they are obligated to minister to Jews in material needs. [28] So when I have finished this and safely delivered the funds[N] to them, I will visit you on the way to Spain. [29] I know that when I come to you, I will come in the fullness of the blessing[O] of Christ.

[30] Now I appeal to you, brothers, through our Lord Jesus Christ and through the love of

---

[A] **15:3** Ps 69:9 [B] **15:5** Lit *God of* [C] **15:8** The Jews [D] **15:9** 2Sm 22:50; Ps 18:49 [E] **15:10** Dt 32:43 [F] **15:11** Ps 117:1 [G] **15:12** Is 11:10 [H] **15:15** Other mss add *brothers* [I] **15:19** A Roman province northwest of Greece on the eastern shore of the Adriatic Sea [J] **15:21** Is 52:15 [K] **15:23** Lit *now, having no longer a place in these parts* [L] **15:24** Other mss add *I will come to you.* [M] **15:26** The churches of these provinces [N] **15:28** Lit *delivered this fruit* [O] **15:29** Other mss add *of the gospel* the Spirit, to join with me in fervent prayers to God on my behalf. ³¹Pray that I may be rescued from the unbelievers in Judea, that the gift I am bringing to^A Jerusalem may be acceptable to the saints, ³²and that, by God's will, I may come to you with joy and be refreshed together with you.

³³The God of peace be with all of you. Amen.

16 I commend to you our sister Phoebe, who is a servant^B of the church in Cenchreae. ²So you should welcome her in the Lord in a manner worthy of the saints and assist her in whatever matter she may require your help. For indeed she has been a benefactor of many—and of me also.

³Give my greetings to Prisca^C and Aquila, my coworkers in Christ Jesus, ⁴who risked their own necks for my life. Not only do I thank them, but so do all the Gentile churches.

⁵Greet also the church that meets in their home.

Greet my dear friend Epaenetus, who is the first convert^D to Christ from Asia.^E

⁶Greet Mary,^F who has worked very hard for you.^G

⁷Greet Andronicus and Junia,^H my fellow countrymen and fellow prisoners. They are noteworthy in the eyes of the apostles,^I,J and they were also in Christ before me.

⁸Greet Ampliatus, my dear friend in the Lord.

⁹Greet Urbanus, our coworker in Christ, and my dear friend Stachys.

¹⁰Greet Apelles, who is approved in Christ.

Greet those who belong to the household of Aristobulus.

¹¹Greet Herodion, my fellow countryman.

Greet those who belong to the household of Narcissus who are in the Lord.

¹²Greet Tryphaena and Tryphosa, who have worked hard in the Lord.

Greet my dear friend Persis, who has worked very hard in the Lord.

¹³Greet Rufus, chosen in the Lord; also his mother—and mine.

¹⁴Greet Asyncritus, Phlegon, Hermes, Patrobas, Hermas, and the brothers who are with them.

¹⁵Greet Philologus and Julia, Nereus and his sister, and Olympas, and all the saints who are with them.

¹⁶Greet one another with a holy kiss. All the churches of Christ send you greetings.

¹⁷Now I urge you, brothers, to watch out for those who cause dissensions and obstacles contrary to the doctrine you have learned. Avoid them, ¹⁸for such people do not serve our Lord Christ but their own appetites.^K They deceive the hearts of the unsuspecting with smooth talk and flattering words.

¹⁹The report of your obedience has reached everyone. Therefore I rejoice over you. But I want you to be wise about what is good, yet innocent about what is evil. ²⁰The God of peace will soon crush Satan under your feet. The grace of our Lord Jesus be with you.

²¹Timothy, my coworker, and Lucius, Jason, and Sosipater, my fellow countrymen, greet you.

²²I Tertius, who wrote this letter, greet you in the Lord.^L

²³Gaius, who is host to me and to the whole church, greets you. Erastus, the city treasurer, and our brother Quartus greet you.

[²⁴The grace of our Lord Jesus Christ be with you all.]^M

²⁵Now to Him who has power to strengthen you according to my gospel and the proclamation about Jesus Christ, according to the revelation of the mystery kept silent for long ages ²⁶but now revealed and made known through the prophetic Scriptures, according to the command of the eternal God to advance the obedience of faith^N among all nations— ²⁷to the only wise God, through Jesus Christ—to Him be the glory forever!^O Amen.

^A15:31 Lit that my service for   ^B16:1 Others interpret this term in a technical sense: deacon, or deaconess, or minister, or courier   ^C16:3 Traditionally, Priscilla, as in Ac 18:2,18,26   ^D16:5 Lit the firstfruits   ^E16:5 Other mss read Achaia   ^F16:6 Or Maria   ^G16:6 Other mss read us   ^H16:7 Either a feminine name or "Junias," a masculine name   ^I16:7 Or are outstanding among   ^J16:7 "The apostles" is not always a technical term referring to the 12; cp. 2Co 8:23; Php 2:25 where this word is translated as "messenger."   ^K16:18 Lit belly   ^L16:22 Or letter in the Lord, greet you   ^M16:24 Other mss omit bracketed text; cp. v. 20   ^N16:26 Or the obedience that is faith, or the faithful obedience, or the obedience that comes from faith; Rm 1:5   ^O16:25-27 Other mss have these vv. at the end of chap 14 or 15.

1 CORINTHIANS

1 Paul, called as an apostle of Christ Jesus by God's will, and Sosthenes our brother: ²To God's church at Corinth, to those who are sanctified in Christ Jesus and called as saints, with all those in every place who call on the name of Jesus Christ our Lord—both their Lord and ours.

³Grace to you and peace from God our Father and the Lord Jesus Christ.

⁴I always thank my God for you because of God's grace given to you in Christ Jesus, ⁵that by Him you were enriched in everything—in all speech and all knowledge. ⁶In this way, the testimony about Christ was confirmed among you, ⁷so that you do not lack any spiritual gift as you eagerly wait for the revelation of our Lord Jesus Christ. ⁸He will also strengthen you to the end, so that you will be blameless in the day of our Lord Jesus Christ. ⁹God is faithful; you were called by Him into fellowship with His Son, Jesus Christ our Lord.

¹⁰Now I urge you, brothers, in the name of our Lord Jesus Christ, that all of you agree in what you say, that there be no divisions among you, and that you be united with the same understanding and the same conviction. ¹¹For it has been reported to me about you, my brothers, by members of Chloe's household, that there is rivalry among you. ¹²What I am saying is this: Each of you says, "I'm with Paul," or "I'm with Apollos," or "I'm with Cephas," or "I'm with Christ." ¹³Is Christ divided? Was it Paul who was crucified for you? Or were you baptized in Paul's name? ¹⁴I thank God^A,B that I baptized none of you except Crispus and Gaius, ¹⁵so that no one can say you were baptized in my name. ¹⁶I did, in fact, baptize the household of Stephanas; beyond that, I don't know if I baptized anyone else. ¹⁷For Christ did not send me to baptize, but to evangelize—not with clever words, so that the cross of Christ will not be emptied of its effect.

¹⁸For the message of the cross is foolishness to those who are perishing, but it is God's power to us who are being saved. ¹⁹For it is written:

> **I will destroy the wisdom**
> **of the wise,**
> **and I will set aside the understanding**
> **of the experts.**^C

²⁰Where is the philosopher?^D Where is the scholar? Where is the debater of this age? Hasn't God made the world's wisdom foolish? ²¹For since, in God's wisdom, the world did not know God through wisdom, God was pleased to save those who believe through the foolishness of the message preached. ²²For the Jews ask for signs and the Greeks seek wisdom, ²³but we preach Christ crucified, a stumbling block to the Jews and foolishness to the Gentiles.^E ²⁴Yet to those who are called, both Jews and Greeks, Christ is God's power and God's wisdom, ²⁵because God's foolishness is wiser than human wisdom, and God's weakness is stronger than human strength.

²⁶Brothers, consider your calling: Not many are wise from a human perspective,^F not many powerful, not many of noble birth. ²⁷Instead, God has chosen what is foolish in the world to shame the wise, and God has chosen what is weak in the world to shame the strong. ²⁸God has chosen what is insignificant and despised in the world—what is viewed as nothing—to bring to nothing what is viewed as something, ²⁹so that no one^G can boast in His presence. ³⁰But it is from Him that you are in Christ Jesus, who became God-given wisdom for us—our righteousness, sanctification, and redemption, ³¹in order that, as it is written: **The one who boasts must boast in the Lord.**^H

2 When I came to you, brothers, announcing the testimony^I of God to you, I did not come with brilliance of speech or wisdom. ²For I didn't think it was a good idea to know anything among you except Jesus Christ and Him crucified. ³I came to you in weakness, in fear, and in much trembling. ⁴My speech and

my proclamation were not with persuasive words of wisdom[A] but with a powerful demonstration by the Spirit, [5]so that your faith might not be based on men's wisdom but on God's power.

[6]However, we do speak a wisdom among the mature, but not a wisdom of this age, or of the rulers of this age, who are coming to nothing. [7]On the contrary, we speak God's hidden wisdom in a mystery, a wisdom God predestined before the ages for our glory. [8]None of the rulers of this age knew this wisdom, for if they had known it, they would not have crucified the Lord of glory. [9]But as it is written:

> **What eye did not see and ear**
> **did not hear,**
> **and what never entered**
> **the human mind—**
> **God prepared this for those**
> **who love Him.**[B]

[10]Now God has revealed these things to us by the Spirit, for the Spirit searches everything, even the depths of God. [11]For who among men knows the thoughts[C] of a man except the spirit of the man that is in him? In the same way, no one knows the thoughts[C] of God except the Spirit of God. [12]Now we have not received the spirit of the world, but the Spirit who comes from God, so that we may understand what has been freely given to us by God. [13]We also speak these things, not in words taught by human wisdom, but in those taught by the Spirit, explaining spiritual things to spiritual people.[D] [14]But the unbeliever[E] does not welcome what comes from God's Spirit, because it is foolishness to him; he is not able to understand it since it is evaluated[F] spiritually. [15]The spiritual person, however, can evaluate[G] everything, yet he himself cannot be evaluated[F] by anyone. [16]For

> **who has known the Lord's mind,**
> **that he may instruct Him?**[H]

But we have the mind of Christ.

3 Brothers, I was not able to speak to you as spiritual people but as people of the flesh, as babies in Christ. [2]I gave you milk to drink, not solid food, because you were not yet ready for it. In fact, you are still not ready, [3]because you are still fleshly. For since there is envy and strife[I] among you, are you not fleshly and living like unbelievers?[J] [4]For whenever someone says, "I'm with Paul," and another, "I'm with Apollos," are you not unspiritual people?[K,L]

[5]What then is Apollos? And what is Paul? They are servants through whom you believed, and each has the role the Lord has given. [6]I planted, Apollos watered, but God gave the growth. [7]So then neither the one who plants nor the one who waters is anything, but only God who gives the growth. [8]Now the one planting and the one watering are one in purpose, and each will receive his own reward according to his own labor. [9]For we are God's coworkers.[M] You are God's field, God's building. [10]According to God's grace that was given to me, I have laid a foundation as a skilled master builder, and another builds on it. But each one must be careful how he builds on it. [11]For no one can lay any other foundation than what has been laid down. That foundation is Jesus Christ. [12]If anyone builds on that foundation with gold, silver, costly stones, wood, hay, or straw, [13]each one's work will become obvious, for the day[N] will disclose it, because it will be revealed by fire; the fire will test the quality of each one's work. [14]If anyone's work that he has built survives, he will receive a reward. [15]If anyone's work is burned up, it will be lost, but he will be saved; yet it will be like an escape through fire.[O]

[16]Don't you yourselves know that you are God's sanctuary and that the Spirit of God lives in you? [17]If anyone destroys God's sanctuary, God will destroy him; for God's sanctuary is holy, and that is what you are.

[18]No one should deceive himself. If anyone among you thinks he is wise in this age, he must become foolish so that he can become wise. [19]For the wisdom of this world is foolishness with God, since it is written: **He**

A2:4 Other mss read human wisdom   B2:9 Is 52:15; 64:4   C2:11 Or things   D2:13 Or things with spiritual words   E2:14 Or unspiritual; lit natural   F2:14,15 Or judged, or discerned   G2:15 Or judge, or discern   H2:16 Is 40:13   I3:3 Other mss add and divisions   J3:3 Lit and walking according to man   K3:4 Other mss read are you not carnal   L3:4 Lit not just human   M3:9 Or are coworkers belonging to God   N3:13 The day of Christ's judgment of believers   O3:15 Lit yet so as through fire catches the wise in their craftiness;[A] [20]and again, **The Lord knows that the reasonings of the wise are meaningless.**[B] [21]So no one should boast in human leaders, for everything is yours— [22]whether Paul or Apollos or Cephas or the world or life or death or things present or things to come—everything is yours, [23]and you belong to Christ, and Christ belongs to God.

4 A person should consider us in this way: as servants of Christ and managers of God's mysteries. [2]In this regard, it is expected of managers that each one of them be found faithful. [3]It is of little importance to me that I should be evaluated by you or by any human court.[C] In fact, I don't even evaluate myself. [4]For I am not conscious of anything against myself, but I am not justified by this. The One who evaluates me is the Lord. [5]Therefore don't judge anything prematurely, before the Lord comes, who will both bring to light what is hidden in darkness and reveal the intentions of the hearts. And then praise will come to each one from God.

[6]Now, brothers, I have applied these things to myself and Apollos for your benefit, so that you may learn from us the saying: "Nothing beyond what is written."[D] The purpose is that none of you will be inflated with pride in favor of one person over another. [7]For who makes you so superior? What do you have that you didn't receive? If, in fact, you did receive it, why do you boast as if you hadn't received it? [8]You are already full! You are already rich! You have begun to reign as kings without us—and I wish you did reign, so that we could also reign with you! [9]For I think God has displayed us, the apostles, in last place, like men condemned to die: We have become a spectacle to the world and to angels and to men. [10]We are fools for Christ, but you are wise in Christ! We are weak, but you are strong! You are distinguished, but we are dishonored! [11]Up to the present hour we are both hungry and thirsty; we are poorly clothed, roughly treated, homeless; [12]we labor, working with our own hands. When we are reviled, we bless; when we are persecuted, we endure it; [13]when we are slandered, we respond graciously. Even now, we are like the world's garbage, like the dirt everyone scrapes off their sandals.

[14]I'm not writing this to shame you, but to warn you as my dear children. [15]For you can have 10,000 instructors in Christ, but you can't have many fathers. For I became your father in Christ Jesus through the gospel. [16]Therefore I urge you to imitate me. [17]This is why I have sent Timothy to you. He is my dearly loved and faithful son in the Lord. He will remind you about my ways in Christ Jesus, just as I teach everywhere in every church. [18]Now some are inflated with pride, as though I were not coming to you. [19]But I will come to you soon, if the Lord wills, and I will know not the talk but the power of those who are inflated with pride. [20]For the kingdom of God is not a matter of talk but of power. [21]What do you want? Should I come to you with a rod, or in love and a spirit of gentleness?

5 It is widely reported that there is sexual immorality among you, and the kind of sexual immorality that is not even tolerated[E] among the Gentiles—a man is living with his father's wife. [2]And you are inflated with pride, instead of filled with grief so that he who has committed this act might be removed from your congregation. [3]For though I am absent in body but present in spirit, I have already decided about the one who has done this thing as though I were present. [4]When you are assembled in the name of our Lord Jesus with my spirit and with the power of our Lord Jesus, [5]turn that one over to Satan for the destruction of the flesh, so that his spirit may be saved in the Day of the Lord.

[6]Your boasting is not good. Don't you know that a little yeast permeates the whole batch of dough? [7]Clean out the old yeast so that you may be a new batch. You are indeed unleavened, for Christ our Passover has been sacrificed.[F] [8]Therefore, let us observe the feast, not with old yeast or with the yeast of malice and evil but with the unleavened bread of sincerity and truth.

[9]I wrote to you in a letter not to associate with sexually immoral people. [10]I did not

---

[A]3:19 Jb 5:13   [B]3:20 Ps 94:11   [C]4:3 Lit *a human day*   [D]4:6 The words in quotation marks could = the OT, a Jewish maxim, or a popular proverb.   [E]5:1 Other mss read *named*   [F]5:7 Other mss add *for us* mean the immoral people of this world or the greedy and swindlers or idolaters; otherwise you would have to leave the world. [11]But now I am writing[A] you not to associate with anyone who claims to be a believer[B] who is sexually immoral or greedy, an idolater or verbally abusive, a drunkard or a swindler. Do not even eat with such a person. [12]For what business is it of mine to judge outsiders? Don't you judge those who are inside? [13]But God judges outsiders. **Put away the evil person from among yourselves.**[C]

6 If any of you has a legal dispute against another, do you dare go to court before the unrighteous,[D] and not before the saints? [2]Or don't you know that the saints will judge the world? And if the world is judged by you, are you unworthy to judge the smallest cases? [3]Don't you know that we will judge angels—not to mention ordinary matters? [4]So if you have cases pertaining to this life, do you select those[E] who have no standing in the church to judge? [5]I say this to your shame! Can it be that there is not one wise person among you who is able to arbitrate between his brothers? [6]Instead, believer[F] goes to court against believer, and that before unbelievers!

[7]Therefore, to have legal disputes against one another is already a moral failure for you. Why not rather put up with injustice? Why not rather be cheated? [8]Instead, you act unjustly and cheat—and you do this to believers! [9]Don't you know that the unrighteous will not inherit God's kingdom? Do not be deceived: No sexually immoral people, idolaters, adulterers, or anyone practicing homosexuality,[G] [10]no thieves, greedy people, drunkards, verbally abusive people, or swindlers will inherit God's kingdom. [11]And some of you used to be like this. But you were washed, you were sanctified, you were justified in the name of the Lord Jesus Christ and by the Spirit of our God.

[12]"Everything is permissible for me,"[H] but not everything is helpful. "Everything is permissible for me," but I will not be brought under the control of anything. [13]"Food for the stomach and the stomach for food," but God will do away with both of them.[I] The body is not for sexual immorality but for the Lord, and the Lord for the body. [14]God raised up the Lord and will also raise us up by His power. [15]Don't you know that your bodies are a part of Christ's body? So should I take a part of Christ's body and make it part of a prostitute? Absolutely not! [16]Don't you know that anyone joined to a prostitute is one body with her? For Scripture says, **The two will become one flesh.**[J] [17]But anyone joined to the Lord is one spirit with Him.

[18]Run from sexual immorality! "Every sin a person can commit is outside the body."[K] On the contrary, the person who is sexually immoral sins against his own body. [19]Don't you know that your body is a sanctuary of the Holy Spirit who is in you, whom you have from God? You are not your own, [20]for you were bought at a price. Therefore glorify God in your body.[L]

7 Now in response to the matters you wrote[M] about: "It is good for a man not to have relations with[N] a woman."[O] [2]But because sexual immorality is so common,[P] each man should have his own wife, and each woman should have her own husband. [3]A husband should fulfill his marital responsibility to his wife, and likewise a wife to her husband. [4]A wife does not have the right over her own body, but her husband does. In the same way, a husband does not have the right over his own body, but his wife does. [5]Do not deprive one another sexually—except when you agree for a time, to devote yourselves to[Q] prayer. Then come together again; otherwise, Satan may tempt you because of your lack of self-control. [6]I say the following[R] as a concession, not as a command. [7]I wish that all people were just like me. But each has his own gift from God, one person in this way and another in that way.

A5:11 Or now I wrote   B5:11 Lit anyone named a brother   C5:13 Dt 17:7   D6:1 Unbelievers; v. 6   E6:4 Or life, appoint those (as a command)   F6:6-8 Lit brothers   G6:9 Lit adulterers, passive homosexual partners, active homosexual partners   H6:12-13 The words in quotation marks are most likely slogans used by some Corinthian Christians and corrected by Paul.   I6:13 Lit both it and them   J6:16 Gn 2:24   K6:18 See note at 1Co 6:12-13.   L6:20 Other mss add and in your spirit, which belong to God.   M7:1 Other mss add to me   N7:1 Lit not to touch   O7:1 The words in quotation marks are a principle that the Corinthians wrote to Paul about to ask for his view.   P7:2 Lit because of immoralities   Q7:5 Other mss add fasting and to   R7:6 Lit say this; some interpret the word as referring to v. 2, vv. 2-5, v. 5 (wholly or in part), or v. 6

⁸I say to the unmarried and to widows: It is good for them if they remain as I am. ⁹But if they do not have self-control, they should marry, for it is better to marry than to burn with desire.

¹⁰I command the married—not I, but the Lord—a wife is not to leaveᴬ her husband. ¹¹But if she does leave, she must remain unmarried or be reconciled to her husband—and a husband is not to leave his wife. ¹²But I (not the Lord)ᴮ say to the rest: If any brother has an unbelieving wife and she is willing to live with him, he must not leave her. ¹³Also, if any woman has an unbelieving husband and he is willing to live with her, she must not leave her husband. ¹⁴For the unbelieving husband is set apart for God by the wife, and the unbelieving wife is set apart for God by the husband.ᶜ Otherwise your children would be corrupt, but now they are set apart for God. ¹⁵But if the unbeliever leaves, let him leave. A brother or a sister is not bound in such cases. God has called youᴰ to live in peace. ¹⁶For you, wife, how do you know whether you will save your husband? Or you, husband, how do you know whether you will save your wife?

¹⁷However, each one must live his life in the situation the Lord assigned when God called him.ᴱ This is what I command in all the churches. ¹⁸Was anyone already circumcised when he was called? He should not undo his circumcision. Was anyone called while uncircumcised? He should not get circumcised. ¹⁹Circumcision does not matter and uncircumcision does not matter, but keeping God's commands does. ²⁰Each person should remain in the life situationᶠ in which he was called. ²¹Were you called while a slave? It should not be a concern to you. But if you can become free, by all means take the opportunity.ᴳ ²²For he who is called by the Lord as a slave is the Lord's freedman.ᴴ Likewise he who is called as a free manᴵ is Christ's slave. ²³You were bought at a price; do not become slaves of men. ²⁴Brothers, each person should remain with God in whatever situation he was called.

²⁵About virgins: I have no command from the Lord, but I do give an opinion as one who by the Lord's mercy is trustworthy. ²⁶Therefore I consider this to be good because of the present distress: It is fine for a man to remain as he is. ²⁷Are you bound to a wife? Do not seek to be loosed. Are you loosed from a wife? Do not seek a wife. ²⁸However, if you do get married, you have not sinned, and if a virgin marries, she has not sinned. But such people will have trouble in this life,ᴶ and I am trying to spare you. ²⁹And I say this, brothers: The time is limited, so from now on those who have wives should be as though they had none, ³⁰those who weep as though they did not weep, those who rejoice as though they did not rejoice, those who buy as though they did not possess, ³¹and those who use the world as though they did not make full use of it. For this world in its current form is passing away.

³²I want you to be without concerns. An unmarried man is concerned about the things of the Lord—how he may please the Lord. ³³But a married man is concerned about the things of the world—how he may please his wife— ³⁴and his interests are divided. An unmarried woman or a virgin is concerned about the things of the Lord, so that she may be holy both in body and in spirit. But a married woman is concerned about the things of the world—how she may please her husband. ³⁵Now I am saying this for your own benefit, not to put a restraint on you, but because of what is proper and so that you may be devoted to the Lord without distraction.

³⁶But if any man thinks he is acting improperly toward his virgin,ᴷ if she is past marriageable age,ᴸ and so it must be, he can do what he wants. He is not sinning; they can get married. ³⁷But he who stands firm in his heart (who is under no compulsion, but has control over his own will) and has decided in his heart to keep his own virgin, will do well. ³⁸So then he who marriesᴹ his virgin

---

ᴬ**7:10** Or *separate from,* or *divorce*   ᴮ**7:12** Jesus did not address the situation of a marriage in the Gentile world where only one person is a believer.   ᶜ**7:14** Lit *the brother*   ᴰ**7:15** Other mss read *us*   ᴱ**7:17** Lit *called each*   ᶠ**7:20** Lit *in the calling*   ᴳ**7:21** Or *But even though you can become free, make the most of your position as a slave.*   ᴴ**7:22** A former slave   ᴵ**7:22** A man who was never a slave   ᴶ**7:28** Lit *in the flesh*   ᴷ**7:36** = a man's fiancée, or his daughter, or his Levirate wife, or a celibate companion   ᴸ**7:36** Or *virgin, if his passions are strong,*   ᴹ**7:38** Or *marries off* does well, but he who does not marry[A] will do better.

[39] A wife is bound[B] as long as her husband is living. But if her husband dies, she is free to be married to anyone she wants—only in the Lord.[C] [40] But she is happier if she remains as she is, in my opinion. And I think that I also have the Spirit of God.

8 About food offered to idols: We know that "we all have knowledge."[D] Knowledge inflates with pride, but love builds up. [2] If anyone thinks he knows anything, he does not yet know it as he ought to know it. [3] But if anyone loves God, he is known by Him.

[4] About eating food offered to idols, then, we know that "an idol is nothing in the world," and that "there is no God but one." [5] For even if there are so-called gods, whether in heaven or on earth—as there are many "gods" and many "lords"—

[6]   yet for us there is one God, the Father.
      All things are from Him,
      and we exist for Him.
      And there is one Lord, Jesus Christ.
      All things are through Him,
      and we exist through Him.

[7] However, not everyone has this knowledge. In fact, some have been so used to idolatry up until now that when they eat food offered to an idol, their conscience, being weak, is defiled. [8] Food will not make us acceptable to God. We are not inferior if we don't eat, and we are not better if we do eat. [9] But be careful that this right of yours in no way becomes a stumbling block to the weak. [10] For if someone sees you, the one who has this knowledge, dining in an idol's temple, won't his weak conscience be encouraged to eat food offered to idols? [11] Then the weak person, the brother for whom Christ died, is ruined[E] by your knowledge. [12] Now when you sin like this against the brothers and wound their weak conscience, you are sinning against Christ. [13] Therefore, if food causes my brother to fall, I will never again eat meat, so that I won't cause my brother to fall.

9 Am I not free? Am I not an apostle? Have I not seen Jesus our Lord? Are you not my work in the Lord? [2] If I am not an apostle to others, at least I am to you, for you are the seal of my apostleship in the Lord. [3] My defense to those who examine me is this: [4] Don't we have the right to eat and drink? [5] Don't we have the right to be accompanied by a Christian wife[F] like the other apostles, the Lord's brothers, and Cephas? [6] Or do Barnabas and I alone have no right to refrain from working? [7] Who ever goes to war at his own expense? Who plants a vineyard and does not eat its fruit? Or who shepherds a flock and does not drink the milk from the flock? [8] Am I saying this from a human perspective? Doesn't the law also say the same thing? [9] For it is written in the law of Moses, **Do not muzzle an ox while it treads out grain.**[G] Is God really concerned with oxen? [10] Or isn't He really saying it for us? Yes, this is written for us, because he who plows ought to plow in hope, and he who threshes should do so in hope of sharing the crop. [11] If we have sown spiritual things for you, is it too much if we reap material benefits from you? [12] If others have this right to receive benefits from you, don't we even more?

However, we have not made use of this right; instead we endure everything so that we will not hinder the gospel of Christ. [13] Don't you know that those who perform the temple services eat the food from the temple, and those who serve at the altar share in the offerings of the altar? [14] In the same way, the Lord has commanded that those who preach the gospel should earn their living by the gospel.

[15] But I have used none of these rights, and I have not written this to make it happen that way for me. For it would be better for me to die than for anyone to deprive me of my boast! [16] For if I preach the gospel, I have no reason to boast, because an obligation is placed on me. And woe to me if I do not preach the gospel! [17] For if I do this willingly, I have a reward, but if unwillingly, I am entrusted with a stewardship. [18] What then is my reward? To preach the gospel and offer it free

of charge and not make full use of my authority in the gospel.

¹⁹Although I am a free man and not anyone's slave, I have made myself a slave to everyone, in order to win more people. ²⁰To the Jews I became like a Jew, to win Jews; to those under the law, like one under the law—though I myself am not under the lawᴬ—to win those under the law. ²¹To those who are without that law, like one without the law—not being without God's law but within Christ's law—to win those without the law. ²²To the weak I became weak, in order to win the weak. I have become all things to all people, so that I may by every possible means save some. ²³Now I do all this because of the gospel, so I may become a partner in its benefits.ᴮ

²⁴Don't you know that the runners in a stadium all race, but only one receives the prize? Run in such a way to win the prize. ²⁵Now everyone who competes exercises self-control in everything. However, they do it to receive a crown that will fade away, but we a crown that will never fade away. ²⁶Therefore I do not run like one who runs aimlessly or box like one beating the air. ²⁷Instead, I discipline my body and bring it under strict control, so that after preaching to others, I myself will not be disqualified.

10 Now I want you to know, brothers, that our fathers were all under the cloud, all passed through the sea, ²and all were baptized into Moses in the cloud and in the sea. ³They all ate the same spiritual food, ⁴and all drank the same spiritual drink. For they drank from a spiritual rock that followed them, and that rock was Christ. ⁵But God was not pleased with most of them, for they were struck down in the wilderness.

⁶Now these things became examples for us, so that we will not desire evil things as they did.ᶜ ⁷Don't become idolaters as some of them were; as it is written, **The people sat down to eat and drink, and got up to play.**ᴰ,ᴱ ⁸Let us not commit sexual immorality as some of them did,ᶠ and in a single day 23,000 people fell dead. ⁹Let us not test Christ

as some of them didᴳ and were destroyed by snakes. ¹⁰Nor should we complain as some of them did,ᴴ and were killed by the destroyer.ᴵ ¹¹Now these things happened to them as examples, and they were written as a warning to us, on whom the ends of the ages have come. ¹²So, whoever thinks he stands must be careful not to fall. ¹³No temptation has overtaken you except what is common to humanity. God is faithful, and He will not allow you to be tempted beyond what you are able, but with the temptation He will also provide a way of escape so that you are able to bear it.

¹⁴Therefore, my dear friends, flee from idolatry. ¹⁵I am speaking as to wise people. Judge for yourselves what I say. ¹⁶The cup of blessing that we give thanks for, is it not a sharing in the blood of Christ? The bread that we break, is it not a sharing in the body of Christ? ¹⁷Because there is one bread, we who are many are one body, for all of us share that one bread. ¹⁸Look at the people of Israel.ᴶ Do not those who eat the sacrifices participate in what is offered on the altar? ¹⁹What am I saying then? That food offered to idols is anything, or that an idol is anything? ²⁰No, but I do say that what theyᴷ sacrifice, they sacrifice to demons and not to God. I do not want you to participate with demons! ²¹You cannot drink the cup of the Lord and the cup of demons. You cannot share in the Lord's table and the table of demons. ²²Or are we provoking the Lord to jealousy? Are we stronger than He?

²³"Everything is permissible,"ᴸ,ᴹ but not everything is helpful. "Everything is permissible,"ᴸ but not everything builds up. ²⁴No one should seek his own good, but the good of the other person.

²⁵Eat everything that is sold in the meat market, asking no questions for conscience' sake, ²⁶for **the earth is the Lord's, and all that is in it.**ᴺ ²⁷If one of the unbelievers invites you over and you want to go, eat everything that is set before you, without raising questions of conscience. ²⁸But if someone says to you, "This is food offered to an idol," do not eat it, out of consideration for the one who told you, and for conscience' sake.ᴼ ²⁹I do not

ᴬ9:20 Other mss omit *though I myself am not under law*   ᴮ9:23 Lit *partner of it*   ᶜ10:6 Lit *they desired*   ᴰ10:7 Or *to dance*   ᴱ10:7 Ex 32:6
ᶠ10:8 Lit *them committed sexual immorality*   ᴳ10:9 Lit *them tested*   ᴴ10:10 Lit *them complained*   ᴵ10:10 Or *the destroying angel*   ᴶ10:18 Lit
Look at Israel according to the flesh   ᴷ10:20 Other mss read *Gentiles*   ᴸ10:23 Other mss add *for me*   ᴹ10:23 See note at 1Co 6:12-13.
ᴺ10:26 Ps 24:1   ᴼ10:28 Other mss add *"For the earth is the Lord's and all that is in it."*

mean your own conscience, but the other person's. For why is my freedom judged by another person's conscience? [30]If I partake with thanks, why am I slandered because of something I give thanks for?

[31]Therefore, whether you eat or drink, or whatever you do, do everything for God's glory. [32]Give no offense to the Jews or the Greeks or the church of God, [33]just as I also try to please all people in all things, not seeking my own profit, but the profit of many, so that they may be saved. [1]Imitate me, as I also imitate Christ.

11

[2]Now I praise you[A] because you always remember me and keep the traditions just as I delivered them to you. [3]But I want you to know that Christ is the head of every man, and the man is the head of the woman,[B] and God is the head of Christ. [4]Every man who prays or prophesies with something on his head dishonors his head. [5]But every woman who prays or prophesies with her head uncovered dishonors her head, since that is one and the same as having her head shaved. [6]So if a woman's head[C] is not covered, her hair should be cut off. But if it is disgraceful for a woman to have her hair cut off or her head shaved, she should be covered.

[7]A man, in fact, should not cover his head, because he is God's image and glory, but woman is man's glory. [8]For man did not come from woman, but woman came from man. [9]And man was not created for woman, but woman for man. [10]This is why a woman should have a symbol of authority on her head, because of the angels. [11]In the Lord, however, woman is not independent of man, and man is not independent of woman. [12]For just as woman came from man, so man comes through woman, and all things come from God.

[13]Judge for yourselves: Is it proper for a woman to pray to God with her head uncovered? [14]Does not even nature itself teach you that if a man has long hair it is a disgrace to him, [15]but that if a woman has long hair, it is her glory? For her hair is given to her[D] as a covering. [16]But if anyone wants to argue about this, we have no other[E] custom, nor do the churches of God.

[17]Now in giving the following instruction I do not praise you, since you come together not for the better but for the worse. [18]For to begin with, I hear that when you come together as a church there are divisions among you, and in part I believe it. [19]There must, indeed, be factions among you, so that those who are approved may be recognized among you. [20]Therefore, when you come together, it is not really to eat the Lord's Supper. [21]For at the meal, each one eats his own supper ahead of others. So one person is hungry while another gets drunk? [22]Don't you have houses to eat and drink in? Or do you look down on the church of God and embarrass those who have nothing? What should I say to you? Should I praise you? I do not praise you for this!

[23]For I received from the Lord what I also passed on to you: On the night when He was betrayed, the Lord Jesus took bread, [24]gave thanks, broke it, and said,[F] "This is My body, which is[G] for you. Do this in remembrance of Me."

[25]In the same way, after supper He also took the cup and said, "This cup is the new covenant established by My blood. Do this, as often as you drink it, in remembrance of Me." [26]For as often as you eat this bread and drink the cup, you proclaim the Lord's death until He comes.

[27]Therefore, whoever eats the bread or drinks the cup of the Lord in an unworthy way will be guilty of sin against the body[H] and blood of the Lord. [28]So a man should examine himself; in this way he should eat the bread and drink from the cup. [29]For whoever eats and drinks without recognizing the body,[I] eats and drinks judgment on himself. [30]This is why many are sick and ill among you, and many have fallen asleep. [31]If we were properly evaluating ourselves, we would not be judged, [32]but when we are judged, we are disciplined by the Lord, so that we may not be condemned with the world.

[33]Therefore, my brothers, when you come together to eat, wait for one another. [34]If any-

[A]11:2 Other mss add brothers,   [B]11:3 Or the husband is the head of the wife   [C]11:6 Lit a woman   [D]11:15 Other mss omit to her   [E]11:16 Or no such   [F]11:24 Other mss add "Take, eat.   [G]11:24 Other mss add broken   [H]11:27 Lit be guilty of the body   [I]11:29 Other mss read drinks unworthily, not discerning the Lord's body one is hungry, he should eat at home, so that when you gather together you will not come under judgment. And I will give instructions about the other matters whenever I come.

12 Now concerning what comes from the Spirit:[A] brothers, I do not want you to be unaware. [2]You know that when you were pagans, you used to be led off to the idols that could not speak. [3]Therefore I am informing you that no one speaking by the Spirit of God says, "Jesus is cursed," and no one can say, "Jesus is Lord," except by the Holy Spirit.

[4]Now there are different gifts, but the same Spirit. [5]There are different ministries, but the same Lord. [6]And there are different activities, but the same God activates each gift in each person.[B] [7]A demonstration of the Spirit is given to each person to produce what is beneficial:

[8] to one is given a message of wisdom
      through the Spirit,
      to another, a message of knowledge
      by the same Spirit,
[9] to another, faith by the same Spirit,
      to another, gifts of healing
      by the one Spirit,
[10] to another, the performing of miracles,
      to another, prophecy,
      to another, distinguishing
      between spirits,
      to another, different kinds
      of languages,
      to another, interpretation
      of languages.

[11]But one and the same Spirit is active in all these, distributing to each person as He wills.

[12]For as the body is one and has many parts, and all the parts of that body, though many, are one body—so also is Christ. [13]For we were all baptized by[C] one Spirit into one body—whether Jews or Greeks, whether slaves or free—and we were all made to drink of one Spirit. [14]So the body is not one part but many. [15]If the foot should say, "Because I'm not a hand, I don't belong to the body," in spite of this it still belongs to the body. [16]And if the ear should say, "Because I'm not an eye, I don't belong to the body," in spite of this it

still belongs to the body. [17]If the whole body were an eye, where would the hearing be? If the whole body were an ear, where would the sense of smell be? [18]But now God has placed each one of the parts in one body just as He wanted. [19]And if they were all the same part, where would the body be? [20]Now there are many parts, yet one body.

[21]So the eye cannot say to the hand, "I don't need you!" Or again, the head can't say to the feet, "I don't need you!" [22]But even more, those parts of the body that seem to be weaker are necessary. [23]And those parts of the body that we think to be less honorable, we clothe these with greater honor, and our unpresentable parts have a better presentation. [24]But our presentable parts have no need of clothing. Instead, God has put the body together, giving greater honor to the less honorable, [25]so that there would be no division in the body, but that the members would have the same concern for each other. [26]So if one member suffers, all the members suffer with it; if one member is honored, all the members rejoice with it.

[27]Now you are the body of Christ, and individual members of it. [28]And God has placed these in the church:

      first apostles, second prophets,
      third teachers, next miracles,
      then gifts of healing, helping,
      managing, various kinds of languages.
[29] Are all apostles? Are all prophets?
      Are all teachers? Do all do miracles?
[30] Do all have gifts of healing?
      Do all speak in other languages?
      Do all interpret?

[31]But desire the greater gifts. And I will show you an even better way.

13 If I speak human or angelic
      languages
      but do not have love,
      I am a sounding gong
      or a clanging cymbal.
[2] If I have the gift of prophecy
      and understand all mysteries
      and all knowledge,

A12:1 Or concerning spiritual things, or spiritual gifts   B12:6 Lit God acts all things in all   C12:13 Or with, or in

and if I have all faith
so that I can move mountains
but do not have love, I am nothing.
³ And if I donate all my goods to feed
   the poor,
and if I give my body in order
   to boast[A]
but do not have love, I gain nothing.
⁴ Love is patient, love is kind.
Love does not envy,
is not boastful, is not conceited,
⁵ does not act improperly,
is not selfish, is not provoked,
and does not keep a record of wrongs.
⁶ Love finds no joy
   in unrighteousness
but rejoices in the truth.
⁷ It bears all things, believes all things,
hopes all things, endures all things.

⁸ Love never ends.
But as for prophecies,
they will come to an end;
as for languages, they will cease;
as for knowledge, it will come
   to an end.
⁹ For we know in part,
and we prophesy in part.
¹⁰ But when the perfect comes,
the partial will come to an end.
¹¹ When I was a child,
I spoke like a child,
I thought like a child,
I reasoned like a child.
When I became a man,
I put aside childish things.
¹² For now we see indistinctly,[B] as
   in a mirror,[C]
but then face to face.
Now I know in part,
but then I will know fully,
as I am fully known.
¹³ Now these three remain:
faith, hope, and love.
But the greatest of these is love.

14 Pursue love and desire spiritual gifts, and above all that you may prophesy. ²For the person who speaks in another language is not speaking to men but to God, since no one understands him; however, he speaks mysteries in the Spirit.[D] ³But the person who prophesies speaks to people for edification, encouragement, and consolation. ⁴The person who speaks in another language builds himself up, but he who prophesies builds up the church. ⁵I wish all of you spoke in other languages, but even more that you prophesied. The person who prophesies is greater than the person who speaks in languages, unless he interprets so that the church may be built up.

⁶But now, brothers, if I come to you speaking in other languages, how will I benefit you unless I speak to you with a revelation or knowledge or prophecy or teaching? ⁷Even inanimate things that produce sounds—whether flute or harp—if they don't make a distinction in the notes, how will what is played on the flute or harp be recognized? ⁸In fact, if the trumpet makes an unclear sound, who will prepare for battle? ⁹In the same way, unless you use your tongue for intelligible speech, how will what is spoken be known? For you will be speaking into the air. ¹⁰There are doubtless many different kinds of languages in the world, and all have meaning.[E] ¹¹Therefore, if I do not know the meaning of the language, I will be a foreigner[F] to the speaker, and the speaker will be a foreigner to me. ¹²So also you—since you are zealous for spiritual gifts,[G] seek to excel in building up the church.

¹³Therefore the person who speaks in another language should pray that he can interpret. ¹⁴For if I pray in another language, my spirit prays, but my understanding is unfruitful. ¹⁵What then? I will pray with the spirit, and I will also pray with my understanding. I will sing with the spirit, and I will also sing with my understanding. ¹⁶Otherwise, if you praise with the spirit,[H] how will the uninformed person[I] say "Amen" at your giving of thanks, since he does not know what you

---

A13:3 Other mss read *body to be burned*   **B13:12** Or *indirectly*   **C13:12** Ancient mirrors were normally made out of polished metals and were not as clear as modern ones.   **D14:2** Or *in spirit*, or *in his spirit*   **E14:10** Lit *and none is without a sound*   **F14:11** Gk *barbaros* = in Eng a "barbarian." To a Gk, a *barbaros* was anyone who did not speak Gk.   **G14:12** Lit *zealous of spirits; spirits* = human spirits, spiritual powers, or the Holy Spirit   **H14:16** Or *praise by the Spirit*   **I14:16** Lit *the one filling the place of the uninformed* are saying? [17]For you may very well be giving thanks, but the other person is not being built up. [18]I thank God that I speak in other languages more than all of you; [19]yet in the church I would rather speak five words with my understanding, in order to teach others also, than 10,000 words in another language.

[20]Brothers, don't be childish in your thinking, but be infants in regard to evil and adult in your thinking. [21]It is written in the law:

> I will speak to these people
> by people of other languages
> and by the lips of foreigners,
> and even then, they will not listen
>   to Me,[A]

says the Lord. [22]It follows that speaking in other languages is intended as a sign,[B] not for believers but for unbelievers. But prophecy is not for unbelievers but for believers. [23]Therefore, if the whole church assembles together and all are speaking in other languages and people who are uninformed or unbelievers come in, will they not say that you are out of your minds? [24]But if all are prophesying and some unbeliever or uninformed person comes in, he is convicted by all and is judged by all. [25]The secrets of his heart will be revealed, and as a result he will fall facedown and worship God, proclaiming, "God is really among you."

[26]What then is the conclusion, brothers? Whenever you come together, each one[C] has a psalm, a teaching, a revelation, another language, or an interpretation. All things must be done for edification. [27]If any person speaks in another language, there should be only two, or at the most three, each in turn, and someone must interpret. [28]But if there is no interpreter, that person should keep silent in the church and speak to himself and to God. [29]Two or three prophets should speak, and the others should evaluate. [30]But if something has been revealed to another person sitting there, the first prophet should be silent. [31]For you can all prophesy one by one, so that everyone may learn and everyone may be encouraged. [32]And the prophets' spirits

are under the control of the prophets, [33]since God is not a God of disorder but of peace.

As in all the churches of the saints, [34]the women[D] should be silent in the churches, for they are not permitted to speak, but should be submissive, as the law also says. [35]And if they want to learn something, they should ask their own husbands at home, for it is disgraceful for a woman to speak in the church meeting. [36]Did the word of God originate from you, or did it come to you only?

[37]If anyone thinks he is a prophet or spiritual, he should recognize that what I write to you is the Lord's command. [38]But if anyone ignores this, he will be ignored.[E] [39]Therefore, my brothers, be eager to prophesy, and do not forbid speaking in other languages. [40]But everything must be done decently and in order.

15 Now brothers, I want to clarify[F] for you the gospel I proclaimed to you; you received it and have taken your stand on it. [2]You are also saved by it, if you hold to the message I proclaimed to you—unless you believed for no purpose.[G] [3]For I passed on to you as most important what I also received:

> that Christ died for our sins
>   according to the Scriptures,
> [4] that He was buried,
>   that He was raised on the third day
>   according to the Scriptures,
> [5] and that He appeared to Cephas,
>   then to the Twelve,
> [6] Then He appeared to over 500 brothers
>   at one time;
>   most of them are still alive,
>   but some have fallen asleep.
> [7] Then He appeared to James,
>   then to all the apostles.
> [8] Last of all, as to one abnormally born,[H]
>   He also appeared to me.

[9]For I am the least of the apostles, unworthy to be called an apostle, because I persecuted the church of God. [10]But by God's grace I am what I am, and His grace toward me was not ineffective. However, I worked more than any of them, yet not I, but God's grace that

A14:21 Is 28:11-12   B14:22 Lit that languages are for a sign   C14:26 Other mss add of you   D14:34 Other mss read your women
E14:38 Other mss read he should be ignored   F15:1 Or I make known   G15:2 Or believed without careful thought, or believed in vain
H15:8 Or one whose birth was unusual, He

was with me. ¹¹Therefore, whether it is I or they, so we proclaim and so you have believed.

¹²Now if Christ is proclaimed as raised from the dead, how can some of you say, "There is no resurrection of the dead"? ¹³But if there is no resurrection of the dead, then Christ has not been raised; ¹⁴and if Christ has not been raised, then our proclamation is without foundation, and so is your faith.ᴬ ¹⁵In addition, we are found to be false witnesses about God, because we have testified about God that He raised up Christ—whom He did not raise up if in fact the dead are not raised. ¹⁶For if the dead are not raised, Christ has not been raised. ¹⁷And if Christ has not been raised, your faith is worthless; you are still in your sins. ¹⁸Therefore, those who have fallen asleep in Christ have also perished. ¹⁹If we have put our hope in Christ for this life only, we should be pitied more than anyone.

²⁰But now Christ has been raised from the dead, the firstfruits of those who have fallen asleep. ²¹For since death came through a man, the resurrection of the dead also comes through a man. ²²For as in Adam all die, so also in Christ all will be made alive. ²³But each in his own order: Christ, the firstfruits; afterward, at His coming, those who belong to Christ. ²⁴Then comes the end, when He hands over the kingdom to God the Father, when He abolishes all rule and all authority and power. ²⁵For He must reign until He puts all His enemies under His feet. ²⁶The last enemy to be abolished is death. ²⁷For **God has put everything under His feet.**ᴮ But when it says "everything" is put under Him, it is obvious that He who puts everything under Him is the exception. ²⁸And when everything is subject to Christ, then the Son Himself will also be subject to the One who subjected everything to Him, so that God may be all in all.

²⁹Otherwise what will they do who are being baptized for the dead? If the dead are not raised at all, then why are people baptized for them?ᶜ ³⁰Why are we in danger every hour? ³¹I affirm by the pride in you that I have in Christ Jesus our Lord: I die every day! ³²If I fought wild animals in Ephesus with only human hope,ᴰ what good did that do me?ᴱ If the dead are not raised, **Let us eat and drink, for tomorrow we die.**ᶠ ³³Do not be deceived: "Bad company corrupts good morals."ᴳ ³⁴Come to your sensesᴴ and stop sinning, for some people are ignorant about God. I say this to your shame.

³⁵But someone will say, "How are the dead raised? What kind of body will they have when they come?" ³⁶Foolish one! What you sow does not come to life unless it dies. ³⁷And as for what you sow—you are not sowing the future body, but only a seed,ᴵ perhaps of wheat or another grain. ³⁸But God gives it a body as He wants, and to each of the seeds its own body. ³⁹Not all flesh is the same flesh; there is one flesh for humans, another for animals, another for birds, and another for fish. ⁴⁰There are heavenly bodies and earthly bodies, but the splendor of the heavenly bodies is different from that of the earthly ones. ⁴¹There is a splendor of the sun, another of the moon, and another of the stars; for one star differs from another star in splendor. ⁴²So it is with the resurrection of the dead:

> Sown in corruption, raised
> in incorruption;
> ⁴³ sown in dishonor, raised in glory;
> sown in weakness, raised
> in power;
> ⁴⁴ sown a natural body, raised
> a spiritual body.

If there is a natural body, there is also a spiritual body. ⁴⁵So it is written: **The first man Adam became a living being;**ᴶ the last Adam became a life-giving Spirit. ⁴⁶However, the spiritual is not first, but the natural, then the spiritual.

> ⁴⁷ The first man was from the earth
> and made of dust;
> the second man isᴷ from heaven.
> ⁴⁸ Like the man made of dust,
> so are those who are made of dust;
> like the heavenly man,
> so are those who are heavenly.

ᴬ**15:14** Or *proclamation is useless, and your faith also is useless,* or *proclamation is empty, and your faith also is empty*   ᴮ**15:27** Ps 8:6
ᶜ**15:29** Other mss read *for the dead*   ᴰ**15:32** Lit *Ephesus according to man*   ᴱ**15:32** Lit *what to me the profit?*   ᶠ**15:32** Is 22:13
ᴳ**15:33** A quotation from the poet Menander, *Thais,* 218   ᴴ**15:34** Lit *Sober up righteously*   ᴵ**15:37** Lit *but a naked seed*   ᴶ**15:45** Gn 2:7
ᴷ**15:47** Other mss add *the Lord*

⁴⁹ And just as we have borne
the image of the man made
of dust,
we will also bear
the image of the heavenly man.

⁵⁰Brothers, I tell you this: Flesh and blood cannot inherit the kingdom of God, and corruption cannot inherit incorruption. ⁵¹Listen! I am telling you a mystery:

We will not all fall asleep,
but we will all be changed,
⁵² in a moment, in the blink
of an eye,
at the last trumpet.
For the trumpet will sound,
and the dead will be
raised incorruptible,
and we will be changed.
⁵³ For this corruptible
must be clothed
with incorruptibility,
and this mortal must be clothed
with immortality.
⁵⁴ When this corruptible is clothed
with incorruptibility,
and this mortal is clothed
with immortality,
then the saying that is written
will take place:
**Death has been swallowed up
in victory.**ᴬ
⁵⁵ **Death, where is your victory?
Death, where is your sting?**ᴮ
⁵⁶ Now the sting of death is sin,
and the power of sin is the law.
⁵⁷ But thanks be to God, who gives us
the victory
through our Lord Jesus Christ!

⁵⁸Therefore, my dear brothers, be steadfast, immovable, always excelling in the Lord's work, knowing that your labor in the Lord is not in vain.

16 Now about the collection for the saints: You should do the same as I instructed the Galatian churches. ²On the first day of the week,ᶜ each of you is to set some-

thing aside and save in keeping with how he prospers, so that no collections will need to be made when I come. ³When I arrive, I will send with letters those you recommend to carry your gracious gift to Jerusalem. ⁴If it is suitable for me to go as well, they can travel with me.

⁵I will come to you after I pass through Macedonia—for I will be traveling through Macedonia— ⁶and perhaps I will remain with you or even spend the winter, so that you may send me on my way wherever I go. ⁷I don't want to see you now just in passing, for I hope to spend some time with you, if the Lord allows. ⁸But I will stay in Ephesus until Pentecost, ⁹because a wide door for effective ministry has opened for meᴰ—yet many oppose me. ¹⁰If Timothy comes, see that he has nothing to fear from you, because he is doing the Lord's work, just as I am. ¹¹Therefore, no one should look down on him. Send him on his way in peace so he can come to me, for I am expecting him with the brothers.ᴱ

¹²About our brother Apollos: I strongly urged him to come to you with the brothers, but he was not at all willing to come now. However, he will come when he has an opportunity.

¹³Be alert, stand firm in the faith, act like a man, be strong. ¹⁴Your every action must be done with love.

¹⁵Brothers, you know the household of Stephanas: They are the firstfruits of Achaia and have devoted themselves to serving the saints. I urge you ¹⁶also to submit to such people, and to everyone who works and labors with them. ¹⁷I am pleased to have Stephanas, Fortunatus, and Achaicus present, because these men have made up for your absence. ¹⁸For they have refreshed my spirit and yours. Therefore recognize such people.

¹⁹The churches of Asia greet you. Aquila and Priscilla greet you warmly in the Lord, along with the church that meets in their home. ²⁰All the brothers greet you. Greet one another with a holy kiss.

²¹ This greeting is in my own handᶠ —Paul. ²²If anyone does not love the Lord, a

ᴬ**15:54** Is 25:8   ᴮ**15:55** Hs 13:14   ᶜ**16:2** Or *Each Sunday*   ᴰ**16:9** Lit *for a door has opened to me, great and effective*   ᴱ**16:11** *With the brothers* may connect with Paul or Timothy.   ᶠ**16:21** Paul normally dictated his letters to a secretary, but signed the end of each letter himself; Rm 16:22; Gl 6:11; Col 4:18; 2Th 3:17.

curse be on him. *Marana tha* that is, Lord, come!^A ²³ The grace of the Lord Jesus be with you. ²⁴ My love be with all of you in Christ Jesus.

2 CORINTHIANS

1 Paul, an apostle of Christ Jesus by God's will, and Timothy our^B brother:

To God's church at Corinth, with all the saints who are throughout Achaia.

² Grace to you and peace from God our Father and the Lord Jesus Christ.

³ Praise the God and Father of our Lord Jesus Christ, the Father of mercies and the God of all comfort. ⁴ He comforts us in all our affliction,^C so that we may be able to comfort those who are in any kind of affliction, through the comfort we ourselves receive from God. ⁵ For as the sufferings of Christ overflow to us, so through Christ our comfort also overflows. ⁶ If we are afflicted, it is for your comfort and salvation. If we are comforted, it is for your comfort, which is experienced in your endurance of the same sufferings that we suffer. ⁷ And our hope for you is firm, because we know that as you share in the sufferings, so you will share in the comfort.

⁸ For we don't want you to be unaware, brothers, of our affliction that took place in Asia: we were completely overwhelmed—beyond our strength—so that we even despaired of life. ⁹ Indeed, we personally had a death sentence within ourselves, so that we would not trust in ourselves but in God who raises the dead. ¹⁰ He has delivered us from such a terrible death, and He will deliver us. We have put our hope in Him that He will deliver us again ¹¹ while you join in helping us by your prayers. Then many will give thanks on our^D behalf for the gift that came to us through the prayers of many.

¹² For this is our confidence: The testimony of our conscience is that we have conducted ourselves in the world, and especially toward you, with God-given sincerity and purity, not by fleshly^E wisdom but by God's grace. ¹³ Now we are writing nothing to you other than what you can read and also understand. I hope you will understand completely— ¹⁴ as you have partially understood us—that we are your reason for pride, as you are ours, in the day of our^F Lord Jesus.

¹⁵ I planned with this confidence to come to you first, so you could have a double benefit,^G ¹⁶ and to go on to Macedonia with your help, then come to you again from Macedonia and be given a start by you on my journey to Judea. ¹⁷ So when I planned this, was I irresponsible? Or what I plan, do I plan in a purely human^H way so that I say "Yes, yes" and "No, no" simultaneously? ¹⁸ As God is faithful, our message to you is not "Yes and no." ¹⁹ For the Son of God, Jesus Christ, who was preached among you by us—by me and Silvanus^I and Timothy—did not become "Yes and no"; on the contrary, a final "Yes" has come in Him. ²⁰ For every one of God's promises is "Yes" in Him. Therefore, the "Amen" is also spoken through Him by us for God's glory. ²¹ Now it is God who strengthens us, with you, in Christ and has anointed us. ²² He has also sealed us and given us the Spirit as a down payment in our hearts.

²³ I call on God as a witness, on my life, that it was to spare you that I did not come to Corinth. ²⁴ I do not mean that we have control of^J your faith, but we are workers with you for your joy, because you stand by 2 faith. ¹ In fact, I made up my mind about this:^K I would not come to you on another painful visit.^L ² For if I cause you pain, then who will cheer me other than the one being hurt by me?^M ³ I wrote this very thing so that when I came I wouldn't have pain from those who ought to give me joy, because I am confident about all of you that my joy will also be

---

^A16:22 Or *Maran atha* (an Aram expression transliterated into Gk) = *Our Lord has come!* ^B1:1 Lit *the* ^C1:4 Or *trouble, or tribulation, or trials, or oppression;* the Gk word has a lit meaning of being under pressure. ^D1:11 Other mss read *your* ^E1:12 The word *fleshly* (characterized by flesh) indicates that the wisdom is natural rather than spiritual. ^F1:14 Other mss omit *our* ^G1:15 Other mss read *a second joy* ^H1:17 Or *a worldly, or a fleshly, or a selfish* ^I1:19 Or *Silas;* Ac 15:22-32; 16:19-40; 17:1-16 ^J1:24 Or *we lord it over, or we rule over* ^K2:1 Lit *I decided this for myself* ^L2:1 Lit *not again in sorrow to come to you* ^M2:2 Lit *the one pained*

yours. ⁴For I wrote to you with many tears out of an extremely troubled and anguished heart—not that you should be hurt, but that you should know the abundant love I have for you.

⁵If anyone has caused pain, he has caused pain not so much to me but to some degree—not to exaggerate—to all of you. ⁶The punishment inflicted by the majority is sufficient for that person. ⁷As a result, you should instead forgive and comfort him. Otherwise, this one may be overwhelmed by excessive grief. ⁸Therefore I urge you to reaffirm your love to him. ⁹I wrote for this purpose: to test your character to see if you are obedient in everything. ¹⁰If you forgive anyone, I do too. For what I have forgiven—if I have forgiven anything—it is for you in the presence of Christ. ¹¹I have done this so that we may not be taken advantage of by Satan. For we are not ignorant of his schemes.

¹²When I came to Troas to preach the gospel of Christ, the Lord opened a door for me. ¹³I had no rest in my spirit because I did not find my brother Titus, but I said good-bye to them and left for Macedonia.

¹⁴But thanks be to God, who always puts us on display^A in Christ^B and through us spreads the aroma of the knowledge of Him in every place. ¹⁵For to God we are the fragrance of Christ among those who are being saved and among those who are perishing. ¹⁶To some we are an aroma of death leading to death, but to others, an aroma of life leading to life. And who is competent for this? ¹⁷For we are not like the many^C who market God's message for profit. On the contrary, we speak with sincerity in Christ, as from God and before God.

3 Are we beginning to commend ourselves again? Or do we need, like some, letters of recommendation to you or from you? ²You yourselves are our letter, written on our hearts, recognized and read by everyone. ³It is clear that you are Christ's letter, produced^D by us, not written with ink but with the Spirit of the living God—not on stone tablets but on tablets that are hearts of flesh.

⁴We have this kind of confidence toward God through Christ. ⁵It is not that we are competent in^E ourselves to consider anything as coming from ourselves, but our competence is from God. ⁶He has made us competent to be ministers of a new covenant, not of the letter, but of the Spirit. For the letter kills, but the Spirit produces life.

⁷Now if the ministry of death, chiseled in letters on stones, came with glory, so that the Israelites were not able to look directly at Moses' face because of the glory from his face—a fading glory— ⁸how will the ministry of the Spirit not be more glorious? ⁹For if the ministry of condemnation had glory, the ministry of righteousness overflows with even more glory. ¹⁰In fact, what had been glorious is not glorious now by comparison because of the glory that surpasses it. ¹¹For if what was fading away was glorious, what endures will be even more glorious.

¹²Therefore, having such a hope, we use great boldness. ¹³We are not like Moses, who used to put a veil over his face so that the Israelites could not stare at the end of what was fading away, ¹⁴but their minds were closed.^F For to this day, at the reading of the old covenant, the same veil remains; it is not lifted, because it is set aside only in Christ. ¹⁵Even to this day, whenever Moses is read, a veil lies over their hearts, ¹⁶but whenever a person turns to the Lord, the veil is removed. ¹⁷Now the Lord is the Spirit, and where the Spirit of the Lord is, there is freedom. ¹⁸We all, with unveiled faces, are looking as in a mirror at^G the glory of the Lord and are being transformed into the same image from glory to glory;^H this is from the Lord who is the Spirit.^I

4 Therefore, since we have this ministry because we were shown mercy, we do not give up. ²Instead, we have renounced shameful secret things, not walking in deceit or distorting God's message, but commending ourselves to every person's conscience in God's sight by an open display of the truth. ³But if our gospel is veiled, it is veiled to those who are perishing. ⁴In their case, the god of

^A2:14 Or always leads us in a triumphal procession, or always causes us to triumph   ^B2:14 Lit in the Christ, or in the Messiah; 1Co 15:22; Eph 1:10,12,20; 3:11   ^C2:17 Other mss read the rest   ^D3:3 Lit ministered to   ^E3:5 Lit from   ^F3:14 Lit their thoughts were hardened   ^G3:18 Or are reflecting   ^H3:18 Progressive glorification or sanctification   ^I3:18 Or from the Spirit of the Lord, or from the Lord, the Spirit this age has blinded the minds of the unbelievers so they cannot see the light of the gospel of the glory of Christ,[A] who is the image of God. [5] For we are not proclaiming ourselves but Jesus Christ as Lord, and ourselves as your slaves because of Jesus. [6] For God who said, "Let light shine out of darkness," has shone in our hearts to give the light of the knowledge of God's glory in the face of Jesus Christ.

[7] Now we have this treasure in clay jars, so that this extraordinary power may be from God and not from us. [8] We are pressured in every way but not crushed; we are perplexed but not in despair; [9] we are persecuted but not abandoned; we are struck down but not destroyed. [10] We always carry the death of Jesus in our body, so that the life of Jesus may also be revealed in our body. [11] For we who live are always given over to death because of Jesus, so that Jesus' life may also be revealed in our mortal flesh. [12] So death works in us, but life in you. [13] And since we have the same spirit of faith in keeping with what is written, **I believed, therefore I spoke,**[B] we also believe, and therefore speak. [14] We know that the One who raised the Lord Jesus will raise us also with Jesus and present us with you. [15] Indeed, everything is for your benefit, so that grace, extended through more and more people, may cause thanksgiving to increase to God's glory.

[16] Therefore we do not give up. Even though our outer person is being destroyed, our inner person is being renewed day by day. [17] For our momentary light affliction[C] is producing for us an absolutely incomparable eternal weight of glory. [18] So we do not focus on what is seen, but on what is unseen. For what is seen is temporary, but what is unseen is eternal.

5 For we know that if our temporary, earthly dwelling[D] is destroyed, we have a building from God, an eternal dwelling[E] in the heavens, not made with hands. [2] Indeed, we groan in this body, desiring to put on our dwelling from heaven, [3] since, when we are clothed,[F] we will not be found naked. [4] Indeed, we groan while we are in this tent, burdened as we are, because we do not want to be un-

clothed but clothed, so that mortality may be swallowed up by life. [5] And the One who prepared us for this very purpose is God, who gave us the Spirit as a down payment.

[6] So, we are always confident and know that while we are at home in the body we are away from the Lord. [7] For we walk by faith, not by sight, [8] and we are confident and satisfied to be out of the body and at home with the Lord. [9] Therefore, whether we are at home or away, we make it our aim to be pleasing to Him. [10] For we must all appear before the tribunal of Christ, so that each may be repaid for what he has done in the body, whether good or worthless.

[11] Therefore, because we know the fear of the Lord, we seek to persuade people. We are completely open before God, and I hope we are completely open to your consciences as well. [12] We are not commending ourselves to you again, but giving you an opportunity to be proud of us, so that you may have a reply for those who take pride in the outward appearance[G] rather than in the heart. [13] For if we are out of our mind, it is for God; if we have a sound mind, it is for you. [14] For Christ's love compels[H] us, since we have reached this conclusion: If One died for all, then all died. [15] And He died for all so that those who live should no longer live for themselves, but for the One who died for them and was raised.

[16] From now on, then, we do not know[I] anyone in a purely human way.[J] Even if we have known[K] Christ in a purely human way,[L] yet now we no longer know[I] Him in this way. [17] Therefore, if anyone is in Christ, he is a new creation; old things have passed away, and look, new things[M] have come. [18] Everything is from God, who reconciled us to Himself through Christ and gave us the ministry of reconciliation: [19] That is, in Christ, God was reconciling the world to Himself, not counting their trespasses against them, and He has committed the message of reconciliation to us. [20] Therefore, we are ambassadors for Christ, certain that God is appealing through us. We plead on Christ's behalf, "Be reconciled to God." [21] He made the One who did not

---

A4:4 Or the gospel of the glorious Christ, or the glorious gospel of Christ   B4:13 Ps 116:10 LXX   C4:17 See note at 2Co 1:4.   D5:1 = our present physical body   E5:1 = our future body   F5:3 Other mss read stripped   G5:12 Lit in face   H5:14 Or For the love of Christ impels, or For the love of Christ controls   I5:16 Or regard   J5:16 Lit anyone according to the flesh   K5:16 Or have regarded   L5:16 Lit Christ according to the flesh   M5:17 Other mss read look, all new things know sin to be sin[A] for us, so that we might become the righteousness of God in Him.

6 Working together[B] with Him, we also appeal to you, "Don't receive God's grace in vain." [2]For He says:

> **I heard you in an acceptable time,**
> **and I helped you in the day**
> **of salvation.**[C]

Look, now is the acceptable time; now is the day of salvation.

[3]We give no opportunity for stumbling to anyone, so that the ministry will not be blamed. [4]But as God's ministers, we commend ourselves in everything:

> by great endurance, by afflictions,
> by hardship, by difficulties,
> [5] by beatings, by imprisonments,
> by riots, by labors,
> by sleepless nights, by times
>   of hunger,
> [6] by purity, by knowledge,
> by patience, by kindness,
> by the Holy Spirit, by sincere love,
> [7] by the message of truth,
> by the power of God;
> through weapons of righteousness
>   on the right hand and the left,
> [8] through glory and dishonor,
> through slander and good report;
> as deceivers yet true;
> [9] as unknown yet recognized;
> as dying and look—we live;
> as being disciplined yet not killed;
> [10] as grieving yet always rejoicing;
> as poor yet enriching many;
> as having nothing yet
>   possessing everything.

[11]We have spoken openly[D] to you, Corinthians; our heart has been opened wide. [12]You are not limited by us, but you are limited by your own affections. [13]I speak as to my children. As a proper response, you should also be open to us.

[14]Do not be mismatched with unbelievers. For what partnership is there between righteousness and lawlessness? Or what fellowship does light have with darkness? [15]What agreement does Christ have with Belial?[E] Or what does a believer have in common with an unbeliever? [16]And what agreement does God's sanctuary have with idols? For we[F] are the sanctuary of the living God, as God said:

> **I will dwell among them**
> **and walk among them,**
> **and I will be their God,**
> **and they will be My people.**[G]
> [17] **Therefore, come out from among them**
> **and be separate, says the Lord;**
> **do not touch any unclean thing,**
> **and I will welcome you.**[H]
> [18] **I will be a Father to you,**
> **and you will be sons and daughters**
> **to Me,**
> **says the Lord Almighty.**[I]

7 Therefore, dear friends, since we have such promises, let us cleanse ourselves from every impurity of the flesh and spirit, completing our sanctification[J] in the fear of God.

[2]Accept us.[K] We have wronged no one, corrupted no one, defrauded no one. [3]I don't say this to condemn you, for I have already said that you are in our hearts, to live together and to die together. [4]I have great confidence in you; I have great pride in you. I am filled with encouragement; I am overcome with joy in all our afflictions.

[5]In fact, when we came into Macedonia, we[L] had no rest. Instead, we were troubled in every way: conflicts on the outside, fears inside. [6]But God, who comforts the humble, comforted us by the arrival of Titus, [7]and not only by his arrival, but also by the comfort he received from you. He told us about your deep longing, your sorrow,[M] and your zeal for me, so that I rejoiced even more. [8]For even if I grieved you with my letter, I do not regret it—even though I did regret it since I saw that the letter grieved you, yet only for a little while. [9]Now I rejoice, not because you were grieved, but because your grief led

---

A5:21 Or be a sin offering   B6:1 Or As we work together   C6:2 Is 49:8   D6:11 Lit Our mouths have been open   E6:15 Or Beliar, a name for the Devil or antichrist in extra-biblical Jewish writings   F6:16 Other mss read you   G6:16 Lv 26:12; Jr 31:33; 32:38; Ezk 37:26   H6:17 Is 52:11   I6:18 2Sm 7:14; Is 43:6; 49:22; 60:4; Hs 1:10   J7:1 Or spirit, perfecting holiness   K7:2 Lit Make room for us   L7:5 Lit our flesh   M7:7 Or lamentation, or mourning to repentance. For you were grieved as God willed, so that you didn't experience any loss from us. [10]For godly grief produces a repentance not to be regretted and leading to salvation, but worldly grief produces death. [11]For consider how much diligence this very thing—this grieving as God wills—has produced in you: what a desire to clear yourselves, what indignation, what fear, what deep longing, what zeal, what justice! In every way you showed yourselves to be pure in this matter. [12]So even though I wrote to you, it was not because of the one who did wrong, or because of the one who was wronged, but in order that your diligence for us might be made plain to you in the sight of God. [13]For this reason we have been comforted.

In addition to our comfort, we rejoiced even more over the joy Titus had,[A] because his spirit was refreshed by all of you. [14]For if I have made any boast to him about you, I have not been embarrassed; but as I have spoken everything to you in truth, so our boasting to Titus has also turned out to be the truth. [15]And his affection toward you is even greater as he remembers the obedience of all of you, and how you received him with fear and trembling. [16]I rejoice that I have complete confidence in you.

8 We want you to know, brothers, about the grace of God granted to the churches of Macedonia: [2]During a severe testing by affliction, their abundance of joy and their deep poverty overflowed into the wealth of their generosity. [3]I testify that, on their own, according to their ability and beyond their ability, [4]they begged us insistently for the privilege of sharing in the ministry to the saints, [5]and not just as we had hoped. Instead, they gave themselves especially to the Lord, then to us by God's will. [6]So we urged Titus that just as he had begun, so he should also complete this grace to you. [7]Now as you excel in everything—faith, speech, knowledge, and in all diligence, and in your love for us[B]—excel also in this grace.

[8]I am not saying this as a command. Rather, by means of the diligence of others, I am testing the genuineness of your love. [9]For you know the grace of our Lord Jesus Christ: Though He was rich, for your sake He became poor, so that by His poverty you might become rich. [10]Now I am giving an opinion on this because it is profitable for you, who a year ago began not only to do something but also to desire it.[C] [11]But now finish the task[D] as well, that just as there was eagerness to desire it, so there may also be a completion from what you have. [12]For if the eagerness is there, it is acceptable according to what one has, not according to what he does not have. [13]It is not that there may be relief for others and hardship for you, but it is a question of equality[E]—[14]at the present time your surplus is available for their need, so their abundance may also become available for our need, so there may be equality. [15]As it has been written:

> **The person who gathered much
> did not have too much,
> and the person who gathered little
> did not have too little.**[F]

[16]Thanks be to God who put the same concern for you into the heart of Titus. [17]For he accepted our urging and, being very diligent, went out to you by his own choice. [18]We have sent with him the brother who is praised throughout the churches for his gospel ministry.[G] [19]And not only that, but he was also appointed by the churches to accompany us with this gift[H] that is being administered by us for the glory of the Lord Himself and to show our eagerness to help. [20]We are taking this precaution so no one can criticize us about this large sum administered by us. [21]For we are making provision for what is right, not only before the Lord but also before men. [22]We have also sent with them our brother. We have often tested him in many circumstances and found him to be diligent—and now even more diligent because of his great confidence in you. [23]As for Titus, he is my partner and coworker serving you; as for our brothers, they are the messengers of the churches, the glory of Christ. [24]Therefore, show them proof before the churches of your love and of our boasting about you.

A7:13 Lit the joy of Titus   B8:7 Other mss read in our love for you   C8:10 Lit to will   D8:11 Lit finish the doing   E8:13 Lit but from equality
F8:15 Ex 16:18   G8:18 Lit churches, in the gospel   H8:19 Or grace

9 Now concerning the ministry to the saints, it is unnecessary for me to write to you. ²For I know your eagerness, and I brag about you to the Macedonians:ᴬ "Achaiaᴮ has been prepared since last year," and your zeal has stirred up most of them. ³But I sent the brothers so our boasting about you in the matter would not prove empty, and so you would be prepared just as I said. ⁴For if any Macedonians come with me and find you unprepared, we, not to mention you, would be embarrassed in that situation.ᶜ ⁵Therefore I considered it necessary to urge the brothers to go on ahead to you and arrange in advance the generous gift you promised, so that it will be ready as a gift and not as an extortion.

⁶Remember this:ᴰ The person who sows sparingly will also reap sparingly, and the person who sows generously will also reap generously. ⁷Each person should do as he has decided in his heart—not reluctantly or out of necessity, for God loves a cheerful giver. ⁸And God is able to make every grace overflow to you, so that in every way, always having everything you need, you may excel in every good work. ⁹As it is written:

He scattered;
He gave to the poor;
His righteousness endures forever.ᴱ

¹⁰Now the One who provides seed for the sower and bread for food will provide and multiply your seed and increase the harvest of your righteousness. ¹¹You will be enriched in every way for all generosity, which produces thanksgiving to God through us. ¹²For the ministry of this service is not only supplying the needs of the saints, but is also overflowing in many acts of thanksgiving to God. ¹³They will glorify God for your obedience to the confession ofᶠ the gospel of Christ, and for your generosity in sharing with them and with others through the proof provided by this service. ¹⁴And they will have deep affection forᴳ you in their prayers on your behalf because of the surpassing grace of God in you. ¹⁵Thanks be to God for His indescribable gift.

10 Now I, Paul, make a personal appeal to you by the gentleness and graciousness of Christ—I who am humble among you in person but bold toward you when absent. ²I beg you that when I am present I will not need to be bold with the confidence by which I plan to challenge certain people who think we are behaving in an unspiritual way.ᴴ ³For though we live in the body,ᴵ we do not wage war in an unspiritual way,ᴶ ⁴since the weapons of our warfare are not worldly,ᴷ but are powerful through God for the demolition of strongholds. We demolish arguments ⁵and every high-minded thing that is raised up against the knowledge of God, taking every thought captive to obey Christ. ⁶And we are ready to punish any disobedience, once your obedience has been confirmed.

⁷Look at what is obvious.ᴸ If anyone is confident that he belongs to Christ, he should remind himself of this: Just as he belongs to Christ, so do we. ⁸For if I boast some more about our authority, which the Lord gave for building you up and not for tearing you down, I am not ashamed. ⁹I don't want to seem as though I am trying to terrify you with my letters. ¹⁰For it is said, "His letters are weighty and powerful, but his physical presence is weak, and his public speaking is despicable." ¹¹Such a person should consider this: What we are in the words of our letters when absent, we will be in actions when present.

¹²For we don't dare classify or compare ourselves with some who commend themselves. But in measuring themselves by themselves and comparing themselves to themselves, they lack understanding. ¹³We, however, will not boast beyond measure but according to the measure of the area of ministry that God has assigned to us, which reaches even to you. ¹⁴For we are not overextending ourselves, as if we had not reached you, since we have come to you with the gospel of Christ. ¹⁵We are not bragging beyond measure about other people's labors. But we have the hope that as your faith increases, our area of ministry will be greatly enlarged, ¹⁶so that we may proclaim the good news to

ᴬ9:2 Macedonia was a Roman province in the northern area of modern Greece.   ᴮ9:2 Achaia was the Roman province, south of Macedonia, where Corinth was located.   ᶜ9:4 Or in this confidence   ᴰ9:6 Lit And this   ᴱ9:9 Ps 112:9   ᶠ9:13 Or your obedient confession to   ᴳ9:14 Or will long for   ᴴ10:2 Or are living as a non-Christian; lit are walking according to flesh   ᴵ10:3 Lit flesh   ᴶ10:3 Lit war according to flesh   ᴷ10:4 Lit fleshly   ᴸ10:7 Or You are looking at things outwardly the regions beyond you, not boasting about what has already been done in someone else's area of ministry. ¹⁷So **the one who boasts must boast in the Lord.**ᴬ ¹⁸For it is not the one commending himself who is approved, but the one the Lord commends.

11 I wish you would put up with a little foolishness from me. Yes, do put up with me.ᴮ ²For I am jealous over you with a godly jealousy, because I have promised you in marriage to one husband—to present a pure virgin to Christ. ³But I fear that, as the serpent deceived Eve by his cunning, your minds may be seduced from a complete and pureᶜ devotion to Christ. ⁴For if a person comes and preaches another Jesus, whom we did not preach, or you receive a different spirit, which you had not received, or a different gospel, which you had not accepted, you put up with it splendidly!

⁵Now I consider myself in no way inferior to the "super-apostles." ⁶Though untrained in public speaking, I am certainly not untrained in knowledge. Indeed, we have always made that clear to you in everything. ⁷Or did I commit a sin by humbling myself so that you might be exalted, because I preached the gospel of God to you free of charge? ⁸I robbed other churches by taking pay from them to minister to you. ⁹When I was present with you and in need, I did not burden anyone, for the brothers who came from Macedonia supplied my needs. I have kept myself, and will keep myself, from burdening you in any way. ¹⁰As the truth of Christ is in me, this boasting of mine will not be stoppedᴰ in the regions of Achaia. ¹¹Why? Because I don't love you? God knows I do!

¹²But I will continue to do what I am doing, in order to denyᴱ the opportunity of those who want an opportunity to be regarded just as our equals in what they boast about. ¹³For such people are false apostles, deceitful workers, disguising themselves as apostles of Christ. ¹⁴And no wonder! For Satan disguises himself as an angel of light. ¹⁵So it is no great thing if his servants also disguise themselves as servants of righteousness. Their destinyᶠ will be according to their works.

¹⁶I repeat: No one should consider me a fool. But if you do, at least accept me as a fool, so I too may boast a little. ¹⁷What I say in this matterᴳ of boasting, I don't speak as the Lord would, but foolishly. ¹⁸Since many boast in an unspiritual way,ᴴ I will also boast. ¹⁹For you, being so wise, gladly put up with fools! ²⁰In fact, you put up with it if someone enslaves you, if someone devours you, if someone captures you, if someone dominates you, or if someone hits you in the face. ²¹I say this to our shame: We have been weak.

But in whatever anyone dares to boast—I am talking foolishly—I also dare:

²² Are they Hebrews? So am I.
Are they Israelites? So am I.
Are they the seed of Abraham?
So am I.

²³ Are they servants of Christ?
I'm talking like a madman—
I'm a better one:
with far more labors,
many more imprisonments,
far worse beatings, near deathᴵ
many times.

²⁴ Five times I received 39 lashes
from Jews.

²⁵ Three times I was beaten with rods
by the Romans.
Once I was stoned by my enemies.ᴶ
Three times I was shipwrecked.
I have spent a night and a day
in the open sea.

²⁶ On frequent journeys, I faced
dangers from rivers,
dangers from robbers,
dangers from my own people,
dangers from the Gentiles,
dangers in the city,
dangers in the open country,
dangers on the sea,
and dangers among false brothers;

²⁷ labor and hardship,
many sleepless nights,
hunger and thirst,

ᴬ10:17 Jr 9:24   ᴮ11:1 Or Yes, you are putting up with me   ᶜ11:3 Other mss omit and pure   ᴰ11:10 Or silenced   ᴱ11:12 Lit cut off   ᶠ11:15 Lit end   ᴳ11:17 Or business, or confidence   ᴴ11:18 Lit boast according to the flesh   ᴵ11:23 Lit and in deaths   ᴶ11:25 A common Jewish method of capital punishment; Ac 14:5

often without food, cold,
and lacking clothing.

[28] Not to mention[A] other things, there is the daily pressure on me: my care for all the churches. [29] Who is weak, and I am not weak? Who is made to stumble, and I do not burn with indignation? [30] If boasting is necessary, I will boast about my weaknesses. [31] The God and Father of the Lord Jesus, who is praised forever, knows I am not lying. [32] In Damascus, the governor under King Aretas[B] guarded the city of the Damascenes in order to arrest me, [33] so I was let down in a basket through a window in the wall and escaped his hands.

12 Boasting is necessary. It is not profitable, but I will move on to visions and revelations of the Lord. [2] I know a man in Christ who was caught up into the third heaven 14 years ago. Whether he was in the body or out of the body, I don't know, God knows. [3] I know that this man—whether in the body or out of the body I don't know, God knows— [4] was caught up into paradise. He heard inexpressible words, which a man is not allowed to speak. [5] I will boast about this person, but not about myself, except of my weaknesses. [6] For if I want to boast, I will not be a fool, because I will be telling the truth. But I will spare you, so that no one can credit me with something beyond what he sees in me or hears from me, [7] especially because of the extraordinary revelations. Therefore, so that I would not exalt myself, a thorn in the flesh was given to me, a messenger[C] of Satan to torment me so I would not exalt myself. [8] Concerning this, I pleaded with the Lord three times to take it away from me. [9] But He said to me, "My grace is sufficient for you, for power[D] is perfected in weakness." Therefore, I will most gladly boast all the more about my weaknesses, so that Christ's power may reside in me. [10] So I take pleasure in weaknesses, insults, catastrophes, persecutions, and in pressures, because of Christ. For when I am weak, then I am strong.

[11] I have become a fool; you forced it on me. I should have been endorsed by you, since I am not in any way inferior to the "super-apostles," even though I am nothing. [12] The signs of an apostle were performed with great endurance among you—not only signs but also wonders and miracles. [13] So in what way were you treated worse than the other churches, except that I personally did not burden you? Forgive me this wrong!

[14] Now I am ready to come to you this third time. I will not burden you, for I am not seeking what is yours, but you. For children are not obligated to save up for their parents, but parents for their children. [15] I will most gladly spend and be spent for you.[E] If I love you more, am I to be loved less? [16] Now granted, I have not burdened you; yet sly as I am, I took you in by deceit! [17] Did I take advantage of you by anyone I sent you? [18] I urged Titus to come, and I sent the brother with him. Did Titus take advantage of you? Didn't we walk in the same spirit and in the same footsteps?

[19] You have thought all along that we were defending ourselves to you.[F] No, in the sight of God we are speaking in Christ, and everything, dear friends, is for building you up. [20] For I fear that perhaps when I come I will not find you to be what I want, and I may not be found by you to be what you want;[G] there may be quarreling, jealousy, outbursts of anger, selfish ambitions, slander, gossip, arrogance, and disorder. [21] I fear that when I come my God will again[H] humiliate me in your presence, and I will grieve for many who sinned before and have not repented of the moral impurity, sexual immorality, and promiscuity they practiced.

13 This is the third time I am coming to you. **Every fact must be established by the testimony[I] of two or three witnesses.**[J] [2] I gave a warning when I was present the second time, and now I give a warning while I am absent to those who sinned before and to all the rest: If I come again, I will not be lenient, [3] since you seek proof of Christ speaking in me. He is not weak toward you, but powerful among you. [4] In fact, He was crucified in weakness, but He lives by God's power. For we

A11:28 Lit *Apart from*   B11:32 Aretus IV (9 B.C.–A.D. 40), a Nabatean Arab king   C12:7 Or *me, an angel*   D12:9 Other mss read *My power*   E12:15 Lit *for your souls,* or *for your lives*   F12:19 Or *Have you thought . . . to you?*   G12:20 Lit *be as you want*   H12:21 Or *come again my God will*   I13:1 Lit *mouth*   J13:1 Dt 17:6; 19:15

also are weak in Him, yet toward you we will live with Him by God's power.

⁵ Test yourselves to see if you are in the faith. Examine yourselves. Or do you yourselves not recognize that Jesus Christ is in you?—unless you fail the test.ᴬ ⁶ And I hope you will recognize that we do not fail the test. ⁷ Now we pray to God that you do nothing wrong—not that we may appear to pass the test, but that you may do what is right, even though we may appear to fail. ⁸ For we are not able to do anything against the truth, but only for the truth. ⁹ In fact, we rejoice when we are weak and you are strong. We also pray

that you become fully mature.ᴮ ¹⁰ This is why I am writing these things while absent, that when I am there I will not use severity, in keeping with the authority the Lord gave me for building up and not for tearing down.

¹¹ Finally, brothers, rejoice. Become mature, be encouraged, be of the same mind, be at peace, and the God of love and peace will be with you. ¹² Greet one another with a holy kiss. All the saints greet you.

¹³ The grace of the Lord Jesus Christ, and the love of God, and the fellowship of the Holy Spirit be with all of you.ᶜ

GALATIANS

1 Paul, an apostle—not from men or by man, but by Jesus Christ and God the Father who raised Him from the dead— ² and all the brothers who are with me:

To the churches of Galatia.ᴰ

³ Grace to you and peace from God the Father and our Lordᴱ Jesus Christ, ⁴ who gave Himself for our sins to rescue us from this present evil age, according to the will of our God and Father. ⁵ To whom be the glory forever and ever. Amen.

⁶ I am amazed that you are so quickly turning away from Him who called you by the grace of Christ and are turning to a different gospel— ⁷ not that there is another gospel, but there are some who are troubling you and want to change the good newsᶠ about the Messiah. ⁸ But even if we or an angel from heaven should preach to you a gospel other than what we have preached to you, a curse be on him!ᴳ ⁹ As we have said before, I now say again: If anyone preaches to you a gospel contrary to what you received, a curse be on him!

¹⁰ For am I now trying to win the favor of people, or God? Or am I striving to please people? If I were still trying to please people, I would not be a slave of Christ.

¹¹ Now I want you to know, brothers, that the gospel preached by me is not based on human thought.ᴴ ¹² For I did not receive it from a human source and I was not taught it, but it came by a revelation from Jesus Christ.

¹³ For you have heard about my former way of life in Judaism: I persecuted God's church to an extreme degree and tried to destroy it. ¹⁴ I advanced in Judaism beyond many contemporaries among my people, because I was extremely zealous for the traditions of my ancestors. ¹⁵ But when God, who from my birth set me apart and called me by His grace, was pleased ¹⁶ to reveal His Son in me, so that I could preach Him among the Gentiles, I did not immediately consult with anyone.ᴵ ¹⁷ I did not go up to Jerusalem to those who had become apostles before me; instead I went to Arabia and came back to Damascus.

¹⁸ Then after three years I did go up to Jerusalem to get to know Cephas,ᴶ and I stayed with him 15 days. ¹⁹ But I didn't see any of the other apostles except James, the Lord's brother. ²⁰ Now I am not lying in what I write to you. God is my witness.ᴷ

²¹ Afterward, I went to the regions of Syria and Cilicia. ²² I remained personally unknown to the Judean churches in Christ; ²³ they simply kept hearing: "He who for-

ᴬ13:5 Or you are disqualified, or you are counterfeit   ᴮ13:9 Or become complete, or be restored   ᶜ13:12-13 Some translations divide these 2 vv. into 3 vv. so that v. 13 begins with All the saints . . . and v. 14 begins with The grace of . . .   ᴰ1:2 A Roman province in what is now Turkey   ᴱ1:3 Other mss read God our Father and the Lord   ᶠ1:7 Or gospel   ᴳ1:8 Or you, let him be condemned, or you, let him be condemned to hell; Gk anathema   ᴴ1:11 Lit not according to man   ᴵ1:16 Lit flesh and blood   ᴶ1:18 Other mss read Peter   ᴷ1:20 Lit Behold, before God merly persecuted us now preaches the faith he once tried to destroy." ²⁴And they glorified God because of me.

2 Then after 14 years I went up again to Jerusalem with Barnabas, taking Titus along also. ²I went up according to a revelation and presented to them the gospel I preach among the Gentiles—but privately to those recognized as leaders—so that I might not be running, or have run the race, in vain. ³But not even Titus who was with me, though he was a Greek, was compelled to be circumcised. ⁴This issue arose because of false brothers smuggled in, who came in secretly to spy on the freedom that we have in Christ Jesus, in order to enslave us. ⁵But we did not give up and submit to these people for even an hour, so that the truth of the gospel would be preserved for you.

⁶Now from those recognized as important (what they really were makes no difference to me; God does not show favoritism^A)—they added nothing to me. ⁷On the contrary, they saw that I had been entrusted with the gospel for the uncircumcised, just as Peter was for the circumcised, ⁸since the One at work in Peter for an apostleship to the circumcised was also at work in me for the Gentiles. ⁹When James, Cephas, and John, recognized as pillars, acknowledged the grace that had been given to me, they gave the right hand of fellowship to me and Barnabas, agreeing that we should go to the Gentiles and they to the circumcised. ¹⁰They asked only that we would remember the poor, which I made every effort to do.

¹¹But when Cephas^B came to Antioch, I opposed him to his face because he stood condemned.^C ¹²For he regularly ate with the Gentiles before certain men came from James. However, when they came, he withdrew and separated himself, because he feared those from the circumcision party. ¹³Then the rest of the Jews joined his hypocrisy, so that even Barnabas was carried away

by their hypocrisy. ¹⁴But when I saw that they were deviating from the truth of the gospel, I told Cephas^B in front of everyone, "If you, who are a Jew, live like a Gentile and not like a Jew, how can you compel Gentiles to live like Jews?"^D

¹⁵We who are Jews by birth and not "Gentile sinners" ¹⁶know that no one is justified by the works of the law but by faith in Jesus Christ.^E And we have believed in Christ Jesus so that we might be justified by faith in Christ^F and not by the works of the law, because by the works of the law no human being will^G be justified. ¹⁷But if we ourselves are also found to be "sinners" while seeking to be justified by Christ, is Christ then a promoter^H of sin? Absolutely not! ¹⁸If I rebuild the system^I I tore down, I show myself to be a lawbreaker. ¹⁹For through the law I have died to the law, so that I might live for God. I have been crucified with Christ^J ²⁰and I no longer live, but Christ lives in me. The life I now live in the body,^K I live by faith in the Son of God, who loved me and gave Himself for me. ²¹I do not set aside the grace of God, for if righteousness comes through the law, then Christ died for nothing.

3 You foolish Galatians! Who has hypnotized you,^L before whose eyes Jesus Christ was vividly portrayed^M as crucified? ²I only want to learn this from you: Did you receive the Spirit by the works of the law or by hearing with faith?^N ³Are you so foolish? After beginning with the Spirit, are you now going to be made complete by the flesh?^O ⁴Did you suffer so much for nothing—if in fact it was for nothing? ⁵So then, does God supply you with the Spirit and work miracles among you by the works of the law or by hearing with faith?^N

⁶Just as Abraham **believed God, and it was credited to him for righteousness,**^P ⁷then understand that those who have faith are Abraham's sons. ⁸Now the Scripture saw in

---

^A**2:6** Or *God is not a respecter of persons;* lit *God does not receive the face of man*   ^B**2:11,14** Other mss read *Peter*   ^C**2:11** Or *he was in the wrong*   ^D**2:14** Some translations continue the quotation through v. 16 or v. 21.   ^E**2:16** Or *by the faithfulness of Jesus Christ*   ^F**2:16** Or *by the faithfulness of Christ*   ^G**2:16** Lit *law all flesh will not*   ^H**2:17** Or *servant*   ^I**2:18** Lit *rebuild those things that*   ^J**2:19** Other textual traditions place *I have been crucified with Christ* in v. 20.   ^K**2:20** Or *flesh*   ^L**3:1** Other mss add *not to obey the truth*   ^M**3:1** Other mss add *among you*   ^N**3:2,5** Lit *by law works or faith hearing or hearing the message*   ^O**3:3** By human effort   ^P**3:6** Gn 15:6

advance that God would justify the Gentiles by faith and told the good news ahead of time to Abraham, saying, **All the nations will be blessed through you.**[A] [9] So those who have faith are blessed with Abraham, who had faith.[B]

[10] For all who rely on the works of the law are under a curse, because it is written: **Everyone who does not continue doing everything written in the book of the law is cursed.**[C] [11] Now it is clear that no one is justified before God by the law, because **the righteous will live by faith.**[D] [12] But the law is not based on faith; instead, **the one who does these things will live by them.**[E] [13] Christ has redeemed us from the curse of the law by becoming a curse for us, because it is written: **Everyone who is hung on a tree is cursed.**[F] [14] The purpose was that the blessing of Abraham would come to the Gentiles by Christ Jesus, so that we could receive the promised Spirit through faith.

[15] Brothers, I'm using a human illustration.[G] No one sets aside or makes additions to even a human covenant[H] that has been ratified. [16] Now the promises were spoken to Abraham and to his seed. He does not say "and to seeds," as though referring to many, but referring to one, **and to your seed,**[I] who is Christ. [17] And I say this: The law, which came 430 years later, does not revoke a covenant that was previously ratified by God[J] and cancel the promise. [18] For if the inheritance is from the law, it is no longer from the promise; but God granted it to Abraham through the promise.

[19] Why then was the law given? It was added because of transgressions until the Seed to whom the promise was made would come. The law was put into effect through angels by means of a mediator. [20] Now a mediator is not for just one person, but God is one. [21] Is the law therefore contrary to God's promises? Absolutely not! For if a law had been given that was able to give life, then righteousness would certainly be by the law.

[22] But the Scripture has imprisoned everything under sin's power,[K] so that the promise by faith in Jesus Christ might be given to those who believe. [23] Before this faith came, we were confined under the law, imprisoned until the coming faith was revealed. [24] The law, then, was our guardian[L] until Christ, so that we could be justified by faith. [25] But since that faith has come, we are no longer under a guardian, [26] for you are all sons of God through faith in Christ Jesus.

[27] For as many of you as have been baptized into Christ have put on Christ like a garment. [28] There is no Jew or Greek, slave or free, male or female; for you are all one in Christ Jesus. [29] And if you belong to Christ, then you are Abraham's seed, heirs according

4 to the promise. [1] Now I say that as long as the heir is a child, he differs in no way from a slave, though he is the owner of everything. [2] Instead, he is under guardians and stewards until the time set by his father. [3] In the same way we also, when we were children, were in slavery under the elemental forces[M] of the world. [4] When the time came to completion, God sent His Son, born of a woman, born under the law, [5] to redeem those under the law, so that we might receive adoption as sons. [6] And because you are sons, God has sent the Spirit of His Son into our[N] hearts, crying, "*Abba*, Father!" [7] So you are no longer a slave but a son, and if a son, then an heir through God.

[8] But in the past, when you didn't know God, you were enslaved to things[O] that by nature are not gods. [9] But now, since you know God, or rather have become known by God, how can you turn back again to the weak and bankrupt elemental forces? Do you want to be enslaved to them all over again? [10] You observe special days, months, seasons, and years. [11] I am fearful for you, that perhaps my labor for you has been wasted.

[12] I beg you, brothers: Become like me, for I also became like you. You have not wronged

A**3:8** Gn 12:3; 18:18   B**3:9** Or *with believing Abraham*   C**3:10** Dt 27:26   D**3:11** Hab 2:4   E**3:12** Lv 18:5   F**3:13** Dt 21:23   G**3:15** Lit *I speak according to man*   H**3:15** Or *will*, or *testament*   I**3:16** Gn 12:7; 13:15; 17:8; 24:7   J**3:17** Other mss add *in Christ*   K**3:22** Lit *under sin*   L**3:24** The word translated *guardian* in vv. 24–25 is different from the word in Gl 4:2. In our culture, we do not have a slave who takes a child to and from school, protecting the child from harm or corruption. In Gk the word *paidogogos* described such a slave. This slave was not a teacher.   M**4:3** Or *spirits*, or *principles*   N**4:6** Other mss read *your*   O**4:8** Or *beings* me; [13] you know that previously I preached the gospel to you because of a physical illness. [14] You did not despise or reject me though my physical condition was a trial for you.[A] On the contrary, you received me as an angel of God, as Christ Jesus Himself.

[15] What happened to this sense of being blessed you had? For I testify to you that, if possible, you would have torn out your eyes and given them to me. [16] Have I now become your enemy by telling you the truth? [17] They[B] are enthusiastic about you, but not for any good. Instead, they want to isolate you so you will be enthusiastic about them. [18] Now it is always good to be enthusiastic about good—and not just when I am with you. [19] My children, I am again suffering labor pains for you until Christ is formed in you. [20] I would like to be with you right now and change my tone of voice, because I don't know what to do about you.

[21] Tell me, those of you who want to be under the law, don't you hear the law? [22] For it is written that Abraham had two sons, one by a slave and the other by a free woman. [23] But the one by the slave was born according to the impulse of the flesh, while the one by the free woman was born as the result of a promise. [24] These things are illustrations,[C] for the women represent the two covenants. One is from Mount Sinai and bears children into slavery—this is Hagar. [25] Now Hagar is Mount Sinai in Arabia and corresponds to the present Jerusalem, for she is in slavery with her children. [26] But the Jerusalem above is free, and she is our mother. [27] For it is written:

> Rejoice, childless woman,
> who does not give birth.
> Burst into song and shout,
> you who are not in labor,
> for the children of the desolate
>   are many,
> more numerous than those
> of the woman who has
>   a husband.[D]

[28] Now you, brothers, like Isaac, are children of promise. [29] But just as then the child born according to the flesh persecuted the one born according to the Spirit, so also now. [30] But what does the Scripture say?

> Drive out the slave and her son, for the son of the slave will never be a coheir with the son of the free woman.[E]

[31] Therefore, brothers, we are not children of the slave but of the free woman.

5 Christ has liberated us to be free. Stand firm then and don't submit again to a yoke of slavery. [2] Take note! I, Paul, tell you that if you get yourselves circumcised, Christ will not benefit you at all. [3] Again I testify to every man who gets himself circumcised that he is obligated to keep the entire law. [4] You who are trying to be justified by the law are alienated from Christ; you have fallen from grace. [5] For through the Spirit, by faith, we eagerly wait for the hope of righteousness. [6] For in Christ Jesus neither circumcision nor uncircumcision accomplishes anything; what matters is faith working through love.

[7] You were running well. Who prevented you from obeying the truth? [8] This persuasion did not come from the One who called you. [9] A little yeast leavens the whole lump of dough. [10] I have confidence in the Lord you will not accept any other view. But whoever it is that is confusing you will pay the penalty. [11] Now brothers, if I still preach circumcision, why am I still persecuted? In that case the offense of the cross has been abolished. [12] I wish those who are disturbing you might also get themselves castrated!

[13] For you were called to be free, brothers; only don't use this freedom as an opportunity for the flesh, but serve one another through love. [14] For the entire law is fulfilled in one statement: **Love your neighbor as yourself.**[F] [15] But if you bite and devour one another, watch out, or you will be consumed by one another.

[16] I say then, walk by the Spirit and you will not carry out the desire of the flesh. [17] For the flesh desires what is against the Spirit, and

A 4:14 Other mss read *me* B 4:17 The false teachers C 4:24 Typology or allegory D 4:27 Is 54:1 E 4:30 Gn 21:10 F 5:14 Lv 19:18

the Spirit desires what is against the flesh; these are opposed to each other, so that you don't do what you want. [18] But if you are led by the Spirit, you are not under the law.

[19] Now the works of the flesh are obvious:[A,B] sexual immorality, moral impurity, promiscuity, [20] idolatry, sorcery, hatreds, strife, jealousy, outbursts of anger, selfish ambitions, dissensions, factions, [21] envy,[C] drunkenness, carousing, and anything similar. I tell you about these things in advance—as I told you before—that those who practice such things will not inherit the kingdom of God.

[22] But the fruit of the Spirit is love, joy, peace, patience, kindness, goodness, faith,[D] [23] gentleness, self-control. Against such things there is no law. [24] Now those who belong to Christ Jesus have crucified the flesh with its passions and desires. [25] Since we live by the Spirit, we must also follow the Spirit. [26] We must not become conceited, provoking one another, envying one another.

6 Brothers, if someone is caught in any wrongdoing, you who are spiritual should restore such a person with a gentle spirit, watching out for yourselves so you also won't be tempted. [2] Carry one another's burdens; in this way you will fulfill the law of Christ. [3] For if anyone considers himself to be something when he is nothing, he deceives himself. [4] But each person should examine his own work, and then he will have a reason for boasting in himself alone, and not in respect to someone else. [5] For each person will have to carry his own load.

[6] The one who is taught the message must share all his good things with the teacher. [7] Don't be deceived: God is not mocked. For whatever a man sows he will also reap, [8] because the one who sows to his flesh will reap corruption from the flesh, but the one who sows to the Spirit will reap eternal life from the Spirit. [9] So we must not get tired of doing good, for we will reap at the proper time if we don't give up. [10] Therefore, as we have opportunity, we must work for the good of all, especially for those who belong to the household of faith.

[11] Look at what large letters I use as I write to you in my own handwriting. [12] Those who want to make a good impression in the flesh are the ones who would compel you to be circumcised—but only to avoid being persecuted for the cross of Christ. [13] For even the circumcised don't keep the law themselves; however, they want you to be circumcised in order to boast about your flesh. [14] But as for me, I will never boast about anything except the cross of our Lord Jesus Christ. The world has been crucified to me through the cross, and I to the world. [15] For[E] both circumcision and uncircumcision mean nothing; what matters instead is a new creation. [16] May peace come to all those who follow this standard, and mercy to the Israel of God!

[17] From now on, let no one cause me trouble, because I bear on my body scars for the cause of Jesus. [18] Brothers, the grace of our Lord Jesus Christ be with your spirit. Amen.

EPHESIANS

1 Paul, an apostle of Christ Jesus by God's will:

To the faithful saints in Christ Jesus at Ephesus.[F]

[2] Grace to you and peace from God our Father and the Lord Jesus Christ.

[3] Praise the God and Father of our Lord Jesus Christ, who has blessed us in Christ with every spiritual blessing in the heavens. [4] For He chose us in Him, before the foundation of the world, to be holy and blameless in His sight.[G] In love[H] [5] He predestined us to be adopted through Jesus Christ for Himself, according to His favor and will, [6] to the praise of His glorious grace that He favored us with in the Beloved.

A5:19 Other mss add *adultery*   B5:19 Lit *obvious, which are:*   C5:21 Other mss add *murders*   D5:22 Or *faithfulness*   E6:15 Other mss add *in Christ Jesus*   F1:1 Other mss omit *at Ephesus*   G1:4 Vv. 3-14 are 1 sentence in Gk.   H1:4 Or *In His sight in love*

[7]We have redemption in Him through His blood, the forgiveness of our trespasses, according to the riches of His grace [8]that He lavished on us with all wisdom and understanding. [9]He made known to us the mystery of His will, according to His good pleasure that He planned in Him [10]for the administration[A] of the days of fulfillment[B]—to bring everything together in the Messiah, both things in heaven and things on earth in Him.

[11]We have also received an inheritance[C] in Him, predestined according to the purpose of the One who works out everything in agreement with the decision of His will, [12]so that we who had already put our hope in the Messiah might bring praise to His glory.

[13]When you heard the message of truth, the gospel of your salvation, and when you believed in Him, you were also sealed with the promised Holy Spirit. [14]He is the down payment of our inheritance, for the redemption of the possession,[D] to the praise of His glory.

[15]This is why, since I heard about your faith in the Lord Jesus and your love for all the saints, [16]I never stop giving thanks for you as I remember you in my prayers. [17]I pray that the God of our Lord Jesus Christ, the glorious Father,[E] would give you a spirit[F] of wisdom and revelation in the knowledge of Him. [18]I pray that the perception of your mind[G] may be enlightened so you may know what is the hope of His calling, what are the glorious riches of His inheritance among the saints, [19]and what is the immeasurable greatness of His power to us who believe, according to the working of His vast strength.

[20]He demonstrated this power in the Messiah by raising Him from the dead and seating Him at His right hand in the heavens— [21]far above every ruler and authority, power and dominion, and every title given,[H] not only in this age but also in the one to come. [22]And **He put everything under His feet**[I] and appointed Him as head over everything for the church, [23]which is His body, the fullness of the One who fills all things in every way.

2 And you were dead in your trespasses and sins [2]in which you previously walked according to the ways of this world, according to the ruler who exercises authority over the lower heavens,[J] the spirit now working in the disobedient.[K] [3]We too all previously lived among them in our fleshly desires, carrying out the inclinations of our flesh and thoughts, and we were by nature children under wrath as the others were also. [4]But God, who is rich in mercy, because of His great love that He had for us,[L] [5]made us alive with the Messiah even though we were dead in trespasses. You are saved by grace! [6]Together with Christ Jesus He also raised us up and seated us in the heavens, [7]so that in the coming ages He might display the immeasurable riches of His grace through His kindness to us in Christ Jesus. [8]For you are saved by grace through faith, and this is not from yourselves; it is God's gift— [9]not from works, so that no one can boast. [10]For we are His creation, created in Christ Jesus for good works, which God prepared ahead of time so that we should walk in them.

[11]So then, remember that at one time you were Gentiles in the flesh—called "the uncircumcised" by those called "the circumcised," which is done in the flesh by human hands. [12]At that time you were without the Messiah, excluded from the citizenship of Israel, and foreigners to the covenants of the promise, without hope and without God in the world. [13]But now in Christ Jesus, you who were far away have been brought near by the blood of the Messiah. [14]For He is our peace, who made both groups one and tore down the dividing wall of hostility. In His flesh, [15]He made of no effect the law consisting of commands and expressed in regulations, so that He might create in Himself one new man from the two, resulting in peace. [16]He did this so that He might reconcile both to God in one body through the cross and put the hostility to death by it.[M] [17]When the Messiah came, He proclaimed the good news of peace to you who were far away and peace to those who were near. [18]For through Him we

---

[A]1:10 Or dispensation; lit house law (Gk oikonomia)   [B]1:10 Lit the fulfillment of times   [C]1:11 Or we also were chosen as an inheritance, or we were also made an inheritance   [D]1:14 The possession could be either man's or God's   [E]1:17 Or the Father of glory   [F]1:17 Or you the Spirit   [G]1:18 Lit the eyes of your heart   [H]1:21 Lit every name named   [I]1:22 Ps 8:6   [J]2:2 Lit ruler of the domain of the air   [K]2:2 Lit sons of disobedience   [L]2:4 Lit love with which He loved us   [M]2:16 Or death in Himself

Turn to page 82 and find John 1:11-13.

both have access by one Spirit to the Father. [19] So then you are no longer foreigners and strangers, but fellow citizens with the saints, and members of God's household, [20] built on the foundation of the apostles and prophets, with Christ Jesus Himself as the cornerstone. [21] The whole building, being put together by Him, grows into a holy sanctuary in the Lord. [22] You also are being built together for God's dwelling in the Spirit.

3 For this reason, I, Paul, the prisoner of Christ Jesus on behalf of you Gentiles— [2] you have heard, haven't you, about the administration of God's grace that He gave to me for you? [3] The mystery was made known to me by revelation, as I have briefly written above. [4] By reading this you are able to understand my insight about the mystery of the Messiah. [5] This was not made known to people[A] in other generations as it is now revealed to His holy apostles and prophets by the Spirit: [6] The Gentiles are coheirs, members of the same body, and partners of the promise in Christ Jesus through the gospel. [7] I was made a servant of this gospel by the gift of God's grace that was given to me by the working of His power.

[8] This grace was given to me—the least of all the saints—to proclaim to the Gentiles the incalculable riches of the Messiah, [9] and to shed light for all about the administration of the mystery hidden for ages in God who created all things. [10] This is so God's multi-faceted wisdom may now be made known through the church to the rulers and authorities in the heavens. [11] This is according to His eternal purpose accomplished in the Messiah, Jesus our Lord. [12] In Him we have boldness and confident access through faith in Him. [B] [13] So then I ask you not to be discouraged over my afflictions on your behalf, for they are your glory.

[14] For this reason I kneel before the Father[C] [15] from whom every family in heaven and on earth is named. [16] I pray that He may grant you, according to the riches of His glory, to be strengthened with power in the inner man through His Spirit, [17] and that the Messiah may dwell in your hearts through faith. I pray

that you, being rooted and firmly established in love, [18] may be able to comprehend with all the saints what is the length and width, height and depth of God's love, [19] and to know the Messiah's love that surpasses knowledge, so you may be filled with all the fullness of God.

[20] Now to Him who is able to do above and beyond all that we ask or think according to the power that works in us— [21] to Him be glory in the church and in Christ Jesus to all generations, forever and ever. Amen.

4 Therefore I, the prisoner for the Lord, urge you to walk worthy of the calling you have received, [2] with all humility and gentleness, with patience, accepting[D] one another in love, [3] diligently keeping the unity of the Spirit with the peace that binds us. [4] There is one body and one Spirit—just as you were called to one hope[E] at your calling— [5] one Lord, one faith, one baptism, [6] one God and Father of all, who is above all and through all and in all.

[7] Now grace was given to each one of us according to the measure of the Messiah's gift. [8] For it says:

> When He ascended on high,
> He took prisoners into captivity;[F]
> He gave gifts to people.[G]

[9] But what does "He ascended" mean except that He[H] descended to the lower parts of the earth?[I] [10] The One who descended is also the One who ascended far above all the heavens, that He might fill[J] all things. [11] And He personally gave some to be apostles, some prophets, some evangelists, some pastors and teachers, [12] for the training of the saints in the work of ministry, to build up the body of Christ, [13] until we all reach unity in the faith and in the knowledge of God's Son, growing into a mature man with a stature measured by Christ's fullness. [14] Then we will no longer be little children, tossed by the waves and blown around by every wind of teaching, by human cunning with cleverness in the techniques of deceit. [15] But speaking the truth in love, let us grow in every way into Him who is the head—Christ. [16] From Him the whole

A3:5 Lit to the sons of men B3:12 Or through His faithfulness C3:14 Other mss add of our Lord Jesus Christ D4:2 Or tolerating E4:4 Lit called in one hope F4:8 Or He led the captives G4:8 Ps 68:18 H4:9 Other mss add first I4:9 Or the lower parts, namely, the earth J4:10 Or fulfill; Eph 1:23

body, fitted and knit together by every supporting ligament, promotes the growth of the body for building up itself in love by the proper working of each individual part.

¹⁷Therefore, I say this and testify in the Lord: You should no longer walk as the Gentiles walk, in the futility of their thoughts. ¹⁸They are darkened in their understanding, excluded from the life of God, because of the ignorance that is in them and because of the hardness of their hearts. ¹⁹They became callous and gave themselves over to promiscuity for the practice of every kind of impurity with a desire for more and more.ᴬ

²⁰But that is not how you learned about the Messiah, ²¹assuming you heard about Him and were taught by Him, because the truth is in Jesus. ²²You took offᴮ your former way of life, the old selfᶜ that is corrupted by deceitful desires; ²³you are being renewedᴰ in the spirit of your minds; ²⁴you put onᴱ the new self, the one created according to God's likeness in righteousness and purity of the truth.

²⁵Since you put away lying, **Speak the truth, each one to his neighbor,**ᶠ because we are members of one another. ²⁶**Be angry and do not sin.**ᴳ Don't let the sun go down on your anger, ²⁷and don't give the Devil an opportunity. ²⁸The thief must no longer steal. Instead, he must do honest work with his own hands, so that he has something to share with anyone in need. ²⁹No foul language is to come from your mouth, but only what is good for building up someone in need,ᴴ so that it gives grace to those who hear. ³⁰And don't grieve God's Holy Spirit. You were sealed by Himᴵ for the day of redemption. ³¹All bitterness, anger and wrath, shouting and slander must be removed from you, along with all malice. ³²And be kind and compassionate to one another, forgiving one another, just as God also forgave youᴶ in Christ.

5 Therefore, be imitators of God, as dearly loved children. ²And walk in love, as the Messiah also loved us and gave Himself for us, a sacrificial and fragrant offering to God. ³But sexual immorality and any impurity or greed

should not even be heard ofᴷ among you, as is proper for saints. ⁴Coarse and foolish talking or crude joking are not suitable, but rather giving thanks. ⁵For know and recognize this: Every sexually immoral or impure or greedy person, who is an idolater, does not have an inheritance in the kingdom of the Messiah and of God.

⁶Let no one deceive you with empty arguments, for God's wrath is coming on the disobedientᴸ because of these things. ⁷Therefore, do not become their partners. ⁸For you were once darkness, but now you are light in the Lord. Walk as children of light— ⁹for the fruit of the lightᴹ results in all goodness, righteousness, and truth— ¹⁰discerning what is pleasing to the Lord. ¹¹Don't participate in the fruitless works of darkness, but instead expose them. ¹²For it is shameful even to mention what is done by them in secret. ¹³Everything exposed by the light is made clear, ¹⁴for what makes everything clear is light. Therefore it is said:

> Get up, sleeper, and rise up
>   from the dead,
>   and the Messiah will shine on you.ᴺ

¹⁵Pay careful attention, then, to how you walk—not as unwise people but as wise— ¹⁶making the most of the time,ᴼ because the days are evil. ¹⁷So don't be foolish, but understand what the Lord's will is. ¹⁸And don't get drunk with wine, which leads to reckless actions, but be filled by the Spirit:

19   speaking to one another
      in psalms, hymns, and spiritual songs,
      singing and making music
      from your heart to the Lord,
20   giving thanks always for everything
      to God the Father
      in the name of our Lord Jesus Christ,
21   submitting to one another
      in the fear of Christ.

²²Wives, submitᴾ to your own husbands as to the Lord, ²³for the husband is the head of

---

ᴬ**4:19** Lit with greediness   ᴮ**4:21-22** Or Jesus. This means: take off (as a command)   ᶜ**4:22** Lit man; = a person before conversion   ᴰ**4:22-23** Or desires; renew (as a command)   ᴱ**4:23-24** Or minds; and put on (as a command)   ᶠ**4:25** Zch 8:16   ᴳ**4:26** Ps 4:4   ᴴ**4:29** Lit for the building up of the need   ᴵ**4:30** Or Spirit, by whom you were sealed   ᴶ**4:32** Other mss read us   ᴷ**5:3** Or be named   ᴸ**5:6** Lit sons of disobedience   ᴹ**5:9** Other mss read fruit of the Spirit   ᴺ**5:14** This poem may have been an early Christian hymn based on several passages in Isaiah; Is 9:2; 26:19; 40:1; 51:17; 52:1; 60:1.   ᴼ**5:16** Lit buying back the time   ᴾ**5:22** Other mss omit submit the wife as Christ is the head of the church. He is the Savior of the body. ²⁴Now as the church submits to Christ, so wives are to submit to their husbands in everything. ²⁵Husbands, love your wives, just as Christ loved the church and gave Himself for her ²⁶to make her holy, cleansingᴬ her with the washing of water by the word. ²⁷He did this to present the church to Himself in splendor, without spot or wrinkle or anything like that, but holy and blameless. ²⁸In the same way, husbands are to love their wives as their own bodies. He who loves his wife loves himself. ²⁹For no one ever hates his own flesh but provides and cares for it, just as Christ does for the church, ³⁰since we are members of His body.ᴮ

³¹ **For this reason a man will leave
his father and mother
and be joined to his wife,
and the two will become one flesh.**ᶜ

³²This mystery is profound, but I am talking about Christ and the church. ³³To sum up, each one of you is to love his wife as himself, and the wife is to respect her husband.

6 Children, obey your parents as you would the Lord,ᴰ because this is right. ²**Honor your father and mother**, which is the first commandmentᴱ with a promise, ³**so that it may go well with you and that you may have a long life in the land.**ᶠ,ᴳ ⁴Fathers, don't stir up anger in your children, but bring them up in the training and instruction of the Lord.

⁵Slaves, obey your humanᴴ masters with fear and trembling, in the sincerity of your heart, as to Christ. ⁶Don't work only while being watched, in order to please men, but as slaves of Christ, do God's will from your heart.ᴵ ⁷Serve with a good attitude, as to the Lord and not to men, ⁸knowing that whatever good each one does, slave or free, he will receive this back from the Lord. ⁹And masters, treat your slaves the same way, without threatening them, because you know that both their Master and yours is in heaven, and there is no favoritism with Him.

¹⁰Finally, be strengthened by the Lord and by His vast strength. ¹¹Put on the full armor of God so that you can stand against the tacticsᴶ of the Devil. ¹²For our battle is not against flesh and blood, but against the rulers, against the authorities, against the world powers of this darkness, against the spiritual forces of evil in the heavens. ¹³This is why you must take up the full armor of God, so that you may be able to resist in the evil day, and having prepared everything, to take your stand. ¹⁴Stand, therefore,

with truth like a belt
    around your waist,
righteousness like armor
    on your chest,
¹⁵ and your feet sandaled with readiness
    for the gospel of peace.ᴷ
¹⁶ In every situation take the shield
    of faith,
and with it you will be able
    to extinguish
all the flaming arrows of the evil one.
¹⁷ Take the helmet of salvation,
    and the sword of the Spirit,
    which is God's word.

¹⁸Pray at all times in the Spirit with every prayer and request, and stay alert in this with all perseverance and intercession for all the saints. ¹⁹Pray also for me, that the message may be given to me when I open my mouth to make known with boldness the mystery of the gospel. ²⁰For this I am an ambassador in chains. Pray that I might be bold enough in Him to speak as I should.

²¹Tychicus, our dearly loved brother and faithful servantᴸ in the Lord, will tell you all the news about me so that you may be informed. ²²I am sending him to you for this very reason, to let you know how we are and to encourage your hearts.

²³Peace to the brothers, and love with faith, from God the Father and the Lord Jesus Christ. ²⁴Grace be with all who have undying love for our Lord Jesus Christ.ᴹ,ᴺ

ᴬ**5:26** Or *having cleansed*   ᴮ**5:30** Other mss add *and of His flesh and of His bones*   ᶜ**5:31** Gn 2:24   ᴰ**6:1** Lit *parents in the Lord*   ᴱ**6:2** Or *is a preeminent commandment*   ᶠ**6:3** Or *life on the earth*   ᴳ**6:2-3** Ex 20:12   ᴴ**6:5** Lit *according to the flesh*   ᴵ**6:6** Lit *from soul*   ᴶ**6:11** Or *schemes, or tricks*   ᴷ**6:15** *Ready to go tell others about the gospel*   ᴸ**6:21** Or *deacon*   ᴹ**6:24** Other mss add *Amen.*   ᴺ**6:24** Lit *all who love our Lord Jesus Christ in incorruption*

PHILIPPIANS

1 Paul and Timothy, slaves of Christ Jesus:
To all the saints in Christ Jesus who are in Philippi, including the overseers and deacons.

² Grace to you and peace from God our Father and the Lord Jesus Christ.

³ I give thanks to my God for every remembrance of you,ᴬ ⁴ always praying with joy for all of you in my every prayer, ⁵ because of your partnership in the gospel from the first day until now. ⁶ I am sure of this, that He who started a good work in youᴮ will carry it on to completion until the day of Christ Jesus. ⁷ It is right for me to think this way about all of you, because I have you in my heart,ᶜ and you are all partners with me in grace, both in my imprisonment and in the defense and establishment of the gospel. ⁸ For God is my witness, how deeply I miss all of you with the affection of Christ Jesus. ⁹ And I pray this: that your love will keep on growing in knowledge and every kind of discernment, ¹⁰ so that you can approve the things that are superior and can be pure and blameless inᴰ the day of Christ, ¹¹ filled with the fruit of righteousness that comes through Jesus Christ to the glory and praise of God.

¹² Now I want you to know, brothers, that what has happened to me has actually resulted in the advance of the gospel, ¹³ so that it has become known throughout the whole imperial guard,ᴱ and to everyone else, that my imprisonment is in the cause of Christ. ¹⁴ Most of the brothers in the Lord have gained confidence from my imprisonment and dare even more to speak the messageᶠ fearlessly. ¹⁵ To be sure, some preach Christ out of envy and strife, but others out of good will.ᴳ ¹⁶ These do so out of love, knowing that I am appointed for the defense of the gospel; ¹⁷ the others proclaim Christ out of rivalry, not sincerely, seeking to cause me anxiety in my imprisonment.ᴴ ¹⁸ What does it matter? Just that in every way, whether out of false motives or true, Christ is proclaimed.

And in this I rejoice. Yes, and I will rejoice ¹⁹ because I know this will lead to my deliveranceᴵ through your prayers and help from the Spirit of Jesus Christ. ²⁰ My eager expectation and hope is that I will not be ashamed about anything, but that now as always, with all boldness, Christ will be highly honored in my body, whether by life or by death.

²¹ For me, living is Christ and dying is gain. ²² Now if I live on in the flesh, this means fruitful work for me; and I don't know which one I should choose. ²³ I am pressured by both. I have the desire to depart and be with Christ—which is far better— ²⁴ but to remain in the flesh is more necessary for you. ²⁵ Since I am persuaded of this, I know that I will remain and continue with all of you for your progress and joy in the faith, ²⁶ so that, because of me, your confidence may grow in Christ Jesus when I come to you again.

²⁷ Just one thing: Live your life in a manner worthy of the gospel of Christ. Then, whether I come and see you or am absent, I will hear about you that you are standing firm in one spirit, with one mind,ᴶ working side by side for the faith that comes from the gospel, ²⁸ not being frightened in any way by your opponents. This is a sign of destruction for them, but of your deliverance—and this is from God. ²⁹ For it has been given to you on Christ's behalf not only to believe in Him, but also to suffer for Him, ³⁰ having the same struggle that you saw I had and now hear that I have.

2 If then there is any encouragement in Christ, if any consolation of love, if any fellowship with the Spirit, if any affection and mercy, ² fulfill my joy by thinking the same way, having the same love, sharing the same feelings, focusing on one goal. ³ Do nothing out of rivalry or conceit, but in humility consider others as more important than yourselves. ⁴ Everyone should look out not only for his own interests, but also for the interests of others.

⁵Make your own attitude that of Christ Jesus,

⁶ who, existing in the form of God,
did not consider
    equality with God
as something to be used
    for His own advantage.ᴬ
⁷ Instead He emptied Himself
by assuming the form of a slave,
taking on the likeness of men.
And when He had come
    as a man
in His external form,
⁸ He humbled Himself
by becoming obedient
to the point of death—
even to death on a cross.
⁹ For this reason God
    highly exalted Him
and gave Him the name
that is above every name,
¹⁰ so that at the name of Jesus
every knee will bow—
of those who are in heaven
    and on earth
and under the earth—
¹¹ and every tongue should confess
that Jesus Christ is Lord,ᴮ
to the glory of God the Father.

¹²So then, my dear friends, just as you have always obeyed, not only in my presence, but now even more in my absence, work out your own salvation with fear and trembling. ¹³For it is God who is working in you, enabling you both to desire and to work out His good purpose. ¹⁴Do everything without grumbling and arguing, ¹⁵so that you may be blameless and pure, children of God who are faultless in a crooked and perverted generation, among whom you shine like stars in the world. ¹⁶Hold firmly toᶜ the message of life. Then I can boast in the day of Christ that I didn't run or labor for nothing. ¹⁷But even if I am poured out as a drink offering on the sacrifice and service of your faith, I am glad and rejoice with all of you. ¹⁸In the same way you should also be glad and rejoice with me.

¹⁹Now I hope in the Lord Jesus to send Timothy to you soon so that I also may be encouraged when I hear news about you. ²⁰For I have no one else like-minded who will genuinely care about your interests; ²¹all seek their own interests, not those of Jesus Christ. ²²But you know his proven character, because he has served with me in the gospel ministry like a son with a father. ²³Therefore, I hope to send him as soon as I see how things go with me. ²⁴I am convinced in the Lord that I myself will also come quickly.

²⁵But I considered it necessary to send you Epaphroditus—my brother, coworker, and fellow soldier, as well as your messenger and minister to my need— ²⁶since he has been longing for all of you and was distressed because you heard that he was sick. ²⁷Indeed, he was so sick that he nearly died. However, God had mercy on him, and not only on him but also on me, so that I would not have one grief on top of another. ²⁸For this reason, I am very eager to send him so that you may rejoice when you see him again and I may be less anxious. ²⁹Therefore, welcome him in the Lord with all joy and hold men like him in honor, ³⁰because he came close to death for the work of Christ, risking his life to make up what was lacking in your ministry to me.

3 Finally, my brothers, rejoice in the Lord. To write to you again about this is no trouble for me and is a protection for you.

²Watch out for "dogs,"ᴰ watch out for evil workers, watch out for those who mutilate the flesh. ³For we are the circumcision, the ones who serve by the Spirit of God, boast in Christ Jesus, and do not put confidence in the flesh— ⁴although I once also had confidence in the flesh. If anyone else thinks he has grounds for confidence in the flesh, I have more: ⁵circumcised the eighth day; of the nation of Israel, of the tribe of Benjamin, a Hebrew born of Hebrews; regarding the law, a Pharisee; ⁶regarding zeal, persecuting the church; regarding the righteousness that is in the law, blameless.

⁷But everything that was a gain to me, I have considered to be a loss because of Christ. ⁸More than that, I also consider everything to be a

ᴬ2:6 Or to be grasped, or to be held on to   ᴮ2:11 Gk kurios = Yahweh; Is 42:8 LXX   ᶜ2:16 Or Offer, or Hold out   ᴰ3:2 An expression of contempt for the unclean, those outside the people of God loss in view of the surpassing value of knowing Christ Jesus my Lord. Because of Him I have suffered the loss of all things and consider them filth, so that I may gain Christ ⁹and be found in Him, not having a righteousness of my own from the law, but one that is through faith in Christ^A—the righteousness from God based on faith. ¹⁰My goal is to know Him and the power of His resurrection and the fellowship of His sufferings, being conformed to His death, ¹¹assuming that I will somehow reach the resurrection from among the dead.

¹²Not that I have already reached the goal or am already fully mature, but I make every effort to take hold of it because I also have been taken hold of by Christ Jesus. ¹³Brothers, I do not^B consider myself to have taken hold of it. But one thing I do: Forgetting what is behind and reaching forward to what is ahead, ¹⁴I pursue as my goal the prize promised by God's heavenly^C call in Christ Jesus. ¹⁵Therefore, all who are mature should think this way. And if you think differently about anything, God will reveal this also to you. ¹⁶In any case, we should live up to whatever truth we have attained. ¹⁷Join in imitating me, brothers, and observe those who live according to the example you have in us. ¹⁸For I have often told you, and now say again with tears, that many live as enemies of the cross of Christ. ¹⁹Their end is destruction; their god is their stomach; their glory is in their shame. They are focused on earthly things, ²⁰but our citizenship is in heaven, from which we also eagerly wait for a Savior, the Lord Jesus Christ. ²¹He will transform the body of our humble condition into the likeness of His glorious body, by the power that enables Him to subject everything to Himself.

4 So then, my brothers, you are dearly loved and longed for—my joy and crown. In this manner stand firm in the Lord, dear friends. ²I urge Euodia and I urge Syntyche to agree in the Lord. ³Yes, I also ask you, true partner,^D to help these women who have contended for the gospel at my side, along with Clement and the rest of my coworkers whose names are in the book of life. ⁴Rejoice in the Lord always. I will say it again: Rejoice! ⁵Let

your graciousness be known to everyone. The Lord is near. ⁶Don't worry about anything, but in everything, through prayer and petition with thanksgiving, let your requests be made known to God. ⁷And the peace of God, which surpasses every thought, will guard your hearts and minds in Christ Jesus.

⁸Finally brothers, whatever is true, whatever is honorable, whatever is just, whatever is pure, whatever is lovely, whatever is commendable—if there is any moral excellence and if there is any praise—dwell on these things. ⁹Do what you have learned and received and heard and seen in me, and the God of peace will be with you.

¹⁰I rejoiced in the Lord greatly that once again you renewed your care for me. You were, in fact, concerned about me but lacked the opportunity to show it. ¹¹I don't say this out of need, for I have learned to be content in whatever circumstances I am. ¹²I know both how to have a little, and I know how to have a lot. In any and all circumstances I have learned the secret of being content—whether well fed or hungry, whether in abundance or in need. ¹³I am able to do all things through Him^E who strengthens me. ¹⁴Still, you did well by sharing with me in my hardship.

¹⁵And you Philippians know that in the early days of the gospel, when I left Macedonia, no church shared with me in the matter of giving and receiving except you alone. ¹⁶For even in Thessalonica you sent gifts for my need several times. ¹⁷Not that I seek the gift, but I seek the profit^F that is increasing to your account. ¹⁸But I have received everything in full, and I have an abundance. I am fully supplied, having received from Epaphroditus what you provided—a fragrant offering, an acceptable sacrifice, pleasing to God. ¹⁹And my God will supply all your needs according to His riches in glory in Christ Jesus. ²⁰Now to our God and Father be glory forever and ever. Amen.

²¹Greet every saint in Christ Jesus. Those brothers who are with me greet you. ²²All the saints greet you, but especially those from Caesar's household. ²³The grace of the Lord Jesus Christ be with your spirit.^G

^A3:9 Or through the faithfulness of Christ   ^B3:13 Other mss read not yet   ^C3:14 Or upward   ^D4:3 Or true Syzygus, possibly a person's name   ^E4:13 Other mss read Christ   ^F4:17 Lit fruit   ^G4:23 Other mss add Amen.

Colossians

1 Paul, an apostle of Christ Jesus by God's will, and Timothy our[A] brother: [2]To the saints in Christ at Colossae, who are faithful brothers.

Grace to you and peace from God our Father.[B]

[3]We always thank God, the Father of our Lord Jesus Christ, when we pray for you, [4]for we have heard of your faith in Christ Jesus and of the love you have for all the saints [5]because of the hope reserved for you in heaven. You have already heard about this hope in the message of truth, the gospel [6]that has come to you. It is bearing fruit and growing all over the world, just as it has among you since the day you heard it and recognized God's grace in the truth.[C] [7]You learned this from Epaphras, our dearly loved fellow slave. He is a faithful servant of the Messiah on your[D] behalf, [8]and he has told us about your love in the Spirit.

[9]For this reason also, since the day we heard this, we haven't stopped praying for you. We are asking that you may be filled with the knowledge of His will in all wisdom and spiritual understanding,[E] [10]so that you may walk worthy of the Lord, fully pleasing to Him, bearing fruit in every good work and growing in the knowledge of God. [11]May you be strengthened with all power, according to His glorious might, for all endurance and patience, with joy [12]giving thanks to the Father, who has enabled you[F] to share in the saints'[G] inheritance in the light. [13]He has rescued us from the domain of darkness and transferred us into the kingdom of the Son He loves. [14]We have redemption,[H] the forgiveness of sins, in Him.

[15] He is the image of the invisible God,
the firstborn over all creation.[I]
[16] For everything was created by Him,
in heaven and on earth,
the visible and the invisible,
whether thrones or dominions
or rulers or authorities—
all things have been created
through Him and for Him.
[17] He is before all things,
and by Him all things
hold together.
[18] He is also the head of the body,
the church;
He is the beginning,
the firstborn from the dead,
so that He might come
to have
first place in everything.
[19] For God was pleased to have
all His fullness dwell in Him,
[20] and through Him to reconcile
everything to Himself
by making peace
through the blood of His cross[J]—
whether things on earth or things
in heaven.

[21]Once you were alienated and hostile in your minds because of your evil actions. [22]But now He has reconciled you by His physical body[K] through His death, to present you holy, faultless, and blameless before Him— [23]if indeed you remain grounded and steadfast in the faith and are not shifted away from the hope of the gospel that you heard. This gospel has been proclaimed in all creation under heaven, and I, Paul, have become a servant of it.

[24]Now I rejoice in my sufferings for you, and I am completing in my flesh what is lacking in Christ's afflictions for His body, that is, the church. [25]I have become its servant, according to God's administration that was given to me for you, to make God's message fully known, [26]the mystery hidden for ages and generations but now revealed to His saints. [27]God wanted to make known among the Gentiles the glorious wealth of this mystery, which is Christ in you, the hope of glory. [28]We proclaim Him, warning and teaching

everyone with all wisdom, so that we may present everyone mature in Christ. [29] I labor for this, striving with His strength that works powerfully in me.

2 For I want you to know how great a struggle I have for you, for those in Laodicea, and for all who have not seen me in person. [2] I want their hearts to be encouraged and joined together in love, so that they may have all the riches of assured understanding and have the knowledge of God's mystery—Christ.[A] [3] All the treasures of wisdom and knowledge are hidden in Him.

[4] I am saying this so that no one will deceive you with persuasive arguments. [5] For I may be absent in body, but I am with you in spirit, rejoicing to see how well ordered you are and the strength of your faith in Christ.

[6] Therefore, as you have received Christ Jesus the Lord, walk in Him, [7] rooted and built up in Him and established in the faith, just as you were taught, overflowing with gratitude.

[8] Be careful that no one takes you captive through philosophy and empty deceit based on human tradition, based on the elemental forces of the world, and not based on Christ. [9] For the entire fullness of God's nature[B] dwells bodily[C] in Christ, [10] and you have been filled by Him, who is the head over every ruler and authority. [11] You were also circumcised in Him with a circumcision not done with hands, by putting off the body of flesh, in the circumcision of the Messiah.[D] [12] Having been buried with Him in baptism, you were also raised with Him through faith in the working of God, who raised Him from the dead. [13] And when you were dead in trespasses and in the uncircumcision of your flesh, He made you alive with Him and forgave us all our trespasses. [14] He erased the certificate of debt, with its obligations, that was against us and opposed to us, and has taken it out of the way by nailing it to the cross. [15] He disarmed the rulers and authorities and disgraced them publicly; He triumphed over them by Him.[E]

[16] Therefore, don't let anyone judge you in regard to food and drink or in the matter of a festival or a new moon or a Sabbath day.[F] [17] These are a shadow of what was to come; the substance is[G] the Messiah. [18] Let no one disqualify you,[H] insisting on ascetic practices and the worship of angels, claiming access to a visionary realm and inflated without cause by his unspiritual[I] mind. [19] He doesn't hold on to the head, from whom the whole body, nourished and held together by its ligaments and tendons, develops with growth from God.

[20] If you died with the Messiah to the elemental forces of this world, why do you live as if you still belonged to the world? Why do you submit to regulations: [21] "Don't handle, don't taste, don't touch"? [22] All these regulations refer to what is destroyed by being used up; they are commands and doctrines of men. [23] Although these have a reputation of wisdom by promoting ascetic practices, humility, and severe treatment of the body, they are not of any value in curbing self-indulgence.[J]

3 So if you have been raised with the Messiah, seek what is above, where the Messiah is, seated at the right hand of God. [2] Set your minds on what is above, not on what is on the earth. [3] For you have died, and your life is hidden with the Messiah in God. [4] When the Messiah, who is your[K] life, is revealed, then you also will be revealed with Him in glory.

[5] Therefore, put to death what belongs to your worldly nature:[L] sexual immorality, impurity, lust, evil desire, and greed, which is idolatry. [6] Because of these, God's wrath comes on the disobedient,[M] [7] and you once walked in these things when you were living in them. [8] But now you must also put away all the following: anger, wrath, malice, slander, and filthy language from your mouth. [9] Do not lie to one another, since you have put off the old self[N] with its practices [10] and have put on the new self. You are being renewed in knowledge according to the image of your[O] Creator. [11] In Christ[P] there is not Greek and Jew, circumcision and uncircumcision, barbarian, Scythian,[Q] slave and free; but Christ is all and in all.

[12] Therefore, God's chosen ones, holy and

A 2:2 Other mss read *mystery of God, both of the Father and of Christ*; other ms variations exist on this v.   B 2:9 Or *of the deity*   C 2:9 Or *nature lives in a human body*   D 2:11 = His death   E 2:15 Or *them through it*; = through the cross   F 2:16 Or *or sabbaths*   G 2:17 Or *substance belongs to*   H 2:18 Or *no one cheat us out of your prize*   I 2:18 Lit *fleshly*   J 2:23 Lit *value against indulgence of the flesh*   K 3:4 Other mss read *our*   L 3:5 Lit *death the members on the earth*   M 3:6 Other mss omit *on the disobedient*   N 3:9 Lit *man*; = a person before conversion   O 3:10 Lit *his*   P 3:11 Lit *Where*   Q 3:11 A term for a savage loved, put on heartfelt compassion, kindness, humility, gentleness, and patience, [13]accepting one another and forgiving one another if anyone has a complaint against another. Just as the Lord has forgiven you, so you must also forgive. [14]Above all, put on love—the perfect bond of unity. [15]And let the peace of the Messiah, to which you were also called in one body, control your hearts. Be thankful. [16]Let the message about the Messiah dwell richly among you, teaching and admonishing one another in all wisdom, and singing psalms, hymns, and spiritual songs, with gratitude in your hearts to God. [17]And whatever you do, in word or in deed, do everything in the name of the Lord Jesus, giving thanks to God the Father through Him.

[18]Wives, be submissive to your husbands, as is fitting in the Lord.
[19]Husbands, love your wives and don't be bitter toward them.
[20]Children, obey your parents in everything, for this pleases the Lord.
[21]Fathers, do not exasperate your children, so they won't become discouraged.
[22]Slaves, obey your human masters in everything. Don't work only while being watched, in order to please men, but work wholeheartedly, fearing the Lord.
[23]Whatever you do, do it enthusiastically,[A] as something done for the Lord and not for men, [24]knowing that you will receive the reward of an inheritance from the Lord. You serve the Lord Christ. [25]For the wrongdoer will be paid back for whatever wrong he has done, and there is no favoritism.

4 Masters, supply your slaves with what is right and fair, since you know that you too have a Master in heaven.

[2]Devote yourselves to prayer; stay alert in it with thanksgiving. [3]At the same time, pray also for us that God may open a door to us for the message, to speak the mystery of the Messiah, for which I am in prison, [4]so that I may reveal it as I am required to speak. [5]Act wisely toward outsiders, making the most of the time. [6]Your speech should always be gracious, seasoned with salt, so that you may know how you should answer each person.

[7]Tychicus, our dearly loved brother, faithful servant, and fellow slave in the Lord, will tell you all the news about me. [8]I have sent him to you for this very purpose, so that you may know how we are[B] and so that he may encourage your hearts. [9]He is with Onesimus, a faithful and dearly loved brother, who is one of you. They will tell you about everything here.

[10]Aristarchus, my fellow prisoner, greets you, as does Mark, Barnabas's cousin (concerning whom you have received instructions: if he comes to you, welcome him), [11]and so does Jesus who is called Justus. These alone of the circumcision are my coworkers for the kingdom of God, and they have been a comfort to me. [12]Epaphras, who is one of you, a slave of Christ Jesus, greets you. He is always contending for you in his prayers, so that you can stand mature and fully assured[C] in everything God wills. [13]For I testify about him that he works hard[D] for you, for those in Laodicea, and for those in Hierapolis. [14]Luke, the dearly loved physician, and Demas greet you. [15]Give my greetings to the brothers in Laodicea, and to Nympha and the church in her home. [16]When this letter has been read among you, have it read also in the church of the Laodiceans; and see that you also read the letter from Laodicea. [17]And tell Archippus, "Pay attention to the ministry you have received in the Lord, so that you can accomplish it."

[18]This greeting is in my own hand—Paul. Remember my imprisonment. Grace be with you.[E]

A3:23 Lit *do it from the soul* B4:8 Other mss read *that he may know how you are* C4:12 Other mss read *and complete* D4:13 Other mss read *he has a great zeal* E4:18 Other mss add *Amen.*

1 THESSALONIANS

1 Paul, Silvanus,[A] and Timothy:
To the church of the Thessalonians in God the Father and the Lord Jesus Christ.
Grace to you and peace.[B]

[2] We always thank God for all of you, remembering you constantly in our prayers. [3] We recall, in the presence of our God and Father, your work of faith, labor of love, and endurance of hope in our Lord Jesus Christ, [4] knowing your election, brothers loved by God. [5] For our gospel did not come to you in word only, but also in power, in the Holy Spirit, and with much assurance. You know what kind of men we were among you for your benefit, [6] and you became imitators of us and of the Lord when, in spite of severe persecution, you welcomed the message with joy from the Holy Spirit. [7] As a result, you became an example to all the believers in Macedonia and Achaia. [8] For the Lord's message rang out from you, not only in Macedonia and Achaia, but in every place that your faith[C] in God has gone out. Therefore, we don't need to say anything, [9] for they themselves report[D] what kind of reception we had from you: how you turned to God from idols to serve the living and true God [10] and to wait for His Son from heaven, whom He raised from the dead—Jesus, who rescues us from the coming wrath.

2 For you yourselves know, brothers, that our visit with you was not without result. [2] On the contrary, after we had previously suffered, and we were treated outrageously in Philippi, as you know, we were emboldened by our God to speak the gospel of God to you in spite of great opposition. [3] For our exhortation didn't come from error or impurity or an intent to deceive. [4] Instead, just as we have been approved by God to be entrusted with the gospel, so we speak, not to please men, but rather God, who examines our hearts. [5] For we never used flattering speech, as you know, or had greedy motives—God is our witness— [6] and we didn't seek glory from people, either from you or from oth-

ers. [7] Although we could have been a burden as Christ's apostles, instead we were gentle[E] among you, as a nursing mother nurtures her own children. [8] We cared so much for you that we were pleased to share with you not only the gospel of God but also our own lives, because you had become dear to us. [9] For you remember our labor and hardship, brothers. Working night and day so that we would not burden any of you, we preached God's gospel to you. [10] You are witnesses, and so is God, of how devoutly, righteously, and blamelessly we conducted ourselves with you believers. [11] As you know, like a father with his own children, [12] we encouraged, comforted, and implored each one of you to walk worthy of God, who calls you into His own kingdom and glory.

[13] This is why we constantly thank God, because when you received the message about God that you heard from us, you welcomed it not as a human message, but as it truly is, the message of God, which also works effectively in you believers. [14] For you, brothers, became imitators of God's churches in Christ Jesus that are in Judea, since you have also suffered the same things from people of your own country, just as they did from the Jews [15] who killed both the Lord Jesus and the prophets and persecuted us; they displease God and are hostile to everyone, [16] hindering us from speaking to the Gentiles so that they may be saved. As a result, they are always completing the number of their sins, and wrath has overtaken them at last.[F]

[17] But as for us, brothers, after we were forced to leave you for a short time (in person, not in heart), we greatly desired and made every effort to return and see you face to face. [18] So we wanted to come to you—even I, Paul, time and again—but Satan hindered us. [19] For who is our hope or joy or crown of boasting in the presence of our Lord Jesus at His coming? Is it not you? [20] For you are our glory and joy!

A1:1 Or *Silas*; Ac 15:22-32; 16:19-40; 17:1-16   B1:1 Other mss add *from God our Father and the Lord Jesus Christ*   C1:8 Or *in every place news of your faith*   D1:9 Lit *report about us*   E2:7 Other mss read *infants*   F2:16 Or *to the end*

3 Therefore, when we could no longer stand it, we thought it was better to be left alone in Athens. ²And we sent Timothy, our brother and God's coworker[A] in the gospel of Christ, to strengthen and encourage you concerning your faith, ³so that no one will be shaken by these persecutions. For you yourselves know that we are appointed to[B] this. ⁴In fact, when we were with you, we told you previously that we were going to suffer persecution, and as you know, it happened. ⁵For this reason, when I could no longer stand it, I also sent him to find out about your faith, fearing that the tempter had tempted you and that our labor might be for nothing.

⁶But now Timothy has come to us from you and brought us good news about your faith and love and reported that you always have good memories of us, wanting to see us, as we also want to see you. ⁷Therefore, brothers, in all our distress and persecution, we were encouraged about you through your faith. ⁸For now we live, if you stand firm in the Lord. ⁹How can we thank God for you in return for all the joy we experience before our God because of you, ¹⁰as we pray very earnestly night and day to see you face to face and to complete what is lacking in your faith?

¹¹Now may our God and Father Himself, and our Lord Jesus, direct our way to you. ¹²And may the Lord cause you to increase and overflow with love for one another and for everyone, just as we also do for you. ¹³May He make your hearts blameless in holiness before our God and Father at the coming of our Lord Jesus with all His saints. Amen.[C]

4 Finally then, brothers, we ask and encourage you in the Lord Jesus, that as you have received from us how you must walk and please God—as you are doing[D]—do so even more. ²For you know what commands we gave you through the Lord Jesus.

³For this is God's will, your sanctification: that you abstain from sexual immorality, ⁴so that each of you knows how to control his own body[E] in sanctification and honor, ⁵not with lustful desires, like the Gentiles who don't know God. ⁶This means one must not trans-

gress against and defraud his brother in this matter, because the Lord is an avenger of all these offenses,[F] as we also previously told and warned you. ⁷For God has not called us to impurity but to sanctification. ⁸Therefore, the person who rejects this does not reject man, but God, who also gives you His Holy Spirit.

⁹About brotherly love: You don't need me to write you because you yourselves are taught by God to love one another. ¹⁰In fact, you are doing this toward all the brothers in the entire region of Macedonia. But we encourage you, brothers, to do so even more, ¹¹to seek to lead a quiet life, to mind your own business,[G] and to work with your own hands, as we commanded you, ¹²so that you may walk properly[H] in the presence of outsiders[I] and not be dependent on anyone.[J]

¹³We do not want you to be uninformed, brothers, concerning those who are asleep, so that you will not grieve like the rest, who have no hope. ¹⁴Since we believe that Jesus died and rose again, in the same way God will bring with Him those who have fallen asleep through[K] Jesus. ¹⁵For we say this to you by a revelation from the Lord:[L] We who are still alive at the Lord's coming will certainly have no advantage over[M] those who have fallen asleep. ¹⁶For the Lord Himself will descend from heaven with a shout,[N] with the archangel's voice, and with the trumpet of God, and the dead in Christ will rise first. ¹⁷Then we who are still alive will be caught up together with them in the clouds to meet the Lord in the air and so we will always be with the Lord. ¹⁸Therefore encourage[O] one another with these words.

5 About the times and the seasons: Brothers, you do not need anything to be written to you. ²For you yourselves know very well that the Day of the Lord will come just like a thief in the night. ³When they say, "Peace and security," then sudden destruction comes on them, like labor pains come on a pregnant woman, and they will not escape. ⁴But you, brothers, are not in the dark, for this day to overtake you like a thief. ⁵For you are all sons of light and sons of the day. We do not belong to the night or the darkness. ⁶So then, we must not sleep,

A3:2 Other mss read servant   B3:3 Or are destined for   C3:13 Other mss omit Amen.   D4:1 Lit walking   E4:4 Or to acquire his own wife; lit to possess his own vessel   F4:6 Lit things   G4:11 Lit to practice one's own things   H4:12 Or may live respectably   I4:12 Non-Christians   J4:12 Or not need anything, or not be in need   K4:14 Or in   L4:15 Or a word of the Lord   M4:15 Or certainly not precede   N4:16 Or command   O4:18 Or comfort like the rest, but we must stay awake and be serious. ⁷For those who sleep, sleep at night, and those who get drunk are drunk at night. ⁸But since we belong to the day, we must be serious and put the armor of faith and love on our chests, and put on a helmet of the hope of salvation. ⁹For God did not appoint us to wrath, but to obtain salvation through our Lord Jesus Christ, ¹⁰who died for us, so that whether we are awake or asleep, we will live together with Him. ¹¹Therefore encourage one another and build each other up as you are already doing.

¹²Now we ask you, brothers, to give recognition to those who labor among you and lead you in the Lord and admonish you, ¹³and to regard them very highly in love because of their work. Be at peace among yourselves. ¹⁴And we exhort you, brothers: warn those who are irresponsible,ᴬ comfort the discouraged, help the weak, be patient with everyone. ¹⁵See to it that no one repays evil for evil to anyone, but always pursue what is good for one another and for all.

¹⁶ Rejoice always!
¹⁷ Pray constantly.
¹⁸ Give thanks
   in everything,
   for this is God's will for you
   in Christ Jesus.
¹⁹ Don't stifle the Spirit.
²⁰ Don't despise prophecies,
²¹ but test all things.
   Hold on to what is good.
²² Stay away from every kind
   of evil.

²³Now may the God of peace Himself sanctify you completely. And may your spirit, soul, and body be kept sound and blameless for the coming of our Lord Jesus Christ. ²⁴He who calls you is faithful, who also will do it. ²⁵Brothers, pray for us also. ²⁶Greet all the brothers with a holy kiss. ²⁷I charge you by the Lord that this letter be read to all the brothers. ²⁸The grace of our Lord Jesus Christ be with you.

2 THESSALONIANS

1 Paul, Silvanus,ᴮ and Timothy:
   To the church of the Thessalonians in God our Father and the Lord Jesus Christ.

²Grace to you and peace from God our Father and the Lord Jesus Christ.

³We must always thank God for you, brothers. This is right, since your faith is flourishing and the love each one of you has for one another is increasing. ⁴Therefore, we ourselves boast about you among God's churches—about your endurance and faith in all the persecutions and afflictions you endure. ⁵It is a clear evidence of God's righteous judgment that you will be counted worthy of God's kingdom, for which you also are suffering, ⁶since it is righteous for God to repay with affliction those who afflict you ⁷and to reward with rest you who are afflicted, along with us. This will take place at the revelation of the Lord Jesus from heaven with His powerful angels, ⁸taking vengeance with flaming fire on those who don't know God and on those who don't obey the gospel of our Lord Jesus. ⁹These will pay the penalty of eternal destruction from the Lord's presence and from His glorious strength ¹⁰in that day when He comes to be glorified by His saints and to be admired by all those who have believed, because our testimony among you was believed. ¹¹And in view of this, we always pray for you that our God will consider you worthy of His calling, and will, by His power, fulfill every desire for goodness and the work of faith, ¹²so that the name of our Lord Jesus will be glorified by you, and you by Him, according to the grace of our God and the Lord Jesus Christ.

2 Now concerning the coming of our Lord Jesus Christ and our being gathered to Him: We ask you, brothers, ²not to be easily upset in mind or troubled, either by a spirit or by a message or by a letter as if from us, alleging that the Day of the Lordᶜ has come. ³Don't let anyone deceive you in any way. For

ᴬ5:14 Or who are disorderly, or who are undisciplined   ᴮ1:1 Or Silas; Ac 15:22-32; 16:19-40; 17:1-16   ᶜ2:2 Other mss read Christ that day will not come unless the apostasy[A] comes first and the man of lawlessness[B] is revealed, the son of destruction. [4] He opposes and exalts himself above every so-called god or object of worship, so that he sits[C] in God's sanctuary,[D] publicizing that he himself is God.

[5] Don't you remember that when I was still with you I told you about this? [6] And you know what currently restrains him, so that he will be revealed in his time. [7] For the mystery of lawlessness is already at work, but the one now restraining will do so until he is out of the way, [8] and then the lawless one will be revealed. The Lord Jesus will destroy him with the breath of His mouth and will bring him to nothing with the brightness of His coming. [9] The coming of the lawless one is based on Satan's working, with all kinds of false miracles, signs, and wonders, [10] and with every unrighteous deception among those who are perishing. They perish because they did not accept the love of the truth in order to be saved. [11] For this reason God sends them a strong delusion so that they will believe what is false, [12] so that all will be condemned—those who did not believe the truth but enjoyed unrighteousness.

[13] But we must always thank God for you, brothers loved by the Lord, because from the beginning[E] God has chosen you for salvation through sanctification by the Spirit and through belief in the truth. [14] He called you to this through our gospel, so that you might obtain the glory of our Lord Jesus Christ. [15] Therefore, brothers, stand firm and hold to the traditions you were taught, either by our message or by our letter.

[16] May our Lord Jesus Christ Himself and God our Father, who has loved us and given us eternal encouragement and good hope by grace, [17] encourage your hearts and strengthen you in every good work and word.

3 Finally, brothers, pray for us that the Lord's message may spread rapidly and be honored, just as it was with you, [2] and that we may be delivered from wicked and evil men, for not all have faith.[F] [3] But the Lord is faithful; He will strengthen and guard you from the evil one. [4] We have confidence in the Lord about you, that you are doing and will do what we command. [5] May the Lord direct your hearts to God's love and Christ's endurance.

[6] Now we command you, brothers, in the name of our Lord Jesus Christ, to keep away from every brother who walks irresponsibly and not according to the tradition received from us. [7] For you yourselves know how you must imitate us: We were not irresponsible among you; [8] we did not eat anyone's food[G] free of charge; instead, we labored and struggled, working night and day, so that we would not be a burden to any of you. [9] It is not that we don't have the right to support, but we did it to make ourselves an example to you so that you would imitate us. [10] In fact, when we were with you, this is what we commanded you: "If anyone isn't willing to work, he should not eat." [11] For we hear that there are some among you who walk irresponsibly, not working at all, but interfering with the work of others. [12] Now we command and exhort such people by the Lord Jesus Christ that quietly working, they may eat their own food.[G] [13] Brothers, do not grow weary in doing good.

[14] And if anyone does not obey our instruction in this letter, take note of that person; don't associate with him, so that he may be ashamed. [15] Yet don't treat him as an enemy, but warn him as a brother.

[16] May the Lord of peace Himself give you peace always in every way. The Lord be with all of you. [17] This greeting is in my own hand—Paul. This is a sign in every letter; this is how I write. [18] The grace of our Lord Jesus Christ be with all of you.

A 2:3 Or rebellion   B 2:3 Other mss read man of sin   C 2:4 Other mss add as God   D 2:4 Or temple   E 2:13 Other mss read because as a firstfruit   F 3:2 Or for the faith is not in everyone   G 3:8,12 Or bread

1 TIMOTHY

1 Paul, an apostle of Christ Jesus by the command of God our Savior and of Christ Jesus our hope:

² To Timothy, my true son in the faith.

Grace, mercy, and peace from God the^A Father and Christ Jesus our Lord.

³ As I urged you when I went to Macedonia, remain in Ephesus so that you may instruct certain people not to teach different doctrine ⁴ or to pay attention to myths and endless genealogies. These promote empty speculations rather than God's plan, which operates by faith. ⁵ Now the goal of our instruction is love that comes from a pure heart, a good conscience, and a sincere faith. ⁶ Some have deviated from these and turned aside to fruitless discussion. ⁷ They want to be teachers of the law, although they don't understand what they are saying or what they are insisting on. ⁸ But we know that the law is good, provided one uses it legitimately. ⁹ We know that the law is not meant for a righteous person, but for the lawless and rebellious, for the ungodly and sinful, for the unholy and irreverent, for those who kill their fathers and mothers, for murderers, ¹⁰ for the sexually immoral and homosexuals, for kidnappers,^B liars, perjurers, and for whatever else is contrary to the sound teaching ¹¹ based on the glorious gospel of the blessed God, which was entrusted to me.

¹² I give thanks to Christ Jesus our Lord who has strengthened me, because He considered me faithful, appointing me to the ministry— ¹³ one who was formerly a blasphemer, a persecutor, and an arrogant man. But I received mercy because I acted out of ignorance in unbelief. ¹⁴ And the grace of our Lord overflowed, along with the faith and love that are in Christ Jesus. ¹⁵ This saying is trustworthy and deserving of full acceptance: "Christ Jesus came into the world to save sinners"—and I am the worst of them. ¹⁶ But I received mercy for this reason, so that in me, the worst of them, Christ Jesus might demonstrate His extraordinary patience as an example to those who would believe in Him for eternal life. ¹⁷ Now to the King eternal, immortal, invisible, the only^C God, be honor and glory forever and ever. Amen.

¹⁸ Timothy, my son, I am giving you this instruction in keeping with the prophecies previously made about you, so that by them you may strongly engage in battle, ¹⁹ having faith and a good conscience. Some have rejected these and have suffered the shipwreck of their faith. ²⁰ Hymenaeus and Alexander are among them, and I have delivered them to Satan, so that they may be taught not to blaspheme.

2 First of all, then, I urge that petitions, prayers, intercessions, and thanksgivings be made for everyone, ² for kings and all those who are in authority, so that we may lead a tranquil and quiet life in all godliness and dignity. ³ This is good, and it pleases God our Savior, ⁴ who wants everyone to be saved and to come to the knowledge of the truth.

⁵   For there is one God
    and one mediator between God
      and humanity,
    Christ Jesus, Himself human,
⁶   who gave Himself—a ransom for all,
    a testimony at the proper time.

⁷ For this I was appointed a herald, an apostle (I am telling the truth;^D I am not lying), and a teacher of the Gentiles in faith and truth.

⁸ Therefore, I want the men in every place to pray, lifting up holy hands without anger or argument. ⁹ Also, the women are to dress themselves in modest clothing, with decency and good sense, not with elaborate hairstyles, gold, pearls, or expensive apparel, ¹⁰ but with good works, as is proper for women who affirm that they worship God. ¹¹ A woman should learn in silence with full submission. ¹² I do not allow a woman to teach or to have authority over a man; instead, she is to be silent. ¹³ For Adam was created first, then Eve. ¹⁴ And Adam was not deceived, but the woman was deceived and transgressed. ¹⁵ But she will be saved through childbearing, if she

continues[A] in faith, love, and holiness, with good judgment.

3 This saying is trustworthy:[B] "If anyone aspires to be an overseer, he desires a noble work." [2]An overseer, therefore, must be above reproach, the husband of one wife, self-controlled, sensible, respectable, hospitable, an able teacher,[C] [3]not addicted to wine, not a bully but gentle, not quarrelsome, not greedy— [4]one who manages his own household competently, having his children under control with all dignity. [5](If anyone does not know how to manage his own household, how will he take care of God's church?) [6]He must not be a new convert, or he might become conceited and fall into the condemnation of the Devil. [7]Furthermore, he must have a good reputation among outsiders, so that he does not fall into disgrace and the Devil's trap.

[8]Deacons, likewise, should be worthy of respect, not hypocritical, not drinking a lot of wine, not greedy for money, [9]holding the mystery of the faith with a clear conscience. [10]And they must also be tested first; if they prove blameless, then they can serve as deacons. [11]Wives, too, must be worthy of respect, not slanderers, self-controlled, faithful in everything. [12]Deacons must be husbands of one wife, managing their children and their own households competently. [13]For those who have served well as deacons acquire a good standing for themselves, and great boldness in the faith that is in Christ Jesus.

[14]I write these things to you, hoping to come to you soon. [15]But if I should be delayed, I have written so that you will know how people ought to act in God's household, which is the church of the living God, the pillar and foundation of the truth. [16]And most certainly, the mystery of godliness is great:

He[D] was manifested in the flesh,
vindicated in the Spirit,
seen by angels,
preached among the nations,
believed on in the world,
taken up in glory.

4 Now the Spirit explicitly says that in later times some will depart from the faith, paying attention to deceitful spirits and the teachings of demons, [2]through the hypocrisy of liars whose consciences are seared. [3]They forbid marriage and demand abstinence from foods that God created to be received with gratitude by those who believe and know the truth. [4]For everything created by God is good, and nothing should be rejected if it is received with thanksgiving, [5]since it is sanctified by the word of God and by prayer.

[6]If you point these things out to the brothers, you will be a good servant of Christ Jesus, nourished by the words of the faith and the good teaching that you have followed. [7]But have nothing to do with irreverent and silly myths. Rather, train yourself in godliness, [8]for

the training of the body has
a limited benefit,
but godliness is beneficial
in every way,
since it holds promise
for the present life
and also for the life to come.

[9]This saying is trustworthy and deserves full acceptance. [10]In fact, we labor and strive[E] for this, because we have put our hope in the living God, who is the Savior of everyone, especially of those who believe.

[11]Command and teach these things. [12]Let no one despise your youth; instead, you should be an example to the believers in speech, in conduct, in love,[F] in faith, in purity. [13]Until I come, give your attention to public reading, exhortation, and teaching. [14]Do not neglect the gift that is in you; it was given to you through prophecy, with the laying on of hands by the council of elders. [15]Practice these things; be committed to them, so that your progress may be evident to all. [16]Pay close attention to your life and your teaching; persevere in these things, for by doing this you will save both yourself and your hearers.

5 Do not rebuke an older man, but exhort him as a father, younger men as brothers, [2]older women as mothers, and with all propriety, the younger women as sisters.

A2:15 Lit *if they continue*   B3:1 "This saying is trustworthy" could refer to 1Tm 2:15.   C3:2 Or *hospitable, skillful in teaching*   D3:16 Other mss read *God*   E4:10 Other mss read *and suffer reproach*   F4:12 Other mss add *in spirit*

³Support[A] widows who are genuinely widows. ⁴But if any widow has children or grandchildren, they must learn to practice godliness toward their own family first and to repay their parents, for this pleases God. ⁵The real widow, left all alone, has put her hope in God and continues night and day in her petitions and prayers; ⁶however, she who is self-indulgent is dead even while she lives. ⁷Command this also, so they won't be blamed. ⁸But if anyone does not provide for his own, that is his own household, he has denied the faith and is worse than an unbeliever.

⁹No widow should be placed on the official support list[B] unless she is at least 60 years old, has been the wife of one husband, ¹⁰and is well known for good works—that is, if she has brought up children, shown hospitality, washed the saints' feet, helped the afflicted, and devoted herself to every good work. ¹¹But refuse to enroll younger widows, for when they are drawn away from Christ by desire, they want to marry ¹²and will therefore receive condemnation because they have renounced their original pledge. ¹³At the same time, they also learn to be idle, going from house to house; they are not only idle, but are also gossips and busybodies, saying things they shouldn't say. ¹⁴Therefore, I want younger women to marry, have children, manage their households, and give the adversary no opportunity to accuse us. ¹⁵For some have already turned away to follow Satan. ¹⁶If any[C] believing woman has widows in her family, she should help them, and the church should not be burdened, so that it can help those who are genuinely widows.

¹⁷The elders who are good leaders should be considered worthy of an ample honorarium,[D] especially those who work hard at preaching and teaching. ¹⁸For the Scripture says:

Do not muzzle an ox
while it is treading out the grain,[E]
and,
the worker is worthy
of his wages.

¹⁹Don't accept an accusation against an elder unless it is supported by two or three witnesses. ²⁰Publicly rebuke those who sin, so that the rest will also be afraid. ²¹I solemnly charge you before God and Christ Jesus and the elect angels to observe these things without prejudice, doing nothing out of favoritism. ²²Don't be too quick to appoint[F] anyone as an elder, and don't share in the sins of others. Keep yourself pure. ²³Don't continue drinking only water, but use a little wine because of your stomach and your frequent illnesses. ²⁴Some people's sins are obvious, going before them to judgment, but the sins of others surface[G] later. ²⁵Likewise, good works are obvious, and those that are not obvious cannot remain hidden.

6 All who are under the yoke as slaves must regard their own masters[H] to be worthy of all respect, so that God's name and His teaching will not be blasphemed. ²Those who have believing masters should not be disrespectful to them because they are brothers, but should serve them better, since those who benefit from their service are believers and dearly loved.

Teach and encourage these things. ³If anyone teaches other doctrine and does not agree with the sound teaching of our Lord Jesus Christ and with the teaching that promotes godliness, ⁴he is conceited, understanding nothing, but has a sick interest in disputes and arguments over words. From these come envy, quarreling, slander, evil suspicions, ⁵and constant disagreement among people whose minds are depraved and deprived of the truth, who imagine that godliness[I] is a way to material gain.[J] ⁶But godliness with contentment is a great gain.

⁷   For we brought nothing into the world,
     and[K] we can take nothing out.
⁸   But if we have food
     and clothing,[L]
     we will be content with these.

⁹But those who want to be rich fall into temptation, a trap, and many foolish and harmful desires, which plunge people into

---

ruin and destruction. [10] For the love of money is a root[A] of all kinds of evil, and by craving it, some have wandered away from the faith and pierced themselves with many pains.

[11] But you, man of God, run
   from these things,
and pursue righteousness,
   godliness, faith,
love, endurance, and gentleness.
[12] Fight the good fight for the faith;
   take hold of eternal life
   that you were called to
   and have made a good
      confession about
   in the presence of
      many witnesses.

[13] In the presence of God, who gives life to all, and of Christ Jesus, who gave a good confession before Pontius Pilate, I charge you [14] to keep the command without fault or failure until the appearing of our Lord Jesus Christ. [15] God will bring this about in His own time. He is

the blessed and only Sovereign,
   the King of kings,
   and the Lord of lords,
[16]   the only One who has immortality,
   dwelling in unapproachable light;
   no one has seen or can see Him,
   to Him be honor and eternal might.
   Amen.

[17] Instruct those who are rich in the present age not to be arrogant or to set their hope on the uncertainty of wealth, but on God,[B] who richly provides us with all things to enjoy. [18] Instruct them to do what is good, to be rich in good works, to be generous, willing to share, [19] storing up for themselves a good reserve[C] for the age to come, so that they may take hold of life that is real.

[20] Timothy, guard what has been entrusted to you, avoiding irreverent, empty speech and contradictions from the "knowledge" that falsely bears that name. [21] By professing it, some people have deviated from the faith.
   Grace be with all of you.

2 TIMOTHY

1 Paul, an apostle of Christ Jesus by God's will, for the promise of life in Christ Jesus: [2] To Timothy, my dearly loved son.
   Grace, mercy, and peace from God the Father and Christ Jesus our Lord.
   [3] I thank God, whom I serve with a clear conscience as my ancestors did, when I constantly remember you in my prayers night and day. [4] Remembering your tears, I long to see you so that I may be filled with joy, [5] clearly recalling your sincere faith that first lived in your grandmother Lois, then in your mother Eunice, and that I am convinced is in you also.
   [6] Therefore, I remind you to keep ablaze[D] the gift of God that is in you through the laying on of my hands. [7] For God has not given us a spirit[E] of fearfulness, but one of power, love, and sound judgment.

[8] So don't be ashamed of the testimony about our Lord, or of me His prisoner. Instead, share in suffering for the gospel, relying on the power of God.

[9]   He has saved us and called us
   with a holy calling,
   not according to our works,
   but according to His own purpose
      and grace,
   which was given to us
      in Christ Jesus
   before time began.
[10]   This has now been made evident
   through the appearing of our Savior
      Christ Jesus,
   who has abolished death
   and has brought life and immortality
      to light
   through the gospel.

A 6:10 Or is the root   B 6:17 Other mss read on the living God   C 6:19 Or foundation   D 1:6 Or to rekindle   E 1:7 Or us the Spirit

¹¹For this gospel I was appointed a herald, apostle, and teacher,^A ¹²and that is why I suffer these things. But I am not ashamed, because I know the One I have believed in and am persuaded that He is able to guard what has been entrusted to me^B until that day.

¹³Hold on to the pattern of sound teaching that you have heard from me, in the faith and love that are in Christ Jesus. ¹⁴Guard, through the Holy Spirit who lives in us, that good thing entrusted to you. ¹⁵This you know: All those in Asia have turned away from me, including Phygelus and Hermogenes. ¹⁶May the Lord grant mercy to the household of Onesiphorus, because he often refreshed me and was not ashamed of my chains. ¹⁷On the contrary, when he was in Rome, he diligently searched for me and found me. ¹⁸May the Lord grant that he obtain mercy from Him on that day. And you know very well how much he ministered at Ephesus.

2 You, therefore, my son, be strong in the grace that is in Christ Jesus. ²And what you have heard from me in the presence of many witnesses, commit to faithful men who will be able to teach others also.

³Share in suffering as a good soldier of Christ Jesus. ⁴No one serving as a soldier gets entangled in the concerns of civilian life; he seeks to please the recruiter. ⁵Also, if anyone competes as an athlete, he is not crowned unless he competes according to the rules. ⁶The hardworking farmer ought to be the first to get a share of the crops. ⁷Consider what I say, for the Lord will give you understanding in everything.

⁸Keep your attention on Jesus Christ as risen from the dead and descended from David. This is according to my gospel. ⁹I suffer for it to the point of being bound like a criminal, but God's message is not bound. ¹⁰This is why I endure all things for the elect: so that they also may obtain salvation, which is in Christ Jesus, with eternal glory. ¹¹This saying is trustworthy:

For if we have died
  with Him,
we will also live with Him;

¹² if we endure,
    we will also reign with Him;
  if we deny Him, He will also deny us;
¹³ if we are faithless, He remains faithful,
    for He cannot deny Himself.

¹⁴Remind them of these things, charging them before God^C not to fight about words; this is in no way profitable and leads to the ruin of the hearers. ¹⁵Be diligent to present yourself approved to God, a worker who doesn't need to be ashamed, correctly teaching the word of truth. ¹⁶But avoid irreverent, empty speech, for this will produce an even greater measure of godlessness. ¹⁷And their word will spread like gangrene; Hymenaeus and Philetus are among them. ¹⁸They have deviated from the truth, saying that the resurrection has already taken place, and are overturning the faith of some. ¹⁹Nevertheless, God's solid foundation stands firm, having this inscription:

**The Lord knows those
  who are His,**^D and
Everyone who names the name
  of the Lord
must turn away
  from unrighteousness.

²⁰Now in a large house there are not only gold and silver bowls, but also those of wood and clay, some for honorable^E use, some for dishonorable.^F ²¹So if anyone purifies himself from anything dishonorable,^G he will be a special^H instrument, set apart, useful to the Master, prepared for every good work.

²²Flee from youthful passions, and pursue righteousness, faith, love, and peace, along with those who call on the Lord from a pure heart. ²³But reject foolish and ignorant disputes, knowing that they breed quarrels. ²⁴The Lord's slave must not quarrel, but must be gentle to everyone, able to teach,^I and patient, ²⁵instructing his opponents with gentleness. Perhaps God will grant them repentance leading them to the knowledge of the truth. ²⁶Then they may come to their senses and escape the Devil's trap, having been captured by him to do his will.

^A1:11 Other mss add of the Gentiles   ^B1:12 Or guard what I have entrusted to Him, or guard my deposit   ^C2:14 Other mss read before the Lord
^D2:19 Nm 16:5   ^E2:20 Or special   ^F2:20 Or ordinary   ^G2:21 Lit from these   ^H2:21 Or an honorable   ^I2:24 Or everyone, skillful in teaching

3 But know this: Difficult times will come in the last days. [2]For people will be lovers of self, lovers of money, boastful, proud, blasphemers, disobedient to parents, ungrateful, unholy, [3]unloving, irreconcilable, slanderers, without self-control, brutal, without love for what is good, [4]traitors, reckless, conceited, lovers of pleasure rather than lovers of God, [5]holding to the form of godliness but denying its power. Avoid these people!

[6]For among them are those who worm their way into households and capture idle women burdened down with sins, led along by a variety of passions, [7]always learning and never able to come to a knowledge of the truth. [8]Just as Jannes and Jambres resisted Moses, so these also resist the truth, men who are corrupt in mind, worthless in regard to the faith. [9]But they will not make further progress, for their lack of understanding will be clear to all, as theirs[A] was also.

[10]But you have followed my teaching, conduct, purpose, faith, patience, love, and endurance, [11]along with the persecutions and sufferings that came to me in Antioch, Iconium, and Lystra. What persecutions I endured! Yet the Lord rescued me from them all. [12]In fact, all those who want to live a godly life in Christ Jesus will be persecuted. [13]Evil people and impostors will become worse, deceiving and being deceived. [14]But as for you, continue in what you have learned and firmly believed. You know those who taught you, [15]and you know that from childhood you have known the sacred Scriptures, which are able to give you wisdom for salvation through faith in Christ Jesus. [16]All Scripture is inspired by God[B] and is profitable for teaching, for rebuking, for correcting, for training in righteousness, [17]so that the man of God may be complete, equipped for every good work.

4 I solemnly charge you before God and Christ Jesus, who is going to judge the living and the dead, and because of His appearing and His kingdom: [2]Proclaim the message; persist in it whether convenient or not; rebuke, correct, and encourage with great patience and teaching. [3]For the time will come when they will not tolerate sound doctrine, but according to their own desires, will multiply teachers for themselves because they have an itch to hear something new.[C] [4]They will turn away from hearing the truth and will turn aside to myths. [5]But as for you, be serious about everything, endure hardship, do the work of an evangelist, fulfill your ministry.

[6]For I am already being poured out as a drink offering, and the time for my departure is close. [7]I have fought the good fight, I have finished the race, I have kept the faith. [8]There is reserved for me in the future the crown of righteousness, which the Lord, the righteous Judge, will give me on that day, and not only to me, but to all those who have loved His appearing.

[9]Make every effort to come to me soon, [10]for Demas has deserted me, because he loved this present world, and has gone to Thessalonica. Crescens has gone to Galatia, Titus to Dalmatia. [11]Only Luke is with me. Bring Mark with you, for he is useful to me in the ministry. [12]I have sent Tychicus to Ephesus. [13]When you come, bring the cloak I left in Troas with Carpus, as well as the scrolls, especially the parchments. [14]Alexander the coppersmith did great harm to me. The Lord will repay him according to his works. [15]Watch out for him yourself because he strongly opposed our words.

[16]At my first defense, no one stood by me, but everyone deserted me. May it not be counted against them. [17]But the Lord stood with me and strengthened me, so that the proclamation might be fully made through me and all the Gentiles might hear. So I was rescued from the lion's mouth. [18]The Lord will rescue me from every evil work and will bring me safely into His heavenly kingdom. To Him be the glory forever and ever! Amen.

[19]Greet Prisca and Aquila, and the household of Onesiphorus. [20]Erastus has remained at Corinth; I left Trophimus sick at Miletus. [21]Make every effort to come before winter. Eubulus greets you, as do Pudens, Linus, Claudia, and all the brothers.

[22]The Lord be with your spirit. Grace be with you.

TITUS

1 Paul, a slave of God and an apostle of Jesus Christ, to build up[A] the faith of God's elect and their knowledge of the truth that leads[B] to godliness, [2] in the hope of eternal life that God, who cannot lie, promised before time began. [3] In His own time He has revealed His message in the proclamation that I was entrusted with by the command of God our Savior:

[4] To Titus, my true son in our common faith.

Grace and peace from God the Father and Christ Jesus our Savior.

[5] The reason I left you in Crete was to set right what was left undone and, as I directed you, to appoint elders in every town: [6] one who is blameless, the husband of one wife, having faithful[C] children not accused of wildness or rebellion. [7] For an overseer, as God's administrator, must be blameless, not arrogant, not hot-tempered, not addicted to wine, not a bully, not greedy for money, [8] but hospitable, loving what is good, sensible, righteous, holy, self-controlled, [9] holding to the faithful message as taught, so that he will be able both to encourage with sound teaching and to refute those who contradict it.

[10] For there are also many rebellious people, full of empty talk and deception, especially those from Judaism.[D] [11] It is necessary to silence them; they overthrow whole households by teaching what they shouldn't in order to get money dishonestly. [12] One of their very own prophets said,

> Cretans are always liars, evil beasts,
> lazy gluttons.[E]

[13] This testimony is true. So, rebuke them sharply, that they may be sound in the faith [14] and may not pay attention to Jewish myths and the commands of men who reject the truth.

[15] To the pure, everything is pure, but to those who are defiled and unbelieving nothing is pure; in fact, both their mind and conscience are defiled. [16] They profess to know God, but they deny Him by their works. They are detestable, disobedient, and disqualified for any good work.

2 But you must say the things that are consistent with sound teaching. [2] Older men are to be level headed, worthy of respect, sensible, and sound in faith, love, and endurance. [3] In the same way, older women are to be reverent in behavior, not slanderers, not addicted to much wine. They are to teach what is good, [4] so they may encourage the young women to love their husbands and to love their children, [5] to be self-controlled, pure, homemakers, kind, and submissive to their husbands, so that God's message will not be slandered.

[6] In the same way, encourage the young men to be self-controlled [7] in everything. Make yourself an example of good works with integrity and dignity[F] in your teaching. [8] Your message is to be sound beyond reproach, so that the opponent will be ashamed, having nothing bad to say about us.

[9] Slaves are to be submissive to their masters in everything, and to be well-pleasing, not talking back [10] or stealing, but demonstrating utter faithfulness, so that they may adorn the teaching of God our Savior in everything.

[11] For the grace of God has appeared with salvation[G] for all people, [12] instructing us to deny godlessness and worldly lusts and to live in a sensible, righteous, and godly way in the present age, [13] while we wait for the blessed hope and appearing of the glory of our great God and Savior, Jesus Christ. [14] He gave Himself for us to redeem us from all lawlessness and to cleanse for Himself a people for His own possession, eager to do good works.

[15] Say these things, and encourage and rebuke with all authority. Let no one disregard[H] you.

3 Remind them to be submissive to rulers and authorities, to obey, to be ready for every good work, [2] to slander no one, to avoid fighting, and to be kind, always showing

---

A1:1 Or according to   **B1:1** Or corresponds   **C1:6** Or believing   **D1:10** Lit the circumcision   **E1:12** This saying is from the Cretan poet Epimenides (6th century B.C.).   **F2:7** Other mss add incorruptibility   **G2:11** Or appeared, bringing salvation; or appeared with saving power   **H2:15** Or despise gentleness to all people. ³For we too were once foolish, disobedient, deceived, enslaved by various passions and pleasures, living in malice and envy, hateful, detesting one another.

⁴ But when the kindness of God
    our Savior and His love
    for mankind appeared,
⁵ He saved us—
    not by works of righteousness
        that we had done,
    but according to His mercy—
    through the washing
        of regeneration
    and renewal by the Holy Spirit.
⁶ He poured out this Spirit
    on us abundantly
    through Jesus Christ our Savior
⁷ so that, having been justified
    by His grace,
    we may become heirs with the hope
    of eternal life.

⁸This saying is trustworthy. I want you to insist on these things, so that those who have believed God might be careful to devote themselves to good works. These are good and profitable for everyone. ⁹But avoid foolish debates, genealogies, quarrels, and disputes about the law, for they are unprofitable and worthless. ¹⁰Reject a divisive person after a first and second warning, ¹¹knowing that such a person is perverted and sins, being self-condemned.

¹²When I send Artemas or Tychicus to you, make every effort to come to me in Nicopolis, for I have decided to spend the winter there. ¹³Diligently help Zenas the lawyer and Apollos on their journey, so that they will lack nothing. ¹⁴And our people must also learn to devote themselves to good works for cases of urgent need, so that they will not be unfruitful. ¹⁵All those who are with me greet you. Greet those who love us in the faith. Grace be with all of you.

PHILEMON

Paul, a prisoner of Christ Jesus, and Timothy our brother:

To Philemon our dear friend and coworker, ²to Apphia our sister,ᴬ to Archippus our fellow soldier, and to the church that meets in your home.

³Grace to you and peace from God our Father and the Lord Jesus Christ.

⁴I always thank my God when I mention you in my prayers, ⁵because I hear of your love and faith towardᴮ the Lord Jesus and for all the saints. ⁶I pray that your participation in the faith may become effective through knowing every good thing that is in usᶜ for the glory of Christ. ⁷For I have great joy and encouragement from your love, because the hearts of the saints have been refreshed through you, brother.

⁸For this reason, although I have great boldness in Christ to command you to do what is right, ⁹I appeal to you, instead, on the basis of love. I, Paul, as an elderly manᴰ and now also as a prisoner of Christ Jesus, ¹⁰appeal to you for my son, Onesimus.ᴱ I fatheredᶠ him while I was in chains. ¹¹Once he was useless to you, but now he is useful both to you and to me. ¹²I am sending him back to you as a part of myself.ᴳ,ᴴ ¹³I wanted to keep him with me, so that in my imprisonment for the gospel he might serve me in your place. ¹⁴But I didn't want to do anything without your consent, so that your good deed might not be out of obligation, but of your own free will. ¹⁵For perhaps this is why he was separated from you for a brief time, so that you might get him back permanently, ¹⁶no longer as a slave, but more than a slave—as a dearly loved brother. He is especially so to me, but even more to you, both in the flesh and in the Lord.ᴵ

¹⁷So if you consider me a partner, accept him as you would me. ¹⁸And if he has wronged you in any way, or owes you any-

thing, charge that to my account. ¹⁹ I, Paul, write this with my own hand: I will repay it—not to mention to you that you owe me even your own self. ²⁰ Yes, brother, may I have joy from you in the Lord; refresh my heart in Christ. ²¹ Since I am confident of your obedience, I am writing to you, knowing that you will do even more than I say. ²² But mean-

while, also prepare a guest room for me, for I hope that through your prayers I will be restored to you.

²³ Epaphras, my fellow prisoner in Christ Jesus, greets you, and so do ²⁴ Mark, Aristarchus, Demas, and Luke, my coworkers.

²⁵ The grace of the Lord^A Jesus Christ be with your spirit.

HEBREWS

1 Long ago God spoke to the fathers by the prophets at different times and in different ways. ² In these last days, He has spoken to us by His Son. God has appointed Him heir of all things and made the universe^B through Him. ³ The Son is the radiance^C of God's glory and the exact expression^D of His nature, sustaining all things by His powerful word. After making purification for sins,^E He sat down at the right hand of the Majesty on high.^F ⁴ So He became higher in rank than the angels, just as the name He inherited is superior to theirs.

⁵ For to which of the angels did He ever say,

You are My Son; today I have become Your Father,^G,H or again, **I will be His Father, and He will be My Son?**^I ⁶ When He again^J brings His firstborn into the world, He says, **And all God's angels must worship Him.**^K ⁷ And about the angels He says:

> **He makes His angels winds,**^L
> **and His servants**^M **a fiery flame,**^N

⁸ but to^O the Son:

> **Your throne, God,**
> **is forever and ever,**
> **and the scepter of Your kingdom**
> **is a scepter of justice.**
> ⁹ **You have loved righteousness**
> **and hated lawlessness;**
> **this is why God, Your God,**
> **has anointed You**
> **with the oil of joy**
> **rather than Your companions.**^P,Q

¹⁰ And:

> **In the beginning, Lord,**
> **You established the earth,**
> **and the heavens are the works**
> **of Your hands;**
> ¹¹ **they will perish, but You remain.**
> **They will all wear out**
> **like clothing;**
> ¹² **You will roll them up like a cloak,**^R
> **and they will be changed**
> **like a robe.**
> **But You are the same,**
> **and Your years will never end.**^S

¹³ Now to which of the angels has He ever said:

> **Sit at My right hand**
> **until I make Your enemies**
> **Your footstool?**^T,U

¹⁴ Are they not all ministering spirits sent out to serve those who are going to inherit salvation?

2 We must, therefore, pay even more attention to what we have heard, so that we will not drift away. ² For if the message spoken through angels was legally binding^V and every transgression and disobedience received a just punishment, ³ how will we escape if we neglect such a great salvation? It was first spoken by the Lord and was confirmed to us by those who heard Him. ⁴ At the same time, God also testified by signs and wonders, various miracles, and distributions of gifts from the Holy Spirit according to His will.

^A2:5 Other mss read *our Lord*   ^B1:2 Lit *ages*   ^C1:3 Or *reflection*   ^D1:3 Or *representation, or copy, or reproduction*   ^E1:3 Other mss read *for our sins by Himself*   ^F1:3 Or *He sat down on high at the right hand of the Majesty*   ^G1:5 Or *have begotten You*   ^H1:5 Ps 2:7   ^I1:5 2Sm 7:14; 1Ch 17:13   ^J1:6 Or *And again, when He*   ^K1:6 Dt 32:43 LXX; Ps 97:7   ^L1:7 Or *spirits*   ^M1:7 Or *ministers*   ^N1:7 Ps 104:4   ^O1:8 Or *about*   ^P1:9 Or *associates*   ^Q1:8-9 Ps 45:6-7   ^R1:12 Other mss omit *like a cloak*   ^S1:10-12 Ps 102:25-27   ^T1:13 Or *enemies a footstool for Your feet*   ^U1:13 Ps 110:1   ^V2:2 Or *valid, or reliable*

⁵For He has not subjected to angels the world to come that we are talking about. ⁶But one has somewhere testified:

> **What is man that You remember him,**
> **or the son of man that You care**
> **for him?**
> ⁷ **You made him lower**
> **than the angels**
> **for a short time;**
> **You crowned him with glory**
> **and honor**ᴬ
> ⁸ **and subjected everything**
> **under his feet.**ᴮ

For in **subjecting everything** to him, He left nothing that is not subject to him. As it is, we do not yet see **everything subjected** to him. ⁹But we do see Jesus—**made lower than the angels for a short time** so that by God's grace He might taste death for everyone—crowned with glory and honor because of His suffering in death.

¹⁰For in bringing many sons to glory, it was entirely appropriate that God—all things exist for Him and through Him—should make the sourceᶜ of their salvation perfect through sufferings. ¹¹For the One who sanctifies and those who are sanctified all have one Father.ᴰ That is why Jesus is not ashamed to call them brothers, ¹²saying:

> **I will proclaim Your name**
> **to My brothers;**
> **I will sing hymns to You**
> **in the congregation.**ᴱ

¹³Again, **I will trust in Him.**ᶠ And again, **Here I am with the children God gave Me.**ᴳ

¹⁴Now since the children have flesh and blood in common, Jesus also shared in these, so that through His death He might destroy the one holding the power of death—that is, the Devil— ¹⁵and free those who were held in slavery all their lives by the fear of death. ¹⁶For it is clear that He does not reach out to help angels, but to help Abraham's offspring. ¹⁷Therefore, He had to be like His brothers in every way, so that He could become a merciful and faithful high priest in serviceᴴ to God, to make propitiation for the sins of the people. ¹⁸For since He Himself was tested and has suffered, He is able to help those who are tested.

3 Therefore, holy brothers and companions in a heavenly calling, consider Jesus, the apostle and high priest of our confession; ²He was faithful to the One who appointed Him, just as Moses was in all God's household. ³For Jesus is considered worthy of more glory than Moses, just as the builder has more honor than the house. ⁴Now every house is built by someone, but the One who built everything is God. ⁵Moses was faithful as a servant in all God's household, as a testimony to what would be said in the future. ⁶But Christ was faithful as a Son over His household. And we are that household if we hold on to the courage and the confidence of our hope.ᴵ

⁷Therefore, as the Holy Spirit says:

> **Today, if you hear His voice,**
> ⁸ **do not harden your hearts**
> **as in the rebellion,**
> **on the day of testing**
> **in the wilderness,**
> ⁹ **where your fathers tested Me, tried Me,**
> **and saw My works** ¹⁰**for 40 years.**
> **Therefore I was provoked**
> **with that generation**
> **and said, "They always go astray**
> **in their hearts,**
> **and they have not known My ways."**
> ¹¹ **So I swore in My anger,**
> **"They will not enter My rest."**ᴶ

¹²Watch out, brothers, so that there won't be in any of you an evil, unbelieving heart that departs from the living God. ¹³But encourage each other daily, while it is still called **today**, so that none of you is hardened by sin's deception. ¹⁴For we have become companions of the Messiah if we hold firmly until the end the realityᴷ that we had at the start. ¹⁵As it is said:

> **Today, if you hear His voice,**
> **do not harden your hearts**
> **as in the rebellion.**ᴸ

ᴬ**2:7** Other mss add *and set him over the works of your hands* ᴮ**2:6-8** Ps 8:5-7 LXX ᶜ**2:10** Or *pioneer, or leader* ᴰ**2:11** Or *father, or origin,* or *all are of one* ᴱ**2:12** Ps 22:22 ᶠ**2:13** 2Sm 22:3 LXX; Is 8:17 LXX; 12:2 LXX ᴳ**2:13** Is 8:18 LXX ᴴ**2:17** Lit *things* ᴵ**3:6** Other mss add *firm to the end* ᴶ**3:7-11** Ps 95:7-11 ᴷ**3:14** Or *confidence* ᴸ**3:15** Ps 95:7-8

[16] For who heard and rebelled? Wasn't it really all who came out of Egypt under Moses? [17] And who was He provoked with for 40 years? Was it not with those who sinned, whose bodies fell in the wilderness? [18] And who did He swear to that they would not enter His rest, if not those who disobeyed? [19] So we see that they were unable to enter because of unbelief.

[4] Therefore, while the promise to enter His rest remains, let us fear that none of you should miss it.[A] [2] For we also have received the good news just as they did; but the message they heard did not benefit them, since they were not united with those who heard it in faith[B] [3] (for we who have believed enter the rest), in keeping with what[C] He has said:

> So I swore in My anger,
> they will not enter My rest.[D]

And yet His works have been finished since the foundation of the world, [4] for somewhere He has spoken about the seventh day in this way:

> And on the seventh day
> God rested from all His works.[E]

[5] Again, in that passage He says, **They will never enter My rest.**[D] [6] Since it remains for some to enter it, and those who formerly received the good news did not enter because of disobedience, [7] again, He specifies a certain day—**today**—speaking through David after such a long time, as previously stated:

> Today, if you hear His voice,
> do not harden your hearts.[F]

[8] For if Joshua had given them rest, God would not have spoken later about another day. [9] Therefore, a Sabbath rest remains for God's people. [10] For the person who has entered His rest has rested from his own works, just as God did from His. [11] Let us then make every effort to enter that rest, so that no one will fall into the same pattern of disobedience.

[12] For the word of God is living and effective and sharper than any double-edged sword, penetrating as far as the separation of soul and spirit, joints and marrow. It is able to judge the ideas and thoughts of the heart. [13] No creature is hidden from Him, but all things are naked and exposed to the eyes of Him to whom we must give an account.

[14] Therefore, since we have a great high priest who has passed through the heavens—Jesus the Son of God—let us hold fast to the confession. [15] For we do not have a high priest who is unable to sympathize with our weaknesses, but One who has been tested in every way as we are, yet without sin. [16] Therefore let us approach the throne of grace with boldness, so that we may receive mercy and find grace to help us at the proper time.

[5] For every high priest taken from men is appointed in service[G] to God for the people, to offer both gifts and sacrifices for sins. [2] He is able to deal gently with those who are ignorant and are going astray, since he is also subject to weakness. [3] Because of this, he must make a sin offering for himself as well as for the people. [4] No one takes this honor on himself; instead, a person is called by God, just as Aaron was. [5] In the same way, the Messiah did not exalt Himself to become a high priest, but the One who said to Him, **You are My Son; today I have become Your Father,**[H] [6] also said in another passage, **You are a priest forever in the order of Melchizedek.**[I]

[7] During His earthly life,[J] He offered prayers and appeals with loud cries and tears to the One who was able to save Him from death, and He was heard because of His reverence. [8] Though He was God's Son, He learned obedience through what He suffered. [9] After He was perfected, He became the source of eternal salvation for all who obey Him, [10] and He was declared by God a high priest in the order of Melchizedek.

[11] We have a great deal to say about this, and it's difficult to explain, since you have become too lazy to understand. [12] Although by this time you ought to be teachers, you need someone to teach you the basic principles of God's revelation again. You need milk, not solid food. [13] Now everyone who lives on milk is inexperienced with the message about righteousness, because he is an infant. [14] But solid food is for the mature—for those whose

---

[A]4:1 Or that any of you might seem to have missed it   [B]4:2 Other mss read since it was not united by faith in those who heard   [C]4:3 Or rest], just as   [D]4:3,5 Ps 95:11   [E]4:4 Gn 2:2   [F]4:7 Ps 95:7-8   [G]5:1 Lit things   [H]5:5 Ps 2:7   [I]5:6 Gn 14:18-20; Ps 110:4   [J]5:7 Lit In the days of His flesh

senses have been trained to distinguish between good and evil.

6 Therefore, leaving the elementary message
about the Messiah, let us go on to maturity,
not laying again the foundation of repentance
from dead works, faith in God, [2] teaching about
ritual washings,[A] laying on of hands, the resurrection of the dead, and eternal judgment. [3] And
we will do this if God permits.

[4] For it is impossible to renew to repentance
those who were once enlightened, who tasted
the heavenly gift, became companions with
the Holy Spirit, [5] tasted God's good word and
the powers of the coming age, [6] and who have
fallen away, because,[B] to their own harm, they
are recrucifying the Son of God and holding
Him up to contempt. [7] For ground that has
drunk the rain that has often fallen on it and
that produces vegetation useful to those it is
cultivated for receives a blessing from God.
[8] But if it produces thorns and thistles, it is
worthless and about to be cursed, and will be
burned at the end.

[9] Even though we are speaking this way,
dear friends, in your case we are confident of
the better things connected with salvation.
[10] For God is not unjust; He will not forget
your work and the love[C] you showed for His
name when you served the saints—and you
continue to serve them. [11] Now we want each
of you to demonstrate the same diligence for
the final realization of your hope, [12] so that
you won't become lazy but will be imitators
of those who inherit the promises through
faith and perseverance.

[13] For when God made a promise to Abraham, since He had no one greater to swear by,
He swore by Himself:

[14] **I will indeed bless you,
   and I will greatly multiply you.**[D]

[15] And so, after waiting patiently, Abraham[E]
obtained the promise. [16] For men swear by
something greater than themselves, and for
them a confirming oath ends every dispute.
[17] Because God wanted to show His unchangeable purpose even more clearly to the heirs
of the promise, He guaranteed it with an
oath, [18] so that through two unchangeable

things, in which it is impossible for God to
lie, we who have fled for refuge might have
strong encouragement to seize the hope set
before us. [19] We have this hope as an anchor
for our lives, safe and secure. It enters the inner sanctuary behind the curtain. [20] Jesus has
entered there on our behalf as a forerunner,
because He has become a high priest forever
in the order of Melchizedek.

7 For this Melchizedek—

> King of Salem, priest of the Most High
>   God,
> who met Abraham and blessed him
> as he returned from defeating
>   the kings,
> [2] and Abraham gave him a tenth
>   of everything;
> first, his name means
>   king of righteousness,
> then also, king of Salem,
> meaning king of peace;
> [3] without father, mother, or genealogy,
> having neither beginning of days
>   nor end of life,
> but resembling the Son of God—

remains a priest forever.
[4] Now consider how great this man was—
even Abraham the patriarch gave a tenth
of the plunder to him! [5] The sons of Levi
who receive the priestly office have a command according to the law to collect a tenth
from the people—that is, from their brothers—though they have also descended from
Abraham.[F] [6] But one without this[G] lineage
collected tenths from Abraham and blessed
the one who had the promises. [7] Without a
doubt,[H] the inferior is blessed by the superior.
[8] In the one case, men who will die receive
tenths, but in the other case, Scripture testifies that he lives. [9] And in a sense Levi himself,
who receives tenths, has paid tenths through
Abraham, [10] for he was still within his ancestor[I] when Melchizedek met him.

[11] If then, perfection came through the Levitical priesthood (for under it the people received the law), what further need was there
for another priest to appear, said to be in the
order of Melchizedek and not in the order of

A6:2 Or about baptisms   B6:6 Or while   C6:10 Other mss read labor of love   D6:14 Gn 22:17   E6:15 Lit he   F7:5 Lit have come out of
Abraham's loins   G7:6 Lit their   H7:7 Or Beyond any dispute   I7:10 Lit still in his father's loins

Aaron? ¹²For when there is a change of the priesthood, there must be a change of law as well. ¹³For the One these things are spoken about belonged to a different tribe. No one from it has served at the altar. ¹⁴Now it is evident that our Lord came from Judah, and Moses said nothing about that tribe concerning priests.

¹⁵And this becomes clearer if another priest like Melchizedek appears, ¹⁶who did not become a priest based on a legal command concerning physical^A descent but based on the power of an indestructible life. ¹⁷For it has been testified:

> **You are a priest forever**
> **in the order of Melchizedek.**^B

¹⁸So the previous command is annulled because it was weak and unprofitable ¹⁹(for the law perfected nothing), but a better hope is introduced, through which we draw near to God. ²⁰None of this happened without an oath. For others became priests without an oath, ²¹but He became a priest with an oath made by the One who said to Him:

> **The Lord has sworn,**
> **and He will not change His mind,**
> **You are a priest forever.**^B

²²So Jesus has also become the guarantee of a better covenant.

²³Now many have become Levitical priests, since they are prevented by death from remaining in office. ²⁴But because He remains forever, He holds His priesthood permanently. ²⁵Therefore, He is always able to save^C those who come to God through Him, since He always lives to intercede for them.

²⁶For this is the kind of high priest we need: holy, innocent, undefiled, separated from sinners, and exalted above the heavens. ²⁷He doesn't need to offer sacrifices every day, as high priests do—first for their own sins, then for those of the people. He did this once for all when He offered Himself. ²⁸For the law appoints as high priests men who are weak, but the promise of the oath, which came after the law, appoints a Son, who has been perfected forever.

8 Now the main point of what is being said is this: We have this kind of high priest, who sat down at the right hand of the throne of the Majesty in the heavens, ²a minister of the sanctuary and the true tabernacle that was set up by the Lord and not man. ³For every high priest is appointed to offer gifts and sacrifices; therefore it was necessary for this priest also to have something to offer. ⁴Now if He were on earth, He wouldn't be a priest, since there are those^D offering the gifts prescribed by the law. ⁵These serve as a copy and shadow of the heavenly things, as Moses was warned when he was about to complete the tabernacle. For God said, **Be careful that you make everything according to the pattern that was shown to you on the mountain.**^E ⁶But Jesus has now obtained a superior ministry, and to that degree He is the mediator of a better covenant, which has been legally enacted on better promises.

⁷For if that first covenant had been faultless, there would have been no occasion for a second one. ⁸But finding fault with His people,^F He says:^G

> **Look, the days are coming,**
> **says the Lord,**
> **when I will make a new covenant**
> **with the house of Israel**
> **and with the house of Judah—**
> ⁹ **not like the covenant**
> **that I made with their ancestors**
> **on the day I took them by their hands**
> **to lead them out of the land of Egypt.**
> **I disregarded them, says the Lord,**
> **because they did not continue**
> **in My covenant.**
> ¹⁰ **But this is the covenant**
> **that I will make with the house**
> **of Israel**
> **after those days, says the Lord:**
> **I will put My laws into their minds**
> **and write them on their hearts.**
> **I will be their God,**
> **and they will be My people.**

---

^A**7:16** Or *fleshly*   ^B**7:17,21** Ps 110:4   ^C**7:25** Or *He is able to save completely*   ^D**8:4** Other mss read *priests*   ^E**8:5** Ex 25:40   ^F**8:8** Lit *with them*   ^G**8:8** Other mss read *finding fault, He says to them*

¹¹ **And each person will not teach
his fellow citizen,**[A]
**and each his brother, saying,
"Know the Lord,"
because they will all know Me,
from the least to the greatest of them.**
¹² **For I will be merciful
to their wrongdoing,
and I will never again remember
their sins.**[B,C]

¹³By saying, **a new covenant**, He has declared that the first is old. And what is old and aging is about to disappear.

9 Now the first covenant also had regulations for ministry and an earthly sanctuary. ²For a tabernacle was set up, and in the first room, which is called the holy place, were the lampstand, the table, and the presentation loaves. ³Behind the second curtain, the tabernacle was called the most holy place. ⁴It contained the gold altar of incense and the ark of the covenant, covered with gold on all sides, in which there was a gold jar containing the manna, Aaron's staff that budded, and the tablets of the covenant. ⁵The cherubim of glory were above it overshadowing the mercy seat. It is not possible to speak about these things in detail right now.

⁶With these things set up this way, the priests enter the first room repeatedly, performing their ministry. ⁷But the high priest alone enters the second room, and he does that only once a year, and never without blood, which he offers for himself and for the sins of the people committed in ignorance. ⁸The Holy Spirit was making it clear that the way into the most holy place had not yet been disclosed while the first tabernacle was still standing. ⁹This is a symbol for the present time, during which gifts and sacrifices are offered that cannot perfect the worshiper's conscience. ¹⁰They are physical regulations and only deal with food, drink, and various washings imposed until the time of restoration.

¹¹But the Messiah has appeared, high priest of the good things that have come.[D] In the greater and more perfect tabernacle not made with hands (that is, not of this creation), ¹²He

entered the most holy place once for all, not by the blood of goats and calves, but by His own blood, having obtained eternal redemption. ¹³For if the blood of goats and bulls and the ashes of a young cow, sprinkling those who are defiled, sanctify for the purification of the flesh, ¹⁴how much more will the blood of the Messiah, who through the eternal Spirit offered Himself without blemish to God, cleanse our[E] consciences from dead works to serve the living God?

¹⁵Therefore, He is the mediator of a new covenant,[F] so that those who are called might receive the promise of the eternal inheritance, because a death has taken place for redemption from the transgressions committed under the first covenant. ¹⁶Where a will exists, the death of the one who made it must be established. ¹⁷For a will is valid only when people die, since it is never in force while the one who made it is living. ¹⁸That is why even the first covenant was inaugurated with blood. ¹⁹For when every command had been proclaimed by Moses to all the people according to the law, he took the blood of calves and goats, along with water, scarlet wool, and hyssop, and sprinkled the scroll itself and all the people, ²⁰saying, **This is the blood of the covenant that God has commanded for you.**[G] ²¹In the same way, he sprinkled the tabernacle and all the articles of worship with blood. ²²According to the law almost everything is purified with blood, and without the shedding of blood there is no forgiveness.

²³Therefore it was necessary for the copies of the things in the heavens to be purified with these sacrifices, but the heavenly things themselves to be purified with better sacrifices than these. ²⁴For the Messiah did not enter a sanctuary made with hands (only a model[H] of the true one) but into heaven itself, so that He might now appear in the presence of God for us. ²⁵He did not do this to offer Himself many times, as the high priest enters the sanctuary yearly with the blood of another. ²⁶Otherwise, He would have had to suffer many times since the foundation of the world. But now He has appeared one time, at the end of the ages, for

A8:11 Other mss read *neighbor*   **B8:12** Other mss add *and their lawless deeds*   **C8:8–12** Jr 31:31-34   **D9:11** Other mss read *that are to come*   **E9:14** Other mss read *your*   **F9:15** The Gk word used here and in vv. 15–18 can be translated covenant, will, or testament.   **G9:20** Ex 24:8   **H9:24** Or *antitype*, or *figure* the removal of sin by the sacrifice of Himself. ²⁷And just as it is appointed for people to die once—and after this, judgment— ²⁸so also the Messiah, having been offered once to bear the sins of many, will appear a second time, not to bear sin, but^A to bring salvation to those who are waiting for Him.

10 Since the law has only a shadow of the good things to come, and not the actual form of those realities, it can never perfect the worshipers by the same sacrifices they continually offer year after year. ²Otherwise, wouldn't they have stopped being offered, since the worshipers, once purified, would no longer have any consciousness of sins? ³But in the sacrifices there is a reminder of sins every year. ⁴For it is impossible for the blood of bulls and goats to take away sins.

⁵Therefore, as He was coming into the world, He said:

> You did not want sacrifice
>   and offering,
> but You prepared a body for Me.
> ⁶ You did not delight
>   in whole burnt offerings
>   and sin offerings.
> ⁷ Then I said, "See—
>   it is written about Me
>   in the volume of the scroll—
>   I have come to do Your will, God!"^B

⁸After He says above, **You did not want or delight in sacrifices and offerings, whole burnt offerings and sin offerings** (which are offered according to the law), ⁹He then says, **See, I have come to do Your will.**^C He takes away the first to establish the second. ¹⁰By this will of God, we have been sanctified through the offering of the body of Jesus Christ once and for all.

¹¹Every priest stands day after day ministering and offering the same sacrifices time after time, which can never take away sins. ¹²But this man, after offering one sacrifice for sins forever, sat down at the right hand of God. ¹³He is now waiting until His enemies are made His footstool. ¹⁴For by one offering He has perfected forever those who are

sanctified. ¹⁵The Holy Spirit also testifies to us about this. For after He says:

> ¹⁶ **This is the covenant I will make**
> **with them**
> **after those days, says the Lord:**
> **I will put My laws on their hearts**
> **and write them on their minds,**

¹⁷He adds:

> **I will never again remember**
> **their sins and their lawless acts.**^D

¹⁸Now where there is forgiveness of these, there is no longer an offering for sin.

¹⁹Therefore, brothers, since we have boldness to enter the sanctuary through the blood of Jesus, ²⁰by a new and living way He has opened for us through the curtain (that is, His flesh), ²¹and since we have a great high priest over the house of God, ²²let us draw near with a true heart in full assurance of faith, our hearts sprinkled clean from an evil conscience and our bodies washed in pure water. ²³Let us hold on to the confession of our hope without wavering, for He who promised is faithful. ²⁴And let us be concerned about one another in order to promote love and good works, ²⁵not staying away from our worship meetings, as some habitually do, but encouraging each other, and all the more as you see the day drawing near.

²⁶For if we deliberately sin after receiving the knowledge of the truth, there no longer remains a sacrifice for sins, ²⁷but a terrifying expectation of judgment and the fury of a fire about to consume the adversaries. ²⁸If anyone disregards Moses' law, he dies without mercy, based on the testimony of two or three witnesses. ²⁹How much worse punishment do you think one will deserve who has trampled on the Son of God, regarded as profane^E the blood of the covenant by which he was sanctified, and insulted the Spirit of grace? ³⁰For we know the One who has said, **Vengeance belongs to Me, I will repay,**^F,G and again, **The Lord will judge His people.**^H ³¹It is a terrifying thing to fall into the hands of the living God!

---

^A9:28 Lit *time, apart from sin,*   ^B10:5-7 Ps 40:6-8   ^C10:9 Other mss add *God*   ^D10:16-17 Jr 31:33-34   ^E10:29 Or *ordinary*   ^F10:30 Other mss add *says the Lord*   ^G10:30 Dt 32:35   ^H10:30 Dt 32:36

³²Remember the earlier days when, after you had been enlightened, you endured a hard struggle with sufferings. ³³Sometimes you were publicly exposed to taunts and afflictions, and at other times you were companions of those who were treated that way. ³⁴For you sympathized with the prisoners[A] and accepted with joy the confiscation of your possessions, knowing that you yourselves have a better and enduring possession.[B] ³⁵So don't throw away your confidence, which has a great reward. ³⁶For you need endurance, so that after you have done God's will, you may receive what was promised.

³⁷ For yet in **a very little while,**
the Coming One will come
and not delay.
³⁸ **But My righteous one**[C]**will live by faith;**
and if he draws back,
I have no pleasure in him.[D]

³⁹But we are not those who draw back and are destroyed, but those who have faith and obtain life.

11 Now faith is the reality[E] of what is hoped for, the proof[F] of what is not seen. ²For our ancestors won God's approval by it.

³By faith we understand that the universe was[G] created by God's command,[H] so that what is seen has been made from things that are not visible.

⁴By faith Abel offered to God a better sacrifice than Cain did. By faith he was approved as a righteous man, because God approved his gifts, and even though he is dead, he still speaks through his faith.

⁵By faith Enoch was taken away so he did not experience death, and **he was not to be found because God took him away.**[I] For prior to his removal he was approved, since he had pleased God. ⁶Now without faith it is impossible to please God, for the one who draws near to Him must believe that He exists and rewards those who seek Him.

⁷By faith Noah, after he was warned about what was not yet seen and motivated by godly

fear, built an ark to deliver his family. By faith he condemned the world and became an heir of the righteousness that comes by faith.

⁸By faith Abraham, when he was called, obeyed and went out to a place he was going to receive as an inheritance. He went out, not knowing where he was going. ⁹By faith he stayed as a foreigner in the land of promise, living in tents with Isaac and Jacob, coheirs of the same promise. ¹⁰For he was looking forward to the city that has foundations, whose architect and builder is God.

¹¹By faith even Sarah herself, when she was unable to have children, received power to conceive offspring, even though she was past the age, since she[J] considered that the One who had promised was faithful. ¹²Therefore from one man—in fact, from one as good as dead—came offspring as numerous as the stars of heaven and as innumerable as the grains of sand by the seashore.

¹³These all died in faith without having received the promises, but they saw them from a distance, greeted them, and confessed that they were foreigners and temporary residents on the earth. ¹⁴Now those who say such things make it clear that they are seeking a homeland. ¹⁵If they were thinking about where they came from, they would have had an opportunity to return. ¹⁶But they now desire a better place—a heavenly one. Therefore God is not ashamed to be called their God, for He has prepared a city for them.

¹⁷By faith Abraham, when he was tested, offered up Isaac. He received the promises and he was offering his unique son, ¹⁸the one it had been said about, **Your seed will be traced**[K] **through Isaac.**[L] ¹⁹He considered God to be able even to raise someone from the dead, and as an illustration,[M] he received him back.

²⁰By faith Isaac blessed Jacob and Esau concerning things to come. ²¹By faith Jacob, when he was dying, blessed each of the sons of Joseph, and **he worshiped, leaning on the top of his staff.**[N] ²²By faith Joseph, as he was nearing the end of his life, mentioned the

A**10:34** Other mss read *sympathized with my imprisonment*   B**10:34** Other mss add *in heaven*   C**10:38** Other mss read *the righteous one*   D**10:37-38** Is 26:20 LXX; Hab 2:3-4   E**11:1** Or *assurance*   F**11:1** Or *conviction*   G**11:3** Or *the worlds were, or the ages were*   H**11:3** Or *word*   I**11:5** Gn 5:21-24   J**11:11** Or *By faith Abraham, even though he was past age—and Sarah herself was barren—received the ability to procreate since he*   K**11:18** Lit *called*   L**11:18** Gn 21:12   M**11:19** Or *a foreshadowing, or a parable, or a type*   N**11:21** Gn 47:31

exodus of the Israelites and gave instructions concerning his bones. ²³By faith, after Moses was born, he was hidden by his parents for three months, because they saw that the child was beautiful, and they didn't fear the king's edict. ²⁴By faith Moses, when he had grown up, refused to be called the son of Pharaoh's daughter ²⁵and chose to suffer with the people of God rather than to enjoy the short-lived pleasure of sin. ²⁶For he considered the reproach because of the Messiah to be greater wealth than the treasures of Egypt, since his attention was on the reward.

²⁷By faith he left Egypt behind, not being afraid of the king's anger, for Moses persevered as one who sees Him who is invisible. ²⁸By faith he instituted the Passover and the sprinkling of the blood, so that the destroyer of the firstborn might not touch the Israelites. ²⁹By faith they crossed the Red Sea as though they were on dry land. When the Egyptians attempted to do this, they were drowned.

³⁰By faith the walls of Jericho fell down after being encircled by the Israelites for seven days. ³¹By faith Rahab the prostitute received the spies in peace and didn't perish with those who disobeyed.

³²And what more can I say? Time is too short for me to tell about Gideon, Barak, Samson, Jephthah, David, Samuel, and the prophets, ³³who by faith conquered kingdoms, administered justice, obtained promises, shut the mouths of lions, ³⁴quenched the raging of fire, escaped the edge of the sword, gained strength after being weak, became mighty in battle, and put foreign armies to flight. ³⁵Women received their dead—they were raised to life again. Some men were tortured, not accepting release, so that they might gain a better resurrection, ³⁶and others experienced mockings and scourgings, as well as bonds and imprisonment. ³⁷They were stoned,ᴬ they were sawed in two, they died by the sword, they wandered about in sheepskins, in goatskins, destitute, afflicted, and mistreated. ³⁸The world was not worthy of them. They wandered in deserts and on mountains, hiding in caves and holes in the ground.

³⁹All these were approved through their faith, but they did not receive what was promised, ⁴⁰since God had provided something better for us, so that they would not be made perfect without us.

12 Therefore, since we also have such a large cloud of witnesses surrounding us, let us lay aside every weight and the sin that so easily ensnares us. Let us run with endurance the race that lies before us, ²keeping our eyes on Jesus,ᴮ the source and perfecterᶜ of our faith, who for the joy that lay before Himᴰ endured a cross and despised the shame and has sat down at the right hand of God's throne.

³For consider Him who endured such hostility from sinners against Himself, so that you won't grow weary and lose heart. ⁴In struggling against sin, you have not yet resisted to the point of shedding your blood. ⁵And you have forgotten the exhortation that addresses you as sons:

> **My son, do not take the Lord's**
> **discipline lightly**
> **or faint when you are**
> **reproved by Him,**
> ⁶ **for the Lord disciplines the one**
> **He loves**
> **and punishes every son He receives.**ᴱ

⁷Endure suffering as discipline: God is dealing with you as sons. For what son is there that a father does not discipline? ⁸But if you are without discipline—which allᶠ receiveᴳ—then you are illegitimate children and not sons. ⁹Furthermore, we had natural fathers discipline us, and we respected them. Shouldn't we submit even more to the Father of spirits and live? ¹⁰For they disciplined us for a short time based on what seemed good to them, but He does it for our benefit, so that we can share His holiness. ¹¹No discipline seems enjoyable at the time, but painful. Later on, however, it yields the fruit of peace and righteousness to those who have been trained by it.

¹²Therefore strengthen your tired hands and weakened knees, ¹³and make straight paths for your feet, so that what is lame may not be dislocated^A but healed instead.

¹⁴Pursue peace with everyone, and holiness—without it no one will see the Lord. ¹⁵Make sure that no one falls short of the grace of God and that no root of bitterness springs up, causing trouble and by it, defiling many. ¹⁶And make sure that there isn't any immoral or irreverent person like Esau, who sold his birthright in exchange for one meal. ¹⁷For you know that later, when he wanted to inherit the blessing, he was rejected because he didn't find any opportunity for repentance, though he sought it with tears.

¹⁸For you have not come to what could be touched, to a blazing fire, to darkness, gloom, and storm, ¹⁹to the blast of a trumpet, and the sound of words. (Those who heard it begged that not another word be spoken to them, ²⁰for they could not bear what was commanded: **And if even an animal touches the mountain, it must be stoned!**^B ²¹The appearance was so terrifying that Moses said, **I am terrified and trembling.**^C) ²²Instead, you have come to Mount Zion, to the city of the living God (the heavenly Jerusalem), to myriads of angels in festive gathering, ²³to the assembly of the firstborn whose names have been written^D in heaven, to God who is the Judge of all, to the spirits of righteous people made perfect, ²⁴to Jesus (mediator of a new covenant), and to the sprinkled blood, which says better things than the blood of Abel.

²⁵Make sure that you do not reject the One who speaks. For if they did not escape when they rejected Him who warned them on earth, even less will we if we turn away from Him who warns us from heaven. ²⁶His voice shook the earth at that time, but now He has promised, **Yet once more I will shake not only the earth but also heaven.**^E ²⁷This expression, "Yet once more," indicates the removal of what can be shaken—that is, created things—so that what is not shaken might remain. ²⁸Therefore, since we are receiving a kingdom that cannot be shaken, let us hold

on to grace.^F By it, we may serve God acceptably, with reverence and awe, ²⁹for our God is a consuming fire.

13 Let brotherly love continue. ²Don't neglect to show hospitality, for by doing this some have welcomed angels as guests without knowing it. ³Remember the prisoners, as though you were in prison with them, and the mistreated, as though you yourselves were suffering bodily.^G ⁴Marriage must be respected by all, and the marriage bed kept undefiled, because God will judge immoral people and adulterers. ⁵Your life should be free from the love of money. Be satisfied with what you have, for He Himself has said, **I will never leave you or forsake you.**^H ⁶Therefore, we may boldly say:

> **The Lord is my helper;**
> **I will not be afraid.**
> **What can man do to me?**^I

⁷Remember your leaders who have spoken God's word to you. As you carefully observe the outcome of their lives, imitate their faith. ⁸Jesus Christ is the same yesterday, today, and forever. ⁹Don't be led astray by various kinds of strange teachings; for it is good for the heart to be established by grace and not by foods, since those involved in them have not benefited. ¹⁰We have an altar from which those who serve the tabernacle do not have a right to eat. ¹¹For the bodies of those animals whose blood is brought into the most holy place by the high priest as a sin offering are burned outside the camp. ¹²Therefore Jesus also suffered outside the gate, so that He might sanctify^J the people by His own blood. ¹³Let us then go to Him outside the camp, bearing His disgrace. ¹⁴For we do not have an enduring city here; instead, we seek the one to come. ¹⁵Therefore, through Him let us continually offer up to God a sacrifice of praise, that is, the fruit of our lips that confess His name. ¹⁶Don't neglect to do what is good and to share, for God is pleased with such sacrifices. ¹⁷Obey your leaders^K and submit to them, for they keep watch over your souls as those who will give an account, so

that they can do this with joy and not with grief, for that would be unprofitable for you. [18]Pray for us; for we are convinced that we have a clear conscience, wanting to conduct ourselves honorably in everything. [19]And I especially urge you to pray[A] that I may be restored to you very soon.

[20]Now may the God of peace, who brought up from the dead our Lord Jesus—the great Shepherd of the sheep—with the blood of the everlasting covenant, [21]equip[B] you with all that is good to do His will, working in us what is pleasing in His sight, through Jesus Christ. Glory belongs to Him forever and ever.[C] Amen.

[22]Brothers, I urge you to receive this message of exhortation, for I have written to you briefly. [23]Be aware that our brother Timothy has been released. If he comes soon enough, he will be with me when I see you. [24]Greet all your leaders and all the saints. Those who are from Italy greet you. [25]Grace be with all of you.

JAMES

1 James, a slave of God and of the Lord Jesus Christ:

To the 12 tribes in the Dispersion.[D]
Greetings.

[2]Consider it a great joy, my brothers, whenever you experience various trials, [3]knowing that the testing of your faith produces endurance. [4]But endurance must do its complete work, so that you may be mature and complete, lacking nothing.

[5]Now if any of you lacks wisdom, he should ask God, who gives to all generously and without criticizing, and it will be given to him. [6]But let him ask in faith without doubting. For the doubter is like the surging sea, driven and tossed by the wind. [7]That person should not expect to receive anything from the Lord. [8]An indecisive[E] man is unstable in all his ways.

[9]The brother of humble circumstances should boast in his exaltation, [10]but the one who is rich should boast in his humiliation because he will pass away like a flower of the field. [11]For the sun rises with its scorching heat and dries up the grass; its flower falls off, and its beautiful appearance is destroyed. In the same way, the rich man will wither away while pursuing his activities.

[12]A man who endures trials[F] is blessed, because when he passes the test he will receive the crown of life that God[G] has promised to those who love Him.

[13]No one undergoing a trial should say, "I am being tempted by God." For God is not tempted by evil,[H] and He Himself doesn't tempt anyone. [14]But each person is tempted when he is drawn away and enticed by his own evil desires. [15]Then after desire has conceived, it gives birth to sin, and when sin is fully grown, it gives birth to death.

[16]Don't be deceived, my dearly loved brothers. [17]Every generous act and every perfect gift is from above, coming down from the Father of lights; with Him there is no variation or shadow cast by turning. [18]By His own choice, He gave us a new birth by the message of truth[I] so that we would be the firstfruits of His creatures.

[19]My dearly loved brothers, understand this: Everyone must be quick to hear, slow to speak, and slow to anger, [20]for man's anger does not accomplish God's righteousness. [21]Therefore, ridding yourselves of all moral filth and evil,[J] humbly receive the implanted word, which is able to save you.[K]

[22]But be doers of the word and not hearers only, deceiving yourselves. [23]Because if anyone is a hearer of the word and not a doer, he is like a man looking at his own face[L] in a mirror. [24]For he looks at himself, goes away, and immediately forgets what kind of man he was. [25]But the one who looks intently into the perfect law of freedom and perseveres in

---

A13:19 Lit *to do this*   B13:21 Or *perfect*   C13:21 Other mss omit *and ever*   D1:1 Jewish people scattered throughout Gentile lands who spoke Gk and were influenced by Gk culture   E1:8 Or *A doubting,* or *A double-minded*   F1:12 Lit *trial,* used as a collective   G1:12 Other mss read *that the Lord*   H1:13 Or *evil persons,* or *evil things*   I1:18 = the gospel   J1:21 Lit *evil excess*   K1:21 Lit *save your souls*   L1:23 Lit *at the face of his birth* it, and is not a forgetful hearer but one who does good works—this person will be blessed in what he does.

²⁶If anyone^A thinks he is religious without controlling his tongue, then his religion is useless and he deceives himself. ²⁷Pure and undefiled religion before our^B God and Father is this: to look after orphans and widows in their distress and to keep oneself unstained by the world.

2 My brothers, do not show favoritism as you hold on to the faith in our glorious Lord Jesus Christ. ²For example, a man comes into your meeting wearing a gold ring and dressed in fine clothes, and a poor man dressed in dirty clothes also comes in. ³If you look with favor on the man wearing the fine clothes and say, "Sit here in a good place," and yet you say to the poor man, "Stand over there," or, "Sit here on the floor by my footstool," ⁴haven't you discriminated among yourselves and become judges with evil thoughts?

⁵Listen, my dear brothers: Didn't God choose the poor in this world to be rich in faith and heirs of the kingdom that He has promised to those who love Him? ⁶Yet you dishonored that poor man. Don't the rich oppress you and drag you into the courts? ⁷Don't they blaspheme the noble name that was pronounced over you at your baptism?

⁸Indeed, if you keep the royal law prescribed in the Scripture, **Love your neighbor as yourself**,^C you are doing well. ⁹But if you show favoritism, you commit sin and are convicted by the law as transgressors. ¹⁰For whoever keeps the entire law, yet fails in one point, is guilty of breaking it all. ¹¹For He who said, **Do not commit adultery**,^D also said, **Do not murder.**^E So if you do not commit adultery, but you do murder, you are a lawbreaker.

¹²Speak and act as those who will be judged by the law of freedom. ¹³For judgment is without mercy to the one who hasn't shown mercy. Mercy triumphs over judgment.

¹⁴What good is it, my brothers, if someone says he has faith^F but does not have works? Can his faith^F save him?

¹⁵If a brother or sister is without clothes and lacks daily food ¹⁶and one of you says to them, "Go in peace, keep warm, and eat well," but you don't give them what the body needs, what good is it? ¹⁷In the same way faith, if it doesn't have works, is dead by itself.

¹⁸But someone will say, "You have faith, and I have works."^G Show me your faith without works, and I will show you faith from my works.^H ¹⁹You believe that God is one; you do well. The demons also believe—and they shudder.

²⁰Foolish man! Are you willing to learn that faith without works is useless? ²¹Wasn't Abraham our father justified by works when he offered Isaac his son on the altar? ²²You see that faith was active together with his works, and by works, faith was perfected. ²³So the Scripture was fulfilled that says, **Abraham believed God, and it was credited to him for righteousness**,^I and he was called God's friend. ²⁴You see that a man is justified by works and not by faith alone. ²⁵And in the same way, wasn't Rahab the prostitute also justified by works when she received the messengers and sent them out by a different route? ²⁶For just as the body without the spirit is dead, so also faith without works is dead.

3 Not many should become teachers, my brothers, knowing that we will receive a stricter judgment, ²for we all stumble in many ways. If anyone does not stumble in what he says,^J he is a mature man who is also able to control his whole body.^K

³Now when we put bits into the mouths of horses to make them obey us, we also guide the whole animal.^L ⁴And consider ships: Though very large and driven by fierce winds, they are guided by a very small rudder wherever the will of the pilot directs. ⁵So too, though the tongue is a small part of the body, it boasts great things. Consider how large a forest a small fire ignites. ⁶And the tongue is a fire. The tongue, a world of unrighteousness, is placed among the parts of our bodies. It pollutes the whole body, sets the course of life on fire, and is set on fire by hell.

^A1:26 Other mss add *among you*   ^B1:27 Or *before the*   ^C2:8 Lv 19:18   ^D2:11 Ex 20:14; Dt 5:18   ^E2:11 Ex 20:13; Dt 5:17   ^F2:14 Or *Can faith*, or *Can that faith*, or *Can such faith*   ^G2:18 The quotation may end here or after v. 18b or v. 19.   ^H2:18 Other mss read *Show me your faith from your works, and from my works I will show you my faith.*   ^I2:23 Gn 15:6   ^J3:2 Lit *in word*   ^K3:2 Lit *to bridle the whole body*   ^L3:3 Lit *whole body*

[7]Every sea creature, reptile, bird, or animal is tamed and has been tamed by man, [8]but no man can tame the tongue. It is a restless evil, full of deadly poison. [9]We praise our[A] Lord and Father with it, and we curse men who are made in God's likeness with it. [10]Praising and cursing come out of the same mouth. My brothers, these things should not be this way. [11]Does a spring pour out sweet and bitter water from the same opening? [12]Can a fig tree produce olives, my brothers, or a grapevine produce figs? Neither can a saltwater spring yield fresh water.

[13]Who is wise and has understanding among you? He should show his works by good conduct with wisdom's gentleness. [14]But if you have bitter envy and selfish ambition in your heart, don't brag and deny the truth. [15]Such wisdom does not come from above but is earthly, unspiritual, demonic. [16]For where envy and selfish ambition exist, there is disorder and every kind of evil. [17]But the wisdom from above is first pure, then peace-loving, gentle, compliant, full of mercy and good fruits, without favoritism and hypocrisy. [18]And the fruit of righteousness is sown in peace by those who cultivate peace.

4 What is the source of wars and fights among you? Don't they come from the cravings that are at war within you?[B] [2]You desire and do not have. You murder and covet and cannot obtain. You fight and war. You do not have because you do not ask. [3]You ask and don't receive because you ask with wrong motives, so that you may spend it on your evil desires.

[4]Adulteresses![C,D] Don't you know that friendship with the world is hostility toward God? So whoever wants to be the world's friend becomes God's enemy. [5]Or do you think it's without reason the Scripture says that the Spirit who lives in us yearns jealously?[E]

[6]But He gives greater grace. Therefore He says:

> **God resists the proud,**
> **but gives grace to the humble.**[F]

[7]Therefore, submit to God. But resist the Devil, and he will flee from you. [8]Draw near to God, and He will draw near to you. Cleanse your hands, sinners, and purify your hearts, double-minded people! [9]Be miserable and mourn and weep. Your laughter must change to mourning and your joy to sorrow. [10]Humble yourselves before the Lord, and He will exalt you.

[11]Don't criticize one another, brothers. He who criticizes a brother or judges his brother criticizes the law and judges the law. But if you judge the law, you are not a doer of the law but a judge. [12]There is one lawgiver and judge[G] who is able to save and to destroy. But who are you to judge your neighbor?

[13]Come now, you who say, "Today or tomorrow we will travel to such and such a city and spend a year there and do business and make a profit." [14]You don't even know what tomorrow will bring—what your life will be! For you are like smoke that appears for a little while, then vanishes.

[15]Instead, you should say, "If the Lord wills, we will live and do this or that." [16]But as it is, you boast in your arrogance. All such boasting is evil. [17]So it is a sin for the person who knows to do what is good and doesn't do it.

5 Come now, you rich people! Weep and wail over the miseries that are coming on you. [2]Your wealth is ruined and your clothes are moth-eaten. [3]Your silver and gold are corroded, and their corrosion will be a witness against you and will eat your flesh like fire. You stored up treasure in the last days! [4]Look! The pay that you withheld from the workers who reaped your fields cries out, and the outcry of the harvesters has reached the ears of the Lord of Hosts.[H] [5]You have lived luxuriously on the land and have indulged yourselves. You have fattened your hearts for[I] the day of slaughter. [6]You have condemned—you have murdered—the righteous man; he does not resist you.

[7]Therefore, brothers, be patient until the Lord's coming. See how the farmer waits for the precious fruit of the earth and is patient

with it until it receives the early and the late rains. [8] You also must be patient. Strengthen your hearts, because the Lord's coming is near.

[9] Brothers, do not complain about one another, so that you will not be judged. Look, the judge stands at the door!

[10] Brothers, take the prophets who spoke in the Lord's name as an example of suffering and patience. [11] See, we count as blessed those who have endured.[A] You have heard of Job's endurance and have seen the outcome from the Lord. The Lord is very compassionate and merciful.

[12] Now above all, my brothers, do not swear, either by heaven or by earth or with any other oath. Your "yes" must be "yes," and your "no" must be "no," so that you won't fall under judgment.[B]

[13] Is anyone among you suffering? He should pray. Is anyone cheerful? He should sing praises. [14] Is anyone among you sick? He should call for the elders of the church, and they should pray over him after anointing him with olive oil in the name of the Lord. [15] The prayer of faith will save the sick person, and the Lord will restore him to health; if he has committed sins, he will be forgiven. [16] Therefore, confess your sins to one another and pray for one another, so that you may be healed. The urgent request of a righteous person is very powerful in its effect. [17] Elijah was a man with a nature like ours; yet he prayed earnestly that it would not rain, and for three years and six months it did not rain on the land. [18] Then he prayed again, and the sky gave rain and the land produced its fruit.

[19] My brothers, if any among you strays from the truth, and someone turns him back, [20] let him know that whoever turns a sinner from the error of his way will save his life from death and cover a multitude of sins.

1 PETER

1 Peter, an apostle of Jesus Christ:
   To the temporary residents dispersed[C] in Pontus, Galatia, Cappadocia, Asia, and Bithynia, chosen [2] according to the foreknowledge of God the Father and set apart by the Spirit for obedience and for sprinkling with the blood of Jesus Christ.

May grace and peace be multiplied to you.

[3] Praise the God and Father of our Lord Jesus Christ. According to His great mercy, He has given us a new birth into a living hope through the resurrection of Jesus Christ from the dead [4] and into an inheritance that is imperishable, uncorrupted, and unfading, kept in heaven for you. [5] You are being protected by God's power through faith for a salvation that is ready to be revealed in the last time. [6] You rejoice in this,[D] though now for a short time you have had to struggle in various trials [7] so that the genuineness of your faith—more valuable than gold, which perishes though refined by fire—may result in[E] praise, glory, and honor at the revelation of Jesus Christ. [8] You love Him, though you have not seen Him. And though not seeing Him now, you believe in Him and rejoice with inexpressible and glorious joy, [9] because you are receiving the goal of your[F] faith, the salvation of your souls.[G]

[10] Concerning this salvation, the prophets who prophesied about the grace that would come to you searched and carefully investigated. [11] They inquired into what time or what circumstances[H] the Spirit of Christ within them was indicating when He testified in advance to the messianic sufferings[I] and the glories that would follow.[J] [12] It was revealed to them that they were not serving themselves but you. These things have now been announced to you through those who preached the gospel to you by the Holy Spirit sent from heaven. Angels desire to look into these things.

A5:11 Or have persevered   B5:12 Other mss read fall into hypocrisy   C1:1 Jewish people scattered throughout Gentile lands who spoke Gk and were influenced by Gk culture   D1:6 Or In this fact rejoice   E1:7 Lit may be found for   F1:9 Other mss read our, or they omit the possessive pronoun   G1:9 Or your lives   H1:11 Or inquired about the person or time   I1:11 Or the sufferings of Christ   J1:11 Lit the glories after that

¹³Therefore, with your minds ready for action,[A] be serious and set your hope completely on the grace to be brought to you at the revelation of Jesus Christ. ¹⁴As obedient children, do not be conformed to the desires of your former ignorance. ¹⁵But as the One who called you is holy, you also are to be holy in all your conduct; ¹⁶for it is written, **Be holy, because I am holy.**[B]

¹⁷And if you address as Father the One who judges impartially based on each one's work, you are to conduct yourselves in fear during the time of your temporary residence. ¹⁸For you know that you were redeemed from your empty way of life inherited from the fathers, not with perishable things like silver or gold, ¹⁹but with the precious blood of Christ, like that of a lamb without defect or blemish. ²⁰He was chosen[C] before the foundation of the world but was revealed at the end of the times for you ²¹who through Him are believers in God, who raised Him from the dead and gave Him glory, so that your faith and hope are in God.

²²By obedience to the truth,[D] having purified yourselves[E] for sincere love of the brothers, love one another earnestly[F] from a pure[G] heart, ²³since you have been born again—not of perishable seed but of imperishable—through the living and enduring word of God. ²⁴For

> **All flesh is like grass,**
> **and all its glory like a flower**
> **of the grass.**
> **The grass withers,**
> **and the flower falls,**
> ²⁵ **but the word of the Lord**
> **endures forever.**[H]

And this is the word that was preached as the gospel to you.

2 So rid yourselves of all malice, all deceit, hypocrisy, envy, and all slander. ²Like newborn infants, desire the pure spiritual milk, so that you may grow by it for your salvation,[I] ³since **you have tasted that the Lord is good.**[J] ⁴Coming to Him, a living stone—rejected by men but chosen and valuable to God— ⁵you yourselves, as living stones, are being built into a spiritual house for a holy priesthood to offer spiritual sacrifices acceptable to God through Jesus Christ. ⁶For it is contained in Scripture:

> **Look! I lay a stone in Zion,**
> **a chosen**
> **and honored[K] cornerstone,[L]**
> **and the one who believes**
> **in Him**
> **will never be put to shame!**[M,N]

⁷So honor will come to you who believe, but for the unbelieving,

> **The stone that the builders**
> **rejected—**
> **this One has become**
> **the cornerstone,**[O]

⁸and

> **A stone to stumble over,**[P]
> **and a rock to trip over.**[Q,R]

They stumble because they disobey the message; they were destined for this.

> ⁹ But you are **a chosen race,**[S,T]
> **a royal priesthood,**[U]
> **a holy nation,**[V] **a people**
> **for His possession,**[W]
> **so that you may proclaim**
> **the praises**[X,Y]
> of the One who called you
> out of darkness
> into His marvelous light.
> ¹⁰ Once you were not a people,
> but now you are God's people;
> you had not received mercy,
> but now you have received mercy.

¹¹Dear friends, I urge you as strangers and temporary residents to abstain from fleshly desires that war against you.[Z] ¹²Conduct yourselves honorably among the Gentiles,[AA]

A1:13 Lit *Therefore, when you have the loins of your mind girded* **B1:16** Lv 11:44-45; 19:2; 20:7 **C1:20** Or *foreknown* **D1:22** Other mss add *through the Spirit* **E1:22** Or *purified your souls* **F 1:22** Or *intensely* **G 1:22** Other mss omit *pure* **H1:24-25** Is 40:6-8 **I2:2** Other mss omit *in your salvation* **J2:3** Ps 34:8 **K2:6** Or *valuable* **L2:6** Lit *head of the corner* **M2:6** Or *be disappointed* **N2:6** Is 28:16 LXX **O2:7** Ps 118:22 **P2:8** Or *a stone causing stumbling* **Q2:8** Or *a rock to trip over* **R2:8** Is 8:14 **S2:9** Or *generation, or nation* **T2:9** Dt 7:6; 10:15; Is 43:20 LXX **U2:9** Ex 19:6; 23:22 LXX; Is 61:6 **V2:9** Ex 19:6; 23:22 LXX **W2:9** Ex 19:5; 23:22 LXX; Dt 4:20; 7:6; Is 43:21 LXX **X2:9** Or *the mighty deeds* **Y2:9** Is 42:12; 43:21 **Z2:11** Or *against the soul* **AA2:12** Or *among the nations, or among the pagans* so that in a case where they speak against you as those who do what is evil, they will, by observing your good works, glorify God on the day of visitation.[A]

[13] Submit to every human authority[B] because of the Lord, whether to the Emperor[C] as the supreme authority [14] or to governors as those sent out by him to punish those who do what is evil and to praise those who do what is good. [15] For it is God's will that you silence the ignorance of foolish people by doing good. [16] As God's slaves, live as free people, but don't use your freedom as a way to conceal evil. [17] Honor everyone. Love the brotherhood. Fear God. Honor the Emperor.[C]

[18] Household slaves, submit with all fear to your masters, not only to the good and gentle but also to the cruel.[D] [19] For it brings favor[E] if, mindful of God's will,[F,G] someone endures grief from suffering unjustly. [20] For what credit is there if you sin and are punished, and you endure it? But when you do what is good and suffer, if you endure it, this brings favor with God.

[21] For you were called to this,
   because Christ also suffered for you,
   leaving you an example,
   so that you should follow
      in His steps.
[22] He **did not commit sin,
   and no deceit was found
   in His mouth;**[H]
[23] when He was reviled,
   He did not revile in return;
   when He was suffering,
   He did not threaten
   but entrusted Himself to the One
      who judges justly.
[24] He Himself bore our sins
   in His body on the tree,
   so that, having died to sins,
   we might live for righteousness;
   you have been healed by His wounds.[I]
[25] For you **were like sheep
   going astray,**[J]
   but you have now returned

to the Shepherd and Guardian[K]
   of your souls.

3 In the same way, wives, submit yourselves to your own husbands so that, even if some disobey the Christian message, they may be won over[L] without a message by the way their wives live [2] when they observe your pure, reverent lives. [3] Your beauty should not consist of outward things like elaborate hairstyles and the wearing of gold ornaments[M] or fine clothes. [4] Instead, it should consist of what is inside[N] the heart with the imperishable quality of a gentle and quiet spirit, which is very valuable in God's eyes. [5] For in the past, the holy women who put their hope in God also beautified themselves in this way, submitting to their own husbands, [6] just as Sarah obeyed Abraham, calling him lord. You have become her children when you do what is good and are not frightened by anything alarming.

[7] Husbands, in the same way, live with your wives with an understanding of their weaker nature[O] yet showing them honor as coheirs of the grace of life, so that your prayers will not be hindered.

[8] Now finally, all of you should be like-minded and sympathetic, should love believers,[P] and be compassionate and humble,[Q] [9] not paying back evil for evil or insult for insult but, on the contrary, giving a blessing, since you were called for this, so that you can inherit a blessing.

[10]   For **the one who wants to love life
      and to see good days
      must keep his tongue from evil
      and his lips from speaking deceit,**
[11]   **and he must turn away from evil
      and do what is good.
      He must seek peace and pursue it,**
[12]   **because the eyes of the Lord are
         on the righteous
      and His ears are open
         to their request.
      But the face of the Lord is against
      those who do what is evil.**[R]

¹³And who will harm[A] you if you are deeply committed to what is good?[B] ¹⁴But even if you should suffer for righteousness, you are blessed. **Do not fear what they fear or be disturbed,**[C] ¹⁵but honor[D] the Messiah[E] as Lord in your hearts. Always be ready to give a defense to anyone who asks you for a reason[F] for the hope that is in you. ¹⁶However, do this with gentleness and respect, keeping your conscience clear,[G,H] so that when you are accused,[I] those who denounce your Christian life[J] will be put to shame. ¹⁷For it is better to suffer for doing good, if that should be God's will,[K] than for doing evil.

¹⁸   For Christ also suffered for sins
        once for all,[L]
        the righteous for the unrighteous,[M]
        that He might bring you[N] to God,
        after being put to death
          in the fleshly realm[O]
        but made alive in the spiritual realm.[P]

¹⁹In that state[Q] He also went and made a proclamation to the spirits in prison[R] ²⁰who in the past were disobedient, when God patiently waited in the days of Noah while an ark was being prepared. In it a few—that is, eight people[S]—were saved through water. ²¹Baptism, which corresponds to this, now saves you (not the removal of the filth of the flesh, but the pledge[T] of a good conscience toward God) through the resurrection of Jesus Christ. ²²Now that He has gone into heaven, He is at God's right hand with angels, authorities, and powers subject to Him.

4 Therefore, since Christ suffered[U] in the flesh,[V] equip[W] yourselves also with the same resolve[X]—because the one who suffered in the flesh has finished with sin[Y]— ²in order to live the remaining time in the flesh, no longer for human desires,[Z] but for God's will. ³For there has already been enough time spent in doing what the pagans choose to do:[AA] carrying on in unrestrained behavior, evil desires, drunkenness, orgies, carousing, and lawless idolatry. ⁴So they are surprised that you don't plunge with them into the same flood[AB] of wild living—and they slander you. ⁵They will give an account to the One who stands ready to judge the living and the dead. ⁶For this reason the gospel was also preached to those who are now dead, so that, although they might be judged by men in the fleshly realm,[O] they might live by God in the spiritual realm.[AC]

⁷Now the end of all things is near; therefore, be serious and disciplined for prayer. ⁸Above all, maintain an intense love for each other, since **love covers a multitude of sins.**[AD] ⁹Be hospitable to one another without complaining. ¹⁰Based on the gift each one has received, use it to serve others, as good managers of the varied grace of God. ¹¹If anyone speaks, it should be as one who speaks God's words; if anyone serves, it should be from the strength God provides, so that God may be glorified through Jesus Christ in everything. To Him belong the glory and the power forever and ever. Amen.

¹²Dear friends, don't be surprised when the fiery ordeal[AE] comes among you to test you as if something unusual were happening to you. ¹³Instead, rejoice as you share in the sufferings of the Messiah, so that you may also rejoice with great joy at the revelation of His glory. ¹⁴If you are ridiculed for the name of Christ, you are blessed, because the Spirit of glory and of God rests on you.[AF] ¹⁵None of you, however, should suffer as a murderer, a thief, an evildoer, or a meddler.[AG] ¹⁶But if anyone suffers as a "Christian," he should not be ashamed but should glorify God in having that name. ¹⁷For the time has come for judgment to begin with God's household, and if it begins with us, what will the outcome be for those who disobey the gospel of God?

A3:13 Or mistreat, or do evil to   B3:13 Or you are partisans for the good; lit you are zealots   C3:14 Is 8:12   D3:15 Or sanctify; lit set apart   E3:15 Other mss read set God   F3:15 Or who demands of you an accounting   G3:16 Lit good   H3:16 Or keeping a clear conscience   I3:16 Other mss read when they speak against you as evildoers   J3:16 Lit your good behavior in Christ   K3:17 Lit if the will of God should will   L3:18 Other mss read died for sins on our behalf; other mss read died for our sins; other mss read died for sins on your behalf   M3:18 Or the Righteous One in the place of the unrighteous many   N3:18 Other mss read us   O3:18; 4:6 Or in the flesh   P3:18 Or in the spirit, or in the Spirit   Q3:19 Or In whom, or At that time, or In which   R3:19 Perhaps fallen supernatural beings or angels; 2Pt 2:4; Jd 6   S3:20 Lit souls   T3:21 Or the appeal   U4:1 Other mss read suffered for us   V4:1 The phrase "in the flesh" probably means in human experience.   W4:1 Or arm   X4:1 Or perspective, or attitude   Y4:1 Or the one who has suffered in the flesh has ceased from sin   Z4:2 Lit for desires of human beings   AA4:3 Or Gentiles   AB4:4 Lit you don't run with them into the same pouring out   AC4:6 Or in the spirit   AD4:8 Pr 10:12   AE4:12 Lit the burning   AF4:14 Other mss add He is blasphemed because of them, but He is glorified because of you.   AG4:15 Or as one who defrauds others

¹⁸ And **if a righteous person is saved
with difficulty,
what will become of the ungodly
and the sinner?**ᴬ

¹⁹So those who suffer according to God's will should, while doing what is good, entrust themselves to a faithful Creator.

5 Therefore, as a fellow elder and witness to the sufferings of the Messiah and also a participant in the glory about to be revealed, I exhort the elders among you: ²Shepherd God's flock among you, not overseeingᴮ out of compulsion but freely, according to God's will;ᶜ not for the money but eagerly; ³not lording it over those entrusted to you, but being examples to the flock. ⁴And when the chief Shepherd appears, you will receive the unfading crown of glory.

⁵In the same way, you younger men, be subject to the elders. And all of you clothe yourselves withᴰ humility toward one another, because

**God resists the proud
but gives grace to the humble.**ᴱ

⁶Humble yourselves, therefore, under the mighty hand of God, so that He may exalt you at the proper time,ᶠ ⁷casting all your care on Him, because He cares about you.

⁸Be serious! Be alert! Your adversary the Devil is prowling around like a roaring lion, looking for anyone he can devour. ⁹Resist him and be firm in the faith, knowing that the same sufferings are being experienced by your fellow believers throughout the world.

¹⁰Now the God of all grace, who called you to His eternal glory in Christ Jesus, will personallyᴳ restore, establish, strengthen, and support you after you have suffered a little.ᴴ ¹¹The dominionᴵ belongs to Him forever.ᴶ Amen.

¹²I have written you this brief letter through Silvanusᴷ (I know him to be a faithful brother) to encourage you and to testify that this is the true grace of God. Take your stand in it! ¹³The church in Babylon,ᴸ also chosen, sends you greetings, as does Mark, my son. ¹⁴Greet one another with a kiss of love. Peace to all of you who are in Christ.ᴹ

2 PETER

1 Simeonᴺ Peter, a slave and an apostle of Jesus Christ:

To those who have obtained a faith of equal privilege with oursᴼ through the righteousness of our God and Savior Jesus Christ.

²May grace and peace be multiplied to you through the knowledge of God and of Jesus our Lord.

³Hisᴾ divine power has given us everything required for life and godliness through the knowledge of Him who called us by� His own glory and goodness. ⁴By these He has given us very great and precious promises, so that through them you may share in the divine nature, escaping the corruption that is in the world because of evil desires. ⁵For this very reason, make every effort to supplement your faith with goodness, goodness with

knowledge, ⁶knowledge with self-control, self-control with endurance, endurance with godliness, ⁷godliness with brotherly affection, and brotherly affection with love. ⁸For if these qualities are yours and are increasing, they will keep you from being useless or unfruitful in the knowledge of our Lord Jesus Christ. ⁹The person who lacks these things is blind and shortsighted and has forgotten the cleansing from his past sins. ¹⁰Therefore, brothers, make every effort to confirm your calling and election, because if you do these things you will never stumble. ¹¹For in this way, entry into the eternal kingdom of our Lord and Savior Jesus Christ will be richly supplied to you.

¹²Therefore I will always remind you about these things, even though you know them

ᴬ4:18 Pr 11:31 LXX   ᴮ5:2 Other mss omit *overseeing*   ᶜ5:2 Other mss omit *according to God's will*   ᴰ5:5 Lit *you tie around yourselves*
ᴱ5:5 Pr 3:34 LXX   ᶠ5:6 Lit *in time*   ᴳ5:10 Lit *Himself*   ᴴ5:10 Or *a little while, or to a small extent*   ᴵ5:11 Other mss read *dominion and glory*;
other mss read *glory and dominion*   ᴶ5:11 Other mss read *forever and ever*   ᴷ5:12 Or *Silas*; Ac 15:22-32; 16:19-40; 17:1-16   ᴸ5:13 Probably
refers to Rome   ᴹ5:14 Other mss read *Christ Jesus. Amen.*   ᴺ1:1 Other mss read *Simon*   ᴼ1:1 Or *obtained a faith of the same kind as ours*
ᴾ1:3 Lit *As His*   globe1:3 Or *to*

and are established in the truth you have. [13]I consider it right, as long as I am in this bodily tent,[A] to wake you up with a reminder, [14]knowing that I will soon lay aside my tent, as our Lord Jesus Christ has also shown me. [15]And I will also make every effort that you may be able to recall these things at any time after my departure.[B]

[16]For we did not follow cleverly contrived myths when we made known to you the power and coming of our Lord Jesus Christ; instead, we were eyewitnesses of His majesty. [17]For when He received honor and glory from God the Father, a voice came to Him from the Majestic Glory:

> This is My beloved Son.[C]
> I take delight in Him![D]

[18]And we heard this voice when it came from heaven while we were with Him on the holy mountain. [19]So we have the prophetic word strongly confirmed. You will do well to pay attention to it, as to a lamp shining in a dismal place, until the day dawns and the morning star rises in your hearts. [20]First of all, you should know this: No prophecy of Scripture comes from one's own interpretation, [21]because no prophecy ever came by the will of man; instead, men spoke from God as they were moved by the Holy Spirit.

2 But there were also false prophets among the people, just as there will be false teachers among you. They will secretly bring in destructive heresies, even denying the Master who bought them, and will bring swift destruction on themselves. [2]Many will follow their unrestrained ways, and the way of truth will be blasphemed because of them. [3]They will exploit you in their greed with deceptive words. Their condemnation, pronounced long ago, is not idle, and their destruction does not sleep.

[4]For if God didn't spare the angels who sinned but threw them down into Tartarus[E] and delivered them to be kept in chains[F] of darkness until judgment; [5]and if He didn't spare the ancient world, but protected Noah,

a preacher of righteousness, and seven others,[G] when He brought a flood on the world of the ungodly; [6]and if He reduced the cities of Sodom and Gomorrah to ashes and condemned them to ruin,[H] making them an example to those who were going to be ungodly;[I] [7]and if He rescued righteous Lot, distressed by the unrestrained behavior of the immoral [8](for as he lived among them, that righteous man tormented himself day by day with the lawless deeds he saw and heard)— [9]then the Lord knows how to rescue the godly from trials and to keep the unrighteous under punishment until the day of judgment, [10]especially those who follow the polluting desires of the flesh and despise authority.

Bold, arrogant people! They do not tremble when they blaspheme the glorious ones; [11]however, angels, who are greater in might and power, do not bring a slanderous charge against them before the Lord.[J] [12]But these people, like irrational animals—creatures of instinct born to be caught and destroyed—speak blasphemies about things they don't understand, and in their destruction they too will be destroyed, [13]suffering harm as the payment for unrighteousness. They consider it a pleasure to carouse in the daytime. They are spots and blemishes, delighting in their deceptions[K] as they feast with you. [14]They have eyes full of adultery and are always looking for sin. They seduce unstable people and have hearts trained in greed. Children under a curse! [15]They have gone astray by abandoning the straight path and have followed the path of Balaam, the son of Bosor,[L] who loved the wages of unrighteousness [16]but received a rebuke for his transgression: A donkey that could not talk spoke with a human voice and restrained the prophet's irrationality.

[17]These people are springs without water, mists driven by a whirlwind. The gloom of darkness has been reserved for them. [18]For by uttering boastful, empty words, they seduce, with fleshly desires and debauchery, people who have barely escaped[M] from those who

---

[A]1:13 = Peter's body   [B]1:15 Or my death   [C]1:17 Other mss read My Son, My Beloved   [D]1:17 = Christ's transfiguration; Mt 17:5   [E]2:4 = Gk name for a place of divine punishment in the underworld.   [F]2:4 Other mss read in pits   [G]2:5 Lit righteousness, as the eighth   [H]2:6 Other mss omit to ruin   [I]2:6 Other mss read an example of what is going to happen to the ungodly   [J]2:11 Other mss read them from the Lord   [K]2:13 Other mss read delighting in the love feasts   [L]2:15 Other mss read Beor   [M]2:18 Or people who are barely escaping live in error. [19] They promise them freedom, but they themselves are slaves of corruption, since people are enslaved to whatever defeats them. [20] For if, having escaped the world's impurity through the knowledge of our Lord and Savior Jesus Christ, they are again entangled in these things and defeated, the last state is worse for them than the first. [21] For it would have been better for them not to have known the way of righteousness than, after knowing it, to turn back from the holy command delivered to them. [22] It has happened to them according to the true proverb: **A dog returns to its own vomit,**[A] and, "a sow, after washing itself, wallows in the mud."

3 Dear friends, this is now the second letter I have written to you; in both letters, I want to develop a genuine understanding with a reminder, [2] so that you can remember the words previously spoken by the holy prophets and the command of our Lord and Savior given through your apostles. [3] First, be aware of this: Scoffers will come in the last days to scoff, living according to their own desires, [4] saying, "Where is the promise of His coming? Ever since the fathers fell asleep, all things continue as they have been since the beginning of creation." [5] They willfully ignore this: Long ago the heavens and the earth were brought about from water and through water by the word of God. [6] Through these waters the world of that time perished when it was flooded. [7] But by the same word, the present heavens and earth are stored up for fire, being kept until the day of judgment and destruction of ungodly men.

[8] Dear friends, don't let this one thing escape you: With the Lord one day is like a thousand years, and a thousand years like one day. [9] The Lord does not delay His promise, as some understand delay, but is patient with you, not wanting any to perish but all to come to repentance.

[10] But the Day of the Lord will come like a thief;[B] on that day the heavens will pass away with a loud noise, the elements will burn and be dissolved, and the earth and the works on it will be disclosed.[C] [11] Since all these things are to be destroyed in this way, it is clear what sort of people you should be in holy conduct and godliness [12] as you wait for and earnestly desire the coming[D] of the day of God. The heavens will be on fire and be dissolved because of it, and the elements will melt with the heat. [13] But based on His promise, we wait for the new heavens and a new earth, where righteousness will dwell.

[14] Therefore, dear friends, while you wait for these things, make every effort to be found at peace with Him without spot or blemish. [15] Also, regard the patience of our Lord as an opportunity for salvation, just as our dear brother Paul has written to you according to the wisdom given to him. [16] He speaks about these things in all his letters in which there are some matters that are hard to understand. The untaught and unstable twist them to their own destruction, as they also do with the rest of the Scriptures.

[17] Therefore, dear friends, since you know this in advance, be on your guard, so that you are not led away by the error of lawless people and fall from your own stability. [18] But grow in the grace and knowledge of our Lord and Savior Jesus Christ. To Him be the glory both now and to the day of eternity.[E] Amen.[F]

A2:22 Pr 26:11   B3:10 Other mss add *in the night*   C3:10 Other mss read *will be burned up*   D3:12 Or *and speed the coming*   E3:18 Or *now and forever*   F3:18 Other mss omit *Amen.*

1 JOHN

1 What was from the beginning,
what we have heard,
what we have seen with our eyes,
what we have observed
and have touched with our hands,
concerning the Word of life—
2 that life was revealed,
and we have seen it
and we testify and declare to you
the eternal life that was
with the Father
and was revealed to us—
3 what we have seen and heard
we also declare to you,
so that you may have fellowship
along with us;
and indeed our fellowship is
with the Father
and with His Son Jesus Christ.
4 We are writing these things[A]
so that our[B] joy may be complete.

5 Now this is the message we have heard from Him and declare to you: God is light, and there is absolutely no darkness in Him. 6 If we say, "We have fellowship with Him," yet we walk in darkness, we are lying and are not practicing[C] the truth. 7 But if we walk in the light as He Himself is in the light, we have fellowship with one another, and the blood of Jesus His Son cleanses us from all sin. 8 If we say, "We have no sin," we are deceiving ourselves, and the truth is not in us. 9 If we confess our sins, He is faithful and righteous to forgive us our sins and to cleanse us from all unrighteousness. 10 If we say, "We don't have any sin," we make Him a liar, and His word is not in us.

2 My little children, I am writing you these things so that you may not sin. But if anyone does sin, we have an advocate with the Father—Jesus Christ the Righteous One. 2 He Himself is the propitiation for our sins, and not only for ours, but also for those of the whole world.

3 This is how we are sure that we have come to know Him: by keeping His commands.

4 The one who says, "I have come to know Him," yet doesn't keep His commands, is a liar, and the truth is not in him. 5 But whoever keeps His word, truly in him the love of God is perfected.[D] This is how we know we are in Him: 6 The one who says he remains in Him should walk just as He walked.

7 Dear friends, I am not writing you a new command but an old command that you have had from the beginning. The old command is the message you have heard. 8 Yet I am writing you a new command, which is true in Him and in you, because the darkness is passing away and the true light is already shining.

9 The one who says he is in the light but hates his brother is in the darkness until now. 10 The one who loves his brother remains in the light, and there is no cause for stumbling in him.[E] 11 But the one who hates his brother is in the darkness, walks in the darkness, and doesn't know where he's going, because the darkness has blinded his eyes.

12 I am writing to you, little children,
because your sins have
been forgiven
because of Jesus' name.
13 I am writing to you, fathers,
because you have come to know
the One who is
from the beginning.
I am writing to you, young men,
because you have had victory
over the evil one.
14 I have written to you, children,
because you have come to know
the Father.
I have written to you, fathers,
because you have come to know
the One who is
from the beginning.
I have written to you, young men,
because you are strong,
God's word remains in you,
and you have had victory
over the evil one.

A1:4 Other mss add to you   B1:4 Other mss read your   C1:6 Or not living according to   D2:5 Or truly completed   E2:10 Or in it

Turn to page 84 and find John 3:16.

¹⁵ Do not love the world or the things that belong to^A the world. If anyone loves the world, love for the Father is not in him. ¹⁶ For everything that belongs to^B the world—the lust of the flesh, the lust of the eyes, and the pride in one's lifestyle—is not from the Father, but is from the world. ¹⁷ And the world with its lust is passing away, but the one who does God's will remains forever.

¹⁸ Children, it is the last hour. And as you have heard, "Antichrist is coming," even now many antichrists have come. We know from this that it is the last hour. ¹⁹ They went out from us, but they did not belong to us; for if they had belonged to us, they would have remained with us. However, they went out so that it might be made clear that none of them belongs to us.

²⁰ But you have an anointing from the Holy One, and all of you have knowledge.^C ²¹ I have not written to you because you don't know the truth, but because you do know it, and because no lie comes from the truth. ²² Who is the liar, if not the one who denies that Jesus is the Messiah? This one is the antichrist: the one who denies the Father and the Son. ²³ No one who denies the Son can have the Father; he who confesses the Son has the Father as well.

²⁴ What you have heard from the beginning must remain in you. If what you have heard from the beginning remains in you, then you will remain in the Son and in the Father. ²⁵ And this is the promise that He Himself made to us: eternal life. ²⁶ I have written these things to you about those who are trying to deceive you.

²⁷ The anointing you received from Him remains in you, and you don't need anyone to teach you. Instead, His anointing teaches you about all things and is true and is not a lie; just as He has taught you, remain in Him.

²⁸ So now, little children, remain in Him, so that when He appears we may have boldness and not be ashamed before Him at His coming. ²⁹ If you know that He is righteous, you know this as well: Everyone who does

what is right has been born of Him. ¹ Look at how great a love^D the Father has given us that we should be called God's children. And we are! The reason the world does not know us is that it didn't know Him. ² Dear friends, we are God's children now, and what we will be has not yet been revealed. We know that when He appears, we will be like Him because we will see Him as He is. ³ And everyone who has this hope in Him purifies himself just as He is pure.

⁴ Everyone who commits sin also breaks the law;^E sin is the breaking of law. ⁵ You know that He was revealed so that He might take away sins,^F and there is no sin in Him. ⁶ Everyone who remains in Him does not sin;^G everyone who^H sins has not seen Him or known Him.

⁷ Little children, let no one deceive you! The one who does what is right is righteous, just as He is righteous. ⁸ The one who commits^I sin is of the Devil, for the Devil has sinned from the beginning. The Son of God was revealed for this purpose: to destroy the Devil's works. ⁹ Everyone who has been born of God does not sin,^J because His^K seed remains in him; he is not able to sin,^L because he has been born of God. ¹⁰ This is how God's children—and the Devil's children—are made evident. Whoever does not do what is right is not of God, especially the one who does not love his brother. ¹¹ For this is the message you have heard from the beginning: We should love one another, ¹² unlike Cain, who was of the evil one and murdered^M his brother. And why did he murder him? Because his works were evil, and his brother's were righteous. ¹³ Do not be surprised, brothers, if the world hates you. ¹⁴ We know that we have passed from death to life because we love our brothers. The one who does not love remains in death. ¹⁵ Everyone who hates his brother is a murderer, and you know that no murderer has eternal life residing in him.

¹⁶ This is how we have come to know love: He laid down His life for us. We should also lay down our lives for our brothers. ¹⁷ If anyone has this world's goods and sees his

brother in need but closes his eyes to his need—how can God's love reside in him?

¹⁸Little children, we must not love with word or speech, but with truth and action. ¹⁹This is how we will know we belong to the truth and will convince our conscience in His presence, ²⁰even if our conscience condemns us, that God is greater than our conscience, and He knows all things.

²¹Dear friends, if our conscience doesn't condemn us, we have confidence before God ²²and can receive whatever we ask from Him because we keep His commands and do what is pleasing in His sight. ²³Now this is His command: that we believe in the name of His Son Jesus Christ, and love one another as He commanded us. ²⁴The one who keeps His commands remains in Him, and He in him. And the way we know that He remains in us is from the Spirit He has given us.

4 Dear friends, do not believe every spirit, but test the spirits to determine if they are from God, because many false prophets have gone out into the world.

²This is how you know the Spirit of God: Every spirit who confesses that Jesus Christ hasᴬ come in the flesh is from God. ³But every spirit who does not confess Jesusᴮ is not from God. This is the spirit of the antichrist; you have heard that he is coming, and he is already in the world now.

⁴You are from God, little children, and you have conquered them, because the One who is in you is greater than the one who is in the world. ⁵They are from the world. Therefore what they say is from the world, and the world listens to them. ⁶We are from God. Anyone who knows God listens to us; anyone who is not from God does not listen to us. From this we know the Spirit of truth and the spirit of deception.

⁷Dear friends, let us love one another, because love is from God, and everyone who loves has been born of God and knows God. ⁸The one who does not love does not know God, because God is love. ⁹God's love was revealed among us in this way:ᶜ God sent His One and Only Son into the world so that we might live through Him. ¹⁰Love consists in this: not that we loved God, but that He loved us and sent His Son to be theᴰ propitiation for our sins. ¹¹Dear friends, if God loved us in this way, we also must love one another. ¹²No one has ever seen God.ᴱ If we love one another, God remains inᶠ us and His love is perfected in us.

¹³This is how we know that we remain in Him and He in us: He has given assurance to us from His Spirit. ¹⁴And we have seen and we testify that the Father has sent His Son as the world's Savior. ¹⁵Whoever confessesᴳ that Jesus is the Son of God—God remains in him and he in God. ¹⁶And we have come to know and to believe the love that God has for us. God is love, and the one who remains in love remains in God, and God remains in him.

¹⁷In this, love is perfected with us so that we may have confidence in the day of judgment, for we are as He is in this world. ¹⁸There is no fear in love; instead, perfect love drives out fear, because fear involves punishment.ᴴ So the one who fears has not reached perfection in love. ¹⁹We loveᴵ because He first loved us.

²⁰If anyone says, "I love God," yet hates his brother, he is a liar. For the person who does not love his brother he has seen cannot love the God he has not seen.ᴶ ²¹And we have this command from Him: The one who loves God must also love his brother.

5 Everyone who believes that Jesus is the Messiah has been born of God, and everyone who loves the Father also loves the one born of Him. ²This is how we know that we love God's children when we love God and obeyᴷ His commands. ³For this is what love for God is: to keep His commands. Now His commands are not a burden, ⁴because whatever has been born of God conquers the world. This is the victory that has conquered the world: our faith. ⁵And who is the one who conquers the world but the one who believes that Jesus is the Son of God?

⁶Jesus Christ—He is the One who came by water and blood, not by water only, but by

ᴬ4:2 Or confesses Jesus to be the Christ   ᴮ4:3 Other mss read confess that Jesus has come in the flesh   ᶜ4:9 Or revealed in us   ᴰ4:10 Or a
ᴱ4:12 Since God is an infinite being, no one can see Him in His absolute essential nature; Ex 33:18-23.   ᶠ4:12 Or remains among   ᴳ4:15 Or
acknowledges   ᴴ4:18 Or fear has its own punishment or torment   ᴵ4:19 Other mss add Him   ᴶ4:20 Other mss read has seen, how is he able to
love ... seen? (as a question)   ᴷ5:2 Other mss read keep

water and by blood. And the Spirit is the One who testifies, because the Spirit is the truth. [7] For there are three that testify:[A] [8] the Spirit, the water, and the blood—and these three are in agreement. [9] If we accept the testimony of men, God's testimony is greater, because it is God's testimony that He has given about His Son. [10] (The one who believes in the Son of God has this testimony within him. The one who does not believe God has made Him a liar, because he has not believed in the testimony God has given about His Son.) [11] And this is the testimony: God has given us eternal life, and this life is in His Son.

[12] The one who has the Son has life. The one who doesn't have the Son of God does not have life. [13] I have written these things to you who believe in the name of the Son of God, so that you may know that you have eternal life.

[14] Now this is the confidence we have before Him: Whenever we ask anything according to His will, He hears us. [15] And if we know that He hears whatever we ask, we know that we have what we have asked Him for.

[16] If anyone sees his brother committing a sin that does not bring death, he should ask, and God[B] will give life to him—to those who commit sin that doesn't bring death. There is sin[C] that brings death. I am not saying he should pray about that. [17] All unrighteousness is sin, and there is sin that does not bring death.

[18] We know that everyone who has been born of God does not sin, but the One[D] who is born of God keeps him,[E,F] and the evil one does not touch him.

[19] We know that we are of God, and the whole world is under the sway of the evil one.

[20] And we know that the Son of God has come and has given us understanding so that we may know the true One.[G] We are in the true One—that is, in His Son Jesus Christ. He is the true God and eternal life.

[21] Little children, guard yourselves from idols.

2 JOHN

The Elder:[H] To the elect lady[I] and her children: I love all of you in the truth—and not only I, but also all who have come to know the truth— [2] because of the truth that remains in us and will be with us forever.

[3] Grace, mercy, and peace will be with us from God the Father and from Jesus Christ, the Son of the Father, in truth and love.

[4] I was very glad to find some of your children walking in the truth, in keeping with a command we have received from the Father. [5] So now I urge you, dear lady—not as if I were writing you a new command, but one we have had from the beginning—that we love one another. [6] And this is love: that we walk according to His commands. This is the command as you have heard it from the beginning: you must walk in love.[J]

[7] Many deceivers have gone out into the world; they do not confess the coming of Jesus Christ in the flesh.[K] This is the deceiver and the antichrist. [8] Watch yourselves so you don't lose what we[L] have worked for, but so that you may receive a full reward. [9] Anyone who does not remain in Christ's teaching but goes beyond it, does not have God. The one who remains in that teaching, this one has both the Father and the Son. [10] If anyone comes to you and does not bring this teaching, do not receive him into your home, and don't say, "Welcome," to him; [11] for the one who says, "Welcome," to him shares in his evil works.

[12] Though I have many things to write to you, I don't want to do so with paper and ink. Instead, I hope to be with you and talk face to face[M] so that our joy may be complete.

[13] The children of your elect sister send you greetings

A5:7-8 Other mss (Vg and a few late Gk mss) read *testify in heaven: the Father, the Word, and the Holy Spirit, and these three are One.* **B***And there are three who bear witness on earth:* **B5:16** Lit *He* **C5:16** Or *is a sin* **D5:18** *Jesus Christ* **E5:18** Other mss read *himself* **F5:18** Or *the one who is born of God keeps himself* **G5:20** Other mss read *the true God* **H1** Or *Presbyter* **I1** Or *Kyria,* a proper name; probably a literary figure for a local church known to John; the children would be its members. **J6** Lit *in it* **K7** Or *confess Jesus Christ as coming in the flesh* **L8** Other mss read *you* **M12** Lit *mouth to mouth*

3 JOHN

The Elder:

To my dear friend[A] Gaius: I love you in the truth.

[2] Dear friend,[B] I pray that you may prosper in every way and be in good health physically just as you are spiritually.[C] [3] For I was very glad when some brothers came and testified to your faithfulness to the truth—how you are walking in the truth. [4] I have no greater joy than this: to hear that my children are walking in the truth.

[5] Dear friend,[B] you are showing faithfulness[D] by whatever you do for the brothers, especially when they are strangers. [6] They have testified to your love in front of the church. You will do well to send them on their journey in a manner worthy of God, [7] since they set out for the sake of the Name, accepting nothing from pagans. [8] Therefore, we ought to support such men so that we can be coworkers with[E] the truth.

[9] I wrote something to the church, but Diotrephes, who loves to have first place among them, does not receive us. [10] This is why, if I come, I will remind him of the works he is doing, slandering us with malicious words. And he is not satisfied with that! He not only refuses to welcome the brothers himself, but he even stops those who want to do so and expels them from the church.

[11] Dear friend,[B] do not imitate what is evil, but what is good. The one who does good is of God; the one who does evil has not seen God. [12] Demetrius has a good testimony from everyone, and from the truth itself. And we also testify for him, and you know that our testimony is true.

[13] I have many things to write you, but I don't want to write to you with pen and ink. [14] I hope to see you soon, and we will talk face to face.[F]

Peace be with you. The friends send you greetings. Greet the friends by name.

JUDE

Jude, a slave of Jesus Christ and a brother of James:

To those who are the called, loved[G] by God the Father and kept by Jesus Christ.

[2] May mercy, peace, and love be multiplied to you.

[3] Dear friends, although I was eager to write you about the salvation we share, I found it necessary to write and exhort you to contend for the faith that was delivered to the saints once for all. [4] For some men, who were designated for this judgment long ago, have come in by stealth; they are ungodly, turning the grace of our God into promiscuity and denying Jesus Christ, our only Master and Lord.

[5] Now I want to remind you, though you know all these things: The Lord[H] first[I] saved a people out of Egypt and later destroyed those who did not believe; [6] and He has kept, with eternal chains in darkness for the judgment of the great day, the angels who did not keep their own position but deserted their proper dwelling. [7] In the same way, Sodom and Gomorrah and the cities around them committed sexual immorality and practiced perversions,[J] just as angels did, and serve as an example by undergoing the punishment of eternal fire.

[8] Nevertheless, these dreamers likewise defile their flesh, reject authority, and blaspheme glorious ones.. [9] Yet Michael the archangel, when he was disputing with the Devil in a debate about Moses' body, did not dare bring an abusive condemnation against him but said, "The Lord rebuke you!" [10] But these people blaspheme anything they don't understand. What they know by instinct like

A1 Or my beloved   B2,5,11 Or Beloved   C2 Lit as your soul prospers   D5 Lit are doing a faithful thing   E8 Or coworkers for   F14 Lit mouth to mouth   G1 Other mss read sanctified   H5 Other mss read Jesus/Joshua, God, or God Christ   I5 Other mss place first after remind you   J7 Lit and went after other flesh unreasoning animals—they destroy themselves with these things. [11] Woe to them! For they have traveled in the way of Cain, have abandoned themselves to the error of Balaam for profit, and have perished in Korah's rebellion.

[12] These are the ones who are like dangerous reefs[A] at your love feasts. They feast with you, nurturing only themselves without fear. They are waterless clouds carried along by winds; trees in late autumn—fruitless, twice dead, pulled out by the roots; [13] wild waves of the sea, foaming up their shameful deeds; wandering stars for whom the blackness of darkness is reserved forever!

[14] And Enoch, in the seventh generation from Adam, prophesied about them:

Look! The Lord comes[B]
with thousands of His holy ones
[15] to execute judgment on all
and to convict them[C]
of all their ungodly acts
that they have done
in an ungodly way,
and of all the harsh things
ungodly sinners
have said against Him.

[16] These people are discontented grumblers, walking according to their desires; their mouths utter arrogant words, flattering people for their own advantage.

[17] But you, dear friends, remember what was predicted by the apostles of our Lord Jesus Christ; [18] they told you, "In the end time there will be scoffers walking according to their own ungodly desires." [19] These people create divisions and are unbelievers,[D] not having the Spirit.

[20] But you, dear friends, as you build yourselves up in your most holy faith and pray in the Holy Spirit, [21] keep yourselves in the love of God, expecting the mercy of our Lord Jesus Christ for eternal life. [22] Have mercy on those who doubt; [23] save others by snatching them from the fire; have mercy on others but with fear, hating even the garment defiled by the flesh.

[24] Now to Him who is able to protect you from stumbling and to make you stand in the presence of His glory, blameless and with great joy, [25] to the only God our Savior, through Jesus Christ our Lord,[E] be glory, majesty, power, and authority before all time,[F] now and forever. Amen.

REVELATION

1 The revelation of[G] Jesus Christ that God gave Him to show His slaves what must quickly[H] take place. He sent it and signified it[I] through His angel to His slave John, [2] who testified to God's word and to the testimony[J] about Jesus Christ, in all he saw.[K] [3] The one who reads this is blessed, and those who hear the words of this prophecy and keep[L] what is written in it are blessed, because the time is near!

[4] John:
To the seven churches in Asia.
Grace and peace to you from[M] the One who is, who was, and who is coming; from the seven spirits[N] before His throne; [5] and from Jesus Christ, the faithful witness, the firstborn from the dead and the ruler of the kings of the earth.

To Him who loves us and has set us free[O] from our sins by His blood, [6] and made us a kingdom,[P] priests[Q] to His God and Father—the glory and dominion are His forever and ever. Amen.

[7]   Look! He is coming
with the clouds,
and every eye will see Him,
including those who pierced[R] Him.
And all the families of the earth[S,T]

A12 Or like spots B14 Or came C15 Lit convict all D19 Or natural E25 Other mss omit through Jesus Christ our Lord F25 Other mss omit before all time G1:1 Or Revelation of, or A revelation of H1:1 Or soon I1:1 Made it known through symbols J1:2 Or witness K1:2 Lit as many as he saw L1:3 Or follow, or obey M1:4 Other mss add God N1:4 Or the sevenfold Spirit O1:5 Other mss read has washed us P1:6 Other mss read kings and Q1:6 Or made us into (or to be) a kingdom of priests; Ex 19:6 R1:7 Or impaled S1:7 Or all the tribes of the land T1:7 Gn 12:3; 28:14; Zch 14:17

will mourn over Him.[A][B]
This is certain. Amen.

[8]"I am the Alpha and the Omega," says the Lord God, "the One who is, who was, and who is coming, the Almighty."

[9]I, John, your brother and partner in the tribulation, kingdom, and endurance that are in Jesus, was on the island called Patmos because of God's word and the testimony about Jesus.[C] [10]I was in the Spirit[D][E] on the Lord's day,[F] and I heard a loud voice behind me like a trumpet [11]saying, "Write on a scroll[G] what you see and send it to the seven churches: Ephesus, Smyrna, Pergamum, Thyatira, Sardis, Philadelphia, and Laodicea."

[12]I turned to see whose voice it was that spoke to me. When I turned I saw seven gold lampstands, [13]and among the lampstands was One like the Son of Man,[H] dressed in a long robe and with a gold sash wrapped around His chest. [14]His head and hair were white like wool—white as snow—and His eyes like a fiery flame. [15]His feet were like fine bronze as it is fired in a furnace, and His voice like the sound of cascading[I] waters. [16]He had seven stars in His right hand; a sharp double-edged sword came from His mouth, and His face was shining like the sun at midday.[J]

[17]When I saw Him, I fell at His feet like a dead man. He laid His right hand on me and said, "Don't be afraid! I am the First and the Last, [18]and the Living One. I was dead, but look—I am alive forever and ever, and I hold the keys of death and Hades. [19]Therefore write what you have seen, what is, and what will take place after this. [20]The secret of the seven stars you saw in My right hand and of the seven gold lampstands is this: The seven stars are the angels[K] of the seven churches, and the seven lampstands[L] are the seven churches.

2 "Write to the angel[M] of the church in Ephesus:

"The One who holds the seven stars in His right hand and who walks among the seven gold lampstands says: [2]I know your works, your labor, and your endurance, and that you

cannot tolerate evil. You have tested those who call themselves apostles and are not, and you have found them to be liars. [3]You also possess endurance and have tolerated many things because of My name and have not grown weary. [4]But I have this against you: You have abandoned the love you had at first. [5]Remember then how far you have fallen; repent, and do the works you did at first. Otherwise, I will come to you[N] and remove your lampstand from its place—unless you repent. [6]Yet you do have this: You hate the practices of the Nicolaitans, which I also hate.

[7]"Anyone who has an ear should listen to what the Spirit says to the churches. I will give the victor the right to eat from the tree of life, which is in[O] God's paradise.

[8]"Write to the angel of the church in Smyrna:

"The First and the Last, the One who was dead and came to life, says: [9]I know your[P] affliction and poverty, yet you are rich. I know the slander of those who say they are Jews and are not, but are a synagogue of Satan. [10]Don't be afraid of what you are about to suffer. Look, the Devil is about to throw some of you into prison to test you, and you will have affliction for 10 days. Be faithful until death, and I will give you the crown[Q] of life.

[11]"Anyone who has an ear should listen to what the Spirit says to the churches. The victor will never be harmed by the second death.

[12]"Write to the angel of the church in Pergamum:

"The One who has the sharp, double-edged sword says: [13]I know[R] where you live—where Satan's throne is! And you are holding on to My name and did not deny your faith in Me,[S] even in the days of Antipas, My faithful witness who was killed among you, where Satan lives. [14]But I have a few things against you. You have some there who hold to the teaching of Balaam, who taught Balak to place a stumbling block[T] in front of the Israelites: to eat meat sacrificed to idols and to commit sexual immorality.[A] [15]In the same way, you also have those who hold to the teaching of the Nicolaitans.[B] [16]Therefore repent! Otherwise, I will come to you quickly and fight against them with the sword of My mouth.

[17]"Anyone who has an ear should listen to what the Spirit says to the churches. I will give the victor some of the hidden manna.[C] I will also give him a white stone, and on the stone a new name is inscribed that no one knows except the one who receives it.

[18]"Write to the angel of the church in Thyatira:

"The Son of God, the One whose eyes are like a fiery flame and whose feet are like fine bronze,[D] says: [19]I know your works—your love, faithfulness,[E] service, and endurance. Your last works are greater than the first. [20]But I have this against you: You tolerate the woman Jezebel, who calls herself a prophetess and teaches and deceives My slaves to commit sexual immorality[A] and to eat meat sacrificed to idols. [21]I gave her time to repent, but she does not want to repent of her sexual immorality.[F] [22]Look! I will throw her into a sickbed and those who commit adultery with her into great tribulation, unless they repent of her[G] practices. [23]I will kill her children with the plague.[H] Then all the churches will know that I am the One who examines minds[I] and hearts, and I will give to each of you according to your works. [24]I say to the rest of you in Thyatira, who do not hold this teaching, who haven't known the deep things[J] of Satan—as they say—I do not put any other burden on you. [25]But hold on to what you have until I come. [26]The one who is victorious and keeps My works to the end: I will give him authority over the nations—

[27]   and he will shepherd[K] them
          with an iron scepter;
      he will shatter them like pottery[L]—

just as I have received this from My Father. [28]I will also give him the morning star.

[29]"Anyone who has an ear should listen to what the Spirit says to the churches.

3 "Write to the angel of the church in Sardis:

"The One who has the seven spirits of God and the seven stars says: I know your works; you have a reputation[M] for being alive, but you are dead. [2]Be alert and strengthen[N] what remains, which is about to die, for I have not found your works complete before My God. [3]Remember, therefore, what you have received and heard; keep it, and repent. But if you are not alert, I will come[O] like a thief, and you have no idea at what hour I will come against you.[P] [4]But you have a few people[Q] in Sardis who have not defiled[R] their clothes, and they will walk with Me in white, because they are worthy. [5]In the same way, the victor will be dressed in white clothes, and I will never erase his name from the book of life but will acknowledge his name before My Father and before His angels.

[6]"Anyone who has an ear should listen to what the Spirit says to the churches.

[7]"Write to the angel of the church in Philadelphia:

"The Holy One, the True One, the One who has the key of David, who opens and no one will close, and closes and no one opens says: [8]I know your works. Because you have limited strength, have kept My word, and have not denied My name, look, I have placed before you an open door that no one is able to close. [9]Take note! I will make those from the synagogue of Satan, who claim to be Jews and are not, but are lying—note this—I will make them come and bow down at your feet, and they will know that I have loved you. [10]Because you have kept My command to endure,[S] I will also keep you from the hour of testing that is going to come over the whole world to test those who live on the earth. [11]I am coming quickly. Hold on to what you have, so that no one takes your crown. [12]The victor: I will make him a pillar in the sanctuary of My God, and he will never go out again. I will write on him the name of My God and the name of the city of My God—the new Jerusalem, which comes down out of heaven from My God—and My new name.

A2:14,20 Or commit fornication   B2:15 Other mss add which I hate   C2:17 Other mss add to eat   D2:18 Probably gleaming white hot; Rv 1:15   E2:19 Or faith   F2:21 Or her fornication   G2:22 Other mss read their   H2:23 Or I will surely kill her children   I2:23 Lit kidneys   J2:24 Or the secret things   K2:27 Or rule; see 19:15   L2:27 Ps 2:9   M3:1 Lit have a name   N3:2 Other mss read guard   O3:3 Other mss add upon you   P3:3 Or upon you   Q3:4 Lit few names   R3:4 Or soiled   S3:10 Lit My word of endurance

[13]"Anyone who has an ear should listen to what the Spirit says to the churches.

[14]"Write to the angel of the church in Laodicea:

"The Amen, the faithful and true Witness, the Originator[A] of God's creation says: [15]I know your works, that you are neither cold nor hot. I wish that you were cold or hot. [16]So, because you are lukewarm, and neither hot nor cold, I am going to vomit[B] you out of My mouth. [17]Because you say, 'I'm rich; I have become wealthy and need nothing,' and you don't know that you are wretched, pitiful, poor, blind, and naked, [18]I advise you to buy from Me gold refined in the fire so that you may be rich, white clothes so that you may be dressed and your shameful nakedness not be exposed, and ointment to spread on your eyes so that you may see. [19]As many as I love, I rebuke and discipline. So be committed[C] and repent. [20]Listen! I stand at the door and knock. If anyone hears My voice and opens the door, I will come in to him and have dinner with him, and he with Me. [21]The victor: I will give him the right to sit with Me on My throne, just as I also won the victory and sat down with My Father on His throne.

[22]"Anyone who has an ear should listen to what the Spirit says to the churches."

4 After this I looked, and there in heaven was an open door. The first voice that I had heard speaking to me like a trumpet said, "Come up here, and I will show you what must take place after this."

[2]Immediately I was in the Spirit,[D] and a throne was set there in heaven. One was seated on the throne, [3]and the One seated[E] looked like jasper[F] and carnelian[G] stone. A rainbow that looked like an emerald surrounded the throne. [4]Around that throne were 24 thrones, and on the thrones sat 24 elders dressed in white clothes, with gold crowns on their heads. [5]Flashes of lightning and rumblings of thunder came from the throne. Seven fiery torches were burning before the throne, which are the seven spirits of God. [6]Something like a sea of glass, similar to crystal, was also before the throne. Four living creatures covered with eyes in front and in back were in the middle[H] and around the throne. [7]The first living creature was like a lion; the second living creature was like a calf; the third living creature had a face like a man; and the fourth living creature was like a flying eagle. [8]Each of the four living creatures had six wings; they were covered with eyes around and inside. Day and night they never stop,[I] saying:

Holy, holy, holy,[J]
Lord God, the Almighty,
who was, who is, and who is coming.

[9]Whenever the living creatures give glory, honor, and thanks to the One seated on the throne, the One who lives forever and ever, [10]the 24 elders fall down before the One seated on the throne, worship the One who lives forever and ever, cast their crowns before the throne, and say:

[11]   Our Lord and God,[K]
    You are worthy to receive
    glory and honor and power,
    because You have created all things,
    and because of Your will
    they exist and were created.

5 Then I saw in the right hand of the One seated on the throne a scroll with writing on the inside and on the back, sealed with seven seals. [2]I also saw a mighty angel proclaiming in a loud voice, "Who is worthy to open the scroll and break its seals?" [3]But no one in heaven or on earth or under the earth was able to open the scroll or even to look in it. [4]And I cried and cried because no one was found worthy to open[L] the scroll or even to look in it.

[5]Then one of the elders said to me, "Stop crying. Look! The Lion from the tribe of Judah, the Root of David, has been victorious so that He may open the scroll and[M] its seven seals." [6]Then I saw One like a slaughtered lamb standing between[N] the throne and the four living creatures and among the elders. He had seven horns and seven eyes, which are the seven spirits of God sent into all the earth.

⁷He came and took the scroll^A out of the right hand of the One seated on the throne.

⁸When He took the scroll, the four living creatures and the 24 elders fell down before the Lamb. Each one had a harp and gold bowls filled with incense, which are the prayers of the saints. ⁹And they sang a new song:

> You are worthy to take the scroll
> and to open its seals,
> because You were slaughtered,
> and You redeemed^B people^C
> for God by Your blood
> from every tribe and language
> and people and nation.
> ¹⁰ You made them a kingdom^D
> and priests to our God,
> and they will reign on the earth.

¹¹Then I looked and heard the voice of many angels around the throne, and also of the living creatures and of the elders. Their number was countless thousands, plus thousands of thousands. ¹²They said with a loud voice:

> The Lamb who was slaughtered
> is worthy
> to receive power and riches
> and wisdom and strength
> and honor and glory and blessing!

¹³I heard every creature in heaven, on earth, under the earth, on the sea, and everything in them say:

> Blessing and honor and glory
> and dominion
> to the One seated on the throne,
> and to the Lamb, forever and ever!

¹⁴The four living creatures said, "Amen," and the elders fell down and worshiped.

6 Then I saw^E the Lamb open one of the seven^F seals, and I heard one of the four living creatures say with a voice like thunder, "Come!"^G,H ²I looked, and there was a white horse. The horseman on it had a bow; a crown

was given to him, and he went out as a victor to conquer.^I

³When He opened the second seal, I heard the second living creature say, "Come!"^G,H ⁴Then another horse went out, a fiery red one, and its horseman was empowered^J to take peace from the earth, so that people would slaughter one another. And a large sword was given to him.

⁵When He opened the third seal, I heard the third living creature say, "Come!"^G,H And I looked, and there was a black horse. The horseman on it had a set of scales in his hand. ⁶Then I heard something like a voice among the four living creatures say, "A quart of wheat for a denarius, and three quarts of barley for a denarius—but do not harm the olive oil and the wine."

⁷When He opened the fourth seal, I heard the voice of the fourth living creature say, "Come!"^G,H ⁸And I looked, and there was a pale green^K horse. The horseman on it was named Death, and Hades was following after him. Authority was given to them^L over a fourth of the earth, to kill by the sword, by famine, by plague, and by the wild animals of the earth.

⁹When He opened the fifth seal, I saw under the altar the people^M slaughtered because of God's word and the testimony they had.^N ¹⁰They cried out with a loud voice: "Lord,^O the One who is holy and true, how long until You judge and avenge our blood from those who live on the earth?" ¹¹So a white robe was given to each of them, and they were told to rest a little while longer until the number would be completed of their fellow slaves and their brothers, who were going to be killed just as they had been.

¹²Then I saw Him open^P the sixth seal. A violent earthquake occurred; the sun turned black like sackcloth made of goat hair; the entire moon^Q became like blood; ¹³the stars^R of heaven fell to the earth as a fig tree drops its unripe figs when shaken by a high wind; ¹⁴the sky separated like a scroll being rolled up; and every mountain and island was moved from its place.

^A5:7 Other mss exclude the scroll   ^B5:9 Or purchased   ^C5:9 Other mss read us   ^D5:10 Other mss read them kings   ^E6:1 Lit saw when   ^F6:1 Other mss omit seven   ^G6:1,3,5,7 Other mss add and see   ^H6:1,3,5,7 Or Go!   ^I6:2 Lit went out conquering and in order to conquer.   ^J6:4 Or was granted; lit was given   ^K6:8 Or a greenish gray   ^L6:8 Other mss read him   ^M6:9 Lit souls   ^N6:9 Other mss add about the Lamb   ^O6:10 Or Master   ^P6:12 Lit I saw when He opened   ^Q6:12 Or the full moon   ^R6:13 Perhaps meteors

¹⁵Then the kings of the earth, the nobles, the military commanders, the rich, the powerful, and every slave and free person hid in the caves and among the rocks of the mountains. ¹⁶And they said to the mountains and to the rocks, "Fall on us and hide us from the face of the One seated on the throne and from the wrath of the Lamb, ¹⁷because the great day of TheirᴬA wrath has come! And who is able to stand?"

7 After this I saw four angels standing at the four corners of the earth, restraining the four winds of the earth so that no wind could blow on the earth or on the sea or on any tree. ²Then I saw another angel, who had the seal of the living God rise up from the east. He cried out in a loud voice to the four angels who were empoweredᴮ to harm the earth and the sea: ³"Don't harm the earth or the sea or the trees until we seal the slaves of our God on their foreheads." ⁴And I heard the number of those who were sealed:

144,000 sealed from every tribe
of the Israelites:
⁵ 12,000 sealed from the tribe of Judah,
12,000ᶜ from the tribe of Reuben,
12,000 from the tribe of Gad,
⁶ 12,000 from the tribe of Asher,
12,000 from the tribe of Naphtali,
12,000 from the tribe of Manasseh,
⁷ 12,000 from the tribe of Simeon,
12,000 from the tribe of Levi,
12,000 from the tribe of Issachar,
⁸ 12,000 from the tribe of Zebulun,
12,000 from the tribe of Joseph,
12,000 sealed from the tribe
of Benjamin.

⁹After this I looked, and there was a vast multitude from every nation, tribe, people, and language, which no one could number, standing before the throne and before the Lamb. They were robed in white with palm branches in their hands. ¹⁰And they cried out in a loud voice:

Salvation belongs to our God,
who is seated on the throne,
and to the Lamb!

¹¹All the angels stood around the throne, the elders, and the four living creatures, and they fell facedown before the throne and worshiped God, ¹²saying:

Amen! Blessing and glory and wisdom
and thanksgiving and honor
and power and strength
be to our God forever and ever. Amen.

¹³Then one of the elders asked me, "Who are these people robed in white, and where did they come from?"
¹⁴I said to him, "Sir,ᴰ you know."
Then he told me:

These are the ones coming out
of the great tribulation.
They washed their robes
and made them white
in the blood of the Lamb.
¹⁵ For this reason they are
before the throne of God,
and they serve Him day and night
in His sanctuary.
The One seated on the throne
will shelterᴱ them:
¹⁶ They will no longer hunger;
they will no longer thirst;
the sun will no longer strike them,
nor will any heat.
¹⁷ For the Lamb who is at the center
of the throne
will shepherd them;
He will guide them to springs
of living waters,
and God will wipe away every tear
from their eyes.

8 When He opened the seventh seal, there was silence in heaven for about half an hour. ²Then I saw the seven angels who stand in the presence of God; seven trumpets were given to them. ³Another angel, with a gold incense burner, came and stood at the altar. He was given a large amount of incense to offer with the prayers of all the saints on the gold altar in front of the throne. ⁴The smoke of the incense, with the prayers of the saints, went up in the presence of God from the angel's

A6:17 Other mss read His   B7:2 Lit angels to whom it was given   C7:5-8 Other mss add sealed after each number   D7:14 Lit My lord
E7:15 Or will spread His tent over

hand. ⁵The angel took the incense burner, filled it with fire from the altar, and hurled it to the earth; there were rumblings of thunder, flashes of lightning, and an earthquake. ⁶And the seven angels who had the seven trumpets prepared to blow them.

⁷The first angel[A] blew his trumpet, and hail and fire, mixed with blood, were hurled to the earth. So a third of the earth was burned up, a third of the trees were burned up, and all the green grass was burned up.

⁸The second angel blew his trumpet, and something like a great mountain ablaze with fire was hurled into the sea. So a third of the sea became blood, ⁹a third of the living creatures in the sea died, and a third of the ships were destroyed.

¹⁰The third angel blew his trumpet, and a great star, blazing like a torch, fell from heaven. It fell on a third of the rivers and springs of water. ¹¹The name of the star is Wormwood, and a third of the waters became wormwood. So, many of the people died from the waters, because they had been made bitter.

¹²The fourth angel blew his trumpet, and a third of the sun was struck, a third of the moon, and a third of the stars, so that a third of them were darkened. A third of the day was without light, and the night as well.

¹³I looked again and heard an eagle[B] flying high overhead, crying out in a loud voice, "Woe! Woe! Woe to those who live on the earth, because of the remaining trumpet blasts that the three angels are about to sound!"

9 The fifth angel blew his trumpet, and I saw a star that had fallen from heaven to earth. The key to the shaft of the abyss was given to him. ²He opened the shaft of the abyss, and smoke came up out of the shaft like smoke from a great[C] furnace so that the sun and the air were darkened by the smoke from the shaft. ³Then locusts came out of the smoke on to the earth, and power[D] was given to them like the power that scorpions have on the earth. ⁴They were told not to harm the grass of the earth, or any green plant, or any tree, but only people who do not have God's seal on their foreheads. ⁵They were not per-

mitted to kill them but were to torment them for five months; their torment is like the torment caused by a scorpion when it strikes a man. ⁶In those days people will seek death and will not find it; they will long to die, but death will flee from them.

⁷The appearance of the locusts was like horses equipped for battle. Something like gold crowns was on their heads; their faces were like men's faces; ⁸they had hair like women's hair; their teeth were like lions' teeth; ⁹they had chests like iron breastplates; the sound of their wings was like the sound of chariots with many horses rushing into battle; ¹⁰and they had tails with stingers like scorpions, so that with their tails they had the power[D] to harm people for five months. ¹¹They had as their king[E] the angel of the abyss; his name in Hebrew is Abaddon,[F] and in Greek he has the name Apollyon.[G] ¹²The first woe has passed. There are still two more woes to come after this.

¹³The sixth angel blew his trumpet. From the four[H] horns of the gold altar that is before God, I heard a voice ¹⁴say to the sixth angel who had the trumpet, "Release the four angels bound at the great river Euphrates." ¹⁵So the four angels who were prepared for the hour, day, month, and year were released to kill a third of the human race. ¹⁶The number of mounted troops was 200 million;[I] I heard their number. ¹⁷This is how I saw the horses in my vision: The horsemen had breastplates that were fiery red, hyacinth blue, and sulfur yellow. The heads of the horses were like lions' heads, and from their mouths came fire, smoke, and sulfur. ¹⁸A third of the human race was killed by these three plagues—by the fire, the smoke, and the sulfur that came from their mouths. ¹⁹For the power of the horses is in their mouths and in their tails, for their tails, which resemble snakes, have heads, and they inflict injury with them.

²⁰The rest of the people, who were not killed by these plagues, did not repent of the works of their hands to stop worshiping demons and idols of gold, silver, bronze, stone, and wood, which are not able to see, hear, or walk. ²¹And they did not repent of their mur-

ders, their sorceries,[A] their sexual immorality, or their thefts.

10 Then I saw another mighty angel coming down from heaven, surrounded by a cloud, with a rainbow over his head.[B] His face was like the sun, his legs[C] were like fiery pillars, ²and he had a little scroll opened in his hand. He put his right foot on the sea, his left on the land, ³and he cried out with a loud voice like a roaring lion. When he cried out, the seven thunders spoke with their voices. ⁴And when the seven thunders spoke, I was about to write. Then I heard a voice from heaven, saying, "Seal up what the seven thunders said, and do not write it down!"

⁵Then the angel that I had seen standing on the sea and on the land raised his right hand to heaven. ⁶He swore an oath by the One who lives forever and ever, who created heaven and what is in it, the earth and what is in it, and the sea and what is in it: "There will no longer be an interval of time,[D] ⁷but in the days of the sound of the seventh angel, when he will blow his trumpet, then God's hidden plan will be completed, as He announced to His servants[E] the prophets."

⁸Now the voice that I heard from heaven spoke to me again and said, "Go, take the scroll that lies open in the hand of the angel who is standing on the sea and on the land."

⁹So I went to the angel and asked him to give me the little scroll. He said to me, "Take and eat it; it will be bitter in your stomach, but it will be as sweet as honey in your mouth."

¹⁰Then I took the little scroll from the angel's hand and ate it. It was as sweet as honey in my mouth, but when I ate it, my stomach became bitter. ¹¹And I was told,[F] "You must prophesy again about[G] many peoples, nations, languages, and kings."

11 Then I was given a measuring reed like a rod,[H] with these words: "Go[I] and measure God's sanctuary and the altar, and count those who worship there. ²But exclude the courtyard outside the sanctuary. Don't measure it, because it is given to the nations,[J] and

they will trample the holy city for 42 months. ³I will empower[K] my two witnesses, and they will prophesy for 1,260 days,[L] dressed in sackcloth."[M] ⁴These are the two olive trees and the two lampstands that stand before the Lord[N] of the earth. ⁵If anyone wants to harm them, fire comes from their mouths and consumes their enemies; if anyone wants to harm them, he must be killed in this way. ⁶These men have the power to close up the sky so that it does not rain during the days of their prophecy. They also have power over the waters to turn them into blood and to strike the earth with every plague whenever they want.

⁷When they finish their testimony, the beast[O] that comes up out of the abyss will make war with them, conquer them, and kill them. ⁸Their dead bodies[P] will lie in the public square[Q] of the great city, which prophetically[R] is called Sodom and Egypt, where also their Lord was crucified. ⁹And representatives from[S] the peoples, tribes, languages, and nations will view their bodies for three and a half days and not permit their bodies to be put into a tomb. ¹⁰Those who live on the earth will gloat over them and celebrate and send gifts to one another because these two prophets brought judgment to those who live on the earth.

¹¹But after 3½ days, the breath[T] of life from God entered them, and they stood on their feet. So great fear fell on those who saw them. ¹²Then they heard[U] a loud voice from heaven saying to them, "Come up here." They went up to heaven in a cloud, while their enemies watched them. ¹³At that moment a violent earthquake took place, a tenth of the city fell, and 7,000 people were killed in the earthquake. The survivors were terrified and gave glory to the God of heaven. ¹⁴The second woe has passed. Take note: The third woe is coming quickly!

¹⁵The seventh angel blew his trumpet, and there were loud voices in heaven saying:

> The kingdom of the world has become
> the kingdom

A9:21 Or magic potions, or drugs; Gk pharmakon   B10:1 Or a halo on his head   C10:1 Or feet   D10:6 Or be a delay   E10:7 Or slaves
F10:11 Lit And they said to me   G10:11 Or prophesy again against   H11:1 Other mss add and the angel stood up   I11:1 Lit Arise   J11:2 Or
Gentiles   K11:3 Lit I will give to   L11:3 = 3½ years of 30-day months   M11:3 Mourning garment of coarse, often black, material
N11:4 Other mss read God   O11:7 Or wild animal   P11:8 Lit Their corpse   Q11:8 Or lie on the broad street   R11:8 Or spiritually, or
symbolically   S11:9 Lit And from   T11:11 Or spirit   U11:12 Other mss read Then I heard

of our Lord and of His Messiah,
and He will reign forever and ever!

¹⁶The 24 elders, who were seated before God on their thrones, fell facedown and worshiped God, ¹⁷saying:

We thank You, Lord God,
  the Almighty,
who is and who was,^A
because You have taken
  Your great power
and have begun to reign.
¹⁸ The nations were angry,
but Your wrath has come.
The time has come
for the dead to be judged
and to give the reward
to Your servants the prophets,
to the saints, and to those who fear
  Your name,
both small and great,
and the time has come to destroy
those who destroy the earth.

¹⁹God's sanctuary in heaven was opened, and the ark of His covenant^B appeared in His sanctuary. There were flashes of lightning, rumblings of thunder, an earthquake,^C and severe hail.

12 A great sign^D appeared in heaven: a woman clothed with the sun, with the moon under her feet and a crown of 12 stars on her head. ²She was pregnant and cried out in labor and agony as she was about to give birth. ³Then another sign^E appeared in heaven: There was a great fiery red dragon having seven heads and 10 horns, and on his heads were seven diadems.^F ⁴His tail swept away a third of the stars in heaven and hurled them to the earth. And the dragon stood in front of the woman who was about to give birth, so that when she did give birth he might devour her child. ⁵But she gave birth to a Son—a male who is going to shepherd^G all nations with an iron scepter—and her child was caught up to God and to His throne. ⁶The woman fled into the wilderness, where she had a place prepared by God, to be fed there^H for 1,260 days.

⁷Then war broke out in heaven: Michael and his angels fought against the dragon. The dragon and his angels also fought, ⁸but he could not prevail, and there was no place for them in heaven any longer. ⁹So the great dragon was thrown out—the ancient serpent, who is called the Devil^I and Satan,^J the one who deceives the whole world. He was thrown to earth, and his angels with him.

¹⁰Then I heard a loud voice in heaven say:

The salvation and the power
and the kingdom of our God
and the authority of His Messiah
have now come,
because the accuser of our brothers
has been thrown out:
the one who accuses them
before our God day and night.
¹¹ They conquered him
by the blood of the Lamb
and by the word of their testimony,
for they did not love their lives
in the face of death.
¹² Therefore rejoice, you heavens,
and you who dwell in them!
Woe to the earth and the sea,
for the Devil has come down to you
with great fury,
because he knows he has a short time.

¹³When the dragon saw that he had been thrown to earth, he persecuted the woman who gave birth to the male child. ¹⁴The woman was given two wings of a great eagle, so that she could fly from the serpent's presence to her place in the wilderness, where she was fed for a time, times, and half a time.^K ¹⁵From his mouth the serpent spewed water like a river flowing after the woman, to sweep her away in a torrent. ¹⁶But the earth helped the woman. The earth opened its mouth and swallowed up the river that the dragon had spewed from his mouth. ¹⁷So the dragon was furious with the woman and left to wage war against the rest of her offspring^L—those who

keep God's commands and have the testimony about Jesus. [18]He[A] stood on the sand of the sea.[B]

13 And I saw a beast coming up out of the sea. He[C] had 10 horns and seven heads. On his horns were 10 diadems, and on his heads were blasphemous names.[D] [2]The beast I saw was like a leopard, his feet were like a bear's, and his mouth was like a lion's mouth. The dragon gave him his power, his throne, and great authority. [3]One of his heads appeared to be fatally wounded,[E] but his fatal wound was healed. The whole earth was amazed and followed the beast.[F] [4]They worshiped the dragon because he gave authority to the beast. And they worshiped the beast, saying, "Who is like the beast? Who is able to wage war against him?"

[5]A mouth was given to him to speak boasts and blasphemies. He was also given authority to act[G,H] for 42 months. [6]He began to speak[I] blasphemies against God: to blaspheme His name and His dwelling—those who dwell in heaven. [7]And he was permitted to wage war against the saints and to conquer them. He was also given authority over every tribe, people, language, and nation. [8]All those who live on the earth will worship him, everyone whose name was not written from the foundation of the world in the book[J] of life of the Lamb who was slaughtered.[K]

[9]If anyone has an ear, he should listen:

10 If anyone is destined for captivity,
   into captivity he goes.
   If anyone is to be killed[L] with a sword,
   with a sword he will be killed.

This demands the perseverance[M] and faith of the saints.

[11]Then I saw another beast coming up out of the earth; he had two horns like a lamb,[N] but he sounded like a dragon. [12]He exercises all the authority of the first beast on his behalf and compels the earth and those who live on it to worship the first beast, whose fatal wound was healed. [13]He also performs great signs, even causing fire to come down from heaven to earth in front of people. [14]He deceives those who live on the earth because of the signs that he is permitted to perform on behalf of the beast, telling those who live on the earth to make an image[O] of the beast who had the sword wound and yet lived. [15]He was permitted to give a spirit[P] to the image of the beast, so that the image of the beast could both speak and cause whoever would not worship the image of the beast to be killed. [16]And he requires everyone—small and great, rich and poor, free and slave—to be given a mark[Q] on his right hand or on his forehead, [17]so that no one can buy or sell unless he has the mark: the beast's name or the number of his name.

[18]Here is wisdom:[R] The one who has understanding must calculate[S] the number of the beast, because it is the number of a man.[T] His number is 666.[U]

14 Then I looked, and there on Mount Zion stood the Lamb, and with Him were 144,000 who had His name and His Father's name written on their foreheads. [2]I heard a sound[V] from heaven like the sound of cascading waters and like the rumbling of loud thunder. The sound I heard was also like harpists playing on their harps. [3]They sang[W] a new song before the throne and before the four living creatures and the elders, but no one could learn the song except the 144,000 who had been redeemed[X] from the earth. [4]These are the ones not defiled with women, for they have kept their virginity. These are the ones who follow the Lamb wherever He goes. They were redeemed[X,Y] from the human race as the firstfruits for God and the Lamb. [5]No lie was found in their mouths; they are blameless.

[6]Then I saw another angel flying high overhead, having the eternal gospel to announce to the inhabitants of the earth—to every nation, tribe, language, and people. [7]He spoke

A12:18 Other mss read I. "He" is apparently a reference to the dragon. B12:18 Some translations put Rv 12:18 either in Rv 12:17 or Rv 13:1. C13:1 The beasts in Rv 13:1,11 are customarily referred to as "he" or "him" rather than "it." The Gk word for a beast (therion) is grammatically neuter. D13:1 Other mss read heads was a blasphemous name E13:3 Lit be slain to death F13:3 Lit amazed after the beast G13:5 Other mss read wage war H13:5 Or to rule I13:6 Lit He opened his mouth in J13:8 Or scroll K13:8 Or written in the book of life of the Lamb who was slaughtered from the foundation of the world L13:10 Other mss read anyone kills M13:10 Lit Here is the perseverance N13:11 Or ram O13:14 Or statue, or likeness P13:15 Or give breath, or give life Q13:16 Or stamp, or brand R13:18 Or This calls for wisdom S13:18 Or count, or figure out T13:18 Or is a man's number, or is the number of a person U13:18 Other Gk mss read 616 V14:2 Or voice W14:3 Other mss add as it were X14:3,4 Or purchased Y14:4 Other mss add by Jesus with a loud voice: "Fear God and give Him glory, because the hour of His judgment has come. Worship the Maker of heaven and earth, the sea and springs of water."

[8] A second angel[A] followed, saying: "It has fallen, Babylon the Great has fallen,[B] who made all nations drink the wine of her sexual immorality,[C] which brings wrath."

[9] And a third angel[D] followed them and spoke with a loud voice: "If anyone worships the beast and his image and receives a mark on his forehead or on his hand, [10] he will also drink the wine of God's wrath, which is mixed full strength in the cup of His anger. He will be tormented with fire and sulfur in the sight of the holy angels and in the sight of the Lamb, [11] and the smoke of their torment will go up forever and ever. There is no rest[E] day or night for those who worship the beast and his image, or anyone who receives the mark of his name. [12] This demands the perseverance[F] of the saints, who keep God's commands and their faith in Jesus."[G]

[13] Then I heard a voice from heaven saying, "Write: The dead who die in the Lord from now on are blessed."

"Yes," says the Spirit, "let them rest from their labors, for their works follow them!"

[14] Then I looked, and there was a white cloud, and One like the Son of Man[H] was seated on the cloud, with a gold crown on His head and a sharp sickle in His hand. [15] Another angel came out of the sanctuary, crying out in a loud voice to the One who was seated on the cloud, "Use your sickle and reap, for the time to reap has come, since the harvest of the earth is ripe." [16] So the One seated on the cloud swung His sickle over the earth, and the earth was harvested.

[17] Then another angel who also had a sharp sickle came out of the sanctuary in heaven. [18] Yet another angel, who had authority over fire, came from the altar, and he called with a loud voice to the one who had the sharp sickle, "Use your sharp sickle and gather the clusters of grapes from earth's vineyard, because its grapes have ripened." [19] So the angel swung his sickle toward earth and gathered the grapes from earth's vineyard, and he threw them into the great winepress of God's wrath. [20] Then the press was trampled outside the city, and blood flowed out of the press up to the horses' bridles for about 180 miles.[I]

15 Then I saw another great and awe-inspiring sign[J] in heaven: seven angels with the seven last plagues, for with them, God's wrath will be completed. [2] I also saw something like a sea of glass mixed with fire, and those who had won the victory over the beast, his image,[K] and the number of his name, were standing on the sea of glass with harps from God.[L] [3] They sang the song of God's servant Moses and the song of the Lamb:

Great and awe-inspiring are
Your works,
Lord God, the Almighty;
righteous and true are
Your ways,
King of the Nations.[M]
[4] Lord, who will not fear
and glorify Your name?
Because You alone are holy,
for all the nations will come
and worship before You
because Your righteous acts
have been revealed.

[5] After this I looked, and the heavenly sanctuary—the tabernacle of testimony—was opened. [6] Out of the sanctuary came the seven angels with the seven plagues, dressed in clean, bright linen, with gold sashes wrapped around their chests. [7] One of the four living creatures gave the seven angels seven gold bowls filled with the wrath of God who lives forever and ever. [8] Then the sanctuary was filled with smoke from God's glory and from His power, and no one could enter the sanctuary until the seven plagues of the seven angels were completed.

16 Then I heard a loud voice from the sanctuary saying to the seven angels, "Go and pour out the seven[N] bowls of God's

A14:8 Lit Another angel, a second   B14:8 Other mss omit the second has fallen   C14:8 Or wine of her passionate immorality   D14:9 Lit Another angel, a third   E14:11 Lit They have no rest   F14:12 Lit Here is the perseverance   G14:12 Or and faith in Jesus, or and faithfulness to Jesus   H14:14 Or like a son of man   I14:20 Lit 1,600 stadia   J15:1 Or and awesome symbolic display   K15:2 Other mss add his mark   L15:2 Or harps of God; = harps belonging to the service of God   M15:3 Other mss read ages   N16:1 Other mss omit seven wrath on the earth." [2]The first went and poured out his bowl on the earth, and severely painful sores[A] broke out on the people who had the mark of the beast and who worshiped his image.

[3]The second[B] poured out his bowl into the sea. It turned to blood like a dead man's, and all life[C] in the sea died.

[4]The third[B] poured out his bowl into the rivers and the springs of water, and they became blood. [5]I heard the angel of the waters say:

> You are righteous,
> who is and who was,
> the Holy One,
> for You have decided
> these things.
> [6] Because they poured out
> the blood of the saints
> and the prophets,
> You also gave them blood
> to drink;
> they deserve it!

[7]Then I heard someone from the altar say:

> Yes, Lord God, the Almighty,
> true and righteous are
> Your judgments.

[8]The fourth[B] poured out his bowl on the sun. He[D] was given the power[E] to burn people with fire, [9]and people were burned by the intense heat. So they blasphemed the name of God, who had the power[E] over these plagues, and they did not repent and give Him glory.

[10]The fifth[B] poured out his bowl on the throne of the beast, and his kingdom was plunged into darkness. People[F] gnawed their tongues because of their pain [11]and blasphemed the God of heaven because of their pains and their sores, yet they did not repent of their actions.

[12]The sixth[B] poured out his bowl on the great river Euphrates, and its water was dried up to prepare the way for the kings from the east. [13]Then I saw three unclean spirits like frogs coming from the dragon's mouth, from the beast's mouth, and from the mouth of the false prophet. [14]For they are spirits of demons performing signs, who travel to the kings of the whole world to assemble them for the battle of the great day of God, the Almighty.

[15]"Look, I am coming like a thief. The one who is alert and remains clothed[G] so that he may not go around naked and people see his shame is blessed."

[16]So they assembled them at the place called in Hebrew, Armagedon.[H,I]

[17]Then the seventh[B] poured out his bowl into the air,[J] and a loud voice came out of the sanctuary[K] from the throne, saying, "It is done!" [18]There were flashes of lightning and rumblings of thunder. And a severe earthquake occurred like no other since man has been on the earth—so great was the quake. [19]The great city split into three parts, and the cities of the nations[L] fell. Babylon the Great was remembered in God's presence; He gave her the cup filled with the wine of His fierce anger. [20]Every island fled, and the mountains disappeared.[M] [21]Enormous hailstones, each weighing about 100 pounds,[N] fell from the sky on people, and they blasphemed God for the plague of hail because that plague was extremely severe.

17 Then one of the seven angels who had the seven bowls came and spoke with me: "Come, I will show you the judgment of the notorious prostitute[O] who sits on many[P] waters. [2]The kings of the earth committed sexual immorality with her, and those who live on the earth became drunk on the wine of her sexual immorality." [3]So he carried me away in the Spirit[Q] to a desert. I saw a woman sitting on a scarlet beast that was covered[R] with blasphemous names and had seven heads and 10 horns. [4]The woman was dressed in purple and scarlet, adorned with gold, precious stones, and pearls. She had a gold cup in her hand filled with everything vile and with

---

[A]16:2 Lit and a severely painful sore   [B]16:3,4,8,10,12,17 Other mss add angel   [C]16:3 Lit and every soul of life   [D]16:8 Or It   [E]16:8,9 Or authority   [F]16:10 Lit They   [G]16:15 Or and guards his clothes   [H]16:16 Other mss read Armageddon; other mss read Harmegedon; other mss read Mageddon; other mss read Magedon   [I]16:16 Traditionally the hill of Megiddo, a great city that guarded the pass between the coast and the valley of Jezreel or Esdraelon; Jdg 5:19; 2Kg 9:27   [J]16:17 Or on the air   [K]16:17 Other mss add of heaven   [L]16:19 Or the Gentile cities   [M]16:20 Lit mountains were not found   [N]16:21 Lit about a talent; talents varied in weight upwards from 75 pounds   [O]16:1 Traditionally translated the great whore   [P]17:1 Or by many   [Q]17:3 Or in spirit   [R]17:3 Lit was filled the impurities of her[A] prostitution. ⁵On her forehead a cryptic name was written:

BABYLON THE GREAT
THE MOTHER OF PROSTITUTES
AND OF THE VILE THINGS
OF THE EARTH.

⁶Then I saw that the woman was drunk on the blood of the saints and on the blood of the witnesses to Jesus. When I saw her, I was greatly astonished.

⁷Then the angel said to me, "Why are you astonished? I will tell you the secret meaning of the woman and of the beast, with the seven heads and the 10 horns, that carries her. ⁸The beast that you saw was, and is not, and is about to come up from the abyss and go to destruction. Those who live on the earth whose names have not been written in the book of life from the foundation of the world will be astonished when they see the beast that was, and is not, and will be present again.

⁹"Here is the mind with wisdom:[B] The seven heads are seven mountains on which the woman is seated. ¹⁰They are also seven kings:[C] Five have fallen, one is, the other has not yet come, and when he comes, he must remain for a little while. ¹¹The beast that was and is not, is himself an eighth king, yet he belongs to the seven and is going to destruction. ¹²The 10 horns you saw are 10 kings who have not yet received a kingdom, but they will receive authority as kings with the beast for one hour. ¹³These have one purpose, and they give their power and authority to the beast. ¹⁴These will make war against the Lamb, but the Lamb will conquer them because He is Lord of lords and King of kings. Those with Him are called, chosen, and faithful."

¹⁵He also said to me, "The waters you saw, where the prostitute was seated, are peoples, multitudes, nations, and languages. ¹⁶The 10 horns you saw, and the beast, will hate the prostitute. They will make her desolate and naked, devour her flesh, and burn her up with fire. ¹⁷For God has put it into their hearts to carry out His plan by having one purpose

and to give their kingdom[D] to the beast until God's words are accomplished. ¹⁸And the woman you saw is the great city that has an empire[E] over the kings of the earth."

18 After this I saw another angel with great authority coming down from heaven, and the earth was illuminated by his splendor. ²He cried in a mighty voice:

It has fallen,[F]
Babylon the Great has fallen!
She has become a dwelling
 for demons,
a haunt for every unclean spirit,
a haunt for every unclean bird,
and a haunt[G] for every unclean
 and despicable beast.[H]
³ For all the nations have drunk[I]
the wine of her sexual immorality,
which brings wrath.
The kings of the earth
have committed sexual immorality
 with her,
and the merchants of the earth
have grown wealthy
 from her excessive luxury.

⁴Then I heard another voice from heaven:

Come out of her, My people,
so that you will not share in her sins
or receive any of her plagues.
⁵ For her sins are piled up[J] to heaven,
and God has remembered her crimes.
⁶ Pay her back the way she also paid,
and double it according to her works.
In the cup in which she mixed,
mix a double portion for her.
⁷ As much as she glorified herself
 and lived luxuriously,
give her that much torment and grief,
for she says in her heart,
"I sit as a queen;
I am not a widow,
and I will never see grief."
⁸ For this reason her plagues will come
 in one day[K]—
death and grief and famine.
She will be burned up with fire,

A17:4 Other mss read of earth's   B17:9 Or This calls for the mind with wisdom   C17:10 Some editors or translators put They are also seven kings: in v. 9.   D17:17 Or sovereignty   E17:18 Or has sovereignty or rulership   F18:2 Other mss omit It has fallen   G18:2 Or prison H18:2 Other mss omit the words and a haunt for every unclean beast. The words and despicable then refer to the bird of the previous line. I18:3 Some mss read have collapsed; other mss read have fallen   J18:5 Or sins have reached up   K18:8 Suddenly

because the Lord God who judges her
is mighty.

⁹The kings of the earth who have committed sexual immorality and lived luxuriously with her will weep and mourn over her when they see the smoke of her burning. ¹⁰They will stand far off in fear of her torment, saying:

> Woe, woe, the great city,
> Babylon, the mighty city!
> For in a single hour^A
> your judgment has come.

¹¹The merchants of the earth will also weep and mourn over her, because no one buys their merchandise any longer— ¹²merchandise of gold, silver, precious stones, and pearls; fine fabrics of linen, purple, silk, and scarlet; all kinds of fragrant wood products; objects of ivory; objects of expensive wood, brass,^B iron, and marble; ¹³cinnamon, spice,^C,D incense, myrrh,^E and frankincense; wine, olive oil, fine wheat flour, and grain; cattle and sheep; horses and carriages; and slaves^F and human lives.^G

> ¹⁴ The fruit you craved has left you.
> All your splendid
>   and glamorous things are gone;
> they will never find them again.

¹⁵The merchants of these things, who became rich from her, will stand far off in fear of her torment, weeping and mourning, ¹⁶saying:

> Woe, woe, the great city,
> dressed in fine linen, purple,
>   and scarlet,
> adorned with gold, precious stones,
>   and pearls,
> ¹⁷ for in a single hour^A
> such fabulous wealth was destroyed!

And every shipmaster, seafarer, the sailors, and all who do business by sea, stood far off ¹⁸as they watched the smoke from her burning and kept crying out: "Who is like the great city?" ¹⁹They threw dust on their heads and kept crying out, weeping, and mourning:

> Woe, woe, the great city,
> where all those who have ships
>   on the sea
> became rich from her wealth,
> for in a single hour^A
>   she was destroyed.
> ²⁰ Rejoice over her, heaven,
> and you saints, apostles, and prophets,
> because God has executed
>   your judgment on her!^H

²¹Then a mighty angel picked up a stone like a large millstone and threw it into the sea, saying:

> In this way, Babylon the great city
> will be thrown down violently
> and never be found again.
> ²² The sound of harpists, musicians,
> flutists, and trumpeters
> will never be heard in you again;
> no craftsman of any trade
> will ever be found in you again;
> the sound of a mill
> will never be heard in you again;
> ²³ the light of a lamp
> will never shine in you again;
> and the voice of a groom and bride
> will never be heard in you again.
> All this will happen
> because your merchants
> were the nobility of the earth,
> because all the nations were deceived
> by your sorcery,^I
> ²⁴ and the blood of prophets and saints,
> and of all those slaughtered on earth,
> was found in you.^J

19 After this I heard something like the loud voice of a vast multitude in heaven, saying:

> Hallelujah!
> Salvation, glory, and power belong
>   to our God,
> ² because His judgments are true^K
>   and righteous,

because He has judged
the notorious prostitute
who corrupted the earth
with her sexual immorality;
and He has avenged the blood
of His slaves
that was on her hands.

³A second time they said:

Hallelujah!
Her smoke ascends forever and ever!

⁴Then the 24 elders and the four living creatures fell down and worshiped God, who is seated on the throne, saying:

Amen! Hallelujah!

⁵A voice came from the throne, saying:

Praise our God,
all His slaves, who fear Him,
both small and great!

⁶Then I heard something like the voice of a vast multitude, like the sound of cascading waters, and like the rumbling of loud thunder, saying:

Hallelujah, because our Lord God,
the Almighty,
has begun to reign!
⁷   Let us be glad, rejoice,
and give Him glory,
because the marriage of the Lamb
has come,
and His wife has prepared herself.
⁸   She was given fine linen to wear, bright
and pure.

For the fine linen represents the righteous acts of the saints.

⁹Then heᴬ said to me, "Write: Those invited to the marriage feast of the Lamb are fortunate!" He also said to me, "These words of God are true." ¹⁰Then I fell at his feet to worship him, but he said to me, "Don't do that! I am a fellow slave with you and your brothers who have the testimony aboutᴮ Jesus. Worship God, because the testimony about Jesus is the spirit of prophecy."ᶜ

¹¹Then I saw heaven opened, and there was a white horse. Its rider is called Faithful and True, and He judges and makes war in righteousness. ¹²His eyes were like a fiery flame, and many crownsᴰ were on His head. He had a name written that no one knows except Himself. ¹³He wore a robe stained with blood,ᴱ and His name is the Word of God. ¹⁴The armies that were in heaven followed Him on white horses, wearing pure white linen. ¹⁵A sharpᶠ sword came from His mouth, so that He might strike the nations with it. He will shepherdᴳ them with an iron scepter. He will also trample the winepress of the fierce anger of God, the Almighty. ¹⁶And He has a name written on His robe and on His thigh:

KING OF KINGS
AND LORD OF LORDS.

¹⁷Then I saw an angel standing onᴴ the sun, and he cried out in a loud voice, saying to all the birds flying high overhead, "Come, gather together for the great supper of God, ¹⁸so that you may eat the flesh of kings, the flesh of commanders, the flesh of mighty men, the flesh of horses and of their riders, and the flesh of everyone, both free and slave, small and great."

¹⁹Then I saw the beast, the kings of the earth, and their armies gathered together to wage war against the rider on the horse and against His army. ²⁰But the beast was taken prisoner, and along with him the false prophet, who had performed the signs in his presence. He deceived those who accepted the mark of the beast and those who worshiped his image with these signs. Both of them were thrown alive into the lake of fire that burns with sulfur. ²¹The rest were killed with the sword that came from the mouth of the rider on the horse, and all the birds were filled with their flesh.

20 Then I saw an angel coming down from heaven with the key to the abyss and a great chain in his hand. ²He seized the dragon, that ancient serpent who is the Devil and Satan,ᴵ and bound him for 1,000 years. ³He threw him into the abyss, closed it, and

put a seal on it so that he would no longer deceive the nations until the 1,000 years were completed. After that, he must be released for a short time.

⁴Then I saw thrones, and people seated on them who were given authority to judge. I also saw the peopleᴬ who had been beheadedᴮ because of their testimony about Jesus and because of God's word, who had not worshiped the beast or his image, and who had not accepted the mark on their foreheads or their hands. They came to life and reigned with the Messiah for 1,000 years. ⁵The rest of the dead did not come to life until the 1,000 years were completed. This is the first resurrection. ⁶Blessed and holy is the one who shares in the first resurrection! The second death has no powerᶜ over them, but they will be priests of God and of the Messiah, and they will reign with Him for 1,000 years.

⁷When the 1,000 years are completed, Satan will be released from his prison ⁸and will go out to deceive the nations at the four corners of the earth, Gog and Magog, to gather them for battle. Their number is like the sand of the sea. ⁹They came up over the surface of the earth and surrounded the encampment of the saints, the beloved city. Then fire came down from heavenᴰ and consumed them. ¹⁰The Devil who deceived them was thrown into the lake of fire and sulfur where the beast and the false prophet are, and they will be tormented day and night forever and ever.

¹¹Then I saw a great white throne and One seated on it. Earth and heaven fled from His presence, and no place was found for them. ¹²I also saw the dead, the great and the small, standing before the throne, and books were opened. Another book was opened, which is the book of life, and the dead were judged according to their works by what was written in the books. ¹³Then the sea gave up its dead, and Death and Hades gave up their dead; allᴱ were judged according to their works. ¹⁴Death and Hades were thrown into the lake of fire. This is the second death, the lake of fire.ᶠ ¹⁵And

anyone not found written in the book of life was thrown into the lake of fire.

21 Then I saw a new heaven and a new earth, for the first heaven and the first earth had passed away, and the sea no longer existed. ²I also saw the Holy City, new Jerusalem, coming down out of heaven from God, prepared like a bride adorned for her husband.

³Then I heard a loud voice from the throne:ᴳ

> Look! God's dwellingᴴ is
>   with humanity,
> and He will live with them.
> They will be His people,
> and God Himself will be with them
>   and be their God.ᴵ
> ⁴ He will wipe away every tear
>   from their eyes.
> Death will no longer exist;
> grief, crying, and pain will exist
>   no longer,
> because the previous thingsᴶ
>   have passed away.

⁵Then the One seated on the throne said, "Look! I am making everything new." He also said, "Write, because these wordsᴷ are faithful and true." ⁶And He said to me, "It is done! I am the Alpha and the Omega, the Beginning and the End. I will give water as a gift to the thirsty from the spring of life. ⁷The victor will inherit these things, and I will be his God, and he will be My son. ⁸But the cowards, unbelievers,ᴸ vile, murderers, sexually immoral, sorcerers, idolaters, and all liars—their share will be in the lake that burns with fire and sulfur, which is the second death."

⁹Then one of the seven angels, who had held the seven bowls filled with the seven last plagues, came and spoke with me: "Come, I will show you the bride, the wife of the Lamb." ¹⁰He then carried me away in the Spiritᴹ to a great and high mountain and showed me the holy city, Jerusalem, coming down out of heaven from God, ¹¹arrayed with God's glory. Her radiance was like a very precious stone, like a jasper stone, bright as crystal. ¹²The city

ᴬ20:4 Lit *souls*   ᴮ20:4 All who had given their lives for their faith in Christ   ᶜ20:6 Or *authority*   ᴰ20:9 Other mss add *from God*   ᴱ20:13 Lit *each*   ᶠ20:14 Other mss omit *the lake of fire*   ᴳ21:3 Other mss read *from heaven*   ᴴ21:3 Or *tent, or tabernacle*   ᴵ21:3 Other mss omit *and be their God*   ᴶ21:4 Or *the first things*   ᴷ21:5 Other mss add *of God*   ᴸ21:8 Other mss add *the sinful*   ᴹ21:10 Or *in spirit* had a massive high wall, with 12 gates. Twelve angels were at the gates; the names of the 12 tribes of Israel's sons were inscribed on the gates. [13] There were three gates on the east, three gates on the north, three gates on the south, and three gates on the west. [14] The city wall had 12 foundations, and the 12 names of the Lamb's 12 apostles were on the foundations.

[15] The one who spoke with me had a gold measuring rod to measure the city, its gates, and its wall. [16] The city is laid out in a square; its length and width are the same. He measured the city with the rod at 12,000 *stadia*.[A] Its length, width, and height are equal. [17] Then he measured its wall, 144 cubits according to human measurement, which the angel used. [18] The building material of its wall was jasper, and the city was pure gold like clear glass.

[19] The foundations of the city wall were adorned with every kind of precious stone:

> the first foundation jasper,
> the second sapphire,
> the third chalcedony,
> the fourth emerald,
> [20] the fifth sardonyx,
> the sixth carnelian,
> the seventh chrysolite,
> the eighth beryl,
> the ninth topaz,
> the tenth chrysoprase,
> the eleventh jacinth,
> the twelfth amethyst.

[21] The 12 gates are 12 pearls; each individual gate was made of a single pearl. The broad street[B] of the city was pure gold, like transparent glass.

[22] I did not see a sanctuary in it, because the Lord God the Almighty and the Lamb are its sanctuary. [23] The city does not need the sun or the moon to shine on it, because God's glory illuminates it, and its lamp is the Lamb. [24] The nations[C] will walk in its light, and the kings of the earth will bring their glory into it.[D] [25] Each day its gates will never close because it will never be night there. [26] They will bring the glory and honor of the nations into it.[E] [27] Nothing profane will ever enter it: no one who does what is vile or false, but only those written in the Lamb's book of life.

22 Then he showed me the river[F] of living water, sparkling like crystal, flowing from the throne of God and of the Lamb [2] down the middle of the broad street of the city. The tree of life[G] was on both sides of the river, bearing 12 kinds of fruit, producing its fruit every month. The leaves of the tree are for healing the nations, [3] and there will no longer be any curse. The throne of God and of the Lamb will be in the city,[H] and His slaves will serve Him. [4] They will see His face, and His name will be on their foreheads. [5] Night will no longer exist, and people will not need lamplight or sunlight, because the Lord God will give them light. And they will reign forever and ever.

[6] Then he said to me, "These words are faithful and true. And the Lord, the God of the spirits of the prophets,[I] has sent His angel to show His slaves what must quickly take place."[J]

[7] "Look, I am coming quickly! The one who keeps the prophetic words of this book is blessed."

[8] I, John, am the one who heard and saw these things. When I heard and saw them, I fell down to worship at the feet of the angel who had shown them to me. [9] But he said to me, "Don't do that! I am a fellow slave with you, your brothers the prophets, and those who keep the words of this book. Worship God." [10] He also said to me, "Don't seal the prophetic words of this book, because the time is near. [11] Let the unrighteous go on in unrighteousness; let the filthy go on being made filthy; let the righteous go on in righteousness; and let the holy go on being made holy."

[12] "Look! I am coming quickly, and My reward is with Me to repay each person according to what he has done. [13] I am the Alpha and

---

[A]21:16 A *stadion* (sg) = about 600 feet; 12,000 *stadia* = 1,400 miles. [B]21:21 Or *The public square* [C]21:24 Other mss add *of those who are saved* [D]21:24 Other mss read *will bring to Him the nations' glory and honor* [E]21:26 Other mss add *in order that they might go in* [F]22:1 Other mss read *pure river* [G]22:2 Or *was a tree of life, or was a tree that gives life* [H]22:3 Lit *in it* [I]22:6 Other mss read *God of the holy prophets* [J]22:6 Or *soon* the Omega, the First and the Last, the Beginning and the End.

¹⁴"Blessed are those who wash their robes,ᴬ so that they may have the right to the tree of life and may enter the city by the gates. ¹⁵Outside are the dogs, the sorcerers, the sexually immoral, the murderers, the idolaters, and everyone who loves and practices lying.

¹⁶"I, Jesus, have sent My angel to attest these things to youᴮ for the churches. I am the Root and the Offspring of David, the Bright Morning Star."

¹⁷Both the Spirit and the bride say, "Come!" Anyone who hears should say, "Come!" And the one who is thirsty should come. Whoever desires should take the living water as a gift.

¹⁸I testify to everyone who hears the prophetic words of this book: If anyone adds to them, God will add to him the plagues that are written in this book. ¹⁹And if anyone takes away from the words of this prophetic book, God will take away his share of the tree of life and the holy city, written in this book.

²⁰He who testifies about these things says, "Yes, I am coming quickly."

Amen! Come, Lord Jesus!

²¹The grace of the Lord Jesusᶜ be with all the saints.ᴰ Amen.ᴱ

ᴬ22:14 Other mss read *who keep His commands*   ᴮ22:16 In Gk, you is pl   ᶜ22:21 Other mss add *Christ*   ᴰ22:21 Other mss omit *the saints*   ᴱ22:21 Other mss omit *Amen.*

PSALMS AND PROVERBS

PSALMS

BOOK I
(Psalms 1–41)

Psalm 1

1 How happy is the man
who does not follow[A] the advice
of the wicked
or take[B] the path of sinners
or join a group[C] of mockers!
2 Instead, his delight is in the LORD's
instruction,
and he meditates on it day
and night.
3 He is like a tree planted beside streams
of water[D]
that bears its fruit in season[E]
and whose leaf does not wither.
Whatever he does prospers.
4 The wicked are not like this;
instead, they are like chaff
that the wind blows away.
5 Therefore the wicked will not survive[B]
the judgment,
and sinners will not be
in the community of the righteous.
6 For the LORD watches over the way
of the righteous,
but the way of the wicked leads to ruin.

Psalm 2

1 Why do the nations rebel[F]
and the peoples plot in vain?
2 The kings of the earth take their stand,
and the rulers conspire together
against the LORD
and His Anointed One:[G]
3 "Let us tear off their chains
and free ourselves from their restraints."[H]
4 The One enthroned[I] in heaven laughs;
the Lord ridicules them.
5 Then He speaks to them in His anger
and terrifies them in His wrath:
6 "I have consecrated My King[J]
on Zion, My holy mountain."
7 I will declare the LORD's decree:
He said to Me, "You are My Son;[K]
today I have become Your[L] Father.
8 Ask of Me,

and I will make the nations
Your[L] inheritance
and the ends of the earth
Your[L] possession.
9 You will break[M] them with a rod of iron;
You[N] will shatter them like pottery."[O]
10 So now, kings, be wise;
receive instruction, you judges
of the earth.
11 Serve the LORD with reverential awe
and rejoice with trembling.
12 Pay homage to[P] the Son or He[Q]
will be angry
and you will perish in your rebellion,[R]
for His[S] anger may ignite
at any moment.
All those who take refuge in Him[T]
are happy.

Psalm 3
A psalm of David when he fled
from his son Absalom.

1 LORD, how my foes increase!
There are many who attack me.
2 Many say about me,
"There is no help for him
in God."   *Selah*
3 But You, LORD, are a shield around me,
my glory, and the One who lifts up
my head.
4 I cry aloud to the LORD,
and He answers me
from His holy mountain.   *Selah*
5 I lie down and sleep;
I wake again because the LORD
sustains me.
6 I am not afraid of the thousands
of people
who have taken their stand against me
on every side.
7 Rise up, LORD!
Save me, my God!
You strike all my enemies on the cheek;
You break the teeth of the wicked.
8 Salvation belongs to the LORD;
may Your blessing be on Your people.
     Selah

A1:1 Lit *not walk in* **B1:1,5** Lit *stand in* **C1:1** Or *or sit in the seat* **D1:3** Or *beside irrigation canals* **E1:3** Lit *in its season* **F2:1** Or *conspire, or rage* **G2:2** Or *anointed one* **H2:3** Lit *and throw their ropes from us* **I2:4** Lit *who sits* **J2:6** Or *king* **K2:7** Or *me, "You are My son* **L2:7,8** Or *your* **M2:9** LXX, Syr, Tg read *shepherd* **N2:9** Or *you* **O2:9** Lit *a potter's vessel* **P2:12** Lit *Kiss* **Q2:12** Or *son, otherwise he* **R2:12** Lit *perish way* **S2:12** Or *his* **T2:12** Or *him*

Psalm 4

For the choir director: with stringed instruments.
A Davidic psalm.

1 Answer me when I call,
   God, who vindicates me.[A]
   You freed me from affliction;
   be gracious to me and hear my prayer.
2 How long, exalted men, will my honor
      be insulted?
   How long will you love
      what is worthless
   and pursue a lie?   *Selah*
3 Know that the LORD has set apart
   the faithful for Himself;
   the LORD will hear when I call to Him.
4 Be angry[B] and do not sin;
   on your bed, reflect in your heart
      and be still.   *Selah*
5 Offer sacrifices in righteousness[C]
   and trust in the LORD.
6 Many are saying, "Who can show us
      anything good?"
   Look on us with favor, LORD.
7 You have put more joy in my heart
   than they have when their grain
      and new wine abound.
8 I will both lie down and sleep in peace,
   for You alone, LORD, make me live
      in safety.

Psalm 5

For the choir director: with the flutes. A Davidic psalm.

1 Listen to my words, LORD;
   consider my sighing.
2 Pay attention to the sound of my cry,
   my King and my God,
   for I pray to You.
3 At daybreak, LORD, You hear my voice;
   at daybreak I plead my case to You
      and watch expectantly.
4 For You are not a God who delights
      in wickedness;
   evil cannot dwell with You.
5 The boastful cannot stand
      in Your presence;
   You hate all evildoers.
6 You destroy those who tell lies;
   the LORD abhors a man of bloodshed
      and treachery.
7 But I enter Your house
   by the abundance of Your faithful love;
   I bow down toward Your holy temple

in reverential awe of You.
8 LORD, lead me in Your righteousness
   because of my adversaries;[D]
   make Your way straight before me.
9 For there is nothing reliable in what
      they say;[E]
   destruction is within them;
   their throat is an open grave;
   they flatter with their tongues.
10 Punish them, God;
   let them fall by their own schemes.
   Drive them out because of
      their many crimes,
   for they rebel against You.
11 But let all who take refuge in You
      rejoice;
   let them shout for joy forever.
   May You shelter them,
   and may those who love Your name
      boast about You.
12 For You, LORD, bless
      the righteous one;
   You surround him with favor
      like a shield.

Psalm 6

For the choir director: with stringed instruments,
according to *Sheminith*. A Davidic psalm.

1 LORD, do not rebuke me in Your anger;
   do not discipline me in Your wrath.
2 Be gracious to me, LORD,
      for I am weak;[F]
   heal me, LORD, for my bones
      are shaking;
3 my whole being is shaken with terror.
   And You, LORD—how long?
4 Turn, LORD! Rescue me;
   save me because of Your faithful love.
5 For there is no remembrance of You
      in death;
   who can thank You in Sheol?
6 I am weary from my groaning;
   with my tears I dampen my pillow[G]
   and drench my bed every night.
7 My eyes are swollen from grief;
   they[H] grow old because of all
      my enemies.
8 Depart from me, all evildoers,
   for the LORD has heard the sound
      of my weeping.
9 The LORD has heard my plea for help;
   the LORD accepts my prayer.

A4:1 Or God of my righteousness   B4:4 Or Tremble   C4:5 Or Offer right sacrifices; lit Sacrifice sacrifices of righteousness   D5:8 Or of those who lie in wait for me   E5:9 Lit in his mouth   F6:2 Or sick   G6:6 Lit bed   H6:7 LXX, Aq, Sym, Jer read I

¹⁰ All my enemies will be ashamed
and shake with terror;
they will turn back and suddenly
be disgraced.

Psalm 7

A *Shiggaion*^A of David, which he sang to the LORD
concerning the words of Cush,^B a Benjaminite.

¹ Yahweh my God, I seek refuge in You;
save me from all my pursuers
and rescue me

² or they^C will tear me like a lion,
ripping me apart with no one
to rescue me.^D

³ Yahweh my God, if I have done this,
if there is injustice on my hands,

⁴ if I have done harm to one at peace
with me
or have plundered^E my adversary
without cause,

⁵ may an enemy pursue
and overtake me;
may he trample me to the ground
and leave my honor in the dust.   *Selah*

⁶ Rise up, LORD, in Your anger;
lift Yourself up against the fury
of my adversaries;
awake for me;^F
You have ordained^G a judgment.

⁷ Let the assembly of peoples gather
around You;
take Your seat^H on high over it.

⁸ The LORD judges the peoples;
vindicate me, LORD,
according to my righteousness
and my integrity.^I

⁹ Let the evil of the wicked come
to an end,
but establish the righteous.
The One who examines the thoughts
and emotions^J
is a righteous God.

¹⁰ My shield is with^K God,
who saves the upright in heart.

¹¹ God is a righteous judge
and a God who shows His wrath
every day.

¹² If anyone does not repent,
God^L will sharpen His sword;

He has strung^M His bow
and made it ready.

¹³ He has prepared His deadly weapons;
He tips His arrows with fire.

¹⁴ See, the wicked one is pregnant
with evil,
conceives trouble, and gives birth
to deceit.

¹⁵ He dug a pit and hollowed it out
but fell into the hole he had made.

¹⁶ His trouble comes back
on his own head,
and his violence falls on the top
of his head.

¹⁷ I will thank the LORD
for His righteousness;
I will sing about the name of Yahweh
the Most High.

Psalm 8

For the choir director: on the *Gittith*. A Davidic psalm.

¹ Yahweh, our Lord,
how magnificent is Your name
throughout the earth!
You have covered the heavens
with Your majesty.^N

² Because of Your adversaries,
You have established a stronghold^O
from the mouths of children
and nursing infants
to silence the enemy and the avenger.

³ When I observe Your heavens,
the work of Your fingers,
the moon and the stars,
which You set in place,

⁴ what is man that You remember him,
the son of man that You look
after him?

⁵ You made him little less than God^{P,Q}
and crowned him with glory
and honor.

⁶ You made him lord over the works
of Your hands;
You put everything under his feet:^R

⁷ all the sheep and oxen,
as well as the animals in the wild,

⁸ the birds of the sky,
and the fish of the sea
that pass through the currents
of the seas.

A7:title Perhaps a passionate song with rapid changes of rhythm, or a dirge   **B7:title** LXX, Aq, Sym, Theod, Jer read *of the Cushite*   **C7:2** Lit *he*   **D7:2** Lit *ripping, and without a rescuer*   **E7:4** Or *me and have spared*   **F7:6** LXX reads *awake, Lord my God*   **G7:6** Or *me; ordain*   **H7:7** MT reads *and return*   **I7:8** Lit *integrity on me*   **J7:9** Lit *examines hearts and kidneys*   **K7:10** Lit *on*   **L7:12** Lit *He*   **M7:12** Lit *bent; that is, bent the bow to string it*   **N8:1** Lit *earth, which has set Your splendor upon the heavens*   **O8:2** LXX reads *established praise*   **P8:5** LXX reads *angels*   **Q8:5** Or *gods, or a god, or heavenly beings*; lit *Elohim*   **R8:6** Or *authority*

⁹ Yahweh, our Lord,
how magnificent is Your name
throughout the earth!

Psalm 9

For the choir director:
according to *Muth-labben*.[A] A Davidic psalm.

¹ I will thank Yahweh with all my heart;
I will declare all Your wonderful works.
² I will rejoice and boast about You;
I will sing about Your name,
Most High.
³ When my enemies retreat,
they stumble and perish before You.
⁴ For You have upheld my just cause;[B]
You are seated on Your throne
as a righteous judge.
⁵ You have rebuked the nations:
You have destroyed the wicked;
You have erased their name forever
and ever.
⁶ The enemy has come to eternal ruin;
You have uprooted the cities,
and the very memory of them
has perished.
⁷ But the LORD sits enthroned forever;
He has established His throne
for judgment.
⁸ He judges the world
with righteousness;
He executes judgment on the nations
with fairness.
⁹ The LORD is a refuge for the oppressed,
a refuge in times of trouble.
¹⁰ Those who know Your name
trust in You
because You have not abandoned
those who seek You, Yahweh.
¹¹ Sing to the LORD, who dwells in Zion;
proclaim His deeds among the nations.
¹² For the One who seeks an accounting
for bloodshed remembers them;
He does not forget the cry
of the afflicted.
¹³ Be gracious to me, LORD;
consider my affliction at the hands
of those who hate me.
Lift me up from the gates of death,
¹⁴ so that I may declare all Your praises.
I will rejoice in Your salvation
within the gates of Daughter Zion.

¹⁵ The nations have fallen into the pit
they made;
their foot is caught in the net
they have concealed.
¹⁶ The LORD has revealed Himself;
He has executed justice,
striking down[C] the wicked[D]
by the work of their hands.
Higgaion. Selah
¹⁷ The wicked will return to Sheol—
all the nations that forget God.
¹⁸ For the oppressed will not always
be forgotten;
the hope of the afflicted[E] will not perish
forever.
¹⁹ Rise up, LORD! Do not let man prevail;
let the nations be judged
in Your presence.
²⁰ Put terror in them, LORD;
let the nations know they are
only men.   *Selah*

Psalm 10

¹ LORD,[F,G] why do You stand so far away?
Why do You hide in times of trouble?
² In arrogance the wicked
relentlessly pursue the afflicted;
let them be caught in the schemes
they have devised.
³ For the wicked one boasts about
his own cravings;
the one who is greedy curses[H]
and despises the LORD.
⁴ In all his scheming,
the wicked arrogantly thinks:[I]
"There is no accountability,
since God does not exist."
⁵ His ways are always secure;[J]
Your lofty judgments are beyond
his sight;
he scoffs at all his adversaries.
⁶ He says to himself, "I will never
be moved—
from generation to generation
without calamity."
⁷ Cursing, deceit, and violence
fill his mouth;
trouble and malice are
under his tongue.
⁸ He waits in ambush near
the villages;

A9:title Perhaps a musical term   B9:4 Lit *my justice and my cause*   C9:16 Or *justice, snaring*   D9:16 LXX, Aq, Syr, Tg read *justice, the wicked is trapped*   E9:18 Alt Hb tradition reads *humble*   F10:1 Some Hb mss, LXX connect Pss 9–10.   G10:1 Together these 2 psalms form a partial acrostic.   H10:3 Or *he blesses the greedy*   I10:4 Lit *wicked according to the height of his nose*   J10:5 Or *prosperous*

he kills the innocent in secret places.
His eyes are on the lookout
  for the helpless;
⁹ he lurks in secret like a lion
  in a thicket.
He lurks in order to seize the afflicted;
he seizes the afflicted and drags him
  in his net.
¹⁰ So he is oppressed and beaten down;
the helpless fall because of
  his strength.
¹¹ He says to himself, "God has forgotten;
He hides His face and will never see."
¹² Rise up, Lord God! Lift up Your hand.
Do not forget the afflicted.
¹³ Why has the wicked person
  despised God?
He says to himself, "You will not
  demand an account."
¹⁴ But You Yourself have seen trouble
  and grief,
observing it in order to take the matter
  into Your hands.
The helpless entrusts himself to You;
You are a helper of the fatherless.
¹⁵ Break the arm of the wicked
  and evil person;
call his wickedness into account
until nothing remains of it.^A
¹⁶ The Lord is King forever and ever;
the nations will perish from His land.
¹⁷ Lord, You have heard the desire
  of the humble;^B
You will strengthen their hearts.
You will listen carefully,
¹⁸ doing justice for the fatherless
  and the oppressed
so that men of the earth
  may terrify them no more.

Psalm 11

For the choir director. Davidic.

¹ I have taken refuge in the Lord.
How can you say to me,
"Escape to the mountain like a bird!^C
² For look, the wicked string the bow;
they put the^D arrow on the bowstring
to shoot from the shadows
  at the upright in heart.
³ When the foundations are destroyed,

what can the righteous do?"
⁴ The Lord is in His holy temple;
the Lord's throne is in heaven.
His eyes watch; He examines^E everyone.
⁵ The Lord examines the righteous
  and the wicked.
He hates the lover of violence.
⁶ He will rain burning coals^F and sulfur
  on the wicked;
a scorching wind will be their portion.^G
⁷ For the Lord is righteous; He loves
  righteous deeds.
The upright will see His face.

Psalm 12

For the choir director: according to *Sheminith.*
A Davidic psalm.

¹ Help, Lord, for no faithful one remains;
the loyal have disappeared
  from the human race.
² They lie to one another;
they speak with flattering lips
  and deceptive hearts.
³ May the Lord cut off all flattering lips
and the tongue that speaks boastfully.
⁴ They say, "Through our tongues
  we have power;^H
our lips are our own—who can be
  our master?"
⁵ "Because of the oppression
  of the afflicted
and the groaning of the poor,
I will now rise up," says the Lord.
"I will put the one who longs for it
  in a safe place."
⁶ The words of the Lord are pure words,
like silver refined
  in an earthen furnace,
purified seven times.
⁷ You, Lord, will guard us;^I
You will protect us^J
  from this generation forever.
⁸ The wicked wander^K everywhere,
and what is worthless is exalted
  by the human race.

Psalm 13

For the choir director. A Davidic psalm.

¹ Lord, how long will You forget me?
Forever?

---

^A**10:15** Lit *account You do not find* ^B**10:17** Some Hb mss, LXX, Syr read *afflicted* ^C**11:1** Lit *to your mountain, bird* ^D**11:2** Lit *their* ^E**11:4** Lit *His eyelids examine* ^F**11:6** Sym; MT reads *rain snares, fire* ^G**11:6** Lit *be the portion of their cup* ^H**12:4** Lit *That say, "By our tongues we are strengthened* ^I**12:7** Some Hb mss, LXX, Jer; other Hb mss read *them* ^J**12:7** Some Hb mss, LXX; other Hb mss read *him* ^K**12:8** Lit *walk about*

How long will You hide Your face
    from me?
2 How long will I store up
    anxious concerns[A] within me,
agony in my mind every day?
How long will my enemy
    dominate me?
3 Consider me and answer, LORD my God.
Restore brightness to my eyes;
    otherwise, I will sleep in death.
4 My enemy will say, "I have triumphed
    over him,"
and my foes will rejoice
    because I am shaken.
5 But I have trusted in Your faithful love;
my heart will rejoice in
    Your deliverance.
6 I will sing to the LORD
because He has treated me generously.

Psalm 14
For the choir director. Davidic.

1 The fool says in his heart,
    "God does not exist."
They are corrupt; they do vile deeds.
There is no one who does good.
2 The LORD looks down from heaven
    on the human race
to see if there is one who is wise,
one who seeks God.
3 All have turned away;
all alike have become corrupt.
There is no one who does good,
    not even one.[B]
4 Will evildoers never understand?
They consume My people
    as they consume bread;
they do not call on the LORD.
5 Then[C] they will be filled with terror,
for God is with those
    who are[D] righteous.
6 You sinners frustrate the plans
    of the afflicted,
but the LORD is his refuge.
7 Oh, that Israel's deliverance
    would come from Zion!
When the LORD restores the fortunes
    of His people,[E]
Jacob will rejoice; Israel will be glad.[F]

Psalm 15
A Davidic psalm.

1 LORD, who can dwell in Your tent?
Who can live on Your holy mountain?
2 The one who lives honestly,
    practices righteousness,
and acknowledges the truth
    in his heart—
3 who does not slander with his tongue,
who does not harm his friend
or discredit his neighbor,
4 who despises the one rejected
    by the LORD[G]
but honors those who fear the LORD,
who keeps his word whatever the cost,
5 who does not lend his money
    at interest
or take a bribe against the innocent—
the one who does these things
    will never be moved.

Psalm 16
A Davidic Miktam.

1 Protect me, God, for I take refuge
    in You.
2 I[H] said to Yahweh, "You are my Lord;
I have nothing good besides You."[I]
3 As for the holy people who are
    in the land,
they are the noble ones.
All my delight is in them.
4 The sorrows of those who take
    another god
for themselves will multiply;
I will not pour out their drink offerings
    of blood,
and I will not speak their names
    with my lips.
5 LORD, You are my portion[J]
and my cup of blessing;
You hold my future.
6 The boundary lines have fallen for me
    in pleasant places;
indeed, I have a beautiful inheritance.
7 I will praise the LORD
    who counsels me—
even at night my conscience
    instructs me.
8 I keep the LORD in mind[K] always.
Because He is at my right hand,
I will not be shaken.

⁹ Therefore my heart is glad
and my spirit rejoices;
my body also rests securely.
¹⁰ For You will not abandon me to Sheol;
You will not allow Your Faithful One
to see decay.
¹¹ You reveal the path of life to me;
in Your presence is abundant joy;
in Your right hand are
eternal pleasures.

Psalm 17
A Davidic prayer.

¹ LORD, hear a just cause;
pay attention to my cry;
listen to my prayer—
from lips free of deceit.
² Let my vindication come from You,
for You see what is right.
³ You have tested my heart;
You have examined me at night.
You have tried me and found
nothing evil;
I have determined that my mouth
will not sin.ᴬ
⁴ Concerning what people do:
by the word of Your lipsᴮ
I have avoided the ways of the violent.
⁵ My steps are on Your paths;
my feet have not slipped.
⁶ I call on You, God,
because You will answer me;
listen closely to me; hear what I say.
⁷ Display the wonders
of Your faithful love,
Savior of all who seek refuge
from those who rebel
against Your right hand.ᶜ
⁸ Protect me as the pupil of Your eye;
hide me in the shadow of Your wings
⁹ fromᴰ the wicked
who treat me violently,ᴱ
my deadly enemies who surround me.
¹⁰ They have become hardened;ᶠ
their mouths speak arrogantly.
¹¹ They advance against me;ᴳ
now they surround me.
They are determinedᴴ
to throw me to the ground.
¹² They areᴵ like a lion eager to tear,
like a young lion lurking in ambush.

¹³ Rise up, LORD!
Confront him; bring him down.
With Your sword, save me
from the wicked.
¹⁴ With Your hand, LORD, save me
from men,
from men of the world
whose portion is in this life:
You fill their bellies with what
You have in store;
their sons are satisfied,
and they leave their surplus
to their children.
¹⁵ But I will see Your face
in righteousness;
when I awake, I will be satisfied
with Your presence.ᴶ

Psalm 18
For the choir director. Of the servant
of the LORD, David, who spoke the words
of this song to the LORD on the day the LORD
rescued him from the hand of all his enemies
and from the hand of Saul. He said:

¹ I love You, LORD, my strength.
² The LORD is my rock,
my fortress, and my deliverer,
my God, my mountain
where I seek refuge,
my shield and the horn of my salvation,
my stronghold.
³ I called to the LORD, who is
worthy of praise,
and I was saved from my enemies.
⁴ The ropes of death were wrapped
around me;
the torrents of destruction terrified me.
⁵ The ropes of Sheol entangled me;
the snares of death confronted me.
⁶ I called to the LORD in my distress,
and I cried to my God for help.
From His temple He heard my voice,
and my cry to Him reached His ears.
⁷ Then the earth shook and quaked;
the foundations of the mountains
trembled;
they shook because He burned
with anger.
⁸ Smoke rose from His nostrils,
and consuming fire came
from His mouth;

ᴬ17:3 Or evil; my mouth will not sin   ᴮ17:4 God's instruction   ᶜ17:7 Or love, You who save with Your right hand those seeking refuge from
adversaries   ᴰ17:9 Lit from the presence of   ᴱ17:9 Or who plunder me   ᶠ17:10 Lit have closed up their fat   ᴳ17:11 Vg; one Hb ms, LXX read
They cast me out; MT reads Our steps   ᴴ17:11 Lit They set their eyes   ᴵ17:12 Lit He is   ᴶ17:15 Lit form

coals were set ablaze by it.[A]

9 He parted the heavens and came down,
a dark cloud beneath His feet.

10 He rode on a cherub and flew,
soaring on the wings of the wind.

11 He made darkness His hiding place,
dark storm clouds His canopy
around Him.

12 From the radiance of His presence,
His clouds swept onward with hail
and blazing coals.

13 The LORD thundered from[B] heaven;
the Most High projected
His voice.[C]

14 He shot His arrows and scattered them;
He hurled[D] lightning bolts
and routed them.

15 The depths of the sea became visible,
the foundations of the world
were exposed,
at Your rebuke, LORD,
at the blast of the breath
of Your nostrils.

16 He reached down from heaven
and took hold of me;
He pulled me out of deep waters.

17 He rescued me
from my powerful enemy
and from those who hated me,
for they were too strong for me.

18 They confronted me in the day
of my distress,
but the LORD was my support.

19 He brought me out to a spacious place;
He rescued me because He delighted
in me.

20 The LORD rewarded me
according to my righteousness;
He repaid me
according to the cleanness
of my hands.

21 For I have kept the ways of the LORD
and have not turned from my God
to wickedness.

22 Indeed, I have kept all His ordinances
in mind[E]
and have not disregarded His statutes.

23 I was blameless toward Him
and kept myself from sinning.

24 So the LORD repaid me
according to my righteousness,

according to the cleanness of my hands
in His sight.

25 With the faithful
You prove Yourself faithful;
with the blameless man
You prove Yourself blameless;

26 with the pure
You prove Yourself pure,
but with the crooked
You prove Yourself shrewd.

27 For You rescue an afflicted people,
but You humble those
with haughty eyes.

28 LORD, You light my lamp;
my God illuminates my darkness.

29 With You I can attack a barrier,[F]
and with my God I can leap over a wall.

30 God—His way is perfect;
the word of the LORD is pure.
He is a shield to all who take refuge
in Him.

31 For who is God besides Yahweh?
And who is a rock? Only our God.

32 God—He clothes me with strength
and makes my way perfect.

33 He makes my feet like the feet of a deer
and sets me securely on the heights.[G]

34 He trains my hands for war;
my arms can bend a bow of bronze.

35 You have given me the shield
of Your salvation;
Your right hand upholds me,
and Your humility exalts me.

36 You widen a place beneath me
for my steps,
and my ankles do not give way.

37 I pursue my enemies
and overtake them;
I do not turn back until they are
wiped out.

38 I crush them, and they cannot get up;
they fall beneath my feet.

39 You have clothed me with strength
for battle;
You subdue my adversaries
beneath me.

40 You have made my enemies retreat
before me;[H]
I annihilate those who hate me.

41 They cry for help, but there is no one
to save them—

A18:8 Or ablaze from Him   B18:13 Some Hb mss, LXX, Tg, Jer; other Hb mss read in   C18:13 Some Hb mss read voice, with hail and fiery coals   D18:14 Or multiplied   E18:22 Lit Indeed, all His ordinances have been in front of me   F18:29 Or ridge   G18:33 Or on my high places   H18:40 Or You gave me the necks of my enemies

they cry to the Lord, but He does not
answer them.
⁴² I pulverize them like dust
before the wind;
I trample them[A] like mud
in the streets.
⁴³ You have freed me from the feuds
among the people;
You have appointed me the head
of nations;
a people I had not known serve me.
⁴⁴ Foreigners submit to me grudgingly;
as soon as they hear,[B] they obey me.
⁴⁵ Foreigners lose heart
and come trembling
from their fortifications.
⁴⁶ The Lord lives—may my rock
be praised!
The God of my salvation is exalted.
⁴⁷ God—He gives me vengeance
and subdues peoples under me.
⁴⁸ He frees me from my enemies.
You exalt me above my adversaries;
You rescue me from violent men.
⁴⁹ Therefore I will praise You, Yahweh,
among the nations;
I will sing about Your name.
⁵⁰ He gives great victories to His king;
He shows loyalty to His anointed,
to David and his descendants forever.

Psalm 19

For the choir director. A Davidic psalm.

¹ The heavens declare the glory of God,
and the sky[C] proclaims the work
of His hands.
² Day after day they pour out speech;
night after night
they communicate knowledge.[D]
³ There is no speech; there are no words;
their voice is not heard.
⁴ Their message[E] has gone out to all
the earth,
and their words to the ends
of the world.
In the heavens[F] He has pitched a tent
for the sun.
⁵ It is like a groom coming from
the[G] bridal chamber;
it rejoices like an athlete
running a course.

⁶ It rises from one end of the heavens
and circles[H] to their other end;
nothing is hidden from its heat.
⁷ The instruction of the Lord is perfect,
renewing one's life;
the testimony of the Lord
is trustworthy,
making the inexperienced wise.
⁸ The precepts of the Lord are right,
making the heart glad;
the command of the Lord is radiant,
making the eyes light up.
⁹ The fear of the Lord is pure,
enduring forever;
the ordinances of the Lord
are reliable
and altogether righteous.
¹⁰ They are more desirable than gold—
than an abundance of pure gold;
and sweeter than honey,
which comes from the honeycomb.
¹¹ In addition, Your servant is warned
by them;
there is great reward in keeping them.
¹² Who perceives his unintentional sins?
Cleanse me from my hidden faults.
¹³ Moreover, keep Your servant
from willful sins;
do not let them rule over me.
Then I will be innocent
and cleansed from blatant rebellion.
¹⁴ May the words of my mouth
and the meditation of my heart
be acceptable to You,
Lord, my rock and my Redeemer.

Psalm 20

For the choir director. A Davidic psalm.

¹ May Yahweh answer you in a day
of trouble;
may the name of Jacob's God
protect you.
² May He send you help
from the sanctuary
and sustain you from Zion.
³ May He remember all your offerings
and accept your burnt offering.   *Selah*
⁴ May He give you what
your heart desires
and fulfill your whole purpose.
⁵ Let us shout for joy at your victory

A18:42 Some Hb mss, LXX, Syr, Tg; other Hb mss read *I poured them out*   B18:44 Lit *At the hearing of the ear*   C19:1 Or *expanse*   D19:2 Or
Day to day pours out speech, and night to night communicates knowledge   E19:4 LXX, Sym, Syr, Vg; MT reads *line*   F19:4 Lit *In them*   G19:5 Lit
his   H19:6 Lit *its circuit is*

and lift the banner in the name
   of our God.
May Yahweh fulfill all your requests.
6 Now I know that the LORD gives victory
   to His anointed;
He will answer him
   from His holy heaven
with mighty victories
   from[A] His right hand.
7 Some take pride in chariots, and others
   in horses,
but we take pride in the name
   of Yahweh our God.
8 They collapse and fall,
   but we rise and stand firm.
9 LORD, give victory to the king!
May He[B] answer us on the day
   that we call.

Psalm 21
For the choir director. A Davidic psalm.

1 LORD, the king finds joy
   in Your strength.
How greatly he rejoices in Your victory!
2 You have given him his heart's desire
and have not denied the request
   of his lips.   *Selah*
3 For You meet him with rich blessings;
You place a crown of pure gold
   on his head.
4 He asked You for life, and You gave it
   to him—
length of days forever and ever.
5 His glory is great through Your victory;
You confer majesty and splendor
   on him.
6 You give him blessings forever;
You cheer him with joy
   in Your presence.
7 For the king relies on the LORD;
through the faithful love
   of the Most High
he is not shaken.
8 Your hand will capture
   all your enemies;
your right hand will seize
   those who hate you.
9 You will make them burn
   like a fiery furnace when you appear;
the LORD will engulf them in His wrath,
   and fire will devour them.

10 You will wipe their descendants
   from the earth
and their offspring
   from the human race.
11 Though they intend to harm[C] you
and devise a wicked plan,
   they will not prevail.
12 Instead, you will put them to flight
   when you aim your bow[D] at their faces;
13 Be exalted, LORD, in Your strength;
   we will sing and praise Your might.

Psalm 22
For the choir director: according to "The Deer
of the Dawn."[E] A Davidic psalm.

1 My God, my God, why have You
   forsaken me?
Why are You so far
   from my deliverance
and from my words of groaning?[F]
2 My God, I cry by day, but You
   do not answer,
by night, yet I have no rest.
3 But You are holy,
   enthroned on the praises of Israel.
4 Our fathers trusted in You;
   they trusted, and You rescued them.
5 They cried to You and were set free;
they trusted in You
   and were not disgraced.
6 But I am a worm and not a man,
scorned by men and despised
   by people.
7 Everyone who sees me mocks me;
   they sneer[G] and shake their heads:
8 "He relies on[H] the LORD;
let Him rescue him;
let the LORD[I] deliver him,
since He takes pleasure in him."
9 You took me from the womb,
making me secure
   while at my mother's breast.
10 I was given over to You at birth;[J]
You have been my God
   from my mother's womb.
11 Do not be far from me, because distress
   is near
and there is no one to help.
12 Many bulls surround me;
   strong ones of Bashan encircle me.
13 They open their mouths against me—

[A]20:6 Some Hb mss, Aq, Sym, Jer, Syr read *with the victorious might of* [B]20:9 Or *LORD, save. May the king* [C]21:11 Lit *they stretch out evil against* [D]21:12 Lit *aim with your bowstrings* [E]22:title Perhaps a musical term [F]22:1 Or *My words of groaning are so far from delivering me* [G]22:7 Lit *separate with the lip* [H]22:8 Or *Rely on* [I]22:8 Lit *let Him* [J]22:10 Lit *it was cast on You from the womb* lions, mauling and roaring.

¹⁴ I am poured out like water,
and all my bones are disjointed;
my heart is like wax,
melting within me.

¹⁵ My strength is dried up like baked clay;
my tongue sticks to the roof
of my mouth.
You put me into the dust of death.

¹⁶ For dogs have surrounded me;
a gang of evildoers has closed in on me;
they pierced[A] my hands and my feet.

¹⁷ I can count all my bones;
people[B] look and stare at me.

¹⁸ They divided my garments
among themselves,
and they cast lots for my clothing.

¹⁹ But You, LORD, don't be far away.
My strength, come quickly to help me.

²⁰ Deliver my life from the sword,
my only life[C] from the power
of these dogs.

²¹ Save me from the mouth of the lion!
You have rescued[D] me
from the horns of the wild oxen.

²² I will proclaim Your name
to my brothers;
I will praise You in the congregation.

²³ You who fear Yahweh, praise Him!
All you descendants of Jacob,
honor Him!
All you descendants of Israel,
revere Him!

²⁴ For He has not despised or detested
the torment of the afflicted.
He did not hide His face from him
but listened when he cried to Him
for help.

²⁵ I will give praise[E]
in the great congregation
because of You;
I will fulfill my vows
before those who fear You.[F]

²⁶ The humble[G] will eat and be satisfied;
those who seek the LORD
will praise Him.
May your hearts live forever!

²⁷ All the ends of the earth will remember
and turn to the LORD.
All the families of the nations

will bow down before You,

²⁸ for kingship belongs to the LORD;
He rules over the nations.

²⁹ All who prosper on earth will eat
and bow down;
all those who go down to the dust
will kneel before Him—
even the one who cannot preserve
his life.

³⁰ Their descendants will serve Him;
the next generation will be told
about the Lord.

³¹ They will come and tell a people
yet to be born
about His righteousness—
what He has done.

Psalm 23
A Davidic psalm.

¹ The LORD is my shepherd;
there is nothing I lack.

² He lets me lie down in green pastures;
He leads me beside quiet waters.

³ He renews my life;
He leads me along the right paths[H]
for His name's sake.

⁴ Even when I go
through the darkest valley,[I]
I fear no danger,
for You are with me;
Your rod
and Your staff[J]—they comfort me.

⁵ You prepare a table before me
in the presence of my enemies;
You anoint my head with oil;
my cup overflows.

⁶ Only goodness and faithful love
will pursue me
all the days of my life,
and I will dwell in[K] the house
of the LORD
as long as I live.[L]

Psalm 24
A Davidic psalm.

¹ The earth and everything in it,
the world and its inhabitants,
belong to the LORD;

² for He laid its foundation on the seas
and established it on the rivers.

3 Who may ascend the mountain
    of the Lord?
  Who may stand in His holy place?
4 The one who has clean hands
    and a pure heart,
  who has not set his mind[A] on
    what is false,
  and who has not sworn deceitfully.
5 He will receive blessing from the Lord,
  and righteousness from the God
    of his salvation.
6 Such is the generation of those
    who seek Him,
  who seek the face of the God of Jacob.[B]
                              Selah

7 Lift up your heads, you gates!
  Rise up, ancient doors!
  Then the King of glory will come in.
8 Who is this King of glory?
  The Lord, strong and mighty,
  the Lord, mighty in battle.
9 Lift up your heads, you gates!
  Rise up, ancient doors!
  Then the King of glory will come in.
10 Who is He, this King of glory?
   The Lord of Hosts,
   He is the King of glory.   *Selah*

Psalm 25
Davidic.

1 Lord,[C] I turn to You.[D]
2 My God, I trust in You.
  Do not let me be disgraced;
  do not let my enemies gloat over me.
3 No one who waits for You
  will be disgraced;
  those who act treacherously
    without cause
  will be disgraced.
4 Make Your ways known to me, Lord;
  teach me Your paths.
5 Guide me in Your truth and teach me,
  for You are the God of my salvation;
  I wait for You all day long.
6 Remember, Lord, Your compassion
  and Your faithful love,
  for they have existed from antiquity.[E]
7 Do not remember the sins of my youth
  or my acts of rebellion;
  in keeping with Your faithful love,
  remember me

because of Your goodness, Lord.
8 The Lord is good and upright;
  therefore He shows sinners the way.
9 He leads the humble in what is right
  and teaches them His way.
10 All the Lord's ways show faithful love
    and truth
   to those who keep His covenant
    and decrees.
11 Because of Your name, Yahweh,
   forgive my sin, for it is great.
12 Who is the man who fears the Lord?
   He will show him the way
    he should choose.
13 He will live a good life,
   and his descendants will inherit
    the land.[F]
14 The secret counsel of the Lord
   is for those who fear Him,
   and He reveals His covenant to them.
15 My eyes are always on the Lord,
   for He will pull my feet out of the net.
16 Turn to me and be gracious to me,
   for I am alone and afflicted.
17 The distresses of my heart increase;[G]
   bring me out of my sufferings.
18 Consider my affliction and trouble,
   and take away all my sins.
19 Consider my enemies;
    they are numerous,
   and they hate me violently.
20 Guard me and deliver me;
   do not let me be put to shame,
   for I take refuge in You.
21 May integrity and what is right
   watch over me,
   for I wait for You.
22 God, redeem Israel, from all
    its distresses.

Psalm 26
Davidic.

1 Vindicate me, Lord,
  because I have lived with integrity
  and have trusted in the Lord
    without wavering.
2 Test me, Lord, and try me;
  examine my heart and mind.
3 For Your faithful love is before my eyes,
  and I live by Your truth.
4 I do not sit with the worthless

A24:4 Or *not lifted up his soul* B24:6 LXX; some Hb mss, Syr read *seek Your face, God of Jacob*; other Hb mss read *seek Your face, Jacob* C25:1 The lines of this poem form an acrostic. D25:1 Or *To You, Lord, I lift up my soul* E25:6 Or *everlasting* F25:13 Or *earth* G25:17 Or *Relieve the distresses of my heart*

or associate with hypocrites.
5 I hate a crowd of evildoers,
and I do not sit with the wicked.
6 I wash my hands[A] in innocence
and go around Your altar, LORD,
7 raising my voice in thanksgiving
and telling about
Your wonderful works.
8 LORD, I love the house where You dwell,
the place where Your glory resides.
9 Do not destroy me along with sinners,
or my life along with men of bloodshed
10 in whose hands are evil schemes
and whose right hands are filled
with bribes.
11 But I live with integrity;
redeem me and be gracious to me.
12 My foot stands on level ground;
I will praise the LORD in the assemblies.

Psalm 27
Davidic.

1 The LORD is my light
and my salvation—
whom should I fear?
The LORD is the stronghold of my life—
of whom should I be afraid?
2 When evildoers came against me
to devour my flesh,
my foes and my enemies stumbled
and fell.
3 Though an army deploys against me,
my heart is not afraid;
though a war breaks out against me,
still I am confident.
4 I have asked one thing from the LORD;
it is what I desire:
to dwell in the house of the LORD
all the days of my life,
gazing on the beauty of the LORD
and seeking Him in His temple.
5 For He will conceal me in His shelter
in the day of adversity;
He will hide me under the cover
of His tent;
He will set me high on a rock.
6 Then my head will be high
above my enemies around me;
I will offer sacrifices in His tent
with shouts of joy.
I will sing and make music to the LORD.
7 LORD, hear my voice when I call;
be gracious to me and answer me.

8 My heart says this about You,
"You[B] are to seek My face."
LORD, I will seek Your face.
9 Do not hide Your face from me;
do not turn Your servant away in anger.
You have been my helper;
do not leave me or abandon me,
God of my salvation.
10 Even if my father and mother
abandon me,
the LORD cares for me.
11 Because of my adversaries,
show me Your way, LORD,
and lead me on a level path.
12 Do not give me over to the will
of my foes,
for false witnesses rise up against me,
breathing violence.
13 I am certain that I will see
the LORD's goodness
in the land of the living.
14 Wait for the LORD;
be strong[C] and courageous.
Wait for the LORD.

Psalm 28
Davidic.

1 LORD, I call to You;
my rock, do not be deaf to me.
If You remain silent to me,
I will be like those going down
to the Pit.
2 Listen to the sound of my pleading
when I cry to You for help,
when I lift up my hands
toward Your holy sanctuary.
3 Do not drag me away with the wicked,
with the evildoers,
who speak in friendly ways
with their neighbors
while malice is in their hearts.
4 Repay them according to what
they have done—
according to the evil of their deeds.
Repay them according to the work
of their hands;
give them back what they deserve.
5 Because they do not consider
what the LORD has done
or the work of His hands,
He will tear them down and not
rebuild them.
6 May the LORD be praised,

A26:6 A ritual or ceremonial washing to express innocence   B27:8 You is plural in Hb   C27:14 Lit LORD; let your heart be strong

for He has heard the sound
of my pleading.
7 The LORD is my strength
and my shield;
my heart trusts in Him,
and I am helped.
Therefore my heart rejoices,
and I praise Him with my song.
8 The LORD is the strength
of His people;[A]
He is a stronghold of salvation
for His anointed.
9 Save Your people,
bless Your possession,
shepherd them, and carry
them forever.

Psalm 29
A Davidic psalm.

1 Ascribe to Yahweh,
you heavenly beings,[B]
ascribe to the LORD glory and strength.
2 Ascribe to Yahweh the glory due
His name;
worship Yahweh
in the splendor of His holiness.[C]
3 The voice of the LORD is
above the waters.
The God of glory thunders—
the LORD, above vast waters,
4 the voice of the LORD in power,
the voice of the LORD in splendor.
5 The voice of the LORD
breaks the cedars;
the LORD shatters the cedars
of Lebanon.
6 He makes Lebanon skip like a calf,
and Sirion,[D] like a young wild ox.
7 The voice of the LORD flashes
flames of fire.
8 The voice of the LORD shakes
the wilderness;
the LORD shakes the wilderness
of Kadesh.
9 The voice of the LORD makes the deer
give birth[E]
and strips the woodlands bare.
In His temple all cry, "Glory!"
10 The LORD sat enthroned at the flood;
the LORD sits enthroned, King forever.
11 The LORD gives His people strength;

the LORD blesses His people
with peace.

Psalm 30
A psalm; a dedication song for the house. Davidic.

1 I will exalt You, LORD,
because You have lifted me up
and have not allowed my enemies
to triumph over me.
2 LORD my God,
I cried to You for help, and You
healed me.
3 LORD, You brought me up from Sheol;
You spared me from among those
going down[F] to the Pit.
4 Sing to Yahweh, you His faithful ones,
and praise His holy name.
5 For His anger lasts only a moment,
but His favor, a lifetime.
Weeping may spend the night,
but there is joy in the morning.
6 When I was secure, I said,
"I will never be shaken."
7 LORD, when You showed Your favor,
You made me stand
like a strong mountain;
when You hid Your face, I was terrified.
8 LORD, I called to You;
I sought favor from my Lord:
9 "What gain is there in my death,
if I go down to the Pit?
Will the dust praise You?
Will it proclaim Your truth?
10 LORD, listen and be gracious to me;
LORD, be my helper."
11 You turned my lament into dancing;
You removed my sackcloth
and clothed me with gladness,
12 so that I can sing to You and not
be silent.
LORD my God, I will praise You forever.

Psalm 31
For the choir director. A Davidic psalm.

1 LORD, I seek refuge in You;
let me never be disgraced.
Save me by Your righteousness.
2 Listen closely to me;
rescue me quickly.
Be a rock of refuge for me,
a mountain fortress to save me.
3 For You are my rock and my fortress;

[A]28:8 Some Hb mss, LXX, Syr; other Hb mss read *strength for them* [B]29:1 Or *you angels*, or *you sons of the mighty*; lit *LORD sons of the gods* [C]29:2 Or *in holy attire*, or *in holy appearance* [D]29:6 = Mount Hermon [E]29:9 Or *the oaks shake* [F]30:3 Some Hb mss, LXX, Theod, Orig, Syr; other Hb mss, Aq, Sym, Tg, Jer read *from going down*

You lead and guide me
    because of Your name.
⁴ You will free me from the net
    that is secretly set for me,
    for You are my refuge.
⁵ Into Your hand I entrust my spirit;
    You redeemᴬ me, Lᴏʀᴅ, God of truth.
⁶ Iᴮ hate those who are devoted
        to worthless idols,
    but I trust in the Lᴏʀᴅ.
⁷ I will rejoice and be glad
    in Your faithful love
    because You have seen my affliction.
    You have known the troubles of my life
⁸ and have not handed me over
    to the enemy.
    You have set my feet
    in a spacious place.
⁹ Be gracious to me, Lᴏʀᴅ,
    because I am in distress;
    my eyes are worn out
        from angry sorrow—
    my whole beingᶜ as well.
¹⁰ Indeed, my life is consumed with grief
    and my years with groaning;
    my strength has failed
    because of my sinfulness,ᴰ
    and my bones waste away.
¹¹ I am ridiculed by all my adversaries
    and even by my neighbors.
    I am dreaded by my acquaintances;
    those who see me in the street
        run from me.
¹² I am forgotten: gone from memory
        like a dead
        person— like broken pottery.
¹³ I have heard the gossip of many;
    terror is on every side.
    When they conspired against me,
    they plotted to take my life.
¹⁴ But I trust in You, Lᴏʀᴅ;
    I say, "You are my God."
¹⁵ The course of my life is in Your power;
    deliver me from the power
        of my enemies
    and from my persecutors.
¹⁶ Show Your favor to Your servant;
    save me by Your faithful love.
¹⁷ Lᴏʀᴅ, do not let me be disgraced
        when I call on You.
    Let the wicked be disgraced;

let them be silentᴱ,ᶠ in Sheol.
¹⁸ Let lying lips be quieted;
    they speak arrogantly
        against the righteous
    with pride and contempt.
¹⁹ How great is Your goodness
    that You have stored up for those
        who fear You
    and accomplished in the sight
        of everyone
    for those who take refuge in You.
²⁰ You hide them in the protection
        of Your presence;
    You conceal them in a shelterᴳ
    from the schemes of men,
    from quarrelsome tongues.
²¹ May the Lᴏʀᴅ be praised,
    for He has wonderfully shown
        His faithful love to me
    in a city under siege.ᴴ
²² In my alarm I had said,
    "I am cut off from Your sight."
    But You heard the sound
        of my pleading
    when I cried to You for help.
²³ Love the Lᴏʀᴅ, all His faithful ones.
    The Lᴏʀᴅ protects the loyal,
    but fully repays the arrogant.
²⁴ Be strongᴵ and courageous,
    all you who put your hope in the Lᴏʀᴅ.

Psalm 32
Davidic. A Maskil.

¹ How joyful is the one
    whose transgression is forgiven,
    whose sin is covered!
² How joyful is the man
    the Lᴏʀᴅ does not charge with sin
    and in whose spirit is no deceit!
³ When I kept silent, my bones
        became brittle
    from my groaning all day long.
⁴ For day and night Your hand was heavy
        on me;
    my strength was drainedᴶ
    as in the summer's heat.   *Selah*
⁵ Then I acknowledged my sin to You
    and did not conceal my iniquity.
    I said,
    "I will confess my transgressions
        to the Lᴏʀᴅ,"

ᴬ31:5 Or *You have redeemed*, or *You will redeem*, or *spirit. Redeem*   ᴮ31:6 One Hb ms, LXX, Syr, Vg, Jer read *You*   ᶜ31:9 Lit *my soul and my belly*   ᴰ31:10 LXX, Syr, Sym read *affliction*   ᴱ31:17 LXX reads *brought down*   ᶠ31:17 Or *them perish*, or *they wail*   ᴳ31:20 Lit *canopy*   ᴴ31:21 Or *a fortified city*   ᴵ31:24 Lit *Let your heart be strong*   ᴶ32:4 Hb obscure

and You took away the guilt
  of my sin.   *Selah*

6 Therefore let everyone who is faithful
  pray to You
at a time that You may be found.[A]
When great floodwaters come,
they will not reach him.

7 You are my hiding place;
You protect me from trouble.
You surround me with joyful shouts
  of deliverance.   *Selah*

8 I will instruct you and show you
  the way to go;
with My eye on you, I will give counsel.

9 Do not be like a horse or mule,
  without understanding,
that must be controlled with bit
  and bridle
or else it will not come near you.

10 Many pains come to the wicked,
but the one who trusts in the LORD
will have faithful love
  surrounding him.

11 Be glad in the LORD and rejoice,
you righteous ones;
shout for joy,
all you upright in heart.

Psalm 33

1 Rejoice in the LORD,
  you righteous ones;
praise from the upright is beautiful.

2 Praise the LORD with the lyre;
make music to Him with a ten-
  stringed harp.

3 Sing a new song to Him;
play skillfully on the strings,
  with a joyful shout.

4 For the word of the LORD is right,
and all His work is trustworthy.

5 He loves righteousness and justice;
the earth is full of the LORD's
  unfailing love.

6 The heavens were made by the word
  of the LORD,
and all the stars, by the breath
  of His mouth.

7 He gathers the waters of the sea
  into a heap;[B]
He puts the depths into storehouses.

8 Let the whole earth tremble
  before the LORD;

let all the inhabitants of the world
  stand in awe of Him.

9 For He spoke, and it came into being;
He commanded, and it came
  into existence.

10 The LORD frustrates the counsel
  of the nations;
He thwarts the plans of the peoples.

11 The counsel of the LORD stands forever,
the plans of His heart from generation
  to generation.

12 Happy is the nation whose God
  is Yahweh—
the people He has chosen to be
  His own possession!

13 The LORD looks down from heaven;
He observes everyone.

14 He gazes on all the inhabitants
  of the earth
from His dwelling place.

15 He alone shapes their hearts;
He considers all their works.

16 A king is not saved by a large army;
a warrior will not be delivered
  by great strength.

17 The horse is a false hope for safety;
it provides no escape by its great power.

18 Now the eye of the LORD is on those
  who fear Him—
those who depend on His faithful love

19 to deliver them from death
and to keep them alive in famine.

20 We wait for Yahweh;
He is our help and shield.

21 For our hearts rejoice in Him
because we trust in His holy name.

22 May Your faithful love rest on us,
  Yahweh,
for we put our hope in You.

Psalm 34

Concerning David, when he pretended to
be insane in the presence of Abimelech,[C]
  who drove him out, and he departed.

1 I[D] will praise the LORD at all times;
His praise will always be on my lips.

2 I will boast in the LORD;
the humble will hear and be glad.

3 Proclaim Yahweh's greatness with me;
let us exalt His name together.

4 I sought the LORD, and He answered me
and delivered me from all my fears.

A32:6 Lit *time of finding* B33:7 LXX, Tg, Syr, Vg, Jer read *sea as in a bottle* C34:title Probably Achish, king of Gath D34:1 The lines of this
poem form an acrostic.

5 Those who look to Him are^A radiant
with joy;
their faces will never be ashamed.
6 This poor man cried, and the LORD
heard him
and saved him from all his troubles.
7 The Angel of the LORD encamps
around those who fear Him,
and rescues them.
8 Taste and see that the LORD is good.
How happy is the man
who takes refuge in Him!
9 You who are His holy ones, fear Yahweh,
for those who fear Him lack nothing.
10 Young lions^B lack food and go hungry,
but those who seek the LORD
will not lack any good thing.
11 Come, children, listen to me;
I will teach you the fear of the LORD.
12 Who is the man who delights in life,
loving a long life to enjoy what is good?
13 Keep your tongue from evil
and your lips from deceitful speech.
14 Turn away from evil and do
what is good;
seek peace and pursue it.
15 The eyes of the LORD are
on the righteous,
and His ears are open to their cry
for help.
16 The face of the LORD is set
against those who do what is evil,
to erase^C all memory of them
from the earth.
17 The righteous^D cry out,
and the LORD hears,
and delivers them from all
their troubles.
18 The LORD is near the brokenhearted;
He saves those crushed in spirit.
19 Many adversities come to the one
who is righteous,
but the LORD delivers him
from them all.
20 He protects all his bones;
not one of them is broken.
21 Evil brings death to the wicked,
and those who hate the righteous
will be punished.
22 The LORD redeems the life
of His servants,

and all who take refuge in Him will not
be punished.

Psalm 35
Davidic.

1 Oppose my opponents, LORD;
fight those who fight me.
2 Take Your shields— large and small—
and come to my aid.
3 Draw the spear and javelin
against my pursuers,
and assure me: "I am
your deliverance."
4 Let those who seek to kill me
be disgraced and humiliated;
let those who plan to harm me
be turned back and ashamed.
5 Let them be like chaff in the wind,
with the angel of the LORD
driving them away.
6 Let their way be dark and slippery,
with the angel of the LORD
pursuing them.
7 They hid their net for me
without cause;
they dug a pit for me without cause.
8 Let ruin come on him unexpectedly,
and let the net that he hid
ensnare him;
let him fall into it—to his ruin.
9 Then I will rejoice in the LORD;
I will delight in His deliverance.
10 My very bones will say,
"LORD, who is like You,
rescuing the poor from one too strong
for him,
the poor or the needy from one
who robs him?"
11 Malicious witnesses come forward;
they question me about things
I do not know.
12 They repay me evil for good,
making me desolate.
13 Yet when they were sick,
my clothing was sackcloth;
I humbled myself with fasting,
and my prayer was genuine.^E
14 I went about grieving as if
for my friend or brother;
I was bowed down with grief,
like one mourning a mother.

^A34:5 Some Hb mss, LXX, Aq, Syr, Jer read Look to Him and be   ^B34:10 LXX, Syr, Vg read The rich   ^C34:16 Or cut off   ^D34:17 Lit They
^E35:13 Lit prayer returned to my chest

15 But when I stumbled, they gathered
        in glee;
     they gathered against me.
     Assailants I did not know
     tore at me and did not stop.
16 With godless mockery[A]
     they gnashed their teeth at me.
17 Lord, how long will You look on?
     Rescue my life from their ravages,
     my only one from the young lions.
18 I will praise You
        in the great congregation;
     I will exalt You among many people.
19 Do not let my deceitful enemies rejoice
        over me;
     do not let those who hate me
        without cause
     look at me maliciously.
20 For they do not speak
        in friendly ways,
     but contrive deceitful schemes[B]
     against those who live peacefully
        in the land.
21 They open their mouths wide
        against me and say,
     "Aha, aha! We saw it!"[C]
22 You saw it, Lord; do not be silent.
     Lord, do not be far from me.
23 Wake up and rise to my defense,
     to my cause, my God and my Lord!
24 Vindicate me, Lord my God,
     in keeping with Your righteousness,
     and do not let them rejoice over me.
25 Do not let them say in their hearts,
     "Aha! Just what we wanted."
     Do not let them say,
     "We have swallowed him up!"
26 Let those who rejoice
        at my misfortune
     be disgraced and humiliated;
     let those who exalt themselves
        over me
     be clothed with shame and reproach.
27 Let those who want my vindication
     shout for joy and be glad;
     let them continually say,
     "The Lord be exalted.
     He takes pleasure in
        His servant's well-being."
28 And my tongue will proclaim
        Your righteousness,
     Your praise all day long.

Psalm 36

For the choir director. A psalm of David,
the Lord's servant.

1 An oracle within my heart
     concerning the transgression of the
        wicked person:
     There is no dread of God
        before his eyes,
2 for in his own eyes he flatters himself
        too much
     to discover and hate his sin.
3 The words of his mouth are malicious
        and deceptive;
     he has stopped acting wisely
        and doing good.
4 Even on his bed he makes
        malicious plans.
     He sets himself on a path
        that is not good
     and does not reject evil.
5 Lord, Your faithful love reaches
        to heaven,
     Your faithfulness to the clouds.
6 Your righteousness is
        like the highest mountains;
     Your judgments, like the deepest sea.
     Lord, You preserve man and beast.
7 God, Your faithful love is so valuable
     that people take refuge in the shadow
        of Your wings.
8 They are filled from the abundance
        of Your house;
     You let them drink
        from Your refreshing stream,
9 for with You is life's fountain.
     In Your light we will see light.
10 Spread Your faithful love over those
        who know You,
     and Your righteousness
        over the upright in heart.
11 Do not let the foot of the arrogant man
        come near me
     or the hand of the wicked one
        drive me away.
12 There the evildoers fall;
     they have been thrown down
        and cannot rise.

Psalm 37

Davidic.

1 Do[D] not be agitated by evildoers;
     do not envy those who do wrong.
2 For they wither quickly like grass

A35:16 Hb obscure   B35:20 Lit but devise deceitful words   C35:21 Lit Our eyes saw!   D37:1 The lines of this poem form an acrostic.

and wilt like tender green plants.

3 Trust in the Lord and do what is good;
dwell in the land and live securely.[A]

4 Take delight in the Lord,
and He will give you
your heart's desires.

5 Commit your way to the Lord;
trust in Him, and He will act,

6 making your righteousness shine
like the dawn,
your justice like the noonday.

7 Be silent before the Lord and wait
expectantly for Him;
do not be agitated by one who prospers
in his way,
by the man who carries out evil plans.

8 Refrain from anger and give up
your rage;
do not be agitated—it can only
bring harm.

9 For evildoers will be destroyed,
but those who put their hope
in the Lord
will inherit the land.[B]

10 A little while, and the wicked person
will be no more;
though you look for him, he will not
be there.

11 But the humble will inherit the land[B]
and will enjoy abundant prosperity.

12 The wicked person schemes
against the righteous
and gnashes his teeth at him.

13 The Lord laughs at him
because He sees that his day is coming.

14 The wicked have drawn the sword
and strung the[C] bow
to bring down the afflicted and needy
and to slaughter those whose way
is upright.

15 Their swords will enter
their own hearts,
and their bows will be broken.

16 The little that the righteous man has
is better
than the abundance
of many wicked people.

17 For the arms[D] of the wicked
will be broken,
but the Lord supports the righteous.

18 The Lord watches over the blameless
all their days,

and their inheritance will last forever.

19 They will not be disgraced in times
of adversity;
they will be satisfied in days of hunger.

20 But the wicked will perish;
the Lord's enemies, like the glory
of the pastures,
will fade away—
they will fade away like smoke.

21 The wicked man borrows
and does not repay,
but the righteous one is gracious
and giving.

22 Those who are blessed by Him
will inherit the land,[B]
but those cursed by Him
will be destroyed.

23 A man's steps are established
by the Lord,
and He takes pleasure in his way.

24 Though he falls, he will not
be overwhelmed,
because the Lord holds his hand.[E]

25 I have been young and now I am old,
yet I have not seen
the righteous abandoned
or his children begging for bread.

26 He is always generous, always lending,
and his children are a blessing.

27 Turn away from evil and do
what is good,
and dwell there[F] forever.

28 For the Lord loves justice
and will not abandon His faithful ones.
They are kept safe forever,
but the children of the wicked
will be destroyed.

29 The righteous will inherit the land[B]
and dwell in it permanently.

30 The mouth of the righteous
utters wisdom;
his tongue speaks what is just.

31 The instruction of his God is
in his heart;
his steps do not falter.

32 The wicked one lies in wait
for the righteous
and seeks to kill him;

33 the Lord will not leave him
in the power of the wicked one
or allow him to be condemned
when he is judged.

A 37:3 Or and cultivate faithfulness   B 37:9,11,22,29 Or earth   C 37:14 Lit their   D 37:17 Or power   E 37:24 Or Lord supports with His hand   F 37:27 = dwell in the land

34 Wait for the LORD and keep His way,
and He will exalt you to inherit
the land.
You will watch when the wicked
are destroyed.
35 I have seen a wicked, violent man
well-rooted[A] like
a flourishing native tree.
36 Then I passed by and[B] noticed
he was gone;
I searched for him, but he could not
be found.
37 Watch the blameless and observe
the upright,
for the man of peace will have
a future.[C]
38 But transgressors will all
be eliminated;
the future[C] of the wicked
will be destroyed.
39 The salvation of the righteous is
from the LORD,
their refuge in a time of distress.
40 The LORD helps and delivers them;
He will deliver them from the wicked
and will save them
because they take refuge in Him.

Psalm 38
A Davidic psalm for remembrance.

1 LORD, do not punish me in Your anger
or discipline me in Your wrath.
2 For Your arrows have sunk into me,
and Your hand has pressed down
on me.
3 There is no health in my body
because of Your indignation;
there is no strength[D] in my bones
because of my sin.
4 For my sins have flooded over my head;
they are a burden too heavy for me
to bear.
5 My wounds are foul and festering
because of my foolishness.
6 I am bent over and brought low;
all day long I go around in mourning.
7 For my loins are full of burning pain,
and there is no health in my body.
8 I am faint and severely crushed;
I groan because of the anguish
of my heart.
9 Lord, my every desire is known to[E] You;

my sighing is not hidden from You.
10 My heart races, my strength leaves me,
and even the light of my eyes
has faded.[F]
11 My loved ones and friends stand back
from my affliction,
and my relatives stand at a distance.
12 Those who seek my life set traps,
and those who want to harm me
threaten to destroy me;
they plot treachery all day long.
13 I am like a deaf person; I do not hear.
I am like a speechless person
who does not open his mouth.
14 I am like a man who does not hear
and has no arguments in his mouth.
15 I put my hope in You, LORD;
You will answer, Lord my God.
16 For I said, "Don't let them rejoice
over me—
those who are arrogant toward me
when I stumble."
17 For I am about to fall,
and my pain is constantly with me.
18 So I confess my guilt;
I am anxious because of my sin.
19 But my enemies are vigorous
and powerful;[G]
many hate me for no reason.
20 Those who repay evil for good
attack me for pursuing good.
21 LORD, do not abandon me;
my God, do not be far from me.
22 Hurry to help me,
Lord, my Savior.

Psalm 39
For the choir director, for Jeduthun.
A Davidic psalm.

1 I said, "I will guard my ways
so that I may not sin with my tongue;
I will guard my mouth with a muzzle
as long as the wicked are
in my presence."
2 I was speechless and quiet;
I kept silent, even from speaking good,
and my pain intensified.
3 My heart grew hot within me;
as I mused, a fire burned.
I spoke with my tongue:
4 "LORD, reveal to me the end of my life
and the number of my days.

A37:35 Hb obscure   B37:36 DSS, LXX, Syr, Vg, Jer; MT reads *Then he passed away, and I*   C37:37,38 Or *posterity*   D38:3 Hb *shalom*   E38:9 Lit *is in front of*   F38:10 Or *and the light of my eyes—even that is not with me*   G38:19 Or *numerous*

Let me know how short-lived I am.
5 You, indeed, have made my days short
      in length,
   and my life span as nothing
      in Your sight.
   Yes, every mortal man is only a vapor.
                                        Selah
6 "Certainly, man walks about
      like a mere shadow.
   Indeed, they frantically rush around
      in vain,
   gathering possessions
      without knowing who will get them.
7 Now, Lord, what do I wait for?
   My hope is in You.
8 Deliver me from all my transgressions;
   do not make me the taunt of fools.
9 I am speechless; I do not open
      my mouth
   because of what You have done.
10 Remove Your torment from me;
   I fade away because of the force
      of Your hand.
11 You discipline a man with punishment
      for sin,
   consuming like a moth
      what is precious to him;
   every man is only a vapor.   *Selah*
12 "Hear my prayer, Lord,
   and listen to my cry for help;
   do not be silent at my tears.
   For I am a foreigner residing with You,
   a temporary resident like all
      my fathers.
13 Turn Your angry gaze from me
   so that I may be cheered up
   before I die and am gone."

Psalm 40
For the choir director. A Davidic psalm.

1 I waited patiently for the Lord,
   and He turned to me and heard my cry
      for help.
2 He brought me up from a desolate^A pit,
   out of the muddy clay,
   and set my feet on a rock,
   making my steps secure.
3 He put a new song in my mouth,
   a hymn of praise to our God.
   Many will see and fear
   and put their trust in the Lord.
4 How happy is the man

who has put his trust in the Lord
and has not turned to the proud
or to those who run after lies!
5 Lord my God, You have done
      many things—
   Your wonderful works and Your plans
      for us;
   none can compare with You.
   If I were to report and speak of them,
   they are more than can be told.
6 You do not delight in sacrifice
      and offering;
   You open my ears to listen.^B
   You do not ask for
      a whole burnt offering
      or a sin offering.
7 Then I said, "See, I have come;
   it is written about me in the volume
      of the scroll.
8 I delight to do Your will, my God;
   Your instruction lives within me."^C
9 I proclaim righteousness
      in the great assembly;
   see, I do not keep my mouth closed^D—
   as You know, Lord.
10 I did not hide Your righteousness
      in my heart;
   I spoke about Your faithfulness
      and salvation;
   I did not conceal Your constant love
      and truth
   from the great assembly.
11 Lord, do not withhold Your compassion
      from me;
   Your constant love and truth
      will always guard me.
12 For troubles without number
      have surrounded me;
   my sins have overtaken me;
      I am unable to see.
   They are more than the hairs
      of my head,
   and my courage leaves me.
13 Lord, be pleased to deliver me;
   hurry to help me, Lord.
14 Let those who seek to take my life
   be disgraced and confounded.
   Let those who wish me harm
   be driven back and humiliated.
15 Let those who say to me, "Aha, aha!"
   be horrified because of their shame.

¹⁶ Let all who seek You rejoice
    and be glad in You;
let those who love Your salvation
    continually say,
"The LORD is great!"

¹⁷ I am afflicted and needy;
the Lord thinks of me.
You are my helper and my deliverer;
my God, do not delay.

Psalm 41
For the choir director. A Davidic psalm.

¹ Happy is one who cares for the poor;
the LORD will save him in a day
    of adversity.

² The LORD will keep him
    and preserve him;
he will be blessed in the land.
You will not give him over to the desire
    of his enemies.

³ The LORD will sustain him
    on his sickbed;
You will heal him on the bed
    where he lies.

⁴ I said, "LORD, be gracious to me;
heal me, for I have sinned against You."

⁵ My enemies speak maliciously
    about me:
"When will he die and be forgotten?"

⁶ When one of them comes to visit,
    he speaks deceitfully;
he stores up evil in his heart;
he goes out and talks.

⁷ All who hate me whisper together
    about me;
they plan to harm me.

⁸ "Lethal poison has been poured
    into him,
and he won't rise again from where
    he lies!"

⁹ Even my friendᴬ in whom I trusted,
one who ate my bread,
has raised his heel against me.

¹⁰ But You, LORD, be gracious to me
    and raise me up;
then I will repay them.

¹¹ By this I know that You delight in me:
my enemy does not shout in triumph
    over me.

¹² You supported me because of
    my integrity
and set me in Your presence forever.

¹³ May Yahweh, the God of Israel,
    be praised
from everlasting to everlasting.
Amen and amen.

BOOK II
(Psalms 42–72)

Psalm 42
For the choir director. A *Maskil*
of the sons of Korah.

¹ As a deer longs for streams of water,
so I long for You, God.

² I thirst for God, the living God.
When can I come and appear
    before God?

³ My tears have been my food
    day and night,
while all day long people say to me,
"Where is your God?"

⁴ I remember this as I pour out
    my heart:
how I walked with many,
leading the festive procession
    to the house of God,
with joyful and thankful shouts.

⁵ Why am I so depressed?
Why this turmoil within me?
Put your hope in God, for I will
    still praise Him,
my Savior and my God.

⁶ Iᴮ am deeply depressed;
therefore I remember You
    from the land of Jordan
and the peaks of Hermon,
    from Mount Mizar.

⁷ Deep calls to deep in the roar
    of Your waterfalls;
all Your breakers and Your billows
    have swept over me.

⁸ The LORD will send His faithful love
    by day;
His song will be with me
    in the night—
a prayer to the God of my life.

⁹ I will say to God, my rock,
"Why have You forgotten me?
Why must I go about in sorrow
because of the enemy's oppression?"

¹⁰ My adversaries taunt me,
as if crushing my bones,
while all day long they say to me,
"Where is your God?"

ᴬ41:9 Lit *Even a man of my peace*   ᴮ42:5-6 Some Hb mss, LXX, Syr; other Hb mss read *Him, the salvation of His presence.* ⁶ *My God, I*

[11] Why am I so depressed?
Why this turmoil within me?
Put your hope in God, for I will
    still praise Him,
my Savior and my God.

Psalm 43[A]

[1] Vindicate me, God, and defend
    my cause
against an ungodly nation;
rescue me from the deceitful
    and unjust man.

[2] For You are the God of my refuge.
Why have You rejected me?
Why must I go about in sorrow
because of the enemy's oppression?

[3] Send Your light and Your truth;
    let them lead me.
Let them bring me
    to Your holy mountain,
to Your dwelling place.

[4] Then I will come to the altar of God,
to God, my greatest joy.
I will praise You with the lyre,
God, my God.

[5] Why am I so depressed?
Why this turmoil within me?
Put your hope in God, for I will
    still praise Him,
my Savior and my God.

Psalm 44

For the choir director. A *Maskil*
of the sons of Korah.

[1] God, we have heard with our ears—
our ancestors have told us—
the work You accomplished
    in their days,
in days long ago:

[2] to plant them,
You drove out the nations
    with Your hand;
to settle them,
You crushed the peoples.

[3] For they did not take the land
    by their sword—
their arm did not bring them victory—
but by Your right hand, Your arm,
and the light of Your face,
for You were pleased with them.

[4] You are my King, my God,
who ordains[B] victories for Jacob.

[5] Through You we drive back our foes;

through Your name we trample
    our enemies.

[6] For I do not trust in my bow,
and my sword does not
    bring me victory.

[7] But You give us victory over our foes
and let those who hate us be disgraced.

[8] We boast in God all day long;
we will praise Your name forever. *Selah*

[9] But You have rejected
    and humiliated us;
You do not march out with our armies.

[10] You make us retreat from the foe,
and those who hate us
    have taken plunder for themselves.

[11] You hand us over to be eaten like sheep
and scatter us among the nations.

[12] You sell Your people for nothing;
You make no profit from selling them.

[13] You make us an object of reproach
    to our neighbors,
a source of mockery and ridicule
    to those around us.

[14] You make us a joke among the nations,
a laughingstock[C] among the peoples.

[15] My disgrace is before me all day long,
and shame has covered my face,

[16] because of the voice of the scorner
    and reviler,
because of the enemy and avenger.

[17] All this has happened to us,
but we have not forgotten You
or betrayed Your covenant.

[18] Our hearts have not turned back;
our steps have not strayed
    from Your path.

[19] But You have crushed us in a haunt
    of jackals
and have covered us
    with deepest darkness.

[20] If we had forgotten the name
    of our God
and spread out our hands
    to a foreign god,

[21] wouldn't God have found this out,
since He knows the secrets
    of the heart?

[22] Because of You we are slain
    all day long;
we are counted as sheep
    to be slaughtered.

[23] Wake up, Lord! Why are You sleeping?

[A]Ps 43 Many Hb mss connect Pss 42–43   [B]44:4 LXX, Syr, Aq; MT reads *King, God; ordain*   [C]44:14 Lit *shaking of the head*

Get up! Don't reject us forever!

24 Why do You hide Yourself
and forget our affliction
and oppression?

25 For we have sunk down to the dust;
our bodies cling to the ground.

26 Rise up! Help us!
Redeem us because of
Your faithful love.

Psalm 45

For the choir director: according to "The Lilies."[A]
[A] Maskil of the sons of Korah. A love song.

1 My heart is moved by a noble theme
as I recite my verses to the king;
my tongue is the pen
of a skillful writer.

2 You are the most handsome of men;
grace flows from your lips.
Therefore God has blessed you forever.

3 Mighty warrior, strap your sword
at your side.
In your majesty and splendor—

4 in your splendor ride triumphantly
in the cause of truth, humility,
and justice.
May your right hand show your awe-
inspiring acts.

5 Your arrows pierce the hearts
of the king's enemies;
the peoples fall under you.

6 Your throne, God, is[B] forever and ever;
the scepter of Your[C] kingdom is
a scepter of justice.

7 You love righteousness
and hate wickedness;
therefore God, your God,
has anointed you with the oil of joy
more than your companions.

8 Myrrh, aloes, and cassia perfume
all your garments;
from ivory palaces harps bring you joy.

9 Kings' daughters are
among your honored women;
the queen, adorned with gold
from Ophir,
stands at your right hand.

10 Listen, daughter, pay attention
and consider:
forget your people
and your father's house,

11 and the king will desire your beauty.

Bow down to him, for he is your lord.

12 The daughter of Tyre,
the wealthy people,
will seek your favor with gifts.

13 In her chamber, the royal daughter
is all glorious,
her clothing embroidered with gold.

14 In colorful garments she is led
to the king;
after her, the virgins, her companions,
are brought to you.

15 They are led in with gladness
and rejoicing;
they enter the king's palace.

16 Your sons will succeed your ancestors;
you will make them princes
throughout the land.

17 I will cause your name
to be remembered
for all generations;
therefore the peoples will praise you
forever and ever.

Psalm 46

For the choir director. A song of the sons of Korah.
According to Alamoth.[D]

1 God is our refuge and strength,
a helper who is always found
in times of trouble.

2 Therefore we will not be afraid,
though the earth trembles
and the mountains topple
into the depths of the seas,

3 though its waters roar and foam
and the mountains quake
with its turmoil.   Selah

4 There is a river—
its streams delight the city of God,
the holy dwelling place
of the Most High.

5 God is within her;
she will not be toppled.
God will help her
when the morning dawns.

6 Nations rage, kingdoms topple;
the earth melts when He lifts His voice.

7 The LORD of Hosts is with us;
the God of Jacob is our stronghold.
                                           Selah

8 Come, see the works of the LORD,
who brings devastation on the earth.

⁹ He makes wars cease
   throughout the earth.
He shatters bows and cuts spears
   to pieces;
He burns up the chariots.ᴬ

¹⁰ "Stop your fighting—and know that
   I am God,
exalted among the nations,
   exalted on the earth."

¹¹ Yahweh of Hosts is with us;
   the God of Jacob is our stronghold.

                              Selah

Psalm 47

For the choir director. A psalm of the sons of Korah.

¹ Clap your hands, all you peoples;
  shout to God with a jubilant cry.

² For Yahweh, the Most High, is awe-
  inspiring,
  a great King over all the earth.

³ He subdues peoples under us
  and nations under our feet.

⁴ He chooses for us our inheritance—
  the pride of Jacob, whom He loves.

                              Selah

⁵ God ascends among shouts of joy,
  the Lᴏʀᴅ, among the sound
     of trumpets.

⁶ Sing praise to God, sing praise;
  sing praise to our King, sing praise!

⁷ Sing a song of wisdom,ᴮ
  for God is King of all the earth.

⁸ God reigns over the nations;
  God is seated on His holy throne.

⁹ The nobles of the peoples
     have assembled
  with the people of the God of Abraham.
  For the leadersᶜ of the earth
     belong to God;
  He is greatly exalted.

Psalm 48

A song. A psalm of the sons of Korah.

¹ The Lᴏʀᴅ is great and highly praised
  in the city of our God.
  His holy mountain, ²rising splendidly,
  is the joy of the whole earth.
  Mount Zion on the slopes of the north
  is the city of the great King.

³ God is known as a stronghold
  in its citadels.

⁴ Look! The kings assembled;
  they advanced together.

⁵ They looked and froze with fear;
  they fled in terror.

⁶ Trembling seized them there,
  agony like that of a woman in labor,

⁷ as You wrecked the ships of Tarshish
  with the east wind.

⁸ Just as we heard, so we have seen
  in the city of Yahweh of Hosts,
  in the city of our God;
  God will establish it forever.   *Selah*

⁹ God, within Your temple,
  we contemplate Your faithful love.

¹⁰ Your name, God, like Your praise,
  reaches to the ends of the earth;
  Your right hand is filled with justice.

¹¹ Mount Zion is glad.
  The townsᴰ of Judah rejoice
  because of Your judgments.

¹² Go around Zion, encircle it;
  count its towers,

¹³ note its ramparts; tour its citadels
  so that you can tell a future generation:

¹⁴ "This God, our God forever and ever—
  He will always lead us."ᴱ

Psalm 49

For the choir director.
A psalm of the sons of Korah.

¹ Hear this, all you peoples;
  listen, all who inhabit the world,

² both low and high,ᶠ
  rich and poor together.

³ My mouth speaks wisdom;
  my heart's meditation
     brings understanding.

⁴ I turn my ear to a proverb;
  I explain my riddle with a lyre.

⁵ Why should I fear in times of trouble?
  The iniquity of my foes surrounds me.

⁶ They trust in their wealth
  and boast of their abundant riches.

⁷ Yet these cannot redeem a personᴳ
  or pay his ransom to God—

⁸ since the price of redeeming him is
     too costly,
  one should forever stop tryingᴴ—

⁹ so that he may live forever
  and not see the Pit.

¹⁰ For one can see that wise men die;

ᴬ46:9 Lit *chariots with fire*   ᴮ47:7 Hb a *Maskil*   ᶜ47:9 Lit *shields*   ᴰ48:11 Lit *daughters*   ᴱ48:14 Some Hb mss, LXX; other Hb mss read *over death*   ᶠ49:2 Lit *both sons of Adam and sons of man*   ᴳ49:7 Or *Certainly he cannot redeem himself*, or *Yet he cannot redeem a brother*   ᴴ49:8 Or *costly, it will cease forever*

foolish and stupid men also pass away.
Then they leave their wealth to others.
11 Their graves are their eternal homes,[A]
their homes from generation
   to generation,
though they have named estates
   after themselves.
12 But despite his assets,[B]
   man will not last;
he is like the animals that perish.
13 This is the way of those
   who are arrogant,
and of their followers,
who approve of their words.[C]   *Selah*
14 Like sheep they are headed for Sheol;
Death will shepherd them.
The upright will rule over them
   in the morning,
and their form will waste away
   in Sheol,[D]
far from their lofty abode.
15 But God will redeem my life
from the power of Sheol,
for He will take me.   *Selah*
16 Do not be afraid when a man gets rich,
   when the wealth[E]
   of his house increases.
17 For when he dies, he will take
   nothing at all;
his wealth[F] will not follow him down.
18 Though he praises himself
   during his lifetime—
and people praise you when you do well
   for yourself—
19 he will go to the generation
   of his fathers;
they will never see the light.
20 A man with valuable possessions[G]
but without understanding
is like the animals that perish.

Psalm 50
A psalm of Asaph.

1 Yahweh, the God of gods[H] speaks;
He summons the earth from east
   to west.[I]
2 From Zion, the perfection of beauty,
God appears in radiance.[J]
3 Our God is coming; He will not
   be silent!
Devouring fire precedes Him,

and a storm rages around Him.
4 On high, He summons heaven
   and earth
in order to judge His people.
5 "Gather My faithful ones to Me,
those who made a covenant with Me
   by sacrifice."
6 The heavens proclaim
   His righteousness,
for God is the Judge.   *Selah*
7 "Listen, My people, and I will speak;
I will testify against you, Israel.
I am God, your God.
8 I do not rebuke you for your sacrifices
or for your burnt offerings,
which are continually before Me.
9 I will not accept a bull
   from your household
or male goats from your pens,
10 for every animal of the forest is Mine,
the cattle on a thousand hills.
11 I know every bird of the mountains,[K]
and the creatures of the field are Mine.
12 If I were hungry, I would not tell you,
for the world and everything in it
   is Mine.
13 Do I eat the flesh of bulls
or drink the blood of goats?
14 Sacrifice a thank offering to God,
and pay your vows to the Most High.
15 Call on Me in a day of trouble;
I will rescue you,
   and you will honor Me."
16 But God says to the wicked:
"What right do you have to recite
   My statutes
and to take My covenant on your lips?
17 You hate instruction
and turn your back on My words.[L]
18 When you see a thief,
you make friends with him,
and you associate with adulterers.
19 You unleash your mouth for evil
and harness your tongue for deceit.
20 You sit, maligning your brother,
slandering your mother's son.
21 You have done these things,
   and I kept silent;
you thought I was just like you.
But I will rebuke you

and lay out the case before you.[A]

22 "Understand this, you who forget God,
    or I will tear you apart,
    and there will be no one to rescue you.
23 Whoever sacrifices a thank offering
        honors Me,
    and whoever orders his conduct,
    I will show him the salvation of God."

Psalm 51

For the choir director. A Davidic psalm,
when Nathan the prophet came to him
after he had gone to Bathsheba.

1 Be gracious to me, God,
    according to Your faithful love;
    according to Your abundant
        compassion,
    blot out my rebellion.
2 Wash away my guilt
    and cleanse me from my sin.
3 For I am conscious of my rebellion,
    and my sin is always before me.
4 Against You—You alone—
        I have sinned
    and done this evil in Your sight.
    So You are right
        when You pass sentence;
    You are blameless when You judge.
5 Indeed, I was guilty when I was born;
    I was sinful when my mother
        conceived me.
6 Surely You desire integrity
        in the inner self,
    and You teach me wisdom deep within.
7 Purify me with hyssop,
        and I will be clean;
    wash me, and I will be
        whiter than snow.
8 Let me hear joy and gladness;
    let the bones You have crushed rejoice.
9 Turn Your face away[B] from my sins
    and blot out all my guilt.
10 God, create a clean heart for me
    and renew a steadfast[C] spirit
        within me.
11 Do not banish me from Your presence
    or take Your Holy Spirit from me.
12 Restore the joy of Your salvation to me,
    and give me a willing spirit.[D]
13 Then I will teach the rebellious
        Your ways,
    and sinners will return to You.

14 Save me from the guilt of bloodshed,
        God,
    the God of my salvation,
    and my tongue will sing
        of Your righteousness.
15 Lord, open my lips,
    and my mouth will declare Your praise.
16 You do not want a sacrifice,
        or I would give it;
    You are not pleased
        with a burnt offering.
17 The sacrifice pleasing to God is[E]
        a broken spirit.
    God, You will not despise a broken
        and humbled heart.
18 In Your good pleasure, cause Zion
        to prosper;
    build[F] the walls of Jerusalem.
19 Then You will delight
        in righteous sacrifices,
    whole burnt offerings;
    then bulls will be offered on Your altar.

Psalm 52

For the choir director. A Davidic *Maskil.*
When Doeg the Edomite went and reported to Saul,
telling him, "David went to Ahimelech's house."

1 Why brag about evil, you hero!
    God's faithful love is constant.
2 Like a sharpened razor,
    your tongue devises destruction,
    working treachery.
3 You love evil instead of good,
    lying instead of speaking truthfully.
                                    Selah
4 You love any words that destroy,
    you treacherous tongue!
5 This is why God will bring
        you down forever.
    He will take you, ripping you out of
        your tent;
    He will uproot you from the land
        of the living.   *Selah*
6 The righteous will look on with awe
    and will ridicule him:
7 "Here is the man
    who would not make God his refuge,
    but trusted in the abundance
        of his riches,
    taking refuge
        in his destructive behavior."[G]
8 But I am like a flourishing olive tree

in the house of God;
I trust in God's faithful love
    forever and ever.
[9] I will praise You forever for what
    You have done.
In the presence of Your faithful people,
I will put my hope in Your name,
    for it is good.

Psalm 53

For the choir director: on *Mahalath.*[A]
A Davidic *Maskil.*

[1] The fool says in his heart,
    "God does not exist."
They are corrupt, and they do
    vile deeds.
There is no one who does good.
[2] God looks down from heaven
    on the human race
to see if there is one who is wise,
    one who seeks God.
[3] All have turned away;
    all alike have become corrupt.
There is no one who does good,
    not even one.
[4] Will evildoers never understand?
They consume My people
    as they consume bread;
they do not call on God.
[5] Then they will be filled with terror—
    terror like no other—
because God will scatter
    the bones of those who besiege you.
You will put them to shame,
    for God has rejected them.
[6] Oh, that Israel's deliverance
    would come from Zion!
When God restores the fortunes
    of His people,[B]
Jacob will rejoice; Israel will be glad.

Psalm 54

For the choir director: with stringed instruments.
A Davidic *Maskil.* When the Ziphites went and said to
    Saul, "Is David not hiding among us?"

[1] God, save me by Your name,
    and vindicate me by Your might!
[2] God, hear my prayer;
    listen to the words of my mouth.
[3] For strangers rise up against me,
    and violent men seek my life.

They have no regard for God.[C]   *Selah*
[4] God is my helper;
    the Lord is the sustainer of my life.[D]
[5] He will repay my adversaries
    for their evil.
Because of Your faithfulness,
    annihilate them.
[6] I will sacrifice a freewill offering
    to You.
I will praise Your name, Yahweh,
    because it is good.
[7] For He has delivered me
    from every trouble,
and my eye has looked down on
    my enemies.

Psalm 55

For the choir director: with stringed instruments.
A Davidic *Maskil.*

[1] God, listen to my prayer
    and do not ignore[E] my plea for help.
[2] Pay attention to me and answer me.
I am restless and in turmoil
    with my complaint,
[3] because of the enemy's voice,
    because of the pressure[F] of the wicked.
For they bring down disaster on me[G]
    and harass me in anger.
[4] My heart shudders within me;
    terrors of death sweep over me.
[5] Fear and trembling grip me;
    horror has overwhelmed me.
[6] I said, "If only I had[H] wings
    like a dove!
I would fly away and find rest.
[7] How far away I would flee;
    I would stay in the wilderness.   *Selah*
[8] I would hurry to my shelter
    from the raging wind and the storm."
[9] Lord, confuse[I] and confound
    their speech,[J]
for I see violence and strife in the city;
[10] day and night they make the rounds
    on its walls.
Crime and trouble are within it;
[11] destruction is inside it;
oppression and deceit never leave
    its marketplace.
[12] Now it is not an enemy
    who insults me—
otherwise I could bear it;

[A]**53:title** Perhaps a tune, a musical instrument, or a dance; this may be related to Hb word for "sickness." [B]**53:6** Or *restores His captive people* [C]**54:3** Lit *They do not set God before them* [D]**54:4** Or *is with those who sustain my life* [E]**55:1** Or *hide Yourself from* [F]**55:3** Or *threat, or oppression* [G]**55:3** LXX, Syr, Sym; MT reads *they cause me to totter* [H]**55:6** Lit *"Who will give to me . . . dove?* [I]**55:9** Or *destroy* [J]**55:9** Lit *and divide their tongue*

it is not a foe who rises up
    against me—
otherwise I could hide from him.
13 But it is you, a man who is my peer,
    my companion and good friend!
14 We used to have close fellowship;
    we walked with the crowd
      into the house of God.
15 Let death take them by surprise;
    let them go down to Sheol alive,
    because evil is in their homes
      and within them.
16 But I call to God,
    and the LORD will save me.
17 I complain and groan morning, noon,
    and night,
    and He hears my voice.
18 Though many are against me,
    He will redeem me
      from my battle unharmed.
19 God, the One enthroned from long ago,
    will hear and will humiliate them *Selah*
    because they do not change
    and do not fear God.
20 My friend acts violently
    against those at peace with him;
    he violates his covenant.
21 His buttery words are smooth,[A]
    but war is in his heart.
    His words are softer than oil,
    but they are drawn swords.
22 Cast your burden on the LORD,
    and He will sustain you;
    He will never allow the righteous
      to be shaken.
23 God, You will bring them down
    to the Pit of destruction;
    men of bloodshed and treachery
    will not live out half their days.
    But I will trust in You.

Psalm 56

For the choir director: according to "A Silent
Dove Far Away."[B] A Davidic *Miktam*. When the
Philistines seized him in Gath.

1 Be gracious to me, God,
    for man tramples me;
    he fights and oppresses me all day
      long.
2 My adversaries trample me all day,
    for many arrogantly fight against me.[C]

3 When I am afraid,
    I will trust in You.
4 In God, whose word I praise,
    in God I trust; I will not fear.
    What can man do to me?
5 They twist my words all day long;
    all their thoughts against me are evil.
6 They stir up strife,[D] they lurk;
    they watch my steps
    while they wait to take my life.
7 Will they escape in spite of such sin?
    God, bring down the nations in wrath.
8 You Yourself have recorded
    my wanderings.[E]
    Put my tears in Your bottle.
    Are they not in Your records?
9 Then my enemies will retreat
    on the day when I call.
    This I know: God is for me.
10 In God, whose word I praise,
    in the LORD, whose word I praise,
11 in God I trust; I will not fear.
    What can man do to me?
12 I am obligated by vows[F] to You, God;
    I will make my thank offerings to You.
13 For You delivered me from death,
    even my feet from stumbling,
    to walk before God in the light of life.

Psalm 57

For the choir director: "Do Not Destroy."[B]
A Davidic *Miktam*. When he fled before Saul
into the cave.

1 Be gracious to me, God, be gracious
    to me,
    for I take refuge in You.
    I will seek refuge in the shadow
      of Your wings
    until danger passes.
2 I call to God Most High,
    to God who fulfills His purpose
      for me.[G]
3 He reaches down from heaven
    and saves me,
    challenging the one who tramples me.
          Selah
    God sends His faithful love and truth.
4 I am surrounded by lions;
    I lie down with those who devour men.
    Their teeth are spears and arrows;
    their tongues are sharp swords.

A55:21 Some Hb mss, Sym, Syr, Tg, Jer read *His speech is smoother than butter*   B56:title, 5:7 title Possibly a tune   C56:2 Or *many fight against me, O exalted One*, or *many fight against me from the heights*   D56:6 Or *They attack*   E56:8 Or *misery*   F56:12 Lit *On me the vows* G57:2 Or *who avenges me*

⁵ God, be exalted above the heavens;
  let Your glory be over the whole earth.
⁶ They prepared a net for my steps;
  I was despondent.
  They dug a pit ahead of me,
  but they fell into it!   *Selah*
⁷ My heart is confident, God, my heart
    is confident.
  I will sing; I will sing praises.
⁸ Wake up, my soul!ᴬ
  Wake up, harp and lyre!
  I will wake up the dawn.
⁹ I will praise You, Lord,
    among the peoples;
  I will sing praises to You
    among the nations.
¹⁰ For Your faithful love is as high as
    the heavens;
  Your faithfulness reaches the clouds.
¹¹ God, be exalted above the heavens;
  let Your glory be
    over the whole earth.

Psalm 58

For the choir director: "Do Not Destroy."ᴮ
A Davidic *Miktam*.

¹ Do you really speak righteously,
    you mighty ones?ᶜ
  Do you judge people fairly?
² No, you practice injustice
    in your hearts;
  with your hands
    you weigh out violence in the land.
³ The wicked go astray from the womb;
  liars err from birth.
⁴ They have venom like the venom
    of a snake,
  like the deaf cobra that stops up
    its ears,
⁵ that does not listen to the sound
    of the charmers
  who skillfully weave spells.
⁶ God, knock the teeth
    out of their mouths;
  Lᴏʀᴅ, tear out the young lions' fangs.
⁷ They will vanish like water
    that flows by;
  they will aim their useless arrows.ᴰ·ᴱ
⁸ Like a slug that moves along in slime,
  like a woman's miscarried child,
  they will not see the sun.

⁹ Before your pots can feel the heat of
    the thorns—
  whether green or burning—
  He will sweep them away.ᶠ
¹⁰ The righteous one will rejoice
    when he sees the retribution;
  he will wash his feet in the blood
    of the wicked.
¹¹ Then people will say,
  "Yes, there is a reward
    for the righteous!
  There is a God who judges on earth!"

Psalm 59

For the choir director: "Do Not Destroy."ᴮ
A Davidic *Miktam*. When Saul sent agents
to watch the house and kill him.

¹ Deliver me from my enemies, my God;
  protect me from those who rise up
    against me.
² Deliver me from those
    who practice sin,
  and save me from men of bloodshed.
³ Lᴏʀᴅ, look! They set an ambush for me.
  Powerful men attack me,
  but not because of any sin or rebellion
    of mine.
⁴ For no fault of mine,
  they run and take up a position.
  Awake to help me, and take notice.
⁵ Lᴏʀᴅ God of Hosts, You are the
    God of Israel,
  rise up to punish all the nations;
  do not show grace
    to any wicked traitors.   *Selah*
⁶ They return at evening,
    snarling like dogs
  and prowling around the city.
⁷ Look, they spew from their mouths—
  sharp words fromᴳ their lips.
  "For who," they say, "will hear?"
⁸ But You laugh at them, Lᴏʀᴅ;
  You ridicule all the nations.
⁹ I will keep watch for You,
    myᴵ strength,
  because God is my stronghold.
¹⁰ My faithful Godᴶ will come to meet me;
  God will let me look down on
    my adversaries.
¹¹ Do not kill them; otherwise, my people
    will forget.

ᴬ57:8 Lit glory   ᴮ58:title; 59 title Possibly a tune   ᶜ58:1 Or Can you really speak righteousness in silence?   ᴰ58:7 Or their arrows as if they were circumcised; Hb obscure   ᴱ58:7 Or they wither like trampled grass   ᶠ58:9 Or thorns, He will sweep it away, whether raw or cooking, or thorns, He will sweep him away alive in fury   ᴳ59:7 Lit swords are on   ᴴ59:9 Some Hb mss, LXX, Vg, Tg; other Hb mss read his   ᴵ59:10 Alt Hb tradition reads My God in His faithful love

By Your power, make them
      homeless wanderers
and bring them down,
Lord, our shield.
¹² For the sin of their mouths and the
      words of their lips,
let them be caught in their pride.
They utter curses and lies.
¹³ Consume them in rage;
consume them until they are gone.
Then people will know
      throughout^A the earth
that God rules over Jacob.   *Selah*
¹⁴ And they return at evening,
      snarling like dogs
and prowling around the city.
¹⁵ They scavenge for food;
they growl if they are not satisfied.
¹⁶ But I will sing of Your strength
and will joyfully proclaim
Your faithful love in the morning.
For You have been a stronghold
      for me,
a refuge in my day of trouble.
¹⁷ To You, my strength, I sing praises,
because God is my stronghold—
my faithful God.

Psalm 60

For the choir director: according to
"The Lily of Testimony."^B A Davidic *Miktam* for teaching.
When he fought with Aram-naharaim and Aram-zobah,
and Joab returned and struck Edom in the Valley
of Salt, killing 12,000.

¹ God, You have rejected us;
You have broken out^C against us;
You have been angry. Restore us!^D
² You have shaken the land
      and split it open.
Heal its fissures, for it shudders.
³ You have made Your people
      suffer hardship;
You have given us wine to drink
that made us stagger.
⁴ You have given a signal flag to those
      who fear You,
so that they can flee
before the archers.^E   *Selah*
⁵ Save with Your right hand,
      and answer me,
so that those You love may be rescued.
⁶ God has spoken in His sanctuary:^F

"I will triumph!
      I will divide up Shechem.
I will apportion the Valley of Succoth.
⁷ Gilead is Mine, Manasseh is Mine,
and Ephraim is My helmet;
Judah is My scepter.
⁸ Moab is My washbasin.
I throw My sandal on Edom;
I shout in triumph over Philistia."
⁹ Who will bring me to the fortified city?
Who will lead me to Edom?
¹⁰ God, haven't You rejected us?
God, You do not march out
      with our armies.
¹¹ Give us aid against the foe,
for human help is worthless.
¹² With God we will perform valiantly;
He will trample our foes.

Psalm 61

For the choir director: on stringed instruments. Davidic.

¹ God, hear my cry;
pay attention to my prayer.
² I call to You from the ends of the earth
when my heart is without strength.
Lead me to a rock that is
      high above me,
³ for You have been a refuge for me,
a strong tower in the face of the enemy.
⁴ I will live in Your tent forever
and take refuge under the shelter
      of Your wings.   *Selah*
⁵ God, You have heard my vows;
You have given a heritage
to those who fear Your name.
⁶ Add days to the king's life;
may his years span many generations.
⁷ May he sit enthroned
      before God forever;
appoint faithful love and truth
      to guard him.
⁸ Then I will continually sing
      of Your name,
fulfilling my vows day by day.

Psalm 62

For the choir director: according to Jeduthun.
A Davidic psalm.

¹ I am at rest in God alone;
my salvation comes from Him.
² He alone is my rock and my salvation,
my stronghold; I will never be shaken.

---

^A59:13 Lit *know to the ends of*   ^B60:title Possibly a tune; Pss 45; 69; 80   ^C60:1 Lit *have burst through*   ^D60:1 Or *Turn back to us*   ^E60:4 Or *can rally before the archers, or can rally because of the truth*   ^F60:6 Or *has promised by His holy nature*

³ How long will you threaten a man?
Will all of you attack[A]
as if he were a leaning wall
or a tottering stone fence?
⁴ They only plan to bring him down
from his high position.
They take pleasure in lying;
they bless with their mouths,
but they curse inwardly.   Selah
⁵ Rest in God alone, my soul,
for my hope comes from Him.
⁶ He alone is my rock and my salvation,
my stronghold; I will not be shaken.
⁷ My salvation and glory depend on God,
my strong rock.
My refuge is in God.
⁸ Trust in Him at all times, you people;
pour out your hearts before Him.
God is our refuge.   Selah
⁹ Men are only a vapor;
exalted men, an illusion.
Weighed in the scales, they go up;
together they are less than a vapor.
¹⁰ Place no trust in oppression,
or false hope in robbery.
If wealth increases,
pay no attention to it.[B]
¹¹ God has spoken once;
I have heard this twice:
strength belongs to God,
¹² and faithful love belongs
to You, Lord.
For You repay each according to
his works.

Psalm 63
A Davidic psalm. When he was
in the Wilderness of Judah.

¹ God, You are my God; I eagerly
seek You.
I thirst for You;
my body faints for You
in a land that is dry, desolate,
and without water.
² So I gaze on You in the sanctuary
to see Your strength and Your glory.
³ My lips will glorify You
because Your faithful love is better
than life.
⁴ So I will praise You as long as I live;
at Your name, I will lift up my hands.
⁵ You satisfy me as with rich food;[C]

my mouth will praise You
with joyful lips.
⁶ When I think of You as I lie on my bed,
I meditate on You
during the night watches
⁷ because You are my helper;
I will rejoice in the shadow
of Your wings.
⁸ I follow close to You;
Your right hand holds on to me.
⁹ But those who seek to destroy my life
will go into the depths of the earth.
¹⁰ They will be given over to the power
of the sword;
they will become the jackals' prey.
¹¹ But the king will rejoice in God;
all who swear by Him[D] will boast,
for the mouths of liars will be shut.

Psalm 64
For the choir director. A Davidic psalm.

¹ God, hear my voice when I complain.
Protect my life from the terror
of the enemy.
² Hide me from the scheming
of wicked people,
from the mob of evildoers,
³ who sharpen their tongues like swords
and aim bitter words like arrows,
⁴ shooting from concealed places
at the innocent.
They shoot at him suddenly
and are not afraid.
⁵ They encourage each other
in an evil plan;[E,F]
they talk about hiding traps and say,
"Who will see them?"[G]
⁶ They devise crimes and say,
"We have perfected a secret plan."
The inner man and the heart
are mysterious.
⁷ But God will shoot them with arrows;
suddenly, they will be wounded.
⁸ They will be made to stumble;
their own tongues work against them.
All who see them will shake
their heads.
⁹ Then everyone will fear
and will tell about God's work,
for they will understand
what He has done.
¹⁰ The righteous one rejoices in the Lord

---

^A62:3 Some Hb mss read *you be struck down* ^B62:10 Lit *increases, do not set heart* ^C63:5 Lit *with fat and fatness* ^D63:11 Or *him* ^E64:5 Or *thing; lit word* ^F64:5 Or *They hold fast to an evil purpose,* or *They establish for themselves an evil purpose* ^G64:5 Or *us,* or *it*

and takes refuge in Him;
all those who are upright in heart
will offer praise.

Psalm 65

For the choir director. A Davidic psalm. A song.

¹ Praise is rightfully Yours,ᴬ
God, in Zion;
vows to You will be fulfilled.
² All humanity will come to You,
the One who hears prayer.
³ Iniquities overwhelm me;
only You can atone forᴮ our rebellions.
⁴ How happy is the one You choose
and bring near to live in Your courts!
We will be satisfied with the goodness
of Your house,
the holiness of Your temple.ᶜ
⁵ You answer us in righteousness,
with awe-inspiring works,
God of our salvation,
the hope of all the ends of the earth
and of the distant seas.
⁶ You establish the mountains
by Yourᴰ power,
robed with strength.
⁷ You silence the roar of the seas,
the roar of their waves,
and the tumult of the nations.
⁸ Those who live far away are awed
by Your signs;
You make east and west shout for joy.
⁹ You visit the earth
and water it abundantly,
enriching it greatly.
God's stream is filled with water,
for You prepare the earthᴱ in this way,
providing people with grain.
¹⁰ You soften it with showers and bless
its growth,
soaking its furrows and leveling
its ridges.
¹¹ You crown the year
with Your goodness;
Your ways overflow with plenty.ᶠ
¹² The wilderness pastures overflow,
and the hills are robed with joy.
¹³ The pastures are clothed with flocks
and the valleys covered with grain.
They shout in triumph; indeed,
they sing.

Psalm 66

For the choir director. A song. A psalm.

¹ Shout joyfully to God, all the earth!
² Sing about the glory of His name;
make His praise glorious.
³ Say to God, "How awe-inspiring
are Your works!
Your enemies will cringe before You
because of Your great strength.
⁴ All the earth will worship You
and sing praise to You.
They will sing praise to Your name."
Selah

⁵ Come and see the wonders of God;
His acts for humanity are awe-
inspiring.
⁶ He turned the sea into dry land,
and they crossed the river on foot.
There we rejoiced in Him.
⁷ He rules forever by His might;
He keeps His eye on the nations.
The rebellious should not
exalt themselves. *Selah*

⁸ Praise our God, you peoples;
let the sound of His praise be heard.
⁹ He keeps us aliveᴳ
and does not allow our feet to slip.
¹⁰ For You, God, tested us;
You refined us as silver is refined.
¹¹ You lured us into a trap;
You placed burdens on our backs.
¹² You let men ride over our heads;
we went through fire and water,
but You brought us out to abundance.ᴴ
¹³ I will enter Your house
with burnt offerings;
I will pay You my vows
¹⁴ that my lips promised
and my mouth spoke
during my distress.
¹⁵ I will offer You fattened sheep
as burnt offerings,
with the fragrant smoke of rams;
I will sacrifice oxen with goats. *Selah*

¹⁶ Come and listen, all who fear God,
and I will tell what He has done for me.
¹⁷ I cried out to Him with my mouth,
and praise was on my tongue.
¹⁸ If I had been aware of malice
in my heart,
the Lord would not have listened.

ᴬ**65:1** Or *Praise is silence to You,* or *Praise awaits You*   ᴮ**65:3** Or *can forgive,* or *can wipe out*   ᶜ**65:4** Or *house, Your holy temple*   ᴰ**65:6** Some LXX mss, Vg; MT reads *His*   ᴱ**65:9** Lit *prepare it*   ᶠ**65:11** Lit *ways drip with fat*   ᴳ**66:9** Lit *He sets our soul in life*   ᴴ**66:12** Or *a place of satisfaction*

¹⁹ However, God has listened;
He has paid attention to the sound
of my prayer.
²⁰ May God be praised!
He has not turned away my prayer
or turned His faithful love from me.

Psalm 67

For the choir director: with stringed instruments.
A psalm. A song.

¹ May God be gracious to us and bless us;
look on us with favor   *Selah*
² so that Your way may be known
on earth,
Your salvation among all nations.
³ Let the peoples praise You, God;
let all the peoples praise You.
⁴ Let the nations rejoice and shout
for joy,
for You judge the peoples with fairness
and lead the nations on earth.   *Selah*
⁵ Let the peoples praise You, God,
let all the peoples praise You.
⁶ The earth has produced its harvest;
God, our God, blesses us.
⁷ God will bless us,
and all the ends of the earth
will fear Him.

Psalm 68

For the choir director. A Davidic psalm. A song.

¹ God arises. His enemies scatter,
and those who hate Him flee
from His presence.
² As smoke is blown away,
so You blow them away.
As wax melts before the fire,
so the wicked are destroyed before God.
³ But the righteous are glad;
they rejoice before God and celebrate
with joy.
⁴ Sing to God! Sing praises to His name.
Exalt Him who rides on the clouds[A] —
His name is Yahweh[B]—and rejoice
before Him.
⁵ God in His holy dwelling is
a father of the fatherless
and a champion of widows.
⁶ God provides homes for those
who are deserted.
He leads out the prisoners
to prosperity,[C]

but the rebellious live
in a scorched land.
⁷ God, when You went out
before Your people,
when You marched through the desert,
Selah
⁸ the earth trembled and the skies
poured down rain
before God, the God of Sinai,[D]
before God, the God of Israel.
⁹ You, God, showered abundant rain;
You revived Your inheritance
when it languished.
¹⁰ Your people settled in it;
God, You provided for the poor
by Your goodness.
¹¹ The Lord gave the command;
a great company of women brought
the good news:
¹² "The kings of the armies
flee—they flee!"
She who stays at home divides
the spoil.
¹³ While[E] you lie among the sheepfolds,[F]
the wings of a dove are covered
with silver,
and its feathers with glistening gold.
¹⁴ When the Almighty scattered kings
in the land,
it snowed on Zalmon.[G]
¹⁵ Mount Bashan is
God's towering mountain;
Mount Bashan is a mountain
of many peaks.
¹⁶ Why gaze with envy,
you mountain peaks,
at the mountain[H] God desired
for His dwelling?
The Lord will live there forever!
¹⁷ God's chariots are tens of thousands,
thousands and thousands;
the Lord is among them
in the sanctuary[I]
as He was at Sinai.
¹⁸ You ascended to the heights,
taking away captives;
You received gifts from[J] people,
even from the rebellious,
so that the Lord God might live there.[K]
¹⁹ May the Lord be praised!
Day after day He bears our burdens;

A68:4 Or rides through the desert   B68:4 Lit Yah   C68:6 Or prisoners with joyous music; Hb uncertain   D68:8 Lit God, this Sinai   E68:13 Or
If   F68:13 Or campfires, or saddlebags; Hb obscure   G68:14 Or Black Mountain   H68:16 = Mount Zion   I68:17 Or in holiness   J68:18 Lit
among   K68:18 Or even those rebelling against the Lord God's living there, or even rebels are living with the Lord God; Hb obscure

God is our salvation.   *Selah*

²⁰ Our God is a God of salvation,
and escape from death belongs
to the Lord God.

²¹ Surely God crushes the heads
of His enemies,
the hairy head of one who goes on
in his guilty acts.

²² The Lord said, "I will bring them back
from Bashan;
I will bring them back from the depths
of the sea

²³ so that your foot may wade^A in blood
and your dogs' tongues may have
their share
from the enemies."

²⁴ People have seen Your procession, God,
the procession of my God,
my King, in the sanctuary.^B

²⁵ Singers^C lead the way,
with musicians following;
among them are young women
playing tambourines.

²⁶ Praise God in the assemblies;
praise the Lord from the fountain
of Israel.

²⁷ There is Benjamin, the youngest,
leading them,
the rulers of Judah in their assembly,^D
the rulers of Zebulun, the rulers
of Naphtali.

²⁸ Your God has decreed your strength.
Show Your strength, God,
You who have acted on our behalf.

²⁹ Because of Your temple at Jerusalem,
kings will bring tribute to You.

³⁰ Rebuke the beast^E in the reeds,
the herd of bulls with the calves
of the peoples.
Trample underfoot those with bars
of silver.^F
Scatter the peoples who take pleasure
in war.

³¹ Ambassadors will come^G from Egypt;
Cush will stretch out its hands^H to God.

³² Sing to God, you kingdoms
of the earth;
sing praise to the Lord,   *Selah*

³³ to Him who rides in the ancient,
highest heavens.

Look, He thunders
with His powerful voice!

³⁴ Ascribe power to God.
His majesty is over Israel,
His power among the clouds.

³⁵ God, You are awe-inspiring
in Your sanctuaries.
The God of Israel gives power
and strength to His people.
May God be praised!

Psalm 69

For the choir director: according to "The Lilies:"^I
Davidic.

¹ Save me, God,
for the water has risen to my neck.

² I have sunk in deep mud, and there is
no footing;
I have come into deep waters,
and a flood sweeps over me.

³ I am weary from my crying;
my throat is parched.
My eyes fail, looking for my God.

⁴ Those who hate me without cause
are more numerous than the hairs
of my head;
my deceitful enemies, who would
destroy me,
are powerful.
Though I did not steal, I must repay.

⁵ God, You know my foolishness,
and my guilty acts are not hidden
from You.

⁶ Do not let those who put their hope
in You
be disgraced because of me,
Lord God of Hosts;
do not let those who seek You
be humiliated because of me,
God of Israel.

⁷ For I have endured insults
because of You,
and shame has covered my face.

⁸ I have become a stranger
to my brothers
and a foreigner to my mother's sons

⁹ because zeal for Your house
has consumed me,
and the insults of those who insult You
have fallen on me.

¹⁰ I mourned and fasted,

---

^A**68:23** LXX, Syr read *dip*   ^B**68:24** Or *in holiness*   ^C**68:25** Some Hb mss, LXX, Syr read *Officials*   ^D**68:27** Hb obscure   ^E**68:30** Probably
Egypt   ^F**68:30** Or *peoples, trampling on those who take pleasure in silver,* or *peoples, trampling on the bars of silver,* or *peoples, who trample each
other for bars of silver*   ^G**68:31** Or *They bring red cloth,* or *They bring bronze*   ^H**68:31** Probably with tribute or in submission   ^I**69:title** Possibly
a tune; Pss 45; 60; 80

but it brought me insults.
11 I wore sackcloth as my clothing,
and I was a joke to them.
12 Those who sit at the city gate
talk about me,
and drunkards make up songs
about me.
13 But as for me, LORD,
my prayer to You is for a time of favor.
In Your abundant, faithful love, God,
answer me with Your sure salvation.
14 Rescue me from the miry mud;
don't let me sink.
Let me be rescued from those
who hate me
and from the deep waters.
15 Don't let the floodwaters sweep over me
or the deep swallow me up;
don't let the Pit close its mouth over me.
16 Answer me, LORD,
for Your faithful love is good;
in keeping with Your great compassion,
turn to me.
17 Don't hide Your face from Your servant,
for I am in distress.
Answer me quickly!
18 Draw near to me and redeem me;
ransom me because of my enemies.
19 You know the insults I endure—
my shame and disgrace.
You are aware of all my adversaries.
20 Insults have broken my heart,
and I am in despair.
I waited for sympathy,
but there was none;
for comforters, but found no one.
21 Instead, they gave me gall[A] for my food,
and for my thirst
they gave me vinegar to drink.
22 Let their table set before them be
a snare,
and let it be a trap for their allies.
23 Let their eyes grow too dim to see,
and let their loins continually shake.
24 Pour out Your rage on them,
and let Your burning anger
overtake them.
25 Make their fortification desolate;
may no one live in their tents.
26 For they persecute the one You struck
and talk about the pain of those
You wounded.

27 Add guilt to their guilt;
do not let them share
in Your righteousness.
28 Let them be erased from the book
of life
and not be recorded with the righteous.
29 But as for me—poor and in pain—
let Your salvation protect me, God.
30 I will praise God's name with song
and exalt Him with thanksgiving.
31 That will please Yahweh more than
an ox,
more than a bull with horns
and hooves.
32 The humble will see it and rejoice.
You who seek God, take heart!
33 For the LORD listens to the needy
and does not despise
His own who are prisoners.
34 Let heaven and earth praise Him,
the seas and everything that moves
in them,
35 for God will save Zion
and build up[B] the cities of Judah.
They will live there and possess it.
36 The descendants of His servants
will inherit it,
and those who love His name will live
in it.

Psalm 70

For the choir director. Davidic. To bring remembrance.

1 God, deliver me.
Hurry to help me, LORD!
2 Let those who seek my life
be disgraced and confounded;
let those who wish me harm
be driven back and humiliated.
3 Let those who say, "Aha, aha!"
retreat because of their shame.
4 Let all who seek You rejoice
and be glad in You;
let those who love Your salvation
continually say, "God is great!"
5 I am afflicted and needy;
hurry to me, God.
You are my help and my deliverer;
LORD, do not delay.

Psalm 71

1 LORD, I seek refuge in You;
let me never be disgraced.
2 In Your justice, rescue and deliver me;

A 69:21 A bitter substance   B 69:35 Or and rebuild

listen closely to me and save me.
3 Be a rock of refuge for me,
where I can always go.
Give the command to save me,
for You are my rock and fortress.
4 Deliver me, my God, from the power
of the wicked,
from the grasp of the unjust
and oppressive.
5 For You are my hope, Lord GOD,
my confidence from my youth.
6 I have leaned on You from birth;
You took me from my mother's womb.
My praise is always about You.
7 I have become an ominous sign
to many,
but You are my strong refuge.
8 My mouth is full of praise
and honor to You all day long.
9 Don't discard me in my old age;
as my strength fails,
do not abandon me.
10 For my enemies talk about me,
and those who spy on me plot together,
11 saying, "God has abandoned him;
chase him and catch him,
for there is no one to rescue him."
12 God, do not be far from me;
my God, hurry to help me.
13 May my adversaries be disgraced
and destroyed;
may those who seek my harm
be covered with disgrace
and humiliation.
14 But I will hope continually
and will praise You more and more.
15 My mouth will tell
about Your righteousness
and Your salvation all day long,
though I cannot sum them up.
16 I come because of the mighty acts
of the Lord GOD;
I will proclaim Your righteousness,
Yours alone.
17 God, You have taught me
from my youth,
and I still proclaim
Your wonderful works.
18 Even when I am old and gray,
God, do not abandon me.
Then I will[A] proclaim Your power
to another generation,

Your strength to all who are to come.
19 Your righteousness
reaches heaven, God,
You who have done great things;
God, who is like You?
20 You caused me to experience
many troubles and misfortunes,
but You will revive me again.
You will bring me up again,
even from the depths of the earth.
21 You will increase my honor
and comfort me once again.
22 Therefore, I will praise You with a harp
for Your faithfulness, my God;
I will sing to You with a lyre,
Holy One of Israel.
23 My lips will shout for joy
when I sing praise to You
because You have redeemed me.
24 Therefore, my tongue will proclaim
Your righteousness all day long,
for those who seek my harm
will be disgraced and confounded.

Psalm 72
Solomonic.

1 God, give Your justice to the king
and Your righteousness
to the king's son.
2 He will judge Your people
with righteousness
and Your afflicted ones with justice.
3 May the mountains bring prosperity[B]
to the people
and the hills, righteousness.
4 May he vindicate the afflicted
among the people,
help the poor,
and crush the oppressor.
5 May he continue[C] while the
sun endures
and as long as the moon,
throughout all generations.
6 May he be like rain that falls
on the cut grass,
like spring showers that water
the earth.
7 May the righteous[D] flourish in his days
and prosperity[B] abound
until the moon is no more.
8 May he rule from sea to sea
and from the Euphrates
to the ends of the earth.

A 71:18 Lit me until I   B 72:3,7 Or peace   C 72:5 LXX; MT reads May they fear you   D 72:7 Some Hb mss, LXX, Syr, Jer read May righteousness

⁹ May desert tribes kneel before him
and his enemies lick the dust.
¹⁰ May the kings of Tarshish
and the coasts and islands
bring tribute,
the kings of Sheba and Seba offer gifts.
¹¹ Let all kings bow down to him,
all nations serve him.
¹² For he will rescue the poor who cry out
and the afflicted who have no helper.
¹³ He will have pity on the poor
and helpless
and save the lives of the poor.
¹⁴ He will redeem them from oppression
and violence,
for their lives are^A precious^B
in his sight.
¹⁵ May he live long!
May gold from Sheba be given to him.
May prayer be offered
for him continually,
and may he be blessed all day long.
¹⁶ May there be plenty of grain
in the land;
may it wave on the tops
of the mountains.
May its crops be like Lebanon.
May people flourish in the cities
like the grass of the field.
¹⁷ May his name endure forever;
as long as the sun shines,
may his fame increase.
May all nations be blessed by him
and call him blessed.
¹⁸ May the LORD God, the God of Israel,
who alone does wonders, be praised.
¹⁹ May His glorious name
be praised forever;
the whole earth is filled with His glory.
Amen and amen.
²⁰ The prayers of David son of Jesse
are concluded.

BOOK III

(Psalms 73–89)

Psalm 73

A psalm of Asaph.

¹ God is indeed good to Israel,
to the pure in heart.
² But as for me, my feet almost slipped;
my steps nearly went astray.

³ For I envied the arrogant;
I saw the prosperity of the wicked.
⁴ They have an easy time until they die,^C
and their bodies are well fed.^D
⁵ They are not in trouble like others;
they are not afflicted like most people.
⁶ Therefore, pride is their necklace,
and violence covers them
like a garment.
⁷ Their eyes bulge out from fatness;
the imaginations of their hearts
run wild.
⁸ They mock, and they speak maliciously;
they arrogantly threaten oppression.
⁹ They set their mouths against heaven,
and their tongues strut
across the earth.
¹⁰ Therefore His people turn to them^E
and drink in their
overflowing words.^F
¹¹ The wicked say, "How can God know?
Does the Most High know everything?"
¹² Look at them—the wicked!
They are always at ease,
and they increase their wealth.
¹³ Did I purify my heart
and wash my hands in innocence
for nothing?
¹⁴ For I am afflicted all day long
and punished every morning.
¹⁵ If I had decided to say
these things aloud,
I would have betrayed Your people.^G
¹⁶ When I tried to understand all this,
it seemed hopeless^H
¹⁷ until I entered God's sanctuary.
Then I understood their destiny.
¹⁸ Indeed, You put them
in slippery places;
You make them fall into ruin.
¹⁹ How suddenly they become a desolation!
They come to an end, swept away
by terrors.
²⁰ Like one waking from a dream,
Lord, when arising, You will despise
their image.
²¹ When I became embittered
and my innermost being^I was wounded,
²² I was stupid and didn't understand;
I was an unthinking animal
toward You.

---

^A**72:14** Lit *their blood is*   ^B**72:14** Or *valuable*   ^C**73:4** Lit *For there are no pangs to their death*   ^D**73:4** Lit *fat*   ^E**73:10** Lit *turn here*   ^F**73:10** Lit
and waters of fullness are drained by them   ^G**73:15** Lit *betrayed the generation of Your sons*   ^H**73:16** Lit *it was trouble in my eyes*   ^I**73:21** Lit *my
kidneys*

²³ Yet I am always with You;
    You hold my right hand.
²⁴ You guide me with Your counsel,
    and afterward You will take me up
        in glory.^A
²⁵ Who do I have in heaven but You?
    And I desire nothing on earth but You.
²⁶ My flesh and my heart may fail,
    but God is the strength^B of my heart,
    my portion forever.
²⁷ Those far from You
        will certainly perish;
    You destroy all who are
        unfaithful to You.
²⁸ But as for me, God's presence is
        my good.
    I have made the Lord GOD my refuge,
    so I can tell about all You do.

Psalm 74
A Maskil of Asaph.

¹ Why have You rejected us forever, God?
    Why does Your anger burn
        against the sheep of Your pasture?
² Remember Your congregation,
    which You purchased long ago
    and redeemed as the tribe
        for Your own possession.
    Remember Mount Zion
        where You dwell.
³ Make Your way^C to the everlasting ruins,
    to all that the enemy has destroyed
        in the sanctuary.
⁴ Your adversaries roared
        in the meeting place
    where You met with us.^D
    They set up their emblems as signs.
⁵ It was like men in a thicket of trees,
        wielding axes,
⁶ then smashing all the carvings
    with hatchets and picks.
⁷ They set Your sanctuary on fire;
    they utterly^E desecrated
    the dwelling place of Your name.
⁸ They said in their hearts,
    "Let us oppress them relentlessly."
    They burned down every place
        throughout the land
    where God met with us.^F
⁹ There are no signs for us to see.
    There is no longer a prophet.

And none of us knows how long
        this will last.
¹⁰ God, how long will the enemy mock?
    Will the foe insult Your name forever?
¹¹ Why do You hold back Your hand?
    Stretch out^G Your right hand
        and destroy them!
¹² God my King is from ancient times,
    performing saving acts on the earth.
¹³ You divided the sea with Your strength;
    You smashed the heads
        of the sea monsters
    in the waters;
¹⁴ You crushed the heads of Leviathan;
    You fed him to the creatures
        of the desert.
¹⁵ You opened up springs and streams;
    You dried up ever-flowing rivers.
¹⁶ The day is Yours, also the night;
    You established the moon and the sun.
¹⁷ You set all the boundaries of the earth;
    You made summer and winter.
¹⁸ Remember this: the enemy
        has mocked Yahweh,
    and a foolish people has insulted
        Your name.
¹⁹ Do not give the life of Your dove
        to beasts;^H
    do not forget the lives
        of Your poor people forever.
²⁰ Consider the covenant,
    for the dark places of the land
        are full of violence.
²¹ Do not let the oppressed turn away
        in shame;
    let the poor and needy praise Your name.
²² Rise up, God, defend Your cause!
    Remember the insults
        that fools bring against You
        all day long.
²³ Do not forget the clamor
        of Your adversaries,
    the tumult of Your opponents
        that goes up constantly.

Psalm 75
For the choir director: "Do Not Destroy."^I
A psalm of Asaph. A song.

¹ We give thanks to You, God;
    we give thanks to You, for Your name
        is near.

---

^A**73:24** Or *will receive me with honor* ^B**73:26** Lit *rock* ^C**74:3** Lit *Lift up Your steps* ^D**74:4** Lit *in Your meeting place* ^E**74:7** Lit *they to the
ground* ^F**74:8** Lit *every meeting place of God in the land* ^G**74:11** Lit *From Your bosom* ^H**74:19** One Hb ms, LXX, Syr read *Do not hand over to
beasts a soul that praises You* ^I**75 title** Possibly a tune

People tell about
Your wonderful works.
2 "When I choose a time,
I will judge fairly.
3 When the earth and all
its inhabitants shake,
I am the One who steadies its pillars.
Selah
4 I say to the boastful, 'Do not boast,'
and to the wicked, 'Do not lift up
your horn.
5 Do not lift up your horn against heaven
or speak arrogantly.'"
6 Exaltation does not come
from the east, the west, or the desert,
7 for God is the Judge:
He brings down one and exalts another.
8 For there is a cup in the LORD's hand,
full of wine blended with spices,
and He pours from it.
All the wicked of the earth will drink,
draining it to the dregs.
9 As for me, I will tell about Him forever;
I will sing praise to the God of Jacob.
10 "I will cut off all the horns
of the wicked,
but the horns of the righteous will be
lifted up."

Psalm 76

For the choir director: with stringed instruments.
A psalm of Asaph. A song.

1 God is known in Judah;
His name is great in Israel.
2 His tent is in Salem,[A]
His dwelling place in Zion.
3 There He shatters the bow's
flaming arrows,
the shield, the sword, and the weapons
of war.   *Selah*
4 You are resplendent and majestic
coming down from the mountains
of prey.
5 The brave-hearted
have been plundered;
they have slipped into their final sleep.
None of the warriors was able to lift
a hand.
6 At Your rebuke, God of Jacob,
both chariot and horse lay still.
7 And You—You are to be feared.[B]
When You are angry,
who can stand before You?

8 From heaven
You pronounced judgment.
The earth feared and grew quiet
9 when God rose up to judge
and to save all the lowly of the earth.
Selah
10 Even human wrath will praise You;
You will clothe Yourself
with their remaining wrath.[C]
11 Make and keep your vows
to the LORD your God;
let all who are around Him
bring tribute
to the awe-inspiring One.[D]
12 He humbles the spirit of leaders;
He is feared by the kings of the earth.

Psalm 77

For the choir director: according
to Jeduthun. Of Asaph. A psalm.

1 I cry aloud to God,
aloud to God, and He will hear me.
2 I sought the Lord in my day of trouble.
My hands were continually lifted up
all night long;
I refused to be comforted.
3 I think of God; I groan;
I meditate; my spirit becomes weak.
Selah
4 You have kept me from closing
my eyes;
I am troubled and cannot speak.
5 I consider days of old,
years long past.
6 At night I remember my music;
I meditate in my heart,
and my spirit ponders.
7 "Will the Lord reject forever
and never again show favor?
8 Has His faithful love ceased forever?
Is His promise at an end
for all generations?
9 Has God forgotten to be gracious?
Has He in anger
withheld His compassion?"   *Selah*
10 So I say, "I am grieved[E]
that the right hand of the Most High
has changed."
11 I will remember the LORD's works;
yes, I will remember
Your ancient wonders.
12 I will reflect on all You have done
and meditate on Your actions.

¹³ God, Your way is holy.
   What god is great like God?
¹⁴ You are the God who works wonders;
   You revealed Your strength
      among the peoples.
¹⁵ With power You redeemed Your people,
   the descendants of Jacob and Joseph.
                                    Selah

¹⁶ The waters saw You, God.
   The waters saw You; they trembled.
   Even the depths shook.
¹⁷ The clouds poured down water.
   The storm clouds thundered;
   Your arrows flashed back and forth.
¹⁸ The sound of Your thunder was
      in the whirlwind;
   lightning lit up the world.
   The earth shook and quaked.
¹⁹ Your way went through the sea
   and Your path through
      the great waters,
   but Your footprints were unseen.
²⁰ You led Your people like a flock
   by the hand of Moses and Aaron.

Psalm 78
A *Maskil* of Asaph.

¹ My people, hear my instruction;
   listen to what I say.
² I will declare wise sayings;
   I will speak mysteries from the past—
³ things we have heard and known
   and that our fathers have passed down
      to us.
⁴ We must not hide them
      from their children,
   but must tell a future generation
   the praises of the Lord,
   His might, and the wonderful works
   He has performed.
⁵ He established a testimony in Jacob
   and set up a law in Israel,
   which He commanded our fathers
   to teach to their children
⁶ so that a future generation—
   children yet to be born— might know.
   They were to rise and tell their children
⁷ so that they might put their confidence
      in God
   and not forget God's works,
   but keep His commands.
⁸ Then they would not be
      like their fathers,

a stubborn and rebellious generation,
a generation whose heart was not loyal
and whose spirit was not faithful
   to God.
⁹ The Ephraimite archers turned back
   on the day of battle.
¹⁰ They did not keep God's covenant
   and refused to live by His law.
¹¹ They forgot what He had done,
   the wonderful works
      He had shown them.
¹² He worked wonders in the sight of
      their fathers
   in the land of Egypt, the region
      of Zoan.
¹³ He split the sea
      and brought them across;
   the water stood firm like a wall.
¹⁴ He led them with a cloud by day
   and with a fiery light
      throughout the night.
¹⁵ He split rocks in the wilderness
   and gave them drink as abundant
      as the depths.
¹⁶ He brought streams out of the stone
   and made water flow down like rivers.
¹⁷ But they continued to sin against Him,
   rebelling in the desert
      against the Most High.
¹⁸ They deliberately^A tested God,
   demanding the food they craved.
¹⁹ They spoke against God, saying,
   "Is God able to provide food
      in the wilderness?
²⁰ Look! He struck the rock and water
      gushed out;
   torrents overflowed.
   But can He also provide bread
   or furnish meat for His people?"
²¹ Therefore, the Lord heard
      and became furious;
   then fire broke out against Jacob,
   and anger flared up against Israel
²² because they did not believe God
   or rely on His salvation.
²³ He gave a command
      to the clouds above
   and opened the doors of heaven.
²⁴ He rained manna for them to eat;
   He gave them grain from heaven.
²⁵ People^B ate the bread of angels.^C

A**78:18** Lit *in their heart*   B**78:25** Lit *Man*   C**78:25** Lit *mighty ones*

He sent them an abundant supply
of food.

26 He made the east wind blow
in the skies
and drove the south wind by His might.

27 He rained meat on them like dust,
and winged birds like the sand
of the seas.

28 He made them fall in His camp,
all around His tent.^A,B

29 They ate and were completely satisfied,
for He gave them what they craved.

30 Before they had satisfied their desire,
while the food was still
in their mouths,

31 God's anger flared up against them,
and He killed some of their best men.
He struck down Israel's choice
young men.

32 Despite all this, they kept sinning
and did not believe
His wonderful works.

33 He made their days end in futility,
their years in sudden disaster.

34 When He killed some of them,
the rest began to seek Him;
they repented and searched for God.

35 They remembered that God was
their rock,
the Most High God, their Redeemer.

36 But they deceived Him
with their mouths,
they lied to Him with their tongues,

37 their hearts were insincere toward Him,
and they were unfaithful
to His covenant.

38 Yet He was compassionate;
He atoned for^C their guilt
and did not destroy them.
He often turned His anger aside
and did not unleash^D all His wrath.

39 He remembered that they were
only flesh,
a wind that passes and does not return.

40 How often they rebelled against Him
in the wilderness
and grieved Him in the desert.

41 They constantly tested God
and provoked the Holy One of Israel.

42 They did not remember
His power shown

on the day He redeemed them
from the foe,

43 when He performed
His miraculous signs in Egypt
and His wonders in the region of Zoan.

44 He turned their rivers into blood,
and they could not drink
from their streams.

45 He sent among them swarms of flies,
which fed on them,
and frogs, which devastated them.

46 He gave their crops to the caterpillar
and the fruit of their labor
to the locust.

47 He killed their vines with hail
and their sycamore fig trees
with a flood.

48 He handed over their livestock to hail
and their cattle to lightning bolts.

49 He sent His burning anger
against them:
fury, indignation, and calamity—
a band of deadly messengers.^E

50 He cleared a path for His anger.
He did not spare them from death
but delivered their lives to the plague.

51 He struck all the firstborn in Egypt,
the first progeny of the tents of Ham.^F

52 He led His people out like sheep
and guided them like a flock
in the wilderness.

53 He led them safely,
and they were not afraid;
but the sea covered their enemies.

54 He brought them to His holy land,
to the mountain
His right hand acquired.

55 He drove out nations before them.
He apportioned their inheritance by lot
and settled the tribes of Israel
in their tents.

56 But they rebelliously tested
the Most High God,
for they did not keep His decrees.

57 They treacherously turned away
like their fathers;
they became warped like a faulty bow.

58 They enraged Him
with their high places
and provoked His jealousy
with their carved images.

---

^A 78:28 LXX, Syr read *in their camp, all around their tents*   ^B 78:28 Or *in its camp, all around its tents*   ^C 78:38 Or *He wiped out*, or *He forgave*   ^D 78:38 Or *stir up*   ^E 78:49 Or *angels*   ^F 78:51 Ham's descendants who settled in Egypt

⁵⁹ God heard and became furious;
    He completely rejected Israel.
⁶⁰ He abandoned the tabernacle at Shiloh,
    the tent where He resided
        among men.ᴬ
⁶¹ He gave up His strengthᴮ to captivity
    and His splendor to the hand of a foe.
⁶² He surrendered His people
        to the sword
    because He was enraged
        with His heritage.
⁶³ Fire consumed His chosen young men,
    and His young women
        had no wedding songs.ᶜ
⁶⁴ His priests fell by the sword,
    but theᴰ widows could not lament.ᴱ
⁶⁵ Then the Lord awoke as if from sleep,
    like a warrior from the effects of wine.
⁶⁶ He beat back His foes;
    He gave them lasting shame.
⁶⁷ He rejected the tent of Joseph
    and did not choose the tribe
        of Ephraim.
⁶⁸ He chose instead the tribe of Judah,
    Mount Zion, which He loved.
⁶⁹ He built His sanctuary
        like the heights,ᶠ
    like the earth that
        He established forever.
⁷⁰ He chose David His servant
    and took him from the sheepfolds;
⁷¹ He brought him from tending ewes
    to be shepherd over His people Jacob—
    over Israel, His inheritance.
⁷² He shepherded them with a pure heart
    and guided them
        with his skillful hands.

Psalm 79
A psalm of Asaph.

¹ God, the nations have invaded
        Your inheritance,
    desecrated Your holy temple,
    and turned Jerusalem into ruins.
² They gave the corpses of Your servants
    to the birds of the sky for food,
    the flesh of Your godly ones
        to the beasts of the earth.
³ They poured out their blood
    like water all around Jerusalem,
    and there was no one to bury them.

⁴ We have become an object of reproach
        to our neighbors,
    a source of mockery and ridicule
        to those around us.
⁵ How long, Yahweh? Will You
        be angry forever?
    Will Your jealousy keep burning
        like fire?
⁶ Pour out Your wrath on the nations
    that don't acknowledge You,
    on the kingdoms that don't call on
        Your name,
⁷ for they have devoured Jacob
    and devastated his homeland.
⁸ Do not hold past sinsᴳ against us;
    let Your compassion come
        to us quickly,
    for we have become weak.
⁹ God of our salvation, help us—
    for the glory of Your name.
    Deliver us and atone forᴴ our sins,
    because of Your name.
¹⁰ Why should the nations ask,
    "Where is their God?"
    Before our eyes,
    let vengeance for the shed blood
        of Your servants
    be known among the nations.
¹¹ Let the groans of the prisoners
        reach You;
    according to Your great power,
    preserve those condemned to die.
¹² Pay back sevenfold to our neighbors
    the reproach they have hurled at You,
        Lord.
¹³ Then we, Your people, the sheep
        of Your pasture,
    will thank You forever;
    we will declare Your praise
    to generation after generation.

Psalm 80
For the choir director: according to "The Lilies."ᴵ
A testimony of Asaph. A psalm.

¹ Listen, Shepherd of Israel,
    who leads Joseph like a flock;
    You who sit enthroned
        on the cherubim,
    rise up
² before Ephraim,
    Benjamin, and Manasseh.ᴶ

ᴬ78:60 Hb *adam*   ᴮ78:61 = the ark of the covenant   ᶜ78:63 Lit *virgins were not praised*   ᴰ78:64 Lit *His*   ᴱ78:64 War probably prevented customary funerals.   ᶠ78:69 Either the heights of heaven or the mountain heights   ᴳ79:8 Or *hold the sins of past generations*   ᴴ79:9 Or *and wipe out, or and forgive*   ᴵ80:title Possibly a tune; Pss 45; 60; 69   ᴶ80:2 This is the marching order for the camp of Israel.

Rally Your power and come
to save us.
³ Restore us, God;
look on us with favor,
and we will be saved.
⁴ LORD God of Hosts,
how long will You be angry
with Your people's prayers?
⁵ You fed them the bread of tears
and gave them a full measure^A
of tears to drink.
⁶ You make us quarrel
with our neighbors;
our enemies make fun of us.
⁷ Restore us, God of Hosts;
look on us with favor, and we will be
saved.
⁸ You uprooted a vine from Egypt;
You drove out the nations
and planted it.
⁹ You cleared a place for it;
it took root and filled the land.
¹⁰ The mountains were covered
by its shade,
and the mighty cedars^B
with its branches.
¹¹ It sent out sprouts toward the Sea^C
and shoots toward the River.^D
¹² Why have You broken down its walls
so that all who pass by pick its fruit?
¹³ The boar from the forest tears it
and creatures of the field feed on it.
¹⁴ Return, God of Hosts.
Look down from heaven and see;
take care of this vine,
¹⁵ the root^E Your right hand has planted,
the shoot^F that You made strong
for Yourself.
¹⁶ It was cut down and burned up;^G
they^H perish at the rebuke
of Your countenance.
¹⁷ Let Your hand be with the man
at Your right hand,
with the son of man
You have made strong for Yourself.
¹⁸ Then we will not turn away from You;
revive us, and we will call
on Your name.
¹⁹ Restore us, Yahweh, the God of Hosts;
look on us with favor, and we will
be saved.

Psalm 81
For the choir director: on the *Gittith*. Of Asaph.

¹ Sing for joy to God our strength;
shout in triumph to the God of Jacob.
² Lift up a song—play the tambourine,
the melodious lyre, and the harp.
³ Blow the horn on the day of
our feasts^I,J
during the new moon
and during the full moon.
⁴ For this is a statute for Israel,
a judgment of the God of Jacob.
⁵ He set it up as an ordinance for Joseph
when He went throughout^K the land
of Egypt.
I heard an unfamiliar language:
⁶ "I relieved his shoulder
from the burden;
his hands were freed from carrying
the basket.
⁷ You called out in distress,
and I rescued you;
I answered you from the thundercloud.
I tested you at the waters of Meribah.
Selah
⁸ Listen, My people, and I will
admonish you.
Israel, if you would only listen to Me!
⁹ There must not be a strange god
among you;
you must not bow down
to a foreign god.
¹⁰ I am Yahweh your God,
who brought you up from the land
of Egypt.
Open your mouth wide, and I will
fill it.
¹¹ "But My people did not listen to Me;
Israel did not obey Me.
¹² So I gave them over
to their stubborn hearts
to follow their own plans.
¹³ If only My people would listen to Me
and Israel would follow My ways,
¹⁴ I would quickly subdue their enemies
and turn My hand against their foes."
¹⁵ Those who hate the LORD
would pretend submission to Him;
their doom would last forever.
¹⁶ But He would feed Israel^L
with the best wheat.

---

^A80:5 Lit *a one-third measure*   ^B80:10 Lit *the cedars of God*   ^C80:11 = the Mediterranean   ^D80:11 = the Euphrates   ^E80:15 Hb obscure   ^F80:15 Or *son*   ^G80:16 Lit *burned with fire*   ^H80:16 Or *may they*   ^I81:3 Lit *feast*   ^J81:3 Either Passover or Tabernacles   ^K81:5 LXX, Syr, Jer read *out of*   ^L81:16 Lit *him*

"I would satisfy you with honey
from the rock."

Psalm 82
A psalm of Asaph.

1 God has taken His place
in the divine assembly;
He judges among the gods:[A]
2 "How long will you judge unjustly
and show partiality to the wicked?
                                                              Selah
3 Provide justice for the needy
and the fatherless;
uphold the rights of the oppressed
and the destitute.
4 Rescue the poor and needy;
save them from the power of
the wicked."
5 They do not know or understand;
they wander in darkness.
All the foundations of the earth
are shaken.
6 I said, "You are gods;
you are all sons of the Most High.
7 However, you will die like men
and fall like any other ruler."
8 Rise up, God, judge the earth,
for all the nations belong to You.

Psalm 83
A song. A psalm of Asaph.

1 God, do not keep silent.
Do not be deaf, God; do not be idle.
2 See how Your enemies make an uproar;
those who hate You
have acted arrogantly.[B]
3 They devise clever schemes
against Your people;
they conspire against
Your treasured ones.
4 They say, "Come, let us wipe them out
as a nation
so that Israel's name will no longer
be remembered."
5 For they have conspired
with one mind;
they form an alliance[C] against You—
6 the tents of Edom and the Ishmaelites,
Moab and the Hagrites,
7 Gebal, Ammon, and Amalek,
Philistia with the inhabitants of Tyre.
8 Even Assyria has joined them;

they lend support[D] to the sons of Lot.[E]
                                                              Selah
9 Deal with them as You did with Midian,
as You did with Sisera
and Jabin at the Kishon River.
10 They were destroyed at En-dor;
they became manure for the ground.
11 Make their nobles like Oreb and Zeeb,
and all their tribal leaders like Zebah
and Zalmunna,
12 who said, "Let us seize God's pastures
for ourselves."
13 Make them like tumbleweed, my God,
like straw before the wind.
14 As fire burns a forest,
as a flame blazes through mountains,
15 so pursue them with Your tempest
and terrify them with Your storm.
16 Cover their faces with shame
so that they will seek
Your name Yahweh.
17 Let them be put to shame
and terrified forever;
let them perish in disgrace.
18 May they know that You alone—
whose name is Yahweh—
are the Most High over all the earth.

Psalm 84
For the choir director: on the *Gittith*.
A psalm of the sons of Korah.

1 How lovely is Your dwelling place,
LORD of Hosts.
2 I long and yearn
for the courts of the LORD;
my heart and flesh cry out
for[F] the living God.
3 Even a sparrow finds a home,
and a swallow, a nest for herself
where she places her young—
near Your altars, LORD of Hosts,
my King and my God.
4 How happy are those who reside
in Your house,
who praise You continually.   *Selah*
5 Happy are the people whose strength is
in You,
whose hearts are set on pilgrimage.
6 As they pass through the Valley
of Baca,[G]
they make it a source of springwater;

A 82:1 Or *the heavenly beings,* or *the earthly rulers;* lit *elohim*   B 83:2 Lit *have lifted their head*   C 83:5 Lit *they cut a covenant*   D 83:8 Lit *they are an arm*   E 83:8 = Moab and Edom   F 84:2 Or *flesh shout for joy to*   G 84:6 Or *Valley of Tears*

even the autumn rain will cover it
    with blessings.^A

7 They go from strength to strength;
    each appears before God in Zion.
8 LORD God of Hosts, hear my prayer;
    listen, God of Jacob.   *Selah*
9 Consider our shield,^B God;
    look on the face of Your anointed one.
10 Better a day in Your courts
    than a thousand anywhere else.
    I would rather be at the door
      of the house of my God
    than to live in the tents
      of wicked people.
11 For the LORD God is a sun and shield.
    The LORD gives grace and glory;
    He does not withhold the good
    from those who live with integrity.
12 Happy is the person who trusts in You,
    LORD of Hosts!

Psalm 85
For the choir director. A psalm of the sons of Korah.

1 LORD, You showed favor to Your land;
    You restored Jacob's prosperity.^C
2 You took away Your people's guilt;
    You covered all their sin.   *Selah*
3 You withdrew all Your fury;
    You turned from Your burning anger.
4 Return to us, God of our salvation,
    and abandon Your displeasure with us.
5 Will You be angry with us forever?
    Will You prolong Your anger for all
      generations?
6 Will You not revive us again
    so that Your people may rejoice
      in You?
7 Show us Your faithful love, LORD,
    and give us Your salvation.
8 I will listen to what God will say;
    surely the LORD will declare peace
    to His people, His godly ones,
    and not let them go back
      to foolish ways.
9 His salvation is very near
    those who fear Him,
    so that glory may dwell in our land.
10 Faithful love and truth
    will join together;
    righteousness and peace will embrace.
11 Truth will spring up from the earth,
    and righteousness will look
      down from heaven.

12 Also, the LORD will provide
    what is good,
    and our land will yield its crops.
13 Righteousness will go before Him
    to prepare the way for His steps.

Psalm 86
A Davidic prayer.

1 Listen, LORD, and answer me,
    for I am poor and needy.
2 Protect my life, for I am faithful.
    You are my God; save Your servant
    who trusts in You.
3 Be gracious to me, Lord,
    for I call to You all day long.
4 Bring joy to Your servant's life,
    because I turn to You, Lord.
5 For You, Lord, are kind and ready
    to forgive,
    rich in faithful love to all who call
    on You.
6 LORD, hear my prayer;
    listen to my plea for mercy.
7 I call on You in the day of my distress,
    for You will answer me.
8 Lord, there is no one like You
    among the gods,
    and there are no works like Yours.
9 All the nations You have made
    will come and bow down
      before You, Lord,
    and will honor Your name.
10 For You are great
    and perform wonders;
    You alone are God.
11 Teach me Your way, Yahweh,
    and I will live by Your truth.
    Give me an undivided mind to fear
    Your name.
12 I will praise You with all my heart,
    Lord my God,
    and will honor Your name forever.
13 For Your faithful love for me is great,
    and You deliver my life from the depths
    of Sheol.
14 God, arrogant people have attacked me;
    a gang of ruthless men seeks my life.
    They have no regard for You.
15 But You, Lord, are a compassionate
    and gracious God,
    slow to anger and rich in faithful love
    and truth.
16 Turn to me and be gracious to me.

Give Your strength to Your servant;
save the son of Your female servant.

17 Show me a sign of Your goodness;
my enemies will see and be put
to shame
because You, LORD, have helped
and comforted me.

Psalm 87
A psalm of the sons of Korah. A song.

1 His foundation is on the holy mountains.
2 The LORD loves the gates of Zion
more than all the dwellings of Jacob.
3 Glorious things are said about you,
city of God. *Selah*
4 "I will mention those who know Me:
Rahab, Babylon, Philistia, Tyre,
and Cush—
each one was born there."
5 And it will be said of Zion,
"This one and that one were born
in her."
The Most High Himself
will establish her.
6 When He registers the peoples,
the LORD will record,
"This one was born there." *Selah*
7 Singers and dancers alike will say,
"My whole source of joy is^A in you."

Psalm 88
A song. A psalm of the sons of Korah.
For the choir director: according to *Mahalath
Leannoth.* A *Maskil* of Heman the Ezrahite.

1 LORD, God of my salvation,
I cry out before You day and night.
2 May my prayer reach Your presence;
listen to my cry.
3 For I have had enough troubles,
and my life is near Sheol.
4 I am counted among those going down
to the Pit.
I am like a man without strength,
5 abandoned^B among the dead.
I am like the slain lying in the grave,
whom You no longer remember,
and who are cut off from Your care.^C
6 You have put me in the lowest part
of the Pit,
in the darkest places, in the depths.
7 Your wrath weighs heavily on me;
You have overwhelmed me with all
Your waves. *Selah*

8 You have distanced my friends
from me;
You have made me repulsive to them.
I am shut in and cannot go out.
9 My eyes are worn out from crying.
LORD, I cry out to You all day long;
I spread out my hands to You.
10 Do You work wonders for the dead?
Do departed spirits rise up
to praise You? *Selah*
11 Will Your faithful love be declared
in the grave,
Your faithfulness in Abaddon?
12 Will Your wonders be known in
the darkness
or Your righteousness in the land
of oblivion?
13 But I call to You for help, LORD;
in the morning my prayer meets You.
14 LORD, why do You reject me?
Why do You hide Your face from me?
15 From my youth,
I have been afflicted and near death.
I suffer Your horrors; I am desperate.
16 Your wrath sweeps over me;
Your terrors destroy me.
17 They surround me like water
all day long;
they close in on me from every side.
18 You have distanced loved one
and neighbor from me;
darkness is my only friend.^D

Psalm 89
A *Maskil* of Ethan the Ezrahite.

1 I will sing about the LORD's
faithful love forever;
I will proclaim Your faithfulness to all
generations
with my mouth.
2 For I will declare,
"Faithful love is built up forever;
You establish Your faithfulness
in the heavens."
3 The LORD said,
"I have made a covenant
with My chosen one;
I have sworn an oath to David
My servant:
4 'I will establish your offspring forever
and build up your throne
for all generations.'" *Selah*

^A87:7 Lit "All my springs, are ^B88:5 Or set free ^C88:5 Or hand ^D88:18 Or from me, my friends. Oh darkness!

⁵ Lᴏʀᴅ, the heavens praise
   Your wonders—
   Your faithfulness also—
   in the assembly of the holy ones.
⁶ For who in the skies can compare
      with the Lᴏʀᴅ?
   Who among the heavenly beings^A is
      like the Lᴏʀᴅ?
⁷ God is greatly feared in the council
      of the holy ones,
   more awe-inspiring than^B
      all who surround Him.
⁸ Lᴏʀᴅ God of Hosts,
   who is strong like You, Lᴏʀᴅ?
   Your faithfulness surrounds You.
⁹ You rule the raging sea;
   when its waves surge, You still them.
¹⁰ You crushed Rahab like one
      who is slain;
   You scattered Your enemies
      with Your powerful arm.
¹¹ The heavens are Yours; the earth also
      is Yours.
   The world and everything
      in it—You founded them.
¹² North and south—You created them.
   Tabor and Hermon shout for joy
      at Your name.
¹³ You have a mighty arm;
   Your hand is powerful;
   Your right hand is lifted high.
¹⁴ Righteousness and justice are
      the foundation
   of Your throne;
   faithful love and truth go before You.
¹⁵ Happy are the people who know
      the joyful shout;
   Yahweh, they walk in the light
      of Your presence.
¹⁶ They rejoice in Your name all day long,
   and they are exalted
      by Your righteousness.
¹⁷ For You are their magnificent strength;
   by Your favor our horn is exalted.
¹⁸ Surely our shield^C belongs to the Lᴏʀᴅ,
   our king to the Holy One of Israel.
¹⁹ You once spoke in a vision
      to Your loyal ones
   and said: "I have granted help
      to a warrior;
   I have exalted one chosen^D
      from the people.

²⁰ I have found David My servant;
   I have anointed him with My sacred oil.
²¹ My hand will always be with him,
   and My arm will strengthen him.
²² The enemy will not afflict^E him;
   no wicked man will oppress him.
²³ I will crush his foes before him
   and strike those who hate him.
²⁴ My faithfulness and love will be
      with him,
   and through My name
   his horn will be exalted.
²⁵ I will extend his power to the sea
   and his right hand to the rivers.
²⁶ He will call to Me, 'You are my Father,
   my God, the rock of my salvation.'
²⁷ I will also make him My firstborn,
   greatest of the kings of the earth.
²⁸ I will always preserve My faithful love
      for him,
   and My covenant with him will endure.
²⁹ I will establish his line forever,
   his throne as long as heaven lasts.^F
³⁰ If his sons forsake My instruction
   and do not live by My ordinances,
³¹ if they dishonor My statutes
   and do not keep My commands,
³² then I will call their rebellion
      to account with the rod,
   their sin with blows.
³³ But I will not withdraw
   My faithful love from him
   or betray My faithfulness.
³⁴ I will not violate My covenant
   or change what My lips have said.
³⁵ Once and for all
   I have sworn an oath by My holiness;
   I will not lie to David.
³⁶ His offspring will continue forever,
   his throne like the sun before Me,
³⁷ like the moon, established forever,
   a faithful witness in the sky."   *Selah*
³⁸ But You have spurned
      and rejected him;
   You have become enraged
      with Your anointed.
³⁹ You have repudiated the covenant
      with Your servant;
   You have completely dishonored
      his crown.^G
⁴⁰ You have broken down all his walls;

You have reduced his fortified cities
to ruins.
⁴¹ All who pass by plunder him;
he has become an object of ridicule
to his neighbors.
⁴² You have lifted high the right hand
of his foes;
You have made all his enemies rejoice.
⁴³ You have also turned back
his sharp sword
and have not let him stand in battle.
⁴⁴ You have made his splendorᴬ cease
and have overturned his throne.
⁴⁵ You have shortened the days
of his youth;
You have covered him with shame.
Selah

⁴⁶ How long, LORD? Will You hide
Yourself forever?
Will Your anger keep burning like fire?
⁴⁷ Remember how short my life is.
Have You created everyone
for nothing?
⁴⁸ What man can live
and never see death?
Who can save himself from the power
of Sheol?   *Selah*

⁴⁹ Lord, where are the former acts
of Your faithful love
that You swore to David
in Your faithfulness?
⁵⁰ Remember, Lord, the ridicule
against Your servants—
in my heart I carry abuse from all
the peoples—
⁵¹ how Your enemies have ridiculed, LORD,
how they have ridiculed every step
of Your anointed.
⁵² May the LORD be praised forever.
Amen and amen.

BOOK IV
(Psalms 90–106)

Psalm 90
A prayer of Moses, the man of God.

¹ Lord, You have been our refugeᴮ
in every generation.
² Before the mountains were born,
before You gave birth to the earth
and the world,
from eternity to eternity, You are God.

³ You return mankind to the dust,
saying, "Return, descendants of Adam."
⁴ For in Your sight a thousand years
are like yesterday that passes by,
like a few hours of the night.
⁵ You end their lives;ᶜ they sleep.
They are like grass that grows
in the morning—
⁶ in the morning it sprouts and grows;
by evening it withers and dries up.
⁷ For we are consumed by Your anger;
we are terrified by Your wrath.
⁸ You have set our unjust ways
before You,
our secret sins in the light
of Your presence.
⁹ For all our days ebb away
under Your wrath;
we end our years like a sigh.
¹⁰ Our lives lastᴰ seventy years
or, if we are strong, eighty years.
Even the best of them areᴱ struggle
and sorrow;
indeed, they pass quickly and we
fly away.
¹¹ Who understands the power
of Your anger?
Your wrath matches the fear that
is due You.
¹² Teach us to number our days carefully
so that we may develop wisdom
in our hearts.ᶠ
¹³ LORD—how long?
Turn and have compassion
on Your servants.
¹⁴ Satisfy us in the morning
with Your faithful love
so that we may shout with joy
and be glad all our days.
¹⁵ Make us rejoice for as many days
as You have humbled us,
for as many years as
we have seen adversity.
¹⁶ Let Your work be seen
by Your servants,
and Your splendor by their children.
¹⁷ Let the favor of the Lord our God be
on us;
establish for us the work
of our hands—
establish the work of our hands!

ᴬ89:44 Hb obscure   ᴮ90:1 Some Hb mss, LXX; other Hb mss read *dwelling place*   ᶜ90:5 Or *You overwhelm them*; Hb obscure   ᴰ90:10 Lit *The days of our years in them*   ᴱ90:10 LXX, Tg, Syr, Vg read *Even their span is*; Hb obscure   ᶠ90:12 Or *develop a heart of wisdom*

Psalm 91

1 The one who lives under the protection
   of the Most High
   dwells in the shadow of the Almighty.
2 I will say[A] to the LORD, "My refuge
   and my fortress,
   my God, in whom I trust."
3 He Himself will deliver you
   from the hunter's net,
   from the destructive plague.
4 He will cover you with His feathers;
   you will take refuge under His wings.
   His faithfulness will be
   a protective shield.
5 You will not fear the terror of the night,
   the arrow that flies by day,
6 the plague that stalks in darkness,
   or the pestilence that ravages at noon.
7 Though a thousand fall at your side
   and ten thousand at your right hand,
   the pestilence will not reach you.
8 You will only see it with your eyes
   and witness the punishment
   of the wicked.
9 Because you have made
   the LORD—my refuge,
   the Most High—your dwelling place,
10 no harm will come to you;
   no plague will come near your tent.
11 For He will give His angels orders
   concerning you,
   to protect you in all your ways.
12 They will support you with their hands
   so that you will not strike your foot
   against a stone.
13 You will tread on the lion and the cobra;
   you will trample the young lion
   and the serpent.
14 Because he is lovingly devoted to Me,
   I will deliver him;
   I will protect him because he knows
   My name.
15 When he calls out to Me,
   I will answer him;
   I will be with him in trouble.
   I will rescue him and give him honor.
16 I will satisfy him with a long life
   and show him My salvation.

Psalm 92

A psalm. A song for the Sabbath day.

1 It is good to praise Yahweh,
   to sing praise to Your name,
   Most High,
2 to declare Your faithful love
   in the morning
   and Your faithfulness at night,
3 with a ten-stringed harp
   and the music of a lyre.
4 For You have made me rejoice, LORD,
   by what You have done;
   I will shout for joy
   because of the works of Your hands.
5 How magnificent are Your works, LORD,
   how profound Your thoughts!
6 A stupid person does not know,
   a fool does not understand this:
7 though the wicked sprout like grass
   and all evildoers flourish,
   they will be eternally destroyed.
8 But You, LORD, are exalted forever.
9 For indeed, LORD, Your enemies—
   indeed, Your enemies will perish;
   all evildoers will be scattered.
10 You have lifted up my horn
   like that of a wild ox;
   I have been anointed[B] with oil.
11 My eyes look down on my enemies;
   my ears hear evildoers when they
   attack me.
12 The righteous thrive like a palm tree
   and grow like a cedar tree in Lebanon.
13 Planted in the house of the LORD,
   they thrive in the courts of our God.
14 They will still bear fruit in old age,
   healthy and green,
15 to declare: "The LORD is just;
   He is my rock,
   and there is no unrighteousness
   in Him."

Psalm 93

1 The LORD reigns! He is robed
   in majesty;
   The LORD is robed,
   enveloped in strength.
   The world is firmly established;
   it cannot be shaken.
2 Your throne has been established
   from the beginning;[C]
   You are from eternity.
3 The floods have lifted up, LORD,
   the floods have lifted up their voice;
   the floods lift up their pounding waves.

A91:1-2 LXX, Syr, Jer read 2 Almighty, saying, or 2 Almighty, he will say   B92:10 Syr reads You have anointed me   C93:2 Lit from then

⁴ Greater than the roar of many waters—
the mighty breakers of the sea—
the LORD on high is majestic.
⁵ LORD, Your testimonies
are completely reliable;
holiness is the beauty of^A Your house
for all the days to come.

Psalm 94

¹ LORD, God of vengeance—
God of vengeance, appear.
² Rise up, Judge of the earth;
repay the proud what they deserve.
³ LORD, how long will the wicked—
how long will the wicked gloat?
⁴ They pour out arrogant words;
all the evildoers boast.
⁵ LORD, they crush Your people;
they afflict Your heritage.
⁶ They kill the widow and the foreigner
and murder the fatherless.
⁷ They say, "The LORD doesn't see it.
The God of Jacob
doesn't pay attention."
⁸ Pay attention, you stupid people!
Fools, when will you be wise?
⁹ Can the One who shaped the ear
not hear,
the One who formed the eye not see?
¹⁰ The One who instructs nations,
the One who teaches
man knowledge—
does He not discipline?
¹¹ The LORD knows man's thoughts;
they are meaningless.
¹² LORD, happy is the man You discipline
and teach from Your law
¹³ to give him relief from troubled times
until a pit is dug for the wicked.
¹⁴ The LORD will not forsake His people
or abandon His heritage,
¹⁵ for justice will again be righteous,
and all the upright in heart
will follow^B it.
¹⁶ Who stands up for me
against the wicked?
Who takes a stand for me
against evildoers?
¹⁷ If the LORD had not been my helper,
I would soon rest in the silence
of death.
¹⁸ If I say, "My foot is slipping,"

Your faithful love
will support me, LORD.
¹⁹ When I am filled with cares,
Your comfort brings me joy.
²⁰ Can a corrupt throne—
one that creates trouble by law—
become Your ally?
²¹ They band together against the life
of the righteous
and condemn the innocent to death.
²² But the LORD is my refuge;
my God is the rock of my protection.
²³ He will pay them back for their sins
and destroy them for their evil.
The LORD our God will destroy them.

Psalm 95

¹ Come, let us shout joyfully to the LORD,
shout triumphantly to the rock
of our salvation!
² Let us enter His presence
with thanksgiving;
let us shout triumphantly to Him
in song.
³ For the LORD is a great God,
a great King above all gods.
⁴ The depths of the earth are
in His hand,
and the mountain peaks are His.
⁵ The sea is His; He made it.
His hands formed the dry land.
⁶ Come, let us worship and bow down;
let us kneel before the LORD our Maker.
⁷ For He is our God,
and we are the people of His pasture,
the sheep under His care.^C
Today, if you hear His voice:
⁸ Do not harden your hearts
as at Meribah,
as on that day at Massah
in the wilderness
⁹ where your fathers tested Me;
they tried Me, though they had seen
what I did.
¹⁰ For 40 years I was disgusted
with that generation;
I said, "They are a people whose hearts
go astray;
they do not know My ways."
¹¹ So I swore in My anger,
"They will not enter My rest."

Psalm 96

1 Sing a new song to the LORD;
   sing to the LORD, all the earth.
2 Sing to Yahweh, praise His name;
   proclaim His salvation from day to day.
3 Declare His glory among the nations,
   His wonderful works
      among all peoples.
4 For the LORD is great and is
      highly praised;
   He is feared above all gods.
5 For all the gods of the peoples are idols,
   but the LORD made the heavens.
6 Splendor and majesty are before Him;
   strength and beauty are
      in His sanctuary.
7 Ascribe to the LORD, you families
      of the peoples,
   ascribe to the LORD glory and strength.
8 Ascribe to Yahweh the glory
      of His name;
   bring an offering and enter His courts.
9 Worship the LORD in the splendor
      of His holiness;
   tremble before Him, all the earth.
10 Say among the nations:
      "The LORD reigns.
   The world is firmly established;
      it cannot be shaken.
   He judges the peoples fairly."
11 Let the heavens be glad
      and the earth rejoice;
   let the sea and all that fills it resound.
12 Let the fields and everything
      in them exult.
   Then all the trees of the forest
      will shout for joy
13 before the LORD, for He is coming—
   for He is coming to judge the earth.
   He will judge the world
      with righteousness
   and the peoples with His faithfulness.

Psalm 97

1 The LORD reigns! Let the earth rejoice;
   let the many coasts and islands be glad.
2 Clouds and thick darkness
      surround Him;
   righteousness and justice are
      the foundation of His throne.
3 Fire goes before Him
   and burns up His foes on every side.

4 His lightning lights up the world;
   the earth sees and trembles.
5 The mountains melt like wax
   at the presence of the LORD—
   at the presence of the Lord of all
      the earth.
6 The heavens proclaim His righteousness;
   all the peoples see His glory.
7 All who serve carved images,
   those who boast in idols, will be
      put to shame.
   All the gods[A] must worship Him.
8 Zion hears and is glad,
   and the towns[B] of Judah rejoice
   because of Your judgments, LORD.
9 For You, LORD,
   are the Most High over all the earth;
   You are exalted above all the gods.
10 You who love the LORD, hate evil!
   He protects the lives of His godly ones;
   He rescues them from the power of
      the wicked.
11 Light dawns[C,D] for the righteous,
   gladness for the upright in heart.
12 Be glad in Yahweh, you righteous ones,
   and praise His holy name.[E]

Psalm 98

A psalm.

1 Sing a new song to the LORD,
   for He has performed wonders;
   His right hand and holy arm
   have won Him victory.
2 The LORD has made His victory known;
   He has revealed His righteousness
   in the sight of the nations.
3 He has remembered His love
   and faithfulness to the house of Israel;
   all the ends of the earth
   have seen our God's victory.
4 Shout to the LORD, all the earth;
   be jubilant, shout for joy, and sing.
5 Sing to the LORD with the lyre,
   with the lyre and melodious song.
6 With trumpets and the blast
      of the ram's horn
   shout triumphantly
   in the presence of the LORD, our King.
7 Let the sea and all that fills it,
   the world and those who live in it,
      resound.
8 Let the rivers clap their hands;

let the mountains shout together
for joy
9 before the LORD,
for He is coming to judge the earth.
He will judge the world righteously
and the peoples fairly.

Psalm 99

1 The LORD reigns! Let
the peoples tremble.
He is enthroned above the cherubim.
Let the earth quake.
2 Yahweh is great in Zion;
He is exalted above all the peoples.
3 Let them praise Your great
and awe-inspiring name.
He is holy.
4 The mighty King loves justice.
You have established fairness;
You have administered justice
and righteousness in Jacob.
5 Exalt the LORD our God;
bow in worship at His footstool.
He is holy.
6 Moses and Aaron were
among His priests;
Samuel also was among
those calling on His name.
They called to Yahweh
and He answered them.
7 He spoke to them in a pillar
of cloud;
they kept His decrees and the statutes
He gave them.
8 LORD our God, You answered them.
You were a forgiving God to them,
an avenger of their sinful actions.
9 Exalt the LORD our God;
bow in worship at His holy mountain,
for the LORD our God is holy.

Psalm 100
A psalm of thanksgiving.

1 Shout triumphantly to the LORD,
all the earth.
2 Serve the LORD with gladness;
come before Him with joyful songs.
3 Acknowledge that Yahweh is God.
He made us, and we are His[A] —
His people, the sheep of His pasture.
4 Enter His gates with thanksgiving
and His courts with praise.

Give thanks to Him and praise
His name.
5 For Yahweh is good, and His love
is eternal;
His faithfulness endures
through all generations.

Psalm 101
A Davidic psalm.

1 I will sing of faithful love and justice;
I will sing praise to You, LORD.
2 I will pay attention to the way
of integrity.
When will You come to me?
I will live with a heart of integrity
in my house.
3 I will not set anything worthless
before my eyes.
I hate the practice of transgression;
it will not cling to me.
4 A devious heart will be far from me;
I will not be involved with[B] evil.
5 I will destroy anyone
who secretly slanders his neighbor;
I cannot tolerate anyone
with haughty eyes or an arrogant heart.
6 My eyes favor the faithful of the land
so that they may sit down with me.
The one who follows the way
of integrity
may serve me.
7 No one who acts deceitfully
will live in my palace;
no one who tells lies
will remain in my presence.[C]
8 Every morning I will destroy
all the wicked of the land,
eliminating all evildoers
from the LORD's city.

Psalm 102
A prayer of an afflicted person who is weak and pours
out his lament before the LORD.

1 LORD, hear my prayer;
let my cry for help come before You.
2 Do not hide Your face from me
in my day of trouble.
Listen closely to me;
answer me quickly when I call.
3 For my days vanish like smoke,
and my bones burn like a furnace.
4 My heart is afflicted,
withered like grass;

A100:3 Alt Hb tradition, some Hb mss, LXX, Syr, Vg read *and not we ourselves*   B101:4 Lit *not know*   C101:7 Lit *in front of my eyes*

I even forget to eat my food.
5 Because of the sound of my groaning,
my flesh sticks to my bones.
6 I am like a desert owl,[A]
like an owl among the ruins.
7 I stay awake;
I am like a solitary bird on a roof.
8 My enemies taunt me all day long;
they ridicule and curse me.
9 I eat ashes like bread
and mingle my drinks with tears
10 because of Your indignation and wrath;
for You have picked me up
and thrown me aside.
11 My days are like a lengthening shadow,
and I wither away like grass.
12 But You, Lord, are enthroned forever;
Your fame endures to all generations.
13 You will rise up and have compassion
on Zion,
for it is time to show favor to her—
the appointed time has come.
14 For Your servants take delight
in its stones
and favor its dust.
15 Then the nations will fear the name
of Yahweh,
and all the kings of the earth
Your glory,
16 for the Lord will rebuild Zion;
He will appear in His glory.
17 He will pay attention to the prayer
of the destitute
and will not despise their prayer.
18 This will be written
for a later generation,
and a newly created people will praise
the Lord:
19 He looked down from
His holy heights—
the Lord gazed out from heaven
to earth—
20 to hear a prisoner's groaning,
to set free those condemned to die,[B]
21 so that they might declare
the name of Yahweh in Zion
and His praise in Jerusalem,
22 when peoples and kingdoms
are assembled
to serve the Lord.
23 He has broken my[C] strength
in midcourse;

He has shortened my days.
24 I say: "My God, do not take me
in the middle of my life![D]
Your years continue
through all generations.
25 Long ago You established the earth,
and the heavens are the work
of Your hands.
26 They will perish, but You will endure;
all of them will wear out like clothing.
You will change them like a garment,
and they will pass away.
27 But You are the same,
and Your years will never end.
28 Your servants' children
will dwell securely,
and their offspring will be established
before You."

Psalm 103
Davidic.

1 My soul, praise Yahweh,
and all that is within me, praise
His holy name.
2 My soul, praise the Lord,
and do not forget all His benefits.
3 He forgives all your sin;
He heals all your diseases.
4 He redeems your life from the Pit;
He crowns you with faithful love
and compassion.
5 He satisfies you[E] with goodness;
your youth is renewed like the eagle.
6 The Lord executes acts
of righteousness
and justice for all the oppressed.
7 He revealed His ways to Moses,
His deeds to the people of Israel.
8 The Lord is compassionate
and gracious,
slow to anger and rich in faithful love.
9 He will not always accuse us
or be angry forever.
10 He has not dealt with us as
our sins deserve
or repaid us according to our offenses.
11 For as high as the heavens are above
the earth,
so great is His faithful love
toward those who fear Him.
12 As far as the east is from the west,
so far has He removed

our transgressions from us.

¹³ As a father has compassion
    on his children,
so the Lᴏʀᴅ has compassion on those
    who fear Him.
¹⁴ For He knows what we are made of,
    remembering that we are dust.
¹⁵ As for man, his days are like grass—
    he blooms like a flower of the field;
¹⁶ when the wind passes over it,
        it vanishes,
    and its place is no longer known.ᴬ
¹⁷ But from eternity to eternity
    the Lᴏʀᴅ's faithful love is toward
        those who fear Him,
    and His righteousness
        toward the grandchildren
¹⁸ of those who keep His covenant,
    who remember to observe His precepts.
¹⁹ The Lᴏʀᴅ has established His throne
        in heaven,
    and His kingdom rules over all.
²⁰ Praise the Lᴏʀᴅ,
    all His angels of great strength,
    who do His word,
    obedient to His command.
²¹ Praise the Lᴏʀᴅ, all His armies,
    His servants who do His will.
²² Praise the Lᴏʀᴅ, all His works
    in all the places where He rules.
    My soul, praise Yahweh!

Psalm 104

¹ My soul, praise Yahweh!
    Lᴏʀᴅ my God, You are very great;
    You are clothed with majesty
        and splendor.
² He wraps Himself in light as if it were
        a robe,
    spreading out the sky like a canopy,
³ laying the beams of His palace
        on the waters above,
    making the clouds His chariot,
    walking on the wings of the wind,
⁴ and making the winds
        His messengers,ᴮ
    flames of fire His servants.
⁵ He established the earth
        on its foundations;
    it will never be shaken.
⁶ You covered it with the deep
        as if it were a garment;

the waters stood above the mountains.
⁷ At Your rebuke the waters fled;
    at the sound of Your thunder
        they hurried away—
⁸ mountains rose and valleys sankᶜ—
    to the place You established for them.
⁹ You set a boundary they cannot cross;
    they will never cover the earth again.
¹⁰ He causes the springs to gush
        into the valleys;
    they flow between the mountains.
¹¹ They supply water for every wild beast;
    the wild donkeys quench their thirst.
¹² The birds of the sky live
        beside the springs;
    they sing among the foliage.
¹³ He waters the mountains
        from His palace;
    the earth is satisfied by the fruit
        of Your labor.
¹⁴ He causes grass to grow
        for the livestock
    and provides crops for man
        to cultivate,
    producing food from the earth,
¹⁵ wine that makes man's heart glad—
    making his face shine with oil—
    and bread that sustains man's heart.
¹⁶ The trees of the Lᴏʀᴅ flourish,ᴰ
    the cedars of Lebanon that He planted.
¹⁷ There the birds make their nests;
    the stork makes its home
        in the pine trees.
¹⁸ The high mountains are
        for the wild goats;
    the cliffs are a refuge for hyraxes.
¹⁹ He made the moon to mark
        theᴱ festivals;ᶠ
    the sun knows when to set.
²⁰ You bring darkness,
        and it becomes night,
    when all the forest animals stir.
²¹ The young lions roar for their prey
    and seek their food from God.
²² The sun rises; they go back
    and lie down in their dens.
²³ Man goes out to his work
    and to his labor until evening.
²⁴ How countless are Your works, Lᴏʀᴅ!
    In wisdom You have made them all;
    the earth is full of Your creatures.ᴳ

ᴬ103:16 Lit place no longer knows it   ᴮ104:4 Or angels   ᶜ104:7-8 Or away. They flowed over the mountains and went down valleys   ᴰ104:16 Lit are satisfied   ᴱ104:19 Lit moon for   ᶠ104:19 Or the appointed times   ᴳ104:24 Lit possessions

25 Here is the sea, vast and wide,
teeming with creatures
   beyond number—
living things both large and small.
26 There the ships move about,
and Leviathan, which You formed
   to play there.
27 All of them wait for You
to give them their food
   at the right time.
28 When You give it to them,
they gather it;
when You open Your hand,
they are satisfied with good things.
29 When You hide Your face,
they are terrified;
when You take away their breath,
they die and return to the dust.
30 When You send Your breath,ᴬ
they are created,
and You renew the face of the earth.
31 May the glory of the Lᴏʀᴅ
   endure forever;
may the Lᴏʀᴅ rejoice in His works.
32 He looks at the earth, and it trembles;
He touches the mountains,
and they pour out smoke.
33 I will sing to the Lᴏʀᴅ all my life;
I will sing praise to my God while I live.
34 May my meditation be pleasing to Him;
I will rejoice in the Lᴏʀᴅ.
35 May sinners vanish from the earth
and wicked people be no more.
My soul, praise Yahweh!
Hallelujah!

Psalm 105

1 Give thanks to Yahweh, call on
   His name;
proclaim His deeds among the peoples.
2 Sing to Him, sing praise to Him;
tell about all His wonderful works!
3 Honor His holy name;
let the hearts of those who seek
   Yahweh rejoice.
4 Search for the Lᴏʀᴅ and for
   His strength;
seek His face always.
5 Remember the wonderful works
   He has done,
His wonders, and the judgments He
has pronounced,ᴮ

6 you offspring of Abraham His servant,
Jacob's descendants—
   His chosen ones.
7 He is the Lᴏʀᴅ our God;
His judgments govern the whole earth.
8 He remembers His covenant forever,
the promise He ordained
for a thousand generations—
9 the covenant He made with Abraham,
sworeᶜ to Isaac,
10 and confirmed to Jacob as a decree
and to Israel
   as an everlasting covenant:
11 "I will give the land of Canaan to you
as your inherited portion."
12 When they were few in number,
very few indeed,
and temporary residents in Canaan,
13 wandering from nation to nation
and from one kingdom to another,
14 He allowed no one to oppress them;
He rebuked kings on their behalf:
15 "Do not touch My anointed ones,
or harm My prophets."
16 He called down famine against the land
and destroyed the entire food supply.
17 He had sent a man ahead of them—
Joseph, who was sold as a slave.
18 They hurt his feet with shackles;
his neck was put in an iron collar.
19 Until the time his prediction
   came true,
the word of the Lᴏʀᴅ tested him.
20 The king sent for him
   and released him;
the ruler of peoples set him free.
21 He made him master of his household,
ruler over all his possessions—
22 bindingᴰ his officials at will
and instructing his elders.
23 Then Israel went to Egypt;
Jacob lived as a foreigner in the land
   of Ham.ᴱ
24 The Lᴏʀᴅᶠ made His people
   very fruitful;
He made them more numerous
   than their foes,
25 whose hearts He turned to hate
   His people
and to deal deceptively
   with His servants.

ᴬ104:30 Or Spirit   ᴮ105:5 Lit judgments of His mouth   ᶜ105:9 Lit and His oath   ᴰ105:22 LXX, Syr, Vg read teaching   ᴱ105:23 = Egypt
ᶠ105:24 Lit He

²⁶ He sent Moses His servant,
and Aaron, whom He had chosen.
²⁷ They performed His miraculous signs
among them,
and wonders in the land of Ham.ᴬ
²⁸ He sent darkness,
and it became dark—
for did they not defyᴮ His commands?
²⁹ He turned their water into blood
and caused their fish to die.
³⁰ Their land was overrun with frogs,
even in their royal chambers.
³¹ He spoke, and insects came—
gnats throughout their country.
³² He gave them hail for rain,
and lightning throughout their land.
³³ He struck their vines and fig trees
and shattered the trees
of their territory.
³⁴ He spoke, and locusts came—
young locusts without number.
³⁵ They devoured all the vegetation
in their land
and consumed the produce
of their land.
³⁶ He struck all the firstborn
in their land,
all their first progeny.
³⁷ Then He brought Israel out with silver
and gold,
and no one among His tribes stumbled.
³⁸ Egypt was glad when they left,
for the dread of Israelᶜ had fallen
on them.
³⁹ He spread a cloud as a covering
and gave a fire to light up the night.
⁴⁰ They asked, and He brought quail
and satisfied them with bread
from heaven.
⁴¹ He opened a rock, and water
gushed out;
it flowed like a stream in the desert.
⁴² For He remembered His holy promise
to Abraham His servant.
⁴³ He brought His people out
with rejoicing,
His chosen ones with shouts of joy.
⁴⁴ He gave them the lands of the nations,
and they inherited
what other peoples had worked for.
⁴⁵ All this happened
so that they might keep His statutes

and obey His instructions.
Hallelujah!

Psalm 106

¹ Hallelujah!
Give thanks to the LORD, for He is good;
His faithful love endures forever.
² Who can declare the LORD's mighty acts
or proclaim all the praise due Him?
³ How happy are those
who uphold justice,
who practice righteousness at all times.
⁴ Remember me, LORD,
when You show favor to Your people.
Come to me with Your salvation
⁵ so that I may enjoy the prosperity
of Your chosen ones,
rejoice in the joy of Your nation,
and boast about Your heritage.
⁶ Both we and our fathers have sinned;
we have done wrong
and have acted wickedly.
⁷ Our fathers in Egypt did not grasp
the significance of
Your wonderful works
or remember Your many acts
of faithful love;
instead, they rebelled
by the sea—the Red Sea.
⁸ Yet He saved them
because of His name,
to make His power known.
⁹ He rebuked the Red Sea,
and it dried up;
He led them through the depths
as through a desert.
¹⁰ He saved them from the hand
of the adversary;
He redeemed them from the hand
of the enemy.
¹¹ Water covered their foes;
not one of them remained.
¹² Then they believed His promises
and sang His praise.
¹³ They soon forgot His works
and would not wait for His counsel.
¹⁴ They were seized with craving
in the wilderness
and tested God in the desert.
¹⁵ He gave them what they asked for,
but sent a wasting disease
among them.

ᴬ105:27 = Egypt   ᴮ105:28 LXX, Syr read for they did defy   ᶜ105:38 Lit them

¹⁶ In the camp they were envious
of Moses
and of Aaron, the LORD's holy one.

¹⁷ The earth opened up
and swallowed Dathan;
it covered the assembly of Abiram.

¹⁸ Fire blazed throughout their assembly;
flames consumed the wicked.

¹⁹ At Horeb they made a calf
and worshiped the cast metal image.

²⁰ They exchanged their glory^{A,B}
for the image of a grass-eating ox.

²¹ They forgot God their Savior,
who did great things in Egypt,

²² wonderful works in the land of Ham,^C
awe-inspiring acts at the Red Sea.

²³ So He said
He would have destroyed them—
if Moses His chosen one
had not stood before Him in the breach
to turn His wrath away
from destroying them.

²⁴ They despised the pleasant land
and did not believe His promise.

²⁵ They grumbled in their tents
and did not listen to the LORD's voice.

²⁶ So He raised His hand against them
with an oath
that He would make them fall
in the desert

²⁷ and would disperse their descendants^D
among the nations,
scattering them throughout the lands.

²⁸ They aligned themselves with Baal
of Peor
and ate sacrifices offered
to lifeless gods.^E

²⁹ They provoked the LORD
with their deeds,
and a plague broke out against them.

³⁰ But Phinehas stood up and intervened,
and the plague was stopped.

³¹ It was credited to him as righteousness
throughout all generations to come.

³² They angered the LORD at the waters
of Meribah,
and Moses suffered^F because of them;

³³ for they embittered his spirit,^G
and he spoke rashly with his lips.

³⁴ They did not destroy the peoples
as the LORD had commanded them

³⁵ but mingled with the nations
and adopted their ways.

³⁶ They served their idols,
which became a snare to them.

³⁷ They sacrificed their sons
and daughters to demons.

³⁸ They shed innocent blood—
the blood of their sons and daughters
whom they sacrificed to the idols
of Canaan;
so the land became polluted
with blood.

³⁹ They defiled themselves
by their actions
and prostituted themselves
by their deeds.

⁴⁰ Therefore the LORD's anger burned
against His people,
and He abhorred His own inheritance.

⁴¹ He handed them over to the nations;
those who hated them ruled them.

⁴² Their enemies oppressed them,
and they were subdued
under their power.

⁴³ He rescued them many times,
but they continued to rebel deliberately
and were beaten down by their sin.

⁴⁴ When He heard their cry,
He took note of their distress,

⁴⁵ remembered His covenant with them,
and relented according to the riches
of His faithful love.

⁴⁶ He caused them to be pitied
before all their captors.

⁴⁷ Save us, Yahweh our God,
and gather us from the nations,
so that we may give thanks
to Your holy name
and rejoice in Your praise.

⁴⁸ May Yahweh, the God of Israel,
be praised
from everlasting to everlasting.
Let all the people say, "Amen!"
Hallelujah!

BOOK V
(Psalms 107–150)

Psalm 107

¹ Give thanks to the LORD, for He is good;
His faithful love endures forever.

^A**106:20** Alt Jewish tradition reads *His* or *My glory*   ^B**106:20** = God   ^C**106:22** = Egypt   ^D**106:27** Syr; MT reads *would make their descendants fall*   ^E**106:28** Lit *sacrifices for dead ones*   ^F**106:32** Lit *and it was evil for Moses*   ^G**106:33** Some Hb mss, LXX, Syr, Jer; other Hb mss read *they rebelled against His Spirit*

2 Let the redeemed of the Lord proclaim
   that He has redeemed them
      from the hand of the foe
3 and has gathered them
      from the lands—
   from the east and the west,
   from the north and the south.
4 Some[A] wandered
      in the desolate wilderness,
   finding no way to a city
      where they could live.
5 They were hungry and thirsty;
   their spirits failed[B] within them.
6 Then they cried out to the Lord
      in their trouble;
   He rescued them from their distress.
7 He led them by the right path
   to go to a city where they could live.
8 Let them give thanks to the Lord
      for His faithful love
   and His wonderful works for
      all humanity.
9 For He has satisfied the thirsty
   and filled the hungry with good things.
10 Others[A] sat in darkness and gloom[C]—
   prisoners in cruel chains—
11 because they rebelled
      against God's commands
   and despised the counsel
      of the Most High.
12 He broke their spirits[D] with hard labor;
   they stumbled, and there was no one
      to help.
13 Then they cried out to the Lord
      in their trouble;
   He saved them from their distress.
14 He brought them out of darkness
      and gloom[C]
   and broke their chains apart.
15 Let them give thanks to the Lord
      for His faithful love
   and His wonderful works for
      all humanity.
16 For He has broken down
      the bronze gates
   and cut through the iron bars.
17 Fools suffered affliction
   because of their rebellious ways
      and their sins.
18 They loathed all food
   and came near the gates of death.

19 Then they cried out to the Lord
      in their trouble;
   He saved them from their distress.
20 He sent His word and healed them;
   He rescued them from the Pit.
21 Let them give thanks to the Lord
      for His faithful love
   and His wonderful works for
      all humanity.
22 Let them offer sacrifices
      of thanksgiving
   and announce His works with shouts
      of joy.
23 Others[A] went to sea in ships,
   conducting trade on the vast waters.
24 They saw the Lord's works,
   His wonderful works in the deep.
25 He spoke and raised a tempest
   that stirred up the waves of the sea.[E]
26 Rising up to the sky, sinking down
      to the depths,
   their courage[F] melting away
      in anguish,
27 they reeled and staggered
      like drunken men,
   and all their skill was useless.
28 Then they cried out to the Lord
      in their trouble,
   and He brought them
      out of their distress.
29 He stilled the storm to a murmur,
   and the waves of the sea[G] were hushed.
30 They rejoiced when the waves[H]
      grew quiet.
   Then He guided them to the harbor
      they longed for.
31 Let them give thanks to the Lord
      for His faithful love
   and His wonderful works for
      all humanity.
32 Let them exalt Him in the assembly
      of the people
   and praise Him in the council
      of the elders.
33 He turns rivers into desert,
   springs of water into thirsty ground,
34 and fruitful land into salty wasteland,
   because of the wickedness
      of its inhabitants.
35 He turns a desert into a pool of water,
   dry land into springs of water.

A107:4,10,23 Lit They   B107:5 Lit their soul fainted   C107:10,14 Or the shadow of death   D107:12 Lit hearts   E107:25 Lit of it   F107:26 Lit
souls   G107:29 Lit of them   H107:30 Lit when they

³⁶ He causes the hungry to settle there,
and they establish a city
where they can live.
³⁷ They sow fields and plant vineyards
that yield a fruitful harvest.
³⁸ He blesses them,
and they multiply greatly;
He does not let their livestock decrease.
³⁹ When they are diminished
and are humbled
by cruel oppression and sorrow,
⁴⁰ He pours contempt on nobles
and makes them wander
in a trackless wasteland.
⁴¹ But He lifts the needy out of
their suffering
and makes their families multiply
like flocks.
⁴² The upright see it and rejoice,
and all injustice shuts its mouth.
⁴³ Let whoever is wise pay attention
to these things
and considerᴬ the LORD's acts
of faithful love.

Psalm 108
A song. A Davidic psalm.

¹ My heart is confident, God;ᴮ
I will sing; I will sing praises
with the whole of my being.ᶜ
² Wake up, harp and lyre!
I will wake up the dawn.
³ I will praise You, LORD,
among the peoples;
I will sing praises to You
among the nations.
⁴ For Your faithful love is higher
than the heavens,
and Your faithfulness reaches to
the clouds.
⁵ God, be exalted above the heavens,
and let Your glory be over
the whole earth.
⁶ Save with Your right hand
and answer me
so that those You love may be rescued.
⁷ God has spoken in His sanctuary:ᴰ
"I will triumph!
I will divide up Shechem.
I will apportion the Valley of Succoth.
⁸ Gilead is Mine, Manasseh is Mine,
and Ephraim is My helmet;

Judah is My scepter.
⁹ Moab is My washbasin;
I throw My sandal on Edom.
I shout in triumph over Philistia."
¹⁰ Who will bring me
to the fortified city?
Who will lead me to Edom?
¹¹ God, haven't You rejected us?
God, You do not march out
with our armies.
¹² Give us aid against the foe,
for human help is worthless.
¹³ With God we will perform valiantly;
He will trample our foes.

Psalm 109
For the choir director. A Davidic psalm.

¹ God of my praise, do not be silent.
² For wicked and deceitful mouths open
against me;
they speak against me
with lying tongues.
³ They surround me with hateful words
and attack me without cause.
⁴ In return for my love they accuse me,
but I continue to pray.ᴱ
⁵ They repay me evil for good,
and hatred for my love.
⁶ Set a wicked person over him;
let an accuserᶠ stand at his right hand.
⁷ When he is judged, let him
be found guilty,
and let his prayer be counted as sin.
⁸ Let his days be few;
let another take over his position.
⁹ Let his children be fatherless
and his wife a widow.
¹⁰ Let his children wander as beggars,
searching for food farᴳ
from their demolished homes.
¹¹ Let a creditor seize all he has;
let strangers plunder what he has
worked for.
¹² Let no one show him kindness,
and let no one be gracious
to his fatherless children.
¹³ Let the line of his descendants
be cut off;
let their name be blotted out
in the next generation.
¹⁴ Let his ancestors' guilt
be remembered before the LORD,

ᴬ107:43 Lit and let them consider   ᴮ108:1 Some Hb mss, LXX, Syr add my heart is confident   ᶜ108:1 Lit praises, even my glory   ᴰ108:7 Or has
promised by His holy nature   ᴱ109:4 Lit but I, prayer   ᶠ109:6 Or adversary   ᴳ109:10 LXX reads beggars, driven far

and do not let his mother's sin
     be blotted out.
15 Let their sins[A] always remain
     before the LORD,
     and let Him erase[B] all memory of them
     from the earth.
16 For he did not think to show kindness,
     but pursued the afflicted, poor, and
     brokenhearted
     in order to put them to death.
17 He loved cursing—let it fall on him;
     he took no delight
     in blessing—let it be far from him.
18 He wore cursing like his coat—
     let it enter his body like water
     and go into his bones like oil.
19 Let it be like a robe he wraps
     around himself,
     like a belt he always wears.
20 Let this be the LORD's payment
     to my accusers,
     to those who speak evil against me.
21 But You, Yahweh my Lord,
     deal kindly with me
     because of Your name;
     deliver me because of the goodness
     of Your faithful love.
22 For I am afflicted and needy;
     my heart is wounded within me.
23 I fade away like a lengthening shadow;
     I am shaken off like a locust.
24 My knees are weak from fasting,
     and my body is emaciated.[C]
25 I have become an object of ridicule
     to my accusers;[D]
     when they see me, they shake
     their heads in scorn.
26 Help me, LORD my God;
     save me according to Your faithful love
27 so they may know that this is Your hand
     and that You, LORD, have done it.
28 Though they curse, You will bless.
     When they rise up, they will be
     put to shame,
     but Your servant will rejoice.
29 My accusers will be clothed
     with disgrace;
     they will wear their shame like a cloak.
30 I will fervently thank the LORD
     with my mouth;
     I will praise Him in the presence
     of many.

31 For He stands at the right hand of
     the needy
     to save him from those who would
     condemn him.

Psalm 110
A Davidic psalm.

1 This is the declaration of the LORD
     to my Lord:
     "Sit at My right hand
     until I make Your enemies
     Your footstool."
2 The LORD will extend
     Your mighty scepter from Zion.
     Rule[E] over Your surrounding[F] enemies.
3 Your people will volunteer
     on Your day of battle.[G]
     In holy splendor, from the womb
     of the dawn,
     the dew of Your youth belongs to You.[H]
4 The LORD has sworn an oath
     and will not take it back:
     "Forever, You are a priest
     like Melchizedek."
5 The Lord is at Your right hand;
     He will crush kings on the day
     of His anger.
6 He will judge the nations,
     heaping up corpses;
     He will crush leaders
     over the entire world.
7 He will drink from the brook
     by the road;
     therefore, He will lift up His head.

Psalm 111

1 Hallelujah![I]
     I will praise the LORD with all my heart
     in the assembly of the upright
     and in the congregation.
2 The LORD's works are great,
     studied by all who delight in them.
3 All that He does is splendid
     and majestic;
     His righteousness endures forever.
4 He has caused His wonderful works
     to be remembered.
     The LORD is gracious
     and compassionate.
5 He has provided food for those
     who fear Him;
     He remembers His covenant forever.

A109:15 Lit *Let them*   B109:15 Or *cut off*   C109:24 Lit *denied from fat*   D109:25 Lit *to them*   E110:2 One Hb ms, LXX, Tg read *You will rule*   F110:2 Lit *Rule in the midst of Your*   G110:3 Lit *power*   H110:3 Hb obscure   I111:1 The lines of this poem form an acrostic.

⁶ He has shown His people the power
   of His works
 by giving them the inheritance
   of the nations.
⁷ The works of His hands are truth
   and justice;
 all His instructions are trustworthy.
⁸ They are established forever and ever,
   enacted in truth and in what is right.
⁹ He has sent redemption to His people.
 He has ordained His covenant forever.
 His name is holy and awe-inspiring.
¹⁰ The fear of the LORD is the beginning
   of wisdom;
 all who follow His instructions[A] have
   good insight.
 His praise endures forever.

Psalm 112

¹ Hallelujah![B]
 Happy is the man who fears the LORD,
 taking great delight in His commands.
² His descendants will be powerful
   in the land;
 the generation of the upright
   will be blessed.
³ Wealth and riches are in his house,
 and his righteousness endures forever.
⁴ Light shines in the darkness
   for the upright.
 He is gracious, compassionate,
   and righteous.
⁵ Good will come to a man
   who lends generously
 and conducts his business fairly.
⁶ He will never be shaken.
 The righteous man will be
   remembered forever.
⁷ He will not fear bad news;
 his heart is confident,
   trusting in the LORD.
⁸ His heart is assured; he will not fear.
 In the end he will look in triumph
   on his foes.
⁹ He distributes freely to the poor;
 his righteousness endures forever.
 His horn will be exalted in honor.
¹⁰ The wicked man will see it
   and be angry;
 he will gnash his teeth in despair.
 The desire of the wicked man will come
   to nothing.

Psalm 113

¹ Hallelujah!
 Give praise, servants of Yahweh;
 praise the name of Yahweh.
² Let the name of Yahweh be praised
 both now and forever.
³ From the rising of the sun
   to its setting,
 let the name of Yahweh be praised.
⁴ Yahweh is exalted above all the nations,
 His glory above the heavens.
⁵ Who is like Yahweh our God—
 the One enthroned on high,
⁶ who stoops down to look
 on the heavens and the earth?
⁷ He raises the poor from the dust
 and lifts the needy
   from the garbage pile
⁸ in order to seat them with nobles—
 with the nobles of His people.
⁹ He gives the childless woman
   a household,
 making her the joyful mother
   of children.
 Hallelujah!

Psalm 114

¹ When Israel came out of Egypt—
 the house of Jacob from a people
 who spoke a foreign language—
² Judah became His sanctuary,
 Israel, His dominion.
³ The sea looked and fled;
 the Jordan turned back.
⁴ The mountains skipped like rams,
 the hills, like lambs.
⁵ Why was it, sea, that you fled?
 Jordan, that you turned back?
⁶ Mountains, that you skipped like rams?
 Hills, like lambs?
⁷ Tremble, earth, at the presence
   of the Lord,
 at the presence of the God of Jacob,
⁸ who turned the rock into a pool
   of water,
 the flint into a spring of water.

Psalm 115

¹ Not to us, Yahweh, not to us,
 but to Your name give glory
 because of Your faithful love,
   because of Your truth.
² Why should the nations say,

"Where is their God?"

³ Our God is in heaven
and does whatever He pleases.
⁴ Their idols are silver and gold,
made by human hands.
⁵ They have mouths but cannot speak,
eyes, but cannot see.
⁶ They have ears but cannot hear,
noses, but cannot smell.
⁷ They have hands but cannot feel,
feet, but cannot walk.
They cannot make a sound
with their throats.
⁸ Those who make them are[A] just
like them,
as are all who trust in them.
⁹ Israel,[B] trust in the LORD!
He is their help and shield.
¹⁰ House of Aaron, trust in the LORD!
He is their help and shield.
¹¹ You who fear the LORD,
trust in the LORD!
He is their help and shield.
¹² The LORD remembers us
and will bless us.
He will bless the house of Israel;
He will bless the house of Aaron;
¹³ He will bless those who fear the LORD—
small and great alike.
¹⁴ May the LORD add to your numbers,
both yours and your children's.
¹⁵ May you be blessed by the LORD,
the Maker of heaven and earth.
¹⁶ The heavens are the LORD's,[C]
but the earth He has given
to the human race.
¹⁷ It is not the dead who praise the LORD,
nor any of those descending
into the silence of death.
¹⁸ But we will praise the LORD,
both now and forever.
Hallelujah!

Psalm 116

¹ I love the LORD because He has heard
my appeal for mercy.
² Because He has turned His ear to me,
I will call out to Him as long as I live.
³ The ropes of death were wrapped
around me,
and the torments of Sheol
overcame me;
I encountered trouble and sorrow.

⁴ Then I called on the name of Yahweh:
"Yahweh, save me!"
⁵ The LORD is gracious and righteous;
our God is compassionate.
⁶ The LORD guards the inexperienced;
I was helpless, and He saved me.
⁷ Return to your rest, my soul,
for the LORD has been good to you.
⁸ For You, LORD, rescued me from death,
my eyes from tears,
my feet from stumbling.
⁹ I will walk before the LORD
in the land of the living.
¹⁰ I believed, even when I said,
"I am severely afflicted."
¹¹ In my alarm I said,
"Everyone is a liar."
¹² How can I repay the LORD
for all the good He has done for me?
¹³ I will take the cup of salvation
and call on the name of Yahweh.
¹⁴ I will fulfill my vows to the LORD
in the presence of all His people.
¹⁵ The death of His faithful ones
is valuable in the LORD's sight.
¹⁶ LORD, I am indeed Your servant;
I am Your servant, the son
of Your female servant.
You have loosened my bonds.
¹⁷ I will offer You a sacrifice
of thanksgiving
and call on the name of Yahweh.
¹⁸ I will fulfill my vows to the LORD
in the presence of all His people,
¹⁹ in the courts of the LORD's house—
within you, Jerusalem.
Hallelujah!

Psalm 117

¹ Praise the LORD, all nations!
Glorify Him, all peoples!
² For His faithful love to us is great;
the LORD's faithfulness endures forever.
Hallelujah!

Psalm 118

¹ Give thanks to the LORD, for He is good;
His faithful love endures forever.
² Let Israel say,
"His faithful love endures forever."
³ Let the house of Aaron say,
"His faithful love endures forever."
⁴ Let those who fear the LORD say,

"His faithful love endures forever."
5 I called to the LORD in distress;
the LORD answered me
and put me in a spacious place.[A]
6 The LORD is for me; I will not be afraid.
What can man do to me?
7 The LORD is my helper,
Therefore, I will look in triumph
on those who hate me.
8 It is better to take refuge in the LORD
than to trust in man.
9 It is better to take refuge in the LORD
than to trust in nobles.
10 All the nations surrounded me;
in the name of Yahweh
I destroyed them.
11 They surrounded me, yes,
they surrounded me;
in the name of Yahweh
I destroyed them.
12 They surrounded me like bees;
they were extinguished like a fire
among thorns;
in the name of Yahweh
I destroyed them.
13 You[B] pushed me[C] hard to make me fall,
but the LORD helped me.
14 The LORD is my strength and my song;
He has become my salvation.
15 There are shouts of joy and victory
in the tents of the righteous:
"The LORD's right hand
performs valiantly!
16 The LORD's right hand is raised.
The LORD's right hand
performs valiantly!"
17 I will not die, but I will live
and proclaim what the LORD has done.
18 The LORD disciplined me severely
but did not give me over to death.
19 Open the gates of righteousness
for me;
I will enter through them
and give thanks to the LORD.
20 This is the gate of the LORD;
the righteous will enter through it.
21 I will give thanks to You
because You have answered me
and have become my salvation.
22 The stone that the builders rejected
has become the cornerstone.
23 This came from the LORD;

it is wonderful in our eyes.
24 This is the day the LORD has made;
let us rejoice and be glad in it.
25 LORD, save us!
LORD, please grant us success!
26 He who comes in the name
of the LORD is blessed.
From the house of the LORD
we bless you.
27 The LORD is God and has given us light.
Bind the festival sacrifice with cords
to the horns of the altar.
28 You are my God, and I will give
You thanks.
You are my God; I will exalt You.
29 Give thanks to the LORD, for He is good;
His faithful love endures forever.

Psalm 119

א Alef

1 How[D] happy are those whose way
is blameless,
who live according to the LORD's
instruction!
2 Happy are those who keep His decrees
and seek Him with all their heart.
3 They do nothing wrong;
they follow His ways.
4 You have commanded
that Your precepts
be diligently kept.
5 If only my ways were committed
to keeping Your statutes!
6 Then I would not be ashamed
when I think about
all Your commands.
7 I will praise You with a sincere heart
when I learn
Your righteous judgments.
8 I will keep Your statutes;
never abandon me.

ב Bet

9 How can a young man keep his way
pure?
By keeping Your[E] word.
10 I have sought You with all my heart;
don't let me wander
from Your commands.
11 I have treasured Your word in my heart
so that I may not sin against You.

[A]118:5 Or *answered me with freedom*   [B]118:13 Perhaps the enemy   [C]118:13 LXX, Syr, Jer read *I was pushed*   [D]119:1 The stanzas of this poem form an acrostic.   [E]119:9 Or *keeping it according to Your*

¹² Lord, may You be praised;
   teach me Your statutes.
¹³ With my lips I proclaim
   all the judgments from Your mouth.
¹⁴ I rejoice in the way revealed by
      Your decrees
   as much as in all riches.
¹⁵ I will meditate on Your precepts
   and think about Your ways.
¹⁶ I will delight in Your statutes;
   I will not forget Your word.

ג Gimel

¹⁷ Deal generously with Your servant
   so that I might live;
   then I will keep Your word.
¹⁸ Open my eyes so that
      I may contemplate
   wonderful things
      from Your instruction.
¹⁹ I am a stranger on earth;
   do not hide Your commands from me.
²⁰ I am continually overcome
   with longing for Your judgments.
²¹ You rebuke the proud,
   the ones under a curse,
   who wander from Your commands.
²² Take insult and contempt away
      from me,
   for I have kept Your decrees.
²³ Though princes sit together speaking
      against me,
   Your servant will think
      about Your statutes;
²⁴ Your decrees are my delight
   and my counselors.

ד Dalet

²⁵ My life is down in the dust;
   give me life through Your word.
²⁶ I told You about my life,
   and You listened to me;
   teach me Your statutes.
²⁷ Help me understand
   the meaning of Your precepts
   so that I can meditate on Your wonders.
²⁸ I am weary^A from grief;
   strengthen me through Your word.
²⁹ Keep me from the way of deceit
   and graciously give me
      Your instruction.

³⁰ I have chosen the way of truth;
   I have set Your ordinances before me.
³¹ I cling to Your decrees;
   Lord, do not put me to shame.
³² I pursue the way of Your commands,
   for You broaden my understanding.^B

ה He

³³ Teach me, Lord, the meaning^C
      of Your statutes,
   and I will always keep them.^D
³⁴ Help me understand Your instruction,
   and I will obey it
   and follow it with all my heart.
³⁵ Help me stay on the path
      of Your commands,
   for I take pleasure in it.
³⁶ Turn my heart to Your decrees
   and not to material gain.
³⁷ Turn my eyes
   from looking at what is worthless;
   give me life in Your ways.^E
³⁸ Confirm what You said to Your servant,
   for it produces reverence for You.
³⁹ Turn away the disgrace I dread;
   indeed, Your judgments are good.
⁴⁰ How I long for Your precepts!
   Give me life through
      Your righteousness.

ו Vav

⁴¹ Let Your faithful love
      come to me, Lord,
   Your salvation, as You promised.
⁴² Then I can answer the one
      who taunts me,
   for I trust in Your word.
⁴³ Never take the word of truth
      from my mouth,
   for I hope in Your judgments.
⁴⁴ I will always obey Your instruction,
   forever and ever.
⁴⁵ I will walk freely in an open place
   because I seek Your precepts.
⁴⁶ I will speak of Your decrees
      before kings
   and not be ashamed.
⁴⁷ I delight in Your commands,
   which I love.
⁴⁸ I will lift up my hands
      to Your commands,

---

^A119:28 Or *I weep*   ^B119:32 Lit *You enlarge my heart*   ^C119:33 Lit *way*   ^D119:33 Or *will keep it as my reward*   ^E119:37 Some Hb mss, Tg read *word*

which I love,
and will meditate on Your statutes.

ז Zayin

49 Remember Your word to Your servant;
You have given me hope through it.
50 This is my comfort in my affliction:
Your promise has given me life.
51 The arrogant constantly ridicule me,
but I do not turn away
from Your instruction.
52 Lord, I remember Your judgments
from long ago
and find comfort.
53 Rage seizes me because of the wicked
who reject Your instruction.
54 Your statutes are the theme of my song
during my earthly life.[A]
55 Yahweh, I remember Your name
in the night,
and I obey Your instruction.
56 This is my practice:
I obey Your precepts.

ח Khet

57 The Lord is my portion;[B]
I have promised to keep Your words.
58 I have sought Your favor with all
my heart;
be gracious to me according to
Your promise.
59 I thought about my ways
and turned my steps back
to Your decrees.
60 I hurried, not hesitating
to keep Your commands.
61 Though the ropes of the wicked
were wrapped around me,
I did not forget Your instruction.
62 I rise at midnight to thank You
for Your righteous judgments.
63 I am a friend to all who fear You,
to those who keep Your precepts.
64 Lord, the earth is filled with
Your faithful love;
teach me Your statutes.

ט Tet

65 Lord, You have treated
Your servant well,
just as You promised.

66 Teach me good judgment
and discernment,
for I rely on Your commands.
67 Before I was afflicted I went astray,
but now I keep Your word.
68 You are good, and You do what is good;
teach me Your statutes.
69 The arrogant have smeared me
with lies,
but I obey Your precepts with all
my heart.
70 Their hearts are hard and insensitive,
but I delight in Your instruction.
71 It was good for me to be afflicted
so that I could learn Your statutes.
72 Instruction from Your lips is better
for me
than thousands of gold
and silver pieces.

י Yod

73 Your hands made me and formed me;
give me understanding
so that I can learn Your commands.
74 Those who fear You will see me
and rejoice,
for I put my hope in Your word.
75 I know, Lord, that Your judgments
are just
and that You have afflicted me fairly.
76 May Your faithful love comfort me
as You promised Your servant.
77 May Your compassion come to me
so that I may live,
for Your instruction is my delight.
78 Let the arrogant be put to shame
for slandering me with lies;
I will meditate on Your precepts.
79 Let those who fear You,
those who know Your decrees,
turn to me.
80 May my heart be blameless
regarding Your statutes
so that I will not be put to shame.

כ Kaf

81 I long for Your salvation;
I put my hope in Your word.
82 My eyes grow weary
looking for what You have promised;
I ask, "When will You comfort me?"

[A]119:54 Lit song in the house of my sojourning [B]119:57 Lit You are my portion, Lord

83 Though I have become like a wineskin
      dried by smoke,
   I do not forget Your statutes.
84 How many days must
      Your servant wait?
   When will You execute judgment
      on my persecutors?
85 The arrogant have dug pits for me;
   they violate Your instruction.
86 All Your commands are true;
   people persecute me
      with lies—help me!
87 They almost ended my life on earth,
   but I did not abandon Your precepts.
88 Give me life in accordance with
      Your faithful love,
   and I will obey the decree
      You have spoken.

ל Lamed

89 LORD, Your word is forever;
   it is firmly fixed in heaven.
90 Your faithfulness is for all generations;
   You established the earth,
      and it stands firm.
91 They stand today in accordance with
      Your judgments,
   for all things are Your servants.
92 If Your instruction had not been
      my delight,
   I would have died in my affliction.
93 I will never forget Your precepts,
   for You have given me life
      through them.
94 I am Yours; save me,
   for I have sought Your precepts.
95 The wicked hope to destroy me,
   but I contemplate Your decrees.
96 I have seen a limit to all perfection,
   but Your command is without limit.

מ Mem

97 How I love Your instruction!
   It is my meditation all day long.
98 Your commands make me wiser
      than my enemies,
   for they are always with me.
99 I have more insight than
      all my teachers
   because Your decrees are
      my meditation.

100 I understand more than the elders
    because I obey Your precepts.
101 I have kept my feet from every evil path
    to follow Your word.
102 I have not turned from Your judgments,
    for You Yourself have instructed me.
103 How sweet Your word is to my taste—
    sweeter than honey in my mouth.
104 I gain understanding
       from Your precepts;
    therefore I hate every false way.

נ Nun

105 Your word is a lamp for my feet
    and a light on my path.
106 I have solemnly sworn
    to keep Your righteous judgments.
107 I am severely afflicted;
    LORD, give me life through Your word.
108 LORD, please accept my willing offerings
       of praise,
    and teach me Your judgments.
109 My life is constantly in danger,^A
    yet I do not forget Your instruction.
110 The wicked have set a trap for me,
    but I have not wandered
       from Your precepts.
111 I have Your decrees as a heritage forever;
    indeed, they are the joy of my heart.
112 I am resolved to obey Your statutes
    to the very end.^B

ס Samek

113 I hate those who are double-minded,
    but I love Your instruction.
114 You are my shelter and my shield;
    I put my hope in Your word.
115 Depart from me, you evil ones,
    so that I may obey
       my God's commands.
116 Sustain me as You promised,
       and I will live;
    do not let me be ashamed of my hope.
117 Sustain me so that I can be safe
    and always be concerned about
       Your statutes.
118 You reject all who stray
       from Your statutes,
    for their deceit is a lie.
119 You remove all the wicked on earth
    as if they were^C dross;

^A119:109 Lit in my hand   ^B119:112 Or statutes; the reward is eternal   ^C119:119 Some Hb mss, DSS, LXX, Aq, Sym, Jer read All the wicked of
the earth You count as

therefore, I love Your decrees.
120 I tremble[A] in awe of You;
I fear Your judgments.

ע Ayin

121 I have done what is just and right;
do not leave me to my oppressors.
122 Guarantee Your servant's well-being;
do not let the arrogant oppress me.
123 My eyes grow weary looking for
Your salvation
and for Your righteous promise.
124 Deal with Your servant based on
Your faithful love;
teach me Your statutes.
125 I am Your servant;
give me understanding
so that I may know Your decrees.
126 It is time for the LORD to act,
for they have violated Your instruction.
127 Since I love Your commands
more than gold, even the purest gold,
128 I carefully follow[B] all Your precepts
and hate every false way.

פ Pe

129 Your decrees are wonderful;
therefore I obey them.
130 The revelation of Your words
brings light
and gives understanding
to the inexperienced.
131 I open my mouth and pant
because I long for Your commands.
132 Turn to me and be gracious to me,
as is Your practice toward those
who love Your name.
133 Make my steps steady
through Your promise;
don't let any sin dominate me.
134 Redeem me from human oppression,
and I will keep Your precepts.
135 Show favor to Your servant,
and teach me Your statutes.
136 My eyes pour out streams of tears
because people do not follow
Your instruction.

צ Tsade

137 You are righteous, LORD,
and Your judgments are just.

138 The decrees You issue are righteous
and altogether trustworthy.
139 My anger overwhelms me
because my foes forget Your words.
140 Your word is completely pure,
and Your servant loves it.
141 I am insignificant and despised,
but I do not forget Your precepts.
142 Your righteousness is
an everlasting righteousness,
and Your instruction is true.
143 Trouble and distress
have overtaken me,
but Your commands are my delight.
144 Your decrees are righteous forever.
Give me understanding, and I will live.

ק Qof

145 I call with all my heart;
answer me, LORD.
I will obey Your statutes.
146 I call to You; save me,
and I will keep Your decrees.
147 I rise before dawn and cry out for help;
I put my hope in Your word.
148 I am awake through each watch
of the night
to meditate on Your promise.
149 In keeping with Your faithful love,
hear my voice.
LORD, give me life in keeping with
Your justice.
150 Those who pursue evil plans[C]
come near;
they are far from Your instruction.
151 You are near, LORD,
and all Your commands are true.
152 Long ago I learned from Your decrees
that You have established them forever.

ר Resh

153 Consider my affliction and rescue me,
for I have not forgotten
Your instruction.
154 Defend my cause and redeem me;
give me life as You promised.
155 Salvation is far from the wicked
because they do not seek Your statutes.
156 Your compassions are many, LORD;
give me life according to
Your judgments.

A 119:120 Lit My flesh shudders   B 119:128 Lit I therefore follow carefully   C 119:150 Some Hb mss, LXX, Sym, Jer read who maliciously persecute me

157 My persecutors and foes are many.
I have not turned from Your decrees.
158 I have seen the disloyal and feel disgust
because they do not keep Your word.
159 Consider how I love Your precepts;
LORD, give me life according to
Your faithful love.
160 The entirety of Your word is truth,
and all Your righteous judgments
endure forever.

ש Sin/ ש Shin

161 Princes have persecuted me
without cause,
but my heart fears only Your word.
162 I rejoice over Your promise
like one who finds vast treasure.
163 I hate and abhor falsehood,
but I love Your instruction.
164 I praise You seven times a day
for Your righteous judgments.
165 Abundant peace belongs to those
who love Your instruction;
nothing makes them stumble.
166 LORD, I hope for Your salvation
and carry out Your commands.
167 I obey Your decrees
and love them greatly.
168 I obey Your precepts and decrees,
for all my ways are before You.

ת Tav

169 Let my cry reach You, LORD;
give me understanding according to
Your word.
170 Let my plea reach You;
rescue me according to
Your promise.
171 My lips pour out praise,
for You teach me Your statutes.
172 My tongue sings about Your promise,
for all Your commands are righteous.
173 May Your hand be ready to help me,
for I have chosen Your precepts.
174 I long for Your salvation, LORD,
and Your instruction is my delight.
175 Let me live, and I will praise You;
may Your judgments help me.
176 I wander like a lost sheep;
seek Your servant,
for I do not forget Your commands.

Psalm 120
A song of ascents.

1 In my distress I called to the LORD,
and He answered me.
2 "LORD, deliver me from lying lips
and a deceitful tongue."
3 What will He give you,
and what will He do to you,
you deceitful tongue?
4 A warrior's sharp arrows
with burning charcoal!A
5 What misery that I have stayed
in Meshech,B
that I have lived among the tents
of Kedar!C
6 I have lived too long
with those who hate peace.
7 I am for peace; but when I speak,
they are for war.

Psalm 121
A song of ascents.

1 I lift my eyes toward the mountains.
Where will my help come from?
2 My help comes from the LORD,
the Maker of heaven and earth.
3 He will not allow your foot to slip;
your Protector will not slumber.
4 Indeed, the Protector of Israel
does not slumber or sleep.
5 The LORD protects you;
the LORD is a shelter right
by your side.D
6 The sun will not strike you by day
or the moon by night.
7 The LORD will protect you
from all harm;
He will protect your life.
8 The LORD will protect your coming
and going
both now and forever.

Psalm 122
A Davidic song of ascents.

1 I rejoiced with those who said to me,
"Let us go to the house of the LORD."
2 Our feet are standing
within your gates, Jerusalem—
3 Jerusalem, built as a city should be,
solidly joined together,
4 where the tribes, Yahweh's tribes,
go up

A120:4 Lit with coals of the broom bush B120:5 = a people far to the north of Palestine C120:5 = a nomadic people of the desert to the southeast D121:5 Lit is your shelter at your right hand

to give thanks to the name of Yahweh.
(This is an ordinance for Israel.)
5 There, thrones for judgment
    are placed,
  thrones of the house of David.
6 Pray for the peace of Jerusalem:
  "May those who love you prosper;
7 may there be peace within your walls,
  prosperity within your fortresses."
8 Because of my brothers and friends,
  I will say, "Peace be with you."
9 Because of the house of the LORD
    our God,
  I will seek your good.

Psalm 123
A song of ascents.

1 I lift my eyes to You,
  the One enthroned in heaven.
2 Like a servant's eyes
    on his master's hand,
  like a servant girl's eyes
    on her mistress's hand,
  so our eyes are on the LORD our God
  until He shows us favor.
3 Show us favor, LORD, show us favor,
  for we've had more than enough
    contempt.
4 We've had more than enough
  scorn from the arrogant
  and contempt from the proud.

Psalm 124
A Davidic song of ascents.

1 If the LORD had not been on our side—
  let Israel say—
2 If the LORD had not been on our side
  when men attacked us,
3 then they would have swallowed us alive
  in their burning anger against us.
4 Then the waters would have
    engulfed us;
  the torrent would have swept over us;
5 the raging waters would have swept
    over us.
6 Praise the LORD,
  who has not let us be ripped apart
    by their teeth.
7 We have escaped like a bird
    from the hunter's net;
  the net is torn, and we have escaped.
8 Our help is in the name of Yahweh,
  the Maker of heaven and earth.

Psalm 125
A song of ascents.

1 Those who trust in the LORD are
    like Mount Zion.
  It cannot be shaken; it remains forever.
2 Jerusalem—the mountains
    surround her.
  And the LORD surrounds His people,
  both now and forever.
3 The scepter of the wicked
    will not remain
  over the land allotted to the righteous,
  so that the righteous will not apply
    their hands to injustice.
4 Do what is good, LORD, to the good,
  to those whose hearts are upright.
5 But as for those who turn aside
    to crooked ways,
  the LORD will banish them
    with the evildoers.
  Peace be with Israel.

Psalm 126
A song of ascents.

1 When the LORD restored the fortunes
    of Zion,A
  we were like those who dream.
2 Our mouths were filled
    with laughter then,
  and our tongues with shouts of joy.
  Then they said among the nations,
  "The LORD has done great things
    for them."
3 The LORD had done great things for us;
  we were joyful.
4 Restore our fortunes,B LORD,
  like watercourses in the Negev.
5 Those who sow in tears
  will reap with shouts of joy.
6 Though one goes along weeping,
  carrying the bag of seed,
  he will surely come back with shouts
    of joy,
  carrying his sheaves.

Psalm 127
A Solomonic song of ascents.

1 Unless the LORD builds a house,
  its builders labor over it in vain;
  unless the LORD watches over a city,
  the watchman stays alert in vain.
2 In vain you get up early
  and stay up late,

A126:1 Or LORD returned those of Zion who had been captives   B126:4 Or Return our captives

working hard to have enough food—
yes, He gives sleep to the one
    He loves.^A

³ Sons are indeed a heritage
    from the LORD,
children, a reward.

⁴ Like arrows in the hand of a warrior
are the sons born in one's youth.

⁵ Happy is the man who has filled
    his quiver with them.
Such men will never be put to shame
when they speak with their enemies
    at the city gate.

Psalm 128
A song of ascents.

¹ How happy is everyone who fears
    the LORD,
who walks in His ways!

² You will surely eat
what your hands have worked for.
You will be happy,
and it will go well for you.

³ Your wife will be like a fruitful vine
within your house,
your sons, like young olive trees
around your table.

⁴ In this very way
the man who fears the LORD
will be blessed.

⁵ May the LORD bless you from Zion,
so that you will see the prosperity
    of Jerusalem
all the days of your life

⁶ and will see your children's children!
Peace be with Israel.

Psalm 129
A song of ascents.

¹ Since my youth they have often
    attacked me—
let Israel say—

² Since my youth they have often
    attacked me,
but they have not prevailed against me.

³ Plowmen plowed over my back;
they made their furrows long.

⁴ The LORD is righteous;
He has cut the ropes of the wicked.

⁵ Let all who hate Zion
be driven back in disgrace.

⁶ Let them be like grass on the rooftops,
which withers before it grows up^B

⁷ and can't even fill the hands
    of the reaper
or the arms of the one
    who binds sheaves.

⁸ Then none who pass by will say,
"May the LORD's blessing be on you."
We bless you in the name of Yahweh.

Psalm 130
A song of ascents.

¹ Out of the depths I call to You, Yahweh!

² Lord, listen to my voice;
let Your ears be attentive
to my cry for help.

³ Yahweh, if You considered sins,
Lord, who could stand?

⁴ But with You there is forgiveness,
so that You may be revered.

⁵ I wait for Yahweh; I wait
and put my hope in His word.

⁶ I wait for the Lord
more than watchmen
    for the morning—
more than watchmen for the morning.

⁷ Israel, put your hope in the LORD.
For there is faithful love with the LORD,
and with Him is redemption
    in abundance.

⁸ And He will redeem Israel
from all its sins.

Psalm 131
A Davidic song of ascents.

¹ LORD, my heart is not proud;
my eyes are not haughty.
I do not get involved with things
too great or too difficult for me.

² Instead, I have calmed
    and quieted myself
like a little weaned child
    with its mother;
I am like a little child.

³ Israel, put your hope in the LORD,
both now and forever.

Psalm 132
A song of ascents.

¹ LORD, remember David
and all the hardships he endured,

² and how he swore an oath to the LORD,
making a vow to the Mighty One
    of Jacob:

³ "I will not enter my house^C

or get into my bed,[A]
4 I will not allow my eyes to sleep
   or my eyelids to slumber
5 until I find a place for the LORD,
   a dwelling for the Mighty One
      of Jacob."
6 We heard of the ark in Ephrathah;[B]
   we found it in the fields of Jaar.[C]
7 Let us go to His dwelling place;
   let us worship at His footstool.
8 Rise up, LORD, come to
      Your resting place,
   You and Your powerful ark.
9 May Your priests be clothed
      with righteousness,
   and may Your godly people shout
      for joy.
10 Because of Your servant David,
   do not reject Your anointed one.[D]
11 The LORD swore an oath to David,
   a promise He will not abandon:
   "I will set one of your descendants[E]
      on your throne.
12 If your sons keep My covenant
   and My decrees that I will teach them,
   their sons will also sit on
      your throne forever."
13 For the LORD has chosen Zion;
   He has desired it for His home:
14 "This is My resting place forever;
   I will make My home here
   because I have desired it.
15 I will abundantly bless its food;
   I will satisfy its needy with bread.
16 I will clothe its priests with salvation,
   and its godly people will shout for joy.
17 There I will make a horn grow
      for David;
   I have prepared a lamp for
      My anointed one.
18 I will clothe his enemies with shame,
   but the crown he wears[F]
      will be glorious."

Psalm 133
A Davidic song of ascents.

1 How good and pleasant it is
   when brothers live together
      in harmony!
2 It is like fine oil on the head,
   running down on the beard,

running down Aaron's beard
   onto his robes.
3 It is like the dew of Hermon[G]
   falling on the mountains of Zion.
   For there the LORD has appointed
      the blessing—
   life forevermore.

Psalm 134
A song of ascents.

1 Now praise the LORD,
   all you servants of the LORD
   who stand in the LORD's house at night!
2 Lift up your hands in the holy place
   and praise the LORD!
3 May the LORD,
   Maker of heaven and earth,
   bless you from Zion.

Psalm 135

1 Hallelujah!
   Praise the name of Yahweh.
   Give praise, you servants of Yahweh
2 who stand in the house of Yahweh,
   in the courts of the house of our God.
3 Praise Yahweh, for Yahweh is good;
   sing praise to His name,
      for it is delightful.
4 For Yahweh has chosen Jacob
      for Himself,
   Israel as His treasured possession.
5 For I know that Yahweh is great;
   our Lord is greater than all gods.
6 Yahweh does whatever He pleases
   in heaven and on earth,
   in the seas and all the depths.
7 He causes the clouds to rise
      from the ends of the earth.
   He makes lightning for the rain
   and brings the wind
      from His storehouses.
8 He struck down the firstborn of Egypt,
   both man and beast.
9 He sent signs and wonders
      against you, Egypt,
   against Pharaoh and all his officials.
10 He struck down many nations
   and slaughtered mighty kings:
11 Sihon king of the Amorites,
   Og king of Bashan,
   and all the kings of Canaan.
12 He gave their land as an inheritance,

A132:3 Lit *into the couch of my bed*   B132:6 = Bethlehem   C132:6 = Kiriath-jearim   D132:10 = the king   E132:11 Lit *set the fruit of your womb*   F132:18 Lit *but on him his crown*   G133:3 The tallest mountain in the region, noted for its abundant precipitation

an inheritance to His people Israel.
13 Yahweh, Your name endures forever,
Your reputation, Yahweh,
through all generations.
14 For Yahweh will vindicate His people
and have compassion on His servants.
15 The idols of the nations are of silver
and gold,
made by human hands.
16 They have mouths but cannot speak,
eyes, but cannot see.
17 They have ears but cannot hear;
indeed, there is no breath
in their mouths.
18 Those who make them are just
like them,
as are all who trust in them.
19 House of Israel, praise Yahweh!
House of Aaron, praise Yahweh!
20 House of Levi, praise Yahweh!
You who revere the Lord,
praise the Lord!
21 May the Lord be praised from Zion;
He dwells in Jerusalem.
Hallelujah!

Psalm 136

1 Give thanks to the Lord, for He is good.
His love is eternal.
2 Give thanks to the God of gods.
His love is eternal.
3 Give thanks to the Lord of lords.
His love is eternal.
4 He alone does great wonders.
His love is eternal.
5 He made the heavens skillfully.
His love is eternal.
6 He spread the land on the waters.
His love is eternal.
7 He made the great lights:
His love is eternal.
8 the sun to rule by day,
His love is eternal.
9 the moon and stars to rule by night.
His love is eternal.
10 He struck the firstborn of the Egyptians
His love is eternal.
11 and brought Israel out from among
them
His love is eternal.
12 with a strong hand
and outstretched arm.
His love is eternal.

13 He divided the Red Sea
His love is eternal.
14 and led Israel through,
His love is eternal.
15 but hurled Pharaoh and his army
into the Red Sea.
His love is eternal.
16 He led His people in the wilderness.
His love is eternal.
17 He struck down great kings
His love is eternal.
18 and slaughtered famous kings—
His love is eternal.
19 Sihon king of the Amorites
His love is eternal.
20 and Og king of Bashan—
His love is eternal.
21 and gave their land as an inheritance,
His love is eternal.
22 an inheritance to Israel His servant.
His love is eternal.
23 He remembered us in our humiliation
His love is eternal.
24 and rescued us from our foes.
His love is eternal.
25 He gives food to every creature.
His love is eternal.
26 Give thanks to the God of heaven!
His love is eternal.

Psalm 137

1 By the rivers of Babylon—
there we sat down and wept
when we remembered Zion.
2 There we hung up our lyres
on the poplar trees,
3 for our captors there asked us
for songs,
and our tormentors, for rejoicing:
"Sing us one of the songs of Zion."
4 How can we sing the Lord's song
on foreign soil?
5 If I forget you, Jerusalem,
may my right hand forget its skill.
6 May my tongue stick to the roof
of my mouth
if I do not remember you,
if I do not exalt Jerusalem
as my greatest joy!
7 Remember, Lord,
what the Edomites said
that day[A] at Jerusalem:
"Destroy it! Destroy it

A137:7 The day Jerusalem fell to the Babylonians in 586 B.C.

down to its foundations!"

8 Daughter Babylon,
   doomed to destruction,
happy is the one who pays you back
   what you have done to us.
9 Happy is he who takes your little ones
   and dashes them against the rocks.

Psalm 138
Davidic.

1 I will give You thanks
   with all my heart;
I will sing Your praise
   before the heavenly beings.^A
2 I will bow down
   toward Your holy temple
and give thanks to Your name
   for Your constant love and truth.
You have exalted Your name
   and Your promise above
   everything else.
3 On the day I called, You answered me;
   You increased strength within me.^B
4 All the kings on earth
   will give You thanks, Lord,
when they hear
   what You have promised.^C
5 They will sing of the Lord's ways,
   for the Lord's glory is great.
6 Though the Lord is exalted,
   He takes note of the humble;
but He knows the haughty
   from a distance.
7 If I walk into the thick of danger,
   You will preserve my life
from the anger of my enemies.
   You will extend Your hand;
Your right hand will save me.
8 The Lord will fulfill His purpose
   for me.
Lord, Your love is eternal;
   do not abandon the work
   of Your hands.

Psalm 139
For the choir director. A Davidic psalm.

1 Lord, You have searched me
   and known me.
2 You know when I sit down and when
   I stand up;
You understand my thoughts
   from far away.

3 You observe my travels and my rest;
   You are aware of all my ways.
4 Before a word is on my tongue,
   You know all about it, Lord.
5 You have encircled me;
   You have placed Your hand on me.
6 This extraordinary knowledge is
   beyond me.
   It is lofty; I am unable to reach it.
7 Where can I go to escape Your Spirit?
   Where can I flee from Your presence?
8 If I go up to heaven, You are there;
   if I make my bed in Sheol,
   You are there.
9 If I live at the eastern horizon
   or settle at the western limits,^D
10 even there Your hand will lead me;
   Your right hand will hold on to me.
11 If I say, "Surely the darkness
   will hide me,
   and the light around me
   will be night"—
12 even the darkness is not dark to You.
   The night shines like the day;
   darkness and light are alike to You.
13 For it was You who created
   my inward parts;^E
You knit me together
   in my mother's womb.
14 I will praise You
   because I have been remarkably
   and wonderfully made.^F,B
Your works are wonderful,
   and I know this very well.
15 My bones were not hidden from You
   when I was made in secret,
   when I was formed in the depths
   of the earth.
16 Your eyes saw me when I was formless;
   all my days were written in Your book
   and planned
   before a single one of them began.
17 God, how difficult^G Your thoughts are
   for me to comprehend;
   how vast their sum is!
18 If I counted them,
   they would outnumber the grains
   of sand;
   when I wake up,^H I am still with You.
19 God, if only You would kill
   the wicked—

---

you bloodthirsty men, stay away
   from me—
20 who invoke You deceitfully.
   Your enemies swear by You falsely.
21 LORD, don't I hate those who hate You,
   and detest those who rebel
      against You?
22 I hate them with extreme hatred;
   I consider them my enemies.
23 Search me, God, and know my heart;
   test me and know my concerns.
24 See if there is any offensive[A] way in me;
   lead me in the everlasting way.

Psalm 140
For the choir director. A Davidic psalm.

1 Rescue me, LORD, from evil men.
   Keep me safe from violent men
2 who plan evil in their hearts.
   They stir up wars all day long.
3 They make their tongues
   as sharp as a snake's bite;
   viper's venom is under their lips. *Selah*
4 Protect me, LORD,
   from the clutches of the wicked.
   Keep me safe from violent men
   who plan to make me stumble.[B]
5 The proud hide a trap with ropes
      for me;
   they spread a net along the path
   and set snares for me.   *Selah*
6 I say to the LORD, "You are my God."
   Listen, LORD, to my cry for help.
7 Lord GOD, my strong Savior,
   You shield my head on the day
      of battle.
8 LORD, do not grant the desires
      of the wicked;
   do not let them achieve their goals.
   Otherwise, they will become proud.
                                  Selah
9 When those who surround me rise up,[C]
   may the trouble their lips cause
      overwhelm them.
10 Let hot coals fall on them.
   Let them be thrown into the fire,
   into the abyss, never again to rise.
11 Do not let a slanderer stay in the land.
   Let evil relentlessly[D] hunt down
      a violent man.
12 I[E] know that the LORD upholds

the just cause of the poor,
   justice for the needy.
13 Surely the righteous will praise
      Your name;
   the upright will live in Your presence.

Psalm 141
A Davidic psalm.

1 LORD, I call on You; hurry to help me.
   Listen to my voice when I call on You.
2 May my prayer be set before You
      as incense,
   the raising of my hands
      as the evening offering.
3 LORD, set up a guard for my mouth;
   keep watch at the door of my lips.
4 Do not let my heart turn
      to any evil thing
   or perform wicked acts
   with men who commit sin.
   Do not let me feast on their delicacies.
5 Let the righteous one strike me—
   it is an act of faithful love;
   let him rebuke me—
   it is oil for my head;
   let me[F] not refuse it.
   Even now my prayer is against
   the evil acts of the wicked.[G]
6 When their rulers[H] will be thrown off
   the sides of a cliff,
   the people[I] will listen to my words,
   for they are pleasing.
7 As when one plows and breaks up
      the soil,
   turning up rocks,
   so our[J] bones have been scattered
   at the mouth of Sheol.
8 But my eyes look to You, Lord GOD.
   I seek refuge in You; do not let me die.[K]
9 Protect me from[L] the trap they have set
      for me,
   and from the snares of evildoers.
10 Let the wicked fall into their own nets,
   while I pass by safely.

Psalm 142
A Davidic *Maskil*. When he was
in the cave. A prayer.

1 I cry aloud to the LORD;
   I plead aloud to the LORD for mercy.
2 I pour out my complaint before Him;
   I reveal my trouble to Him.

A139:24 Or *idolatrous*   B140:4 Lit *to trip up my steps*   C140:9 Lit *Head of those who surround me*   D140:11 Hb obscure   E140:12 Alt Hb
tradition reads *You*   F141:5 Lit *my head*   G141:5 Lit *of them*   H141:6 Or *judges*   I141:6 Lit *cliff, and they*   J141:7 DSS reads *my;* some LXX
mss, Syr read *their*   K141:8 Or *not pour out my life*   L141:9 Lit *from the hands of*

³ Although my spirit is weak within me,
You know my way.
Along this path I travel
they have hidden a trap for me.
⁴ Look to the right and see:ᴬ
no one stands up for me;
there is no refuge for me;
no one cares about me.
⁵ I cry to You, Lᴏʀᴅ;
I say, "You are my shelter,
my portion in the land of the living."
⁶ Listen to my cry,
for I am very weak.
Rescue me from those who pursue me,
for they are too strong for me.
⁷ Free me from prison
so that I can praise Your name.
The righteous will gather around me
because You deal generously with me.

Psalm 143
A Davidic psalm.

¹ Lᴏʀᴅ, hear my prayer.
In Your faithfulness listen to my plea,
and in Your righteousness answer me.
² Do not bring Your servant
into judgment,
for no one alive is righteous
in Your sight.
³ For the enemy has pursued me,
crushing me to the ground,
making me live in darkness
like those long dead.
⁴ My spirit is weak within me;
my heart is overcome with dismay.
⁵ I remember the days of old;
I meditate on all You have done;
I reflect on the work of Your hands.
⁶ I spread out my hands to You;
I am like parched land before You.
Selah
⁷ Answer me quickly, Lᴏʀᴅ;
my spirit fails.
Don't hide Your face from me,
or I will be like those
going down to the Pit.
⁸ Let me experience
Your faithful love in the morning,
for I trust in You.
Reveal to me the way I should go
because I long for You.
⁹ Rescue me from my enemies, Lᴏʀᴅ;

I come to You for protection.ᴮ
¹⁰ Teach me to do Your will,
for You are my God.
May Your gracious Spirit
lead me on level ground.
¹¹ Because of Your name, Yahweh,
let me live.
In Your righteousness deliver me
from trouble,
¹² and in Your faithful love
destroy my enemies.
Wipe out all those who attack me,
for I am Your servant.

Psalm 144
Davidic.

¹ May the Lᴏʀᴅ, my rock, be praised,
who trains my hands for battle
and my fingers for warfare.
² He is my faithful love and my fortress,
my stronghold and my deliverer.
He is my shield, and I take refuge
in Him;
He subdues my peopleᶜ under me.
³ Lᴏʀᴅ, what is man,
that You care for him,
the son of man, that You think of him?
⁴ Man is like a breath;
his days are like a passing shadow.
⁵ Lᴏʀᴅ, part Your heavens
and come down.
Touch the mountains,
and they will smoke.
⁶ Flash Your lightning and scatter
the foe;ᴰ
shoot Your arrows and rout them.
⁷ Reach downᴱ from heaven;
rescue me from deep water,
and set me free
from the grasp of foreigners
⁸ whose mouths speak lies,
whose right hands are deceptive.
⁹ God, I will sing a new song to You;
I will play on a ten-stringed harp
for You—
¹⁰ the One who gives victory to kings,
who frees His servant David
from the deadly sword.
¹¹ Set me free and rescue me
from the grasp of foreigners
whose mouths speak lies,
whose right hands are deceptive.

¹² Then our sons will be like plants
    nurtured in their youth,
    our daughters, like corner pillars
    that are carved in the palace style.
¹³ Our storehouses will be full,
    supplying all kinds of produce;
    our flocks will increase by thousands
    and tens of thousands in
    our open fields.
¹⁴ Our cattle will be well fed.ᴬ
    There will be no breach in the walls,
    no going into captivity,ᴮ
    and no cry of lament in
    our public squares.
¹⁵ Happy are the people with
    such blessings.
    Happy are the people
    whose God is Yahweh.

Psalm 145
A Davidic hymn.

¹ Iᶜ exalt You, my God the King,
    and praise Your name forever and ever.
² I will praise You every day;
    I will honor Your name
    forever and ever.
³ Yahweh is great and is highly praised;
    His greatness is unsearchable.
⁴ One generation will declare Your works
    to the next
    and will proclaim Your mighty acts.
⁵ Iᴰ will speak of Your splendor and
    glorious majesty
    andᴱ Your wonderful works.
⁶ They will proclaim the power
    of Your awe-inspiring acts,
    and I will declare Your greatness.ᶠ
⁷ They will give a testimony
    of Your great goodness
    and will joyfully sing
    of Your righteousness.
⁸ The Lord is gracious
    and compassionate,
    slow to anger and great in faithful love.
⁹ The Lord is good to everyone;
    His compassion rests
    on all He has made.
¹⁰ All You have made
    will thank You, Lord;
    theᴳ godly will praise You.

¹¹ They will speak of the glory
    of Your kingdom
    and will declare Your might,
¹² informing all people
    of Your mighty acts
    and of the glorious splendor
    of Yourᴴ kingdom.
¹³ Your kingdom is
    an everlasting kingdom;
    Your rule is for all generations.
    The Lord is faithful in all His words
    and gracious in all His actions.ᴵ
¹⁴ The Lord helps all who fall;
    He raises up all who are oppressed.ᴶ
¹⁵ All eyes look to You,
    and You give them their food at the
    proper time.
¹⁶ You open Your hand
    and satisfy the desire
    of every living thing.
¹⁷ The Lord is righteous in all His ways
    and gracious in all His acts.
¹⁸ The Lord is near all who call out
    to Him,
    all who call out to Him with integrity.
¹⁹ He fulfills the desires of those
    who fear Him;
    He hears their cry for help
    and saves them.
²⁰ The Lord guards all those
    who love Him,
    but He destroys all the wicked.
²¹ My mouth will declare Yahweh's praise;
    let every living thing
    praise His holy name forever and ever.

Psalm 146

¹ Hallelujah!
    My soul, praise the Lord.
² I will praise the Lord all my life;
    I will sing to my God as long as I live.
³ Do not trust in nobles,
    in man, who cannot save.
⁴ When his breathᴷ leaves him,
    he returns to the ground;
    on that day his plans die.
⁵ Happy is the one whose help is the God
    of Jacob,
    whose hope is in the Lord his God,
⁶ the Maker of heaven and earth,
    the sea and everything in them.

ᴬ144:14 Or will bear heavy loads, or will be pregnant   ᴮ144:14 Or be no plague, no miscarriage   ᶜ145:1 The lines of this poem form an acrostic.   ᴰ145:5 LXX, Syr read They   ᴱ145:5 LXX, Syr read and they will tell of   ᶠ145:6 Alt Hb tradition, Jer read great deeds   ᴳ145:10 Lit Your   ᴴ145:12 LXX, Syr, Jer; MT reads His   ᴵ145:13 One Hb ms, DSS, LXX, Syr; some Hb mss omit The Lord is faithful in all His words and gracious in all His actions.   ᴶ145:14 Lit bowed down   ᴷ146:4 Or spirit

He remains faithful forever,
7 executing justice for the exploited
and giving food to the hungry.
The LORD frees prisoners.
8 The LORD opens the eyes of the blind.
The LORD raises up those
who are oppressed.[A]
The LORD loves the righteous.
9 The LORD protects foreigners
and helps the fatherless and the widow,
but He frustrates the ways
of the wicked.
10 The LORD reigns forever;
Zion, your God reigns
for all generations.
Hallelujah!

Psalm 147

1 Hallelujah!
How good it is to sing to our God,
for praise is pleasant and lovely.
2 The LORD rebuilds Jerusalem;
He gathers Israel's exiled people.
3 He heals the brokenhearted
and binds up their wounds.
4 He counts the number of the stars;
He gives names to all of them.
5 Our Lord is great, vast in power;
His understanding is infinite.[B]
6 The LORD helps the afflicted
but brings the wicked to the ground.
7 Sing to the LORD with thanksgiving;
play the lyre to our God,
8 who covers the sky with clouds,
prepares rain for the earth,
and causes grass to grow on the hills.
9 He provides the animals
with their food,
and the young ravens, what they cry for.
10 He is not impressed by the strength
of a horse;
He does not value the power[C] of a man.
11 The LORD values those who fear Him,
those who put their hope
in His faithful love.
12 Exalt the LORD, Jerusalem;
praise your God, Zion!
13 For He strengthens the bars
of your gates
and blesses your children within you.
14 He endows your territory
with prosperity;[D]

He satisfies you with the finest wheat.
15 He sends His command
throughout the earth;
His word runs swiftly.
16 He spreads snow like wool;
He scatters frost like ashes;
17 He throws His hailstones like crumbs.
Who can withstand His cold?
18 He sends His word and melts them;
He unleashes His winds,[E]
and the waters flow.
19 He declares His word to Jacob,
His statutes and judgments to Israel.
20 He has not done this for any nation;
they do not know[F] His judgments.
Hallelujah!

Psalm 148

1 Hallelujah!
Praise the LORD from the heavens;
praise Him in the heights.
2 Praise Him, all His angels;
praise Him, all His hosts.
3 Praise Him, sun and moon;
praise Him, all you shining stars.
4 Praise Him, highest heavens,
and you waters above the heavens.
5 Let them praise the name of Yahweh,
for He commanded,
and they were created.
6 He set them in position forever and ever;
He gave an order that will never
pass away.
7 Praise the LORD from the earth,
all sea monsters and ocean depths,
8 lightning[G] and hail, snow and cloud,
powerful wind that executes
His command,
9 mountains and all hills,
fruit trees and all cedars,
10 wild animals and all cattle,
creatures that crawl and flying birds,
11 kings of the earth and all peoples,
princes and all judges of the earth,
12 young men as well as young women,
old and young together.
13 Let them praise the name of Yahweh,
for His name alone is exalted.
His majesty covers heaven and earth.
14 He has raised up a horn for His people,
resulting in praise to all
His godly ones,

A146:8 Lit bowed down   B147:5 Lit understanding has no number   C147:10 Lit legs   D147:14 Or peace   E147:18 Or breath   F147:20 DSS, LXX, Syr, Tg read He has not made known to them   G148:8 Or fire

to the Israelites, the people
   close to Him.
Hallelujah!

Psalm 149

1 Hallelujah!
Sing to the LORD a new song,
His praise in the assembly of the godly.
2 Let Israel celebrate its Maker;
let the children of Zion rejoice
   in their King.
3 Let them praise His name with dancing
and make music to Him
   with tambourine and lyre.
4 For Yahweh takes pleasure
   in His people;
He adorns the humble with salvation.
5 Let the godly celebrate
   in triumphal glory;
let them shout for joy on their beds.
6 Let the exaltation of God be
   in their mouths[A]
and a double-edged sword
   in their hands,
7 inflicting vengeance on the nations

and punishment on the peoples,
8 binding their kings with chains
and their dignitaries
   with iron shackles,
9 carrying out the judgment
   decreed against them.
This honor is for all His godly people.
Hallelujah!

Psalm 150

1 Hallelujah!
Praise God in His sanctuary.
Praise Him in His mighty heavens.
2 Praise Him for His powerful acts;
praise Him for His abundant greatness.
3 Praise Him with trumpet blast;
praise Him with harp and lyre.
4 Praise Him with tambourine
   and dance;
praise Him with flute and strings.
5 Praise Him with resounding cymbals;
praise Him with clashing cymbals.
6 Let everything that breathes
   praise the LORD.
Hallelujah!

PROVERBS

1 The proverbs of Solomon
son of David, king of Israel:
2 For learning what wisdom
   and discipline are;
for understanding insightful sayings;
3 for receiving wise instruction
in righteousness, justice, and integrity;
4 for teaching shrewdness
   to the inexperienced,[B]
knowledge and discretion
   to a young man—
5 a wise man will listen and increase
   his learning,
and a discerning man
   will obtain guidance—
6 for understanding a proverb
   or a parable,[C]
the words of the wise,
   and their riddles.
7 The fear of the LORD
is the beginning of knowledge;
fools despise wisdom and discipline.

8 Listen, my son,
   to your father's instruction,
and don't reject
   your mother's teaching,
9 for they will be a garland of grace
   on your head
and a gold chain around your neck.
10 My son, if sinners entice you,
   don't be persuaded.
11 If they say—"Come with us!
Let's set an ambush and kill someone.[D]
Let's attack some innocent person
   just for fun![E]
12 Let's swallow them alive, like Sheol,
still healthy as they go down to the Pit.
13 We'll find all kinds of valuable property
and fill our houses with plunder.
14 Throw in your lot with us,
and we'll all share our money"[F]—
15 my son, don't travel that road
   with them
or set foot on their path,

A149:6 Lit *throat*   B1:4 Or *simple, or gullible*   C1:6 Or *an enigma*   D1:11 Lit *Let's ambush for blood*   E1:11 Lit *person for no reason*   F1:14 Lit
us; one bag will be for all of us

¹⁶ because their feet run toward trouble
  and they hurry to commit murder.ᴬ
¹⁷ It is foolish to spread a net
  where any bird can see it,
¹⁸ but they set an ambush
    to kill themselves;ᴮ
  they attack their own lives.
¹⁹ Such are the paths of all who make
    profit dishonestly;
  it takes the lives of those
    who receive it.ᶜ
²⁰ Wisdom calls out in the street;
  she raises her voice
    in the public squares.
²¹ She cries out aboveᴰ the commotion;
  she speaks at the entrance
    of the city gates:
²² "How long, foolish ones, will you
    love ignorance?
  How long will you mockers
    enjoy mocking
  and you fools hate knowledge?
²³ If you respond to my warning,ᴱ
  then I will pour out my spirit on you
  and teach you my words.
²⁴ Since I called out and you refused,
    extended my hand and no one
    paid attention,
²⁵ since you neglected all my counsel
  and did not accept my correction,
²⁶ I, in turn, will laugh at your calamity.
  I will mock when terror strikes you,
²⁷ when terror strikes you like a storm
  and your calamity comes
    like a whirlwind,
  when trouble and stress overcome you.
²⁸ Then they will call me,
    but I won't answer;
  they will search for me, but won't
    find me.
²⁹ Because they hated knowledge,
    didn't choose to fear the LORD,
³⁰ were not interested in my counsel,
  and rejected all my correction,
³¹ they will eat the fruit of their way
  and be glutted with their own schemes.
³² For the turning away
    of the inexperienced will kill them,
  and the complacency of fools
    will destroy them.
³³ But whoever listens to me
    will live securely

2

and be free from the fear of danger."
My son, if you accept my words
and store up my commands
    within you,
² listening closelyᶠ to wisdom
  and directing your heart
    to understanding;
³ furthermore, if you call out to insight
  and lift your voice to understanding,
⁴ if you seek it like silver
  and search for it like hidden treasure,
⁵ then you will understand the fear
    of the LORD
  and discover the knowledge of God.
⁶ For the LORD gives wisdom;
  from His mouth come knowledge
    and understanding.
⁷ He stores up successᴳ for the upright;
  He is a shield for those who live
    with integrity
⁸ so that He may guard the paths
    of justice
  and protect the way
    of His loyal followers.
⁹ Then you will understand
    righteousness, justice,
  and integrity—every good path.
¹⁰ For wisdom will enter your mind,
  and knowledge will delight your heart.
¹¹ Discretion will watch over you,
  and understanding will guard you,
¹² rescuing you from the way of evil—
  from the one who says perverse things,
¹³ from those who abandon
    the right paths
  to walk in ways of darkness,
¹⁴ from those who enjoy doing evil
  and celebrate perversion,
¹⁵ whose paths are crooked,
  and whose ways are devious.
¹⁶ It will rescue you
    from a forbidden woman,
  from a strangerᴴ
    with her flattering talk,
¹⁷ who abandons the companion
    of her youth
  and forgets the covenant of her God;
¹⁸ for her house sinks down to death
  and her ways to the land
    of the departed spirits.
¹⁹ None return who go to her;
  none reach the paths of life.

ᴬ**1:16** Lit to shed blood   ᴮ**1:18** Lit they ambush for their blood   ᶜ**1:19** Lit takes the life of its masters   ᴰ**1:21** Lit at the head of   ᴱ**1:23** Lit back to my reprimand   ᶠ**2:2** Lit you, stretching out your ear   ᴳ**2:7** Or resourcefulness   ᴴ**2:16** Or foreign woman

20 So follow the way of good people,
   and keep to the paths of the righteous.
21 For the upright will inhabit the land,
   and those of integrity will remain in it;
22 but the wicked will be cut off
     from the land,
   and the treacherous uprooted from it.

3

My son, don't forget my teaching,
   but let your heart keep my commands;
2 for they will bring you
   many days, a full life,[A] and well-being.
3 Never let loyalty and faithfulness
     leave you.
   Tie them around your neck;
   write them on the tablet of your heart.
4 Then you will find favor
     and high regard
   in the sight of God and man.
5 Trust in the LORD with all your heart,
   and do not rely on
     your own understanding;
6 think about Him in all your ways,
   and He will guide you
     on the right paths.[B]
7 Don't consider yourself to be wise;
   fear the LORD and turn away from evil.
8 This will be healing for your body[C]
   and strengthening for your bones.
9 Honor the LORD with your possessions
   and with the first produce
     of your entire harvest;
10 then your barns will be
     completely filled,
   and your vats will overflow
     with new wine.
11 Do not despise the LORD's instruction,
     my son,
   and do not loathe His discipline;
12 for the LORD disciplines the one
     He loves,
   just as a father, the son he delights in.
13 Happy is a man who finds wisdom
   and who acquires understanding,
14 for she is more profitable than silver,
   and her revenue is better than gold.
15 She is more precious than jewels;
   nothing you desire compares with her.
16 Long life[D] is in her right hand;
   in her left, riches and honor.
17 Her ways are pleasant,
   and all her paths, peaceful.

18 She is a tree of life to those
     who embrace her,
   and those who hold on to her
     are happy.
19 The LORD founded the earth by wisdom
   and established the heavens
     by understanding.
20 By His knowledge the watery depths
     broke open,
   and the clouds dripped with dew.
21 Maintain your competence
     and discretion.
   My son, don't lose sight of them.
22 They will be life for you[E,F]
   and adornment[G] for your neck.
23 Then you will go safely on your way;
   your foot will not stumble.
24 When you lie[H] down, you will not
     be afraid;
   you will lie down, and your sleep
     will be pleasant.
25 Don't fear sudden danger
   or the ruin of the wicked
     when it comes,
26 for the LORD will be your confidence[I]
   and will keep your foot from a snare.
27 When it is in your power,[J]
   don't withhold good from the one
     it belongs to.
28 Don't say to your neighbor, "Go away!
     Come back later.
   I'll give it
     tomorrow"— when it is there
     with you.
29 Don't plan any harm
     against your neighbor,
   for he trusts you and lives near you.
30 Don't accuse anyone without cause,
   when he has done you no harm.
31 Don't envy a violent man
   or choose any of his ways;
32 for the devious are detestable
     to the LORD,
   but He is a friend[K] to the upright.
33 The LORD's curse is on the household
     of the wicked,
   but He blesses the home
     of the righteous;
34 He mocks those who mock,
   but gives grace to the humble.
35 The wise will inherit honor,

A3:2 Lit days, years of life   B3:6 Lit will make your paths straight   C3:8 Lit navel   D3:16 Lit Length of days   E3:22 Or be your throat   F3:22 In
Hb, nephesh can mean throat, soul, or life.   G3:22 Or grace   H3:24 LXX reads sit   I3:26 Or be at your side   J3:27 Lit in the power of your hands
K3:32 Or confidential counsel

but He holds up fools to dishonor.[A]

4 Listen, my sons,
to a father's discipline,
and pay attention so that
you may gain understanding,

2 for I am giving you good instruction.
Don't abandon my teaching.

3 When I was a son with my father,
tender and precious to my mother,

4 he taught me and said:
"Your heart must hold on to my words.
Keep my commands and live.

5 Get wisdom, get understanding;
don't forget or turn away
from the words of my mouth.

6 Don't abandon wisdom, and she will
watch over you;
love her, and she will guard you.

7 Wisdom is supreme—so get wisdom.
And whatever else you get,
get understanding.

8 Cherish her, and she will exalt you;
if you embrace her, she will honor you.

9 She will place a garland of grace
on your head;
she will give you a crown of beauty."

10 Listen, my son. Accept my words,
and you will live many years.

11 I am teaching you the way of wisdom;
I am guiding you on straight paths.

12 When you walk, your steps will not
be hindered;
when you run, you will not stumble.

13 Hold on to instruction; don't let go.
Guard it, for it is your life.

14 Don't set foot on the path
of the wicked;
don't proceed in the way of evil ones.

15 Avoid it; don't travel on it.
Turn away from it, and pass it by.

16 For they can't sleep
unless they have done what is evil;
they are robbed of sleep
unless they make someone stumble.

17 They eat the bread of wickedness
and drink the wine of violence.

18 The path of the righteous is
like the light of dawn,
shining brighter and brighter
until midday.

19 But the way of the wicked is
like the darkest gloom;

they don't know what makes
them stumble.

20 My son, pay attention to my words;
listen closely to my sayings.

21 Don't lose sight of them;
keep them within your heart.

22 For they are life to those
who find them,
and health to one's whole body.

23 Guard your heart above all else,[B]
for it is the source of life.

24 Don't let your mouth
speak dishonestly,
and don't let your lips talk deviously.

25 Let your eyes look forward;
fix your gaze[C] straight ahead.

26 Carefully consider the path[D]
for your feet,
and all your ways will be established.

27 Don't turn to the right or to the left;
keep your feet away from evil.

5 My son, pay attention to my wisdom;
listen closely[E] to my understanding

2 so that you may maintain discretion
and your lips safeguard knowledge.

3 Though the lips
of the forbidden woman drip honey
and her words are[F] smoother than oil,

4 in the end she's as bitter as wormwood
and as sharp as a double-edged sword.

5 Her feet go down to death;
her steps head straight for Sheol.

6 She doesn't consider the path of life;
she doesn't know that her ways
are unstable.

7 So now, my sons, listen to me,
and don't turn away from the words
of my mouth.

8 Keep your way far from her.
Don't go near the door of her house.

9 Otherwise, you will give up
your vitality to others
and your years to someone cruel;

10 strangers will drain your resources,
and your earnings will end up
in a foreigner's house.

11 At the end of your life, you will lament
when your physical body
has been consumed,

12 and you will say,
"How I hated discipline,
and how my heart despised correction.

[A]3:35 Or but haughty fools dishonor, or but fools exalt dishonor   [B]4:23 Or heart with all diligence   [C]4:25 Lit eyelids   [D]4:26 Or Clear a
path   [E]5:1 Lit wisdom; stretch out your ear   [F]5:3 Lit her palate is

¹³ I didn't obey my teachers
   or listen closely[A] to my mentors.
¹⁴ I am on the verge of complete ruin
   before the entire community."
¹⁵ Drink water from your own cistern,
   water flowing from your own well.
¹⁶ Should your springs flow in the streets,
   streams of water in the public squares?
¹⁷ They should be for you alone
   and not for you to share with strangers.
¹⁸ Let your fountain be blessed,
   and take pleasure in the wife
      of your youth.
¹⁹ A loving doe, a graceful fawn—
   let her breasts always satisfy you;
   be lost in her love forever.
²⁰ Why, my son, would you be infatuated
   with a forbidden woman
   or embrace the breast of a stranger?
²¹ For a man's ways are
      before the LORD's eyes,
   and He considers all his paths.
²² A wicked man's iniquities entrap him;
   he is entangled in the ropes
      of his own sin.
²³ He will die because there is
      no discipline,
   and be lost because of
      his great stupidity.

6 My son, if you have put up security
   for your neighbor[B]
   or entered into an agreement
      with[C] a stranger,[D]
² you have been trapped by the words
      of your lips[E]—
   ensnared by the words of your mouth.
³ Do this, then, my son,
      and free yourself,
   for you have put yourself
      in your neighbor's power:
   Go, humble yourself, and plead
      with your neighbor.
⁴ Don't give sleep to your eyes
   or slumber to your eyelids.
⁵ Escape like a gazelle from a hunter,[F]
   like a bird from a fowler's trap.[G]
⁶ Go to the ant, you slacker!
   Observe its ways and become wise.
⁷ Without leader, administrator, or ruler,
⁸ it prepares its provisions in summer;
   it gathers its food during harvest.

⁹ How long will you stay in bed,
      you slacker?
   When will you get up
      from your sleep?
¹⁰ A little sleep, a little slumber,
   a little folding of the arms to rest,
¹¹ and your poverty will come like
      a robber,
   your need, like a bandit.
¹² A worthless person, a wicked man
   goes around speaking dishonestly,
¹³ winking his eyes, signaling
      with his feet,
   and gesturing with his fingers.
¹⁴ He always plots evil with perversity
      in his heart—
   he stirs up trouble.
¹⁵ Therefore calamity
      will strike him suddenly;
   he will be shattered
      instantly—beyond recovery.
¹⁶ The LORD hates six things;
   in fact, seven are detestable to Him:
¹⁷ arrogant eyes, a lying tongue,
   hands that shed innocent blood,
¹⁸ a heart that plots wicked schemes,
   feet eager to run to evil,
¹⁹ a lying witness who gives
      false testimony,
   and one who stirs up trouble
      among brothers.
²⁰ My son, keep your father's command,
   and don't reject
      your mother's teaching.
²¹ Always bind them to your heart;
   tie them around your neck.
²² When you walk here and there,
      they will guide you;
   when you lie down, they will
      watch over you;
   when you wake up, they will
      talk to you.
²³ For a command is a lamp,
      teaching is a light,
   and corrective discipline is the way
      to life.
²⁴ They will protect you
      from an evil woman,[H]
   from the flattering[I] tongue
      of a stranger.
²⁵ Don't lust in your heart for her beauty

[A]5:13 Lit *or turn my ear* [B]6:1 Or *friend* [C]6:1 Lit *or shaken hands for or with* [D]6:1 The Hb word for *stranger* can refer to a foreigner, an Israelite outside one's family, or simply to another person. [E]6:2 Lit *mouth* [F]6:5 Lit *hand* [G]6:24 LXX reads *from a married woman* [H]6:24 Lit *smooth*

or let her captivate you
    with her eyelashes.
26 For a prostitute's fee is only a loaf
    of bread,[A]
but an adulteress[B] goes after
    a precious life.
27 Can a man embrace fire[C]
    and his clothes not be burned?
28 Can a man walk on burning coals
    without scorching his feet?
29 So it is with the one who sleeps with
    another man's wife;
no one who touches her
    will go unpunished.
30 People don't despise the thief
    if he steals
to satisfy himself when he is hungry.
31 Still, if caught, he must pay
    seven times as much;
he must give up all the wealth
    in his house.
32 The one who commits adultery[D]
    lacks sense;
whoever does so destroys himself.
33 He will get a beating[E] and dishonor,
    and his disgrace will never be removed.
34 For jealousy enrages a husband,
    and he will show no mercy
    when he takes revenge.
35 He will not be appeased by anything
    or be persuaded by lavish gifts.

7 My son, obey my words,
    and treasure my commands.
2 Keep my commands and live;
    protect my teachings
    as the pupil of your eye.
3 Tie them to your fingers;
    write them on the tablet of your heart.
4 Say to wisdom, "You are my sister,"
    and call understanding your relative.
5 She will keep you
    from a forbidden woman,
a stranger with her flattering talk.
6 At the window of my house
    I looked through my lattice.
7 I saw among the inexperienced,[F]
I noticed among the youths,
    a young man lacking sense.
8 Crossing the street near her corner,

he strolled down the road to her house
9 at twilight, in the evening,
    in the dark of the night.
10 A woman came to meet him
    dressed like a prostitute,
    having a hidden agenda.[G]
11 She is loud and defiant;
    her feet do not stay at home.
12 Now in the street, now in the squares,
    she lurks at every corner.
13 She grabs him and kisses him;
    she brazenly says[H] to him,
14 "I've made fellowship offerings;[I]
    today I've fulfilled my vows.
15 So I came out to meet you,
    to search for you, and I've found you.
16 I've spread coverings on my bed—
    richly colored linen from Egypt.
17 I've perfumed my bed
    with myrrh, aloes, and cinnamon.
18 Come, let's drink deeply of lovemaking
    until morning.
Let's feast on each other's love!
19 My husband isn't home;
    he went on a long journey.
20 He took a bag of money with him
    and will come home at the time
    of the full moon."
21 She seduces him
    with her persistent pleading;
she lures with her flattering[J] talk.
22 He follows her impulsively
    like an ox going to the slaughter,
like a deer bounding toward a trap[K]
23 until an arrow pierces its[L] liver,
    like a bird darting into a snare—
he doesn't know it will cost him
    his life.
24 Now, my sons, listen to me,
    and pay attention to the words
    of my mouth.
25 Don't let your heart turn aside
    to her ways;
don't stray onto her paths.
26 For she has brought many
    down to death;
her victims are countless.[M]
27 Her house is the road to Sheol,
    descending to the chambers of death.

---

8 Doesn't Wisdom call out?
Doesn't Understanding make her voice
heard?
² At the heights overlooking the road,
at the crossroads, she takes her stand.
³ Beside the gates at the entry
toᴬ the city,
at the main entrance, she cries out:
⁴ "People, I call out to you;
my cry is to mankind.
⁵ Learn to be shrewd,
you who are inexperienced;
develop common sense,
you who are foolish.
⁶ Listen, for I speak of noble things,
and what my lips say is right.
⁷ For my mouth tells the truth,
and wickedness is detestable to my lips.
⁸ All the words of my mouth
are righteous;
none of them are deceptive or perverse.
⁹ All of them are clear to the perceptive,
and right to those
who discover knowledge.
¹⁰ Accept my instruction instead of silver,
and knowledge rather than pure gold.
¹¹ For wisdom is better than jewels,
and nothing desirable can compare
with it.
¹² I, Wisdom, share a home
with shrewdness
and have knowledge and discretion.
¹³ To fear the LORD is to hate evil.
I hate arrogant pride, evil conduct,
and perverse speech.
¹⁴ I possess good advice and competence;ᴮ
I have understanding and strength.
¹⁵ It is by me that kings reign
and rulers enact just law;
¹⁶ by me, princes lead,
as do nobles and all righteous judges.ᶜ
¹⁷ I love those who love me,
and those who search for me find me.
¹⁸ With me are riches and honor,
lasting wealth and righteousness.
¹⁹ My fruit is better than solid gold,
and my harvest than pure silver.
²⁰ I walk in the way of righteousness,
along the paths of justice,
²¹ giving wealth as an inheritance
to those who love me,

and filling their treasuries.
²² "The LORD madeᴰ me
at the beginning of His creation,ᴱ
before His works of long ago.
²³ I was formed before ancient times,
from the beginning,
before the earth began.
²⁴ I was born
when there were no watery depths
and no springs filled with water.
²⁵ I was delivered
before the mountains and hills
were established,
²⁶ before He made the land, the fields,
or the first soil on earth.
²⁷ I was there when He established
the heavens,
when He laid out the horizon
on the surface of the ocean,
²⁸ when He placed the skies above,
when the fountains of the ocean
gushed out,
²⁹ when He set a limit for the sea
so that the waters would not violate
His command,
when He laid out the foundations
of the earth.
³⁰ I was a skilled craftsmanᶠ beside Him.
I was Hisᴳ delight every day,
always rejoicing before Him.
³¹ I was rejoicing in His inhabited world,
delighting in the human race.
³² "And now, my sons, listen to me;
those who keep my ways are happy.
³³ Listen to instruction and be wise;
don't ignore it.
³⁴ Anyone who listens to me is happy,
watching at my doors every day,
waiting by the posts of my doorway.
³⁵ For the one who finds me finds life
and obtains favor from the LORD,
³⁶ but the one who misses meᴴ
harms himself;
all who hate me love death."

9 Wisdom has built her house;
she has carved out her seven pillars.
² She has prepared her meat;
she has mixed her wine;
she has also set her table.
³ She has sent out
her female servants;

ᴬ8:3 Lit *the mouth of*   ᴮ8:14 Or *resourcefulness*   ᶜ8:16 Some Hb mss, LXX read *nobles who judge the earth*   ᴰ8:22 Or *possessed, or begot*
ᴱ8:22 Lit *way*   ᶠ8:30 Or *a confidant, or a child,* or *was constantly*   ᴳ8:30 LXX; MT omits *His*   ᴴ8:36 Or *who sins against me*

she calls out from the highest points
  of the city:
4 "Whoever is inexperienced,
    enter here!"
  To the one who lacks sense, she says,
5 "Come, eat my bread,
  and drink the wine I have mixed.
6 Leave inexperience behind,
    and you will live;
  pursue the way of understanding.
7 The one who corrects a mocker
  will bring dishonor on himself;
  the one who rebukes a wicked man
    will get hurt.[A]
8 Don't rebuke a mocker, or he will
    hate you;
  rebuke a wise man, and he will
    love you.
9 Instruct a wise man, and he will be
    wiser still;
  teach a righteous man, and he will
    learn more.
10 "The fear of the LORD is the beginning
    of wisdom,
  and the knowledge of the Holy One
    is understanding.
11 For by Wisdom your days will be many,
  and years will be added to your life.
12 If you are wise, you are wise
    for your own benefit;
  if you mock, you alone will bear
    the consequences."
13 The woman Folly is rowdy;
  she is gullible and knows nothing.
14 She sits by the doorway of her house,
  on a seat at the highest point
    of the city,
15 calling to those who pass by,
  who go straight ahead on their paths:
16 "Whoever is inexperienced,
    enter here!"
  To the one who lacks sense, she says,
17 "Stolen water is sweet,
  and bread eaten secretly is tasty!"
18 But he doesn't know
    that the departed spirits are there,
  that her guests are in the depths
    of Sheol.

10 Solomon's proverbs:
  A wise son brings joy to his father,
  but a foolish son, heartache
    to his mother.

2 Ill-gotten gains do not profit anyone,
  but righteousness rescues from death.
3 The LORD will not let the righteous
    go hungry,
  but He denies the wicked
    what they crave.
4 Idle hands make one poor,
  but diligent hands bring riches.
5 The son who gathers during summer
    is prudent;
  the son who sleeps during harvest
    is disgraceful.
6 Blessings are on the head
    of the righteous,
  but the mouth of the wicked
    conceals violence.
7 The remembrance of the righteous is
    a blessing,
  but the name of the wicked will rot.
8 A wise heart accepts commands,
  but foolish lips will be destroyed.
9 The one who lives with integrity
    lives securely,
  but whoever perverts his ways will be
    found out.
10 A sly wink of the eye causes grief,
  and foolish lips will be destroyed.
11 The mouth of the righteous is
    a fountain of life,
  but the mouth of the wicked
    conceals violence.
12 Hatred stirs up conflicts,
  but love covers all offenses.
13 Wisdom is found on the lips
    of the discerning,
  but a rod is for the back of the one
    who lacks sense.
14 The wise store up knowledge,
  but the mouth of the fool
    hastens destruction.
15 A rich man's wealth is his fortified city;
  the poverty of the poor is
    their destruction.
16 The labor of the righteous leads to life;
  the activity of the wicked leads to sin.
17 The one who follows instruction is
    on the path to life,
  but the one who rejects correction
    goes astray.
18 The one who conceals hatred has
    lying lips,
  and whoever spreads slander is a fool.

A 9:7 Lit man his blemish

¹⁹ When there are many words,
   sin is unavoidable,
but the one who controls his lips
   is wise.
²⁰ The tongue of the righteous is
   pure silver;
the heart of the wicked is of little value.
²¹ The lips of the righteous feed many,
but fools die for lack of sense.
²² The LORD's blessing enriches,
and struggle adds nothing to it.ᴬ
²³ As shameful conduct is pleasure
   for a fool,
so wisdom is for a man of understanding.
²⁴ What the wicked dreads will come
   to him,
but what the righteous desire
   will be given to them.
²⁵ When the whirlwind passes,
   the wicked are no more,
but the righteous are secure forever.
²⁶ Like vinegar to the teeth and smoke
   to the eyes,
so the slacker is to the one
   who sends him on an errand.
²⁷ The fear of the LORD prolongs life,ᴮ
but the years of the wicked
   are cut short.
²⁸ The hope of the righteous is joy,
but the expectation of the wicked
   comes to nothing.
²⁹ The way of the LORD is a stronghold
   for the honorable,
but destruction awaits the malicious.
³⁰ The righteous will never be shaken,
but the wicked will not remain
   on the earth.
³¹ The mouth of the righteous
   produces wisdom,
but a perverse tongue will be cut out.
³² The lips of the righteous know
   what is appropriate,
but the mouth of the wicked,
   only what is perverse.

11 Dishonest scales are detestable
   to the LORD,
but an accurate weight is His delight.
² When pride comes, disgrace follows,
but with humility comes wisdom.
³ The integrity of the upright
   guides them,

but the perversity of the treacherous
   destroys them.
⁴ Wealth is not profitable on a day
   of wrath,
but righteousness rescues from death.
⁵ The righteousness of the blameless
   clears his path,
but the wicked person will fall
   because of his wickedness.
⁶ The righteousness of the upright
   rescues them,
but the treacherous are trapped
   by their own desires.
⁷ When the wicked man dies,
his expectation comes to nothing,
and hope placed in wealthᶜ,ᴰ vanishes.
⁸ The righteous one is rescued
   from trouble;
in his place, the wicked one goes in.
⁹ With his mouth the ungodly
   destroys his neighbor,
but through knowledge the righteous
   are rescued.
¹⁰ When the righteous thrive,
   a city rejoices,
and when the wicked die, there is
   joyful shouting.
¹¹ A city is built up by the blessing
   of the upright,
but it is torn down by the mouth
   of the wicked.
¹² Whoever shows contempt
   for his neighbor lacks sense,
but a man with understanding
   keeps silent.
¹³ A gossip goes around revealing
   a secret,
but a trustworthy person keeps
   a confidence.
¹⁴ Without guidance, people fall,
but with many counselors
   there is deliverance.
¹⁵ If someone puts up security
   for a stranger,
he will suffer for it,
but the one who hates
   such agreements is protected.
¹⁶ A gracious woman gains honor,
but violentᴱ men gain only riches.
¹⁷ A kind man benefits himself,
but a cruel man brings disaster
   on himself.

ᴬ10:22 Or and He adds no trouble to it   ᴮ10:27 Lit LORD adds to days   ᶜ11:7 LXX reads hope of the ungodly   ᴰ11:7 Or strength   ᴱ11:16 Or ruthless

18 The wicked man earns an empty wage,
but the one who sows righteousness,
a true reward.
19 Genuine righteousness leads to life,
but pursuing evil leads to death.
20 Those with twisted minds
are detestable to the LORD,
but those with blameless conduct are
His delight.
21 Be assured[A] that the wicked
will not go unpunished,
but the offspring of the righteous
will escape.
22 A beautiful woman who rejects
good sense
is like a gold ring in a pig's snout.
23 The desire of the righteous
turns out well,
but the hope of the wicked
leads to wrath.
24 One person gives freely,
yet gains more;
another withholds what is right,
only to become poor.
25 A generous person will be enriched,
and the one who gives a drink of water
will receive water.
26 People will curse anyone
who hoards grain,
but a blessing will come to the one
who sells it.
27 The one who searches for what is good
finds favor,
but if someone looks for trouble,
it will come to him.
28 Anyone trusting in his riches will fall,
but the righteous will flourish
like foliage.
29 The one who brings ruin
on his household
will inherit the wind,
and a fool will be a slave
to someone whose heart is wise.
30 The fruit of the righteous is a tree
of life,
but violence[B] takes lives.
31 If the righteous will be repaid on earth,
how much more the wicked and sinful.

12 Whoever loves discipline
loves knowledge,
but one who hates correction is stupid.

2 The good person obtains favor
from the LORD,
but He condemns a man who schemes.
3 Man cannot be made secure
by wickedness,
but the root of the righteous
is immovable.
4 A capable wife[C] is her husband's crown,
but a wife who causes shame
is like rottenness in his bones.
5 The thoughts of the righteous are just,
but guidance from the wicked
leads to deceit.
6 The words of the wicked are
a deadly ambush,
but the speech of the upright
rescues them.
7 The wicked are overthrown and perish,
but the house of the righteous
will stand.
8 A man is praised for his insight,
but a twisted mind is despised.
9 Better to be dishonored, yet have
a servant,
than to act important but have no food.
10 A righteous man cares about
his animal's health,
but even the merciful acts
of the wicked are cruel.
11 The one who works his land will have
plenty of food,
but whoever chases fantasies
lacks sense.
12 The wicked desire what evil men have,[D]
but the root of the righteous
produces fruit.
13 An evil man is trapped
by his rebellious speech,
but a righteous one escapes
from trouble.
14 A man will be satisfied with good
by the words of his mouth,
and the work of a man's hands
will reward him.
15 A fool's way is right in his own eyes,
but whoever listens to counsel is wise.
16 A fool's displeasure is known at once,
but whoever ignores an insult
is sensible.
17 Whoever speaks the truth declares
what is right,
but a false witness, deceit.

A11:21 Lit *Hand to hand*   B11:30 LXX, Syr; MT reads *but a wise one*   C12:4 Or *A wife of quality*, or *A wife of good character*   D12:12 Or *desire a stronghold of evil*

18 There is one who speaks rashly,
   like a piercing sword;
   but the tongue of the wise
   brings healing.

19 Truthful lips endure forever,
   but a lying tongue, only a moment.

20 Deceit is in the hearts of those
   who plot evil,
   but those who promote peace have joy.

21 No disaster overcomes the righteous,
   but the wicked are full of misery.

22 Lying lips are detestable to the Lord,
   but faithful people are His delight.

23 A shrewd person conceals knowledge,
   but a foolish heart publicizes stupidity.

24 The diligent hand will rule,
   but laziness will lead to forced labor.

25 Anxiety in a man's heart
   weighs it down,
   but a good word cheers it up.

26 A righteous man is careful in dealing
   with his neighbor,[A]
   but the ways of the wicked
   lead them astray.

27 A lazy man doesn't roast his game,
   but to a diligent man, his wealth
   is precious.

28 There is life in the path
   of righteousness,
   but another path leads to death.[B]

13 A wise son responds to his
   father's discipline,
   but a mocker doesn't listen to rebuke.

2 From the words of his mouth,
   a man will enjoy good things,
   but treacherous people have
   an appetite for violence.

3 The one who guards his mouth
   protects his life;
   the one who opens his lips invites
   his own ruin.

4 The slacker craves, yet has nothing,
   but the diligent is fully satisfied.

5 The righteous hate lying,
   but the wicked act disgustingly
   and disgracefully.

6 Righteousness guards people
   of integrity,[C]
   but wickedness undermines the sinner.

7 One man pretends to be rich
   but has nothing;
   another pretends to be poor but has
   great wealth.

8 Riches are a ransom for a man's life,
   but a poor man hears no threat.

9 The light of the righteous
   shines brightly,
   but the lamp of the wicked is put out.

10 Arrogance leads to nothing but strife,
   but wisdom is gained by those
   who take advice.

11 Wealth obtained by fraud will dwindle,
   but whoever earns it through labor[D]
   will multiply it.

12 Delayed hope makes the heart sick,
   but fulfilled desire is a tree of life.

13 The one who has contempt
   for instruction will pay the penalty,
   but the one who respects a command
   will be rewarded.

14 A wise man's instruction is a fountain
   of life,
   turning people away from the snares
   of death.

15 Good sense wins favor,
   but the way of the treacherous
   never changes.[E]

16 Every sensible person
   acts knowledgeably,
   but a fool displays his stupidity.

17 A wicked messenger falls into trouble,
   but a trustworthy courier
   brings healing.

18 Poverty and disgrace come to those
   who ignore discipline,
   but the one who accepts correction
   will be honored.

19 Desire fulfilled is sweet to the taste,
   but to turn from evil
   is an abomination to fools.

20 The one who walks with the wise
   will become wise,
   but a companion of fools
   will suffer harm.

21 Disaster pursues sinners,
   but good rewards the righteous.

22 A good man leaves an inheritance
   to his[F] grandchildren,
   but the sinner's wealth is stored up
   for the righteous.

23 The uncultivated field of the poor
   yields abundant food,
   but without justice, it is swept away.

A12:26 Or man guides his neighbor   B12:28 Or righteousness, and in its path there is no death   C13:6 Lit guards integrity of way   D13:11 Lit whoever gathers upon his hand   E13:15 LXX, Syr, Tg read treacherous will perish   F13:22 Or inheritance: his

24 The one who will not use the rod hates
his son,
but the one who loves him disciplines
him diligently.

25 A righteous man eats until he is satisfied,
but the stomach of the wicked is empty.

14 Every wise woman builds her house,
but a foolish one tears it down
with her own hands.

2 Whoever lives with integrity
fears the LORD,
but the one who is devious in his ways
despises Him.

3 The proud speech of a fool brings a rod
of discipline,[A]
but the lips of the wise protect them.

4 Where there are no oxen, the
feeding trough is empty,[B]
but an abundant harvest comes
through the strength of an ox.

5 An honest witness does not deceive,
but a dishonest witness utters lies.

6 A mocker seeks wisdom
and doesn't find it,
but knowledge comes easily
to the perceptive.

7 Stay away from a foolish man;
you will gain no knowledge
from his speech.

8 The sensible man's wisdom is
to consider his way,
but the stupidity of fools
deceives them.

9 Fools mock at making restitution,[C]
but there is goodwill
among the upright.

10 The heart knows its own bitterness,
and no outsider shares in its joy.

11 The house of the wicked
will be destroyed,
but the tent of the upright will stand.[D]

12 There is a way that seems right
to a man,
but its end is the way to death.

13 Even in laughter a heart may be sad,
and joy may end in grief.

14 The disloyal one will get
what his conduct deserves,
and a good man, what his deeds deserve.

15 The inexperienced one believes
anything,
but the sensible one watches[E] his steps.

16 A wise man is cautious and turns
from evil,
but a fool is easily angered
and is careless.[F]

17 A quick-tempered man acts foolishly,
and a man who schemes is hated.

18 The inexperienced inherit foolishness,
but the sensible are crowned
with knowledge.

19 The evil bow before those
who are good,
the wicked, at the gates
of the righteous.

20 A poor man is hated even
by his neighbor,
but there are many who love the rich.

21 The one who despises his neighbor sins,
but whoever shows kindness
to the poor will be happy.

22 Don't those who plan evil go astray?
But those who plan good find loyalty
and faithfulness.

23 There is profit in all hard work,
but endless talk[G] leads only to poverty.

24 The crown of the wise is their wealth,
but the foolishness of fools
produces foolishness.

25 A truthful witness rescues lives,
but one who utters lies is deceitful.

26 In the fear of the LORD one has
strong confidence
and his children have a refuge.

27 The fear of the LORD is a fountain
of life,
turning people away from the snares
of death.

28 A large population is a king's splendor,
but a shortage of people is
a ruler's devastation.

29 A patient person shows great
understanding,
but a quick-tempered one
promotes foolishness.

30 A tranquil heart is life to the body,
but jealousy is rottenness to the bones.

31 The one who oppresses the poor person
insults his Maker,
but one who is kind to the needy
honors Him.

32 The wicked one is thrown down
by his own sin,

A14:3 Some emend to *In the mouth of a fool is a rod for his back*   B14:4 Or *clean*   C14:9 Or *at guilt offerings*   D14:11 Lit *flourish*   E14:15 Lit *the prudent understand*   F14:16 Or *and falls*   G14:23 Lit *but word of lips*

but the righteous one has a refuge
in his death.
³³ Wisdom resides in the heart
of the discerning;
she is known^A even among fools.
³⁴ Righteousness exalts a nation,
but sin is a disgrace to any people.
³⁵ A king favors a wise servant,
but his anger falls on a disgraceful one.

15 A gentle answer turns away anger,
but a harsh word stirs up wrath.
² The tongue of the wise
makes knowledge attractive,
but the mouth of fools
blurts out foolishness.
³ The eyes of the LORD are everywhere,
observing the wicked and the good.
⁴ The tongue that heals is a tree of life,
but a devious tongue^B breaks the spirit.
⁵ A fool despises his father's discipline,
but a person who accepts correction
is sensible.
⁶ The house of the righteous
has great wealth,
but trouble accompanies the income
of the wicked.
⁷ The lips of the wise
broadcast knowledge,
but not so the heart of fools.
⁸ The sacrifice of the wicked is detestable
to the LORD,
but the prayer of the upright is
His delight.
⁹ The LORD detests the way of the wicked,
but He loves the one
who pursues righteousness.
¹⁰ Discipline is harsh for the one
who leaves the path;
the one who hates correction will die.
¹¹ Sheol and Abaddon lie open
before the LORD—
how much more, human hearts.
¹² A mocker doesn't love one
who corrects him;
he will not consult the wise.
¹³ A joyful heart makes a face cheerful,
but a sad heart produces
a broken spirit.
¹⁴ A discerning mind seeks knowledge,
but the mouth of fools feeds
on foolishness.

¹⁵ All the days of the oppressed
are miserable,
but a cheerful heart has
a continual feast.
¹⁶ Better a little with the fear of the LORD
than great treasure with turmoil.
¹⁷ Better a meal of vegetables
where there is love
than a fattened ox with hatred.
¹⁸ A hot-tempered man stirs up conflict,
but a man slow to anger calms strife.
¹⁹ A slacker's way is like a thorny hedge,
but the path of the upright is
a highway.
²⁰ A wise son brings joy to his father,
but a foolish man despises his mother.
²¹ Foolishness brings joy to one
without sense,
but a man with understanding walks
a straight path.
²² Plans fail when there is no counsel,
but with many advisers they succeed.
²³ A man takes joy in giving an answer;^C
and a timely word—how good that is!
²⁴ For the discerning the path of life
leads upward,
so that he may avoid going down
to Sheol.
²⁵ The LORD destroys the house
of the proud,
but He protects the widow's territory.
²⁶ The LORD detests the plans
of an evil man,
but pleasant words are pure.
²⁷ The one who profits dishonestly
troubles his household,
but the one who hates bribes will live.
²⁸ The mind of the righteous person
thinks before answering,
but the mouth of the wicked blurts out
evil things.
²⁹ The LORD is far from the wicked,
but He hears the prayer
of the righteous.
³⁰ Bright eyes cheer the heart;
good news strengthens^D the bones.
³¹ One who^E listens to life-giving rebukes
will be at home among the wise.
³² Anyone who ignores discipline
despises himself,
but whoever listens to correction
acquires good sense.^F

A14:33 LXX reads unknown   B15:4 Lit but crookedness in it   C15:23 Lit in an answer of his mouth   D15:30 Lit makes fat   E15:31 Lit An ear
that   F15:32 Lit acquires a heart

³³ The fear of the Lord is what
wisdom teaches,
and humility comes before honor.

16

The reflections of the heart
belong to man,
but the answer of the tongue is
from the Lord.

² All a man's ways seem right to him,
but the Lord evaluates the motives.^A

³ Commit your activities to the Lord,
and your plans will be achieved.

⁴ The Lord has prepared everything
for His purpose—
even the wicked for the day of disaster.

⁵ Everyone with a proud heart is
detestable to the Lord;
be assured,^B he will not go unpunished.

⁶ Wickedness is atoned for by loyalty
and faithfulness,
and one turns from evil by the fear
of the Lord.

⁷ When a man's ways please the Lord,
He^C makes even his enemies to be
at peace with him.

⁸ Better a little with righteousness
than great income with injustice.

⁹ A man's heart plans his way,
but the Lord determines his steps.

¹⁰ God's verdict is on the lips of a king;^D
his mouth should not give
an unfair judgment.

¹¹ Honest balances and scales are
the Lord's;
all the weights in the bag^E are
His concern.

¹² Wicked behavior^F is detestable to kings,
since a throne is established
through righteousness.

¹³ Righteous lips are a king's delight,
and he loves one who speaks honestly.

¹⁴ A king's fury is a messenger of death,
but a wise man appeases it.

¹⁵ When a king's face lights up,
there is life;
his favor is like a cloud
with spring rain.

¹⁶ Get wisdom—
how much better it is than gold!
And get understanding—
it is preferable to silver.

¹⁷ The highway of the upright avoids evil;
the one who guards his way protects
his life.

¹⁸ Pride comes before destruction,
and an arrogant spirit before a fall.

¹⁹ Better to be lowly of spirit
with the humble^G
than to divide plunder with the proud.

²⁰ The one who understands a matter
finds success,
and the one who trusts in the Lord
will be happy.

²¹ Anyone with a wise heart
is called discerning,
and pleasant speech^H
increases learning.

²² Insight is a fountain of life
for its possessor,
but the discipline of fools is folly.

²³ A wise heart instructs its mouth
and increases learning with its speech.^I

²⁴ Pleasant words are a honeycomb:
sweet to the taste^J and health
to the body.^K

²⁵ There is a way that seems right
to a man,
but its end is the way to death.

²⁶ A worker's appetite works for him
because his hunger^L urges him on.

²⁷ A worthless man digs up evil,
and his speech is like a scorching fire.

²⁸ A contrary man spreads conflict,
and a gossip separates close friends.

²⁹ A violent man lures his neighbor,
leading him in a way that is not good.

³⁰ The one who narrows his eyes
is planning deceptions;
the one who compresses his lips
brings about evil.

³¹ Gray hair is a glorious crown;
it is found in the way of righteousness.

³² Patience is better than power,
and controlling one's temper,^M
than capturing a city.

³³ The lot is cast into the lap,
but its every decision is from the Lord.

17

Better a dry crust with peace
than a house full of feasting with strife.

² A wise servant will rule over
a disgraceful son

A16:2 Lit weighs spirits   B16:5 Lit hand to hand   C16:7 Or he   D16:10 Or A divination is on the lips of a king   E16:11 Merchants kept the
stones for their scales in a bag.   F16:12 Either the king's or someone else's behavior   G16:19 Alt Hb tradition reads afflicted   H16:21 Lit and
sweetness of lips   I16:23 Lit learning upon his lips   J16:24 Lit throat   K16:24 Lit bones   L16:26 Lit mouth   M16:32 Lit and ruling over one's
spirit

and share an inheritance
    among brothers.
3 A crucible for silver, and a smelter
    for gold,
and the LORD is the tester of hearts.
4 A wicked person listens to
    malicious talk;[A]
a liar pays attention to
    a destructive tongue.
5 The one who mocks the poor insults
    his Maker,
and one who rejoices over calamity
    will not go unpunished.
6 Grandchildren are the crown
    of the elderly,
and the pride of sons is their fathers.
7 Eloquent words are not appropriate
    on a fool's lips;
how much worse are lies for a ruler.
8 A bribe seems like a magic stone
    to its owner;
wherever he turns, he succeeds.
9 Whoever conceals an offense
    promotes love,
but whoever gossips about it
    separates friends.
10 A rebuke cuts into a perceptive person
    more than a hundred lashes into a fool.
11 An evil man seeks only rebellion;
a cruel messenger[B] will be sent
    against him.
12 Better for a man to meet a bear robbed
    of her cubs
than a fool in his foolishness.
13 If anyone returns evil for good,
evil will never depart from his house.
14 To start a conflict is to release a flood;
stop the dispute before it breaks out.
15 Acquitting the guilty and condemning
    the just—
both are detestable to the LORD.
16 Why does a fool have money
    in his hand
with no intention of buying wisdom?
17 A friend loves at all times,
and a brother is born for a difficult time.
18 One without sense enters
    an agreement[C]
and puts up security for his friend.
19 One who loves to offend loves strife;
one who builds a high threshold
    invites injury.

20 One with a twisted mind
    will not succeed,
and one with deceitful speech will fall
    into ruin.
21 A man fathers a fool to his own sorrow;
the father of a fool has no joy.
22 A joyful heart is good medicine,
but a broken spirit dries up the bones.
23 A wicked man secretly takes a bribe
to subvert the course of justice.
24 Wisdom is the focus of the perceptive,
but a fool's eyes roam to the ends
    of the earth.
25 A foolish son is grief to his father
and bitterness to the one
    who bore him.
26 It is certainly not good to fine
    an innocent person
or to beat a noble for his honesty.[D]
27 The intelligent person restrains
    his words,
and one who keeps a cool head[E]
is a man of understanding.
28 Even a fool is considered wise
    when he keeps silent,
discerning when he seals his lips.

18 One who isolates himself pursues
    selfish desires;
he rebels against all sound judgment.
2 A fool does not delight
    in understanding,
but only wants to show off
    his opinions.[F]
3 When a wicked man comes,
    contempt also does,
and along with dishonor, disgrace.
4 The words of a man's mouth
    are deep waters,
a flowing river, a fountain of wisdom.[G]
5 It is not good to show partiality
    to the guilty
by perverting the justice
    due the innocent.
6 A fool's lips lead to strife,
and his mouth provokes a beating.
7 A fool's mouth is his devastation,
and his lips are a trap for his life.
8 A gossip's words are like choice food
    that goes down
to one's innermost being.[H]
9 The one who is truly lazy in his work

A17:4 Lit to lips of iniquity   B17:11 Or a merciless angel   C17:18 Lit sense shakes hands   D17:26 Or noble unfairly   E17:27 Lit spirit   F18:2 Lit
to uncover his heart   G18:4 Or waters; a fountain of wisdom is a flowing river.   H18:8 Lit to the chambers of the belly

is brother to a vandal.^A

¹⁰ The name of Yahweh is a strong tower;
the righteous run to it
and are protected.^B

¹¹ A rich man's wealth is his fortified city;
in his imagination it is like a high wall.

¹² Before his downfall a man's heart
is proud,
but humility comes before honor.

¹³ The one who gives an answer
before he listens—
this is foolishness and disgrace for him.

¹⁴ A man's spirit can endure sickness,
but who can survive a broken spirit?

¹⁵ The mind of the discerning
acquires knowledge,
and the ear of the wise seeks it.

¹⁶ A gift opens doors^C for a man
and brings him before the great.

¹⁷ The first to state his case seems right
until another comes and cross-
examines him.

¹⁸ Casting the lot ends quarrels
and separates powerful opponents.

¹⁹ An offended brother is harder to reach^D
than a fortified city,
and quarrels are like the bars
of a fortress.

²⁰ From the fruit of his mouth
a man's stomach is satisfied;
he is filled with the product of his lips.

²¹ Life and death are in the power
of the tongue,
and those who love it will eat its fruit.

²² A man who finds a wife finds
a good thing
and obtains favor from the LORD.

²³ The poor man pleads,
but the rich one answers roughly.

²⁴ A man with many friends
may be harmed,^E
but there is a friend who stays closer
than a brother.

19

Better a poor man who lives
with integrity
than someone who has deceitful lips
and is a fool.

² Even zeal is not good
without knowledge,
and the one who acts hastily^F sins.

³ A man's own foolishness leads
him astray,
yet his heart rages against the LORD.

⁴ Wealth attracts many friends,
but a poor man is separated
from his friend.

⁵ A false witness will not go unpunished,
and one who utters lies will not escape.

⁶ Many seek a ruler's favor,
and everyone is a friend of one
who gives gifts.

⁷ All the brothers of a poor man
hate him;
how much more do his friends
keep their distance from him!
He may pursue them with words,
but they are not there.^G

⁸ The one who acquires good sense^H
loves himself;
one who safeguards understanding
finds success.

⁹ A false witness will not go unpunished,
and one who utters lies perishes.

¹⁰ Luxury is not appropriate for a fool—
how much less for a slave to rule
over princes!

¹¹ A person's insight gives him patience,
and his virtue is to overlook an offense.

¹² A king's rage is like the roaring
of a lion,
but his favor is like dew on the grass.

¹³ A foolish son is his father's ruin,
and a wife's nagging is
an endless dripping.

¹⁴ A house and wealth are inherited
from fathers,
but a sensible wife is from the LORD.

¹⁵ Laziness induces deep sleep,
and a lazy person will go hungry.

¹⁶ The one who keeps commands
preserves himself;
one who disregards^I his ways will die.

¹⁷ Kindness to the poor is a loan
to the LORD,
and He will give a reward to the lender.^J

¹⁸ Discipline your son while there is hope;
don't be intent on killing him.^K

¹⁹ A person with great anger bears
the penalty;
if you rescue him, you'll have to do
it again.

A18:9 Lit master of destruction   B18:10 Lit raised high   C18:16 Lit gift makes room   D18:19 LXX, Syr, Tg, Vg read is stronger   E18:24 Some LXX mss, Syr, Tg, Vg read friends must be friendly   F19:2 Lit who is hasty with feet   G19:7 Hb uncertain   H19:8 Lit acquires a heart   I19:16 Or despises, or treats lightly   J19:17 Lit to him   K19:18 Lit don't lift up your soul to his death

20 Listen to counsel
and receive instruction
so that you may be wise later in life.^A

21 Many plans are in a man's heart,
but the Lord's decree will prevail.

22 What is desirable in a man is
his fidelity;
better to be a poor man than a liar.

23 The fear of the Lord leads to life;
one will sleep at night^B without danger.

24 The slacker buries his hand
in the bowl;
he doesn't even bring it back
to his mouth.

25 Strike a mocker, and the inexperienced
learn a lesson;
rebuke the discerning,
and he gains knowledge.

26 The one who assaults his father
and evicts his mother
is a disgraceful and shameful son.

27 If you stop listening to correction,
my son,
you will stray from the words
of knowledge.

28 A worthless witness mocks justice,
and a wicked mouth swallows iniquity.

29 Judgments are prepared for mockers,
and beatings for the backs of fools.

20 Wine is a mocker, beer is a brawler,
and whoever staggers because of them
is not wise.

2 A king's terrible wrath is
like the roaring of a lion;
anyone who provokes him
endangers himself.

3 It is honorable for a man to resolve
a dispute,
but any fool can get himself
into a quarrel.

4 The slacker does not plow
during planting season;^C
at harvest time he looks,^D and there is
nothing.

5 Counsel in a man's heart is deep water;
but a man of understanding
draws it out.

6 Many a man proclaims his own loyalty,
but who can find a trustworthy man?

7 The one who lives with integrity
is righteous;

his children^E who come after him
will be happy.

8 A king sitting on a throne to judge
sifts out all evil with his eyes.

9 Who can say, "I have kept
my heart pure;
I am cleansed from my sin"?

10 Differing weights
and varying measures^F—
both are detestable to the Lord.

11 Even a young man is known
by his actions—
if his behavior is pure and upright.

12 The hearing ear and the seeing eye—
the Lord made them both.

13 Don't love sleep, or you will
become poor;
open your eyes, and you'll have
enough to eat.

14 "It's worthless, it's worthless!"
the buyer says,
but after he is on his way, he gloats.

15 There is gold and a multitude of jewels,
but knowledgeable lips are
a rare treasure.

16 Take his garment,^G
for he has put up security for a stranger;
get collateral if it is for foreigners.

17 Food gained by fraud is sweet to a man,
but afterward his mouth is full
of gravel.

18 Finalize plans with counsel,
and wage war with sound guidance.

19 The one who reveals secrets is
a constant gossip;
avoid someone with a big mouth.

20 Whoever curses his father or mother—
his lamp will go out in deep darkness.

21 An inheritance gained prematurely
will not be blessed ultimately.

22 Don't say, "I will avenge this evil!"
Wait on the Lord, and He will
rescue you.

23 Differing weights^H are detestable
to the Lord,
and dishonest scales are unfair.

24 A man's steps are determined
by the Lord,
so how can anyone understand
his own way?

25 It is a trap for anyone to dedicate
something rashly

---

^A 19:20 Lit in your end   ^B 19:23 Lit will spend the night satisfied   ^C 20:4 Lit plow in winter   ^D 20:4 Lit inquires   ^E 20:7 Lit sons   ^F 20:10 Lit Stone
and stone, measure and measure   ^G 20:16 A debtor's outer garment was held as collateral.   ^H 20:23 Lit A stone and a stone

and later to reconsider his vows.

26 A wise king separates out the wicked
and drives the threshing wheel
over them.

27 The LORD's lamp sheds light on
a person's life,[A]
searching the innermost parts.[B]

28 Loyalty and faithfulness deliver a king;
through loyalty he maintains
his throne.

29 The glory of young men is
their strength,
and the splendor of old men is
gray hair.

30 Lashes and wounds purge away evil,
and beatings cleanse
the innermost parts.[C]

21 A king's heart is like streams of water
in the LORD's hand:
He directs it wherever He chooses.

2 All a man's ways seem right to him,
but the LORD evaluates the motives.[D]

3 Doing what is righteous and just
is more acceptable to the LORD
than sacrifice.

4 The lamp[E] that guides the wicked—
haughty eyes
and an arrogant heart—is sin.

5 The plans of the diligent certainly lead
to profit,
but anyone who is reckless
certainly becomes poor.

6 Making a fortune
through a lying tongue
is a vanishing mist,[F] a pursuit
of death.[G,H]

7 The violence of the wicked
sweeps them away
because they refuse to act justly.

8 A guilty man's conduct is crooked,
but the behavior of the innocent
is upright.

9 Better to live on the corner of a roof
than to share a house
with a nagging wife.

10 A wicked person desires evil;
he has no consideration[I]
for his neighbor.

11 When a mocker is punished,
the inexperienced become wiser;

when one teaches a wise man,
he acquires knowledge.

12 The Righteous One considers
the house of the wicked;
He brings the wicked to ruin.

13 The one who shuts his ears to the cry
of the poor
will himself also call out
and not be answered.

14 A secret gift soothes anger,
and a covert bribe,[J] fierce rage.

15 Justice executed is a joy
to the righteous
but a terror to those
who practice iniquity.

16 The man who strays from the way
of wisdom
will come to rest
in the assembly
of the departed spirits.

17 The one who loves pleasure
will become a poor man;
whoever loves wine and oil will not
get rich.

18 The wicked are a ransom
for the righteous,
and the treacherous, for[K] the upright.

19 Better to live in a wilderness
than with a nagging and hot-
tempered wife.

20 Precious treasure and oil are
in the dwelling of a wise person,
but a foolish man consumes them.[L]

21 The one who pursues righteousness
and faithful love
will find life, righteousness, and honor.

22 A wise person went up against a city
of warriors
and brought down its secure fortress.

23 The one who guards his mouth
and tongue
keeps himself out of trouble.

24 The proud and arrogant person,
named "Mocker,"
acts with excessive pride.

25 A slacker's craving will kill him
because his hands refuse to work.

26 He is filled with craving[M] all day long,
but the righteous give and don't
hold back.

²⁷ The sacrifice of a wicked person
    is detestable—
how much more so
when he brings it
    with ulterior motives!
²⁸ A lying witness will perish,
but the one who listens
    will speak successfully.
²⁹ A wicked man puts on a bold face,
but the upright man considers his way.
³⁰ No wisdom, no understanding,
    and no counsel
will prevail against the LORD.
³¹ A horse is prepared for the day
    of battle,
but victory comes from the LORD.

22 A good name is to be chosen
over great wealth;
favor is better than silver and gold.
² The rich and the poor have this
    in common:ᴬ
the LORD made them both.ᴮ
³ A sensible person sees danger
    and takes cover,
but the inexperienced keep going
    and are punished.
⁴ The result of humility is fear
    of the LORD,
along with wealth, honor, and life.
⁵ There are thorns and snares
    on the path of the crooked;
the one who guards himself stays
    far from them.
⁶ Teach a youth about the way
    he should go;
even when he is old he will not depart
    from it.
⁷ The rich rule over the poor,
and the borrower is a slave
    to the lender.
⁸ The one who sows injustice
    will reap disaster,
and the rod of his fury
    will be destroyed.
⁹ A generous personᶜ will be blessed,
for he shares his food with the poor.
¹⁰ Drive out a mocker, and conflict
    goes too;
then quarreling and dishonor
    will cease.

¹¹ The one who loves a pure heart
and gracious lips—the king is
    his friend.
¹² The LORD's eyes keep watch
    over knowledge,
but He overthrows the words
    of the treacherous.
¹³ The slacker says,
    "There's a lion outside!
I'll be killed in the public square!"
¹⁴ The mouth of the forbidden woman is
    a deep pit;
a man cursed by the LORD will fall
    into it.
¹⁵ Foolishness is tangled up in the heart
    of a youth;
the rod of discipline will drive it away
    from him.
¹⁶ Oppressing the poor to enrich oneself,
and giving to the rich—both lead
    only to poverty.

Words of the Wise

¹⁷ Listen closely,ᴰ pay attention
    to the words of the wise,
and apply your mind to my knowledge.
¹⁸ For it is pleasing if you keep them
    within you
and ifᴱ they are constantly on your lips.
¹⁹ I have instructed you
    today—even you—
so that your confidence may be
    in the LORD.
²⁰ Haven't I written for you
    thirty sayingsᶠ
about counsel and knowledge,
²¹ in order to teach you true
    and reliable words,
so that you may give
    a dependable reportᴳ
to those who sent you?
²² Don't rob a poor man
    because he is poor,
and don't crush the oppressed
    at the gate,
²³ for the LORD will take up their case
and will plunder those
    who plunder them.
²⁴ Don't make friends
    with an angry man,ᴴ
and don't be a companion of a
    hot-tempered man,

ᴬ22:2 Lit poor meet   ᴮ22:2 Lit all   ᶜ22:9 Lit Good of eye   ᴰ22:17 Lit Stretch out your ear   ᴱ22:18 Or you; let them be, or you, so that
ᶠ22:20 Text emended; one Hb tradition reads you previously; alt Hb tradition reads you excellent things; LXX, Syr, Vg read you three times
ᴳ22:21 Lit give dependable words   ᴴ22:24 Lit with a master of anger

²⁵ or you will learn his ways
and entangle yourself in a snare.
²⁶ Don't be one of those
who enter agreements,ᴬ
who put up security for loans.
²⁷ If you have no money to pay,
even your bed will be taken
from under you.
²⁸ Don't move
an ancient boundary marker
that your fathers set up.
²⁹ Do you see a man skilled in his work?
He will stand in the presence of kings.
He will not stand in the presence
of unknown men.

23 When you sit down to dine
with a ruler,
consider carefully whatᴮ is before you,
² and put a knife to your throat
if you have a bigᶜ appetite;
³ don't desire his choice food,
for that food is deceptive.
⁴ Don't wear yourself out to get rich;
stop giving your attention to it.
⁵ As soon as your eyes fly to it,
it disappears,
for it makes wings for itself
and flies like an eagle to the sky.
⁶ Don't eat a stingy person's bread,ᴰ
and don't desire his choice food,
⁷ for it's like someone calculating
inwardly.ᴱ
"Eat and drink," he says to you,
but his heart is not with you.
⁸ You will vomit the little you've eaten
and waste your pleasant words.
⁹ Don't speak toᶠ a fool,
for he will despise the insight
of your words.
¹⁰ Don't move
an ancient boundary marker,
and don't encroach on the fields
of the fatherless,
¹¹ for their Redeemer is strong,
and He will take up their case
against you.
¹² Apply yourself to discipline
and listen to words of knowledge.
¹³ Don't withhold discipline from a youth;
if you beat him with a rod,
he will not die.

¹⁴ Strike him with a rod,
and you will rescue his life from Sheol.
¹⁵ My son, if your heart is wise,
my heart will indeed rejoice.
¹⁶ My innermost being will cheer
when your lips say what is right.
¹⁷ Don't let your heart envy sinners;
instead, always fear the Lᴏʀᴅ.
¹⁸ For then you will have a future,
and your hope will never fade.
¹⁹ Listen, my son, and be wise;
keep your mind on the right course.
²⁰ Don't associate with those who drink
too much wine
or with those who gorge themselves
on meat.
²¹ For the drunkard and the glutton
will become poor,
and grogginess will clothe them
in rags.
²² Listen to your father who gave you life,
and don't despise your mother
whenᴳ she is old.
²³ Buy—and do not sell—truth,
wisdom, instruction,
and understanding.
²⁴ The father of a righteous son
will rejoice greatly,
and one who fathers a wise son
will delight in him.
²⁵ Let your father and mother have joy,
and let her who gave birth to you
rejoice.
²⁶ My son, give me your heart,
and let your eyes observe my ways.
²⁷ For a prostitute is a deep pit,
and a stranger is a narrow well;
²⁸ indeed, she sets an ambush
like a robber
and increases those among men
who are unfaithful.
²⁹ Who has woe? Who has sorrow?
Who has conflicts?
Who has complaints?
Who has wounds for no reason?
Who has red eyes?
³⁰ Those who linger over wine,
those who go looking for mixed wine.
³¹ Don't gaze at wine because it is red,
when it gleams in the cup
and goes down smoothly.

ᴬ**22:26** Lit who shakes hands   ᴮ**23:1** Or who   ᶜ**23:2** Lit you are the master of an   ᴰ**23:6** Lit eat bread of an evil eye   ᴱ**23:7** LXX reads it is like
someone swallowing a hair in the throat   ᶠ**23:9** Lit in the ears of   ᴳ**23:22** Or because

³² In the end it bites like a snake
and stings like a viper.
³³ Your eyes will see strange things,
and you will say absurd things.^A
³⁴ You'll be like someone sleeping
out at sea
or lying down on the top
of a ship's mast.
³⁵ "They struck me, but^B I feel no pain!
They beat me, but I didn't know it!
When will I wake up?
I'll look for another drink."

24

Don't envy evil men
or desire to be with them,
² for their hearts plan violence,
and their words stir up trouble.
³ A house is built by wisdom,
and it is established by understanding;
⁴ by knowledge the rooms are filled
with every precious
and beautiful treasure.
⁵ A wise warrior is better
than a strong one,^C
and a man of knowledge than one
of strength;^D
⁶ for you should wage war
with sound guidance—
victory comes with many counselors.
⁷ Wisdom is inaccessible to^E a fool;
he does not open his mouth at the gate.
⁸ The one who plots evil
will be called a schemer.
⁹ A foolish scheme is sin,
and a mocker is detestable to people.
¹⁰ If you do nothing in a difficult time,
your strength is limited.
¹¹ Rescue those being taken off to death,
and save those stumbling
toward slaughter.
¹² If you say, "But we didn't know
about this,"
won't He who weighs hearts
consider it?
Won't He who protects your life know?
Won't He repay a person according to
his work?
¹³ Eat honey, my son, for it is good,
and the honeycomb is sweet
to your palate;
¹⁴ realize that wisdom is the same
for you.

If you find it, you will have a future,
and your hope will never fade.
¹⁵ Wicked man, don't set an ambush,
at the camp of the righteous man;
don't destroy his dwelling.
¹⁶ Though a righteous man falls
seven times,
he will get up,
but the wicked will stumble into ruin.
¹⁷ Don't gloat when your enemy falls,
and don't let your heart rejoice
when he stumbles,
¹⁸ or the LORD will see, be displeased,
and turn His wrath away from him.
¹⁹ Don't be agitated by evildoers,
and don't envy the wicked.
²⁰ For the evil have no future;
the lamp of the wicked will be put out.
²¹ My son, fear the LORD, as well as
the king,
and don't associate with rebels,^F
²² for destruction from them
will come suddenly;
who knows what distress these two
can bring?
²³ These sayings also belong to the wise:
It is not good to show partiality
in judgment.
²⁴ Whoever says to the guilty,
"You are innocent"—
people will curse him, and tribes
will denounce him;
²⁵ but it will go well with those
who convict the guilty,
and a generous blessing will come
to them.
²⁶ He who gives an honest answer
gives a kiss on the lips.
²⁷ Complete your outdoor work,
and prepare your field;
afterward, build your house.
²⁸ Don't testify against your neighbor
without cause.
Don't deceive with your lips.
²⁹ Don't say, "I'll do to him what he did
to me;
I'll repay the man for what
he has done."
³⁰ I went by the field of a slacker
and by the vineyard of a man
lacking sense.

³¹ Thistles had come up everywhere,
 weeds covered the ground,
 and the stone wall was ruined.
³² I saw, and took it to heart;
 I looked, and received instruction:
³³ a little sleep, a little slumber,
 a little folding of the arms to rest,
³⁴ and your poverty will come
  like a robber,
 your need, like a bandit.

25 These too are proverbs of Solomon,
 which the men of Hezekiah,
  king of Judah, copied.
² It is the glory of God to conceal
  a matter
 and the glory of kings to investigate
  a matter.
³ As the heaven is high and the earth
  is deep,
 so the hearts of kings cannot
  be investigated.
⁴ Remove impurities from silver,
 and a vessel will be produced^A
  for a silversmith.
⁵ Remove the wicked
  from the king's presence,
 and his throne will be established
  in righteousness.
⁶ Don't brag about yourself
  before the king,
 and don't stand in the place
  of the great;
⁷ for it is better for him to say to you,
  "Come up here!"
 than to demote you in plain view
  of a noble.^B
⁸ Don't take a matter to court hastily.
 Otherwise, what will you do afterward
 if your opponent^C humiliates you?
⁹ Make your case with your opponent^C
 without revealing another's secret;
¹⁰ otherwise, the one who hears
  will disgrace you,
 and you'll never live it down.^D
¹¹ A word spoken at the right time
 is like gold apples on a silver tray.^E
¹² A wise correction to a receptive ear
 is like a gold ring or an ornament
  of gold.
¹³ To those who send him,
 a trustworthy messenger

is like the coolness of snow
 on a harvest day;
he refreshes the life of his masters.
¹⁴ The man who boasts about a gift
 that does not exist
is like clouds and wind without rain.
¹⁵ A ruler can be persuaded
 through patience,
and a gentle tongue can break a bone.
¹⁶ If you find honey, eat only
 what you need;
otherwise, you'll get sick from it
 and vomit.
¹⁷ Seldom set foot
 in your neighbor's house;
otherwise, he'll get sick of you
 and hate you.
¹⁸ A man giving false testimony
 against his neighbor
is like a club, a sword, or a sharp arrow.
¹⁹ Trusting an unreliable person in a
 difficult time
is like a rotten tooth or a faltering foot.
²⁰ Singing songs to a troubled heart
 is like taking off clothing on a cold day
or like pouring vinegar on soda.^F
²¹ If your enemy is hungry, give him food
 to eat,
and if he is thirsty, give him water
 to drink;
²² for you will heap burning coals
 on his head,
and the LORD will reward you.
²³ The north wind produces rain,
 and a backbiting tongue, angry looks.
²⁴ Better to live on the corner of a roof
 than to share a house
  with a nagging wife.
²⁵ Good news from a distant land
 is like cold water to a parched throat.^G
²⁶ A righteous person who yields
  to the wicked
 is like a muddied spring
  or a polluted well.
²⁷ It is not good to eat too much honey
 or to seek glory after glory.^H
²⁸ A man who does not control his temper
 is like a city whose wall is broken down.

26 Like snow in summer and rain
 at harvest,

---

^A**25:4** Lit will come out; Ex 32:24 ^B**25:7** Lit you before a noble whom your eyes see ^C**25:8,9** Or neighbor ^D**25:10** Lit and your evil report will not turn back ^E**25:11** Or like apples of gold in settings of silver ^F**25:20** Lit natron, or sodium carbonate ^G**25:25** Or a weary person ^H**25:27** Lit seek their glory, glory honor is inappropriate for a fool.

2 Like a flitting sparrow
    or a fluttering swallow,
  an undeserved curse goes nowhere.

3 A whip for the horse, a bridle
      for the donkey,
  and a rod for the backs of fools.

4 Don't answer a fool according to
      his foolishness
  or you'll be like him yourself.

5 Answer a fool according to
      his foolishness
  or he'll become wise in his own eyes.

6 The one who sends a message
      by a fool's hand
  cuts off his own feet and drinks violence.

7 A proverb in the mouth of a fool
  is like lame legs that hang limp.

8 Giving honor to a fool
  is like binding a stone in a sling.[A]

9 A proverb in the mouth of a fool
  is like a stick with thorns,
  brandished by[B] the hand of a drunkard.

10 The one who hires a fool or who hires
        those passing by
   is like an archer who wounds everyone.

11 As a dog returns to its vomit,
   so a fool repeats his foolishness.

12 Do you see a man who is wise
        in his own eyes?
   There is more hope for a fool
        than for him.

13 The slacker says, "There's a lion
        in the road—
   a lion in the public square!"

14 A door turns on its hinges,
   and a slacker, on his bed.

15 The slacker buries his hand in the bowl;
   he is too weary to bring it to his mouth.

16 In his own eyes, a slacker is wiser
        than seven men
        who can answer sensibly.

17 A person who is passing by and meddles
        in a quarrel that's not his
   is like one who grabs a dog by the ears.

18 Like a madman who throws
        flaming darts and deadly arrows,

19 so is the man who deceives his neighbor
   and says, "I was only joking!"

20 Without wood, fire goes out;
   without a gossip, conflict dies down.

21 As charcoal for embers and wood
        for fire,
   so is a quarrelsome man
        for kindling strife.

22 A gossip's words are like choice food
   that goes down to
        one's innermost being.[C]

23 Smooth[D] lips with an evil heart
   are like glaze on an earthen vessel.

24 A hateful person disguises himself
        with his speech
   and harbors deceit within.

25 When he speaks graciously,
        don't believe him,
   for there are seven abominations
        in his heart.

26 Though his hatred is concealed
        by deception,
   his evil will be revealed in the assembly.

27 The one who digs a pit will fall into it,
   and whoever rolls a stone—
   it will come back on him.

28 A lying tongue hates those it crushes,
   and a flattering mouth causes ruin.

27 Don't boast about tomorrow,
   for you don't know what a day
        might bring.

2 Let another praise you, and not
        your own mouth—
  a stranger, and not your own lips.

3 A stone is heavy and sand, a burden,
  but aggravation from a fool
        outweighs them both.

4 Fury is cruel, and anger a flood,
  but who can withstand jealousy?

5 Better an open reprimand
        than concealed love.

6 The wounds of a friend are trustworthy,
  but the kisses of an enemy are excessive.

7 A person who is full tramples
        on a honeycomb,
  but to a hungry person, any bitter thing
        is sweet.

8 A man wandering from his home
  is like a bird wandering from its nest.

9 Oil and incense bring joy to the heart,
  and the sweetness of a friend is better
        than self-counsel.[E]

10 Don't abandon your friend
   or your father's friend,

A26:8 A stone bound in a sling would not release and could harm the person using the sling. A modern equivalent is jamming a cork in a gun barrel. B26:9 Lit thorn that goes up into C26:22 Lit to the chambers of the belly D26:23 LXX; MT reads Burning E27:9 LXX reads heart, but the soul is torn up by affliction

and don't go to your brother's house
in your time of calamity;
better a neighbor nearby than a brother
far away.

11 Be wise, my son, and bring my heart joy,
so that I can answer anyone
who taunts me.

12 A sensible person sees danger
and takes cover;
the inexperienced keep going
and are punished.

13 Take his garment,[A]
for he has put up security for a stranger;
get collateral if it is for foreigners.[B]

14 If one blesses his neighbor
with a loud voice early in the morning,
it will be counted as a curse to him.

15 An endless dripping on a rainy day
and a nagging wife are alike.

16 The one who controls her controls
the wind
and grasps oil with his right hand.

17 Iron sharpens iron,
and one man sharpens another.[C]

18 Whoever tends a fig tree will eat its fruit,
and whoever looks after his master
will be honored.

19 As water reflects the face,
so the heart reflects the person.

20 Sheol and Abaddon are never satisfied,
and people's eyes are never satisfied.

21 A crucible for silver, and a smelter
for gold,
and a man for the words of his praise.[D]

22 Though you grind a fool
in a mortar with a pestle
along with grain,
you will not separate his foolishness
from him.

23 Know well the condition of your flock,
and pay attention to your herds,

24 for wealth is not forever;
not even a crown lasts for all time.

25 When hay is removed
and new growth appears
and the grain from the hills
is gathered in,

26 lambs will provide your clothing,
and goats, the price of a field;

27 there will be enough goat's milk
for your food—

food for your household
and nourishment for your
female servants.

28

The wicked flee when no one
is pursuing them,
but the righteous are as bold as a lion.

2 When a land is in rebellion, it has
many rulers,
but with a discerning
and knowledgeable person,
it endures.

3 A destitute leader[E] who oppresses
the poor
is like a driving rain that leaves no food.

4 Those who reject the law
praise the wicked,
but those who keep the law battle
against them.

5 Evil men do not understand justice,
but those who seek the LORD
understand everything.

6 Better a poor man who lives
with integrity
than a rich man who distorts right
and wrong.[F]

7 A discerning son keeps the law,
but a companion of gluttons humiliates
his father.

8 Whoever increases his wealth
through excessive interest
collects it for one who is kind
to the poor.

9 Anyone who turns his ear
away from hearing the law—
even his prayer is detestable.

10 The one who leads the upright
into an evil way
will fall into his own pit,
but the blameless will inherit
what is good.

11 A rich man is wise in his own eyes,
but a poor man who has discernment
sees through him.

12 When the righteous triumph,
there is great rejoicing,[G]
but when the wicked come to power,
people hide themselves.

13 The one who conceals his sins
will not prosper,

A27:13 A debtor's outer garment held as collateral; Dt 24:12-13,17; Jb 22:6; Am 2:8   B27:13 Lit a foreign woman   C27:17 Lit and a man
sharpens his friend's face   D27:21 Or gold, but a man is tested by his praise   E28:3 LXX reads A wicked man   F28:6 Lit who twists two
ways   G28:12 Lit glory

but whoever confesses
  and renounces them
will find mercy.
14 Happy is the one who is always reverent,
but one who hardens his heart falls
  into trouble.
15 A wicked ruler over a helpless people
is like a roaring lion or a charging bear.
16 A leader who lacks understanding
is very oppressive,
but one who hates dishonest profit
prolongs his life.
17 A man burdened by bloodguilt[A]
will be a fugitive until death.
Let no one help him.
18 The one who lives with integrity
  will be helped,
but one who distorts right and wrong[B]
will suddenly fall.
19 The one who works his land
will have plenty of food,
but whoever chases fantasies
will have his fill of poverty.
20 A faithful man will have many blessings,
but one in a hurry to get rich
will not go unpunished.
21 It is not good to show partiality—
yet a man may sin for a piece of bread.
22 A greedy man[C] is in a hurry for wealth;
he doesn't know that poverty will come
  to him.
23 One who rebukes a person will later find
  more favor
than one who flatters[D] with his tongue.
24 The one who robs his father or mother
and says, "That's no sin,"
is a companion to a man who destroys.
25 A greedy person provokes conflict,
but whoever trusts in the Lord
  will prosper.
26 The one who trusts in himself[E] is
  a fool,
but one who walks in wisdom
  will be safe.
27 The one who gives to the poor
will not be in need,
but one who turns his eyes away[F]
will receive many curses.
28 When the wicked come to power,
people hide,

but when they are destroyed,
the righteous flourish.

29 One who becomes stiff-necked,
after many reprimands
will be shattered instantly—
beyond recovery.
2 When the righteous flourish,
  the people rejoice,
but when the wicked rule, people groan.
3 A man who loves wisdom brings joy
  to his father,
but one who consorts with prostitutes
  destroys his wealth.
4 By justice a king brings stability
  to a land,
but a man who demands
  "contributions"[G]
demolishes it.
5 A man who flatters[H] his neighbor
spreads a net for his feet.
6 An evil man is caught by sin,
but the righteous one sings
  and rejoices.
7 The righteous person knows the rights[I]
  of the poor,
but the wicked one does not
  understand these concerns.
8 Mockers inflame a city,
but the wise turn away anger.
9 If a wise man goes to court with a fool,
there will be ranting and raving
  but no resolution.[J]
10 Bloodthirsty men hate
  an honest person,
but the upright care about him.[K]
11 A fool gives full vent to his anger,[L]
but a wise man holds it in check.
12 If a ruler listens to lies,
all his officials will be wicked.
13 The poor and the oppressor have this
  in common:[M]
the Lord gives light to the eyes of both.
14 A king who judges the poor
  with fairness—
his throne will be established forever.
15 A rod of correction imparts wisdom,
but a youth left to himself[N]
is a disgrace to his mother.
16 When the wicked increase,
  rebellion increases,

---

but the righteous will see
their downfall.

17 Discipline your son, and it will bring
you peace of mind
and give you delight.

18 Without revelation[A] people run wild,
but one who listens to instruction
will be happy.

19 A slave cannot be disciplined by words;
though he understands,
he doesn't respond.

20 Do you see a man who speaks
too soon?
There is more hope for a fool
than for him.

21 A slave pampered from his youth
will become arrogant[B] later on.

22 An angry man stirs up conflict,
and a hot-tempered man[C]
increases rebellion.

23 A person's pride will humble him,
but a humble spirit will gain honor.

24 To be a thief's partner is to hate oneself;
he hears the curse but will not testify.[D]

25 The fear of man is a snare,
but the one who trusts in the LORD
is protected.[E]

26 Many seek a ruler's favor,
but a man receives justice
from the LORD.

27 An unjust man is detestable
to the righteous,
and one whose way is upright
is detestable to the wicked.

30 The words of Agur son of Jakeh.
The oracle.[F]
The man's oration to Ithiel, to Ithiel
and Ucal:[G]

2 I am more stupid than any other man,[H]
and I lack man's ability to understand.

3 I have not gained wisdom,
and I have no knowledge
of the Holy One.

4 Who has gone up to heaven
and come down?
Who has gathered the wind
in His hands?
Who has bound up the waters
in a cloak?

Who has established all the ends
of the earth?
What is His name,
and what is the name of His Son—
if you know?

5 Every word of God is pure;[I]
He is a shield to those who take refuge
in Him.

6 Don't add to His words,
or He will rebuke you, and you will be
proved a liar.

7 Two things I ask of You;
don't deny them to me before I die:

8 Keep falsehood and deceitful words
far from me.
Give me neither poverty nor wealth;
feed me with the food I need.

9 Otherwise, I might have too much
and deny You, saying,
"Who is the LORD?"
or I might have nothing and steal,
profaning[J] the name of my God.

10 Don't slander a servant to his master
or he will curse you, and you will
become guilty.

11 There is a generation that curses
its father
and does not bless its mother.

12 There is a generation that is pure
in its own eyes,
yet is not washed from its filth.

13 There is a generation—how haughty
its eyes
and pretentious its looks.[K]

14 There is a generation whose teeth
are swords,
whose fangs are knives,
devouring the oppressed from the land
and the needy from among mankind.

15 The leech has two daughters:
"Give, Give!"
Three things are never satisfied;
four never say, "Enough!":

16 Sheol; a childless womb;
earth, which is never satisfied
with water;
and fire, which never says, "Enough!"

17 As for the eye that ridicules a father
and despises obedience to a mother,

A29:18 Lit vision B29:21 Hb obscure C29:22 Lit a master of rage D29:24 When a call for witnesses was made public, anyone with
information who did not submit his testimony was under a curse. E29:25 Lit raised high F30:1 Or son of Jakeh from Massa; Pr 31:1
G30:1 Hb uncertain. Sometimes read with different word division as oration: I am weary, God, I am weary, God, and I am exhausted, or oration:
I am not God, I am not God, that I should prevail. LXX reads My son, fear my words and when you have received them repent. The man says these
things to the believers in God, and I pause. H30:2 Lit I am more stupid than a man I30:5 Lit refined J30:9 Lit grabbing K30:13 Lit and its
eyelids lifted up

may ravens of the valley pluck it out
and young vultures eat it.

18 Three things are beyond me;
four I can't understand:

19 the way of an eagle in the sky,
the way of a snake on a rock,
the way of a ship at sea,
and the way of a man
with a young woman.

20 This is the way of an adulteress:
she eats and wipes her mouth
and says, "I've done nothing wrong."

21 The earth trembles under three things;
it cannot bear up under four:

22 a servant when he becomes king,
a fool when he is stuffed with food,

23 an unloved woman when she marries,
and a servant girl when she ousts
her queen.

24 Four things on earth are small,
yet they are extremely wise:

25 the ants are not a strong people,
yet they store up their food
in the summer;

26 hyraxes are not a mighty people,
yet they make their homes in the cliffs;

27 locusts have no king,
yet all of them march in ranks;

28 a lizard^A can be caught in your hands,
yet it lives in kings' palaces.

29 Three things are stately in their stride,
even four are stately in their walk:

30 a lion, which is mightiest among beasts
and doesn't retreat before anything,

31 a strutting rooster,^B a goat,
and a king at the head of his army.^C

32 If you have been foolish
by exalting yourself
or if you've been scheming,
put your hand over your mouth.

33 For the churning of milk
produces butter,
and twisting a nose draws blood,
and stirring up anger produces strife.

31 The words of King Lemuel,
an oracle^D that his mother taught him:

2 What should I say, my son?
What, son of my womb?
What, son of my vows?

3 Don't spend your energy on women
or your efforts on those
who destroy kings.

4 It is not for kings, Lemuel,
it is not for kings to drink wine
or for rulers to desire beer.

5 Otherwise, they^E will drink,
forget what is decreed,
and pervert justice for all
the oppressed.^F

6 Give beer to one who is dying
and wine to one whose life is bitter.

7 Let him drink so that he can forget
his poverty
and remember his trouble no more.

8 Speak up^G for those who have no voice,^H
for the justice of all
who are dispossessed.^I

9 Speak up,^G judge righteously,
and defend the cause of^J the oppressed
and needy.

10 Who can find a capable wife?^K
She is far more precious than jewels.^L

11 The heart of her husband trusts in her,
and he will not lack anything good.

12 She rewards him with good, not evil,
all the days of her life.

13 She selects wool and flax
and works with willing hands.

14 She is like the merchant ships,
bringing her food from far away.

15 She rises while it is still night
and provides food for her household
and portions^M for her female servants.

16 She evaluates a field and buys it;
she plants a vineyard
with her earnings.^N

17 She draws on her strength^O
and reveals that her arms are strong.

18 She sees that her profits are good,
and her lamp never goes out at night.

19 She extends her hands
to the spinning staff,
and her hands hold the spindle.

20 Her hands reach^P out to the poor,
and she extends her hands
to the needy.

21 She is not afraid for her household
when it snows,

---

^A30:28 Or spider ^B30:31 Or a greyhound ^C30:31 LXX reads king addressing his people ^D31:1 Or of Lemuel, king of Massa, or of King
Lemuel, a burden ^E31:5 Lit he ^F31:5 Lit sons of affliction ^G31:8,9 Lit Open your mouth ^H31:8 Lit who are mute ^I31:8 Lit all the sons of
passing away ^J31:9 Lit and justice for ^K31:10 Or a wife of quality, or a wife of noble character ^L31:10 Vv. 10-31 form an acrostic. ^M31:15 Or
tasks ^N31:16 Or vineyard by her own labors ^O31:17 Lit She wraps strength around her like a belt ^P31:20 Lit Her hand reaches

for all in her household
   are doubly clothed.[A]

²² She makes her own bed coverings;
   her clothing is fine linen and purple.

²³ Her husband is known at the city gates,
   where he sits among the elders
      of the land.

²⁴ She makes and sells linen garments;
   she delivers belts[B] to the merchants.

²⁵ Strength and honor are her clothing,
   and she can laugh at the time to come.

²⁶ She opens her mouth with wisdom
   and loving instruction[C] is
      on her tongue.

²⁷ She watches over the activities
   of her household
   and is never idle.[D]

²⁸ Her sons rise up and call her blessed.
   Her husband also praises her:

²⁹ "Many women[E] are capable,
   but you surpass them all!"

³⁰ Charm is deceptive and beauty
   is fleeting,
   but a woman who fears the LORD
      will be praised.

³¹ Give her the reward of her labor,[F]
   and let her works praise her
      at the city gates.

A31:21 LXX, Vg; MT reads *are dressed in scarlet* B31:24 Or *sashes* C31:26 Or *and the teaching of kindness* D31:27 Lit *and does not eat the bread of idleness* E31:29 Lit *daughters* F31:31 Lit *the fruit of her hands*

Asking Jesus to be your Savior is the most important decision you can make. What does the Bible say about becoming a Christian?

God loves you.

Love consists in this: not that we loved God,
but that He loved us.

1 John 4:10

Sin separates you from God.

Sin is choosing your way instead of God's way.

Sin separates people from God.

For all have sinned and fall short of the glory of God.

Romans 3:23

Everyone sins—even people who have already become Christians.

But God will forgive you and help you obey Him if you ask.

If we confess our sins, He is faithful and righteous to forgive
us our sins and to cleanse us from all unrighteousness.

1 John 1:9

God sent Jesus so you could have eternal life.

**God sent Jesus so you would not have to die for your sin. Jesus
died on the cross, He was buried, and He rose from the dead.**

For God loved the world in this way: He gave His One
and Only Son, so that everyone who believes in Him
will not perish but have eternal life.

John 3:16

Want to know more?

Just remember the ABCs of Becoming a Christian.
You can find them at the front of this Bible. Follow the
directions at the bottom of that page to discover
how to become a Christian.

God's Holy Spirit will help you know when you are ready to become a Christian. If it is time for you to become a Christian, pray a prayer like the one below.

Dear God,

I know I have sinned and that my sin separates me from You. I am sorry for my sin. Please forgive me. I believe Jesus died on the cross for me so my sin can be forgiven. I believe Jesus rose from the dead and is alive.

I ask Jesus to come into my life to be my Savior and Lord. I will obey You and live for You the rest of my life. Thank You for loving and saving me from my sin.

Amen.

Now you can be baptized to show others that you are a Christian, participate in the Lord's Supper to remember what Jesus did for you, and tell others that Jesus is your Savior and Lord.

Secret Mission

Use the evidence below to decode the secret message.
It's a special mission God has given you!

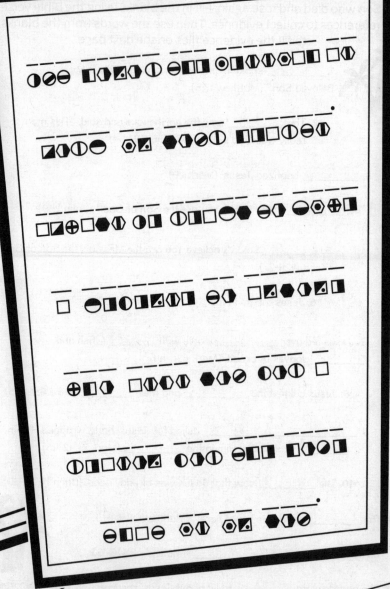

Journey of Evidence

It's time to investigate! Let's collect evidence that shows Jesus is God's Son who died and rose again. Fill in the blanks using the Bible verse references to collect evidence. Then use the words from the blanks to fill the evidence files on the next page.

1. _____ spoke from heaven, saying: "This is My Beloved Son." (Matthew 17:5)

2. The _____ saw the earthquake and said, "This man really was God's Son!" (Matthew 27:54)

3. _____ baptized Jesus. (Mark 1:9)

4. _____ said, "Rabbi, You are the Son of God!" (John 1:49)

5. _____ said, "I believe You are the Messiah, the Son of God." (John 11:24-27)

6. Jesus taught in the _____. (Mark 6:1-2)

7. Jesus fed over _____ people with _____ fish and _____ loaves of bread. (Mark 6:41-44)

8. Jesus calmed the _____ and the _____. (Luke 8:24-25)

9. _____ _____ _____ asked for Jesus' body, wrapped Him in _____, and placed Him in the _____. (Mark 15:42-46)

10. The _____ saw that Jesus was already dead. (John 19:32-33)

11. The _____ said, "He is not here!" (Matthew 28:5-6)

12. Jesus appeared to the _____. (Matthew 28:16-18)

13. The guards were _____ to lie about Jesus' resurrection. (Matthew 28:11-13)

Evidence Files

Eyewitnesses **Miracles of Jesus** **Jesus' Resurrection**

Answers: 1. God; 2. centurion; 3. John; 4. Nathanael; 5. Martha;
6. synagogue, 7. 5,000, 2, 5; 8. wind, waves, 9. Joseph of Arimathea, linen, tomb;
10. soldiers; 11. angel; 12. disciples; 13. bribed

358

Jumbled Case Files

Uh-oh! Some evidence is missing from these case files.
Your help is needed, Special Agent! Draw a line
from the evidence (picture)
to the correct case file.

Loaf of bread
and cup

Earthquake

5 small loaves of
bread and 2 fish

Temple

Storm

Cloud

Soldiers

Perfume
bottle

Spear